MW00390207

 BASEBALLHQ.COM'S **2019**

MINOR LEAGUE
BASEBALL
ANALYST

PRESENTED BY BASEBALLHQ.COM | BRENT HERSHEY, EDITOR | 14TH EDITION

TRIUMPH
BOOKS

Copyright © 2019, USA TODAY Sports Media Group LLC.
No part of this publication may be reproduced, stored in a retrieval system, or transmitted in any form by any means, electronic, mechanical, photocopying, or otherwise, without the prior written permission of the publisher, Triumph Books LLC, 814 North Franklin Street, Chicago, Illinois 60610.

Triumph Books and colophon are registered trademarks of Random House, Inc.

This book is available in quantity at special discounts for your group or organization. For further information, contact:

Triumph Books LLC
814 North Franklin Street
Chicago, Illinois 60610
(312) 337-0747
www.triumphbooks.com

Printed in U.S.A.
ISBN: 978-1-62937-614-1

Data provided by TheBaseballCube.com and Baseball Info Solutions

Cover design by Brent Hershey
Front cover photograph by Kim Klement/USA TODAY Sports

TABLE OF CONTENTS

Juan Soto: An MLBA Timeline

by Brent Hershey

> *"Far away, but one to dream on."*
> *"His polished hit tool is the story."*
> *"Still a teenager but the skills to move quickly."*

Such read excerpts from the three years Juan Soto (OF, WAS) appeared in previous versions of the *Minor League Baseball Analyst* (MLBA). The above quotes are in chronological order—from our 2016, 2017, and 2018 editions of this book.

As we all know, there will be no 2019 entry. Soto's emergence as a baseball star—and fantasy baseball building-block—was one of the most improbable and exciting stories of the 2018 MLB season. Let's take a look back at his brief minor league career in conjunction with the progression of coverage of him in this publication. In doing so, we seek both how to identify similar players, as well as how to employ the MLBA's scouting reports and metrics into fantasy baseball success.

Caveats

Before we get in too deep, there are several caveats to keep in mind.

Juan Soto's rise in 2019 was freakish. We will likely not see another situation like his, where a teenage player started the year in Low-A, and progressed through High-A and Double-A before making his MLB debut in May. Sure, it was talent-based (in 152 combined MiLB AB in 2018, he went .362/.462/.757), but injuries in the Washington outfield played a role as well.

Related, most "9" prospects don't follow such a path. While this examination references our grading system (more on that below), it is not an attempt to say that all 9s could follow this journey. Rather, here are the tools you can use to evaluate any of the prospects in this book.

Reminder: Hindsight is 20/20, and no one likes a navel-gazer. We acknowledge the real risk that this essay could come off as a "We told you so!" piece—*after* Soto was the just the third teenager in MLB history to hit 20+ HR in his rookie season (among his many other feats). In the vein of transparency, here is the complete list of the other teenage hitting prospects who received the same 8E grade as Soto did in our 2016 book and were Top-15 prospects in their organizations: Trent Clark (OF, MIL), Gilbert Lara (SS, MIL), Ali Sanchez (C, NYM), Jahmai Jones (OF, LAA), Isael Soto (OF, MIA), Isaiah White (OF, MIA), Julio Garcia (SS, LAA), Marcus Wilson OF, ARI), Jalen Miller (SS, SF) Gareth Morgan (OF, SEA) and Ti'quan Forbes (3B, TEX). We're here to learn a bit why Soto achieved and these others didn't—not to pat ourselves on the back because one of a dozen *did*.

What we're most interested in is Soto's quick adjustment to MLB. One of the remaining puzzles in terms of prospects and fantasy baseball is how to identify which players will hit the ground running (can be counted on for production soon after) and which ones are likely to have an adjustment period of some sort. The fact that Soto epitomizes the "hit the ground running" end of the continuum—and that he did so as a teenager—is the kernel of

what we'd like to explore. Should we have known that Soto's case would be different—that he would become a fantasy force from the time he set foot on an MLB diamond?

The question is meant to be rhetorical, but one plausible answer, after looking back at our timeline of Juan Soto's appearances in the Minor League Baseball Analyst is … perhaps.

2016 Minor League Baseball Analyst

Soto debuted in this year's book, fresh off inking his $1.5M bonus for signing with Washington the previous July. He had not yet played a game in the U.S. when the book went to press.

Whether or not to include players such as these—just-signed teenagers, without any pro experience—in the MLBA's player-box section is an annual conundrum for our authors. On the one hand, there is so much development to still take place, it's easy to "punt" the player to the next edition, when there's conceivably more data (and in-person looks) to work with and ultimately evaluate. In most cases, that will still provide at least 3-4 years in which the player will be covered in future editions.

On other hand, given the investment that MLB teams make to these players, they are an important part of the team's future. In addition, we ask authors (who are assigned organizations to cover) to submit their initial list of players to include in the book, and usually suggest they go 30-35 players deep. Many times one can make the argument that someone in Soto's case is certainly one of that organization's Top 35 prospects. There are usually a handful of these players who get assigned a player box each year (the best of that class gets covered in the International Prospects article).

In 2016, given the reports on the uniqueness of his skill set, Soto did get a player box and was ranked the #15 prospect in the Washington system. His entire entry said this:

> *Seen as one of the top all-around hitters in the 2015 international draft class due to advanced approach and superior contact skills. Still needs to grow into his power, but has the size and the acumen to adjust. Likely limited to an OF corner spot due to below-average arm and speed. Far away, but one to dream on.*

It was lofty praise, to be sure, but not that different than other Latin teenagers who would play the next year at 17 years old—at this point in their development, many, if not all, of these prospects are ones "to dream on."

We assigned Soto an "8E" grade in this edition—again, not that different than other players of his age/experience. If you're not familiar with our grading system, there's some more detail later in this column, but a quick reference is that we graded Soto with a ceiling of a solid regular MLB player (8), but with a lot of risk attached in reaching that ceiling (E). Players without much (or any) pro experience routinely get "E"s; there's just no substitute for pro experience. To claim to know with any amount of certainty how a prospect will react to the pro game, including facing world-class competition and, likely, some sense of failure, is folly. An 8E was a perfectly justifiable score for someone with Soto's draft standing, age and experience.

We also rate each player's component skills—and had him right at average for both power and batting average in 2016.

2017 Minor League Baseball Analyst

After attending extended spring training in the spring of 2016, Soto exploded in his first pro stops that summer. He spent most of his time in rookie ball in the Gulf Coast League, and then a six-game cameo in the short-season New York Penn League. The combined results were, umm, quite good: .368/.420/.553 with 17 walks and just 29 strikeouts in 190 AB. And scouting reports were just as effusive: he could hit just about anything, knew the strike zone, and could make adjustments during his at-bats. And remember, he's a 17-year-old competing against players sometimes 3-4 years older. Our 2017 snapshot from his player box:

> *A top international signee from 2015, Soto raked his way through rookie ball and won the MVP of the GCL. Has strong hands and an impeccable approach for a teenager, using the whole field and barreling up all types of pitches. Power is emerging, but his polished hit tool is the story. Average defense will limit him to an OF corner.*

On that basis, Soto had jumped to #2 on the Nationals list. Though the following only was published online, in our BaseballHQ.com Organization Report that winter, Soto's Development Path and Fantasy Impact entries fleshed out further the potential impact player we were dealing with:

> *Development Path: He'll report to full-season Hagerstown as an 18-year-old. His advanced hitting acumen, led by excellent strike-zone judgment, hints he could move through the minors quickly if he continues to hit. If not, there's no reason to rush him.*
>
> *Fantasy Impact: Given his age, Soto has a high ceiling on his hitting skills alone. And if a power stroke develops over the course of the next couple of seasons, he could approach superstar potential. Lower risk than most rookie-ball fantasy selections.*

As often happens, the grades we gave in the book adjusted. We bumped Soto up to a 9D in 2017, feeling confident about a hit-tool centered teenager who blew up rookie ball as the type of profile that could develop into a 9; in our mind, an "elite player." Given that he still had not faced full-season competition, there was still considerable risk connected to his profile. Though because he succeeded with what was presented him so far, we lowered his risk to a "D" level. We also adjusted his batting average component skill grade to "plus" (four of out five plus marks) for those same reasons. We looked forward with anticipation to what would certainly be a full-season assignment in 2017 and the next challenge in his development.

2018 Minor League Baseball Analyst

Little did we know one year ago that 2018 would be Soto's final appearance in player box section of the *Minor League Baseball Analyst*. Especially when one considers what happened in Soto's 2017 season.

Soto indeed started out 2017 in full-season Low-A ball, reporting to Hagerstown. It was no match for him; he scalded

South Atlantic League pitching to the tune of .360/.427/.523 through May 2 (86 AB in 23 games). But in the May 2 game, he sprained his right ankle sliding into home plate, and the injury sidelined him for two months. While rehabbing in July back in the Gulf Coast League, Soto's wrist became a problem, and he ended up having hamate surgery. He returned in late August for four GCL games before his season ended.

Soto's overall line from 2017, though abbreviated, still stood out: .351/.415/.505, with more walks (12) than strikeouts (9) in 123 AB. But more than the impressive statistics, it was my first in-person look at Soto in mid-April that convinced me further that something special was at work here.

In batting practice, the ball jumped off his bat: both to his pull side, but just as importantly, to the opposite field. In his first AB, he took two consecutive borderline pitches to work a walk, and later in the game, was aggressive and just missed sending a pitch out. Moreover, he played with a quiet, confident energy incongruent for a 18-year-old Latin teenager just a couple weeks into a cold-weather April game in the Northeast.

The combined stats and in-person look led to this evaluation, even with his injury troubles, in the 2018 MLBA:

> *Well-proportioned with some additional room for muscle, he plays with energy but under control. Has an innate feel to hit, and an approach to put himself into favorable counts. All-fields power that will only improve as he gets stronger. Strong arm but fringy range, but enough for RF. Still a teenager but the tools to move quickly.*

And the added online-only text last offseason:

> *Development Path: Leg and hand injuries wiped out most of 2017, but showed enough that he will take his well-rounded game to Hi-A in 2018. With health, not out of the question that he could rise to AA by the end of the season, putting an MLB debut in 2019.*
>
> *Fantasy Impact: The package is enticing, both the physical and mental (approach) side. Reps should only make him better. He makes the adjustments necessary to hit .300 in the big leagues some years, with 25+ HR thrown in, as well a stellar OBP. In other words, a top-tier fantasy outfielder at his peak.*

This was enough to bump his overall grade up even a bit further. We rarely give out "10"s, but seeing the damage and controlled AB in-person made us feel more comfortable about again lowering his risk, as we assigned a "9C" in last year's edition. Also, the pop in his bat was starting to show, and so he was the rare plus-BA, plus-power player in the 2018 edition.

In addition, he was getting more publicity, and made his first and only appearance on our HQ100 prospect list, coming in at #28. Were we smitten? Yeah, a bit. But in some ways, it made the 2018 season not quite the outlier it may have seemed.

Of course, we know the rest of the 2018 Soto story, but it warrants a quick recap, if only to be reminded of his glorious four-month run. As a 19-year old, he started back at Low-A Hagerstown, spent 16 games there and decimated the Sally as his game power flourished (59 AB, 5 HR, 1.300 OPS). Promoted to

High-A Potomac in late April, he similarly spent 15 games there and further pillaged better pitching (62 AB, 7 HR, 1.256 OPS). Then a short 8-game pit-stop at AA-Harrisburg (35 AB, 2 HR, .981 OPS) before getting the call to Washington for good (thank you, Howie Kendrick) on May 20. There, he raked the rest of the season, finished with 22 MLB HR, a .923 OPS, and came in second in the NL Rookie of the Year voting. Juan Soto is here to stay.

Conclusion

But back to May 20 and Juan Soto's surprising MLB callup. For us fantasy players, the question in the ensuing days was some form of "How confident should we be in this 19-year-old minor league star?" As in, should we pursue Soto hard with our FAAB budgets or high free-agent pool picks, or is the best-case here going to be, say, Austin Meadows (OF, PIT)? (Meadows, to save you the trouble, was called up just a few days earlier than Soto, had a similar 9D grade, is three-plus years older … and finished the year with a .287 BA and 6 HR over 178 AB. Not bad, but obviously not Soto level.)

Our suggestion here (again, 20/20 hindsight) is that the 2018 version of the book you hold in our hands could have helped you with your answer. You ultimately know your league, your own penchant for risk and your competitors' level of prospect savvy. But even only armed with the 2018 book, one could have come to the defendable conclusion that Juan Soto was a special player, a rare rookie that could serve as an in-season boost towards fantasy contention. And if you had the 2017 and/or the 2016 versions, you could have felt even more justified in gathering up that FAAB and putting it behind Soto. No owner who did this regretted it.

Is this year's Juan Soto in the pages that follow? In a literal sense, no—the conflux of talent, experience, skill set, age and (importantly) MLB opportunity was likely a one-time event. But in a more general sense of helping you identify the impactors from the imposters in your fantasy future?

Why, my friend, that's what the pages that follow are all about.

•

Long-time readers of the *Minor League Baseball Analyst* will no doubt recognize most of the elements of the pages that follow in this 14th Edition. For both new and old, let's quickly run through the features and structure.

The Insights section provides some narrative details and tools you can use as you prepare for getting the most out of your farm system and the rookies that will emerge during the 2019 baseball season. All the essays are designed to help you assemble your teams, as well as give you some food for thought on the prospect landscape. This year's topics include the catching conundrum; the top international players; reviews of the 2018 Arizona Fall League and the First Year Player Draft; and a preview of the 2019 college baseball season. If the past is any indication, no doubt many of these players mentioned in the essays will soon be fantasy cornerstones. For keeper leagues, the time to get on board is now.

Up next is the HQ100—our signature list of the top 100 fantasy baseball prospects for 2019. The HQ100 is a compilation of six individual lists (MLBA authors Chris Blessing, Rob Gordon, Alec Dopp, Brent Hershey, as well as BaseballHQ.com prospect-savvy writers Nick Richards and Matthew St-Germain). This list is ranked by overall fantasy value, in an attempt to balance raw skill level, level of polish/refinement, risk in terms of age/level, and overall potential impact value. And then Dopp suggests 10 more "Sleepers" just outside the HQ100, players who just missed in 2019 or who could make the jump to the list in 2020. Last year's column included the likes of Peter Alonso, Carter Kieboom and Jesus Luzardo, so it's worth paying attention to.

While the HQ100 is a collaborative exercise, the player profiles—including the skills grades, commentaries and player ratings—are the primary work of one analyst. Assignments are divided up by organization, so that our analysts get to know an MLB team's system from top to bottom. Our roster is the most diverse and talented that we've ever assembled. As for returnees there's Chris Blessing (responsible for ATL, MIA, CIN, SF, TAM, BAL, NYY, CHW, MIN, KC and SEA), Rob Gordon (CHC, STL, LA, COL and TOR), Alec Dopp (MIL, SD, ARI and OAK), and Brent Hershey (PHI, WAS and TEX). We had a stellar group of newcomers in 2019 that included Kimball Crossley (NYM, PIT, BOS), Emily Waldon (DET, LAA), Craig Goldstein (HOU), and Tanner Smith (CLE). Given our emphasis on seeing players in person—and the daunting task when the book covers 1000+ players—we did share information and insights with each other, tapping the strength of our team. In addition, each writer filled in the gaps with the various scouting and front-office contacts.

As noted at the beginning of the Batters and Pitchers sections, our Potential Ratings have two parts. The first is on upside, graded on a 10-1 scale, with 10 being Hall of Fame potential; 1 is minor league roster filler. A "5" (MLB reserve) is the lowest grade you'll find in the book, as these are the least likely players to have an impact on your fantasy team.

But potential and actualization are two different things, and the A-E letter grades attempt to assess the likelihood of reaching that potential. It's a proxy for risk, which may or may not include age, ability and/or willingness to improve, current grasp of fundamental skills (fastball command, strike zone judgement), experience, and success in the high minors, among other factors.

In the end, these Potential Ratings are carefully considered by the author, and there is no one "correct" grade. One can make the argument that in a sense, an 8B player can at the same time be a 9D—higher ceiling, but much less likely to reach it. It is up to the author to decide which rating will give the clearest picture of this prospect at this point in time. The most valuable information to fantasy players cannot be encapsulated in one rating, but in the combination of skills grades, statistics, biographical information and commentary that the MLBA provides.

Though the player profiles make up the bulk of the book, don't miss the tools that follow: the Major League Equivalencies; the Organization Grades; the Top Prospects by organization, by position, and by specific skills; the Top 75 prospects for 2019 only; an archive of our Top 100 lists; the glossary and a list of minor league affiliates. Whew … there's a lot of information in these pages.

But for now—if you have a suggestion to share, email us at support@baseballhq.com. Otherwise, grab a shovel and dig in. A better fantasy farm system awaits.

The State of the Prospect Catcher

by Chris Blessing

The quality of the MLB catcher pool is at an all-time low. In fact, it has rarely been good over the last decade.

BaseballHQ.com's own Ray Murphy tackled the subject of "Innovating Around the Catcher Pool", an essay first published at BaseballHQ.com during the summer of 2018 and then revised for the *2019 Baseball Forecaster*. He proposed altering the traditional 14-man active hitting roster by taking the second catcher slot and converting it into a second utility slot. His rationale is that only six catchers in 2018 were worth $5 or more; only one catcher eclipsed $10 in value. Murphy is correct; leagues should alter the traditional 14-man active hitting roster. However, some owners are resistant to change, which will cause others to be stuck competing in two-catcher formats. Fear not, help is on the way.

Catcher's Renaissance

At First Pitch Arizona 2018, Eric Longenhagen of FanGraphs coined the phrase "Catcher's Renaissance" when describing the current prospect catching pool. In that vein, one speaker suggested attendees "load up on catching prospects" due to the current catcher pool deficiencies outlined in Murphy's article. While it's easy to scroll down a prospect list and pick catchers based on rankings, it's better to look for markers of successful fantasy catchers. Unfortunately, the public doesn't have access to the Statcast/Trackman data for minor league players since the individual teams own their data. Still, owners can look for skills in the prospect catcher pool that are similar to the minor league skills of some of today's and yesteryear's most successful fantasy catchers. Doing so will help mitigate risk at an incredibly risky position.

Prospect List Risk

Every year, this publication includes a top 100 overall prospect list, the HQ100 (see page 17), and top prospect by position lists, which can be found starting on page 132. Looking at the HQ100 and other prominent media prospect lists from 2011-2015, the industry did a poor job identifying future fantasy contributors. Of the 11 catchers listed as either Stars, Regulars, or Mid-Level fantasy options in the 2019 Forecaster's Universal Draft Guide, only four of the nine catchers who qualified as a prospect between 2011-2015 appeared on the HQ100. The BaseballHQ Minors Team ranked 17 catchers during that time on the HQ100 and only four projected to be Mid-Level or better fantasy contributors in 2019.

We weren't the only ones who were wrong. Everyone had Travis d'Arnaud (injuries), Wil Myers (moved off position), Jesus Montero, Wilin Rosario, Christian Bethancourt, and others ranked highly. However, we were mostly missing catchers like J.T. Realmuto, Willson Contreras, and Salvador Perez until they were practically knocking on the door and ready to become MLB regulars. In other words, as an industry, we only elevated the Realmutos and Contrerases of the world until it was a near certainty they would produce in the big leagues.

Both Realmuto and Contreras were in my coverage area as prospects. While I projected Realmuto as a second-division starter during the 2013 and 2014 seasons, I never considered him for Top 100 inclusion. Contreras came close to making our 2016 HQ100. I liked him more than others, but he was mostly overshadowed by his Double-A teammate (and fellow catcher at the time) Kyle Schwarber.

Don't get me wrong, lists serve a great purpose for fantasy owners. We evaluators at BaseballHQ, like others, put a lot of thought behind our prospect rankings. It's a team effort where we try to eliminate each other's biases to come up with a comprehensive ranking of potential prospect skill sets. However, you're not buying this book just for the rankings. You purchased this book for the analysis, the skill grades, the sabermetric categories, and the player capsule commentaries in constructing your rosters. So let's dig in.

Parameters

I identified 40 catching prospects with a realistic chance at becoming a starting MLB catcher. I narrowed my analysis down by removing every catcher who has yet to make his full-season Class A debut. I wanted a significant sample size to compare future contributors to their past and present counterparts. The biggest names not included are Giants prospect Joey Bart and Dodgers prospect Diego Cartaya. This cut my list down to 28 catching prospects.

The next step was to comb the MLB catcher pool and research their minor league development, looking for attributes or skills that are the backbone of their MLB success. For instance, Yadier Molina, J.T. Realmuto, and Salvador Perez posted elite contact (ct%) at some point in their MiLB careers. I wanted to find current minor league catchers with elite ct% because my research of current MLB catchers, which mostly consisted of catchers who were prospects between 2011 and 2015, indicated ct% was the biggest marker for sustainable success.

My MLB research also looked for attributes not often seen in the catcher pool, like a catcher with a run tool or a catcher with a high walk rate (bb%). Through this research, I was able to identify 12 catchers I believe have a 50% or better probability to become mid-level fantasy contributors.

There are some big catching prospects omitted from this list, like Royals prospect M.J. Melendez. His Single-A ct% was 66% and his bb% was just better than average at 9%. While his potential dwarfs many other catchers, it's hard to project with 50% or more probability that his minor league skills will translate into a mid-level or better contributor.

Elite Skills

For the purposes of this exercise, three catchers carry elite skills: Dodgers prospect Keibert Ruiz (91% ct%), White Sox prospect Zack Collins (19% bb%), and Diamondbacks prospect Daulton Varsho (19 SB in 83 games last season).

Ruiz's skill is the most favorable for future reliability and is most comparable to Double-A versions of Salvador Perez (90% ct%) and Yadier Molina (88% ct%). It doesn't hurt that Ruiz is a premium defender, too. Given the current catcher pool and his ability on both sides of the ball, Ruiz is a Top 10 overall prospect in baseball. As a fantasy prospect, (SPOILER ALERT!) we have him ranked in the Top 30 in our 2019 HQ100.

Collins' skill set comparable players were harder to find, especially factoring in Collins' dismal 62% ct%. The closest comparable catcher I could find was Mike Napoli (68% ct%, 17% bb% in Double-A). The difference is, Collins' raw plus-plus power hasn't developed like Napoli's did (Napoli had 31 HR to Collins' 15 at the same level). This, plus a lacking defensive skill, omits Collins from the 50%-or-better probability list.

The comp people elicit with Varsho and his elite SB skill is Jason Kendall. Though Kendall stole 20+ bases in three consecutive MLB seasons, he wasn't the base-stealing threat Varsho has been in the minors. Kendall never came close to Varsho's 18-SB pace. Outside of being an SB threat, Varsho isn't very comparable to Kendall, with Kendall having an elite ct% (94%) and a better bb% (11%) at the same age and level. Still, Varsho, while factoring in his SB skill, is included on the 50%-or-better probability list because of his SB ability.

Can He Catch?

With the accuracy of defensive metrics improving, the question of "Can he catch?" becomes more and more important. However, MLB organizations value defensive metrics differently, which makes it more difficult to find common ground. Take the 2018 mid-season trade between Cleveland and San Diego. Cleveland made Francisco Mejia expendable because they place a high value on defensive metrics. Mejia is viewed as a complete butcher behind the plate by some around the game, including the Indians, who tried Mejia at multiple positions. San Diego, who acquired Mejia, pledged to keep him at the position. While San Diego may change their mind, they represent a franchise willing to trade off defense for greater offensive skill at catcher. Keep organizational philosophy in mind when looking to acquire a fantasy catcher.

Conclusions

Through my research, I found that catching prospects with an 80% ct% or higher have a greater chance of contributing in fantasy. In most cases, catchers—outside of Gary Sanchez and Mike Zunino—don't develop their power tool until they get to MLB. A great majority of the catchers have outhit their projected HR totals as big leaguers. While ct% has been a good future indicator of MLB production, some catchers, like Kevin Plawecki (88% ct% in Double-A), haven't quite worked out.

Keiburt Ruiz (91% ct%) and Cardinals prospect Andrew Knizner (86%) were the only catchers who produced a ct% greater than 85% in 2018. Blue Jays prospect Danny Jansen (84% ct% prior to MLB stint) was close and should probably be included in the elite ct% group because his 13% bb% is the third-highest bb% among the catchers researched. The two ahead of Jansen, Zack Collins and Orioles prospect Brett Cumberland, have low ct% without an additional carry tool like present HR power.

Below is a list of catchers who have a 50% or better chance of becoming mid-level or better fantasy contributors, ranked by 2018 ct%. Three catchers with a ct% below 80% were close enough with supporting skills to make the list:

Name	ct%	bb%	AB	XBH	SB	2018 Level
Keibert Ruiz, LA	91	6	377	26	0	AA
Andrew Knizner, STL	86	7	361	25	0	AA/AAA
Jose Trevino, TEX	85	6	192	11	0	AA/MLB
Danny Jansen, TOR	83	12	379	43	5	AAA/MLB
Ronaldo Hernandez, TAM	83	7	405	42	10	A
Luis Campusano, SD	83	7	260	14	0	A
Sean Murphy, OAK	81	9	270	37	3	R/AA/AAA
Raudy Read, WAS	81	6	197	16	0	AA/AAA
Ben Rortvedt, MIN	80	9	317	24	1	A/A+
Francisco Mejia, SD	79	6	483	51	0	AAA/MLB
Miguel Amaya, CHC	78	11	414	35	1	A
Daulton Varsho, ARI	77	9	316	29	19	R/A+

May your keeper/dynasty league teams "receive" at least one of these catchers in 2019.

Top 20 International Prospects for 2019

by Chris Blessing

Every July, Christmas comes to dynasty player pools everywhere with an influx of talented prospects from Latin America. As always, this year's class was made up of some incredibly raw, athletic players, including more Cuban players than we've seen before due to the relaxing of government regulations between Cuba and the United States. Of course, with an ever-changing political environment, this could be a one-year thing or the new normal. Listed below are international prospects who signed contracts during the international signing period in 2018.

Please note that some players eligible for this list have player boxes in this book. For the purposes of space, those players aren't profiled in this section. These prospects include Diego Cartaya (C, LA) and Richard Gallardo (RHP, CHC).

In alphabetical order:

Kevin Alcantara (OF, NYY) is a 6'5" speedster with long legs and a plus-plus run tool. Scouts dream on his long, lanky frame, which packs serious power potential. His right-handed swing is long, though Alcantara has a knack for hard contact and a surprisingly good contact rate despite his swing issues. Signed for $1 million, Alcantara is a natural in CF. His plus-plus speed and natural route-running ability push the glove tool toward plus levels, even though his height may someday force him off the position.

Francisco Alvarez (C, NYM) is a powerful, stocky (5'11", 220 lbs) catcher with an advanced hit tool and solid power potential. Signed for $2.7 million out of Venezuela, the Mets are betting his work ethic and surprising athletic ability will aid with defensive improvement, despite his size. At the plate, the right-handed hitting Alvarez has solid contact skills and the ability to spray the field with line drives. There's raw plus power in his frame, which is close to projection. Some scouts fear Alvarez will struggle with size issues as he gets older. The body isn't terrible, but it will need careful TLC. Defensively, his skills project out as below average. However, he's not limited laterally and doesn't stab at the ball. There's a chance he'll be more than passable behind the plate.

Starlyn Castillo (RHP, PHI) signed with the Phillies for $1.6 million despite not fitting the mold of the prototypical bonus baby prospect. The Dominican righty is under 6 feet tall and is filled out with good muscle definition. He's also one of the hardest throwers in the class, sitting in the low-to-mid 90s with his fastball. Castillo was up to 98 mph before signing with Philadelphia. He also has a good idea of how to spin the ball, featuring a sharp, two-plane slider. Castillo also has a feel for a change-up. While there are concerns about his height, he uses his delivery, especially his lower half, to generate velocity and lessen the stress he puts on his arm.

Jose De La Cruz (OF, DET) is a CF prospect who signed with the Tigers for 1.8 million. Scouts love his athleticism and power projection, they don't care so much for his swing mechanics. On the bright side, De La Cruz, a right-handed hitter, has plus bat speed and incorporates good leverage in his lower half. He struggles to get his hands firing from the load position and also struggles with pitch recognition. When he makes contact, he finds the barrel more times than not. There is plus power potential in the profile. Scouts are split on whether he sticks in CF, however, his arm and power should play in either corner OF position.

Sandy Gaston (RHP, TAM) is a hard-throwing Cuban RHP who signed with the Rays in the fall for $2.6 million. Gaston played at an advanced level at a very early age in Cuba, however, he struggled with control, posting an even K/BB ratio. Those concerns have not gone away, even as his fastball has ticked up. It sits in the mid-90s but has been clocked as high as 100 mph. Gaston is athletic with good size and room to grow muscle mass. He doesn't repeat his delivery well and puts significant stress on his upper half to generate velocity, despite achieving good extension. He also has a pronounced head whip, which prevents him from staying online with his delivery.

Antonio Gomez (C, NYY) is a budding defensive prospect with an incredible arm behind the plate. Signed by the Yankees for $600k, Gomez wowed scouts at the MLB International Showcase with his strong throwing arm, quick feet, and online throws. He's also an agile receiver with emerging receiving abilities. At the plate, the Venezuelan has been a late bloomer, as the right-handed hitting Gomez began to barrel velocity with a short, compact swing. His swing trajectory and frame could grow into above-average power potential. The glove will push the profile, but don't sleep on his offensive potential.

Juan Guerrero (SS, COL) is a toolsy infield prospect who signed with the Rockies for $650k out of the Dominican Republic. Guerrero's bat finds the barrel, even though his high leg kick and lower-half mechanics are rough looks. The exaggerated leg kick has proven to be a good timing mechanism and the lower-half mechanics create enough power to thump the ball. It will be interesting to see how the Rockies progress with his swing. Will they try to change his mechanics? One thing is for sure, the leg kick will likely be cut down before his pro debut. Defensively, scouts are split on Guerrero's long-term position. His hands rate out highly and he could end up at either 2B, 3B, or SS.

Alvin Guzman (OF, ARI) is an athletic specimen with room to grow into his frame. Signed by the Diamondbacks for $1.85 million, Guzman has a tool shed to dream on. There's above-average potential with all five tools, though his hit and power tools both lag way behind his defensive skill and running instincts. His right-handed swing is very uneven, as he tends to over-extend early, which causes his swing to go around the baseball. The hope is that under the organization's watchful eye, the athleticism will play up and Guzman's will be able to clean up his swing. The Diamondbacks are likely to bring him along slower than other July 2 studs.

Eduardo Lopez (OF, BOS) is the rare high-floor prospect on the international market. Signed by the Red Sox for $1.15 million, the switch-hitting Dominican OF showcased an advanced approach and swing in the run-up to signing day. Lopez has a smooth, compact swing from the LH side, peppering the gaps with line drives due to advanced barrel control. From the RH side, the swing is geared toward fly ball contact, which should aid in his over-the-fence abilities at maturity. Defensively, he lacks the top-flight speed of other international CF prospects featured in this article, which will likely cause Lopez to eventually move off the position. Luckily, his power potential and arm play in the corner OF.

Marco Luciano (SS/OF, SF) is the top Dominican prospect in this class, receiving a $2.6 million signing bonus. While his future position is up for debate, no one can deny the 17-year-old's desire to be the best he can be. The Giants love his makeup. A tireless worker, Luciano's body and ability is beyond his years. At the plate, the right-handed hitting Luciano is a line drive machine with big power potential. He has quick wrists and hands with a solid swing path, limiting swing-and-miss issues. A quick-twitch athlete, Luciano is only an average runner. While he possesses solid range at SS, most evaluators think his future is in the OF. The Giants are comfortable trying Luciano at SS until he outgrows the position.

Noelvi Marte (SS, SEA) has the potential to become a big power right-handed hitter. While his frame is still wiry, Marte possesses incredible strength, especially in his lower half. Signed for $1.55 million, the 17-year-old Dominican's swing is geared for fly-ball contact. The ball explodes with significant carry off his bat. Marte struggles to get his hands to the hitting zone, causing some swing-and-miss risk. However, with adjustments, there is enough bat speed in the profile to minimize the risk of getting beat in his kitchen. He's presently a below-average runner and could get slower. Defensively, Marte has an outside shot to stick at SS, but is likely a 3B long-term. With his ability and strength, Marte could be a middle-of-the-order bat at maturity.

Orelvis Martinez (SS, TOR) has already been comped to Adrian Beltre at the same age. Sure, a Beltre comp is a lofty expectation for a 17-year-old, however, the Blue Jays believe in Martinez, signing him to a $3.5 million signing bonus. As expected, the right-handed hitting Dominican has crazy power potential. From an open stance with a big leg kick, Martinez's swing trajectory is geared for fly balls. He has quick wrists and a short, compact swing, finding barrel more often than not. With a lot of moving parts in his swing and some noise in his load, there are concerns that Martinez's hit tool may be below average at maturity. The power plays regardless. Currently a SS, he'll likely move off the position to 3B as he adds bulk to his frame.

Victor Victor Mesa (OF, MIA) headlined this year's July 2 Caribbean class, which was considerably weaker than last year's class. The 22-year-old Mesa is an athletic OF prospect with bloodlines (Victor Mesa Sr. was a star in Cuba) who was signed in October for $5.25 million. A right-handed hitter, his bat is behind some of the more recent older Cuban prospects. While guys like Luis Robert have lightning quick bats, Mesa's hands aren't as loose and quick, which has led to concerns against premium velocity. His strength is his athletic ability, and his plus run tool should help him create havoc on the base paths. Victor Victor Mesa wasn't the only Mesa to sign with the Marlins. 17-year old Victor Mesa Jr. also signed with the club for $1 million.

Alejandro Pie (SS, TAM) is a glove-over-hit prospect coming out of the Dominican Republic. Scouts love his tall, lanky size and believe there is tons of physical projection left, which they hope turns into plus power at maturity. A right-handed hitter, Pie is extremely aggressive but has solid hand/eye coordination, which points towards a high contact rate. He also has a quick-twitch swing, even if the swing path needs some work. Signed for $1.4 million, the Rays believe Pie will stick at SS because of his smooth hands, athleticism, and natural instincts, even if his body completely fills out his 6'4" frame.

Jairo Pomares (OF, SF) was a year older (17) than most of the international prospects who signed this year. However, scouts love his athleticism, frame, and hit tool potential. A left-handed hitter, Pomares has one of the smoothest swings in the class. He has quick wrists and strong forearms, which create good bat speed. His bat path is consistent and he has advanced barrel control. The hope here is the power will develop in time, especially as the frame thickens up. Pomares' athleticism and foot speed give him a chance to start in CF at maturity.

Gabriel Rodriguez (SS, CLE) is the best non-catching prospect out of Venezuela this signing period, inking a $2.1 million bonus with the Indians. The 16-year-old right-handed hitter is an impactful player on both sides of the ball. Likely to stick at the SS long-term, Rodriguez has solid instincts and good footwork, enabling him to have solid range despite fringe-average speed. At the plate, Rodriguez has an innate ability to find the barrel. He has a good physique to add strength and could possess above-average

power at projection. Overall, he may be the best all-around prospect in the class with no single tool standing out above another.

Osiel Rodriguez (RHP, NYY) is a Cuban pitcher with an unorthodox delivery who signed with the Yankees for $600k. Rodriguez loves to vary his arm slot, a la Cuban legend Orlando "El Duque" Hernandez. He has good height and an athletic body, which should fill out nicely by projection. The delivery has some effort and violence towards the end of the pitch progression. Despite this, Rodriguez lives in the zone. His fastball sits in the low 90s and has been as high as 97 on the showcase circuit. His slider receives high marks, especially when he's able to vary his arm slot to manipulate the spin. His feel for mixing his repertoire of pitches and his sequencing give him a chance to move quicker than other Bonus Babies.

Junior Sanquintin (SS, CLE) brings an offensive-oriented game to a premium defensive position. Signed for $1.25 million out of the Dominican Republic, the switch-hitting Sanquintin likely fits best at 3B due to his lacking defensive ability at SS and his potential body mass at maturity. He has a quick bat from both sides of the plate with a consistent swing path compared to other teenage prospects. The belief among scouts is his body will fill out with lean muscle and his swing from both sides of the plate is geared towards maximizing loft, thus possibly providing for plus power at maturity. The hit tool will carry the rest of the profile early; his power development will carry the profile late in development.

Miguel Urbina's (OF, MIN) overall game is ahead of pretty much every other position player in this class. He is an instinctual player who has a track record of putting in the work to be successful in all phases of his game. Signed by the Twins for $2.75 million out of Venezuela, there are concerns about Urbina's inability to maintain a consistent swing path. Regardless, his right-handed bat has a knack for hard contact. Urbina's advanced spray approach signals high batting average potential, too. Power should develop as his frame bulks up, and as a plus runner, Urbina carries himself well on the bases and in CF.

Alexander Vargas (SS, NYY) is a switch-hitting Cuban SS who was a late entry to this year's international prospect list. Signed by the Yankees for $2.5 million, Vargas is a plus athlete who presents a potentially plus hit tool from the LH side, which is compact with advanced bat control. His hit tool lags a bit from the RH side with increased length compared to the LH swing. Defensively, he has good instincts at SS and soft hands. A plus runner, his SB instincts are advanced compared to the rest of the class. The run and glove tool may carry the profile.

Top 10 Prospects from the Arizona Fall League

For more than 25 years, the Arizona Fall League (AFL) has been a critical tool for scouts and evaluators to assess prospects at the end of the minor league season and heading into the Winter Meetings. As First Pitch Arizona attendees know, though, it can also be a valuable means for fantasy owners to gain a first-hand perspective on future contributors, as most of the participants are only a year or two away from getting their shot at the big leagues.

For this year's *Minor League Baseball Analyst's* coverage of the AFL, we turn to our friends at 2080Baseball.com. 2080 Baseball had evaluators in Phoenix for the entire AFL season, and they have compiled an ebook with scouting reports of participants in the Fall League. This is their Top 10 from the 2018 AFL, with a summary, strengths, weaknesses, MLB ceiling and risk level for each. Use these reports along with our player boxes as you prepare your fantasy rosters for 2019 and beyond.

The entire 2080 AFL ebook (featuring 50 players) can be downloaded for free at www.2080baseball.com/2019/01/2018aflebook/

1. Vladimir Guerrero, Jr. (3B, TOR)

Baseball's #1 prospect looked the part across 19 games with Surprise. Guerrero has the tools to be an impact bat who hits for plus average and power in the heart of a lineup. Surprisingly agile for his size with a cannon arm, he has the tools to remain at 3B early in his career. Regardless of the position, Guerrero's offensive ceiling makes him a potential all-star.
Strengths: Elite bat speed, strength, and bat-to-ball skill; mature approach; runs surprisingly well
Weaknesses: Thick lower half limits defensive range; likely moves off 3B as frame matures
MLB ceiling: All-Star
Risk: Moderate

2. Forrest Whitley (RHP, HOU)

Whitley missed most of 2018 between serving a suspension to start the year and a minor injury mid-season. Still regarded as one of the game's best pitching prospects entering Fall League, he cemented himself as the #1 arm in the minors with an excellent performance for Scottsdale. Whitley has the tools to become a frontline starter and can impact the big leagues soon.
Strengths: Imposing frame, numerous plus pitches, unhittable stuff when he's locating
Weaknesses: Still ironing out control; has injury red flags in his delivery
MLB ceiling: Frontline Starter
Risk: High

3. Keston Hiura (2B, MIL)

Hiura was named Arizona Fall League MVP after producing in the heart of Peoria's lineup throughout the season. He has the tools to hit for plus average and at least 16-20 HR power. Hiura

is quieting concerns about his ability to remain at 2B, showing rapidly improving defensive tools at the keystone. His bat can carry him to the big leagues at some point in 2019.
Strengths: Pure hitter, plus contact ability; mix of power and contact; improving glove at 2B
Weaknesses: Limited to 2B; power-focused approach comes with more swing-and-miss
MLB ceiling: Top 10 at Position/Occasional All-Star
Risk: Moderate

4. Cristian Pache (OF, ATL)

The most dynamic two-way player on this list, Pache is a true five-tool talent. An elite CF defender, he shows power potential at the plate with the chance for above-average offensive outputs for the position. There's star potential if he hits enough, and even if a streaky bat never fully produces at the level we're projecting, Pache's speed and defense still make him an asset.
Strengths: Excellent athlete, impacts on offense and defense; high-ceiling power/speed toolset
Weaknesses: Still raw at the plate, shows a youthful and swing-happy approach at times
MLB ceiling: Top 10 at Position/Occasional All-Star
Risk: High

5. Carter Kieboom (SS, WAS)

Washington picked Kieboom in the first round in 2016, and he has rocketed through the system since. Kieboom reached Double-A as a 20-year-old last year, then headed to the Fall League for some last-minute polishing. That speaks to how confident the organization is in his ability to contribute soon, possibly by early 2019. A well-rounded player who does a bit of everything, Kieboom profiles safely as a solid big league contributor.
Strengths: Mix of contact and power; chance to stay up the middle; well-rounded player
Weaknesses: Lacks one truly plus tool; might move off SS down the road but stay at 2B
MLB ceiling: Above-Average Player
Risk: Moderate

6. Peter Alonso (1B, NYM)

Alonso hit 36 home runs during the regular season, then established himself as the Fall League's most feared slugger as an encore. He's a masher of the first-degree, a 1B-only who only brings value with the bat. Alonso strikes out a lot (and always will), but his power is excellent and there's enough ability to draw walks to buoy the hit tool. He's ready to step into the middle of a major league lineup right now and has the ceiling of a 30 home run power producer.
Strengths: Excellent power potential, could hit 30+ HRs; patient approach, draws walks
Weaknesses: 1B-only defender, bat must carry profile; power will always come with strikeouts
MLB ceiling: Above-Average Player
Risk: Moderate

7. Taylor Trammell (OF, CIN)

Trammell's 2018 season was highlighted by being named the MVP of the Futures Game, though his stats in A-ball were a bit more pedestrian. His flashes of plus raw power didn't translate to game action during the regular season or Fall League. He has the speed for CF, but his routes and below-average arm make him a fringy fit there right now. With projection on the bat, Trammell could be an above-average contributor if he stays up the middle. If not, he'll finish closer to a regular in LF.

Strengths: Plus athlete with speed and power; patient approach at the plate; stolen base threat

Weaknesses: Power hasn't fully come into games; might be more of a LF than true CF

MLB ceiling: Above-Average Player

Risk: Moderate

8. Jazz Chisholm (SS, ARI)

Chisholm had a breakout regular season in 2018, mashing 25 home runs between two levels. He starred for Salt River in the Fall League, cementing himself as one of the better shortstop prospects in the minors. Chisholm projects as an above-average defensive SS, showing soft hands, good range, and a plus throwing arm. There's more pop in his bat than you're expecting, giving him enticing offensive upside for a center-diamond player if he's able to tone down an over-aggressive approach.

Strengths: Plus athlete, will stick at SS; above-average offensive upside for the position

Weaknesses: Youthful approach, toning down over-aggressiveness at the plate

MLB ceiling: Top 10 at Position/Occasional All-Star

Risk: Extreme

9. Jon Duplantier (RHP, ARI)

Staying healthy has been a struggle for Duplantier, who missed two months in 2018 and came to Fall League to get work in. He was excellent when healthy last season, looking similarly dominant at times this fall for Salt River. He's close to big league ready, and a plus fastball and slider (part of a workable four-pitch mix) give the ceiling of a mid-rotation starter down the road. Duplantier's lengthy injury history and durability concerns are behind the extreme risk tag.

Strengths: Heavy fastball, nasty slider; has weapons to miss bats; flashes three above-average pitches

Weaknesses: Track record of injuries, effort in delivery; change-up still developing

MLB ceiling: Mid-Rotation Starter

Risk: Extreme

10. Luis Robert (OF, CHW)

Signed for a whopping $26M amateur bonus from Cuba, Robert continually battled injuries during his first full pro season in 2018. He suited up for Glendale this fall to make up for lost time, flashing tantalizing tools paired with plenty of present rawness at the plate. Robert has true five-tool potential, with speed and power in a physical frame. His pitch recognition and ability to control the zone have a long way to go. Robert's unrefined offensive game is the largest threat to him not reaching what's otherwise a very lofty ceiling.

Strengths: Excellent athlete, five tool upside; light tower raw power; can remain in CF long-term

Weaknesses: Limited present instincts on both sides of the ball; expands the zone, whiffs often

MLB ceiling: Top 10 at Position/Occasional All-Star

Risk: Extreme

2018 First-Year Player Draft Recap

by Chris Blessing (AL) and Rob Gordon (NL)

AMERICAN LEAGUE

BALTIMORE ORIOLES

For the second season in a row, the Orioles grabbed a prep pitcher with their first selection. Texas prep RHP Grayson Rodriguez (1) is one of the highest upside pitchers in this draft class with a devastating fastball and projectable secondaries. In the CBA round, Baltimore reached for a defensive-oriented SS in Oregon State's Cadyn Grenier (S-1), followed by drafting two pitchers, University of Arkansas RHP Blaine Knight (3) and Kentucky prep LHP Drew Rom (4). University of Iowa OF Robert Neustrom (5), represents the power potential play that Baltimore seemingly targets in the first few rounds in every draft. Otherwise, the organization targeted signable players with limited upside.

Sleeper: University of North Carolina C Cody Roberts (11) brings a fantastic defensive profile and a plus-plus arm. Roberts adjusted well enough to pro ball to assume there may be some offensive skill in his profile.

Grade: C

BOSTON RED SOX

The Red Sox targeted 17-year-old Triston Casas (1), a Florida prep star with significant upside. Boston then took a chance on a Northeast kid, selecting New Jersey prep OF Nick Decker (2), who represents a power bat with some hit tool concerns. TCU RHP Durbin Feltman (3) is undersized, but projects with two potentially plus pitches. Because of his size, Feltman likely profiles best in the bullpen. Boston snagged two catchers in the next few rounds, University of Kentucky's Kole Cottam (4) and St Thomas Elih Marrero (8), son of former MLB catcher Eli Marrero. Boston also shelled out a $565k bonus for Ohio prep 3B Nicholas Northcut (11), signing him out of a commitment to Vanderbilt.

Sleeper: RHP Chris Machamer (16) was the closer at University of Kentucky, and Boston believes Machamer has the stuff, the physique, and the command to start.

Grade: C

CHICAGO WHITE SOX

Contact issues have plagued recent White Sox drafts. This year, they plucked the best hit tool in the entire draft with Oregon State SS Nick Madrigal (1) at fourth overall. He also did well in his pro debut and could start 2019 in Double-A. Then the Sox targeted Oklahoma OF Steele Walker (2), who's had significant success in wood bat leagues. Mississippi State RHP Konnor Pilkington (3) offers three solid pitches from an innings-eating physical frame. In the fifth round, Chicago targeted a command/control type with Indiana RHP Jonathan Stiever.

Sleeper: Several candidates, but Michigan prep 3B Bryce Bush (33) may be the best of the sleeper bunch. He has quick hands and finds plenty of barrels, but there is concern how he will he do against advanced competition.

Grade: B

CLEVELAND INDIANS

The Indians hit the prep ranks hard early: Canadian C Bo Naylor (1) is the brother of Padres prospect Josh Naylor, and a power hitter with a solid chance to stick behind the plate. Then in the compensation round, they took Georgia Prep RHP Ethan Hankins (S-1), who had 1.1 potential entering the spring, followed by New York prep LHP Lenny Torres (CB-1), who had a spectacular pro debut in Arizona flashing three plus pitches. Cleveland targeted undersized Southern Mississippi RHP Nick Sandlin (2), banking on analytical data that suggests Sandlin will pitch well in pro ball. The Indians also shelled out a second-round signing bonus to Raynal Delgado (6). A Florida prep switch-hitting IF, Delgado is an advanced high school bat without a defensive home.

Sleeper: Korey Holland (14) was viewed to be a hard sign out of Langham Creek HS in Texas. The CF prospect fits Cleveland's profile of targeting premium athletes up the middle.

Grade: B

DETROIT TIGERS

Sitting at 1.1, the Tigers toyed a bit with picking someone other than Auburn RHP Casey Mize, but cashed in and took the best arm in the draft, despite some physical risks. Detroit stayed in the Southeast next, selecting Georgia prep OF Parker Meadows (2), brother of Rays OF Austin Meadows, despite some hit tool concerns. Continuing the theme of bloodline players, Detroit selected 2B Kody Clemens (3) out of Texas. OF Kingston Liniak (5) is an extremely toolsy, unrefined California prep player with a frame to dream on. Louisville LHP Adam Wolf (6) is a high-floor play with limited upside.

Sleeper: Detroit failed to sign some of their late round picks, but Maddux Conger (22) is a RHP out of Vanderbilt who could be a hard-thrower out of the pen. Conger's fastball is difficult to elevate, and his slider has two-plane, swing-and-miss potential.

Grade: A-

HOUSTON ASTROS

In the first year running the draft with a limited scout presence, relying heavily on scouting analysts in Houston to filter through analytical data and video, the Astros took an analytically-pleasing hitter with their first-round selection. All Clemson OF Seth Beer (1) does is hit. The Astros are banking on Beer's power potential pushing the profile since he lacks a defensive home. Then they reached for Washington Prep RHP Jayson Schroeder (2), who has a chance at three above-average-or-better pitches from a physically mature frame. Houston then targeted two position players: Jeremy Pina (3) from University of Maine-Orono profiles as a plus defender at SS, though some scouts don't believe he will hit enough to profile as a starter. Alex McKenna (4) from Cal Poly-San Luis Obispo has a terrific approach and high ct% potential. Houston's fifth-round pick, Cody Deason, was Arizona's Friday starter but will likely work best in a RP role.

Sleeper: Jonathan Bermudez (23) may be one of their higher upside day-three college picks. An NAIA standout LHP at Southeastern University, Bermudez has a solid command/control, playing up average overall stuff.

Grade: C+

KANSAS CITY ROYALS

With six picks in the top 100, the Royals revamped their depleted farm system by targeting several collegiate pitchers. Florida RHP Brady Singer (1) fell to them at 19th overall. Then they targeted another Florida RHP, Jackson Kowar (S-1), and a Virginia LHP Daniel Lynch (S-1), with back-to-back picks in the compensation round. Lynch may be the best of the bunch with advanced control of three above-average or better pitches. In the CBA round, Kansas City targeted another LHP, Stanford's Kris Bubic (CB-1), who profiles as a solid back-of-the-rotation starter. They reached for Memphis RHP Mark Bowlan (2), which enabled them to go over slot to sign Singer and other players further down in the draft. Kyle Isbel (3) was second-round value in the third round.

Sleeper: San Jacinto JC LHP Rylan Kaufman (12) signed for second-round money after a velocity jump during the spring. Tall and lean, the Royals are banking on Kaufman adding strength and velocity to his fastball.

Grade: A

LOS ANGELES ANGELS

The Angels continued aggressively targeting prep players at the top of the draft, picking up some of the draft's best athletes with their first two picks. OF Jordyn Adams (1) was committed to play football at UNC before signing with the Angels. The team stayed in the Southeast with their next pick, selecting Alabama prep SS Jeremiah Jackson (2). Hard-throwing Texas A&M-Corpus Christi RHP Aaron Hernandez (3) signaled the start of a pitching run; it wasn't until the 14th round before the Angels selected another position player. They handed out a second-round signing bonus to Michigan Prep RHP William English (5). To sign Adams, English, and others later in the draft, Los Angeles went severely under slot in rounds six through ten.

Sleeper: The Angels handed out a fifth-round signing bonus to sign away Iowa prep RHP Connor Van Scoyoc (11) from his Arizona State commitment. The Angels are banking on Van Scoyoc adding velocity to his heavy fastball.

Grade: C

MINNESOTA TWINS

With only two picks in the top 100, the Twins targeted two collegiate hitters they hope can move quickly through their system. They selected high-floor Oregon State OF Trevor Larnach (1), and hope he can help the parent club sometime during the 2020 season. Then the team targeted C Ryan Jeffers (2) out of UNC-Wilmington, banking on his power potential and presence behind the plate. Saving close to a million dollars going under slot for those two, the Twins went over slot on several other players, such as Utah OF DaShawn Keirsey (4), Florida State RHP Cole Sands (5), and New York prep SS Charles Mack (6), which made up for the lack of talent missing out on a third-round pick.

Sleeper: 2B Michael Helman (11) flew under the radar when he won the NJCAA Player of the Year at Hutchinson JC before transferring to Texas A&. Helman tore the cover off the ball in his pro debut, just as he had done at Hutchinson and Texas A&M.

Grade: B-

NEW YORK YANKEES

With the state of catching in baseball, the Yankees targeted backstops with their first two picks. They chose ambidextrous Georgia prep C Anthony Seigler (1) and followed him up with McLennan CC C Josh Breaux (2). Seigler is seen as the better athlete while Breaux projects as the better power prospect. New York then got a steal with Tennessee prep OF Ryder Green (3), who was considered one of the best power prep bats in the draft. To close out the first 10 rounds, the Yankees selected several pitching prospects, including RHP Frank German (4) from the University of North Florida and RHP Rodney Hutchinson (6) of UNC.

Sleeper: RHP Tanner Myatt (11) was plucked out of Florence-Darlington Tech (SC), has great size (6'7") and sits in the mid-90s with a heavy FB. He struggles with control and likely works best in the pen, but his delivery and velocity give hitters fits.

Grade: C

OAKLAND ATHLETICS

Oakland shook the fabric of the draft by selecting Oklahoma OF Kyler Murray ninth overall. Murray, the Heisman-Trophy-winning QB, says he will forgo his football career to concentrate on baseball. The Athletics targeted two collegiate position players who were teammates on the same travel ball team in high school with their next two picks. Dallas Baptist OF Jameson Hannah (2), and Missouri State SS Jeremy Eierman (CB-2) were all over-slot grabs. Louisiana-Lafayette LHP Hogan Harris (3) was the first pitcher the A's selected. Harris took a step forward this spring, adding velocity and tightening up his 11-to-5 curveball. Oakland hopes Arizona 1B Alfonso Rivas (4) can develop his power stroke as a professional. Ole Miss RHP Brady Feigl (5) has good size and four pitches to attack hitters with.

Sleeper: OF Alonzo Jones (25) struggled with injury and poor production throughout his college career. However, Jones was one of baseball's toolsiest prospects at Columbus HS in Georgia.

Grade: A-

SEATTLE MARINERS

As the Mariners continue to revamp their scouting department and farm system, they hit the college ranks hard in the draft: 18 of their first 20 picks were collegians. Stetson RHP Logan Gilbert (1) instantly became the organization's top homegrown pitching prospect. The Mariners reached a bit in Rounds 2 through 4, targeting higher floor prospects. Louisville OF Josh Stowers (2) is a solid hitter with the potential of becoming a solid regular. Florida State C Cal Raleigh (3) projects as a bat-first catcher. Missouri LHP Michael Plassmeyer (4) was traded to Tampa in the Mike Zunino deal. A few pro scouts identified Plassmeyer as the Mariners second-best pitching prospect prior to the trade. Illinois RHP Joey Gerber (8) could move quickly as a RP-only prospect with two potentially plus pitches.

Sleeper: The Mariners only signed two prep players, both pitchers. Damon Casetta-Stubbs (11) signed for fifth-round money out of Kings Way Christian School in Vancouver, Washington. Casetta-Stubbs struggled in his pro debut, but has ideal size and projection for the Mariners to gamble on.

Grade: B

TAMPA BAY RAYS

With six of the first 100 picks in the draft, the Rays were able to load up on some high-upside plays. Arizona prep LHP Matthew Liberatore (1) was a consensus Top 10 pick who fell to the Rays at #16 overall. Then they selected South Florida LHP Shane McClanahan (S-1) and Indiana prep OF Nick Schnell (S-1) with consecutive picks to open the compensation round. Then the Rays targeted high-floor MIF Tyler Frank (2) out of Florida Atlantic, and a year after drafting two-way player Brendan McKay, the Rays took another two-way player, Cal-Berkley's Tanner Dodson (CB-2). Dodson is a pure CF who could move quickly as an RHP out of the pen. The Rays also dished out a big bonus to Georgia Prep RHP Taj Bradley (5) who saw his velocity tick up significantly in his senior season.

Sleeper: University of Portland's Beau Brundage (33) has grown up around the game since his father is a minor league manager. Although he didn't show it in his pro debut, Brundage has a solid hit tool and is a plus runner.

Grade: A+

TEXAS RANGERS

The Rangers attacked the preps heavily in the first five rounds of the draft. Texas targeted one of the biggest pop-up names of the spring, California prep RHP Cole Winn (1). Winn projects as a mid-rotation starter with three potentially quality pitches. Owen White (2) was plucked out of the North Carolina prep ranks. A RHP, White could have four pitches at projection. Then they selected Arizona prep SS Jonathan Ornelas (3) and bought him out of a strong commitment to Tennessee. Texas prep RHP Mason Englert (4) signed for a second-round signing bonus. Englert's athleticism pushes his pitching profile. The Rangers went back to the prep ranks by selecting undersized SS Jayce Easley (5).

Sleeper: LHP Destin Dotson (12) signed for fifth-round money. Expected to honor his commitment to Tulane, the Rangers took a chance by selecting the tall LHP with physical projection and a heavy fastball without assurances he would sign.

Grade: B+

TORONTO BLUE JAYS

Toronto reached a bit in the first round to get a Texas prep player they really liked and to save money for later in the draft. 3B Jordan Groshans (1) has a solid hit tool. The Blue Jays hope he adds muscle mass to his frame and hits for big power. In the third round, Toronto picked Groshans' high school teammate, RHP Adam Kloffenstein. Kloffenstein's size and heavy sinker make him an attractive starting option. Sandwiched between the two high school picks was Duke OF Griffin Conine (2), son of Jeff Conine, who has an advanced power bat. The Jays expect former TCU reliever-turned-starter Sean Wymer (4) to develop back into a starting pitcher.

Sleeper: The Blue Jays plucked 10th round pick OF Cal Stevenson out of Arizona as a senior sign. Stevenson knocked the snot out of the ball in the Appy League while also displaying an advanced approach and SB potential. He may have been the league's most promising senior sign.

Grade: B

NATIONAL LEAGUE

ARIZONA DIAMONDBACKS

The Diamondbacks selected California prep SS Matt McLain with the 25th overall pick. Ultimately, McLain and his agent Scott Boras were unable to come to terms and instead McLain enrolled at UCLA. The club landed two athletic OF with their competitive balance agreement (CBA) picks: Jake McCarthy and high school OF Alek Thomas (2). The Snakes then went college-pitching heavy in Rounds 3-7, landing RHP Jackson Goddard (3), RHP Ryan Weiss (4), RHP Matt Mercer (5), RHP Ryan Miller, and RHP Travis Moths (7). Mercer had the most impressive debut, posting a 3.10 ERA with 38 K/7 BB in 29 IP between rookie and short-season ball and has a plus 92-94 FB that tops out at 97 mph.

Sleeper: SS Blaze Alexander (11) turned down a scholarship to SEC powerhouse South Carolina, agreeing to an above-slot $500,000 instead. Alexander has a plus arm and all-around skills and should head to full-season ball as a teenager in 2019.

Grade: C

ATLANTA BRAVES

The Braves took a chance on high school hurler Carter Stewart at #8 overall, but his physical showed ligament issues in his right wrist and the two sides were not able to reach an agreement. The Braves did manage to sign their next two picks: 1B Greyson Jenista (2) and RHP Tristan Beck (4). Beck, a three-year starter at Stanford, signed for an over-slot $900,000 and has a solid three-pitch mix, highlighted by a plus swing-and-miss change-up. The Braves lost their third-round pick as a penalty for violating MLB signing rules for international players. In total, the Braves landed only four top 200 prospects and spent just $3.3 million of their $8.3 million allotted budget. This draft has to be considered a huge bust.

Sleeper: C.J. Alexander 3B (20) has plus power and transferred from Bowling Green to State JC of Florida, where he hit .405/.488/.785 with 15 HR. At 6'5", 215 he will have to work hard to stick at 3B, but he has a nice bat.

Grade: D

CHICAGO CUBS

The Cubs have taken just five prep picks in Rounds 1-5 since 2014, coveting versatile offensive-minded players like Stanford SS Nico Horner (1). Hoerner has a profile similar to Ian Happ and fared well in his pro debut before injuring his left elbow. The Cubs had three second-round picks and landed two prep OFs in Brennen Davis and Cole Roederer, and also added San Diego RHP Paul Richan (2-C) and Duke OF Jimmy Heron (3). Richan isn't overpowering, but has a solid four-pitch mix and posted a 2.12 ERA with 31 K/5 BB in 29.2 IP in short-season ball. Overall, this was a solid if unspectacular haul for a system thin on elite-level talent.

Sleeper: Riley Thompson RHP (11) was drafted twice previously before finally signing with the Cubs. He comes after hitters with two plus offerings, highlighted by a mid-90s heater and knee-buckling power curve.

Grade: B

CINCINNATI REDS

The Reds used the fifth overall pick to land Florida standout 3B Jonathan India. India struggled to make consistent contact in his pro debut, but has the tools and plate discipline to hit for power and average. The Reds went over-slot for second-rounder RHP Lyon Richardson, then added Le Moyne College RHP Josiah Gray (CB-2) and University of Illinois OF Bren Spillane (3) before going over slot again to add prep OF Mike Siani (4). Richardson struggled in his debut, but has a plus mid-90s fastball. Siani played on the USA 18U team and was considered a possible late first-round pick, and the team bought him out of a commitment to the University of Virginia. The Reds went under slot in Rounds 5-10, but ended up with five potential impact players and a nice balance of hitting and pitching.

Sleeper: Michael Byrne RHP (13) was the closer for the Florida Gators in 2018. Byrne has a solid 90-92 mph fastball and gets swing-and-misses with his plus slider.

Grade: A-

COLORADO ROCKIES

The Rockies drafted Ole Miss LHP Ryan Rolison at #22 overall. The 21-year-old Rolison doesn't blow hitters away, but pounds the strike zone with a four-pitch mix and impressed in his debut. The Rockies went over slot to add prep 1B Grant Lavigne (CB-1), who at 6'4" 220, had some of the best raw power in the high school ranks. Then the team added Texas A&M RHP Mitchell Kilkenny (2) and Minnesota SS Terrin Vavra, who hit well in short-season ball (.302/.396/.467), and found a mid-round gem in Niko Decolati (6). While this draft class lacks a clear stud, the organization added eight top 200 prospects (three of whom cracked the Rockies top 15) with a nice mix of hitting and pitching, and helped replenish a deep farm system.

Sleeper: RHP Shelby Lackey (18) was a redshirt sophomore at Pacific University who earned All-West Coast Conference honors in 2018, going 6-3 with a 3.48 ERA. His best weapon is an above-average fastball that hits 97 mph in relief.

Grade: A-

LOS ANGELES DODGERS

The Dodgers have a fairly enviable track record of finding quality prospects, and their selection of high school RHP J.T. Ginn could have been another gem. Unfortunately, the team and Ginn were not able to reach an agreement and Ginn opted to head to Mississippi State. The Dodgers were able to sign the rest of their bonus-round picks. That group was highlighted by West Virginia RHP Michael Grove (2), Hofstra LHP John Rooney (3), and high school RHP Braydon Fisher (4). The 22-year-old Grove had Tommy John surgery at the beginning of 2018, but has a plus fastball that sits at 92-96 when healthy. Rooney doesn't have overpowering stuff, but does have a good three-pitch mix. Fisher has good size and some projection left and already works in the low-90s. The loss of Ginn makes the Dodgers' draft class underwhelming.

Sleeper: Niko Hulsizer 1B (18) has plus raw power and smashed 44 home runs in his three years at Morehead State. Hulsizer also has above-average speed but an overly aggressive approach at the plate.

Grade: D

MIAMI MARLINS

The Marlins entered the draft with one of the weaker farm systems in baseball and went the high school route with their first three picks. With the 13th pick, the Marlins added OF Connor Scott who was considered one of the more athletic players in the draft with top-of-the-scale speed, a plus OF arm, and a lean, projectable 6'4", 180 frame. Then they added prep SS Osiris Johnson (2) and C Will Banfield (CB-2), before taking University of Kentucky OF Tristan Pompey (3). Johnson, has plus raw tools and started well in rookie ball (.301/.333/.447). The Marlins went more than double over slot to land Banfield, who was regarded as the best defensive backstop in the draft class. Pompey had the best pro debut, hitting .299/.408/.397 with 32 BB and 10 SB and finished the year at High-A.

Sleeper: Davis Bradshaw OF (11) showed enough in one year of community college ball to get noticed by the Marlins. The 19-year-old Bradshaw has plus-plus speed and showed well in his debut, hitting a combined .354/.418/.427 with 10 BB/13 K and 15 SB.

Grade: B+

MILWAUKEE BREWERS

The Brewers have done a nice job building from within and that continued in 2018. The Crew landed prep SS Brice Turang with the 21st pick and went above slot to get the job done. The 19-year-old Turang does everything well with a quick LH stroke, plus speed, and an advanced approach at the plate. The Brewers went with position players for their next two picks, adding high school OF Joe Gray (2) and Micah Bellow (CBA). The Brewers took pitchers in Rounds 4-6, adding LHP Aaron Ashby (4), RHP Justin Jarvis (5) and Oregon State RHP Drew Rasmussen (6). Gray is a raw, toolsy player with tremendous upside but needs to figure out how to make consistent contact to reach his potential. Ashby struggled initially, but was lights out when moved up to Low-A Wisconsin, thanks in part to a plus curveball. Gray and Turang are years away from the majors, but have the potential to be top 100 prospects.

Sleeper: Clayton Andrews RHP (17) has a plus change-up and was unhittable in his debut, going 6-1 with a 2.18 ERA, 54 K/7 BB, and a .198 BAA in 33 IP.

Grade: B+

NEW YORK METS

The Mets had the sixth pick in the draft and opted to take high school OF Jarred Kelenic. The 19-year-old has an advanced approach at the plate and projects to hit for average and power and is a legit five-tool player, though he may shift to a corner slot as he matures. In the winter, he was shipped to the Mariners as the key piece of the Robinson Cano and Edwin Diaz deal. The Mets then took RHP Simeon Woods-Richardson (2), before landing University of South Carolina standouts 2B Carlos Cortes (3) and RHP Adam Hill (4; traded to Milwaukee in Keon Broxton trade), and Clemson RHP Ryley Gilliam (5). The trade of Kelenic robs this class of its star power.

Sleeper: Ross Adolph OF (12) was a standout at the University of Toledo and has solid offensive upside, hitting .276/.348/.509 with 9 doubles, 12 triples, 7 home runs, and 14 SB in short-season ball and projects as a possible 4th OF.

Grade: A-

PHILADELPHIA PHILLIES

The Phillies had the third pick and opted for Wichita State 3B Alec Bohm. The 22-year-old Bohm has the tools to hit for power and average. The Phillies were able to sign Bohm for $1.1 million under slot and used the extra money to go over slot with high school SS Logan Simmons (6) and prep RHP Dominic Pipkin (9). At 6'4" 160, Pipkin has a lean projectable frame and already has a plus 92-94 mph fastball that tops out at 96. The Phillies didn't have second or third round picks, but then added Cal State Fullerton RHP Colton Eastman (4) and Notre Dame OF Matt Vierling (5). Bohm is the only impact player in this draft class and will need to work hard to stick at 3B. Overall, this was a relatively thin haul.

Sleeper: James McArthur RHP (12) has a huge (6'7") frame and proved durable in three years at Mississippi. His fastball sits at 92-94 and he had an impressive debut, going 2-0 with a 0.54 ERA and 35 K/11 BB in 33.1 IP across three levels.

Grade: C-

PITTSBURGH PIRATES

The Pirates had the 10th pick and landed University of South Alabama OF Travis Swaggerty. The 21-year-old was a three-year starter for the Jaguars, where he hit .319/.457/.504 with 27 HR, 48 SB, and more walks than strikeouts. The club picked high school LHPs Gunnar Hoglund (CB-1) and Braxton Ashcraft (2) with their next two picks, but were unable to sign Hoglund, who instead opted to enroll at Mississippi. Ashcroft has a solid three-pitch mix and profiles as a viable mid-rotation lefty. The Bucs then added collegiate players with their next eight picks, highlighted by Vanderbilt SS Connor Kaiser (3), Cal RHP Aaron Shortridge (4), Arkansas backstop Grant Koch (5), Arizona RHP Michael Flynn (6), and North Carolina State OF Brett Kinneman (7). The inability to sign Hoglund away from Mississippi means Swaggerty is the only player from the 2018 draft to crack the Pirates top 15.

Sleeper: Jonah Davis (15) has plus raw power and hit .321/.446/.606 as a junior for the Cal Bears. Davis has a complicated swing that led to a 75% contact rate in his debut, but he was still able to slash .306/.398/.612 with 15 doubles and 12 HR in 206 rookie ball AB.

Grade: B-

SAN DIEGO PADRES

The Padres added to one of the deepest and most talented farm systems in baseball by nabbing high school LHP Ryan Weathers with the seventh pick. Weathers already has three above-average offerings, highlighted by a good 90-93 mph fastball that holds its plane through the zone. The Padres used two compensation round picks on high school SS Xavier Edwards and Texas Tech OF Grant Little. The Padres went well over slot to land Edwards, who is a dynamic player with double-plus speed and an advanced approach at the plate. They also added Illinois State SS Owen Miller (3), Missouri State RHP Dylan Coleman (4), and East Carolina OF Dwanya Williams-Sutton (5). Miller hit .336/.386/.460 in his debut and should be able to stick at short.

Sleeper: Nick Thwaits RHP (15) agreed to an over-slot bonus of $450,000 instead of going to college at Kent State. The 6'2" Ohio native has a good 91-93 mph and an above-average breaking ball, but his change-up needs work.

Grade: A-

SAN FRANCISCO GIANTS

The Giants had the second pick and wasted little time in selecting Georgia Tech backstop Joey Bart. The 21-year-old Bart led the ACC in hitting in 2018 and impressed in his pro debut, hitting .294/.364/.588 at two rookie league stops and is a plus defender behind the plate. The Giants signed Bart for an under-slot $7 million, allowing them to go above slot to land their second round pick, RHP Sean Hjelle, who has a solid four-pitch mix and at 6'11" is one of the tallest players in MLB history. The club also went over slot on their next three picks RHP Blake Rivera (4), RHP Keaton Win (5), and OF Patrick Hilson (6), who has 70-grade speed and a plus OF arm. Overall, this was an excellent haul for the retooling Giants.

Sleeper: Sean Roby 3B (12) is an offensive-minded 3B from the JuCo circuit in Arizona. The 19-year-old has an aggressive approach at the plate, but slashed .288/.360/.442 with 5 HR in his pro debut and has some interesting upside.

Grade: A

ST. LOUIS CARDINALS

Few teams can match the success the Cardinals have had in acquiring MLB talent via the draft, and they look to have hit the jackpot again, landing prep 3B Nolan Gorman with the 19th pick. Gorman had the best raw power in the draft, and hit .291/.380/.570 with 17 HR in 237 AB between rookie ball and Low-A. After Gorman, the Cardinals added Wake Forest RHP Griffin Roberts (CB-1) and TCU 1B Luken Baker. Baker has a huge frame and hit .319/.386/.460 with 22 HR in 163 AB, while Roberts has a plus slider and a 90-95 mph fastball. The Cardinals took only one other high school player until Round 22—SS Mateo Gill (3). Gill is a plus defender, but has questions about his ability to hit for power or average. Texas Tech LHP Steven Gingery has a plus change-up, a good three-pitch mix, and profiles as a possible back-end starter.

Sleeper: Justin Toerner OF (28) had a solid collegiate career at Cal State Northridge, but did nothing to suggest he was worthy of an early-round pick. The 21-year-old Toerner tore through three levels, compiling a line of .312/.410/.385.

Grade: A

WASHINGTON NATIONALS

The Nationals didn't have a pick until near the end of the first round, when they added high school RHP Mason Denaburg with the 27th pick. Denaburg has an above-average to plus 90-94 mph fastball that tops out at 97 and a curve ball that flashes above average. The Nats then went to college and didn't take another prep player until Round 33. Connecticut LHP Time Cate (2), Vanderbilt RHP Reid Schaller (3), Oklahoma RHP Jake Irvin (4), and Arizona State OF Gage Canning (5) were all pre-draft top 200 prospects and add much-needed organizational depth. Irvin had the best pro debut, going 1-0 with a 1.74 ERA in 20.2 IP. Canning hit well in rookie ball, but struggled when moved up to Low-A Hagerstown.

Sleeper: Pablo O'Connor (27) has above-average power and was a beast at D-2 Azusa Pacific, slashing .337/.455/.691 with 17 HR in just 48 games. His aggressive approach results in significant contact issues, however.

Grade: C

College Players to Watch in 2019

by Chris Lee

Here's our list of 2019 draft-eligible college players who project as top MLB fantasy prospects heading into the 2019 season, which begins the weekend of Feb. 15-17 and ends with the College World Series (June 15-27).

It's the weakest crop of college arms we've seen in years. As for the bats, Vaughn and Rutchman have big upside with high floors, followed by a list of players tough to order.

All stats are from the 2018 college season unless noted.

1. Andrew Vaughn, 1B — *California, R/R, 5-11, 214*
Vaughn was the 2017 Pac 12 Freshman of the Year, then the nation's Golden Spikes Award winner in 2018. The top hitter in the draft, Vaughn combined elite ct% (91%) and Eye (2.40), using the whole field to hit .402/.531/.812 with 23 HR in 199 ABs, followed by 5 HR in 52 Cape Cod League ABs. A mediocre summer for Team USA didn't concern scouts. He won't run, but could hit .300 with 30-plus homers and triple-digit RBIs in MLB.

2. Adley Rutchman, C — *Oregon St., S/R, 6-2, 216*
Rutchman was MVP of the 2018 College World Series. He's a a polished switch-hitter (.408/.505/.628, 1.30 Eye) with gap power and some pop (9 HR in 250 ABs). Catchers are high-risk fantasy investments, especially this far out, but Rutchman's advanced hitting and receiving skills, plus his athleticism—he was OSU football's kickoff man as a freshman—could vault him to 1.1 in the draft. He could easily project as a .280 hitter with 20 HR.

3. Kameron Misner, OF — *Missouri, L/L, 6-4, 219*
Misner draws above-average scouting grades across the board, combining a good approach (20 bb%,) with 60-grade speed and big raw power. He missed the second half of conference play with a broken foot, and his swing may be a bit long, but a .378/.479/.652, 8 HR, 14 SB line in 135 New England Collegiate League ABs shows the upside.

4. Michael Busch, 1B — *North Carolina, L/R, 6-0, 207*
Busch hit .317/465.521 with 13 HR in 240 sophomore ABs, with nice supporting skills (1.80 Eye, 19 bb%, 88 ct%), and even flashed a running ability (8-9 SB), though that may not translate. He could provide 20-plus home-run power and scouts like his ability to control the zone.

5. J.J. Bleday, OF — *Vanderbilt, L/L, 6-3, 205*
A line-drive hitter with an advanced approach (1.50 Eye, 19 bb%) Bleday had a terrific 2018 (.364/.494/.511). He lost six weeks to an oblique injury, but mashed upon his return and hit .311/.374/.500 with 5 HR in 148 AB in the Cape, earning best pro prospect honors. He won't run, but his tools project well in right and there's projectable power as he's not reached his physical peak. He's drawn some Trevor Larnach/Michael Conforto comps.

6. Bryson Stott, SS — *UNLV, L/R, 6-3, 195*
Stott's scouting grades and stolen base output from last season (14 of 16), plus four SB in 40 Cape Cod AB, suggest he could provide considerable base-stealing prowess. His power grades below average, but scouts believe in his hit tool, which is backed by great ct% (93%).

7. Dominic Fletcher, OF — *Arkansas, L/L, 5-10, 185*
Fletcher doesn't run (2 for 4 SB in his career) and probably won't hit for average. But the rising junior has mashed 22 HR over 487 career ABs and scouts think the power projects. Though he's probably a corner outfielder, he has defensive tools that some compare to Jackie Bradley, which should help him stick.

8. Nick Lodolo, LHP — *TCU, L/L, 6-6, 185*
Lodolo was the highest-drafted player in 2016 (41st overall) not to go pro. He took a big step in Dom (10.9) while maintaining already-acceptable Ctl (3.3). He has three quality pitches, headlined by a fastball that tops out at 96. His command needs refining and he's probably not the first college arm off the board, but, his combination of health, ceiling and floor make him tops on this list.

9. Matt Wallner, OF — *Southern Miss, L/R, 6-5, 220*
The 2017 National Freshman of the Year was relatively the same player in 2018 (.351/.474/.618, 16 HR, 77 ct%) as he was the year before (.336/.463/.655, 79 ct%). The power (35 career HR) should translate, but scouts are split on his defense. A stiff swing elevates his risk.

10. Shea Langeliers, C — *Baylor, R/R, 6-0, 195*
He's first an elite catch-and-throw guy, and could go top-five overall. But Langeliers showed consistent home-run power (21 HR) over two seasons at Baylor, and hit 6 HR over 128 AB in the Cape in 2017. Scouts see growth in the bat, and his ct% (82%) provides encouragement.

11. Greg Jones, SS/OF — *UNC Wilmington, S/R, 5-11, 180*
A draft-eligible sophomore, Jones is the highest-risk/reward player here. He's athletic, has 70-80 grade speed, and will play in the middle of the diamond. He's got a line-drive swing with some HR pop (3 HR in 116 Cape ABs) but a terrible ct% (69%) is a major obstacle.

12. Josh Jung, 3B — *Texas Tech, R/R, 6-2, 215*
The 2017 Big 12 Freshman of the Year had a great follow-up (.392/491/.639, 12 HR) with solid underlying skills (88 ct%, 1.20 Eye), then, a respectable summer for Team USA. He's a typical third baseman—he should hit for power and some average, but won't help in steals—and should field well enough to stick there.

More to watch:

Will Holland, SS, Auburn—power-speed combo, but consistency issues

Will Wilson, SS, N.C. State—high power upside, perhaps at 2B

Graeme Stinson, LHP, Duke—considered top college arm, but not athletic and worked mostly out of the bullpen

Braden Shewmake, SS, Texas A&M—potential utility man with double-digit HR/SB

Zack Thompson, LHP, Kentucky—top-10 overall potential, major injury history

Ryne Nelson, RHP, Oregon—reliever has touched 100, could start

Carter Stewart, RHP, Eastern Florida State CC—last year's No. 8 didn't sign due to injury issues

George Kirby, RHP, Elon—24:1 K:BB in 13 Cape Cod IP

Mike Toglia, 1B, UCLA—solid hit/power tools but contact issues

1	Vladimir Guerrero Jr.	3B	TOR		51	Danny Jansen	C	TOR
2	Eloy Jimenez	OF	CHW		52	Alec Bohm	3B	PHI
3	Fernando Tatis Jr.	SS	SD		53	Justus Sheffield	LHP	SEA
4	Victor Robles	OF	WAS		54	Yusinel Diaz	OF	BAL
5	Royce Lewis	SS	MIN		55	Jarred Kelenic	OF	SEA
6	Kyle Tucker	OF	HOU		56	Andres Gimenez	SS	NYM
7	Forrest Whitley	RHP	HOU		57	Estevan Florial	OF	NYY
8	Bo Bichette	SS	TOR		58	Luis Garcia	SS/3B	WAS
9	Nick Senzel	2B	CIN		59	Jon Duplantier	RHP	ARI
10	Alex Kirilloff	OF	MIN		60	Luis Patino	RHP	SD
11	Jo Adell	OF	LAA		61	Leody Taveras	OF	TEX
12	Wander Franco	SS	TAM		62	Nolan Jones	3B	CLE
13	Jesus Luzardo	LHP	OAK		63	Gavin Lux	SS	LA
14	Brendan Rodgers	SS	COL		64	Adonis Medina	RHP	PHI
15	Michael Kopech	RHP	CHW		65	Michel Baez	RHP	SD
16	MacKenzie Gore	LHP	SD		66	Brusdar Graterol	RHP	MIN
17	Taylor Trammell	OF	CIN		67	Julio Pablo Martinez	OF	TEX
18	Keston Hiura	2B	MIL		68	Matthew Liberatore	LHP	TAM
19	Sixto Sanchez	RHP	PHI		69	Cristian Pache	OF	ATL
20	Casey Mize	RHP	DET		70	Dustin May	RHP	LA
21	Dylan Cease	RHP	CHW		71	Josh James	RHP	HOU
22	Mike Soroka	RHP	ATL		72	Jonathan Loaisiga	RHP	NYY
23	Joey Bart	C	SF		73	Sean Murphy	C	OAK
24	Carter Kieboom	SS	WAS		74	Brady Singer	RHP	KC
25	Alex Reyes	RHP	STL		75	Dane Dunning	RHP	CHW
26	Luis Urias	2B	SD		76	Khalil Lee	OF	KC
27	Ian Anderson	RHP	ATL		77	Ryan Mountcastle	3B	BAL
28	Brent Honeywell	RHP	TAM		78	Heliot Ramos	OF	SF
29	Mitch Keller	RHP	PIT		79	Nate Pearson	RHP	TOR
30	Keibert Ruiz	C	LA		80	Drew Waters	OF	ATL
31	Peter Alonso	1B	NYM		81	Jazz Chisholm	SS	ARI
32	Chris Paddack	RHP	SD		82	Hans Crouse	RHP	TEX
33	Hunter Greene	RHP	CIN		83	DL Hall	LHP	BAL
34	A.J. Puk	LHP	OAK		84	MJ Melendez	C	KC
35	Austin Riley	3B	ATL		85	Oneil Cruz	SS	PIT
36	Kyle Wright	RHP	ATL		86	Kristian Robinson	OF	ARI
37	Alex Verdugo	OF	LA		87	Ronaldo Hernandez	C	TAM
38	Luis Robert	OF	CHW		88	Vidal Brujan	2B	TAM
39	Jesus Sanchez	OF	TAM		89	Colton Welker	3B	COL
40	Nick Madrigal	SS	CHW		90	Franklin Perez	RHP	DET
41	Triston McKenzie	RHP	CLE		91	Travis Swaggerty	OF	PIT
42	Yordan Alvarez	OF	HOU		92	Daz Cameron	OF	DET
43	Brendan McKay	1B/LHP	TAM		93	Griffin Canning	RHP	LAA
44	Jonathan India	3B	CIN		94	Bryse Wilson	RHP	ATL
45	Touki Toussaint	RHP	ATL		95	Brandon Marsh	OF	LAA
46	Matt Manning	RHP	DET		96	Bubba Thompson	OF	TEX
47	Francisco Mejia	C	SD		97	Logan Allen	LHP	SD
48	Ke'Bryan Hayes	3B	PIT		98	Justin Dunn	RHP	SEA
49	Nolan Gorman	3B	STL		99	Miguel Amaya	C	CHC
50	Adrian Morejon	LHP	SD		100	Dakota Hudson	RHP	STL

Sleepers Outside the HQ100

by Alec Dopp

BaseballHQ.com's annual HQ100 list serves as a quality jumping-off point for fantasy owners looking for help from prospects both in the short term and in long-term dynasty formats. As most successful owners know, though, we need to dig a bit deeper to find value from minor league players to remain competitive in our leagues each year—and that's where our Sleepers Column comes in.

Last year, we successfully pinpointed a handful of prospects who subsequently exploded onto the scene in 2018—Peter Alonso (1B, NYM), Jesus Luzardo (LHP, OAK) and Carter Kieboom (SS, WAS) all appear on the 2019 list. The goal is to do that once again here. The following are 10 prospects who were outside the 2019 HQ100 but could easily find themselves included in our list a year from now.

Hudson Potts (3B, SD): One of the youngest position players to appear in Double-A in 2018, Potts spent the majority of last summer in the High-A California League, where he slashed .281/.350/.498 with 17 HR in 106 games before capping off his year with a cup of coffee in AA-San Antonio and a trip to the Arizona Fall League. The former first round draft pick creates plus raw power to all fields from a tall, strong frame that, appealingly, might still have some projection left to it. He'll need to sort out some contact issues and iron out a fairly aggressive approach at the plate, but he plays a quality hot corner and has big upside if some things break in the right direction.

Kyler Murray (OF, OAK): A dynamic two-sport athlete at the University of Oklahoma, Murray has yet to set foot on the diamond in the A's system but promises to produce once he does. As just a sophomore in the Big 12 last spring, Murray slashed .296/.398/.556 with 10 HR and 10 SB in 51 games with the Sooners. His best chance to contribute in fantasy formats is with his speed, as he is a plus runner with a burst out of the box. His power and hit tool grade as average right now but his strength and bat speed suggest he'll be a contributor in both categories. The ninth overall pick just last summer, Murray could move up quickly.

Seuly Matias (OF, KC): A long, lean outfielder signed from the Dominican in 2015, Matias burst onto the scene in Low-A ball in 2018 by way of mashing 31 HR with a 57% x/h% across 94 games in the South Atlantic League. The 20-year-old outfielder's raw power is legit, as he produces natural loft and tons of leverage through the zone for big fly-ball power down the road. His approach is uber-aggressive (0.18 Eye) and his swing is quite lengthy, often resulting in whiffs. He has work to do against quality off-speed stuff and could be a BA/OBP burden if those issues aren't addressed, but he still has physical projection and should have monster HR/RBI value.

Jahmai Jones (2B, LAA): A former outfielder, Jones transitioned to second base full time in 2018 whilst breaking through to the upper minors for the first time, eventually winding up with a .239/.337/.380 slash with 10 HR and 24 SB in 123 games in A+/AA. The 21-year-old figures to provide most of his value in SB, as he is a quality athlete and a plus runner. He has a keen eye at the plate and makes solid-average contact from a compact, short stroke through the zone. Though he does not possess a ton of raw power, he has enough to pepper the gaps and eventually provide 18-20 HR annually from a valuable, up-the-middle position on the diamond.

Corey Ray (OF, MIL): The fifth overall pick from 2016's amateur draft, Ray's bat sputtered a bit in the low minors before a major breakthrough in AA last summer, as he muscled 27 HR and slashed .239/.323/.477 with 37 SB in the Southern League. Ray is a premium athlete whose plus speed should morph into SB value in the majors, while the bat speed and added leverage to his swing projects to at least 22-25 HR annually. The concern is that Ray did not make many significant strides with his overall contact ability during his AA breakout, which could be a major roadblock once his debuts. If things break right, though, the HR/SB upside here is real.

Taylor Widener (RHP, ARI): Acquired by the Diamondbacks via trade last February, Widener's introduction to the system included running an impressive 2.75 ERA and 11.5 Dom/2.8 Ctl split across 137 innings in AA in 2018. The 24-year-old is around the plate with all three of his pitches and shows good command of his 91-94 mph fastball that has slight arm-side running action. He will flash an above-average slider that is effective against right-handed batters and he isn't afraid to neutralize lefties with a solid-average change-up with fading action. Strong and physical, Widener could join Arizona's rotation as early as 2019 with a solid spring.

Cole Winn (RHP, TEX): The 15th overall pick from last summer, Winn pitched only during instructional league this fall and did not log any official pro innings after signing with Texas. He has a chance to move quickly, however, due to an advanced repertoire and polish. He owns a low-90s fastball that he commands well and blends in a plus downer curveball with quality depth and 12-to-6 action. His slider and change-up are complementary, and he has some feel for both of them. He has a projectable 6-foot-2 frame and could add a tick of velocity as he adds muscle, and he is a good athlete and shows aptitude for sequencing his pitches well.

Peter Lambert (RHP, COL): Colorado's second-round pick from 2015, Lambert spent time in both AA/AAA last season and posted solid peripherals at both stops, eventually ending 2018 with a 3.28 ERA and 6.4 Dom/1.6 Ctl split across 26 starts. Lambert lacks a premier pitch and doesn't have a sky-high upside, but projects to be effective. He shows plus command of his 92-94 mph fastball and blends in an above-average curveball and average change-up. He throws strikes and is an effective ground-ball pitcher (50% GB% in the upper minors), which should help him as he develops into a back-end type starter for a first-division club down the road.

Albert Abreu (RHP, NYY): A high-upside arm acquired from Houston back in 2016, Abreu has dealt with various injuries as a pro but shows premium stuff when he's on. The 23-year-old righty will sit 93-96 mph with his plus fastball and flashes both an above-average curveball and change-up that allows him to miss bats and produce ground balls at a solid rate. Abreu is strong throughout and has minimal physical projection remaining, and he is a good athlete. Along with injuries, Abreu's ceiling could ultimately be capped by a lack of command, as he struggles to repeat his release point. But if everything comes together, this could be #2 type horse.

Beau Burrows (RHP, DET): Detroit's first round pick from 2015, Burrows' first full season in the upper minors yielded solid but not spectacular returns, including a 4.10 ERA and 8.5 Dom/3.8 Ctl split across 134 innings in the Eastern League. The 6-foot-2 righty gathered Top 100 consideration for his quality four-pitch mix that includes a 91-94 mph fastball and above-average curveball. His change-up and slider act as average pace-changing offerings right now and will be useable at the next level. Burrows will need to work on throwing strikes and keeping the ball on the ground (32% GB% last year), but he misses bats well enough and has some back-end starter upside.

BATTERS

POSITIONS: Up to four positions are listed for each batter and represent those for which he appeared (in order) the most games at in 2018. Positions are shown with their numeric designation (2=CA, 3=1B, 7=LF, 0=DH, etc.)

BATS: Shows which side of the plate he bats from—right (R), left (L) or switch-hitter (S).

AGE: Player's age, as of April 1, 2019.

DRAFTED: The year, round, and school that the player performed at as an amateur if drafted, or where the player was signed from, if a free agent.

EXP MLB DEBUT: The year a player is expected to debut in the major leagues.

H/W: The player's height and weight.

FUT: The role that the batter is expected to have for the majority of his major league career, not necessarily his greatest upside.

SKILLS: Each skill a player possesses is graded and designated with a "+", indicating the quality of the skills, taking into context the batter's age and level played. An average skill will receive three "+" marks.

- **PWR:** Measures the player's ability to drive the ball and hit for power.
- **BAVG:** Measures the player's ability to hit for batting average and judge the strike zone.
- **SPD:** Measures the player's raw speed and base-running ability. When we've measured run times (point of bat-to-ball contact to foot hitting first base), we've included these next to the SPD box.
- **DEF:** Measures the player's overall defense, which includes arm strength, arm accuracy, range, agility, hands, and defensive instincts.

PLAYER STAT LINES: Player statistics for the last five teams that he played for (if applicable), including college and the major leagues.

TEAM DESIGNATIONS: Each team that the player performed for during a given year is included.

LEVEL DESIGNATIONS: The level for each team a player performed is included. "AAA" means Triple-A, "AA" means Double-A, "A+" means high Class-A, "A-" means low Class-A, and "Rk" means rookie level.

SABERMETRIC CATEGORIES: Descriptions of all the sabermetric categories appear in the glossary.

CAPSULE COMMENTARIES: For each player, a brief analysis of their skills/statistics, and their future potential is provided.

ELIGIBILITY: Eligibility for inclusion is the standard for which Major League Baseball adheres to; 130 at-bats or 45 days on the 25-man roster, not including the month of September.

POTENTIAL RATINGS: The Potential Ratings are a two-part system in which a player is assigned a number rating based on his upside potential (1-10) and a letter rating based on the probability of reaching that potential (A-E).

Potential

10:	Hall of Famer	5:	MLB reserve
9:	Elite player	4:	Top minor leaguer
8:	Solid regular	3:	Average minor leaguer
7:	Average regular	2:	Minor league reserve
6:	Platoon player	1:	Minor league roster filler

Probability Rating

- A: 90% probability of reaching potential
- B: 70% probability of reaching potential
- C: 50% probability of reaching potential
- D: 30% probability of reaching potential
- E: 10% probability of reaching potential

SKILLS: Scouts usually grade a player's skills on the 20-80 scale, and while most of the grades are subjective, there are grades that can be given to represent a certain hitting statistic or running speed. These are indicated on this chart:

Scout Grade	HR	BA	Speed (L)	Speed (R)
80	39+	.320+	3.9	4.0
70	32-38	.300-.319	4.0	4.1
60	25-31	.286-.299	4.1	4.2
50 (avg)	17-24	.270-.285	4.2	4.3
40	11-16	.250-.269	4.3	4.4
30	6-10	.220-.249	4.4	4.5
20	0-5	.219-	4.5	4.6

CATCHER POP TIMES: Catchers are timed (in seconds) from the moment the pitch reaches the catcher's mitt until the time that the middle infielder receives the baseball at second base. This number assists both teams in assessing whether a base-runner should steal second base or not.

1.85	+
1.95	MLB average
2.05	–

Adams,Jordyn — 789 — Los Angeles (A)

EXP MLB DEBUT: 2022 | H/W: 6-2 180 | FUT: Starting OF | 8E

Bats R Age 19
2018 (1) HS (NC)

- Pwr ++
- BAvg ++
- Spd ++++
- Def +++

Year	Lev	Team	AB	R	H	HR	RBI	Avg	OB	Slg	OPS	bb%	ct%	Eye	SB	CS	x/h%	Iso	RC/G
2018	Rk	AZL Angels	70	8	17	0	5	243	338	329	666	13	67	0.43	5	2	24	86	4.10
2018	Rk	Orem	35	5	11	0	8	314	385	486	870	10	80	0.57	0	1	45	171	6.68

Wide receiver-turned-outfielder with speed that flashes 80-grade at times. Arm is below average, but speed and instincts combine to balance that out a bit. Spent first year in center, but fringy arm could move him to a corner. Minimal raw power, but looks to project for 15+ home runs in the future as he grows into his body.

Adams,Riley — 2 — Toronto

EXP MLB DEBUT: 2021 | H/W: 6-5 190 | FUT: Reserve C | 6C

Bats R Age 22
2017 (3) San Diego

- Pwr +
- BAvg ++
- Spd +
- Def +++

Year	Lev	Team	AB	R	H	HR	RBI	Avg	OB	Slg	OPS	bb%	ct%	Eye	SB	CS	x/h%	Iso	RC/G
2017	NCAA	San Diego	202	45	63	13	47	312	409	564	973	14	72	0.58	2	0	40	252	8.06
2017	A-	Vancouver	203	26	62	3	35	305	362	438	800	8	75	0.36	1	1	32	133	5.54
2018	A+	Dunedin	349	49	86	4	43	246	341	361	702	13	73	0.54	3	0	36	115	4.47

Tall, big-bodied backstop posted a modest full-season debut. Wide, spread-out stance results in good balance, but limits weight transfer and saps natural power. Good strike zone awareness led to a .352 OB%, but ct% limits BA upside. Has worked hard to make himself a capable receiver with a strong arm, but size limits agility and pop time.

Adell,Jo — 8 — Los Angeles (A)

EXP MLB DEBUT: 2019 | H/W: 6-2 195 | FUT: Starting OF | 9D

Bats R Age 19
2017 (1) HS (KY)

- Pwr +++
- BAvg +++
- Spd ++++
- Def +++

Year	Lev	Team	AB	R	H	HR	RBI	Avg	OB	Slg	OPS	bb%	ct%	Eye	SB	CS	x/h%	Iso	RC/G
2017	Rk	Orem	85	25	32	1	9	376	404	518	922	4	80	0.24	3	2	25	141	6.76
2017	Rk	AZL Angels	118	18	34	4	21	288	344	542	886	8	73	0.31	5	0	47	254	6.81
2018	A	Burlington	95	23	31	6	29	326	396	611	1007	10	73	0.42	4	1	45	284	8.36
2018	A+	Inland Empire	238	46	69	12	42	290	332	546	878	6	74	0.24	9	2	49	256	6.40
2018	AA	Mobile	63	14	15	2	6	238	304	429	733	9	65	0.27	2	0	53	190	4.91

Insanely athletic outfielder with deceptive power at the plate. Body is still developing, but raw power is already grabbing attention. There's work to be done with the mid-20s strikeout percentage, but with his instincts where they are at 19, there's still time. Lethal speed and plus range defensively make him a lock for major league centerfield.

Ademan,Aramis — 6 — Chicago (N)

EXP MLB DEBUT: 2021 | H/W: 5-11 160 | FUT: Starting SS | 7B

Bats L Age 20
2015 FA (DR)

- Pwr ++
- BAvg +++
- Spd +++
- Def +++

Year	Lev	Team	AB	R	H	HR	RBI	Avg	OB	Slg	OPS	bb%	ct%	Eye	SB	CS	x/h%	Iso	RC/G
2017	A-	Eugene	161	23	46	4	27	286	343	466	809	8	81	0.47	10	6	37	180	5.54
2017	A	South Bend	127	13	31	3	15	244	267	378	645	3	81	0.17	4	2	32	134	3.20
2018	A+	Myrtle Beach	396	49	82	3	38	207	276	273	549	9	76	0.40	9	5	21	66	2.23

Was challenged with an assignment to A+ despite being just 19. Proved over-matched, posting just 17 XBH and an anemic sub-.600 OPS. Uses a compact stroke and an all-fields approach that should yield positive results with 12-15 HR power at maturity. Uses plus instincts and a strong arm and should be able to stick at SS over the long-term.

Adolfo,Micker — 79 — Chicago (A)

EXP MLB DEBUT: 2020 | H/W: 6-3 200 | FUT: Starting OF | 8C

Bats R Age 22
2013 FA (DR)

- Pwr ++++
- BAvg ++
- Spd +++
- Def +++

Year	Lev	Team	AB	R	H	HR	RBI	Avg	OB	Slg	OPS	bb%	ct%	Eye	SB	CS	x/h%	Iso	RC/G
2015	Rk	AZL White Sox	83	14	21	0	10	253	303	313	617	7	70	0.24	3	2	19	60	3.07
2016	Rk	AZL White Sox	16	2	4	1	2	250	294	563	857	6	50	0.13	0	0	75	313	8.68
2016	A	Kannapolis	247	30	54	5	21	219	261	340	601	5	64	0.16	0	1	35	121	2.79
2017	A	Kannapolis	424	60	112	16	68	264	314	453	767	7	65	0.21	2	0	41	189	5.30
2018	A+	Winston-Salem	291	48	82	11	50	282	357	464	821	10	68	0.37	2	1	37	182	6.04

Muscular OF continues to struggle staying healthy. Missed 2nd half after Tommy John surgery on right elbow. Plus-plus power plays to all fields. Improved pitch recognition has helped his tool, but still likely low-BA power hitter. A fringe-average runner, doesn't get good jumps on the bases.

Agustin,Telmito — 7 — Washington

EXP MLB DEBUT: 2021 | H/W: 5-10 160 | FUT: Starting OF | 7C

Bats L Age 22
2013 FA (VG)

- Pwr ++
- BAvg ++++
- Spd ++
- Def ++

Year	Lev	Team	AB	R	H	HR	RBI	Avg	OB	Slg	OPS	bb%	ct%	Eye	SB	CS	x/h%	Iso	RC/G
2016	A	Hagerstown	238	35	63	5	30	265	311	387	698	6	70	0.23	14	9	29	122	4.09
2017	A	Hagerstown	296	45	82	9	37	277	307	456	764	4	75	0.18	9	4	38	179	4.79
2017	A+	Potomac	101	12	21	1	14	208	252	277	530	6	74	0.23	3	2	24	69	1.77
2018	A-	Auburn	70	7	13	1	5	186	240	257	497	7	71	0.25	1	0	23	71	1.28
2018	A+	Potomac	205	31	62	5	30	302	364	454	818	9	79	0.47	7	3	29	151	5.69

Improved in his second tour of High-A, showing off his compact swing and solid contact ability. Short, stocky frame unlikely to produce much power, and only a few steals, but sees a lot of pitches and stays against offspeed. Limited to left field.

Alcantara,Sergio — 6 — Detroit

EXP MLB DEBUT: 2020 | H/W: 5-10 150 | FUT: Starting SS | 7C

Bats B Age 22
2012 FA (DR)

- Pwr +
- BAvg ++
- Spd +
- Def ++++

Year	Lev	Team	AB	R	H	HR	RBI	Avg	OB	Slg	OPS	bb%	ct%	Eye	SB	CS	x/h%	Iso	RC/G
2016	A	Kane County	180	15	48	1	16	267	320	328	647	7	86	0.54	3	2	17	61	3.59
2016	A+	Visalia	15	2	4	0	0	267	389	333	722	17	87	1.50	0	1	25	67	5.14
2017	A+	Visalia	340	44	95	3	28	279	345	362	707	9	83	0.60	11	10	21	82	4.36
2017	A+	Lakeland	126	18	29	0	7	230	307	278	585	10	82	0.61	4	3	17	48	2.93
2018	AA	Erie	441	53	120	1	37	272	335	333	669	9	79	0.45	8	5	18	61	3.84

Compact, plus-plus defender with one of the strongest arms in the organization. Fluid actions at shortstop with advanced footwork and accuracy to first that continues to improve. Surpassed offensive expectation in Double-A with solid contact rate, but doesn't project to add much more in the way of power. Able to steal bases, but lacks discipline.

Alemais,Stephen — 46 — Pittsburgh

EXP MLB DEBUT: 2020 | H/W: 6-0 180 | FUT: Utility player | 6C

Bats B Age 23
2016 (3) Tulane

- Pwr +
- BAvg +++
- Spd +++ (4.25)
- Def +++

Year	Lev	Team	AB	R	H	HR	RBI	Avg	OB	Slg	OPS	bb%	ct%	Eye	SB	CS	x/h%	Iso	RC/G
2016	A	West Virginia	37	2	7	0	2	189	231	270	501	5	70	0.18	1	3	29	81	1.44
2017	Rk	GCL Pirates	27	6	7	0	2	259	355	370	725	13	81	0.80	0	0	43	111	4.92
2017	A	West Virginia	121	14	27	3	12	223	254	380	634	4	74	0.16	5	3	41	157	3.12
2017	A+	Bradenton	101	10	32	1	20	317	400	406	806	12	86	1.00	5	2	22	89	5.78
2018	AA	Altoona	402	56	112	1	34	279	350	346	696	10	83	0.64	16	9	19	67	4.30

Solid defensive SS who played 2B a lot this year because of the presence of Cole Tucker. Very smooth and confident in the field, but lacks plus range. Should have no trouble moving all over the diamond in future. Weak, contact bat with little chance for upside or impact. Can run some but not a big SB threat.

Alexander,Blaze — 6 — Arizona

EXP MLB DEBUT: 2022 | H/W: 6-0 160 | FUT: Starting SS | 7C

Bats R Age 19
2018 (11) HS (FL)

- Pwr ++
- BAvg ++
- Spd +++
- Def +++

Year	Lev	Team	AB	R	H	HR	RBI	Avg	OB	Slg	OPS	bb%	ct%	Eye	SB	CS	x/h%	Iso	RC/G
2018	Rk	AZL DBacks	94	25	34	2	25	362	469	574	1043	17	78	0.90	7	3	41	213	9.26
2018	Rk	Missoula	116	27	35	3	17	302	367	509	876	9	73	0.39	3	0	43	207	6.72

Slick-fielding, strong-armed SS who signed for above-slot value in 11th round of 2018 draft. Lean, wiry frame produces good bat speed, but lacks barrel control for impact BA and ct%. Chance for average HR output as he adds strength to his lean frame. Has smooth actions and arm to stick at SS long-term.

Alexander,C.J. — 5 — Atlanta

EXP MLB DEBUT: 2020 | H/W: 6-5 215 | FUT: Starting OF | 8E

Bats L Age 22
2018 (20) Ball St

- Pwr +++
- BAvg +++
- Spd +++
- Def ++

Year	Lev	Team	AB	R	H	HR	RBI	Avg	OB	Slg	OPS	bb%	ct%	Eye	SB	CS	x/h%	Iso	RC/G
2018	Rk	Danville	82	10	29	0	12	354	442	488	930	14	74	0.62	1	1	24	134	7.79
2018	Rk	GCL Braves	34	6	14	1	8	412	500	618	1118	15	88	1.50	0	0	21	206	9.60
2018	A+	Florida	80	5	26	1	7	325	386	450	836	9	79	0.47	3	1	27	125	6.00

Put up stellar numbers at 3 stops in pro debut. Patient hitter with spray approach. Made swing adjustments last off-season, now fluid and compact, leading to ct% improvement. Raw plus power didn't show up in pro debut. Below average defender at 3B. Most scouts project a corner OF long term.

Alfonzo,Eliezer — 2 — Detroit

EXP MLB DEBUT: 2022 | H/W: 5-10 155 | FUT: Reserve C | 6B

Bats B Age 19
2016 FA (VZ)

- Pwr +
- BAvg ++
- Spd +
- Def +++

Year	Lev	Team	AB	R	H	HR	RBI	Avg	OB	Slg	OPS	bb%	ct%	Eye	SB	CS	x/h%	Iso	RC/G
2018	Rk	DSL Tigers 2	110	22	43	0	21	391	485	500	985	15	93	2.50	3	1	26	109	8.20
2018	Rk	GCL Tigers W	69	7	15	1	12	217	308	275	583	12	87	1.00	3	1	13	58	3.07

Solid frame behind the plate with average arm and cat-like defensive reflexes. Natural leadership ability and solid framing through his brief career. Valuable switch-hitter with ability to barrel the ball from both sides of the plate. Swing path can be spotty, but showing improvement.

Alford,Anthony — 789 — Toronto

EXP MLB DEBUT: 2017 | H/W: 6-1 205 | FUT: Starting OF | 8C

Bats R Age 24
2012 (3) HS (MS)
Pwr +++
BAvg ++
Spd +++++
Def ++++

Year	Lev	Team	AB	R	H	HR	RBI	Avg	OB	Slg	OPS	bb%	ct%	Eye	SB	CS	x/h%	Iso	RC/G
2017	AAA	Buffalo	12	1	4	0	0	333	385	417	801	8	83	0.50	0	0	25	83	5.48
2017	MLB	Toronto	8	0	1	0	0	125	125	250	375	0	63	0.00	0	0	100	125	-0.48
2018	A+	Dunedin	20	2	4	0	2	200	304	250	554	13	60	0.38	0	1	25	50	2.40
2018	AAA	Buffalo	375	52	90	5	34	240	296	344	640	7	70	0.27	17	7	31	104	3.38
2018	MLB	Toronto	19	3	2	0	1	105	190	105	296	10	53	0.22	1	0	0	0	-2.37

Ulta-athletic OF had a sub-par season at AAA. Was more aggressive at the plate, chasing out of the zone when previously showed a disciplined approach. Plus raw power has yet to show up in games with a career .385 SLG%. Plus speed and range give him a change to be an elite defender, but needs to get on base to tap into plus speed.

Allen,Austin — 2 — San Diego

EXP MLB DEBUT: 2019 | H/W: 6-4 225 | FUT: Starting 1B | 7C

Bats L Age 25
2015 (4) FL Instute/Technolog
Pwr +++
BAvg +++
Spd +
Def +++

Year	Lev	Team	AB	R	H	HR	RBI	Avg	OB	Slg	OPS	bb%	ct%	Eye	SB	CS	x/h%	Iso	RC/G
2016	A	Fort Wayne	409	52	131	7	61	320	365	425	791	7	83	0.42	0	0	22	105	5.17
2016	AA	San Antonio	11	1	3	1	1	273	273	545	818	0	100		0	0	33	273	4.93
2017	A+	Lake Elsinore	463	71	131	22	81	283	345	497	842	9	76	0.40	0	1	41	214	5.92
2018	AA	San Antonio	451	59	131	22	56	290	344	506	850	8	78	0.38	0	3	40	215	5.90

Strong, stocky catcher who hit 22 HR in two consecutive seasons. Has above-average raw power with natural fly-ball ability and pairs it with solid-average ct% via smooth LH stroke. Questions about glove, arm behind plate persist and will likely move to 1B long term, where his bat profiles well.

Allen,Nick — 6 — Oakland

EXP MLB DEBUT: 2021 | H/W: 5-9 155 | FUT: Starting SS | 7D

Bats B Age 20
2017 (3) HS (CA)
Pwr +
BAvg +++
Spd ++++
Def ++++

Year	Lev	Team	AB	R	H	HR	RBI	Avg	OB	Slg	OPS	bb%	ct%	Eye	SB	CS	x/h%	Iso	RC/G
2017	Rk	AZL Athletics	138	26	35	1	14	254	318	326	644	9	80	0.46	7	3	17	72	3.51
2018	A	Beloit	460	51	110	0	34	239	291	302	594	7	82	0.40	24	8	21	63	2.89

Slick-fielding SS who stands out with his range, running ability and acumen. Short, skinny frame yields poor raw power but shows gap power at present. Makes solid contact via compact, simple swing conducive to line drives and ground balls. Good athlete who picks his SB spots well on the bases.

Alonso,Peter — 3 — New York (N)

EXP MLB DEBUT: 2019 | H/W: 6-2 225 | FUT: Starting 1B | 9C

Bats R Age 24
2016 (2) Florida
Pwr +++++
BAvg ++++
4.60 Spd +
Def +

Year	Lev	Team	AB	R	H	HR	RBI	Avg	OB	Slg	OPS	bb%	ct%	Eye	SB	CS	x/h%	Iso	RC/G
2016	A-	Brooklyn	109	20	35	5	21	321	383	587	970	9	80	0.50	0	1	51	266	7.60
2017	A+	St. Lucie	308	45	88	16	58	286	339	516	856	8	79	0.39	3	4	44	231	5.96
2017	AA	Binghamton	45	7	14	2	5	311	340	578	918	4	84	0.29	0	0	50	267	6.54
2018	AA	Binghamton	220	42	69	15	52	314	426	573	999	16	77	0.86	0	2	39	259	8.25
2018	AAA	Las Vegas	258	50	67	21	67	260	344	585	929	11	70	0.42	0	1	61	326	7.37

Slugger shot to the top of the Mets prospect list with a monster 2018, and figures to be their starting 1B not long into 2019. Paul Konerko type, who despite a lack of athleticism, has a great feel for hitting for power and average. Not the liveliest bat, but strong and has a great approach. Sits on pitches and drives the ball well to all fields.

Alvarez,Yordan — 7 — Houston

EXP MLB DEBUT: 2019 | H/W: 6-5 225 | FUT: Starting 1B | 8C

Bats R Age 23
2015 FA (CU)
Pwr ++++
BAvg +++
Spd +
Def ++

Year	Lev	Team	AB	R	H	HR	RBI	Avg	OB	Slg	OPS	bb%	ct%	Eye	SB	CS	x/h%	Iso	RC/G
2017	A	Quad Cities	111	26	40	9	33	360	470	658	1128	17	68	0.64	2	0	38	297	10.74
2017	A+	Buies Creek	224	19	62	3	36	277	333	393	726	8	82	0.46	6	1	27	116	4.52
2018	AA	Corpus Christi	169	39	55	12	46	325	394	615	1009	10	73	0.42	5	2	45	290	8.26
2018	AAA	Fresno	166	24	43	8	28	259	349	452	801	12	72	0.49	1	0	37	193	5.61

A hulking 6-foot-5, Alvarez annihilated Corpus Christi before receiving a mid-season promotion to AAA. He combines plus raw strength with explosive hips, plus bat speed and feel for the ball to drive the ball consistently. He moves well for his size but is a below-average runner and should end up at first base.

Amaya,Miguel — 2 — Chicago (N)

EXP MLB DEBUT: 2021 | H/W: 6-1 185 | FUT: Starting C | 8C

Bats R Age 20
2015 FA (PN)
Pwr +++
BAvg ++
Spd +
Def ++++

Year	Lev	Team	AB	R	H	HR	RBI	Avg	OB	Slg	OPS	bb%	ct%	Eye	SB	CS	x/h%	Iso	RC/G
2017	A-	Eugene	228	21	52	3	26	228	264	338	601	5	79	0.22	1	0	35	110	2.77
2018	A	South Bend	414	54	106	12	52	256	336	403	740	11	78	0.55	1	0	33	147	4.75

Plus defensive backstop (34% CS%) who moves well behind the plate with soft hands and advanced game calling. Improved pitch recognition gives him a chance to hit, but 2nd half fade (.223 BA) shows there is work to be done. Defense will be carrying tool, but the bat should play enough to have value.

Antuna,Yasel — 6 — Washington

EXP MLB DEBUT: 2023 | H/W: 6-0 170 | FUT: Starting SS | 8E

Bats B Age 19
2016 FA (DR)
Pwr ++
BAvg +++
4.25 Spd ++
Def ++

Year	Lev	Team	AB	R	H	HR	RBI	Avg	OB	Slg	OPS	bb%	ct%	Eye	SB	CS	x/h%	Iso	RC/G
2017	Rk	GCL Nationals	173	25	52	1	17	301	383	399	781	12	83	0.79	5	5	23	98	5.48
2018	A	Hagerstown	323	44	71	6	27	220	290	331	621	9	76	0.41	8	7	31	111	3.15

Lean and projectable athletic SS with some potential with the bat from both sides. Easy, smooth swing from left side; more polish needed from right. Ingredients there for power as he fills out; tools louder than 2018 stats; also solid defender. Underwent Tommy John surgery that will keep him out until mid-2019.

Aparicio,Miguel — 79 — Texas

EXP MLB DEBUT: 2022 | H/W: 6-0 165 | FUT: Starting OF | 8D

Bats L Age 20
2015 FA (VZ)
Pwr ++
BAvg +++
Spd ++
Def +++

Year	Lev	Team	AB	R	H	HR	RBI	Avg	OB	Slg	OPS	bb%	ct%	Eye	SB	CS	x/h%	Iso	RC/G
2017	A-	Spokane	294	47	86	4	33	293	329	395	724	5	87	0.41	2	8	22	102	4.35
2017	A	Hickory	85	6	15	0	9	176	239	247	486	8	79	0.39	1	2	27	71	1.54
2018	A-	Spokane	45	5	11	1	4	244	261	333	594	2	82	0.13	0	1	18	89	2.49
2018	A	Hickory	294	37	63	8	28	214	255	361	615	5	78	0.25	4	6	35	146	2.90

Young and raw player who has yet to put it together. Lean, could add some strength, but at its best, stroke is short and compact. Has a dash of power and speed, but results have been inconsistent. Rangers have pushed him against older competition due to his plus makeup and tools profile, but needs to produce. Can handle CF, but more likely to end up in a corner.

Apostel,Sherten — 5 — Texas

EXP MLB DEBUT: 2022 | H/W: 6-4 198 | FUT: Starting 3B | 9D

Bats R Age 20
2015 FA (CC)
Pwr ++++
BAvg ++
Spd ++
Def ++

Year	Lev	Team	AB	R	H	HR	RBI	Avg	OB	Slg	OPS	bb%	ct%	Eye	SB	CS	x/h%	Iso	RC/G
2018	Rk	Bristol	139	28	36	7	26	259	398	460	858	19	70	0.76	3	1	39	201	6.76
2018	A-	Spokane	37	7	13	1	10	351	478	459	938	20	78	1.13	0	1	15	108	7.81

Big-framed third baseman is a better athlete than one would expect. Huge power is the main attraction, but swing can get long and strikeouts are likely a part of his future. Lays off pitches out of the zone, so will have some OBP value. A raw defender with a strong arm, he may have to move across the diamond at some point in his future.

Aquino,Aristides — 9 — Cincinnati

EXP MLB DEBUT: 2018 | H/W: 6-4 190 | FUT: Starting OF | 7C

Bats R Age 24
2011 FA (DR)
Pwr ++++
BAvg ++
Spd +++
Def ++++

Year	Lev	Team	AB	R	H	HR	RBI	Avg	OB	Slg	OPS	bb%	ct%	Eye	SB	CS	x/h%	Iso	RC/G
2015	A	Dayton	231	25	54	5	27	234	269	364	632	5	77	0.21	6	1	31	130	3.10
2016	A+	Daytona	484	69	132	23	79	273	320	519	839	7	79	0.33	11	7	46	246	5.78
2017	AA	Pensacola	459	54	99	17	56	216	277	397	674	8	68	0.27	9	3	43	181	3.80
2018	AA	Pensacola	404	49	97	20	55	240	301	448	749	8	72	0.31	4	5	43	208	4.70
2018	MLB	Cincinnati	1	0	0	0	0	0	0	0	0	0	0	0.00	0	0		0	

Toolsy, athletic OF was better in 2nd tour of Double-A. Shortened up load and swing is more refined. However, still struggles with breaking ball recognition and swing path issues. Plus raw power potential continues to materialize. Pull-to-CF power. Has lost a step and is an average runner now. 70-grade arm in RF.

Arauz,Jonathan — 6 — Houston

EXP MLB DEBUT: 2021 | H/W: 6-0 147 | FUT: Utility player | 7D

Bats L Age 20
2014 FA (PN)
Pwr ++
BAvg +++
Spd ++
Def +++

Year	Lev	Team	AB	R	H	HR	RBI	Avg	OB	Slg	OPS	bb%	ct%	Eye	SB	CS	x/h%	Iso	RC/G
2016	Rk	Greeneville	201	26	50	2	18	249	314	338	652	9	78	0.42	1	3	26	90	3.60
2017	A-	Tri City	121	16	32	1	11	264	331	364	694	9	76	0.41	1	0	28	99	4.19
2017	A	Quad Cities	127	23	28	0	4	220	327	276	602	14	86	1.11	0	1	18	55	3.49
2018	A	Quad Cities	204	31	61	4	29	299	389	471	859	13	81	0.79	7	6	34	172	6.50
2018	A+	Buies Creek	233	25	39	4	18	167	221	288	508	6	85	0.44	1	2	44	120	1.91

Rough statistical season for the young SS. He flashes feel for contact and has fringy raw power in there but is going to need to hit consistently to get to all of it. Age relative to level is important here, as he played 2018 at 19, and still has time to fill out. He should stick at the six defensively due to a solid glove and plus arm.

Arias,Diosbel | 56 | Texas | EXP MLB DEBUT: 2021 | H/W: 6-2 190 | FUT: Starting 3B | 8D

Bats R Age 22 — 2018 FA (CU) — Pwr +++ / BAvg +++ / Spd + / Def ++

Year	Lev	Team	AB	R	H	HR	RBI	Avg	OB	Slg	OPS	bb%	ct%	Eye	SB	CS	x/h%	Iso	RC/G
2018	A-	Spokane	224	43	82	3	44	366	447	491	939	13	83	0.85	5	1	24	125	7.45

Former Cuban national team member who led the Northwest League in hitting while blistering line drives from gap to gap. Broad-shouldered and strong, he's growing into frame and could have 20-HR potential. A below-average runner, he has SS experience but his quickness well suited to 3B or perhaps 2B. Solid plate approach.

Arias,Gabriel | 6 | San Diego | EXP MLB DEBUT: 2020 | H/W: 6-1 185 | FUT: Starting SS | 7C

Bats R Age 19 — 2016 FA (VZ) — Pwr ++ / BAvg +++ / Spd +++ / Def +++

Year	Lev	Team	AB	R	H	HR	RBI	Avg	OB	Slg	OPS	bb%	ct%	Eye	SB	CS	x/h%	Iso	RC/G
2017	Rk	AZL Padres 2	153	18	42	0	13	275	319	353	672	6	67	0.20	4	6	21	78	3.94
2017	A	Fort Wayne	62	8	15	0	4	242	266	258	524	3	74	0.13	1	0	7	16	1.56
2018	A	Fort Wayne	455	54	109	6	55	240	302	352	654	8	67	0.28	3	3	33	112	3.68

Lean, athletic glove-first SS with well-rounded skillset and offensive upside. Possesses footwork and feel to play plus SS down the road and quality arm to stick. Smooth RH swing and has feel for barrel. Below-average power is mostly gap oriented right now; perhaps more to come as he fills out. Runs well but isn't likely a SB source.

Armenteros,Lazaro | 78 | Oakland | EXP MLB DEBUT: 2021 | H/W: 6-0 182 | FUT: Starting OF | 8D

Bats R Age 19 — 2016 FA (CU) — Pwr +++ / BAvg +++ / Spd +++ / Def ++

Year	Lev	Team	AB	R	H	HR	RBI	Avg	OB	Slg	OPS	bb%	ct%	Eye	SB	CS	x/h%	Iso	RC/G
2017	Rk	AZL Athletics	156	24	45	4	22	288	355	474	829	9	69	0.33	10	1	38	186	6.21
2018	A	Beloit	292	43	81	8	39	277	357	401	757	11	61	0.31	8	6	22	123	5.54

Lean, young athlete who flashed well-rounded skillset in MWL debut. Possesses plus speed but may lose a step as he fills out; should have moderate SB ability. Creates plus bat speed through the zone for hard contact and gap power. Working out kinks in swing and will need to be more disciplined. Chance to stick in CF but has fringe arm for LF.

Arozarena,Randy | 79 | St. Louis | EXP MLB DEBUT: 2019 | H/W: 5-11 170 | FUT: Starting OF | 8D

Bats R Age 24 — 2016 FA (CU) — Pwr +++ / BAvg +++ / Spd +++ / Def +++

Year	Lev	Team	AB	R	H	HR	RBI	Avg	OB	Slg	OPS	bb%	ct%	Eye	SB	CS	x/h%	Iso	RC/G
2017	A+	Palm Beach	265	38	73	8	40	275	309	472	781	5	80	0.25	10	4	45	196	5.00
2017	AA	Springfield	163	34	41	3	9	252	358	380	738	14	79	0.79	8	3	34	129	4.99
2018	AA	Springfield	91	22	36	7	21	396	433	681	1114	6	73	0.24	9	3	33	286	9.44
2018	AAA	Memphis	267	42	62	5	28	232	305	348	653	9	78	0.47	17	5	34	116	3.62

Athletic OF put together a solid season and can do a bit of everything. Can be overly aggressive at the plate, but was more selective as the season progressed. The jump to AAA proved challenging but his base skills remained intact. Above-average defender in LF with a good arm and plus speed.

Arraez,Luis | 4 | Minnesota | EXP MLB DEBUT: 2019 | H/W: 5-10 155 | FUT: Utility player | 6B

Bats L Age 21 — 2013 FA (VZ) — Pwr + / BAvg ++++ / Spd ++ / Def ++

Year	Lev	Team	AB	R	H	HR	RBI	Avg	OB	Slg	OPS	bb%	ct%	Eye	SB	CS	x/h%	Iso	RC/G
2015	Rk	GCL Twins	206	23	63	0	19	306	367	388	756	9	95	2.00	8	8	25	83	5.24
2016	A	Cedar Rapids	475	67	165	3	66	347	387	444	832	6	89	0.61	3	3	22	97	5.70
2017	A+	Fort Myers	13	1	5	0	1	385	385	538	923	0	100		0	0	20	154	6.39
2018	A+	Fort Myers	228	27	73	1	20	320	372	421	794	8	88	0.68	2	3	25	101	5.40
2018	AA	Chattanooga	178	25	53	2	16	298	346	365	711	7	91	0.81	2	0	15	67	4.37

Contact-oriented UT player continued to hit after mid-season Double-A debut. Missed most of 2017 with ACL injury. Incredible bat control. Sprays soft line drives and hard ground balls to all fields with short, punch-and-Judy swing. Difficult to defend. Little power projection in swing and frame. Bellow average runner and defender.

Avelino,Abiatal | 6 | San Francisco | EXP MLB DEBUT: 2018 | H/W: 5-11 186 | FUT: Starting 2B | 7B

Bats R Age 24 — 2011 FA (DR) — Pwr ++ / BAvg +++ / Spd ++++ / Def +++

Year	Lev	Team	AB	R	H	HR	RBI	Avg	OB	Slg	OPS	bb%	ct%	Eye	SB	CS	x/h%	Iso	RC/G
2017	AAA	Scranton/WB	61	5	13	0	6	213	273	262	535	8	84	0.50	3	1	15	49	2.27
2018	AA	Trenton	190	32	64	10	28	337	394	553	947	9	81	0.49	15	4	30	216	7.10
2018	AAA	Scranton/WB	274	33	69	5	38	252	288	372	660	5	78	0.23	10	2	25	120	3.48
2018	AAA	Sacramento	13	2	2	0	1	154	154	154	308	0	77	0.00	2	0	0	0	-1.26
2018	MLB	SF Giants	11	1	3	0	0	273	273	273	545	0	73	0.00	0	0	0	0	1.63

Consistently steady producer, acquired in mid-season trade with NYY, made MLB debut. Contact-oriented hitter who tries to spray ball across the diamond. Average raw power translating in games, mostly pull-oriented. Attacked RCF gap with great authority in 2018. Plus runner with SB skill. Natural SS, but lacks the arm to stick. Likely 2B or UT.

Baddoo,Akil | 8 | Minnesota | EXP MLB DEBUT: 2021 | H/W: 5-11 185 | FUT: Starting CF | 8E

Bats L Age 20 — 2016 (2) HS (MD) — Pwr +++ / BAvg ++ / Spd ++++ / Def +++

Year	Lev	Team	AB	R	H	HR	RBI	Avg	OB	Slg	OPS	bb%	ct%	Eye	SB	CS	x/h%	Iso	RC/G
2016	Rk	GCL Twins	107	15	19	2	15	178	296	271	567	14	66	0.50	8	1	21	93	2.45
2017	Rk	Elizabethton	126	39	45	3	19	357	471	579	1050	18	85	1.42	5	4	44	222	9.14
2017	Rk	GCL Twins	75	18	20	1	10	267	345	440	785	11	83	0.69	4	0	40	173	5.52
2018	A	Cedar Rapids	437	83	106	11	40	243	352	419	771	14	72	0.60	24	5	42	176	5.50

Quick-twitch, athletic OF took step back in full-season debut. Appy Lg darling in 2017, ct% dipped due to unorthodox swing path against advanced competition. Maintained bb% while adjusting approach. Average power potential, especially to the pull side. Plus runner with instincts, and a raw defender in CF.

Bae,Ji-Hwan | 6 | Pittsburgh | EXP MLB DEBUT: 2023 | H/W: 6-1 170 | FUT: Starting SS | 8E

Bats L Age 19 — 2018 FA (KR) — Pwr ++ / BAvg +++ / Spd +++ / Def +++

Year	Lev	Team	AB	R	H	HR	RBI	Avg	OB	Slg	OPS	bb%	ct%	Eye	SB	CS	x/h%	Iso	RC/G
2018	Rk	GCL Pirates	129	24	35	0	13	271	347	349	696	10	88	0.94	10	4	23	78	4.48

Big money Korean signing. Not that physical but has good actions and decent tools. Pirates think he can be a good all-around SS. Has shown good bat-to-ball skills in limited low-level AB, but not a lot of power or plus speed.

Baker,Luken | 3 | St. Louis | EXP MLB DEBUT: 2021 | H/W: 6-4 240 | FUT: Starting 1B | 7C

Bats R Age 22 — 2018 (2) Texas Christian — Pwr ++++ / BAvg +++ / Spd + / Def ++

Year	Lev	Team	AB	R	H	HR	RBI	Avg	OB	Slg	OPS	bb%	ct%	Eye	SB	CS	x/h%	Iso	RC/G
2018	Rk	GCL Cardinals	24	10	12	1	7	500	556	708	1264	11	83	0.75	0	0	25	208	11.11
2018	A	Peoria	139	16	40	3	15	288	361	417	779	10	78	0.52	0	0	30	129	5.27

Massive player had some of the best raw power in the draft and pro debut was impressive. Solid understanding of the strike zone and above-average bat speed, but at his size there is length to his swing and he will have to work hard for the power to remain game-usable. Plus arm and decent glove, but bottom-of-the-scale speed limits him to 1B.

Baldwin,Roldani | 2 | Boston | EXP MLB DEBUT: 2022 | H/W: 5-11 180 | FUT: Reserve C | 6D

Bats R Age 23 — 2013 FA (DR) — Pwr +++ / BAvg ++ / 4.60 Spd + / Def ++

Year	Lev	Team	AB	R	H	HR	RBI	Avg	OB	Slg	OPS	bb%	ct%	Eye	SB	CS	x/h%	Iso	RC/G
2015	A-	Lowell	7	0	2	0	0	286	286	429	714	0	86	0.00	0	0	50	143	4.08
2016	A-	Lowell	95	10	29	1	14	305	347	442	789	6	78	0.29	0	0	34	137	5.26
2016	A	Greenville	225	26	56	3	23	249	278	342	620	4	75	0.16	1	1	27	93	2.89
2017	A	Greenville	368	45	101	14	66	274	310	489	799	5	80	0.26	1	0	50	215	5.20
2018	A+	Salem	202	21	47	7	27	233	269	371	640	5	78	0.23	2	0	30	139	3.11

Hit-first C who lacks athleticism, and whose big swing and overaggressive approach caught up with him some in 2018. Needs to hit because he lacks agility and good hands behind plate. Strength and power there, but holes in swing and approach were exploited once got to Hi-A. Does have arm strength and power to get better on both sides of ball.

Banfield,Will | 2 | Miami | EXP MLB DEBUT: 2022 | H/W: 6-0 200 | FUT: Starting C | 8E

Bats R Age 19 — 2018 (2) HS (GA) — Pwr ++++ / BAvg ++ / Spd ++ / Def ++++

Year	Lev	Team	AB	R	H	HR	RBI	Avg	OB	Slg	OPS	bb%	ct%	Eye	SB	CS	x/h%	Iso	RC/G
2018	Rk	GCL Marlins	82	7	21	0	14	256	315	378	693	8	66	0.25	0	1	43	122	4.45
2018	A	Greensboro	48	5	10	3	4	208	269	396	665	8	69	0.27	0	0	30	188	3.40

Defensive-oriented, athletic C made his pro debut. Quick wrists, strong forearms aid bat speed. Patient approach, doesn't expand zone. Struggles with swing path and extending bat early, selling out for power. Plus raw power profile, will reach it if ct% doesn't dip any further. Superb defender. Glove plays now in upper-minors.

Banks,Nick

789 | **Washington** | EXP MLB DEBUT: 2020 | H/W: 6-0 190 | FUT: Starting OF | **7D**

Bats L Age 24
2016 (4) Texas A&M
Pwr ++
BAvg ++
Spd +++
Def +++

Year	Lev	Team	AB	R	H	HR	RBI	Avg	OB	Sig	OPS	bb%	ct%	Eye	SB	CS	x/h%	Iso	RC/G
2016	NCAA	Texas A&M	239	48	67	9	49	280	346	473	819	9	80	0.51	7	0	37	192	5.65
2016	A-	Auburn	231	18	64	0	19	277	310	320	630	5	84	0.30	7	2	14	43	3.20
2017	A	Hagerstown	440	52	111	7	58	252	301	373	674	7	80	0.34	14	7	32	120	3.78
2018	A	Hagerstown	200	25	52	6	27	260	305	395	700	6	78	0.29	10	4	29	135	3.97
2018	A+	Potomac	232	27	61	4	30	263	305	379	684	6	78	0.27	1	0	28	116	3.83

Split season between two A-ball levels with similar results. Power a tick higher previous seasons, and runs enough for double-digit steals. But doesn't pull the ball for power and lacks a standout tool. Needs to improve vs. LHP to secure a role at higher levels.

Bannon,Rylan

46 | **Baltimore** | EXP MLB DEBUT: 2020 | H/W: 5-10 165 | FUT: Utility player | **7D**

Bats R Age 22
2017 (8) Xavier
Pwr ++
BAvg +++
Spd +++
Def +++

Year	Lev	Team	AB	R	H	HR	RBI	Avg	OB	Sig	OPS	bb%	ct%	Eye	SB	CS	x/h%	Iso	RC/G
2017	NCAA	Xavier	221	45	75	15	50	339	436	633	1070	15	79	0.83	17	0	43	294	9.07
2017	Rk	Ogden	149	39	50	10	30	336	411	591	1001	11	81	0.66	5	0	36	255	7.88
2018	A+	Rancho Cuca	338	58	100	20	61	296	401	559	960	15	70	0.57	4	4	43	263	8.12
2018	AA	Bowie	98	16	20	2	11	204	350	327	677	18	76	0.92	0	0	40	122	4.28

Solid, super-utility type, who provides AB at 2B and 3B, was acquired in mid-season trade from LA. Patient hitter, work counts. Makes lots of hard contact, though so far mostly against younger competition. Has average power potential, which could play up due to pull tendencies. Expectation is that swing-and-miss tendencies likely push bat to bench.

Barley,Jordy

46 | **San Diego** | EXP MLB DEBUT: 2021 | H/W: 6-0 175 | FUT: Starting SS | **8E**

Bats R Age 19
2016 FA (DR)
Pwr ++
BAvg +++
Spd ++++
Def +++

Year	Lev	Team	AB	R	H	HR	RBI	Avg	OB	Sig	OPS	bb%	ct%	Eye	SB	CS	x/h%	Iso	RC/G
2017	Rk	AZL Padres	182	34	44	4	28	242	285	434	719	6	64	0.17	7	2	48	192	4.76
2018	Rk	AZL Padres 2	195	30	39	4	20	200	257	328	585	7	70	0.25	12	7	38	128	2.57

Lean, toolsy SS with upside but requires a lot of refinement. Quality athlete with burst out of the box and has plus speed for some SB impact. Often free-swinging approach and struggles making consistent contact. Ball carries well when he connects; potential for average HR output. Has arm for SS but fringe glove could land him at 2B.

Barrosa,Jorge

8 | **Arizona** | EXP MLB DEBUT: 2023 | H/W: 5-9 165 | FUT: Starting OF | **8E**

Bats B Age 18
2017 FA (VZ)
Pwr +
BAvg +++
Spd +++
Def +++

Year	Lev	Team	AB	R	H	HR	RBI	Avg	OB	Sig	OPS	bb%	ct%	Eye	SB	CS	x/h%	Iso	RC/G
2018	Rk	DSL DBacks	204	57	61	3	21	299	376	412	787	11	83	0.74	37	6	23	113	5.44
2018	Rk	AZL DBacks	43	4	10	0	1	233	283	326	608	7	86	0.50	2	2	20	93	3.22
2018	Rk	Missoula	18	3	3	0	1	167	211	278	488	5	72	0.20	0	0	33	111	1.37

Shorter, wiry OF who moved up three levels in low minors in 2018. Chance for SB returns via solid athleticism and quick first-step despite shorter strides. Switch-hitter who utilizes slap approach at present. Works counts well and has advanced approach. Lacks ideal strength and projects for single-digit HR at maturity.

Bart,Joey

2 | **San Francisco** | EXP MLB DEBUT: 2021 | H/W: 6-3 230 | FUT: Starting C | **9C**

Bats R Age 22
2018 (1) Georgia Tech
Pwr +++++
BAvg ++
Spd ++
Def ++++

Year	Lev	Team	AB	R	H	HR	RBI	Avg	OB	Sig	OPS	bb%	ct%	Eye	SB	CS	x/h%	Iso	RC/G
2018	NCAA	Georgia Tech	220	55	79	16	38	359	460	632	1092	16	75	0.73	3	0	35	273	9.59
2018	Rk	AZL Giants O	23	3	6	0	1	261	292	391	683	4	70	0.14	0	0	33	130	4.05
2018	A-	Salem-Keizer	181	35	54	13	39	298	342	613	955	6	78	0.30	2	1	54	315	7.14

Rare catching prospect with plus offensive and defensive skills. Shortened swing mechanics and became more complete hitter with spray approach. Some ct% concerns hurt hit tool. Raw plus-plus power to all fields. Hit 29 HR split between college and pros; has 30+ HR potential at projection in majors. Neutralizes SB game behind plate.

Basabe,Luis Alexander

789 | **Chicago (A)** | EXP MLB DEBUT: 2020 | H/W: 6-0 160 | FUT: Starting OF | **8D**

Bats B Age 22
2013 FA (VZ)
Pwr +++
BAvg ++
Spd ++++
Def ++++

Year	Lev	Team	AB	R	H	HR	RBI	Avg	OB	Sig	OPS	bb%	ct%	Eye	SB	CS	x/h%	Iso	RC/G
2016	A	Greenville	403	61	104	12	52	258	325	447	772	9	71	0.34	25	5	42	189	5.27
2016	A+	Salem	22	5	8	0	1	364	391	545	937	4	86	0.33	0	0	38	182	6.96
2017	A+	Winston-Salem	375	52	83	5	36	221	311	320	631	12	72	0.47	17	6	27	99	3.40
2018	A+	Winston-Salem	207	36	55	9	30	266	369	502	872	14	69	0.53	7	8	47	237	6.94
2018	AA	Birmingham	231	41	58	6	26	251	337	394	731	11	67	0.39	9	4	31	143	4.86

Quick-twitch, switch-hitting OF has struggled to refine his plus offensive tool shed. Short, compact swing from both sides. Has ability to let ball travel deep, but still get the barrel to it. Poor pitch recognition depresses his ct%. Plus raw power, though swing trajectory geared towards line drives. Plus runner, but corner OF profile.

Bautista,Mariel

8 | **Cincinnati** | EXP MLB DEBUT: 2021 | H/W: 6-3 170 | FUT: Starting OF | **9E**

Bats R Age 21
2014 FA (DR)
Pwr ++++
BAvg +++
Spd ++++
Def +++

Year	Lev	Team	AB	R	H	HR	RBI	Avg	OB	Sig	OPS	bb%	ct%	Eye	SB	CS	x/h%	Iso	RC/G
2017	Rk	AZL Reds	147	29	47	0	20	320	342	395	737	3	84	0.21	16	1	21	75	4.40
2018	Rk	Billings	209	43	69	8	37	330	378	541	918	7	86	0.55	16	3	35	211	6.67

Toolsy, quick twitch athlete with raw tool set. Room to grow into frame. Quick wrists and strong forearms aid in plus bat speed, which minimizes concerns about his length in load. Consistent swing path and good hand/eye lend self to high contact rates. Extreme pull power tendency with 20-25 HR potential, and has a plus run tool.

Bautista,Rafael

8 | **Washington** | EXP MLB DEBUT: 2017 | H/W: 6-2 165 | FUT: Reserve OF | **6A**

Bats R Age 26
2012 FA (DR)
Pwr +
BAvg ++
Spd ++++
Def +++

Year	Lev	Team	AB	R	H	HR	RBI	Avg	OB	Sig	OPS	bb%	ct%	Eye	SB	CS	x/h%	Iso	RC/G
2017	AAA	Syracuse	176	23	44	0	11	250	286	313	599	5	85	0.35	7	4	23	63	2.93
2017	MLB	Washington	25	2	4	0	0	160	222	160	382	7	80	0.40	0	0	0	0	0.16
2018	AA	Harrisburg	27	0	3	0	3	111	200	111	311	10	81	0.60	1	1	0	0	-0.51
2018	AAA	Syracuse	82	11	30	1	4	366	395	463	859	5	72	0.17	5	1	17	98	6.18
2018	MLB	Washington	6	1	0	0	0	0	0	0	0	0	83	0.00	0	0		0	-4.39

Was off to fantastic start at AAA until blew out a knee and had season-ending surgery. That news is even worse than usual since his best skill is his plus-plus speed. A lean singles hitter that relies his hands, he makes solid contact but struggles to drive the ball. Some defensive/ baserunning value if knee comes back healthy.

Beaty,Matt

35 | **Los Angeles (N)** | EXP MLB DEBUT: 2019 | H/W: 6-0 195 | FUT: Utility player | **6C**

Bats L Age 25
2015 (12) Belmont
Pwr +++
BAvg ++
Spd ++
Def ++

Year	Lev	Team	AB	R	H	HR	RBI	Avg	OB	Sig	OPS	bb%	ct%	Eye	SB	CS	x/h%	Iso	RC/G
2015	A	Great Lakes	246	37	73	4	25	297	352	390	742	8	89	0.75	2	1	18	93	4.74
2016	A+	Rancho Cuca	489	66	145	11	88	297	350	425	775	8	85	0.54	6	1	28	129	5.05
2017	AA	Tulsa	438	61	143	15	69	326	376	505	881	7	88	0.65	3	3	33	178	6.24
2018	Rk	AZL Dodgers	8	0	3	0	2	375	375	375	750	0	100		0	0	0	0	4.46
2018	AAA	Oklahoma City	101	13	28	1	12	277	354	406	760	11	83	0.71	0	0	39	129	5.16

Overlooked corner IF was limited to just 34 games due to torn thumb ligament. Prior to the injury showed a quick left-handed bat, average power, and excellent bat-to-ball skills. Now onws a career slash line of 309/.366/.445. Below average speed and defense limits him to a utility role.

Beck,Austin

8 | **Oakland** | EXP MLB DEBUT: 2021 | H/W: 5-11 175 | FUT: Starting OF | **8D**

Bats R Age 20
2017 (1) HS (NC)
Pwr +++
BAvg ++
Spd +++
Def +++

Year	Lev	Team	AB	R	H	HR	RBI	Avg	OB	Sig	OPS	bb%	ct%	Eye	SB	CS	x/h%	Iso	RC/G
2017	Rk	AZL Athletics	152	23	32	2	28	211	290	349	639	10	66	0.33	7	1	41	138	3.58
2018	A	Beloit	493	58	146	2	60	296	337	383	720	6	76	0.26	8	6	24	87	4.36

Young, toolsy OF taken sixth overall in 2017 draft. Possesses plus bat speed and fluid RH stroke; nearly hit .300 in full-season debut. Will flash plus raw power to all fields and doubles will turn into HRs as he fills out. Has over-aggressive approach and swings over breaking stuff regularly. Runs well and plus arm profiles well in RF should he have to move out of CF.

Beer,Seth

7 | **Houston** | EXP MLB DEBUT: 2021 | H/W: 6-2 195 | FUT: Starting 1B | **7C**

Bats L Age 22
2018 (1) Clemson
Pwr ++++
BAvg ++
Spd +
Def +

Year	Lev	Team	AB	R	H	HR	RBI	Avg	OB	Sig	OPS	bb%	ct%	Eye	SB	CS	x/h%	Iso	RC/G
2018	NCAA	Clemson	226	64	68	22	54	301	436	642	1077	19	84	1.50	1	0	49	341	9.07
2018	A-	Tri City	41	9	12	4	7	293	383	659	1042	13	76	0.60	0	0	58	366	8.58
2018	A	Quad Cities	112	15	39	3	16	348	425	491	916	12	85	0.88	1	0	26	143	6.98
2018	A+	Buies Creek	107	15	28	5	19	262	288	439	728	4	79	0.18	0	1	32	178	4.09

The big man boasts plus power and an advanced approach, which was tested significantly in High-A. His swing can get a bit long, and make him susceptible to hard inside pitches. There's no speed to speak of, which makes his future at first base or DH more likely than the outfield.

Bello,Micah — 8 — Milwaukee

EXP MLB DEBUT: 2022 | H/W: 5-11 165 | FUT: Starting OF | 8D

Bats R Age 18 — 2018 (2) HS (HI)

Pwr ++ | BAvg +++ | Spd ++++ | Def +++

Year	Lev	Team	AB	R	H	HR	RBI	Avg	OB	Slg	OPS	bb%	ct%	Eye	SB	CS	x/h%	Iso	RC/G
2018	Rk	AZL Brewers	154	25	37	1	15	240	320	325	644	10	73	0.44	10	1	22	84	3.58

Speed-first OF with athletic tools a'plenty. Runs well out of the box and picks his spots well on bases for SB impact. Makes solid contact against heat and off-speed for top-of-the order profile. Lacks raw power for HR impact, but will have time to add strength to his lean frame.

Beltre,Michael — 789 — Cincinnati

EXP MLB DEBUT: 2020 | H/W: 6-3 180 | FUT: Starting OF | 7D

Bats B Age 23 — 2013 FA (DR)

Pwr ++ | BAvg +++ | Spd ++++ | Def +++

Year	Lev	Team	AB	R	H	HR	RBI	Avg	OB	Slg	OPS	bb%	ct%	Eye	SB	CS	x/h%	Iso	RC/G
2016	Rk	Billings	81	14	25	3	13	309	417	531	948	16	84	1.15	4	1	48	222	7.65
2016	Rk	AZL Reds	106	23	31	0	10	292	359	443	802	9	76	0.44	9	0	32	151	5.80
2017	A	Dayton	407	51	97	3	36	238	320	324	644	11	78	0.55	9	9	24	86	3.63
2018	A	Dayton	165	27	49	4	19	297	402	448	851	15	78	0.78	12	1	29	152	6.48
2018	A+	Daytona	188	28	49	1	18	261	390	362	752	18	74	0.83	10	4	24	101	5.42

Toolsy, athletic switch-hitting OF continues to exhibit good patience and solid contact skills, especially from the LH side. Sluggish load, makes up for poor start by whipping bat quickly through zone. Doesn't utilize lower half for leverage, depressing power potential despite frame built for pop. A plus runner and very adapt base stealer.

Benson,Will — 9 — Cleveland

EXP MLB DEBUT: 2022 | H/W: 6-5 215 | FUT: Starting OF | 8E

Bats L Age 20 — 2016 (1) HS (GA)

Pwr ++++ | BAvg + | Spd +++ | Def +++

Year	Lev	Team	AB	R	H	HR	RBI	Avg	OB	Slg	OPS	bb%	ct%	Eye	SB	CS	x/h%	Iso	RC/G
2016	Rk	AZL Indians	158	31	33	6	27	209	306	424	730	12	62	0.37	10	2	58	215	5.09
2017	A-	Mahoning Val	202	29	48	10	36	238	339	475	814	13	60	0.39	7	1	48	238	6.53
2018	A	Lake County	416	54	75	22	58	180	315	370	685	16	63	0.54	12	6	45	190	4.15

One of those prospects who is easy to dream on, as he has long levers, huge raw power, a propensity for walks and a gun for an arm. While the power has shown up so far in his short pro career, the hit tool has not. His swing is currently too long and uphill, reminiscent of recent Jason Heyward. Has defensive skills for RF.

Bichette,Bo — 6 — Toronto

EXP MLB DEBUT: 2019 | H/W: 5-11 201 | FUT: Starting 2B | 9C

Bats R Age 21 — 2016 (2) HS (FL)

Pwr ++++ | BAvg +++++ | Spd +++ | Def +++

Year	Lev	Team	AB	R	H	HR	RBI	Avg	OB	Slg	OPS	bb%	ct%	Eye	SB	CS	x/h%	Iso	RC/G
2016	Rk	GCL Blue Jays	82	21	35	4	36	427	466	732	1198	7	79	0.35	3	0	43	305	10.33
2017	A	Lansing	284	60	109	10	51	384	439	623	1062	9	81	0.51	12	3	41	239	8.74
2017	A+	Dunedin	164	28	53	4	23	323	376	463	840	8	84	0.54	10	4	26	140	5.83
2018	AA	New Hampshire	539	95	154	11	74	286	344	453	797	8	81	0.48	32	11	40	167	5.43

Advanced hitting prospect with discerning eye at the plate. Good bat speed allows for plenty of hard contact, but aggressive approach limits OB%. Willing to work counts looking for ball he can attack and should develop average to above power. Solid defender with an average arm will need to work hard to stick at SS, but the bat is near elite level.

Biggio,Cavan — 45 — Toronto

EXP MLB DEBUT: 2020 | H/W: 6-2 185 | FUT: Starting 2B | 8D

Bats L Age 23 — 2016 (5) Notre Dame

Pwr ++ | BAvg ++++ | Spd ++ | Def ++

Year	Lev	Team	AB	R	H	HR	RBI	Avg	OB	Slg	OPS	bb%	ct%	Eye	SB	CS	x/h%	Iso	RC/G
2016	NCAA	Notre Dame	196	43	61	4	28	311	460	454	914	22	84	1.69	14	0	30	143	7.66
2016	A-	Vancouver	202	24	57	0	21	282	372	366	739	13	86	1.04	9	3	25	84	5.09
2016	A	Lansing	36	3	8	0	5	222	300	250	550	10	81	0.57	2	0	13	28	2.43
2017	A+	Dunedin	463	75	108	11	60	233	339	363	702	14	70	0.53	11	7	31	130	4.45
2018	AA	New Hampshire	449	80	113	26	99	252	388	499	887	18	67	0.68	20	8	48	247	7.29

Son of Craig Biggio has plus raw power but aggressive approach resulted in plenty of swing-and-missin 2018 and raises concerns about BA. Advanced understanding of strike zone and mechanical adjustment led to plenty of hard contact. Good glove and footwork, but fringe arm and range could push him to a UT role.

Bishop,Braden — 8 — Seattle

EXP MLB DEBUT: 2019 | H/W: 6-1 180 | FUT: Starting CF | 8D

Bats R Age 25 — 2015 (3) Washington

Pwr ++ | BAvg +++ | Spd ++++ | Def +++++

Year	Lev	Team	AB	R	H	HR	RBI	Avg	OB	Slg	OPS	bb%	ct%	Eye	SB	CS	x/h%	Iso	RC/G
2016	A	Clinton	248	38	72	1	21	290	355	331	686	9	81	0.52	6	1	10	40	4.05
2016	A+	Bakersfield	166	19	41	2	22	247	294	319	613	6	77	0.28	2	0	20	72	2.91
2017	A+	Modesto	355	71	105	2	32	296	375	400	775	11	82	0.69	16	4	29	104	5.38
2017	AA	Arkansas	125	18	42	1	11	336	407	448	855	11	88	1.00	6	1	26	112	6.31
2018	AA	Arkansas	345	70	98	8	33	284	353	412	765	10	80	0.54	5	2	29	128	5.03

Exceptionally athletic CF improved power without losing hit tool effectiveness, before hand fracture ended season. Changed trajectory of swing to help with lift without trading much ct%. Patience and line-drive approach yields high OBP. Below-average power plays due to other tools. Plus-plus CF, will stick and get ABs as defensive neutralizer.

Blankenhorn,Travis — 45 — Minnesota

EXP MLB DEBUT: 2020 | H/W: 6-1 195 | FUT: Starting 2B | 7D

Bats L Age 22 — 2015 (3) HS (PA)

Pwr +++ | BAvg ++ | Spd ++ | Def +++

Year	Lev	Team	AB	R	H	HR	RBI	Avg	OB	Slg	OPS	bb%	ct%	Eye	SB	CS	x/h%	Iso	RC/G
2015	Rk	Elizabethton	144	14	35	3	20	243	297	326	623	7	78	0.34	1	0	17	83	3.03
2016	Rk	Elizabethton	138	30	41	9	29	297	336	558	894	5	76	0.24	3	0	41	261	6.33
2016	A	Cedar Rapids	91	11	26	1	12	286	343	418	761	8	69	0.29	2	1	31	132	5.22
2017	A	Cedar Rapids	438	68	110	13	69	251	324	441	764	10	73	0.39	13	2	42	189	5.15
2018	A+	Fort Myers	442	52	102	11	57	231	286	387	673	7	71	0.27	6	4	40	156	3.79

Strong, husky IF struggled at first taste of High-A. Former top 15 MIN prospect, developed slight bat wrap in load, contributing to issues with hard contact and ct%. Uber-aggressive early in counts, works way out of ABs. Average power, doesn't play up due to timing issues. Big-bodied for 2B; 3B didn't take. Instinctual base runner.

Bohm,Alec — 5 — Philadelphia

EXP MLB DEBUT: 2021 | H/W: 6-5 240 | FUT: Starting 3B | 9D

Bats R Age 22 — 2018 (1) Wichita St

Pwr +++++ | BAvg +++ | Spd ++ | Def ++

Year	Lev	Team	AB	R	H	HR	RBI	Avg	OB	Slg	OPS	bb%	ct%	Eye	SB	CS	x/h%	Iso	RC/G
2018	NCAA	Wichita State	224	57	76	16	55	339	437	625	1062	15	88	1.39	9	3	41	286	8.70
2018	Rk	GCL Phillies W	32	8	11	0	5	344	382	438	820	6	88	0.50	2	0	18	94	5.59
2018	Rk	GCL Phillies	27	7	11	0	5	407	429	519	947	4	85	0.25	2	0	18	111	6.89
2018	A-	Williamsport	107	9	24	0	12	224	291	290	580	9	82	0.53	1	0	25	65	2.84

Loads of natural strength that lead to plus-plus power grades, along with an advanced plate approach that improved throughout college career. Hits with a plan; great athlete even with large frame. Some feel that fielding will require future move to 1B, where bat will still play. Nerve issue after a HBP on his knee clouded his short-season debut.

Boldt,Ryan — 789 — Tampa Bay

EXP MLB DEBUT: 2019 | H/W: 6-2 185 | FUT: Starting OF | 7D

Bats L Age 24 — 2016 (2) Nebraska

Pwr ++ | BAvg +++ | Spd +++ | Def +++

Year	Lev	Team	AB	R	H	HR	RBI	Avg	OB	Slg	OPS	bb%	ct%	Eye	SB	CS	x/h%	Iso	RC/G
2016	NCAA	Nebraska	257	48	74	5	30	288	339	416	756	7	86	0.56	20	9	28	128	4.84
2016	A-	Hudson Valley	170	17	37	1	15	218	261	276	538	6	86	0.42	8	9	19	59	2.24
2017	A+	Charlotte	440	60	130	5	62	295	353	407	760	8	80	0.44	23	6	25	111	4.96
2018	AA	Montgomery	241	40	66	7	34	274	340	461	800	9	76	0.41	12	2	38	187	5.54

Athletic, strong OF is tough out but has yet to tap into above-average power potential. Heady player. Battles every AB and sprays line drives to all fields. Swing trajectory and powerful frame suggests higher HR outputs. Little evidence of plus power potential in BP or game. Still, keep eye out for sudden HR barrage. Above-average runnner.

Bolt,Skye — 8 — Oakland

EXP MLB DEBUT: 2019 | H/W: 6-3 190 | FUT: Starting OF | 7D

Bats B Age 25 — 2015 (4) North Carolina

Pwr +++ | BAvg ++ | Spd +++ | Def +++

Year	Lev	Team	AB	R	H	HR	RBI	Avg	OB	Slg	OPS	bb%	ct%	Eye	SB	CS	x/h%	Iso	RC/G
2015	A-	Vermont	181	26	43	4	19	238	327	381	708	12	76	0.55	2	1	37	144	4.45
2016	A	Beloit	342	34	79	5	37	231	315	345	660	11	74	0.48	10	5	34	114	3.79
2017	A+	Stockton	432	76	105	15	66	243	326	435	761	11	69	0.40	9	8	44	192	5.22
2018	A+	Stockton	169	28	45	9	32	266	380	521	901	16	72	0.66	9	3	47	254	7.20
2018	AA	Midland	285	41	73	10	37	256	321	446	766	9	74	0.36	10	1	42	189	5.05

Switch-hitting OF who set career marks in HR and SB in 2018. Tall, lean frame and long levers create plus bat head speed as LHH, where he makes the most impact. Swing path can get long and often chases pitches in the dirt; ct% remains a question mark. Has up-the-middle value as CF with enough range and arm to stick there long-term.

Booker,Joel — 78 — Chicago (A)

EXP MLB DEBUT: 2020 | H/W: 6-2 180 | FUT: Starting OF | 7C

Bats R Age 25 — 2016 (22) Iowa

Pwr ++ | BAvg +++ | Spd ++++ | Def +++

Year	Lev	Team	AB	R	H	HR	RBI	Avg	OB	Slg	OPS	bb%	ct%	Eye	SB	CS	x/h%	Iso	RC/G
2016	Rk	AZL White Sox	135	30	40	1	18	296	358	393	751	9	80	0.48	26	1	25	96	4.89
2017	A	Kannapolis	286	53	86	3	29	301	340	385	725	6	77	0.26	14	5	19	84	4.33
2017	A+	Winston-Salem	189	23	44	2	15	233	271	296	568	5	78	0.24	9	3	18	63	2.30
2018	A+	Winston-Salem	192	39	57	5	21	297	369	469	838	10	78	0.52	14	9	37	172	6.06
2018	AA	Birmingham	267	43	71	2	17	266	322	348	670	8	71	0.29	12	8	23	82	3.81

Sleeper OF prospect struggled after 2nd half promotion to Double-A. Quick-twitch athlete with solid hand/eye coordination & plate discipline, struggles with swing path issues. Swing geared to groundball and line-drive contact. Will sell out for power on middle-in FB; pull power only in BP. A plus runner, struggled with SB efficiency. Tweener risk.

Boswell,Bret | 45 | **Colorado** | EXP MLB DEBUT: 2020 | H/W: 5-11 170 | FUT: Starting 2B | **7D**

Bats L Age 24	Year	Lev	Team	AB	R	H	HR	RBI	Avg	OB	Slg	OPS	bb%	ct%	Eye	SB	CS	x/h%	Iso	RC/G
2017 (8) Texas																				
Pwr ++++	2017	NCAA	Texas	198	34	54	7	33	273	379	444	824	15	80	0.87	5	0	37	172	6.01
BAvg ++	2017	A-	Boise	229	46	67	11	42	293	336	515	851	6	76	0.27	3	3	36	223	5.92
Spd +++	2018	A	Asheville	379	69	109	17	50	288	325	496	821	5	73	0.20	7	5	38	208	5.58
Def +++	2018	A+	Lancaster	118	28	38	10	28	322	389	636	1025	10	65	0.32	2	0	42	314	9.06

Underrated player has some of the best power in the system and blasted a career-high 27 HR between Low and High-A. Sells out for it, though, and low ct% and bb% could be exploited as he moves up, but hard to argue with the results. Moves well on defense with good range and a strong arm, but speed is not part of his game and was old for this level.

Bracho,Aaron | 6 | **Cleveland** | EXP MLB DEBUT: 2023 | H/W: 5-11 175 | FUT: Starting MIF | **8E**

Bats B Age 17	Year	Lev	Team	AB	R	H	HR	RBI	Avg	OB	Slg	OPS	bb%	ct%	Eye	SB	CS	x/h%	Iso	RC/G
2017 FA (VZ)																				
Pwr +++																				
BAvg ++++																				
Spd +++																				
Def ++	2018		(did not play in US)																	

A switch-hitting bat-first infielder that may have to shift to second base later in his pro career. Possesses two hard, but short and compact swings that should be able to produce a lot of hard contact stateside. Does not project to be a plus runner.

Bradley,Bobby | 3 | **Cleveland** | EXP MLB DEBUT: 2020 | H/W: 6-1 225 | FUT: Starting 1B | **7C**

Bats L Age 22	Year	Lev	Team	AB	R	H	HR	RBI	Avg	OB	Slg	OPS	bb%	ct%	Eye	SB	CS	x/h%	Iso	RC/G
2014 (3) HS (MS)	2015	A+	Lynchburg	8	0	0	0	0	0	111	0	111	11	75	0.50	0	0		0	-3.61
Pwr ++++	2016	A+	Lynchburg	485	82	114	29	102	235	338	466	803	13	65	0.44	3	0	46	231	5.90
BAvg ++	2017	AA	Akron	467	66	117	23	89	251	330	465	794	11	74	0.45	3	3	44	214	5.42
Spd +	2018	AA	Akron	369	49	79	24	64	214	300	477	776	11	72	0.43	1	0	58	263	5.17
Def ++	2018	AAA	Columbus	114	11	29	3	19	254	320	430	750	9	62	0.26	0	0	41	175	5.37

The big power hitter largely struggled in 2018, especially in his small sample in AAA. His carrying tool is the long ball, as even in a down 2018 he hit 27 HRs in 129 games across two levels. Despite a feel for the strike zone and ability to take a walk, his 33.6 K% at AAA will not get it done for a bat-only player.

Breaux,Josh | 2 | **New York (A)** | EXP MLB DEBUT: 2022 | H/W: 6-1 220 | FUT: Starting C | **8E**

Bats R Age 21	Year	Lev	Team	AB	R	H	HR	RBI	Avg	OB	Slg	OPS	bb%	ct%	Eye	SB	CS	x/h%	Iso	RC/G
2018 (2) McLennan CC																				
Pwr +++																				
BAvg ++																				
Spd +++	2018	Rk	GCL Yankees	8	0	1	0	0	125	222	125	347	11	88	1.00	0	0	0	0	0.40
Def ++	2018	A-	Staten Island	100	6	28	0	13	280	301	370	671	3	80	0.15	0	0	32	90	3.62

Strong, bat-first CA had solid pro debut. Big-bodied physique at physical projection. Aggressive hit tool with solid bat-to-ball skills. Makes consistent hard contact but is susceptible to quality breaking pitches. Raw plus power potential. Has had success in wood bat leagues with over-the-fence power. 20-25 HR hitter at maturity. Defense is a struggle.

Brigman,Bryson | 46 | **Miami** | EXP MLB DEBUT: 2020 | H/W: 5-11 170 | FUT: Starting 2B | **7D**

Bats R Age 23	Year	Lev	Team	AB	R	H	HR	RBI	Avg	OB	Slg	OPS	bb%	ct%	Eye	SB	CS	x/h%	Iso	RC/G
2016 (3) San Diego	2016	A-	Everett	265	51	69	0	19	260	359	291	650	13	84	0.95	17	12	10	30	3.95
Pwr +	2017	A	Clinton	463	55	109	2	36	235	302	296	598	9	84	0.59	16	8	18	60	3.07
BAvg +++	2018	A+	Modesto	381	47	116	2	38	304	366	391	757	9	85	0.64	15	6	19	87	5.00
Spd +++	2018	A+	Jupiter	71	9	24	0	5	338	365	394	759	4	82	0.23	4	0	17	56	4.68
Def +++	2018	AA	Jacksonville	42	1	13	1	6	310	341	429	769	5	86	0.33	2	0	23	119	4.75

Athletic, contact-oriented MIF was acquired in mid-season trade with SEA. Hit well at multiple-stops in 2018. Uses spray approach to pepper all fields with ground balls and line drives. Solid hand/eye skills but struggles going after pitches, which results in lots of soft contact. Minimal power potential in frame and swing. SB threat.

Brito,Daniel | 4 | **Philadelphia** | EXP MLB DEBUT: 2021 | H/W: 6-1 155 | FUT: Starting 2B | **7D**

Bats L Age 21	Year	Lev	Team	AB	R	H	HR	RBI	Avg	OB	Slg	OPS	bb%	ct%	Eye	SB	CS	x/h%	Iso	RC/G
2014 FA (VZ)																				
Pwr ++	2016	Rk	GCL Phillies	190	35	54	2	25	284	355	421	777	10	86	0.78	7	2	31	137	5.35
BAvg +++	2017	A	Lakewood	447	54	107	6	32	239	292	318	609	7	79	0.35	12	9	21	78	2.92
4.18 Spd +++	2018	A	Lakewood	329	33	83	4	31	252	309	340	649	8	81	0.42	15	6	23	88	3.52
Def +++	2018	A+	Clearwater	92	8	23	0	7	250	296	348	644	6	79	0.32	1	1	30	98	3.49

Inconsistency has plagued him: at his best, exhibits exquisite balance and bat control, can hit breaking stuff has a solid LD stroke. Possesses a live, projectable body that could gain some strength and additional power. But also gives away AB, misses hittable pitches and has gone through long slumps. Very good range and hands in the field.

Brito,Marcos | 4 | **Oakland** | EXP MLB DEBUT: 2021 | H/W: 6-0 160 | FUT: Starting MIF | **8E**

Bats B Age 19	Year	Lev	Team	AB	R	H	HR	RBI	Avg	OB	Slg	OPS	bb%	ct%	Eye	SB	CS	x/h%	Iso	RC/G
2016 FA (DR)																				
Pwr +																				
BAvg +++																				
Spd +++	2017	Rk	AZL Athletics	171	30	40	1	17	234	318	298	616	11	75	0.50	4	1	18	64	3.21
Def +++	2018	A-	Vermont	212	29	51	1	20	241	326	288	614	11	76	0.54	7	6	14	47	3.20

Athletic, switch-hitting INF with loose hands, easy swing and barrel control give him BA upside and plus ct% ability. Power is gap-oriented now but will add strength to lean frame down the road. Advanced approach for age. Versatile defender with arm for SS but has smooth footwork and quick transfer for 2B.

Brito,Ronny | 6 | **Los Angeles (N)** | EXP MLB DEBUT: 2021 | H/W: 6-0 165 | FUT: Starting SS | **7D**

Bats B Age 20	Year	Lev	Team	AB	R	H	HR	RBI	Avg	OB	Slg	OPS	bb%	ct%	Eye	SB	CS	x/h%	Iso	RC/G
2015 FA (DR)																				
Pwr ++	2017	Rk	AZL Dodgers	54	10	13	2	12	241	281	444	725	5	65	0.16	0	0	54	204	4.66
BAvg ++	2017	Rk	Ogden	63	12	15	1	7	238	262	349	611	3	65	0.09	6	0	27	111	2.87
Spd ++++	2018	Rk	DSL Dodgers	15	3	6	0	3	400	471	600	1071	12	73	0.50	0	0	50	200	9.77
Def ++++	2018	Rk	Ogden	219	37	63	11	52	288	350	489	839	9	66	0.28	1	6	35	201	6.25

Switch-hitting shortstop is a plus-plus defender with excellent range, good hands, and a strong arm. Had his best season as a pro. Average bat speed and below-average power limit long-term potential, but the glove and defense is good enough to get him to the majors.

Brujan,Vidal | 4 | **Tampa Bay** | EXP MLB DEBUT: 2020 | H/W: 5-10 150 | FUT: Utility player | **9D**

Bats B Age 21	Year	Lev	Team	AB	R	H	HR	RBI	Avg	OB	Slg	OPS	bb%	ct%	Eye	SB	CS	x/h%	Iso	RC/G
2014 FA (DR)	2016	Rk	GCL Rays	202	41	57	1	8	282	329	406	735	6	93	0.93	8	5	32	124	4.80
Pwr +++	2016	A-	Hudson Valley	8	1	0	0	0	0	111	0	111	11	88	1.00	2	0		0	-2.31
BAvg ++++	2017	A-	Hudson Valley	260	51	74	3	20	285	367	415	783	12	86	0.94	16	8	31	131	5.51
Spd +++++	2018	A	Bowling Green	377	86	118	5	41	313	391	427	818	11	86	0.91	43	15	24	114	5.86
Def +++	2018	A+	Charlotte	98	26	34	4	12	347	434	582	1015	13	85	1.00	12	4	38	235	8.28

Super-athletic, contact-oriented switch-hitting MIF had huge season. Lean, athletic physique with some room to grow into body without compromising run tool. Patient hitter with plus ct% skills. Better from LH side than RH. Power tied with exploiting middle-in pitches as LHH. 15-20 HR at maturity. Second in MiLB with 55 SB. Versatile; future CF a possibility.

Burger,Jake | 35 | **Chicago (A)** | EXP MLB DEBUT: 2020 | H/W: 6-2 210 | FUT: Starting 3B | **8D**

Bats R Age 22	Year	Lev	Team	AB	R	H	HR	RBI	Avg	OB	Slg	OPS	bb%	ct%	Eye	SB	CS	x/h%	Iso	RC/G
2017 (1) Missouri St																				
Pwr ++++	2017	NCAA	Missouri State	247	69	81	22	65	328	428	648	1075	15	85	1.13	3	1	43	320	8.80
BAvg +++	2017	Rk	AZL White Sox	13	4	2	1	2	154	214	462	676	7	85	0.50	0	0	100	308	3.70
Spd ++	2017	A	Kannapolis	181	21	49	4	27	271	320	409	728	7	85	0.46	0	1	31	138	4.47
Def +++	2018		Did not play - injury																	

Physically strong power hitting corner IF missed all of 2018 after tearing left Achilles tendon twice in 3 month period. Patient hitter with high ct%, should settle in at .250-.275 BA. Plus-plus raw power shows up to pull-side during games. Uses lower half well to generate power. Run tool below average on best days. Scouts split on 1B or 3B.

Burt,D.J. | 45 | **Kansas City** | EXP MLB DEBUT: 2020 | H/W: 5-9 160 | FUT: Utility player | **6B**

Bats R Age 23	Year	Lev	Team	AB	R	H	HR	RBI	Avg	OB	Slg	OPS	bb%	ct%	Eye	SB	CS	x/h%	Iso	RC/G
2014 (4) HS (NC)	2014	Rk	Burlington	144	17	31	2	9	215	289	264	553	9	83	0.60	7	3	10	49	2.42
Pwr +	2015	Rk	Idaho Falls	248	56	72	1	28	290	389	391	780	14	77	0.69	20	7	21	101	5.62
BAvg +++	2016	A	Lexington	474	74	122	4	59	257	330	338	667	10	77	0.47	43	17	20	80	3.84
4.05 Spd +++	2017	A+	Wilmington	365	52	83	0	29	227	343	307	650	15	72	0.63	32	13	29	79	3.90
Def +++	2018	A+	Wilmington	410	72	115	3	46	280	371	371	742	13	76	0.60	32	10	21	90	5.00

Lean, small-statured MIF had his best season since rookie ball. Improved ct% and hard hit rate behind improvements. Spray hitter with inside-out swing. Minimal power, completely pull-oriented. Above-average runner with plus instincts. 30-plus SB for third straight season. Rangy defender. Arm suited for 2B.

Cabello, Antonio — 8 — New York (A)

EXP MLB DEBUT: 2022 | **H/W:** 5-10 160 | **FUT:** Starting OF | **9E**

Bats R Age 18
2017 FA (VZ)

	Pwr	+++
	BAvg	++++
	Spd	++++
	Def	+++

Year	Lev	Team	AB	R	H	HR	RBI	Avg	OB	Slg	OPS	bb%	ct%	Eye	SB	CS	x/h%	Iso	RC/G
2018	Rk	GCL Yankees W	137	21	44	5	20	321	411	555	966	13	75	0.62	5	5	41	234	8.01
2018	Rk	DSL Yankees	22	5	5	0	1	227	393	318	711	21	73	1.00	5	1	20	91	5.04

Athletic OF had North American debut cut short by a shoulder injury. Five-tool potential. Advanced approach with some spray skills. Quick hands and strong forearms aid plus bat speed. Strong, stocky frame. Average raw power in frame and bat. Could hit 20 HR at projection. Plus runner who doesn't utilize speed well. Raw defender, likely corner OF.

Cameron, Daz — 8 — Detroit

EXP MLB DEBUT: 2019 | **H/W:** 6-2 185 | **FUT:** Starting OF | **8B**

Bats R Age 22
2015 (1) HS (GA)

	Pwr	++
	BAvg	+++
	Spd	+++
	Def	++

Year	Lev	Team	AB	R	H	HR	RBI	Avg	OB	Slg	OPS	bb%	ct%	Eye	SB	CS	x/h%	Iso	RC/G
2017	A	West Michigan	8	1	2	0	1	250	455	250	705	27	50	0.75	0	1	0	0	5.68
2017	A	Quad Cities	446	79	121	14	73	271	338	466	804	9	76	0.42	32	12	42	195	5.60
2018	A+	Lakeland	216	35	56	3	20	259	336	370	706	10	68	0.36	10	4	27	111	4.50
2018	AA	Erie	200	32	57	5	35	285	364	470	834	11	74	0.47	12	5	39	185	6.20
2018	AAA	Toledo	57	8	12	0	6	211	237	316	553	3	74	0.13	2	2	42	105	2.16

Athletic outfielder who saw exponential growth on both sides of the ball in 2018. Maximizes above-average speed and arm to hold down centerfield with little issue. Produced elevated rate of hard contact over three levels. Keen eye for pitch recognition and level of raw power that projects to increase later on.

Campos, Alexander — 6 — Oakland

EXP MLB DEBUT: 2021 | **H/W:** 6-0 178 | **FUT:** Starting MIF | **7E**

Bats R Age 19
2016 FA (VZ)

	Pwr	+
	BAvg	++
	Spd	++
	Def	+++

Year	Lev	Team	AB	R	H	HR	RBI	Avg	OB	Slg	OPS	bb%	ct%	Eye	SB	CS	x/h%	Iso	RC/G
2017		Did not play in the US																	
2018	Rk	AZL Athletics	71	11	9	0	4	127	244	183	427	13	61	0.39	4	1	33	56	0.27

Short and stocky, he has a well-rounded skillset but lacks elite tool. Swing is simple and compact and has some feel for the barrel. Solid athlete but showed fringe straight-line speed in AZL. Owns plus arm required for SS and looks like he'll stick there long-term.

Campusano, Luis — 2 — San Diego

EXP MLB DEBUT: 2021 | **H/W:** 6-0 200 | **FUT:** Starting C | **7D**

Bats R Age 20
2017 (2) HS (GA)

	Pwr	+++
	BAvg	+++
	Spd	++
	Def	+++

Year	Lev	Team	AB	R	H	HR	RBI	Avg	OB	Slg	OPS	bb%	ct%	Eye	SB	CS	x/h%	Iso	RC/G
2017	Rk	AZL Padres	121	7	34	4	24	281	360	413	774	11	80	0.63	0	2	24	132	5.13
2017	Rk	AZL Padres 2	13	1	2	0	1	154	154	154	308	0	92	0.00	0	0	0	0	-0.30
2018	A	Fort Wayne	260	26	75	3	40	288	337	365	702	7	83	0.44	0	1	19	77	4.14

Strong, hulking CA with potential for HR impact but lacks current feel for the barrel. Flashes massive raw power to pull side when he times pitches right, but over-aggressive approach limits his opportunities for contact. Owns big-time arm strength but could stand to improve his blocking and pitch calling. Move to 1B could be on horizon.

Canario, Alexander — 8 — San Francisco

EXP MLB DEBUT: 2022 | **H/W:** 6-1 165 | **FUT:** Starting OF | **8E**

Bats R Age 18
2016 FA (DR)

	Pwr	++++
	BAvg	+++
	Spd	++++
	Def	+++

Year	Lev	Team	AB	R	H	HR	RBI	Avg	OB	Slg	OPS	bb%	ct%	Eye	SB	CS	x/h%	Iso	RC/G
2018	Rk	AZL Giants	176	36	44	6	19	250	350	403	753	13	71	0.53	8	5	30	153	5.08

Quick-twitch, athletic OF prospect made stateside debut. Showed patient approach with natural ability to find the barrel. Swing is long; will need to shorten up to succeed. Plus raw power potential and hits to all fields in BP; but pull-heavy in games. Plus runner who is likely to lose a step as bulk is added to frame. Likely corner OF long term.

Canning, Gage — 8 — Washington

EXP MLB DEBUT: 2021 | **H/W:** 5-10 175 | **FUT:** Starting OF | **7D**

Bats L Age 20
2018 (5) Arizona St

	Pwr	++
	BAvg	+++
	Spd	+++
	Def	++

Year	Lev	Team	AB	R	H	HR	RBI	Avg	OB	Slg	OPS	bb%	ct%	Eye	SB	CS	x/h%	Iso	RC/G
2018	NCAA	Arizona State	236	47	87	9	45	369	427	648	1075	9	77	0.44	8	7	43	280	9.16
2018	A-	Auburn	54	13	17	2	7	315	373	593	965	8	67	0.28	0	2	47	278	8.42
2018	A	Hagerstown	112	15	25	4	16	223	293	411	703	9	68	0.31	2	0	52	188	4.32

Hits from a wide base and with quick hands and good bat speed. Mainly a line-drive hitter with some gap power and foot speed, though not a huge base-stealer to this point. Will take a walk, but has more contact issues that one might expect. Good first step and adequate arm in OF.

Capel, Conner — 8 — St. Louis

EXP MLB DEBUT: 2020 | **H/W:** 6-1 185 | **FUT:** Starting OF | **7D**

Bats L Age 21
2016 (5) HS (TX)

	Pwr	+++
	BAvg	++
	Spd	+++
	Def	+++

Year	Lev	Team	AB	R	H	HR	RBI	Avg	OB	Slg	OPS	bb%	ct%	Eye	SB	CS	x/h%	Iso	RC/G
2016	Rk	AZL Indians	138	22	29	0	13	210	268	290	558	7	86	0.55	10	3	28	80	2.66
2017	A	Lake County	439	73	108	22	61	246	313	478	792	9	75	0.40	15	10	47	232	5.31
2018	A+	Palm Beach	117	11	29	1	19	248	290	342	632	6	74	0.23	0	1	28	94	3.19
2018	A+	Lynchburg	322	47	84	6	44	261	358	388	747	13	78	0.68	15	10	31	127	5.04

Athletic player was part of the Oscar Mercado deal. Quick lefty stroke shows solid average power, but results regressed after breakout in 2017. Pull-side approach limits opposite field pop. Above-average runner covers ground well in CF with a strong arm, but needs to take more efficient routes.

Carlson, Dylan — 79 — St. Louis

EXP MLB DEBUT: 2021 | **H/W:** 6-3 195 | **FUT:** Starting OF | **8D**

Bats B Age 20
2016 (1) HS (CA)

	Pwr	+++
	BAvg	+++
	Spd	++
	Def	++

Year	Lev	Team	AB	R	H	HR	RBI	Avg	OB	Slg	OPS	bb%	ct%	Eye	SB	CS	x/h%	Iso	RC/G
2016	Rk	GCL Cardinals	183	30	46	3	22	251	312	404	716	8	72	0.31	4	2	41	153	4.51
2017	A	Peoria	383	63	92	7	42	240	331	347	678	12	70	0.45	6	6	28	107	4.06
2018	A	Peoria	47	5	11	2	9	234	368	426	794	18	79	1.00	2	0	45	191	5.73
2018	A+	Palm Beach	376	47	93	9	53	247	339	386	724	12	79	0.67	6	3	33	138	4.67

Switch-hitting OF has above-average raw power, but is just starting to get to it in game action. Pushed aggressively as a teenager in the Florida State League. Showed an improved understanding of the strike zone and made more contact. Smart, hard worker with solid across-the-board tools.

Carmona, Jean — 6 — Baltimore

EXP MLB DEBUT: 2022 | **H/W:** 6-1 183 | **FUT:** Utility player | **7D**

Bats B Age 18
2016 FA (DR)

	Pwr	++
	BAvg	++
	Spd	+++
	Def	+++

Year	Lev	Team	AB	R	H	HR	RBI	Avg	OB	Slg	OPS	bb%	ct%	Eye	SB	CS	x/h%	Iso	RC/G
2017	Rk	AZL Brewers	48	5	7	1	6	146	241	271	512	11	75	0.50	2	1	43	125	1.77
2018	Rk	Helena	155	28	37	4	24	239	298	406	704	8	71	0.29	5	3	41	168	4.27
2018	A-	Aberdeen	93	9	21	0	7	226	273	301	574	6	73	0.24	0	1	33	75	2.48

Strong, athletic switch-hitting IF with raw hit tool. Quick, compact swing with some load and swing path concerns. Over-aggressive with pitch recognition issues. Average raw power, doesn't use lower half in swing. Likely below average HR output at projection. Average runner and versatile defender on IF. Has athleticism to play LF/RF to complete UT profile.

Cartaya, Diego — 2 — Los Angeles (N)

EXP MLB DEBUT: 2023 | **H/W:** 6-2 199 | **FUT:** Starting C | **8D**

Bats R Age 17
2018 FA (VZ)

	Pwr	++
	BAvg	+++
	Spd	+
	Def	++++

Year	Lev	Team	AB	R	H	HR	RBI	Avg	OB	Slg	OPS	bb%	ct%	Eye	SB	CS	x/h%	Iso	RC/G
2018		Did not play in US																	

Top-rated Latin American player signed in July 2018 for $2.5M. Strong, physically mature teenager has a quick bat, a good understanding of the strike zone, and should develop average to above power. He moves well behind the plate with a plus arm and solid receiving skills for his age and has been compared to Salvador Perez.

Casas, Triston — 5 — Boston

EXP MLB DEBUT: 2022 | **H/W:** 6-4 238 | **FUT:** Starting 1B | **9D**

Bats L Age 19
2018 (1) HS (FL)

	Pwr	++++
	BAvg	+++
	Spd	++
	Def	+++

Year	Lev	Team	AB	R	H	HR	RBI	Avg	OB	Slg	OPS	bb%	ct%	Eye	SB	CS	x/h%	Iso	RC/G
2018	Rk	GCL Red Sox	4	0	0	0	0	0	200	0	200	20	50	0.50	0	0		0	-4.89

Boston's first pick in the 2018 draft out of HS. Has the size and power to be a top corner infield power threat. He tore a ligament in his thumb after just four pro AB, but should be fine going forward. He has a very strong, mature body for his age and a simple, quiet swing. Defense may be a concern, if for no other reason than his size.

Castro,Willi — 6 — Detroit

EXP MLB DEBUT: 2019 | H/W: 6-1 165 | FUT: Starting SS | 8C

Bats B Age 21	Year	Lev	Team	AB	R	H	HR	RBI	Avg	OB	Slg	OPS	bb%	ct%	Eye	SB	CS	x/h%	Iso	RC/G
2013 FA (PR)	2016	A+	Lynchburg	9	0	2	0	0	222	222	222	444	0	78	0.00	0	1	0	0	0.46
Pwr +	2017	A+	Lynchburg	469	69	136	11	58	290	330	424	754	6	81	0.31	19	9	28	134	4.67
BAvg ++	2018	AA	Erie	476	67	125	9	52	263	312	397	709	7	77	0.31	17	5	34	134	4.21
Spd ++	2018	AA	Akron	371	55	91	5	39	245	298	350	649	7	77	0.33	13	4	30	105	3.46
Def ++	2018	AAA	Toledo	21	0	6	0	2	286	286	286	571	0	76	0.00	1	0	0	0	1.99

Pure shortstop with feel to hold his post into the future. Quick hands and feet work well, but errors indicate he needs polish. Valuable switch-hitter with handful of Triple-A experience at a young age. Above-average runner who has taken 15-20 stolen bases over his last four seasons. Ability to drive to the gaps with developing power.

Cecchini,Gavin — 4 — New York (N)

EXP MLB DEBUT: 2016 | H/W: 6-2 180 | FUT: Reserve IF | 6C

Bats R Age 25	Year	Lev	Team	AB	R	H	HR	RBI	Avg	OB	Slg	OPS	bb%	ct%	Eye	SB	CS	x/h%	Iso	RC/G
2012 (1) HS (LA)	2016	MLB	NY Mets	6	2	2	0	2	333	333	667	1000	0	67	0.00	0	0	100	333	9.06
Pwr ++	2017	AAA	Las Vegas	453	68	121	6	39	267	327	380	706	8	87	0.66	5	4	30	113	4.37
BAvg +++	2017	MLB	NY Mets	77	4	16	1	7	208	247	273	520	5	75	0.21	0	1	19	65	1.60
4.40 Spd ++	2018	A+	St. Lucie	4	1	2	0	0	500	500	500	1000	0	100		0	0	0	0	6.83
Def ++	2018	AAA	Las Vegas	109	14	32	2	9	294	336	468	804	6	86	0.47	1	1	44	174	5.41

Looking like a tweener at this point. Not enough glove to be a regular SS or 2B and not enough bat to be a regular at 3B. Been trying to get more lower half into his swing to add power, but the result has been less bat control and command of the strike zone. Lacks range and agility for a quality MI. A mediocre utility infield option.

Celestino,Gilberto — 8 — Minnesota

EXP MLB DEBUT: 2021 | H/W: 6-2 175 | FUT: Starting CF | 8D

Bats R Age 20	Year	Lev	Team	AB	R	H	HR	RBI	Avg	OB	Slg	OPS	bb%	ct%	Eye	SB	CS	x/h%	Iso	RC/G
2015 FA (DR)	2016	Rk	GCL Astros	55	7	11	0	2	200	302	291	592	13	71	0.50	6	1	36	91	3.01
Pwr +++	2017	Rk	Greeneville	235	38	63	4	24	268	331	379	709	9	75	0.37	10	2	25	111	4.31
BAvg +++	2018	Rk	Elizabethton	109	13	29	1	13	266	304	349	653	5	85	0.38	8	2	21	83	3.53
Spd ++++	2018	A-	Tri City	127	18	41	4	21	323	372	480	853	7	80	0.40	14	0	29	157	5.94
Def ++++	2018	AA	Corpus Christi	8	0	0	0	0	0	0	0	0	0	38	0.00	0	0		0	-9.15

Defensively skilled, toolsy CF was acquired in deadline deal with HOU. Shortened up elongated swing, but still has work to do. Quiet load with solid bat-to-ball skills. Still raw in recognizing spin. Swing trajectory naturally geared for fly ball contact. Needs to add strength to get to power. A speedster, was 22 for 24 in SB attempts.

Chang,Yu-Cheng — 6 — Cleveland

EXP MLB DEBUT: 2019 | H/W: 6-1 175 | FUT: Starting MIF | 7B

Bats R Age 23	Year	Lev	Team	AB	R	H	HR	RBI	Avg	OB	Slg	OPS	bb%	ct%	Eye	SB	CS	x/h%	Iso	RC/G
2013 FA (TW)	2014	Rk	AZL Indians	159	39	55	6	25	346	412	566	978	10	82	0.64	6	1	35	220	7.68
Pwr ++++	2015	A	Lake County	393	52	91	9	52	232	281	361	642	6	74	0.26	5	6	32	130	3.29
BAvg ++	2016	A+	Lynchburg	417	78	108	13	70	259	331	463	794	10	74	0.41	11	3	47	204	5.55
Spd ++++	2017	AA	Akron	440	72	97	24	66	220	303	461	764	11	70	0.39	11	4	55	241	5.11
Def ++	2018	AAA	Columbus	457	56	117	13	62	256	321	411	733	9	68	0.31	4	3	37	155	4.73

Power took a step back in 2018, but has uppercut swing designed for it. Bat path causes more swing and miss than you would want for someone of his size. Has plus speed and previously displayed the ability for double-digit steals, although those also declined in 2018.

Chatham,CJ — 6 — Boston

EXP MLB DEBUT: 2021 | H/W: 6-4 185 | FUT: Reserve IF | 7D

Bats R Age 24	Year	Lev	Team	AB	R	H	HR	RBI	Avg	OB	Slg	OPS	bb%	ct%	Eye	SB	CS	x/h%	Iso	RC/G
2016 (2) Florida Atlantic	2016	A-	Lowell	108	19	28	4	19	259	310	426	736	7	81	0.40	0	1	32	167	4.46
Pwr ++	2017	Rk	GCL Red Sox	16	5	5	1	3	313	389	500	889	11	94	2.00	0	0	20	188	6.43
BAvg +++	2017	A	Greenville	3	0	1	0	2	333	333	333	667	0	100		0	1	0	0	3.67
4.30 Spd +++	2018	A	Greenville	75	13	23	0	9	307	333	413	747	4	81	0.21	1	1	30	107	4.62
Def +++	2018	A+	Salem	362	42	114	3	43	315	352	384	736	5	80	0.29	10	4	16	69	4.45

Long, thin SS who will do enough with the bat and glove to be MLB utilityman. Injuries have held him back the last two years. Overcame sore arm in 2018 and eventually got back to SS, where he showed he can hold his own at the position. Posted good numbers, but there are some concerns with naturally long levers to swing and overaggressiveness.

Chavis,Michael — 53 — Boston

EXP MLB DEBUT: 2019 | H/W: 5-10 190 | FUT: Starting 3B | 7B

Bats R Age 23	Year	Lev	Team	AB	R	H	HR	RBI	Avg	OB	Slg	OPS	bb%	ct%	Eye	SB	CS	x/h%	Iso	RC/G
2014 (1) HS (GA)	2017	A+	Salem	223	50	71	17	55	318	372	641	1013	8	74	0.33	1	0	51	323	8.13
Pwr ++++	2017	AA	Portland	248	39	62	14	39	250	306	492	798	7	77	0.36	1	0	52	242	5.24
BAvg ++++	2018	A-	Lowell	16	5	5	1	3	313	476	750	1226	24	69	1.00	0	0	100	438	12.81
4.50 Spd +	2018	AA	Portland	122	23	37	6	17	303	370	508	879	10	71	0.37	3	1	35	205	6.61
Def ++	2018	AAA	Pawtucket	33	8	9	2	7	273	294	545	840	3	64	0.08	0	0	56	273	6.29

Would have slotted well into the Steve Pearce role with the Red Sox, had Pearce not re-signed. Does have a chance to stay at 3B, which gives him some upside, but the bat is his best tool. Strong with a natural feel for hitting, but not a good athlete. Hard to say if will hit enough to be quality corner IF.

Chisholm,Jazz — 6 — Arizona

EXP MLB DEBUT: 2020 | H/W: 5-11 165 | FUT: Starting SS | 8C

Bats L Age 21	Year	Lev	Team	AB	R	H	HR	RBI	Avg	OB	Slg	OPS	bb%	ct%	Eye	SB	CS	x/h%	Iso	RC/G
2015 FA (BM)																				
Pwr +++	2016	Rk	Missoula	249	42	70	9	37	281	332	446	778	7	71	0.26	13	4	31	165	5.16
BAvg ++	2017	A	Kane County	109	14	27	1	12	248	311	358	669	8	64	0.26	3	0	30	110	4.04
Spd +++	2018	A	Kane County	307	52	75	15	43	244	312	472	784	9	68	0.31	8	2	48	228	5.41
Def +++	2018	A+	Visalia	149	27	49	10	27	329	367	597	964	6	65	0.17	9	2	37	268	8.06

Athletic, wiry SS who had full 2018 breakout across two levels and in AFL. Combines plus bat speed with natural loft in swing for above-average in-game power despite shorter, slender frame. Often a free-swinger whose poor ct% could be issue in upper minors. Mans solid SS and has just enough arm for left side of INF. Runs well and could have SB value.

Ciuffo,Nick — 2 — Tampa Bay

EXP MLB DEBUT: 2018 | H/W: 6-1 205 | FUT: Reserve C | 6C

Bats L Age 24	Year	Lev	Team	AB	R	H	HR	RBI	Avg	OB	Slg	OPS	bb%	ct%	Eye	SB	CS	x/h%	Iso	RC/G
2013 (1) HS (SC)	2016	A+	Charlotte	229	16	60	0	15	262	290	297	587	4	80	0.20	2	3	13	35	2.54
Pwr ++	2017	AA	Montgomery	371	42	91	7	42	245	322	385	707	10	74	0.44	2	0	41	140	4.40
BAvg ++	2018	A+	Charlotte	8	1	1	0	1	125	125	250	375	0	63	0.00	0	0	100	125	-0.48
Spd +	2018	AAA	Durham	221	26	58	5	28	262	303	380	684	6	72	0.21	0	0	28	118	3.80
Def ++++	2018	MLB	Tampa Bay	37	3	7	1	5	189	250	297	547	8	68	0.25	0	0	29	108	1.92

Former 1st Rd pick made MLB debut after recent offensive struggles. At best, works CF-to-RF with line drive approach. Swing has lengthened and has lost ct%. Power production limited due to poor use of leveraging lower half. Glove carries profile, as he neutralizes the running game.

Clemens,Kody — 4 — Detroit

EXP MLB DEBUT: 2020 | H/W: 6-1 170 | FUT: Starting 2B | 7B

Bats L Age 22	Year	Lev	Team	AB	R	H	HR	RBI	Avg	OB	Slg	OPS	bb%	ct%	Eye	SB	CS	x/h%	Iso	RC/G
2018 (3) Texas																				
Pwr ++																				
BAvg ++	2018	NCAA	Texas	248	58	87	24	72	351	443	726	1169	14	80	0.82	5	0	48	375	10.12
Spd ++	2018	A	West Michigan	149	18	45	4	17	302	388	477	865	12	82	0.78	3	1	36	174	6.47
Def ++	2018	A+	Lakeland	42	6	10	1	3	238	273	357	630	5	71	0.17	1	0	30	119	3.02

Gritty infielder with exceptional defensive instincts. Aggressive play helps to hide limited speed and range. Has history at third base, but shows enough feel to be able to stick at second. Made improvements to swing path and ability to pull the ball. Power has improved steadily with improving eye for pitch recognition.

Clement,Ernie — 6 — Cleveland

EXP MLB DEBUT: 2021 | H/W: 6-0 160 | FUT: Utility player | 5B

Bats R Age 23	Year	Lev	Team	AB	R	H	HR	RBI	Avg	OB	Slg	OPS	bb%	ct%	Eye	SB	CS	x/h%	Iso	RC/G
2017 (4) Virginia	2017	NCAA	Virginia	254	56	80	2	34	315	348	366	714	5	97	1.86	14	2	10	51	4.46
Pwr +	2017	A-	Mahoning Val	175	32	49	0	13	280	304	343	647	3	93	0.50	6	2	20	63	3.59
BAvg ++++	2018	A	Lake County	221	34	59	1	15	267	336	353	689	9	90	1.10	11	6	27	86	4.39
4.23 Spd ++++	2018	A+	Lynchburg	133	29	46	1	13	346	412	421	833	10	95	2.14	5	3	17	75	6.07
Def ++	2018	AA	Akron	65	9	16	0	5	246	279	354	633	4	89	0.43	2	1	38	108	3.49

An old-school type of baseball player, as his game is to put the ball in play and run. His swing is geared for line drive contact to right center field, and that has been something he has consistently been able to do in his minor league career so far. Almost no loft in his swing, limiting his potential for growing into power.

Coca,Yeison — 46 — Milwaukee

EXP MLB DEBUT: 2022 | H/W: 5-10 155 | FUT: Starting 2B | 8E

Bats R Age 19	Year	Lev	Team	AB	R	H	HR	RBI	Avg	OB	Slg	OPS	bb%	ct%	Eye	SB	CS	x/h%	Iso	RC/G
2015 FA (DR)																				
Pwr ++																				
BAvg +++																				
Spd +++	2017	Rk	AZL Brewers	126	14	30	0	15	238	284	262	545	6	71	0.22	6	2	10	24	1.96
Def +++	2018	Rk	Helena	281	49	79	3	21	281	313	413	726	4	77	0.20	16	9	30	132	4.38

Shorter, lean athlete who flashed speed and some power in the short-season Pioneer League. Above-average runner who will have a chance at SB impact at next level. Shows feel for hitting as LH/RH and smooth stroke produces ct% from both sides. Lacks ideal loft for HR output. Ideal range, footwork and soft hands to man a quality 2B.

Collins,Zack — 2 — Chicago (A)

EXP MLB DEBUT: 2019 | H/W: 6-2 210 | FUT: Starting C | 7B

Bats L Age 24
2016 (1) Miami
Pwr +++
BAvg ++
Spd ++
Def +

Year	Lev	Team	AB	R	H	HR	RBI	Avg	OB	Slg	OPS	bb%	ct%	Eye	SB	CS	x/h%	Iso	RC/G
2016	Rk	AZL White Sox	11	1	1	0	0	91	91	91	182	0	36	0.00	0	0	0	0	-4.52
2016	A+	Winston-Salem	120	24	31	6	18	258	418	467	885	22	68	0.85	0	0	42	208	7.38
2017	A+	Winston-Salem	341	63	76	17	48	223	365	443	807	18	65	0.64	0	2	50	220	6.17
2017	AA	Birmingham	34	7	8	2	5	235	422	471	893	24	68	1.00	0	0	50	235	7.50
2018	AA	Birmingham	418	58	98	15	68	234	383	404	788	19	62	0.64	5	0	41	170	6.12

Strong, patient lefty CA continues to struggle with ct% and hard-hit rate in upper minors. A hitch in load prevents barrel from getting out in front of the plate, resulting in soft contact. Plus-plus strike zone discipline; 100-BB potential. Plus-plus raw power hasn't translated to game action due to swing and miss. Poor defender.

Conine,Griffin — 9 — Toronto

EXP MLB DEBUT: 2021 | H/W: 6-1 195 | FUT: Starting OF | 8D

Bats L Age 21
2018 (2) Duke
Pwr ++++
BAvg ++
Spd ++
Def +++

Year	Lev	Team	AB	R	H	HR	RBI	Avg	OB	Slg	OPS	bb%	ct%	Eye	SB	CS	x/h%	Iso	RC/G
2018	NCAA	Duke	227	54	65	18	52	286	400	608	1008	16	67	0.58	0	1	54	322	8.92
2018	Rk	GCL Blue Jays	8	1	3	0	3	375	444	500	944	11	75	0.50	0	0	33	125	7.78
2018	A-	Vancouver	206	24	49	7	30	238	302	427	729	8	69	0.30	5	0	47	189	4.65

Son of Jeff Conine has a quick bat and above-average raw power. Starts with an open LH stance with hands high and uses small leg-kick for timing. Good bat speed and has natural loft to swing, but does have some contact issues and swing can get long. Solid defender with an above-average arm, but speed limits him to a corner slot.

Contreras,Mc Gregory — 7 — Toronto

EXP MLB DEBUT: 2022 | H/W: 6-1 170 | FUT: Starting OF | 7D

Bats R Age 20
2015 FA (VZ)
Pwr +++
BAvg ++
Spd +++
Def +++

Year	Lev	Team	AB	R	H	HR	RBI	Avg	OB	Slg	OPS	bb%	ct%	Eye	SB	CS	x/h%	Iso	RC/G
2017	Rk	Bluefield	190	36	53	5	33	279	322	421	743	6	71	0.22	4	3	28	142	4.66
2018	A-	Vancouver	215	27	56	8	30	260	290	460	751	4	68	0.13	6	4	41	200	4.82

Lean, athletic OF continues to develop into a solid, if not spectacular, prospect. Quick bat and an aggressive approach results in above-average power, but also significant contact issues. Speed is a tick above-average and has the size and raw power to hit 20+ HR at his peak. Corner outfield is his future.

Contreras,William — 2 — Atlanta

EXP MLB DEBUT: 2021 | H/W: 6-0 180 | FUT: Starting C | 8C

Bats R Age 21
2015 FA (VZ)
Pwr ++++
BAvg +++
Spd ++
Def ++

Year	Lev	Team	AB	R	H	HR	RBI	Avg	OB	Slg	OPS	bb%	ct%	Eye	SB	CS	x/h%	Iso	RC/G
2016	Rk	GCL Braves	72	8	19	1	8	264	329	375	704	9	79	0.47	0	1	32	111	4.28
2017	Rk	Danville	169	29	49	4	25	290	378	432	810	12	82	0.80	1	0	31	142	5.78
2018	A	Rome	307	54	90	11	39	293	354	463	817	9	76	0.40	1	1	32	169	5.62
2018	A+	Florida	83	3	21	0	10	253	303	337	641	7	81	0.38	0	0	33	84	3.48

Brother of Willson Contreras is a raw, athletic bat-first CA who advanced to High-A. Compact, raw but patient hitter with spray power approach. Some tinkering needed to load & swing path. Raw plus power, plays to all fields. Athletic behind plate still learning nuances of position. Plus throw tool.

Cozens,Dylan — 9 — Philadelphia

EXP MLB DEBUT: 2018 | H/W: 6-6 235 | FUT: Reserve OF | 7D

Bats L Age 24
2012 (2) HS (AZ)
Pwr +++++
BAvg +
Spd +++
Def ++

Year	Lev	Team	AB	R	H	HR	RBI	Avg	OB	Slg	OPS	bb%	ct%	Eye	SB	CS	x/h%	Iso	RC/G
2015	AA	Reading	40	6	14	3	9	350	395	625	1020	7	83	0.43	2	1	36	275	7.71
2016	AA	Reading	521	106	144	40	125	276	352	591	943	10	64	0.33	21	1	56	315	8.01
2017	AAA	Lehigh Valley	476	68	100	27	75	210	296	418	714	11	59	0.30	8	3	42	208	4.72
2018	AAA	Lehigh Valley	297	49	73	21	58	246	347	529	876	13	58	0.37	9	6	55	283	7.61
2018	MLB	Philadelphia	38	2	6	1	2	158	273	289	562	14	37	0.25	1	0	50	132	4.46

Second try at AAA was better, and made his MLB debut. Swing was shorter; able to cover the plate better, and still crushed fastballs. But well-placed breaking stuff still exposed his holes, and an established sub-60% ct% is too large a burden. Can hit mistake pitches, steal a couple bases and be a COR OF reserve with a strong arm.

Craig,Will — 3 — Pittsburgh

EXP MLB DEBUT: 2020 | H/W: 6-3 212 | FUT: Reserve 1B | 6C

Bats R Age 24
2016 (1) Wake Forest
Pwr +++
BAvg +++
4.60 Spd +
Def +++

Year	Lev	Team	AB	R	H	HR	RBI	Avg	OB	Slg	OPS	bb%	ct%	Eye	SB	CS	x/h%	Iso	RC/G
2016	NCAA	Wake Forest	182	53	69	16	66	379	507	731	1237	21	81	1.34	0	1	46	352	11.42
2016	A-	West Virginia	218	28	61	2	23	280	394	362	756	16	83	1.11	2	0	23	83	5.37
2017	A+	Bradenton	458	59	124	6	61	271	358	371	729	12	77	0.58	1	3	27	100	4.75
2018	AA	Altoona	480	73	119	20	102	248	308	448	756	8	73	0.33	6	3	45	200	4.85

Wide-body who really cheated for power at AA, and the result was a drop in BA. Some length to swing and lack of plus batspeed and athleticism really limits what he can do. Hard to see him hitting well enough to be everyday MLB 1B. May need to go back to 3B some to increase versatility. Has plus arm to do so, but not the feet.

Cron,Kevin — 3 — Arizona

EXP MLB DEBUT: 2019 | H/W: 6-5 245 | FUT: Starting 1B | 7B

Bats R Age 26
2014 (14) Texas Christian
Pwr ++++
BAvg ++
Spd +
Def +++

Year	Lev	Team	AB	R	H	HR	RBI	Avg	OB	Slg	OPS	bb%	ct%	Eye	SB	CS	x/h%	Iso	RC/G
2014	A-	Hillsboro	129	23	37	6	17	287	338	488	827	7	78	0.34	0	0	38	202	5.60
2015	A+	Visalia	518	71	141	27	97	272	310	494	804	5	75	0.21	0	0	43	222	5.24
2016	AA	Mobile	465	60	103	26	88	222	273	437	710	7	71	0.25	3	1	46	215	4.08
2017	AA	Jackson	515	76	146	25	91	283	354	497	851	10	74	0.42	1	0	41	214	6.15
2018	AAA	Reno	392	57	121	22	97	309	367	554	920	8	74	0.36	1	0	42	245	6.97

Tall, hulking 1B with plus raw power and swing geared for fly-ball contact. Strength derived from mass rather than lean muscle that cut into his overall athleticism and swing. Makes fringe contact but shows ability to use all fields. Not a SB source. Ideal frame and build for 1B and has shown flashes of being a solid defender there.

Cruz,Oneil — 6 — Pittsburgh

EXP MLB DEBUT: 2022 | H/W: 6-6 175 | FUT: Starting SS | 9D

Bats L Age 20
2015 FA (DR)
Pwr ++++
BAvg +++
4.10 Spd ++++
Def ++

Year	Lev	Team	AB	R	H	HR	RBI	Avg	OB	Slg	OPS	bb%	ct%	Eye	SB	CS	x/h%	Iso	RC/G
2017	A	Great Lakes	342	51	82	8	36	240	297	342	639	8	68	0.25	8	7	22	102	3.29
2017	A	West Virginia	55	9	12	2	8	218	317	400	717	13	60	0.36	0	0	42	182	4.96
2018	A	West Virginia	402	66	115	14	59	286	342	488	829	8	75	0.34	11	5	40	201	5.84

A freak. At a legit 6-6, has the chance to be perhaps the tallest regular SS ever, and manages to play the position surprisingly well. The bat is going to play somewhere; made strides in 2018. Plus raw power and improving BA and OBP skills. Think Gregory Polanco at SS. Some concerns, but could be a major impact player.

Cumberland,Brett — 2 — Baltimore

EXP MLB DEBUT: 2020 | H/W: 5-10 181 | FUT: Starting C | 7D

Bats B Age 23
2016 (2) California
Pwr +++
BAvg ++
Spd ++
Def ++

Year	Lev	Team	AB	R	H	HR	RBI	Avg	OB	Slg	OPS	bb%	ct%	Eye	SB	CS	x/h%	Iso	RC/G
2017	A	Rome	175	34	46	10	48	263	374	531	905	15	65	0.51	1	0	57	269	7.64
2017	A+	Florida	182	14	49	1	21	269	335	363	698	9	66	0.29	0	2	29	93	4.44
2018	A+	Florida	280	40	66	11	39	236	355	407	763	16	70	0.61	0	1	39	171	5.31
2018	AA	Mississippi	18	1	2	0	0	111	158	111	269	5	72	0.20	0	0	0	0	-1.84
2018	AA	Bowie	42	6	8	3	7	190	261	405	666	9	71	0.33	0	0	38	214	3.38

Strong-bodied, offense-oriented switch hitting CA acquired from ATL mid-season. Power-first approach, as elongated swing limits ct% and hard hit skills. Works walks. Raw plus-power in frame; reaches better for it from LH side. Below-average runner and defender. Has made improvements behind plate to save profile.

Dalbec,Bobby — 5 — Boston

EXP MLB DEBUT: 2020 | H/W: 6-4 219 | FUT: Starting 3B | 9C

Bats R Age 23
2016 (4) Arizona
Pwr +++++
BAvg ++
4.50 Spd +
Def ++++

Year	Lev	Team	AB	R	H	HR	RBI	Avg	OB	Slg	OPS	bb%	ct%	Eye	SB	CS	x/h%	Iso	RC/G
2016	A-	Lowell	132	25	51	7	33	386	426	674	1100	6	75	0.27	2	2	43	288	9.30
2017	Rk	GCL Red Sox	27	3	7	0	2	259	375	296	671	16	67	0.56	1	0	14	37	4.21
2017	A	Greenville	284	48	70	13	39	246	331	437	768	11	57	0.29	4	5	40	190	5.97
2018	A+	Salem	344	59	88	26	85	256	366	573	939	15	62	0.46	3	1	63	317	8.30
2018	AA	Portland	111	14	29	6	24	261	299	514	813	5	59	0.13	0	0	52	252	6.47

The next Troy Glaus. Should be good at 3B with a top-notch arm, and capable of 40 HRs. BA and strikeouts are concerns, but he made great strides in 2018, improving his approach, and earning a promotion to AA. Can drive ball out easily to all fields and will lay off pitches he has trouble handling. Plus makeup will lead to more improvement in 2019.

Davis,Brendon — 56 — Texas

EXP MLB DEBUT: 2021 | H/W: 6-4 155 | FUT: Starting 3B | 7D

Bats R Age 21
2015 (5) HS (CA)
Pwr ++
BAvg ++
4.60 Spd +
Def +++

Year	Lev	Team	AB	R	H	HR	RBI	Avg	OB	Slg	OPS	bb%	ct%	Eye	SB	CS	x/h%	Iso	RC/G
2016	A	Great Lakes	398	51	96	5	49	241	293	334	627	7	70	0.25	8	3	26	93	3.15
2017	A	Hickory	77	8	14	2	6	182	292	273	565	13	64	0.43	0	0	21	91	2.30
2017	A	Great Lakes	310	39	76	8	35	245	345	403	748	13	65	0.44	3	7	39	158	5.26
2017	A+	Rancho Cuca	30	2	6	1	8	200	273	400	673	9	57	0.23	0	0	67	200	4.46
2018	A+	Down East	406	49	103	6	40	254	330	365	694	10	74	0.44	6	2	30	111	4.21

Lean and athletic infielder, made much better contact in 2018. But doesn't run particularly well, and swing is geared to opposite field, which nicks his power projection. Can handle SS, but has arm strength for 3B. Needs to prove he can pull the ball to tap into HR.

Davis,Brennen	8	Chicago (N)	EXP MLB DEBUT: 2022	H/W: 6-4 175	FUT: Starting CF	9E

Bats R Age 19	Year	Lev	Team	AB	R	H	HR	RBI	Avg	OB	Slg	OPS	bb%	ct%	Eye	SB	CS	x/h%	Iso	RC/G
2018 (2) HS (AZ)																				
Pwr +++																				
BAvg ++																				
Spd ++++																				
Def ++++	2018	Rk	AZL Cubs 2	57	9	17	0	3	298	403	333	736	15	79	0.83	6	1	12	35	5.04

Two-sport high school star is raw, but athletic and projectable. Quick bat, strong wrists, and natural raw power give him potential and he showed well in his pro debut. Plus-plus runner with a strong arm, good range, and the instincts to stick in CF. At his height he will need to work hard to keep his swing intact, but the upside is exciting.

Davis,Jaylin	9	Minnesota	EXP MLB DEBUT: 2020	H/W: 6-1 197	FUT: Reserve OF	6B

Bats R Age 24	Year	Lev	Team	AB	R	H	HR	RBI	Avg	OB	Slg	OPS	bb%	ct%	Eye	SB	CS	x/h%	Iso	RC/G
2015 (24) Appalachian St	2016	A	Cedar Rapids	192	32	48	9	29	250	324	469	793	10	67	0.33	3	0	48	219	5.66
Pwr ++	2017	A	Cedar Rapids	251	36	67	12	41	267	311	486	797	6	69	0.21	9	2	42	219	5.43
BAvg ++	2017	A+	Fort Myers	215	26	51	3	25	237	278	335	612	5	67	0.17	1	1	25	98	2.91
Spd +++	2018	A+	Fort Myers	199	23	54	5	19	271	347	397	744	10	71	0.40	3	2	28	126	4.86
Def +++	2018	AA	Chattanooga	240	30	66	6	34	275	333	425	758	8	71	0.30	5	2	33	150	5.00

Physically mature, sleeper OF prospect continues to hit at every stop. Tweener profile with some swing and miss mixed in. Gets to velocity, especially against LHP, despite swing deficiencies in his load and extending too early. Below-average power potential. Corner OF profile with plus arm and average speed.

Dawson,Ronnie	8	Houston	EXP MLB DEBUT: 2020	H/W: 6-2 225	FUT: Reserve OF	8D

Bats L Age 23	Year	Lev	Team	AB	R	H	HR	RBI	Avg	OB	Slg	OPS	bb%	ct%	Eye	SB	CS	x/h%	Iso	RC/G
2016 (2) Ohio St	2016	A-	Tri City	244	41	55	7	36	225	337	373	710	14	73	0.62	12	6	38	148	4.53
Pwr +++	2017	A	Quad Cities	438	81	119	14	62	272	353	438	791	11	77	0.54	17	8	34	167	5.45
BAvg ++	2017	A+	Buies Creek	52	7	17	0	5	327	375	423	798	7	83	0.44	1	3	24	96	5.43
Spd +++	2018	A+	Buies Creek	332	51	82	10	49	247	326	398	724	11	71	0.41	29	11	35	151	4.58
Def +++	2018	AA	Corpus Christi	114	18	33	6	14	289	325	518	843	5	70	0.18	6	3	39	228	5.95

A left-field only prospect, Dawson's bat is going to have to make the case for him to stay on prospect radars. He has plus raw power but struggled to get it into games consistently until his extra-base outburst in AA. He has relatively gaudy stolen base totals but is more of an average runner and those should decline as he approaches the majors.

Daza,Yonathan	789	Colorado	EXP MLB DEBUT: 2020	H/W: 6-2 190	FUT: Reserve OF	6B

Bats R Age 25	Year	Lev	Team	AB	R	H	HR	RBI	Avg	OB	Slg	OPS	bb%	ct%	Eye	SB	CS	x/h%	Iso	RC/G
2011 FA (VZ)	2015	A	Asheville	259	27	78	1	39	301	317	394	711	2	86	0.17	6	11	23	93	4.06
Pwr +	2016	A	Asheville	475	63	146	3	58	307	339	408	748	5	84	0.29	2	7	27	101	4.62
BAvg +++	2016	A+	Modesto	33	1	8	0	3	242	265	303	568	3	79	0.14	1	1	25	61	2.29
Spd ++++	2017	A+	Lancaster	519	93	177	3	87	341	377	466	843	5	83	0.34	31	8	27	125	5.85
Def ++++	2018	AA	Hartford	219	27	67	4	29	306	327	461	789	3	89	0.29	4	5	36	155	5.01

Late developing prospect proved his breakout in 2017 was no fluke. Advanced bat-to-ball skills allows him to make plus contact despite a minuscule bb%. Opposite field approach limits power, but he's a plus defender with a cannon for an arm. Missed seven weeks of action with a hamstring injury that limited his running game.

De La Guerra,Chad	456	Boston	EXP MLB DEBUT: 2020	H/W: 5-10 180	FUT: Utility player	6B

Bats L Age 26	Year	Lev	Team	AB	R	H	HR	RBI	Avg	OB	Slg	OPS	bb%	ct%	Eye	SB	CS	x/h%	Iso	RC/G
2015 (17) Grand Canyon	2016	A	Greenville	240	40	60	1	20	250	336	329	665	11	76	0.54	7	2	22	79	3.93
Pwr ++	2017	A+	Salem	218	47	64	5	36	294	366	463	830	10	82	0.63	5	2	38	170	5.94
BAvg ++++	2017	AA	Portland	196	34	53	4	23	270	347	408	755	11	76	0.48	2	1	36	138	5.02
4.30 Spd ++	2018	AA	Portland	316	51	84	15	54	266	333	462	795	9	70	0.33	4	1	36	196	5.49
Def +++	2018	AAA	Pawtucket	73	6	10	1	4	137	149	205	354	1	71	0.05	2	0	30	68	-0.85

Short infielder who lacks athleticism but can hit the FB and catch the ball all over the diamond. Really reads the ball well on defense, which makes up for a lack of range and agility. Double-A pitchers figured him out some and started to mix in more offspeed. He also started to go for power too much. But skills there to be a tough out at MLB level.

Dean,Austin	79	Miami	EXP MLB DEBUT: 2018	H/W: 6-1 190	FUT: Starting OF	7D

Bats R Age 25	Year	Lev	Team	AB	R	H	HR	RBI	Avg	OB	Slg	OPS	bb%	ct%	Eye	SB	CS	x/h%	Iso	RC/G
2012 (4) HS (TX)	2017	Rk	GCL Marlins	17	3	7	1	7	412	412	706	1118	0	88	0.00	0	0	43	294	8.27
Pwr +++	2017	AA	Jacksonville	234	29	66	4	30	282	323	427	750	6	80	0.30	3	1	33	145	4.70
BAvg +++	2018	AA	Jacksonville	81	13	34	3	14	420	460	654	1114	7	91	0.86	0	0	35	235	8.80
Spd +++	2018	AAA	New Orleans	316	58	103	9	54	326	390	475	864	9	84	0.67	2	2	24	149	6.20
Def +++	2018	MLB	Miami	113	16	25	4	14	221	267	363	629	6	81	0.32	1	0	32	142	3.07

Athletic, contact-oriented OF road a season long hot streak to his MLB debut. Average all-around tool shed. Healthy for full season, found success with gap-to-gap approach and high ct%. Raw plus power in frame, depressed somewhat because of heavy top-spin-generating swing. Doesn't run much but can handle himself defensively.

Dearden,Tyler	9	Boston	EXP MLB DEBUT: 2023	H/W: 6-1 155	FUT: Reserve OF	7D

Bats L Age 20	Year	Lev	Team	AB	R	H	HR	RBI	Avg	OB	Slg	OPS	bb%	ct%	Eye	SB	CS	x/h%	Iso	RC/G
2017 (29) Marist College																				
Pwr +++																				
BAvg +++																				
4.40 Spd +	2017	Rk	GCL Red Sox	74	9	19	2	15	257	375	405	780	16	62	0.50	1	1	37	149	6.00
Def +++	2018	A-	Lowell	170	30	52	4	23	306	352	459	810	7	65	0.20	0	1	33	153	6.04

Michael Saunders type corner OF who has upside but is inexperienced and raw. Swing has some length and he gets out on his front foot too much. Also lacks good pitch recognition. Lower body not that live and does not move well enough for CF. All that said, can get a lot better at the plate, and could still come a long way.

Deatherage,Brock	789	Detroit	EXP MLB DEBUT: 2020	H/W: 6-1 176	FUT: Starting OF	7B

Bats L Age 23	Year	Lev	Team	AB	R	H	HR	RBI	Avg	OB	Slg	OPS	bb%	ct%	Eye	SB	CS	x/h%	Iso	RC/G
2018 (10) North Carolina St																				
Pwr +	2018	NCAA	NC State	228	47	70	14	41	307	383	548	931	11	67	0.37	18	8	34	241	7.66
BAvg ++	2018	Rk	GCL Tigers W	9	6	5	4	7	556	600	1889	2489	10	89	1.00	0	0	80	1333	22.82
Spd +++	2018	A	West Michigan	176	25	55	2	18	313	363	443	806	7	72	0.28	15	3	25	131	5.73
Def ++	2018	A+	Lakeland	45	12	15	1	5	333	412	467	878	12	71	0.46	4	0	20	133	6.88

Aggressive outfielder with plus-plus speed and above-average overall defensive profile. Light footwork, stemming from high school football career. Thrives off speed in the outfield and on the basepaths. Produced deceptive power in debut season. Swing path is good, but over-aggression leads to too much swing-and-miss and needs to be slowed down.

Decker,Nick	789	Boston	EXP MLB DEBUT: 2023	H/W: 6-0 200	FUT: Starting OF	7D

Bats L Age 19	Year	Lev	Team	AB	R	H	HR	RBI	Avg	OB	Slg	OPS	bb%	ct%	Eye	SB	CS	x/h%	Iso	RC/G
2018 (2) HS (NJ)																				
Pwr ++++																				
BAvg +++																				
Spd ++																				
Def +++	2018	Rk	GCL Red Sox	4	1	1	0	0	250	400	500	900	20	75	1.00	0	0	100	250	7.83

Second round pick out of HS in 2018. Short, solid lefty hitter who figures to hit for some power and probably play a corner OF spot. Swing looks good, but involves a lot of lower body action with a big leg lift. Remains to be seen how it plays at pro levels.

Decolati,Niko	789	Colorado	EXP MLB DEBUT: 2021	H/W: 6-1 205	FUT: Starting OF	7D

Bats R Age 21	Year	Lev	Team	AB	R	H	HR	RBI	Avg	OB	Slg	OPS	bb%	ct%	Eye	SB	CS	x/h%	Iso	RC/G
2018 (6) Loyola Marymount																				
Pwr ++++																				
BAvg ++																				
Spd +++	2018	NCAA	Loyola Marymt	207	38	56	6	21	271	343	444	788	10	71	0.38	8	5	38	174	5.52
Def +++	2018	Rk	Grand Junction	263	55	86	11	56	327	404	532	936	11	79	0.61	17	5	34	205	7.28

Strong, physical player surprised in his pro debut. Generates natural loft to swing with plus bat speed and an improved approach. Showed lots of swing-and-miss in college, but made more contact in Rookie Ball. Above-average speed and a solid defender with a strong arm. Plus raw power is best asset, but needs to repeat new found plate discipline.

Deichmann,Greg	789	Oakland	EXP MLB DEBUT: 2020	H/W: 6-2 185	FUT: Starting OF	7C

Bats L Age 23	Year	Lev	Team	AB	R	H	HR	RBI	Avg	OB	Slg	OPS	bb%	ct%	Eye	SB	CS	x/h%	Iso	RC/G
2017 (2) Louisiana St																				
Pwr +++	2017	NCAA	LSU	266	54	82	19	73	308	420	579	999	16	77	0.82	7	3	41	271	8.24
BAvg +++	2017	A-	Vermont	164	31	45	8	30	274	380	530	911	15	76	0.70	4	1	49	256	7.22
Spd ++	2018	Rk	AZL Athletics	38	9	11	1	7	289	372	526	898	12	79	0.63	0	0	45	237	7.00
Def ++	2018	A+	Stockton	166	18	33	6	21	199	273	392	665	9	62	0.27	0	1	61	193	3.95

Tall, lean OF with smooth LH stroke and chance for power impact. Hands work well in swing and generates plus bat head speed at point of contact. Has struggled with quality breaking balls and ct% ability vs. LHP is questionable. Average overall athlete who won't be an SB threat at next level. Likely destined for corner OF role with fringe range.

Delgado, Raynel — 456 — Cleveland

EXP MLB DEBUT: 2023 H/W: 6-2 185 FUT: Starting MIF **7C**

Bats B Age 19
2018 (6) HS (FL)

Pwr +++
BAvg +++
Spd +++
Def +++

Year	Lev	Team	AB	R	H	HR	RBI	Avg	OB	Slg	OPS	bb%	ct%	Eye	SB	CS	x/h%	Iso	RC/G
2018	Rk	AZL Indians 2	173	34	53	1	21	306	409	382	790	15	75	0.68	10	2	21	75	5.78

A switch-hitting infielder with pop from both sides of the plate, he fell down draft boards last spring with a mediocre senior year performance-wise. Possesses two smooth swings with good rhythm and uses his legs well to generate power. He has good barrel control and is a solid average runner.

Deveaux, Trent — 8 — Los Angeles (A)

EXP MLB DEBUT: 2022 H/W: 6-0 160 FUT: Starting OF **8E**

Bats   Age 18
2017 FA (BA)

Pwr ++
BAvg ++
Spd +++++
Def ++++

Year	Lev	Team	AB	R	H	HR	RBI	Avg	OB	Slg	OPS	bb%	ct%	Eye	SB	CS	x/h%	Iso	RC/G
2018	Rk	AZL Angels	166	20	33	1	11	199	300	247	547	13	59	0.35	7	4	18	48	2.20

Advanced defender flirting with premium status. 80-grade speed, plus range and strong arm couple with enough advanced instincts to make him a lock as a starter. Body is still developing, preventing him from showing much power, but already holds good feel for the strike zone. Capitalizes on strong line-drive contact. Some swing-and-miss to polish out.

Devers, Jose — 6 — Miami

EXP MLB DEBUT: 2021 H/W: 6-0 155 FUT: Starting SS **8E**

Bats L Age 19
2016 FA (DR)

Pwr ++
BAvg +++
Spd ++++
Def ++++

Year	Lev	Team	AB	R	H	HR	RBI	Avg	OB	Slg	OPS	bb%	ct%	Eye	SB	CS	x/h%	Iso	RC/G
2017	Rk	GCL Yankees	138	17	34	1	9	246	333	348	681	12	85	0.86	15	3	29	101	4.28
2018	A	Greensboro	337	46	92	0	24	273	304	332	636	4	85	0.31	13	6	17	59	3.32
2018	A+	Jupiter	8	1	2	0	2	250	333	250	583	11	100		0	0	0	0	3.73

Athletic, toolsy LHH SS had successful full-season debut. Improved hit tool pushes profile. Line drive approach with plus bat-to-ball skills. Showed advanced ability to find barrel. Aggressive hitter, expands zone but still makes solid contact. Has not reached for power yet, but 10-15 HR in frame and swing at projection. Excellent defender.

Diaz, Danny — 5 — Boston

EXP MLB DEBUT: 2023 H/W: 6-1 170 FUT: Starting 1B **8D**

Bats R Age 18
2017 FA (VZ)

Pwr ++++
BAvg ++
Spd +
Def ++

Year	Lev	Team	AB	R	H	HR	RBI	Avg	OB	Slg	OPS	bb%	ct%	Eye	SB	CS	x/h%	Iso	RC/G
2018	Rk	DSL Red Sox	105	17	25	6	27	238	273	476	749	5	74	0.19	0	3	52	238	4.49

Was limited to 26 games in rookie ball after breaking a bone in his play. Showed some power when he did play, but not a great command of the zone. Has the big, rangy frame to fill out and be quite strong. Has a strong arm, but he's not smooth or agile, which could make it hard for him to stay at 3B.

Diaz, Eduardo — 789 — Arizona

EXP MLB DEBUT: 2022 H/W: 6-2 175 FUT: Starting OF **7D**

Bats R Age 21
2015 FA (VZ)

Pwr ++
BAvg +++
Spd +++
Def +++

Year	Lev	Team	AB	R	H	HR	RBI	Avg	OB	Slg	OPS	bb%	ct%	Eye	SB	CS	x/h%	Iso	RC/G
2016	Rk	Missoula	2	0	0	0	0	0	0	0	0	0	50	0.00	0	0		0	-7.85
2016	Rk	AZL DBacks	96	7	22	0	7	229	302	271	573	9	75	0.42	4	2	14	42	2.57
2017	Rk	Missoula	247	58	77	7	44	312	341	510	851	4	81	0.23	11	2	39	198	5.83
2018	A	Kane County	120	12	27	2	11	225	244	350	594	2	67	0.08	3	0	33	125	2.59

Athletic, wiry OF with a chance for average tools across the board. Plus runner who is quick to full speed, can steal bases and will man any OF position. Has aggressive approach at plate and will require refinement against quality offspeed. Possesses some bat speed and current gap power could grow into HR as his matures.

Diaz, Isan — 4 — Miami

EXP MLB DEBUT: 2019 H/W: 5-10 185 FUT: Starting 2B **8D**

Bats L Age 22
2014 (2) HS (MA)

Pwr +++
BAvg ++
Spd +++
Def +++

Year	Lev	Team	AB	R	H	HR	RBI	Avg	OB	Slg	OPS	bb%	ct%	Eye	SB	CS	x/h%	Iso	RC/G
2015	Rk	Missoula	272	58	98	13	51	360	431	640	1071	11	76	0.52	12	7	45	279	9.20
2016	A	Wisconsin	507	71	134	20	75	264	356	469	825	12	71	0.49	11	8	44	205	6.11
2017	A+	Carolina	383	59	85	13	54	222	330	376	706	14	68	0.51	9	3	39	154	4.47
2018	AA	Jacksonville	294	44	72	10	42	245	360	418	779	15	68	0.56	10	3	42	173	5.65
2018	AAA	New Orleans	137	19	28	3	14	204	283	358	641	10	67	0.33	4	0	39	153	3.52

Patient, power-first 2B bat struggled with consistent hard-contact rate in 2018. Big, lumbering swing with solid hand/eye coordination. Sells out to plus raw power. Works counts and takes BB. Potential 25-HR power is in stocky frame and uppercut swing. Will struggle with contact, especially against premium velocity. Above-average runner.

Diaz, Lewin — 3 — Minnesota

EXP MLB DEBUT: 2020 H/W: 6-3 180 FUT: Starting 1B **7E**

Bats L Age 22
2013 FA (DR)

Pwr +++
BAvg ++
Spd +
Def +++

Year	Lev	Team	AB	R	H	HR	RBI	Avg	OB	Slg	OPS	bb%	ct%	Eye	SB	CS	x/h%	Iso	RC/G
2015	Rk	GCL Twins	111	12	29	1	15	261	344	369	713	11	78	0.58	2	0	31	108	4.56
2015	Rk	Elizabethton	48	7	8	3	5	167	216	375	591	6	65	0.18	0	0	50	208	2.37
2016	Rk	Elizabethton	174	26	54	9	37	310	355	575	930	6	80	0.34	0	0	48	264	6.86
2017	A	Cedar Rapids	466	47	136	12	68	292	328	444	772	5	83	0.31	2	1	34	152	4.86
2018	A+	Fort Myers	294	21	66	6	35	224	250	344	594	3	81	0.18	1	0	30	119	2.60

Tall, strong 1B-only prospect struggled with low hard-contact rate in High-A. Open stance with slight load, struggles reacting to pitches. Swing is elongated and gets out around the ball. Gets beaten in by average velocity. Plus power in frame but hasn't reached it in-game. Broke thumb in August, missed rest of season. Not a fast runner.

Diaz, Yusniel — 789 — Baltimore

EXP MLB DEBUT: 2019 H/W: 6-1 195 FUT: Starting OF **8B**

Bats R Age 22
2015 FA (CU)

Pwr +++
BAvg ++++
Spd +++
Def +++

Year	Lev	Team	AB	R	H	HR	RBI	Avg	OB	Slg	OPS	bb%	ct%	Eye	SB	CS	x/h%	Iso	RC/G
2016	A+	Rancho Cuca	316	47	86	8	54	272	333	418	751	8	78	0.41	7	8	27	146	4.81
2017	A+	Rancho Cuca	331	42	92	8	39	278	347	414	761	10	78	0.48	7	9	28	136	4.99
2017	AA	Tulsa	108	15	36	3	13	333	390	491	881	8	73	0.34	2	5	31	157	6.62
2018	AA	Tulsa	220	36	69	6	30	314	421	477	899	16	82	1.05	8	8	29	164	7.08
2018	AA	Bowie	134	23	32	5	15	239	329	403	732	12	79	0.64	4	5	34	164	4.66

Contact-oriented, athletic OF struggled after mid-season trade. Employs patient, spray approach. Lower half swing mechanics isn't conducive to power stroke yet, but raw plus power in frame. Above-average runner, gets caught stealing often. Likely a corner OF, where hit tool will drive his profile.

Didder, Ray-Patrick — 6 — Atlanta

EXP MLB DEBUT: 2020 H/W: 6-0 170 FUT: Utility player **6C**

Bats R Age 24
2013 FA (AA)

Pwr +
BAvg ++
Spd ++++
Def ++

Year	Lev	Team	AB	R	H	HR	RBI	Avg	OB	Slg	OPS	bb%	ct%	Eye	SB	CS	x/h%	Iso	RC/G
2016	A	Rome	478	95	131	6	35	274	343	381	724	9	79	0.50	37	12	23	107	4.56
2017	A+	Florida	418	51	96	5	44	230	303	330	633	10	71	0.36	25	13	28	100	3.37
2018	A+	Florida	244	37	51	3	22	209	290	299	590	10	66	0.36	18	3	22	90	2.75
2018	AA	Mississippi	131	17	36	1	17	275	354	374	728	11	72	0.43	9	2	25	99	4.78

Athletic, RHH who played SS in 2018 but has ultimate position versatility. Patient hitter with pull-oriented approach. His swing struggles catching up to velocity and pitches elevated in the zone. Flat swing trajectory not conducive to fly ball contact. Speedy runner with SB history. Arm plays everywhere.

Dodson, Tanner — 8 — Tampa Bay

EXP MLB DEBUT: 2022 H/W: 6-1 160 FUT: Starting CF **7E**

Bats B Age 21
2017 (CBB) California

Pwr +
BAvg +++
Spd ++++
Def ++++

Year	Lev	Team	AB	R	H	HR	RBI	Avg	OB	Slg	OPS	bb%	ct%	Eye	SB	CS	x/h%	Iso	RC/G
2018	A-	Hudson Valley	198	30	54	2	19	273	339	369	708	9	83	0.59	8	3	22	96	4.39

Athletic, switch-hitting 2-way player most scouts like as RHP out of pen. Still a chance he develops as CF. Unorthodox, open set up from both sides of plate. Swing geared towards ground ball and soft line-drive contact, taking advantage of plus run tool. Patient approach, unlikely to develop power. Excellent CF with solid routes and covers ground.

Downs, Jeter — 46 — Los Angeles (N)

EXP MLB DEBUT: 2021 H/W: 5-11 180 FUT: Starting 2B **8D**

Bats R Age 20
2017 (1) HS (FL)

Pwr +++
BAvg +++
Spd +++
Def +++

Year	Lev	Team	AB	R	H	HR	RBI	Avg	OB	Slg	OPS	bb%	ct%	Eye	SB	CS	x/h%	Iso	RC/G
2017	Rk	Billings	172	31	46	6	29	267	367	424	791	14	81	0.84	8	5	26	157	5.53
2018	A	Dayton	455	63	117	13	47	257	333	402	736	10	77	0.50	37	10	32	145	4.67

Solid, athletic MIF performed as expected in full-season debut. A pull-oriented RHH hitter with a solid swing path, he struggled with pitch recognition. With a swing trajectory geared towards generating loft, he has plus instincts and above-average speed on the bases. Has 20/20 potential, though likely a 2B rather than SS. Was shipped to LA in offseason Puig/Kemp trade.

Dubon,Mauricio — 6 — Milwaukee

EXP MLB DEBUT: 2019 | H/W: 6-0 160 | FUT: Starting MIF | 8C

Bats R Age 24
2013 (26) HS (CA)
Pwr ++
BAvg +++
Spd ++++
Def +++

Year	Lev	Team	AB	R	H	HR	RBI	Avg	OB	Slg	OPS	bb%	ct%	Eye	SB	CS	x/h%	Iso	RC/G
2016	A+	Salem	235	53	72	0	29	306	392	379	771	12	89	1.32	24	4	19	72	5.49
2016	AA	Portland	251	48	85	6	40	339	366	538	904	4	86	0.31	6	3	38	199	6.41
2017	AA	Biloxi	268	34	74	2	24	276	338	351	689	9	84	0.60	31	9	22	75	4.13
2017	AAA	Col Springs	224	40	61	6	33	272	315	420	735	6	85	0.41	7	6	34	147	4.47
2018	AAA	Col Springs	108	18	37	4	18	343	355	574	929	2	82	0.11	6	3	41	231	6.53

Versatile athlete who missed most of 2018 after tearing his ACL. Brings plus speed, potential SB impact and positional versatility to the table. Has feel to hit and demonstrates quality ct% skill; sprays the ball to all fields. Does not lift the ball consistently enough for HR impact but will drive gaps and leg out triples. High BA/SB type profile.

Dunand,Joe — 6 — Miami

EXP MLB DEBUT: 2020 | H/W: 6-2 205 | FUT: Starting 3B | 7D

Bats R Age 23
2017 (2) North Carolina St
Pwr +++
BAvg ++
Spd ++
Def +++

Year	Lev	Team	AB	R	H	HR	RBI	Avg	OB	Slg	OPS	bb%	ct%	Eye	SB	CS	x/h%	Iso	RC/G
2017	NCAA	NC State	209	42	60	18	51	287	346	632	978	8	78	0.42	2	0	55	344	7.45
2017	Rk	GCL Marlins	16	4	6	1	3	375	474	750	1224	16	75	0.75	0	0	67	375	11.63
2017	A+	Jupiter	11	1	4	0	1	364	462	545	1007	15	64	0.50	0	1	50	182	9.94
2018	A+	Jupiter	243	39	64	7	42	263	319	391	710	8	78	0.37	2	0	25	128	4.17
2018	AA	Jacksonville	217	25	46	7	28	212	266	369	635	7	67	0.23	0	1	43	157	3.23

Solid, power-first prospect struggled after mid-season promotion to Double-A. Minimal load with slight bat wrap, attacks the FB. Contact rate took a hit in Double-A due to extending early and elongating his swing. Plus raw power, though pull-heavy and likely average power at projection. A SS now, but likely 3B long term due to bulkiness.

Duran,Jarren — 487 — Boston

EXP MLB DEBUT: 2021 | H/W: 6-1 170 | FUT: Starting OF | 8D

Bats L Age 22
2018 (7) Long Beach St
Pwr +++
BAvg ++++
4.10 Spd ++++
Def +++

Year	Lev	Team	AB	R	H	HR	RBI	Avg	OB	Slg	OPS	bb%	ct%	Eye	SB	CS	x/h%	Iso	RC/G
2018	NCAA	Long Beach St	222	42	67	2	22	302	362	392	754	9	86	0.66	17	2	19	90	4.94
2018	A-	Lowell	155	28	54	2	20	348	392	548	940	7	83	0.42	12	4	31	200	7.14
2018	A	Greenville	128	24	47	1	15	367	391	477	868	4	83	0.23	12	6	23	109	5.96

Just-drafted athlete who can run and hit but needs to find a place to play. Did not look great at 2B or CF in limited pro innings at low levels of minors, but has tools to be at least solid OF option down the line. The bat should play somewhere. The swing is good and he should be able to hit for average and some power. Can also run.

Duran,Rodolfo — 2 — Philadelphia

EXP MLB DEBUT: 2022 | H/W: 5-9 170 | FUT: Starting C | 7D

Bats R Age 21
2014 FA (DR)
Pwr ++++
BAvg ++
4.60 Spd +
Def ++

Year	Lev	Team	AB	R	H	HR	RBI	Avg	OB	Slg	OPS	bb%	ct%	Eye	SB	CS	x/h%	Iso	RC/G
2016	Rk	GCL Phillies	73	14	23	3	14	315	351	493	844	5	81	0.29	1	1	26	178	5.64
2016	A-	Williamsport	9	1	2	0	0	222	222	222	444	0	89	0.00	0	0	0	0	0.93
2017	A-	Williamsport	159	14	40	0	6	252	287	346	633	5	77	0.22	0	1	30	94	3.26
2018	A	Lakewood	311	44	81	18	46	260	305	495	800	6	76	0.27	1	1	44	235	5.19

Showed some HR thump from the CA position, though mostly in two one-month spurts. Still a good amount of swing-and-miss in his profile, so questions on how the hit tool will translate to higher levels. Quick feet and strong arm; threw out 42% of SB attemptees, though blocking at times an issue. Seeks additional consistency on both sides of the ball.

Edwards,Xavier — 6 — San Diego

EXP MLB DEBUT: 2022 | H/W: 5-10 155 | FUT: Starting SS | 8D

Bats R Age 19
2018 (1) HS (FL)
Pwr +
BAvg +++
Spd ++++
Def +++

Year	Lev	Team	AB	R	H	HR	RBI	Avg	OB	Slg	OPS	bb%	ct%	Eye	SB	CS	x/h%	Iso	RC/G
2018	Rk	AZL Padres	73	19	28	0	11	384	477	466	942	15	86	1.30	12	1	18	82	7.68
2018	A-	Tri-City	86	21	27	0	5	314	433	360	793	17	83	1.20	10	0	15	47	5.95

Shorter, lean athlete whose glove stands above his bat at present. Mans a plus SS and shows elite footwork and range and has plenty of arm to stick. Offense is predicated on high-volume contact as switch hitter. Will not be HR threat; mostly gaps at next level. Works counts well and spits on pitches in the dirt. Plus-plus speed; will be SB threat.

Eierman,Jeremy — 6 — Oakland

EXP MLB DEBUT: 2021 | H/W: 6-0 195 | FUT: Starting SS | 7C

Bats R Age 22
2018 (2) Missouri St
Pwr +++
BAvg ++
Spd +++
Def +++

Year	Lev	Team	AB	R	H	HR	RBI	Avg	OB	Slg	OPS	bb%	ct%	Eye	SB	CS	x/h%	Iso	RC/G
2018	NCAA	Missouri State	223	48	64	10	49	287	364	516	880	11	79	0.57	21	3	45	229	6.52
2018	A-	Vermont	247	36	58	8	26	235	273	381	654	5	72	0.19	10	4	31	146	3.33

Stocky, strong collegiate INF who made pro debut in short-season NYPL. Strong-armed defender who will have defensive versatility at next level. Owns above-average raw power but swing lacks fluidity for consistent ct%. Aggressive approach limits in-game raw and could be BA burden. Decent athlete who is better runner underway.

Ellis,Drew — 5 — Arizona

EXP MLB DEBUT: 2020 | H/W: 6-3 210 | FUT: Starting 3B | 7C

Bats R Age 23
2017 (2) Louisville
Pwr +++
BAvg +++
Spd ++
Def +++

Year	Lev	Team	AB	R	H	HR	RBI	Avg	OB	Slg	OPS	bb%	ct%	Eye	SB	CS	x/h%	Iso	RC/G
2017	NCAA	Louisville	231	56	82	20	61	355	450	701	1151	15	83	1.00	6	0	48	346	9.85
2017	A-	Hillsboro	181	35	41	8	23	227	317	403	720	12	75	0.53	3	1	39	177	4.45
2018	A+	Visalia	443	57	109	15	71	246	325	429	754	11	78	0.53	2	6	46	183	4.94

Tall, strong 3B who owns big-time raw power that has yet to fully manifest in games. Pop plays to all fields and ball jumps off bat with ease. Displays solid ct% ability and has track record of drawing walks. Not the best athlete and won't be an SB threat. Defensive home is likely 3B despite otherwise average arm and range.

Encarnacion,Jean Carlos — 5 — Baltimore

EXP MLB DEBUT: 2021 | H/W: 6-3 195 | FUT: Starting 3B | 8E

Bats R Age 21
2016 FA (DR)
Pwr +++
BAvg ++
Spd +++
Def +

Year	Lev	Team	AB	R	H	HR	RBI	Avg	OB	Slg	OPS	bb%	ct%	Eye	SB	CS	x/h%	Iso	RC/G
2017	Rk	GCL Braves	103	16	36	2	16	350	374	563	937	4	79	0.18	4	2	39	214	7.02
2017	Rk	Danville	93	14	27	1	6	290	313	355	667	3	77	0.14	3	5	15	65	3.42
2018	A	Rome	361	45	104	10	57	288	313	463	775	3	72	0.13	5	5	37	175	5.00
2018	A	Delmarva	462	55	126	12	64	273	297	439	736	3	71	0.12	5	5	37	167	4.51

Lanky, athletic 3B prospect enjoyed solid full-season debut. Acquired from ATL mid-season. Uber-aggressive, hands-to-ball hitter with poor pitch recognition skills. Raw plus power with swing trajectory geared for game power strides. Struggles finding barrel, muscling bloopers. Unrefined defender with strong arm. Lacks baseball instincts.

Erceg,Lucas — 5 — Milwaukee

EXP MLB DEBUT: 2019 | H/W: 6-3 200 | FUT: Starting 3B | 8C

Bats L Age 23
2016 (2) California
Pwr +++
BAvg +++
Spd +++
Def +++

Year	Lev	Team	AB	R	H	HR	RBI	Avg	OB	Slg	OPS	bb%	ct%	Eye	SB	CS	x/h%	Iso	RC/G
2016	Rk	Helena	105	17	42	2	22	400	442	552	995	7	85	0.50	8	1	26	152	7.64
2016	A	Wisconsin	167	17	47	7	29	281	330	497	827	7	77	0.32	1	3	40	216	5.65
2017	A+	Carolina	496	66	127	15	81	256	305	417	722	7	81	0.37	2	3	39	161	4.33
2017	AAA	Col Springs	10	2	4	0	2	400	455	600	1055	9	90	1.00	0	0	50	200	8.61
2018	AA	Biloxi	463	52	115	13	51	248	304	382	686	7	82	0.45	3	1	30	134	3.92

Tall, lanky 3B with plus raw power and some feel to hit from left side. Employs uppercut bat plane and is pull-oriented, but shows plus ct% ability with smooth swing. Former college closer with plus arm strength required for 3B; will have solid-average range for the hot corner. Still waiting for the tools to materialize into on-field production.

Ernesto,Larry — 789 — Milwaukee

EXP MLB DEBUT: 2023 | H/W: 6-2 175 | FUT: Starting OF | 8C

Bats B Age 18
2018 FA (DR)
Pwr +++
BAvg ++
Spd +++
Def +++

Year	Lev	Team	AB	R	H	HR	RBI	Avg	OB	Slg	OPS	bb%	ct%	Eye	SB	CS	x/h%	Iso	RC/G
2018	Rk	AZL Brewers	20	4	7	0	2	350	381	450	831	5	70	0.17	0	1	29	100	6.05
2018	Rk	DSL Brewers	203	38	48	5	20	236	286	394	680	6	67	0.21	9	4	42	158	3.99

Athletic, high-waisted Dominican OF with quality tools, but remains very raw. Employs smooth swing from both sides but will require work against quality off-speed stuff. Gap power at present and should have at least average power at maturity. Plus runner who should play above-average CF with refined routes; SB impact upon making his debut.

Espinal,Santiago — 6 — Toronto

EXP MLB DEBUT: 2019 | H/W: 5-10 175 | FUT: Reserve SS | 6B

Bats R Age 24
2016 (10) Miami-Dade Coll
Pwr ++
BAvg +++
Spd +++
Def +++

Year	Lev	Team	AB	R	H	HR	RBI	Avg	OB	Slg	OPS	bb%	ct%	Eye	SB	CS	x/h%	Iso	RC/G
2016	Rk	GCL Red Sox	86	8	21	0	10	244	323	267	590	10	87	0.91	1	0	10	23	3.17
2017	A	Greenville	492	64	138	4	46	280	333	358	691	7	86	0.58	20	6	19	77	4.12
2018	A+	Salem	256	53	80	7	32	313	358	477	834	7	86	0.51	9	1	31	164	5.69
2018	A+	Dunedin	65	9	17	2	8	262	324	431	755	8	85	0.60	0	3	35	169	4.86
2018	AA	New Hampshire	147	17	42	1	20	286	348	395	742	9	85	0.64	2	1	29	109	4.85

Athletic infielder was part of the S. Pearce deal. Uses short leg kick to start swing. Quick bat with solid plate discipline as he hunts for pitches he can drive. Makes solid, hard contact. Above-average speed results in good range. Hands work well and has the arm to stick at SS. At 24 the clock is ticking, but has some interesting tools.

Estevez,Omar

46 | **Los Angeles (N)** | EXP MLB DEBUT: 2021 | H/W: 5-10 168 | FUT: Starting 2B | **7D**

Bats R Age 20
2015 FA (CU)
Pwr +++
BAvg +++
Spd +++
Def +++

Year	Lev	Team	AB	R	H	HR	RBI	Avg	OB	Slg	OPS	bb%	ct%	Eye	SB	CS	x/h%	Iso	RC/G
2016	A	Great Lakes	471	46	120	9	61	255	294	389	682	5	74	0.21	3	6	36	134	3.81
2017	A+	Rancho Cuca	457	56	117	4	47	256	306	348	654	7	79	0.34	2	2	26	92	3.55
2018	A+	Rancho Cuca	515	87	143	15	84	278	336	456	792	8	73	0.33	3	1	42	179	5.42

Athletic infielder has a quick stroke and generates surprising pop. Good barrel awareness and plate discipline, but high leg kick results in timing issues and swing-and-miss. Good range with soft hands, but an average arm likely limits him to 2B as he moves up. Strong 2nd half shows upside (.308/.374/.515).

Estrada,Thairo

6 | **New York (A)** | EXP MLB DEBUT: 2019 | H/W: 5-10 154 | FUT: Reserve IF | **6B**

Bats R Age 23
2012 FA (VZ)
Pwr +
BAvg +++
Spd +++
Def ++++

Year	Lev	Team	AB	R	H	HR	RBI	Avg	OB	Slg	OPS	bb%	ct%	Eye	SB	CS	x/h%	Iso	RC/G
2016	A	Charleston (Sc)	140	11	40	5	19	286	324	429	753	5	85	0.38	11	3	23	143	4.56
2016	A+	Tampa	315	52	92	3	30	292	352	375	726	8	85	0.63	7	5	21	83	4.58
2017	AA	Trenton	495	72	149	6	48	301	346	392	738	6	89	0.61	8	11	19	91	4.62
2018	A+	Tampa	45	4	10	0	5	222	222	267	489	0	80	0.00	0	0	20	44	1.17
2018	AAA	Scranton/WB	33	1	5	0	3	152	152	182	333	0	76	0.00	0	0	20	30	-0.92

Utility IF with chance to fill bench role in big leagues starting in 2019. Short, compact swing geared towards line-drive contact. Sprays the field, but is short of stature with limited strength, so isn't a power threat. Is solid at SS with above-average range and soft hands. Could play across the infield. Athletic enough for OF reps too.

Evans,Phillip

456 | **New York (N)** | EXP MLB DEBUT: 2017 | H/W: 5-10 185 | FUT: Utility player | **6D**

Bats R Age 26
2011 (15) HS (CA)
Pwr ++
BAvg ++
4.40 Spd ++
Def +++

Year	Lev	Team	AB	R	H	HR	RBI	Avg	OB	Slg	OPS	bb%	ct%	Eye	SB	CS	x/h%	Iso	RC/G
2016	AA	Binghamton	361	50	121	8	39	335	368	485	853	5	83	0.32	1	1	31	150	5.83
2017	AAA	Las Vegas	466	58	130	11	56	279	339	418	757	8	83	0.53	2	3	31	139	4.88
2017	MLB	NY Mets	33	4	10	0	1	303	378	364	742	11	76	0.50	0	0	20	61	4.93
2018	AAA	Las Vegas	219	34	56	14	39	256	321	493	814	9	81	0.50	4	3	41	237	5.40
2018	MLB	NY Mets	21	1	3	0	1	143	217	143	360	9	62	0.25	1	0	0	0	-0.95

Plus makeup older guy whose defensive versatility has given him MLB value. Does have some pop in his bat, an idea and some patience, but swing gets long around the ball, which limits his value. Though he can play all over the field and works to hold his own at the corner OF and infield positions, is not a plus defender anywhere. Depth piece.

Fabian,Sandro

9 | **San Francisco** | EXP MLB DEBUT: 2020 | H/W: 6-1 180 | FUT: Starting OF | **8E**

Bats R Age 21
2014 FA (DR)
Pwr +++
BAvg ++
Spd ++
Def +++

Year	Lev	Team	AB	R	H	HR	RBI	Avg	OB	Slg	OPS	bb%	ct%	Eye	SB	CS	x/h%	Iso	RC/G
2016	Rk	AZL Giants	159	30	54	2	35	340	367	522	889	4	82	0.25	3	1	37	182	6.37
2017	A	Augusta	480	51	133	11	61	277	292	408	700	2	82	0.11	5	4	31	131	3.80
2018	A+	San Jose	406	47	81	10	35	200	248	325	573	6	74	0.24	1	2	37	126	2.33

Toolsy, slugging OF struggled in aggressive High-A assignment. Contact and hard hit rate took dramatic drop, especially in 2nd half when his slash line cratered to a .167/.253/.276. Only positive sign was increased BB%. Pull-oriented raw-average power; 15-22 HR at maturity. Has lost step defensively since debut. Solid defender in RF with plus arm.

Fairchild,Stuart

8 | **Cincinnati** | EXP MLB DEBUT: 2020 | H/W: 6-0 195 | FUT: Starting CF | **8E**

Bats R Age 23
2017 (2) Wake Forest
Pwr +++
BAvg +++
Spd ++++
Def +++

Year	Lev	Team	AB	R	H	HR	RBI	Avg	OB	Slg	OPS	bb%	ct%	Eye	SB	CS	x/h%	Iso	RC/G
2017	NCAA	Wake Forest	261	65	94	17	67	360	428	636	1064	11	79	0.57	21	5	39	276	8.72
2017	Rk	Billings	204	36	62	3	23	304	363	412	775	9	83	0.54	12	4	19	108	5.13
2018	A	Dayton	235	40	65	7	37	277	361	460	820	12	72	0.48	17	4	37	183	6.02
2018	A+	Daytona	220	25	55	2	20	250	304	350	654	7	71	0.27	6	2	31	100	3.58

Athletic CF prospect made it to High-A in his full-season debut. A high-contact hitter in college, has struggled with breaking ball recognition. Short, compact swing, covers the plate. Lets ball travel deep and sprays to all fields. Average power potential; 20/20 a possibility due to plus run tool. Solid defender, will stick in CF.

Farrar,Logan

7 | **Oakland** | EXP MLB DEBUT: 2020 | H/W: 5-11 200 | FUT: Starting OF | **7D**

Bats L Age 23
2017 (36) VA Commwlth
Pwr +++
BAvg ++
Spd ++
Def ++

Year	Lev	Team	AB	R	H	HR	RBI	Avg	OB	Slg	OPS	bb%	ct%	Eye	SB	CS	x/h%	Iso	RC/G
2017	NCAA	Va. Commonwlth	230	50	84	8	32	365	432	543	975	11	90	1.17	4	4	30	178	7.52
2017	Rk	AZL Athletics	35	10	17	1	6	486	550	800	1350	13	86	1.00	0	0	47	314	12.39
2017	A-	Vermont	179	27	56	3	26	313	363	436	798	7	82	0.42	5	0	29	123	5.34
2018	A	Beloit	421	50	99	12	57	235	309	378	687	10	76	0.44	2	1	31	143	4.00

Stocky, strong-bodied OF who grew into power in MWL debut. Hunts fastballs and muscles balls to pull side, showing plus raw power. Shows willingness to walk and makes solid-average contact despite an otherwise stiff swing. Poor athleticism and lack of defensive home drives his value down, but could be a HR-heavy DH type at the next level.

Feliciano,Mario

2 | **Milwaukee** | EXP MLB DEBUT: 2020 | H/W: 6-1 200 | FUT: Starting C | **8D**

Bats R Age 20
2016 (2) HS (PR)
Pwr ++
BAvg +++
Spd ++
Def +++

Year	Lev	Team	AB	R	H	HR	RBI	Avg	OB	Slg	OPS	bb%	ct%	Eye	SB	CS	x/h%	Iso	RC/G
2016	Rk	AZL Brewers	117	16	31	0	16	265	306	359	665	6	84	0.37	2	2	26	94	3.77
2017	A	Wisconsin	402	47	101	4	36	251	310	331	640	8	82	0.47	10	2	22	80	3.46
2018	Rk	AZL Brewers	14	0	4	0	2	286	375	357	732	13	79	0.67	0	1	25	71	4.90
2018	A+	Carolina	146	20	30	3	12	205	270	329	599	8	60	0.22	2	0	37	123	3.00

Compact, strong CA with potential for modest fantasy impact. Smooth, simple swing lends itself above-average ct% and shows ability to spray the ball to all fields. Lacks sufficient hand separation and bat speed for raw power but should grow into mostly doubles pop. Flashes quality arm behind plate and is good enough athlete to shore up the glove.

Fernandez,Eduarqui

789 | **Milwaukee** | EXP MLB DEBUT: 2023 | H/W: 6-2 176 | FUT: Starting OF | **8E**

Bats B Age 17
2018 FA (DR)
Pwr +++
BAvg +++
Spd +++
Def +++

Year	Lev	Team	AB	R	H	HR	RBI	Avg	OB	Slg	OPS	bb%	ct%	Eye	SB	CS	x/h%	Iso	RC/G
2018		Did not play in US																	

Young Dominican OF who was July signee for $1.1 million. Possesses bevy of raw tools, including loose wrists, a smooth swing and feel to hit from the right side. Thin frame leaves room for added muscle and more power with age. Plus runner with good overall athleticism and arm for either CF/RF. A name to watch.

Fernandez,Vince

79 | **Colorado** | EXP MLB DEBUT: 2020 | H/W: 6-4 205 | FUT: Reserve OF | **7C**

Bats R Age 23
2016 (10) UC-Riverside
Pwr ++++
BAvg ++
Spd ++
Def ++

Year	Lev	Team	AB	R	H	HR	RBI	Avg	OB	Slg	OPS	bb%	ct%	Eye	SB	CS	x/h%	Iso	RC/G
2016	NCAA	UC Riverside	220	40	77	8	42	350	428	509	937	12	74	0.52	4	3	23	159	7.49
2016	Rk	Grand Junction	203	36	63	5	31	310	372	527	899	9	70	0.33	6	2	44	217	7.23
2017	A	Asheville	375	57	101	16	59	269	346	464	810	11	67	0.36	12	8	40	195	5.90
2018	A+	Lancaster	423	82	112	24	75	265	363	532	895	13	59	0.38	10	5	51	267	7.96

Physical OF has some of the best raw power in the system, blasting 40 HR over the past two years. Aggressive lefty stroke with good bat speed, but can be enticed to expand up in the zone raising questions about hit tool. Will need to make more contact and draw walks as he moves up. Average speed with a below-average arm limits him to LF or 4th OF.

Filia,Eric

379 | **Seattle** | EXP MLB DEBUT: 2019 | H/W: 6-0 180 | FUT: Reserve OF | **6B**

Bats L Age 26
2016 (20) UCLA
Pwr +
BAvg ++++
Spd +++
Def ++

Year	Lev	Team	AB	R	H	HR	RBI	Avg	OB	Slg	OPS	bb%	ct%	Eye	SB	CS	x/h%	Iso	RC/G
2016	NCAA	UCLA	207	36	61	3	32	295	411	411	822	17	90	2.05	8	5	26	116	6.32
2016	A-	Everett	246	43	89	4	46	362	449	496	945	14	92	2.05	10	5	27	134	7.53
2016	AAA	Tacoma	1	1	0	0	0	0	500	0	500	50	100		0	0		0	4.75
2017	A+	Modesto	491	63	160	5	59	326	405	434	838	12	91	1.44	9	6	24	108	6.20
2018	AA	Arkansas	296	44	81	2	38	274	368	348	716	13	90	1.47	1	0	21	74	4.87

Extreme pull-oriented contact hitter had solid 2018 season in Double-A, minus power. Patient, high CT% approach. Swing geared towards ground ball and line drive contact. Liners have lots of top spin, depressing power. Single digit HR hitter. Average runner, not a SB threat. Defensively limited to 1B & corner OF.

Flores,Antoni

6 | **Boston** | EXP MLB DEBUT: 2022 | H/W: 6-1 190 | FUT: Reserve IF | **8D**

Bats R Age 18
2017 FA (VZ)
Pwr ++
BAvg ++++
Spd +++
Def +++

Year	Lev	Team	AB	R	H	HR	RBI	Avg	OB	Slg	OPS	bb%	ct%	Eye	SB	CS	x/h%	Iso	RC/G
2018	Rk	DSL Red Sox 2	49	10	17	1	14	347	439	510	949	14	86	1.14	0	1	29	163	7.61
2018	Rk	GCL Red Sox	4	0	1	0	0	250	400	750	1150	20	75	1.00	0	0	100	500	11.63

Thrived in limited DSL ball AB, but did not play much in US because of some minor injuries. Has wiry build with some natural length to his swing so he will have to get stronger to make sure he is not overpowered at the higher levels. He has just okay athleticism at SS so will have to work to stay there.

Florial,Estevan | 789 | New York (A)

EXP MLB DEBUT: 2020 | H/W: 6-1 185 | FUT: Starting OF | **9D**

Bats L Age 21
2014 FA (HT)
Pwr ++++
BAvg ++
Spd ++++
Def ++++

Year	Lev	Team	AB	R	H	HR	RBI	Avg	OB	Slg	OPS	bb%	ct%	Eye	SB	CS	x/h%	Iso	RC/G
2017	A	Charleston (Sc)	344	64	102	11	43	297	371	483	854	11	64	0.33	17	7	36	186	6.91
2017	A+	Tampa	76	13	23	2	14	303	376	461	837	11	68	0.38	6	1	26	158	6.36
2018	Rk	GCL Yankees W	31	10	17	3	8	548	600	1000	1600	11	84	0.80	5	0	41	452	15.02
2018	Rk	GCL Yankees	17	5	11	2	5	647	684	1294	1978	11	88	1.00	3	0	55	647	18.94
2018	A+	Tampa	294	45	75	3	27	255	352	361	713	13	70	0.51	11	10	29	105	4.67

Top OF prospect struggled with broken wrist during lost 2018 season. Has patient approach and plus-plus bat speed; swing shortened up in AFL look. Struggles maintaining swing path and chasing breaking balls. Raw plus power; he will likely reach it by maturity. Swing path is geared towards generating increased loft. A future plus CF.

Forbes,Ti'Quan | 45 | Chicago (A)

EXP MLB DEBUT: 2020 | H/W: 6-3 180 | FUT: Utility player | **6C**

Bats R Age 22
2014 (2) HS (MS)
Pwr ++
BAvg +++
Spd +++
Def +++

Year	Lev	Team	AB	R	H	HR	RBI	Avg	OB	Slg	OPS	bb%	ct%	Eye	SB	CS	x/h%	Iso	RC/G
2016	A	Hickory	427	50	107	4	44	251	292	335	627	6	75	0.24	6	5	22	84	3.09
2017	A	Hickory	302	36	73	8	34	242	271	368	638	4	75	0.16	3	0	27	126	3.07
2017	A+	Winston-Salem	13	3	2	0	0	154	214	231	445	7	100		0	1	50	77	2.19
2017	A+	Down East	185	20	42	3	11	227	278	308	586	7	71	0.24	2	4	21	81	2.50
2018	A+	Winston-Salem	432	59	118	6	51	273	307	391	698	5	83	0.28	4	9	28	118	4.00

Former TEX prospect rallied in second chance at High-A. Acquired in August 2017 trade, was considered a busted prospect. Began hitting for contact in 2018 by reducing swings and misses, but power took step back. Once a plus-runner, has lost speed and doesn't get reads on the bases. Likely utility profile.

Fox,Lucius | 6 | Tampa Bay

EXP MLB DEBUT: 2020 | H/W: 6-1 165 | FUT: Starting SS | **8C**

Bats B Age 21
2015 FA (BM)
Pwr ++
BAvg +++
Spd +++++
Def ++++

Year	Lev	Team	AB	R	H	HR	RBI	Avg	OB	Slg	OPS	bb%	ct%	Eye	SB	CS	x/h%	Iso	RC/G
2016	A	Augusta	285	46	59	2	16	207	298	277	575	11	73	0.49	25	7	20	70	2.65
2017	A	Bowling Green	302	45	84	2	27	278	349	361	710	10	74	0.41	27	10	21	83	4.44
2017	A+	Charlotte	115	19	27	1	12	235	307	287	594	9	71	0.36	3	3	15	52	2.75
2018	A+	Charlotte	351	54	99	2	30	282	359	353	712	11	77	0.53	23	7	20	71	4.49
2018	AA	Montgomery	104	14	23	1	9	221	277	298	575	7	81	0.40	6	2	22	77	2.59

Super-athletic SS made gains with the bat in 2018, which continued in the AFL. Patient switch-hitter with clean swing mechanics, especially from RH side. Swing geared towards top-spin generating line drives. Strong despite lean build. Double-digit HR possible. Plus-plus runner with 25+ SB ability.

Fraley,Jake | 78 | Seattle

EXP MLB DEBUT: 2020 | H/W: 6-0 190 | FUT: Starting CF | **7B**

Bats L Age 23
2016 (2) Louisiana St
Pwr ++
BAvg +++
Spd ++++
Def ++++

Year	Lev	Team	AB	R	H	HR	RBI	Avg	OB	Slg	OPS	bb%	ct%	Eye	SB	CS	x/h%	Iso	RC/G
2016	NCAA	LSU	267	61	87	5	36	326	408	464	872	12	88	1.12	28	10	24	139	6.55
2016	A-	Hudson Valley	206	34	49	1	18	238	323	364	687	11	83	0.76	33	9	35	126	4.37
2017	Rk	GCL Rays	15	6	7	1	2	467	529	867	1396	12	80	0.67	3	1	57	400	13.14
2017	A+	Charlotte	94	6	16	1	12	170	228	255	483	7	74	0.29	1	3	31	85	1.25
2018	A+	Charlotte	225	39	78	4	41	347	414	547	961	10	80	0.59	11	8	38	200	7.69

Oft-injured, athletic OF was acquired in mid-season trade with TAM. Quiet, compact swing with consistent path. Swing trajectory geared towards top-spin generating, line drive contact. Average raw power in swing and frame, likely 10-15 HR at projection. Plus defender in CF. Uses borderline plus-plus run tool well. Struggled with SB% in 2018.

Franco,Anderson | 35 | Washington

EXP MLB DEBUT: 2022 | H/W: 6-3 190 | FUT: Starting 3B | **7D**

Bats R Age 21
2013 FA (DR)
Pwr +++
BAvg ++
Spd +
Def ++

Year	Lev	Team	AB	R	H	HR	RBI	Avg	OB	Slg	OPS	bb%	ct%	Eye	SB	CS	x/h%	Iso	RC/G
2015	A-	Auburn	40	0	9	0	4	225	340	300	640	15	95	3.50	0	0	22	75	4.42
2016	Rk	GCL Nationals	83	9	23	1	9	277	310	349	660	5	87	0.36	1	0	17	72	3.55
2017	A	Hagerstown	408	57	82	11	63	201	274	348	622	9	75	0.41	3	1	44	147	3.15
2018	Rk	GCL Nationals	43	7	15	2	12	349	404	558	962	9	93	1.33	0	0	27	209	7.18
2018	A	Hagerstown	228	21	54	3	34	237	312	338	650	10	80	0.56	2	1	31	101	3.66

Thick, big-framed corner infielder with power, but lacks current hit tool to get to it. Has shown patience and can see a lot of pitches, but in-game adjustments have proven tough to come by. No speed and minimal agility likely moves him to 1B long term, where he will have a tough time carving out full-time AB.

Franco,Wander | 6 | Tampa Bay

EXP MLB DEBUT: 2021 | H/W: 5-10 190 | FUT: Starting 2B | **9C**

Bats B Age 18
2017 FA (DR)
Pwr ++++
BAvg +++++
Spd +++
Def +++

Year	Lev	Team	AB	R	H	HR	RBI	Avg	OB	Slg	OPS	bb%	ct%	Eye	SB	CS	x/h%	Iso	RC/G
2018	Rk	Princeton	242	46	85	11	57	351	416	587	1003	10	92	1.42	4	3	33	236	7.78

Dynamic, switch-hitting phenom destroyed Appy League pitching with elite-level ct% and barrel rate. Advanced approach with a short, compact and lightning-quick swing. Has advanced barrel control and knack for hard contact. Raw plus power. Will reach, especially if swing trajectory begins producing loft. Scouts agree staying at SS unlikely; either 2B or 3B is his future home.

Frank,Tyler | 46 | Tampa Bay

EXP MLB DEBUT: 2022 | H/W: 6-0 170 | FUT: Utility player | **7E**

Bats R Age 22
2018 (2) Florida Atlantic
Pwr ++
BAvg +++
Spd ++
Def +++

Year	Lev	Team	AB	R	H	HR	RBI	Avg	OB	Slg	OPS	bb%	ct%	Eye	SB	CS	x/h%	Iso	RC/G
2018	NCAA	Florida Atlantic	247	70	74	13	35	300	421	547	968	17	85	1.44	4	2	46	247	7.88
2018	A-	Hudson Valley	177	37	51	2	22	288	400	412	812	16	84	1.18	3	3	33	124	6.10

Solid, all-around 2nd round pick carried on amateur success to pro ranks. Hard-nosed player with versatility. Has played C, 2B, 3B, SS and LF in last few years. Patient, contact-oriented hitter. Has good feel for barrel. Not a big power hitter but could project to 10-15 HRs at maturity. Average runner with solid instincts.

Freeman,Tyler | 6 | Cleveland

EXP MLB DEBUT: 2022 | H/W: 6-0 165 | FUT: Starting MIF | **8D**

Bats R Age 19
2017 (2) HS (CA)
Pwr ++
BAvg ++++
Spd ++++
Def ++

Year	Lev	Team	AB	R	H	HR	RBI	Avg	OB	Slg	OPS	bb%	ct%	Eye	SB	CS	x/h%	Iso	RC/G
2017	Rk	AZL Indians	128	19	38	2	14	297	333	414	747	5	91	0.58	5	1	29	117	4.69
2018	A-	Mahoning Val	270	49	95	2	38	352	371	511	882	3	92	0.36	14	3	37	159	6.10

A middle infielder with an aggressive approach and a high aptitude for making contact, he tore up the New York Penn League in his first full season of pro ball. His swing is geared more towards line drive contact than power, though could be a launch angle project in the future. He also runs well, but is a below-average defender.

Friedl,TJ | 789 | Cincinnati

EXP MLB DEBUT: 2019 | H/W: 5-10 170 | FUT: Starting OF | **7C**

Bats L Age 23
2019 FA (UNevada)
Pwr ++
BAvg ++
Spd ++++
Def +++

Year	Lev	Team	AB	R	H	HR	RBI	Avg	OB	Slg	OPS	bb%	ct%	Eye	SB	CS	x/h%	Iso	RC/G
2016	Rk	Billings	121	24	42	3	17	347	410	545	956	10	79	0.52	7	2	38	198	7.55
2017	A	Dayton	250	47	71	5	25	284	358	472	830	10	82	0.63	14	8	44	188	6.01
2017	A+	Daytona	179	15	46	2	13	257	296	346	643	5	78	0.26	2	1	22	89	3.29
2018	A+	Daytona	228	40	67	3	35	294	395	412	807	14	81	0.86	11	4	25	118	5.91
2018	AA	Pensacola	261	47	72	2	16	276	346	360	706	10	79	0.50	19	5	21	84	4.36

An athletic, contact-oriented hitter continues to produce high BA and OBP. A mostly spray hitter, relies on low line drives and ground balls, taking advantage of plus run tool. Swing and lower half not suitable for double-digit HR numbers. Power completely pull dominate. Stole 30 bases split between two levels.

Gamboa,Arquimendes | 6 | Philadelphia

EXP MLB DEBUT: 2021 | H/W: 6-0 175 | FUT: Starting SS | **7D**

Bats B Age 21
2014 FA (vZ)
Pwr ++
BAvg +++
Spd +++
Def ++++

Year	Lev	Team	AB	R	H	HR	RBI	Avg	OB	Slg	OPS	bb%	ct%	Eye	SB	CS	x/h%	Iso	RC/G
2016	A-	Williamsport	130	15	26	2	15	200	252	292	544	6	78	0.32	5	1	31	92	2.09
2017	A	Lakewood	307	44	80	6	29	261	332	378	710	10	83	0.63	8	0	26	117	4.40
2018	A+	Clearwater	434	49	93	2	37	214	300	279	579	11	74	0.48	6	4	22	65	2.70

A very good defender, with hand/range/arm for SS, but optimism about a bat to match took at hit in Hi-A. Switch-hitter who didn't look comfortable vs. LHP; and doesn't seem to have enough juice from either side to drive the ball successfully. Added strength may help as he faded down the stretch again. Still young for the level.

Garcia,Adolis | 9 | St. Louis

EXP MLB DEBUT: 2018 | H/W: 6-1 180 | FUT: Starting OF | **8D**

Bats R Age 26
2017 FA (CU)
Pwr +++
BAvg +++
Spd ++++
Def ++++

Year	Lev	Team	AB	R	H	HR	RBI	Avg	OB	Slg	OPS	bb%	ct%	Eye	SB	CS	x/h%	Iso	RC/G
2017	AA	Springfield	309	43	88	12	55	285	340	476	816	8	75	0.34	12	8	40	191	5.61
2017	AAA	Memphis	136	21	41	3	10	301	336	478	814	5	77	0.23	3	1	39	176	5.50
2018	AAA	Memphis	406	62	104	22	71	256	281	500	781	3	76	0.14	10	3	49	244	4.86
2018	MLB	St. Louis	17	3	2	0	1	118	118	176	294	0	59	0.00	0	0	50	59	-2.00

Finally made his MLB debut after a solid season at AAA. Flashes above-average tools, including power and speed, but approach at the plate leaves much to be desired. Did launch a career-high 22 HR but his walk and strikeout rates limit his upside. Tools are still exciting, but the maturation and polish have been slow to materialize.

Garcia, Anthony — 9 — New York (A)

EXP MLB DEBUT: 2022 | H/W: 6-5 204 | FUT: Starting 1B | 8E
Bats B | Age 18 | 2017 FA (DR)
Pwr ++++ | BAvg ++ | Spd +++ | Def ++

Year	Lev	Team	AB	R	H	HR	RBI	Avg	OB	Slg	OPS	bb%	ct%	Eye	SB	CS	x/h%	Iso	RC/G
2018	Rk	GCL Yankees W	156	18	38	10	20	244	322	513	835	10	53	0.25	3	0	50	269	7.55
2018	Rk	DSL Yankees	16	3	2	0	4	125	313	313	576	16	50	0.38	0	0	100	188	3.50
2018	Rk	Pulaski	21	4	2	0	0	95	174	143	317	9	67	0.29	0	0	50	48	-1.31

Powerful, raw hitting prospect has tremendous size and power potential. A switch-hitter, struggles with approach. Reads FB well and location but struggles with breaking ball. Poor contact skills, especially from RH side. Plus-plus raw power. Plays to all fields in BP but pull-oriented currently in games. Size may move him to 1B defensively.

Garcia, Aramis — 2 — San Francisco

EXP MLB DEBUT: 2018 | H/W: 6-2 195 | FUT: Starting C | 7C
Bats R | Age 26 | 2014 (2) Florida Int'l
Pwr +++ | BAvg ++ | Spd + | Def +++

Year	Lev	Team	AB	R	H	HR	RBI	Avg	OB	Slg	OPS	bb%	ct%	Eye	SB	CS	x/h%	Iso	RC/G
2017	A+	San Jose	324	43	88	17	65	272	304	497	801	4	77	0.21	0	0	43	225	5.11
2017	AA	Richmond	78	11	22	0	8	282	356	436	792	10	73	0.43	0	0	55	154	5.80
2018	AA	Richmond	301	36	70	11	33	233	280	395	676	6	75	0.26	0	1	37	163	3.66
2018	AAA	Sacramento	38	5	9	0	4	237	275	263	538	5	68	0.17	0	0	11	26	1.81
2018	MLB	SF Giants	63	8	18	4	9	286	308	492	800	3	51	0.06	0	0	28	206	7.04

Strong-bodied, bat-first receiver struggled in high minors before enjoying success late in MLB campaign. Aggressive approach with swing-and-miss in profile. Sells out to pull side but best working a spray approach. Raw plus power to all fields in BP. Mostly pull-oriented in game. Improved as receiver, especially with lateral movements. Will stick.

Garcia, Dermis — 35 — New York (A)

EXP MLB DEBUT: 2020 | H/W: 6-3 200 | FUT: Starting 1B | 7E
Bats R | Age 21 | 2014 FA (DR)
Pwr ++++ | BAvg ++ | Spd ++ | Def ++

Year	Lev	Team	AB	R	H	HR	RBI	Avg	OB	Slg	OPS	bb%	ct%	Eye	SB	CS	x/h%	Iso	RC/G
2017	Rk	Pulaski	115	24	31	9	25	270	396	565	961	17	66	0.62	6	0	48	296	8.31
2017	A	Charleston (Sc)	110	12	25	8	20	227	315	518	833	11	62	0.33	0	0	60	291	6.49
2018	A	Charleston (Sc)	324	37	78	15	50	241	317	444	761	10	66	0.32	3	2	44	204	5.21

Former top international prospect has struggled as a professional. Athletic 3B has been in organization since 2014. Struggles getting bat head out and tapping into plus power. Has a solid approach at the plate and doesn't try to do too much. Plus power at projection. NYY is converting 3B into two-way player. Should begin appearing on mound in 2019.

Garcia, Eduardo — 46 — Milwaukee

EXP MLB DEBUT: 2023 | H/W: 6-2 160 | FUT: Starting SS | 8E
Bats R | Age 16 | 2018 FA (VZ)
Pwr ++ | BAvg +++ | Spd +++ | Def +++

Year	Lev	Team	AB	R	H	HR	RBI	Avg	OB	Slg	OPS	bb%	ct%	Eye	SB	CS	x/h%	Iso	RC/G
2018		Did not play in US																	

July 2 signee from Venezuela who has yet to make pro debut. Rail-thin frame requires physical projection, but has tools for impact. Smooth swing lends itself to contact around the zone and could develop average in-game power. Good athlete but only an average runner, he figures to offer limited SB impact.

Garcia, Jose — 46 — Cincinnati

EXP MLB DEBUT: 2021 | H/W: 6-2 175 | FUT: Starting 2B | 8E
Bats R | Age 21 | 2017 FA (CU)
Pwr ++ | BAvg +++ | Spd ++++ | Def ++

Year	Lev	Team	AB	R	H	HR	RBI	Avg	OB	Slg	OPS	bb%	ct%	Eye	SB	CS	x/h%	Iso	RC/G
2018	A	Dayton	482	61	118	6	53	245	273	344	618	4	77	0.17	13	9	27	100	2.90

Athletic, bat-first MIF struggled in US debut. Contact-oriented hitter with short, compact swing. Doesn't utilize lower half well, struggles to tap into average raw power in frame. A bit wiry and may struggle to add bulk to upper half. A plus runner, struggled on the base paths reading moves and pitchers. Likely 2B or utility long term.

Garcia, Luis V. — 56 — Washington

EXP MLB DEBUT: 2021 | H/W: 6-0 190 | FUT: Starting 2B | 9D
Bats L | Age 18 | 2016 FA (DR)
Pwr +++ | BAvg ++++ | Spd +++ (4.30) | Def ++++

Year	Lev	Team	AB	R	H	HR	RBI	Avg	OB	Slg	OPS	bb%	ct%	Eye	SB	CS	x/h%	Iso	RC/G
2017	Rk	GCL Nationals	199	25	60	1	22	302	332	387	719	4	84	0.28	11	2	20	85	4.24
2018	A	Hagerstown	296	48	88	3	31	297	340	402	742	6	83	0.39	8	5	24	105	4.61
2018	A+	Potomac	204	34	61	4	23	299	338	412	750	6	84	0.36	4	1	21	113	4.61

Breakout player as a teenager in two levels of A-ball. Wide and slightly open setup in the box, bat speed and balance result in above average contact, has solid approach. Strong lower half indicates power to come, though speed and SS range will take a hit. Makes in-AB adjustments of a veteran. High upside off a start like this.

Garcia, Luis J. — 6 — Philadelphia

EXP MLB DEBUT: 2022 | H/W: 5-11 170 | FUT: Starting SS | 9E
Bats B | Age 18 | 2017 FA (VZ)
Pwr ++ | BAvg ++++ | Spd +++ | Def ++++

Year	Lev	Team	AB	R	H	HR	RBI	Avg	OB	Slg	OPS	bb%	ct%	Eye	SB	CS	x/h%	Iso	RC/G
2018	Rk	GCL Phillies W	168	33	62	1	32	369	421	488	909	8	88	0.71	12	8	24	119	6.76

A big-money international signee from 2017, he wasted no time dominating his stateside debut. Plate approach is advanced far beyond his years—waits on hittable pitches, sprays line drives into the gaps with quick hands and a short swing. Bat speed and youth hint at more power to come. SB ability; graceful on defense with strong arm.

Gatewood, Jake — 3 — Milwaukee

EXP MLB DEBUT: 2019 | H/W: 6-5 190 | FUT: Starting 1B | 7B
Bats R | Age 23 | 2014 (1) HS (CA)
Pwr ++++ | BAvg ++ | Spd ++ | Def ++

Year	Lev	Team	AB	R	H	HR	RBI	Avg	OB	Slg	OPS	bb%	ct%	Eye	SB	CS	x/h%	Iso	RC/G
2016	A	Wisconsin	496	70	119	14	64	240	267	391	658	4	72	0.13	3	2	39	151	3.38
2017	A+	Carolina	420	66	113	11	53	269	337	438	775	9	69	0.33	7	5	42	169	5.42
2017	AA	Biloxi	92	9	22	4	9	239	300	457	757	8	68	0.28	3	0	45	217	5.01
2018	AA	Biloxi	352	45	86	19	59	244	300	466	766	7	68	0.25	2	0	45	222	5.05

Former SS draftee turned to 1B in upper minors. Long, leveraged swing produces massive raw power to all fields but also eats away at his ability to make sufficient contact. Has become more patient in upper minors; solid bb% makes him more valuable in OBP formats. Glove works well at 1B, where he profiles best long-term.

Gerber, Mike — 89 — San Francisco

EXP MLB DEBUT: 2018 | H/W: 6-2 175 | FUT: Starting OF | 7C
Bats L | Age 26 | 2014 Creighton
Pwr ++ | BAvg + | Spd ++ | Def +++

Year	Lev	Team	AB	R	H	HR	RBI	Avg	OB	Slg	OPS	bb%	ct%	Eye	SB	CS	x/h%	Iso	RC/G
2017	A+	Lakeland	18	3	8	0	2	444	500	667	1167	6	61	0.29	0	0	38	222	12.73
2017	AA	Erie	350	62	102	13	45	291	362	477	840	10	76	0.46	10	6	36	186	6.03
2018	AAA	Toledo	17	4	7	1	3	412	444	706	1150	6	65	0.17	0	0	43	294	11.06
2018	AAA	Toledo	287	35	61	13	34	213	269	411	680	7	64	0.21	2	2	48	199	3.95
2018	MLB	Detroit	42	2	4	0	2	95	174	119	293	9	50	0.19	0	0	25	24	-2.40

Defense-first outfielder with well-rounded profile. Fringy speed, but impressive defensive instincts play to his advantage. Plays well enough. Isn't built to grab many bags, but will tag some off instinct alone. Ability to hit for limited power. Strikeouts bit him in 2018, forcing him to fight for position in 2019.

Gigliotti, Michael — 8 — Kansas City

EXP MLB DEBUT: 2021 | H/W: 6-2 173 | FUT: Starting CF | 8D
Bats R | Age 22 | 2017 (4) Lipscomb
Pwr ++ | BAvg +++ | Spd ++++ | Def ++++

Year	Lev	Team	AB	R	H	HR	RBI	Avg	OB	Slg	OPS	bb%	ct%	Eye	SB	CS	x/h%	Iso	RC/G
2017	NCAA	Lipscomb	202	60	58	3	17	287	431	411	842	20	80	1.24	31	5	31	124	6.68
2017	Rk	Burlington	155	30	51	3	30	329	444	477	921	17	86	1.52	15	5	27	148	7.48
2017	A	Lexington	86	14	26	1	8	302	362	419	780	9	77	0.40	7	5	27	116	5.27
2018	A	Lexington	17	3	4	1	2	235	435	471	905	26	71	1.20	1	0	50	235	7.64

Speedy, contact-oriented OF missed most of season after tearing ACL. Patient hitter with an up-the-middle approach, though some say he's too patient. Short, line-drive stroke oriented to take advantage of plus-plus run tool. Pull-oriented below-average power not much of a factor in profile. Plus defender in CF.

Gilliam, Isiah — 79 — New York (A)

EXP MLB DEBUT: 2021 | H/W: 6-2 215 | FUT: Starting OF | 7E
Bats B | Age 22 | 2015 (20) Chipola College
Pwr +++ | BAvg ++ | Spd +++ | Def ++

Year	Lev	Team	AB	R	H	HR	RBI	Avg	OB	Slg	OPS	bb%	ct%	Eye	SB	CS	x/h%	Iso	RC/G
2016	Rk	Pulaski	218	32	52	10	33	239	294	440	734	7	71	0.27	3	0	46	202	4.53
2017	A	Charleston (Sc)	444	80	122	15	85	275	355	468	823	11	75	0.50	9	5	43	194	5.93
2018	A+	Tampa	474	59	123	13	71	259	312	397	708	7	68	0.24	4	5	30	137	4.29

Athletic, muscular switch-hitting OF struggled to maintain 2017 hit tool strides into 2018. Approach took a step back after previous bb% and ct%. Better hitter from RH side; LH swing is longer and struggles to maintain swing plane. Contact is harder from RH side. Plus raw power in frame and BP. Not a SB threat.

Gimenez,Andres

6 | New York (N) | EXP MLB DEBUT: 2020 | H/W: 5-11 165 | FUT: Starting SS | 8B

Bats L Age 20
2015 FA (VZ)

- Pwr ++
- BAvg +++
- 4.10 Spd ++++
- Def ++++

Year	Lev	Team	AB	R	H	HR	RBI	Avg	OB	Slg	OPS	bb%	ct%	Eye	SB	CS	x/h%	Iso	RC/G
2017	A	Columbia	347	49	92	4	31	265	320	349	669	7	82	0.46	14	8	18	84	3.78
2018	A+	St. Lucie	308	43	87	6	30	282	330	432	762	7	77	0.31	28	11	34	149	4.92
2018	AA	Binghamton	137	19	38	0	16	277	322	358	680	6	84	0.41	10	3	26	80	3.95

Good defensive SS with good, but not great, tools across the board. Upside limited by relatively small frame and size. But should hit and field well enough to be at least solid everyday SS. Some power may come with age and added strength, but gets in trouble now when tries to hit for power. A good base runner, but not a burner.

Gomez,Moises

7 | Tampa Bay | EXP MLB DEBUT: 2021 | H/W: 5-11 196 | FUT: Starting OF | 8D

Bats R Age 20
2015 FA (VZ)

- Pwr ++++
- BAvg ++
- Spd ++
- Def +++

Year	Lev	Team	AB	R	H	HR	RBI	Avg	OB	Slg	OPS	bb%	ct%	Eye	SB	CS	x/h%	Iso	RC/G
2016	Rk	GCL Rays	168	20	37	1	10	220	272	327	600	7	78	0.32	4	3	35	107	2.91
2017	Rk	Princeton	211	37	58	5	28	275	317	398	715	6	75	0.25	10	1	28	123	4.19
2018	A	Bowling Green	471	67	132	19	82	280	329	503	832	7	71	0.25	4	3	45	223	5.97

Strong-bodied, emerging OF led Midwest Lg in XBH, playing on prospect loaded Single-A club. Aggressive approach with swing-and-miss in profile. Swing geared towards fly ball contact. Hit 19 HR, mostly to pull side but began to tap into opposite field power late. 25-30 HR potential at maturity. Below average runner. LF only profile due to arm.

Gonzalez,Brayan

4 | Philadelphia | EXP MLB DEBUT: 2023 | H/W: 5-11 172 | FUT: Starting 2B | 7C

Bats R Age 19
2016 FA (VZ)

- Pwr ++
- BAvg ++
- Spd +++
- Def ++++

Year	Lev	Team	AB	R	H	HR	RBI	Avg	OB	Slg	OPS	bb%	ct%	Eye	SB	CS	x/h%	Iso	RC/G
2017	Rk	GCL Phillies	134	23	36	2	24	269	329	388	717	8	75	0.36	6	0	33	119	4.42
2018	A-	Williamsport	197	21	39	1	24	198	251	274	525	7	56	0.16	3	1	31	76	1.95

Big-money international signee is a plus defender with good arm strength and outstanding internal clock. Natural SS, but has played and will likely settle in at 2B. Surprising raw power from a solid swing from both sides, but strikeouts have mounted. Good pitch recognition, but so far has struggled to hit velocity. Still a pup.

Gonzalez,Jacob

5 | San Francisco | EXP MLB DEBUT: 2021 | H/W: 6-4 206 | FUT: Starting 3B | 7D

Bats R Age 20
2017 (2) HS (AZ)

- Pwr +++
- BAvg ++
- Spd ++
- Def ++

Year	Lev	Team	AB	R	H	HR	RBI	Avg	OB	Slg	OPS	bb%	ct%	Eye	SB	CS	x/h%	Iso	RC/G
2017	Rk	AZL Giants	168	23	57	1	21	339	397	458	855	9	86	0.70	0	1	30	119	6.19
2018	A	Augusta	459	54	104	8	45	227	276	331	607	6	77	0.29	7	5	29	105	2.85

Son of Luis Gonzalez. Bat pushes overall profile. Struggled with elongated swing in first taste of Single-A, causing pitchers to live in his kitchen, but enough skill here to recover. Plus raw power in profile, completely to the pull-side; 18-23 HR at projection. Limited athletically. May not stick at 3B. Currently passable.

Gonzalez,Luis

89 | Chicago (A) | EXP MLB DEBUT: 2020 | H/W: 6-0 185 | FUT: Starting OF | 8C

Bats L Age 23
2017 (3) New Mexico

- Pwr +++
- BAvg +++
- Spd +++
- Def ++++

Year	Lev	Team	AB	R	H	HR	RBI	Avg	OB	Slg	OPS	bb%	ct%	Eye	SB	CS	x/h%	Iso	RC/G
2017	NCAA	New Mexico	219	62	79	8	42	361	495	589	1084	21	85	1.81	14	0	41	228	9.66
2017	Rk	Great Falls	17	3	2	0	3	118	286	176	462	19	82	1.33	0	0	50	59	1.85
2017	A	Kannapolis	233	26	57	2	12	245	351	361	711	14	79	0.76	2	3	33	116	4.70
2018	A	Kannapolis	230	35	69	8	26	300	359	491	850	8	75	0.37	7	2	38	191	6.12
2018	A+	Winston-Salem	252	50	79	6	45	313	380	504	884	10	82	0.59	3	5	42	190	6.59

Former collegiate 2-way player has come into own as a hitter. Made incredible strides in 2018. Has a compact swing geared towards line-drive contact. Works all fields, though power is currently pull-oriented. As swing develops, expect power to top out in the 20-25 HR range. Average speed limits SB potential.

Gonzalez,Oscar

79 | Cleveland | EXP MLB DEBUT: 2022 | H/W: 6-2 180 | FUT: Starting OF | 7E

Bats R Age 21
2014 FA (DR)

- Pwr ++++
- BAvg ++
- Spd +++
- Def ++++

Year	Lev	Team	AB	R	H	HR	RBI	Avg	OB	Slg	OPS	bb%	ct%	Eye	SB	CS	x/h%	Iso	RC/G
2016	Rk	AZL Indians	145	30	44	8	26	303	340	566	905	5	61	0.14	4	0	45	262	7.75
2016	A-	Mahoning Val	3	0	0	0	0	0	250	0	250	25	67	1.00	0	0		0	-2.42
2017	A-	Mahoning Val	237	20	67	3	34	283	298	388	686	2	74	0.08	0	0	28	105	3.69
2018	A	Lake County	462	52	135	13	52	292	310	435	745	3	77	0.11	5	6	29	143	4.37

His calling card is his above-average raw power. He does not fully tap into it, however, due to his tendency to bail with his front side and reach for balls. At this point in his career he has not quite figured out his strike zone. Plus corner outfield defender who can run.

Gonzalez,Pedro

8 | Texas | EXP MLB DEBUT: 2022 | H/W: 6-3 160 | FUT: Reserve OF | 7D

Bats R Age 21
2014 FA (DR)

- Pwr +++
- BAvg +
- Spd +++
- Def +++

Year	Lev	Team	AB	R	H	HR	RBI	Avg	OB	Slg	OPS	bb%	ct%	Eye	SB	CS	x/h%	Iso	RC/G
2016	Rk	Grand Junction	226	32	52	2	19	230	275	394	669	6	66	0.18	6	7	48	164	4.02
2017	Rk	Grand Junction	187	28	60	3	28	321	380	519	899	9	72	0.34	11	6	42	198	7.17
2017	A-	Spokane	17	2	0	0	0	0	105	0	105	11	53	0.25	0	0		0	-5.99
2018	A	Hickory	337	47	79	12	46	234	293	421	715	8	67	0.25	9	5	43	187	4.45

Physically gifted, and power/speed tools, but struggled in his first crack at full-season ball. Way too many holes in his swing will depress BA and keep raw power under wraps. Plus speed and defense give him some value, but contact needs to take a step forward.

Gordon,Miles

78 | Cincinnati | EXP MLB DEBUT: 2021 | H/W: 6-1 185 | FUT: Reserve OF | 7D

Bats L Age 21
2015 (4) HS (ON)

- Pwr ++
- BAvg +++
- Spd ++++
- Def +++

Year	Lev	Team	AB	R	H	HR	RBI	Avg	OB	Slg	OPS	bb%	ct%	Eye	SB	CS	x/h%	Iso	RC/G
2015	Rk	AZL Reds	118	15	26	0	12	220	264	305	569	6	78	0.27	5	3	27	85	2.48
2016	Rk	Billings	65	11	17	0	11	262	368	369	738	14	78	0.79	3	2	29	108	5.14
2017	Rk	Billings	232	40	74	8	37	319	390	530	920	10	76	0.49	7	3	38	211	7.17
2018	A	Dayton	204	37	43	2	8	211	291	324	614	10	77	0.50	17	6	30	113	3.23

Athletic Canadian LHH OF struggled through injury and slow start in first full season look. Tweener profile. Unorthodox short, compact swing conducive to hard contact but a raw swing plane. Power potential in frame; likely 10-15 HR at maturity. Ran a lot in 2018; was on a 40+ SB pace. Gave up hockey to sign in 2015.

Gordon,Nick

46 | Minnesota | EXP MLB DEBUT: 2019 | H/W: 6-2 175 | FUT: Starting MIF | 7B

Bats L Age 23
2014 (1) HS (FL)

- Pwr ++
- BAvg +++
- Spd +++
- Def +++

Year	Lev	Team	AB	R	H	HR	RBI	Avg	OB	Slg	OPS	bb%	ct%	Eye	SB	CS	x/h%	Iso	RC/G
2015	A	Cedar Rapids	481	79	133	1	58	277	331	360	690	8	82	0.44	25	8	23	83	4.11
2016	A+	Fort Myers	461	56	134	3	52	291	324	386	710	5	81	0.26	19	13	24	95	4.16
2017	AA	Chattanooga	519	80	140	9	66	270	337	408	746	9	74	0.40	13	7	33	139	4.89
2018	AA	Chattanooga	162	22	54	5	20	333	376	525	900	6	83	0.41	7	2	33	191	6.48
2018	AAA	Rochester	382	40	81	2	29	212	257	283	540	6	79	0.28	13	3	23	71	2.05

Former high pick improved ct% but struggled with hard contact. Simple line drive swing, but struggles with pitch recognition that leads to indecision. More pull-oriented in 2018 but failed to cash in with HR total and still has below average power. An above-average runner, he is adequate at SS, though 2B is his long-term home.

Gorman,Nolan

5 | St. Louis | EXP MLB DEBUT: 2021 | H/W: 6-1 210 | FUT: Starting 3B | 9C

Bats L Age 18
2018 (1) HS (AZ)

- Pwr +++++
- BAvg +++
- Spd +
- Def +++

Year	Lev	Team	AB	R	H	HR	RBI	Avg	OB	Slg	OPS	bb%	ct%	Eye	SB	CS	x/h%	Iso	RC/G
2018	Rk	Johnson City	143	41	50	11	28	350	443	664	1107	14	74	0.65	1	3	44	315	9.78
2018	A	Peoria	94	8	19	6	16	202	279	426	704	10	59	0.26	0	2	47	223	4.53

Advanced prep hitter had the best combination of hit and power tools in the draft. Plus bat speed with a good understanding of the strike zone. Does have some swing-and-miss as he hunts balls he can crush. Played SS in HS but moved to 3B as a pro where he shows good instincts and an average arm. Below-average speed is only negative.

Graffanino,A.J.

6 | Atlanta | EXP MLB DEBUT: 2021 | H/W: 6-2 170 | FUT: Utility player | 6C

Bats B Age 21
2018 (8) Washington

- Pwr +
- BAvg ++
- Spd +++
- Def +++

Year	Lev	Team	AB	R	H	HR	RBI	Avg	OB	Slg	OPS	bb%	ct%	Eye	SB	CS	x/h%	Iso	RC/G
2018	NCAA	Washington	110	16	40	0	19	364	435	455	890	11	91	1.40	5	2	20	91	6.80
2018	Rk	Danville	27	2	11	0	6	407	429	407	836	4	89	0.33	1	0	0	0	5.41
2018	A	Rome	143	19	43	1	11	301	338	378	715	5	83	0.33	4	3	21	77	4.23

Son of Tony Graffanino, and a scrappy, LHH UT player. Spray, punch-and-Judy hitter with high ct%. Was a bit aggressive expanding zone in pro debut. Lean frame, swing isn't optimal for power development. Solid IF with good actions at SS. Average runner with baserunning instincts.

Granite,Zack

8 | Minnesota | EXP MLB DEBUT: 2017 | H/W: 6-0 175 | FUT: Reserve OF | 6A

Bats L Age 26	Year	Lev	Team	AB	R	H	HR	RBI	Avg	OB	Slg	OPS	bb%	ct%	Eye	SB	CS	x/h%	Iso	RC/G
2013 (14) Seton Hall	2016	AA	Chattanooga	526	86	155	4	52	295	347	382	729	7	92	0.98	56	14	19	87	4.70
Pwr +	2017	A+	Fort Myers	19	2	7	0	1	368	429	526	955	10	89	1.00	3	0	29	158	7.48
BAvg +++	2017	AAA	Rochester	284	46	96	5	29	338	390	475	865	8	88	0.71	15	6	26	137	6.16
Spd ++++	2017	MLB	Minnesota	93	14	22	1	13	237	324	290	614	11	90	1.33	2	2	14	54	3.59
Def ++++	2018	AAA	Rochester	237	28	50	0	4	211	278	245	523	8	88	0.79	9	4	16	34	2.35

Speedy, contact-oriented OF struggled through an injury-marred '18 season. A right shoulder injury sapped bat speed, contributing to poor BA despite ct% in line with career numbers. No power to speak of. Sprays field with line-drives, utilizing plus running speed. Limited playing time limits SB opportunities. 20-SB threat in right situation.

Gray,Joe

8 | Milwaukee | EXP MLB DEBUT: 2022 | H/W: 6-1 195 | FUT: Starting OF | 9E

Bats R Age 19	Year	Lev	Team	AB	R	H	HR	RBI	Avg	OB	Slg	OPS	bb%	ct%	Eye	SB	CS	x/h%	Iso	RC/G
2018 (2) HS (MS)																				
Pwr +++																				
BAvg ++																				
Spd ++++																				
Def +++	2018	Rk	AZL Brewers	77	14	14	2	9	182	337	325	662	19	68	0.72	6	0	50	143	4.00

Lanky, athletic OF with loud tools but requires maturation. Has quick-twitch qualities and bat speed through the zone for future HR value. Contact has been an issue and will require fine-tuning. Runs very well underway and will steal some bases. Cannon arm and good range profile him best to RF long-term.

Green,Ryder

8 | New York (A) | EXP MLB DEBUT: 2022 | H/W: 6-0 200 | FUT: Starting OF | 8E

Bats R Age 18	Year	Lev	Team	AB	R	H	HR	RBI	Avg	OB	Slg	OPS	bb%	ct%	Eye	SB	CS	x/h%	Iso	RC/G
2018 (3) HS (TN)																				
Pwr ++++																				
BAvg ++																				
Spd +++																				
Def +++	2018	Rk	GCL Yankees	79	11	16	3	10	203	300	392	692	12	56	0.31	3	2	44	190	4.82

Strong, athletic OF hopes to develop into power hitter at maturity. Long, lumbering swing and poor pitch recognition skills may hold back power potential. Struggled with ct% in GCL debut. Profiles as a pull-oriented hitter. Power in frame and swing. Steep uppercut conducive to big over-the-fence power potential. Above-average run tool.

Gregorio,Osmy

5 | Tampa Bay | EXP MLB DEBUT: 2022 | H/W: 6-2 175 | FUT: Starting SS | 7E

Bats R Age 20	Year	Lev	Team	AB	R	H	HR	RBI	Avg	OB	Slg	OPS	bb%	ct%	Eye	SB	CS	x/h%	Iso	RC/G
2016 FA (DR)																				
Pwr ++																				
BAvg +++	2017	Rk	AZL Mariners	191	28	42	2	23	220	284	319	603	8	63	0.24	14	1	29	99	3.00
Spd +++	2017	A-	Everett	18	1	4	0	3	222	300	222	522	10	44	0.20	1	0	0	0	2.54
Def +++	2018	Rk	Princeton	143	25	35	3	21	245	316	378	694	9	78	0.48	6	2	31	133	4.16

Lean, athletic IF prospect showed signs of life in Appy Lg stint. Raw hitter, improved swing path to ball by shortening up, leading to significant ct% gains. Swing still has length, and struggles with consistent hard contact. Average raw power in swing and physique. Natural SS, moved off to accommodate Wander Franco.

Grenier,Cadyn

6 | Baltimore | EXP MLB DEBUT: 2021 | H/W: 5-11 180 | FUT: Starting SS | 7E

Bats R Age 22	Year	Lev	Team	AB	R	H	HR	RBI	Avg	OB	Slg	OPS	bb%	ct%	Eye	SB	CS	x/h%	Iso	RC/G
2018 (1) Oregon St																				
Pwr ++																				
BAvg ++																				
Spd +++	2018	NCAA	Oregon State	273	70	87	6	47	319	394	462	856	11	79	0.60	9	1	29	143	6.30
Def ++++	2018	A	Delmarva	162	23	35	1	13	216	291	333	624	9	67	0.32	3	2	43	117	3.36

Defensive-oriented 2018 draftee struggled with Ks in pro debut. Patient approach, but swing length and pitch recognition were concerns. Extended early, minimizing swing trajectory geared towards fly balls. Pull-oriented power; likely 10-15 HR at projection. Tremendous defender with plus arm. Above-average runner. Defense caries profile.

Grisham,Trent

789 | Milwaukee | EXP MLB DEBUT: 2020 | H/W: 6-0 205 | FUT: Starting OF | 7C

Bats L Age 22	Year	Lev	Team	AB	R	H	HR	RBI	Avg	OB	Slg	OPS	bb%	ct%	Eye	SB	CS	x/h%	Iso	RC/G
2015 (1) HS (TX)	2015	Rk	Helena	42	5	13	1	5	310	431	381	812	18	81	1.13	5	3	8	71	6.01
Pwr +++	2015	Rk	AZL Brewers	165	34	51	1	16	309	415	442	858	15	78	0.83	20	5	27	133	6.74
BAvg ++	2016	A	Wisconsin	221	27	51	2	24	231	341	344	685	14	69	0.54	5	10	37	113	4.36
Spd +++	2017	A+	Carolina	457	78	102	8	45	223	360	348	708	18	69	0.70	37	5	34	125	4.74
Def +++	2018	AA	Biloxi	335	45	78	7	31	233	354	337	692	16	74	0.72	10	3	24	104	4.35

Former 1st round pick whose stock has fallen considerably since turning pro. Still a good athlete with range for CF but lacks arm for RF; runs well enough to have most impact in SB. Producing consistent hard contact has been a struggle, though he continues to walk at an elite rate. With lack of an elite tool, his upside is limited.

Groshans,Jordan

65 | Toronto | EXP MLB DEBUT: 2022 | H/W: 6-3 178 | FUT: Starting 3B | 8D

Bats R Age 19	Year	Lev	Team	AB	R	H	HR	RBI	Avg	OB	Slg	OPS	bb%	ct%	Eye	SB	CS	x/h%	Iso	RC/G
2018 (1) HS (TX)																				
Pwr +++																				
BAvg +++																				
Spd ++	2018	Rk	Bluefield	44	4	8	1	4	182	217	273	490	4	82	0.25	0	0	25	91	1.37
Def +++	2018	Rk	GCL Blue Jays	142	17	47	4	39	331	387	500	887	8	80	0.45	0	0	34	169	6.51

Rangy, athletic player has an advanced feel for hitting and projects to have above-average power once he fills. Plus bat speed allows him to catch up to elite velocity and all-fields line drive swing should lead to .280+ BA. Average speed and range with an above-average arm. Split time at SS/3B in pro debut, but size and arm profile better at 3B.

Guerrero,Gregory

45 | New York (N) | EXP MLB DEBUT: 2023 | H/W: 6-0 186 | FUT: Reserve IF | 6D

Bats R Age 20	Year	Lev	Team	AB	R	H	HR	RBI	Avg	OB	Slg	OPS	bb%	ct%	Eye	SB	CS	x/h%	Iso	RC/G
2015 FA (DR)																				
Pwr +++																				
BAvg ++																				
Spd +	2017	Rk	GCL Mets	143	17	31	0	12	217	253	252	505	5	81	0.26	1	3	13	35	1.63
Def ++	2018		Did not play - injury																	

Had a lost season due to a shoulder injury in 2018, not logging any official pro ABs. Did not look good in limited time in extended spring training, pulling off the ball frequently. Strong, hitter's body who really needs to hit to have a chance because he is limited at 2B and 3B, but the early returns on the bat are not great.

Guerrero,Vladimir

5 | Toronto | EXP MLB DEBUT: 2019 | H/W: 6-1 200 | FUT: Starting 3B | 10C

Bats R Age 20	Year	Lev	Team	AB	R	H	HR	RBI	Avg	OB	Slg	OPS	bb%	ct%	Eye	SB	CS	x/h%	Iso	RC/G
2015 FA (QC)	2017	A+	Dunedin	168	31	56	6	31	333	451	494	945	18	83	1.29	2	2	25	161	7.69
Pwr +++++	2018	Rk	GCL Blue Jays	9	3	3	0	0	333	400	556	956	10	89	1.00	0	0	67	222	7.63
BAvg +++++	2018	A+	Dunedin	4	1	2	0	2	500	500	750	1250	0	100		0	0	50	250	9.68
Spd ++	2018	AA	New Hampshire	234	48	94	14	60	402	451	671	1122	8	88	0.78	3	3	36	269	8.93
Def ++	2018	AAA	Buffalo	110	15	37	6	16	336	416	564	980	12	91	1.50	0	0	35	227	7.59

Elite hit tool combined with plate discipline and high baseball IQ to create a generational talent. Ability to tell balls from strikes allows him to hunt for pitches he can mash. Plus raw power should continue to develop and blasted 20 HR in 357 AB. Solid defender, but will have to work hard to stick on the dirt and conditioning is a priority.

Guillorme,Luis

6 | New York (N) | EXP MLB DEBUT: 2018 | H/W: 5-10 170 | FUT: Utility player | 6B

Bats L Age 24	Year	Lev	Team	AB	R	H	HR	RBI	Avg	OB	Slg	OPS	bb%	ct%	Eye	SB	CS	x/h%	Iso	RC/G
2013 (10) HS (FL)	2015	A	Savannah	446	67	142	0	55	318	392	354	746	11	84	0.77	18	8	11	36	4.96
Pwr +	2016	A+	St. Lucie	441	47	116	1	46	263	329	315	644	9	86	0.68	4	2	16	52	3.67
BAvg ++	2017	AA	Binghamton	481	70	136	1	43	283	376	331	707	13	89	1.31	4	3	15	48	4.74
4.40 Spd +	2018	AAA	Las Vegas	247	41	75	3	33	304	379	417	796	11	84	0.77	2	1	27	113	5.57
Def +++	2018	MLB	NY Mets	67	4	14	0	5	209	284	239	523	9	96	2.33	1	0	14	30	2.78

Middle infielder who is limited by his lack of size and athleticism. Hands and hand/eye are his best attributes. Mediocre range and agility at SS and 2B, but plus arm, reads and feel for the game. Sees ball well at plate and makes contact. Some pull power there, but when goes for it he loses a lot of contact ability. A below average runner.

Gutierrez,Kelvin

5 | Kansas City | EXP MLB DEBUT: 2019 | H/W: 6-3 185 | FUT: Starting 3B | 7C

Bats R Age 24	Year	Lev	Team	AB	R	H	HR	RBI	Avg	OB	Slg	OPS	bb%	ct%	Eye	SB	CS	x/h%	Iso	RC/G
2013 FA (DR)	2016	A+	Potomac	38	7	9	1	2	237	293	342	635	7	87	0.60	2	2	22	105	3.38
Pwr +++	2017	Rk	GCL Nationals	33	6	7	0	1	212	297	364	661	11	79	0.57	2	0	57	152	4.04
BAvg +++	2017	A+	Potomac	222	34	64	2	16	288	344	414	759	8	73	0.32	3	0	28	126	5.06
Spd +++	2018	AA	NW Arkansas	242	29	67	6	40	277	332	409	741	8	81	0.43	10	3	25	132	4.61
Def ++++	2018	AA	Harrisburg	230	36	63	5	26	274	321	391	712	7	73	0.26	10	1	22	117	4.23

Late-blooming, athletic 3B prospect acquired in mid-season trade with WAS. Filled out physique and tapped into raw plus power while also improving ct%. Extreme pull-hitter. Changed swing trajectory to improve fly ball rate. Underrated runner due to poor home-to-first times but was 20 for 24 in SB attempts.

Guzman,Jeison — 6 — Kansas City

EXP MLB DEBUT: 2021 | H/W: 6-2 180 | FUT: Starting SS | 7E

Bats L Age 20 | 2015 FA (DR)

Skills	Year	Lev	Team	AB	R	H	HR	RBI	Avg	OB	Slg	OPS	bb%	ct%	Eye	SB	CS	x/h%	Iso	RC/G
Pwr ++	2016	Rk	AZL Royals	188	35	49	1	19	261	325	378	703	9	77	0.41	5	3	31	117	4.35
BAvg ++	2017	Rk	Burlington	193	21	40	0	15	207	285	249	534	10	77	0.47	3	3	15	41	2.12
Spd +++	2018	Rk	Burlington	106	17	30	2	8	283	356	368	724	10	85	0.75	14	1	13	85	4.58
Def ++++	2018	A	Lexington	209	27	50	2	21	239	300	349	649	8	72	0.31	12	4	32	110	3.55

Tremendous defender with raw hitting tools, showed some life with bat in second go of Appy Lg, then made leap to full-season ball. Contact-oriented approach with swing trajectory geared towards ground ball contact. Pull-heavy spray chart with below-average power. Frame has room to grow into strength. Plus runner with solid instincts.

Guzman,Jonathan — 6 — Philadelphia

EXP MLB DEBUT: 2023 | H/W: 6-0 156 | FUT: Starting SS | 8D

Bats R Age 19 | 2015 FA (DR)

Skills	Year	Lev	Team	AB	R	H	HR	RBI	Avg	OB	Slg	OPS	bb%	ct%	Eye	SB	CS	x/h%	Iso	RC/G
Pwr ++	2017	Rk	GCL Phillies	153	17	38	1	13	248	299	320	619	7	84	0.46	5	1	18	72	3.21
BAvg +++	2017	A-	Williamsport	19	2	5	1	2	263	391	421	812	17	84	1.33	0	1	20	158	5.87
Spd ++	2017	A+	Clearwater	3	0	0	0	0	0	0	0	0	0	0	0.00	0	0		0	
Def ++++	2018	A-	Williamsport	243	28	51	2	14	210	241	272	513	4	75	0.16	3	4	20	62	1.49

Thin-framed MIF with a feel for contact, but too often swung himself into outs. A dose of patience and better swing selection could go a long way. Has a bit of power, but needs to add strength. Some speed, but not efficient baserunner. A plus defensive SS who will stick at the position with soft hands, plus arm and elite range.

Haase,Eric — 2 — Cleveland

EXP MLB DEBUT: 2018 | H/W: 5-10 180 | FUT: Reserve C | 6B

Bats R Age 26 | 2011 (7) HS (MI)

Skills	Year	Lev	Team	AB	R	H	HR	RBI	Avg	OB	Slg	OPS	bb%	ct%	Eye	SB	CS	x/h%	Iso	RC/G
	2016	AA	Akron	226	28	47	12	33	208	263	438	701	7	67	0.23	0	2	57	230	4.16
Pwr ++++	2017	AA	Akron	333	59	86	26	59	258	345	574	918	12	65	0.38	4	2	56	315	7.58
BAvg +	2017	AAA	Columbus	6	1	2	1	2	333	429	833	1262	14	67	0.50	0	0	50	500	12.13
Spd +	2018	AAA	Columbus	433	54	102	20	71	236	287	443	730	7	67	0.22	3	1	46	208	4.59
Def ++	2018	MLB	Cleveland	16	0	2	0	1	125	125	125	250	0	63	0.00	0	0	0	0	-2.76

Got a cup of coffee and his first MLB hit in September. An MLB-ready catcher with big power; two 20-HR seasons. A bit older for a prospect, he also has some swing and miss issues. Defensively he is below average, although he does receive pretty well.

Haggery,Sam — 456 — New York (N)

EXP MLB DEBUT: 2020 | H/W: 5-11 175 | FUT: Utility player | 6C

Bats B Age 24 | 2015 (24) New Mexico

Skills	Year	Lev	Team	AB	R	H	HR	RBI	Avg	OB	Slg	OPS	bb%	ct%	Eye	SB	CS	x/h%	Iso	RC/G
Pwr +	2016	A	Lake County	344	56	79	4	39	230	319	320	639	12	69	0.43	12	2	27	90	3.51
BAvg +++	2017	A+	Lynchburg	427	72	108	3	32	253	354	398	752	14	76	0.65	49	13	40	145	5.28
Spd ++++	2018	AA	Akron	280	44	68	4	37	243	371	396	767	17	73	0.74	24	7	44	154	5.61
Def +++	2018	AAA	Columbus	17	3	3	0	2	176	263	176	440	11	65	0.33	2	0	0	0	0.41

A leadoff or nine-type of switch hitter who can get on base and run, but possesses very little power. Has shown great proficiency for stealing bases in the minors and is seen as a very smart player. Grinder type who has worked his way up the ladder after very little hype as an amateur.

Hall,Adam — 6 — Baltimore

EXP MLB DEBUT: 2022 | H/W: 5-11 165 | FUT: Starting 2B | 8E

Bats R Age 19 | 2017 (2) HS (ON)

Skills	Year	Lev	Team	AB	R	H	HR	RBI	Avg	OB	Slg	OPS	bb%	ct%	Eye	SB	CS	x/h%	Iso	RC/G
Pwr ++																				
BAvg +++																				
Spd ++++	2017	Rk	GCL Orioles	9	4	6	0	2	667	667	1000	1667	0	78	0.00	1	0	33	333	16.18
Def +++	2018	A-	Aberdeen	222	35	65	1	24	293	343	374	717	7	74	0.29	22	5	20	81	4.41

Lean athletic Canadian hish schooler made strides in 2018. Feel for contact but lacks matured pitch recognition skills. Short, compact-oriented swing geared towards ground ball and line drive contact. A plus runner and a natural SS, though questionable arm moves to 2B long term.

Hampson,Garrett — 46 — Colorado

EXP MLB DEBUT: 2018 | H/W: 6-0 165 | FUT: Starting 2B | 8C

Bats R Age 24 | 2016 (3) Long Beach St

Skills	Year	Lev	Team	AB	R	H	HR	RBI	Avg	OB	Slg	OPS	bb%	ct%	Eye	SB	CS	x/h%	Iso	RC/G
	2016	A-	Boise	256	43	77	2	44	301	411	441	853	16	78	0.86	36	4	31	141	6.69
Pwr ++	2017	A+	Lancaster	533	113	174	8	70	326	390	462	852	10	86	0.73	51	14	25	135	6.16
BAvg +++	2018	AA	Hartford	148	28	45	4	15	304	391	466	857	12	89	1.24	19	1	31	162	6.36
Spd ++++	2018	AAA	Albuquerque	296	53	93	6	25	314	377	459	837	9	80	0.52	17	4	29	145	5.95
Def +++	2018	MLB	Colorado	40	3	11	0	4	275	383	400	783	15	70	0.58	2	0	36	125	5.92

Had a stellar campaign and contributed to the Rockies late-season playoff run. Advanced hit tool and plus speed. Patient approach at the plate, barrels the ball consistently, and draws plenty of walks to take advantage of speed. Has below-average power limits his HR appeal, but has defensive versatility.

Hannah,Jameson — 789 — Oakland

EXP MLB DEBUT: 2021 | H/W: 5-9 184 | FUT: Starting OF | 8D

Bats L Age 21 | 2018 (2) Dallas Baptist

Skills	Year	Lev	Team	AB	R	H	HR	RBI	Avg	OB	Slg	OPS	bb%	ct%	Eye	SB	CS	x/h%	Iso	RC/G
Pwr ++																				
BAvg +++																				
Spd ++++	2018	NCAA	Dallas Baptist	236	62	85	6	45	360	443	555	998	13	85	1.00	8	1	36	195	8.12
Def +++	2018	A-	Vermont	86	14	24	1	10	279	347	384	731	9	72	0.38	6	0	25	105	4.72

Shorter, compact OF who signed for above-slot value in 2018's second round. Quality athlete who moves well and has speed for above-average SB impact. Swing is geared for contact and all-fields approach and power is more gap-oriented than HR. Shows good discipline and should reflect in future OBP value. LF is his landing spot with fringe arm.

Harrison,KJ — 2 — Milwaukee

EXP MLB DEBUT: 2020 | H/W: 6-0 208 | FUT: Starting C | 7C

Bats R Age 22 | 2017 (3) Oregon St

Skills	Year	Lev	Team	AB	R	H	HR	RBI	Avg	OB	Slg	OPS	bb%	ct%	Eye	SB	CS	x/h%	Iso	RC/G
Pwr +++																				
BAvg ++																				
Spd +	2017	Rk	Helena	185	38	57	10	33	308	385	546	931	11	70	0.42	0	0	42	238	7.48
Def ++	2018	A	Wisconsin	417	45	95	12	51	228	294	384	678	9	65	0.27	2	2	43	156	4.03

Strong, durable CA drafted in 2017's third round. Has leveraged swing that produces fly-ball trajectories and plus raw power, though over-aggressive approach limits him to pitcher-friendly counts and poor ct%. Has above-average arm for a backstop but remains raw with transfer and blocking skills. Should stick at CA with more reps.

Harrison,Monte — 89 — Miami

EXP MLB DEBUT: 2019 | H/W: 6-3 200 | FUT: Starting OF | 9E

Bats R Age 23 | 2014 (2) HS (MO)

Skills	Year	Lev	Team	AB	R	H	HR	RBI	Avg	OB	Slg	OPS	bb%	ct%	Eye	SB	CS	x/h%	Iso	RC/G
	2016	Rk	AZL Brewers	19	4	4	0	1	211	348	368	716	17	79	1.00	0	0	50	158	5.07
Pwr ++++	2016	A	Wisconsin	267	34	59	6	37	221	275	337	612	7	64	0.21	8	3	31	116	3.00
BAvg ++	2017	A	Wisconsin	223	32	59	11	32	265	349	475	825	12	69	0.41	11	3	41	211	6.06
Spd ++++	2017	A+	Carolina	230	41	64	10	35	278	320	487	807	6	70	0.20	16	1	42	209	5.54
Def ++++	2018	AA	Jacksonville	521	85	125	19	48	240	299	399	698	8	59	0.20	28	9	34	159	4.58

Toolsy, athletic OF struggled mightly to make contact in first taste of Double-A. Still, there's a lot to like. Quick twitch swing with plus power potential. Could hit 30 HR with more bat-to-ball. Plus runner, plus defender with plus-plus arm. Could profile defensively anywhere in OF.

Haseley,Adam — 78 — Philadelphia

EXP MLB DEBUT: 2019 | H/W: 6-1 195 | FUT: Starting OF | 8C

Bats L Age 22 | 2017 (1) Virginia

Skills	Year	Lev	Team	AB	R	H	HR	RBI	Avg	OB	Slg	OPS	bb%	ct%	Eye	SB	CS	x/h%	Iso	RC/G
	2017	Rk	GCL Phillies	12	3	7	0	4	583	643	833	1476	14	75	0.67	1	1	29	250	15.42
Pwr ++	2017	A-	Williamsport	137	18	37	2	18	270	338	380	717	9	80	0.50	5	3	30	109	4.46
BAvg +++	2017	A	Lakewood	66	15	17	1	6	258	319	379	698	8	80	0.46	0	1	29	121	4.19
Spd ++	2018	A+	Clearwater	330	54	99	5	38	300	338	415	753	5	84	0.35	7	3	23	115	4.69
Def +++	2018	AA	Reading	136	23	43	6	17	316	388	478	866	11	86	0.84	0	1	23	162	6.18

Adjusted well to first full year of pro ball; some mechanical tweaks teased our more patience and hard contact. Uses the whole field and began to turn on some balls, but still only 15-18 HR power at peak. Excellent hit tool; can run and handle CF, but likely moves to LF long-term.

Hayes,Ke'Bryan — 5 — Pittsburgh

EXP MLB DEBUT: 2020 | H/W: 6-1 210 | FUT: Starting 3B | 8B

Bats R Age 22 | 2015 (1) HS (TX)

Skills	Year	Lev	Team	AB	R	H	HR	RBI	Avg	OB	Slg	OPS	bb%	ct%	Eye	SB	CS	x/h%	Iso	RC/G
	2015	A-	West Virginia	41	8	9	0	7	220	319	244	563	13	83	0.86	1	1	11	24	2.82
Pwr +++	2016	Rk	GCL Pirates	5	0	2	0	0	400	500	600	1100	17	80	1.00	0	0	50	200	10.07
BAvg ++++	2016	A	West Virginia	247	27	65	6	37	263	308	393	701	6	79	0.31	6	5	29	130	4.02
4.30 Spd +++	2017	A+	Bradenton	421	66	117	2	43	278	342	363	705	9	82	0.54	27	5	21	86	4.36
Def ++++	2018	AA	Altoona	437	64	128	7	47	293	374	444	818	12	81	0.68	12	5	35	151	5.91

The son of Charlie Hayes, and should up being a sleeker, more athletic version of his father. Has always had good bat-to-ball skills but starting to find his power, as he made a determined effort to use his lower half more. How much impact he will have with the bat is the question. His defense at 3B is a plus; probably could hold his own at SS.

Hays,Austin | 9 | Baltimore | EXP MLB DEBUT: 2017 | H/W: 6-1 195 | FUT: Starting OF | 8C

Bats R Age 23	Year	Lev	Team	AB	R	H	HR	RBI	Avg	OB	Slg	OPS	bb%	ct%	Eye	SB	CS	x/h%	Iso	RC/G
2016 (3) Jacksonville	2017	A+	Frederick	262	42	86	16	41	328	358	592	949	4	85	0.30	4	6	40	263	6.75
Pwr ++++	2017	AA	Bowie	261	39	86	16	54	330	361	594	955	5	83	0.29	1	1	41	264	6.89
BAvg +++	2017	MLB	Baltimore	60	4	13	1	8	217	242	317	559	3	73	0.13	0	0	31	100	2.04
Spd +++	2018	A-	Aberdeen	37	6	7	0	3	189	231	243	474	5	81	0.29	0	0	29	54	1.32
Def +++	2018	AA	Bowie	273	34	66	12	43	242	274	432	706	4	78	0.20	6	3	39	190	3.92

Strong, athletic OF struggled in 2018 with injury and selling out for pull-power instead of relying on natural spray approach. Corrected issues late, salvaging season. Patient approach with short, compact swing. Knack for barrel. Swing trajectory geared towards creating loft. Plus-power plays. Solid runner, not a blazer.

Henry,Payton | 2 | Milwaukee | EXP MLB DEBUT: 2021 | H/W: 6-2 215 | FUT: Starting C | 8E

Bats R Age 21	Year	Lev	Team	AB	R	H	HR	RBI	Avg	OB	Slg	OPS	bb%	ct%	Eye	SB	CS	x/h%	Iso	RC/G
2016 (6) HS (UT)																				
Pwr +++																				
BAvg ++	2016	Rk	AZL Brewers	82	15	21	0	17	256	307	341	648	7	77	0.32	0	1	33	85	3.54
Spd ++	2017	Rk	Helena	207	38	50	7	33	242	338	435	772	13	67	0.43	1	0	50	193	5.55
Def +++	2018	A	Wisconsin	337	44	79	10	41	234	312	380	692	10	63	0.31	1	3	34	145	4.32

Offense-minded CA prospect who mashed 27 XBH but also posted 63% ct% in full-season debut. Flashes plus raw power but has struggles making contact against quality offspeed. Still refining footwork and blocking skills behind the plate but should have enough arm to stick there long-term.

Heredia,Starling | 789 | Los Angeles (N) | EXP MLB DEBUT: 2022 | H/W: 6-0 215 | FUT: Starting OF | 8E

Bats R Age 20	Year	Lev	Team	AB	R	H	HR	RBI	Avg	OB	Slg	OPS	bb%	ct%	Eye	SB	CS	x/h%	Iso	RC/G
2015 FA (DR)	2017	Rk	Ogden	82	21	35	4	17	427	489	732	1221	11	71	0.42	5	4	46	305	11.75
Pwr +++	2017	Rk	AZL Dodgers	28	8	12	2	9	429	500	857	1357	13	75	0.57	0	0	50	429	13.23
BAvg +	2017	A	Great Lakes	99	14	21	1	8	212	284	323	608	9	62	0.26	5	1	38	111	3.18
Spd ++	2018	Rk	AZL Dodgers	26	6	7	1	2	269	367	385	751	13	58	0.36	1	0	14	115	5.55
Def ++	2018	A	Great Lakes	203	18	37	6	26	182	242	325	567	7	60	0.20	3	0	43	143	2.37

Strong-bodied player has plus bat speed and above-average to plus power, but ultra aggressive approach results in tons of swing-and-miss. Stiff hands and limited feel for hitting. Average to above speed and arm allow him to play all three OF slots. Hard to see this profile translating at higher levels.

Hermosillo,Michael | 789 | Los Angeles (A) | EXP MLB DEBUT: 2018 | H/W: 5-9 189 | FUT: Reserve OF | 7D

Bats R Age 24	Year	Lev	Team	AB	R	H	HR	RBI	Avg	OB	Slg	OPS	bb%	ct%	Eye	SB	CS	x/h%	Iso	RC/G
2013 (28) HS (IL)	2017	A+	Inland Empire	53	5	17	0	2	321	419	434	853	15	72	0.60	5	2	35	113	6.84
Pwr +	2017	AA	Mobile	278	40	69	4	26	248	343	353	695	13	74	0.55	21	9	28	104	4.33
BAvg ++	2017	AAA	Salt Lake	115	20	33	5	16	287	328	487	815	6	76	0.25	9	2	36	200	5.44
Spd +++	2018	AAA	Salt Lake	273	43	73	12	46	267	340	480	820	10	68	0.34	10	5	41	212	6.01
Def ++	2018	MLB	LA Angels	57	7	12	1	1	211	250	333	583	5	70	0.18	0	1	42	123	2.48

Deceptive outfielder who leveraged breakout in 2018 to launch to MLB debut. Experience at all three outfield posts, although primarily a centerfielder with plus speed and above-average arm. Power spiked at the plate in 2018, but doesn't project as a high-power bat long term. Speed plays up well on the basepaths.

Hernandez,Brayan | 789 | Miami | EXP MLB DEBUT: 2021 | H/W: 6-2 175 | FUT: Reserve OF | 6C

Bats B Age 21	Year	Lev	Team	AB	R	H	HR	RBI	Avg	OB	Slg	OPS	bb%	ct%	Eye	SB	CS	x/h%	Iso	RC/G
2014 FA (VZ)	2017	Rk	GCL Marlins	8	2	2	0	0	250	333	375	708	11	75	0.50	0	0	50	125	4.62
Pwr ++	2017	A-	Everett	103	9	26	2	15	252	300	408	708	6	75	0.27	4	1	31	155	4.24
BAvg ++	2017	A-	Batavia	59	9	16	0	3	271	295	407	702	3	76	0.14	0	0	31	136	4.14
Spd ++++	2017	AAA	Tacoma	5	0	2	0	0	400	400	400	800	0	100		1	0	0	0	4.93
Def ++++	2018	A-	Batavia	219	28	47	3	18	215	280	342	623	8	74	0.34	10	2	40	128	3.21

Toolsy, athletic OF prospect continues to struggle in short-season ball. Top international FA in 2014, acquired in 2017 trade with SEA. Enjoyed better success with patience this season but struggled with hard contact. Swing is long-winded and lacks consistent bat path. Speedy. but not on base enough to take advantage. Raw plus power in frame.

Hernandez,Ronaldo | 2 | Tampa Bay | EXP MLB DEBUT: 2021 | H/W: 6-1 185 | FUT: Starting C | 9D

Bats R Age 21	Year	Lev	Team	AB	R	H	HR	RBI	Avg	OB	Slg	OPS	bb%	ct%	Eye	SB	CS	x/h%	Iso	RC/G
2014 FA (CB)																				
Pwr ++++																				
BAvg ++++																				
Spd ++	2017	Rk	Princeton	223	42	74	5	40	332	377	507	883	7	83	0.41	2	2	38	175	6.36
Def ++	2018	A	Bowling Green	405	68	115	21	79	284	335	494	829	7	83	0.45	10	4	37	210	5.53

Athletic, converted IF continues to carry bat-first label despite significant in-season improvements behind the plate. Raw plus hit and power tool. Instincts beyond his years at the plate. Adjusts his swing based on situation. Uses lower half well with power stroke. Defense still question mark despite plus-plus arm. Sneaky SB threat.

Hernandez,Yadiel | 7 | Washington | EXP MLB DEBUT: 2019 | H/W: 5-9 185 | FUT: Reserve OF | 6A

Bats L Age 31	Year	Lev	Team	AB	R	H	HR	RBI	Avg	OB	Slg	OPS	bb%	ct%	Eye	SB	CS	x/h%	Iso	RC/G
2016 FA (CU)																				
Pwr +++																				
BAvg ++++	2017	AA	Harrisburg	397	57	116	12	59	292	380	441	820	12	83	0.85	5	2	29	149	5.85
Spd ++	2018	AA	Harrisburg	108	17	34	7	22	315	422	537	959	16	83	1.11	2	1	29	222	7.54
Def ++	2018	AAA	Syracuse	325	45	90	11	46	277	349	431	780	10	73	0.41	2	1	30	154	5.26

Maintains great balance at the plate and can drive the ball effectively to the opposite field—even with power. Short but strong, he's also patient and waits on a good pitch. And older Cuban defector, there is no projection left, but could be a COR OF bat off the bench.

Herrera,Ivan | 2 | St. Louis | EXP MLB DEBUT: 2022 | H/W: 6-0 180 | FUT: Starting C | 8D

Bats R Age 18	Year	Lev	Team	AB	R	H	HR	RBI	Avg	OB	Slg	OPS	bb%	ct%	Eye	SB	CS	x/h%	Iso	RC/G
2016 FA (PN)																				
Pwr +++																				
BAvg +++																				
Spd ++	2018	Rk	GCL Cardinals	112	23	39	1	25	348	407	500	907	9	82	0.55	1	1	28	152	6.88
Def +++	2018	AA	Springfield	4	0	0	0	0	0	0	0	0	0	50	0.00	0	0		0	-7.85

Offensive-minded backstop had an impressive stateside debut. Short, compact stroke and a good understanding of the strike zone resulted in plenty of hard contact. In-game power is limited for now, but has the size and bat speed to hit 15-20 HR down the road, but will have to work hard to stick at the position.

Herron,Jimmy | 8 | Chicago (N) | EXP MLB DEBUT: 2022 | H/W: 6-1 185 | FUT: Reserve OF | 7D

Bats R Age 22	Year	Lev	Team	AB	R	H	HR	RBI	Avg	OB	Slg	OPS	bb%	ct%	Eye	SB	CS	x/h%	Iso	RC/G
2018 (3) Duke																				
Pwr +																				
BAvg +++	2018	NCAA	Duke	250	61	76	5	36	304	404	460	864	14	89	1.50	23	4	34	156	6.63
Spd +++	2018	Rk	AZL Cubs	29	6	9	1	2	310	459	517	977	22	93	4.00	0	0	44	207	8.40
Def +++	2018	A	South Bend	110	12	27	3	17	245	320	345	665	10	78	0.50	1	3	19	100	3.68

Uses a short, compact stroke and line-drive approach to shoot balls to all fields. Spreads out at the plate, but the lack of bat speed leaves him vulnerable to plus velo and likely prevents him from above-average power. Smart, gritty player who draws walks and has the speed and range for CF, but an arm injury limits him to LF down the road.

Heyward,Jacob | 79 | San Francisco | EXP MLB DEBUT: 2020 | H/W: 6-1 191 | FUT: Reserve OF | 6C

Bats R Age 23	Year	Lev	Team	AB	R	H	HR	RBI	Avg	OB	Slg	OPS	bb%	ct%	Eye	SB	CS	x/h%	Iso	RC/G
2016 (18) Miami	2016	Rk	AZL Giants	95	27	32	1	21	337	471	579	1050	20	68	0.80	10	2	50	242	10.31
Pwr ++	2016	A-	Salem-Keizer	14	4	4	0	4	286	412	429	840	18	79	1.00	1	0	50	143	6.70
BAvg ++	2017	A	Augusta	359	40	80	10	45	223	304	351	655	10	69	0.38	5	7	33	128	3.61
Spd +++	2018	A+	San Jose	407	61	105	12	47	258	355	415	770	13	74	0.59	14	8	37	157	5.30
Def +++	2018	AAA	Sacramento	5	1	2	0	0	400	500	600	1100	17	40	0.33	0	0	50	200	18.25

Brother of Jason Heyward. Has similar approach and history of patience at plate. Lacks bat speed and average-or-better physical tool to take advantage of approach. Although improved in Double-A, struggles making consistent hard-contact and selling out to pull-power. An above-average runner; will end up as COR OF.

Hicklen,Brewer | 78 | Kansas City | EXP MLB DEBUT: 2021 | H/W: 6-2 194 | FUT: Starting OF | 7D

Bats R Age 23	Year	Lev	Team	AB	R	H	HR	RBI	Avg	OB	Slg	OPS	bb%	ct%	Eye	SB	CS	x/h%	Iso	RC/G
2017 (7) Alabama-Birmingh	2017	NCAA	Alabama-Birmhm	186	43	61	8	31	328	408	586	994	12	72	0.48	17	4	43	258	8.46
Pwr +++	2017	Rk	Idaho Falls	87	19	26	1	10	299	365	471	836	9	75	0.41	3	1	42	172	6.21
BAvg ++	2017	Rk	AZL Royals	69	19	24	3	13	348	423	609	1032	12	65	0.38	13	3	38	261	9.61
Spd ++++	2018	A	Lexington	306	59	94	17	65	307	358	552	910	7	68	0.24	29	6	40	245	7.16
Def ++	2018	A+	Wilmington	71	11	15	1	3	211	253	310	563	5	63	0.15	6	0	33	99	2.26

Former 2-sport collegiate player made significant strides in first full pro season. Athletic OF with raw hit tool. Cut down swing length to post respectable ct%. Struggled with hard contat after aggressive promotion to High-A. Raw above-average power to all fields. Plus-plus runner; 35 for 41 SB attempts. Incredibly raw defender.

Hilliard,Sam — 9 — Colorado

EXP MLB DEBUT: 2020 | H/W: 6-5 225 | FUT: Starting OF | **8D**

Bats L Age 25 — 2015 (15) Crowder Coll

Pwr ++++ | BAvg ++ | Spd ++++ | Def +++

Year	Lev	Team	AB	R	H	HR	RBI	Avg	OB	Slg	OPS	bb%	ct%	Eye	SB	CS	x/h%	Iso	RC/G
2015	Rk	Grand Junction	222	45	68	7	42	306	403	532	935	14	75	0.65	12	4	41	225	7.65
2016	A	Asheville	461	71	123	17	83	267	346	449	795	11	67	0.37	30	12	37	182	5.73
2017	A+	Lancaster	536	95	161	21	92	300	360	487	847	9	71	0.32	37	17	32	187	6.18
2018	AA	Hartford	435	58	114	9	40	262	326	389	714	9	65	0.27	23	14	30	126	4.60

Impressive raw tools, but failed to repeat breakout of 2017. Uses large frame to generate leverage and plus raw power, but lingering contact issues resulted in a HR drop. Plus speed is most game-ready tool and should continue to play as he moves up. Range, arm strength, and size are ideal for RF, but needs to shorten stroke and make more contact.

Hinojosa,C.J. — 46 — San Francisco

EXP MLB DEBUT: 2020 | H/W: 5-11 185 | FUT: Reserve IF | **6B**

Bats R Age 24 — 2015 (11) Texas

Pwr + | BAvg +++ | Spd ++ | Def +++

Year	Lev	Team	AB	R	H	HR	RBI	Avg	OB	Slg	OPS	bb%	ct%	Eye	SB	CS	x/h%	Iso	RC/G
2016	A+	San Jose	260	45	77	6	34	296	382	442	824	12	82	0.78	1	4	30	146	5.94
2016	AA	Richmond	226	27	56	3	19	248	309	336	645	8	81	0.47	1	0	21	88	3.50
2017	AA	Richmond	373	47	99	4	35	265	322	340	662	8	89	0.74	5	4	20	75	3.86
2018	A+	San Jose	26	2	8	0	2	308	357	346	703	7	77	0.33	1	0	13	38	4.16
2018	AA	Richmond	253	26	66	3	26	261	325	360	685	9	89	0.86	5	3	27	99	4.21

Contact-oriented IF worked way back after Achilles injury and drug suspension. Scrappy hitter, works counts. Relies on spray approach to take advantage of high ct%. Doesn't consistently hit ball hard in air. Below-average raw power likely fair as pro. Fringe runner, but picks spots to create SB opportunities.

Hiraldo,Miguel — 5 — Toronto

EXP MLB DEBUT: 2022 | H/W: 5-11 170 | FUT: Starting 3B | **7D**

Bats R Age 18 — 2017 FA (DR)

Pwr +++ | BAvg +++ | Spd +++ | Def ++

Year	Lev	Team	AB	R	H	HR	RBI	Avg	OB	Slg	OPS	bb%	ct%	Eye	SB	CS	x/h%	Iso	RC/G
2018	Rk	DSL Blue Jays	214	41	67	2	33	313	380	453	833	10	86	0.77	15	6	34	140	6.01
2018	Rk	GCL Blue Jays	39	3	9	0	3	231	250	333	583	3	69	0.08	3	0	44	103	2.53

Physically mature teen signed for $750,000. Advanced hitter with a good understanding of the strike zone and above-average bat speed and raw power. Moved to 3B as a pro where he shows good hands and a strong, accurate arm. Thick frame and will have to work on conditioning to remain at 3B. Solid offensive upside and an impressive pro debut.

Hiura,Keston — 4 — Milwaukee

EXP MLB DEBUT: 2019 | H/W: 5-11 185 | FUT: Starting 2B | **9C**

Bats R Age 22 — 2017 (1) UC-Irvine

Pwr +++ | BAvg +++++ | Spd +++ | Def +++

Year	Lev	Team	AB	R	H	HR	RBI	Avg	OB	Slg	OPS	bb%	ct%	Eye	SB	CS	x/h%	Iso	RC/G
2017	NCAA	UC Irvine	199	48	88	8	42	442	554	693	1248	20	81	1.32	9	6	38	251	11.87
2017	Rk	AZL Brewers	62	18	27	4	18	435	485	839	1324	9	79	0.46	0	2	44	403	12.12
2017	A	Wisconsin	105	14	35	0	15	333	375	476	851	6	77	0.29	2	0	37	143	6.20
2018	A+	Carolina	206	38	66	7	23	320	364	529	893	6	77	0.30	4	6	39	209	6.54
2018	AA	Biloxi	279	36	76	6	20	272	326	416	741	7	80	0.39	11	5	34	143	4.65

Pure-hitting 2B with tons of BA upside and solid overall skillset. Quick, strong wrists result in hard line-drive trajectories and gap power with potentially more to come. Aggressive but makes above-average contact. Compact, stocky frame; average runner at best; SB impact likely limited. Working on glovework at 2B, which is his future home.

Hoerner,Nico — 6 — Chicago (N)

EXP MLB DEBUT: 2021 | H/W: 5-11 190 | FUT: Starting 2B | **8C**

Bats R Age 21 — 2018 (1) Stanford

Pwr ++ | BAvg ++++ | Spd +++ | Def ++

Year	Lev	Team	AB	R	H	HR	RBI	Avg	OB	Slg	OPS	bb%	ct%	Eye	SB	CS	x/h%	Iso	RC/G
2018	NCAA	Stanford	229	44	80	2	40	349	399	502	901	8	90	0.86	15	4	31	153	6.66
2018	Rk	AZL Cubs	12	3	3	0	1	250	357	500	857	14	100		2	0	67	250	7.05
2018	A-	Eugene	22	6	7	1	2	318	444	545	990	19	86	1.67	4	1	29	227	8.26
2018	A	South Bend	15	1	6	1	3	400	471	667	1137	12	93	2.00	0	0	33	267	9.24

Contact-oriented IF had some of the best barrel control in the draft. Elbow injury limited him to just 49 pro AB. Average speed with a strong arm and good hands on defense, but lacks first step quickness and range to stick at short. Showed impressive pop with wood bats in the summer Cape Cod League and should develop at least average power.

Holmes,Quentin — 8 — Cleveland

EXP MLB DEBUT: 2023 | H/W: 6-1 175 | FUT: Starting CF | **8E**

Bats R Age 19 — 2017 (2) HS (NY)

Pwr ++ | BAvg ++ | Spd ++++ | Def ++++

Year	Lev	Team	AB	R	H	HR	RBI	Avg	OB	Slg	OPS	bb%	ct%	Eye	SB	CS	x/h%	Iso	RC/G
2017	Rk	AZL Indians	159	22	29	2	15	182	222	289	511	5	62	0.13	5	4	34	107	1.50
2018	Rk	AZL Indians 2	21	5	3	0	1	143	280	190	470	16	62	0.50	2	1	33	48	1.01
2018	Rk	AZL Indians	2	0	0	0	0	0	0	0	0	0	50	0.00	0	0		0	-7.85

Can fly and in time he should be a plus defensive center fielder, but his swing, approach and footwork still need a lot of work. His current toe tap and lack of pitch recognition lead to a lot of off-balance hacks. He struggled in his 2018 pro debut, but still has a lot of time to be able to develop his offensive game.

Holmes,Tra — 789 — Arizona

EXP MLB DEBUT: 2021 | H/W: 6-0 165 | FUT: Starting OF | **7D**

Bats B Age 22 — 2017 (11) Faulkner U

Pwr ++ | BAvg ++ | Spd ++++ | Def +++

Year	Lev	Team	AB	R	H	HR	RBI	Avg	OB	Slg	OPS	bb%	ct%	Eye	SB	CS	x/h%	Iso	RC/G
2017	NCAA	Faulkner Univ	212	74	69	8	43	325	448	528	976	18	74	0.85	59	69	33	203	8.41
2017	A-	Hillsboro	181	32	35	3	23	193	277	271	548	10	65	0.33	12	5	23	77	2.06
2018	A-	Hillsboro	134	29	38	4	13	284	333	463	796	7	76	0.31	19	6	37	179	5.34
2018	A	Kane County	104	10	16	0	7	154	254	202	456	12	63	0.37	9	3	31	48	0.77

Pure athlete who struggled in first taste of full-season ball in 2018. Shows patient, calculated approach and is willing to walk. Level bat path yields GB/LD contact but overall bat-to-ball skills could be major hurdle for him. HR upside limited to single-digits. Quick to full speed; plus underway runner; could provide SB value if ct% improves.

Howard,Ryan — 46 — San Francisco

EXP MLB DEBUT: 2019 | H/W: 6-2 195 | FUT: Reserve IF | **6B**

Bats R Age 24 — 2016 (5) Missouri

Pwr + | BAvg +++ | Spd +++ | Def ++++

Year	Lev	Team	AB	R	H	HR	RBI	Avg	OB	Slg	OPS	bb%	ct%	Eye	SB	CS	x/h%	Iso	RC/G
2016	NCAA	Missouri	217	40	64	5	27	295	378	433	811	12	85	0.88	10	0	30	138	5.76
2016	Rk	AZL Giants	8	1	2	0	0	250	400	250	650	20	100		0	0	0	0	5.05
2016	A-	Salem-Keizer	224	33	61	4	31	272	312	371	683	5	89	0.54	2	2	23	98	3.93
2017	A+	San Jose	526	59	161	9	50	306	335	397	732	4	85	0.28	7	2	19	91	4.30
2018	AA	Richmond	422	44	115	4	50	273	334	396	730	8	87	0.71	9	5	35	123	4.72

Defensive-oriented MIF with contact skills had solid Double-A campaign. Short, compact swing with level swing trajectory. Plus bat-to-ball skills. Trying to curb aggressiveness at plate. Doubled bb% but still concern against better competition. Doesn't generate leverage in lower half for power. Average runner with plus instincts. Natural SS.

Howlett,Brandon — 5 — Boston

EXP MLB DEBUT: 2023 | H/W: 6-1 205 | FUT: Starting 3B | **8D**

Bats R Age 19 — 2018 (21) HS (FL)

Pwr +++ | BAvg +++ | Spd + | Def +++

Year	Lev	Team	AB	R	H	HR	RBI	Avg	OB	Slg	OPS	bb%	ct%	Eye	SB	CS	x/h%	Iso	RC/G
2018	Rk	GCL Red Sox	137	24	42	5	25	307	403	526	928	14	72	0.58	0	1	48	219	7.63
2018	A-	Lowell	15	5	2	1	2	133	381	400	781	29	80	2.00	1	0	100	267	5.82

Was outstanding in the rookie level Gulf Coast League, showing patience. Tools are there to hit, hit for power and play 3B. Solid body and good actions, although not a runner. Swing looks sound and generates a lot of power. Still, a long way away and a lot to prove against higher level pitching.

Huff,Sam — 2 — Texas

EXP MLB DEBUT: 2021 | H/W: 6-4 190 | FUT: Starting C | **8D**

Bats R Age 21 — 2016 (7) HS (AZ)

Pwr +++ | BAvg ++ | Spd + | Def +++

Year	Lev	Team	AB	R	H	HR	RBI	Avg	OB	Slg	OPS	bb%	ct%	Eye	SB	CS	x/h%	Iso	RC/G
2016	Rk	AZL Rangers	97	19	32	1	17	330	425	485	909	14	70	0.55	0	0	38	155	7.67
2017	Rk	AZL Rangers	197	34	49	9	31	249	330	452	782	11	66	0.36	3	2	41	203	5.53
2018	A	Hickory	415	53	100	18	55	241	281	439	719	5	66	0.16	9	1	43	198	4.42

His size stands out for a CA, but has shown the agility and strong arm to say at the position. All which makes his raw strength so intriguing. Strikeouts have been a problem, and he's not patient, but he has a powerful swing which resulted in an impressive HR total for a teenager's first crack at full-season ball. Watchable.

Hurst,Scott — 89 — St. Louis

EXP MLB DEBUT: 2020 | H/W: 5-10 175 | FUT: Reserve OF | **7D**

Bats L Age 23 — 2017 (3) Cal St Fullerton

Pwr ++ | BAvg +++ | Spd +++ | Def +++

Year	Lev	Team	AB	R	H	HR	RBI	Avg	OB	Slg	OPS	bb%	ct%	Eye	SB	CS	x/h%	Iso	RC/G
2017	NCAA	Cal St Fullerton	247	56	81	12	40	328	411	575	986	12	85	0.97	7	1	40	247	7.81
2017	A-	State College	213	36	60	3	21	282	349	432	781	9	73	0.38	6	4	33	150	5.45
2018	Rk	GCL Cardinals	15	5	6	0	2	400	550	600	1150	25	87	2.50	2	0	50	200	11.05
2018	A	Peoria	190	28	56	3	25	295	359	411	769	9	78	0.46	7	4	27	116	5.11
2018	A+	Palm Beach	48	10	17	1	9	354	446	542	988	14	79	0.80	1	0	41	188	8.28

Undersized but athletic CF missed a month of action with a hamstring injury, but has a solid season before and after. Short, compact stroke and a solid understanding of the strike zone results in an above-average bat and he should continue to hit for average. Covers ground well in CF. Small frame and line-drive approach limits power upside.

Ibanez,Andy — 45 — Texas

EXP MLB DEBUT: 2019 | H/W: 5-9 183 | FUT: Reserve IF | 7D

Bats R Age 26 — 2015 FA (CU)

Skills	Year	Lev	Team	AB	R	H	HR	RBI	Avg	OB	Sig	OPS	bb%	ct%	Eye	SB	CS	x/h%	Iso	RC/G
Pwr +++	2016	A	Hickory	185	28	60	7	35	324	416	546	962	14	85	1.04	10	8	43	222	7.66
BAvg +++	2016	AA	Frisco	307	39	80	6	31	261	316	391	707	8	85	0.53	5	2	33	130	4.28
Spd ++	2017	AA	Frisco	310	33	82	8	29	265	319	400	719	7	85	0.52	6	1	29	135	4.37
Def ++	2018	AAA	Round Rock	463	62	131	12	55	283	340	410	750	8	84	0.54	1	6	26	127	4.74

Finished most productive season at Triple-A, where he spent most of his time at 3B after several years at 2B. Doesn't have typical 3B power; projects to HR more in the 12-15 range. But makes good contact and can take a walk, but no real standout tool. Running game has left him as he's aged.

India,Jonathan — 5 — Cincinnati

EXP MLB DEBUT: 2021 | H/W: 6-0 185 | FUT: Starting 3B | 9C

Bats R Age 22 — 2018 (1) Florida

Skills	Year	Lev	Team	AB	R	H	HR	RBI	Avg	OB	Sig	OPS	bb%	ct%	Eye	SB	CS	x/h%	Iso	RC/G
Pwr ++++	2018	NCAA	Florida	226	66	79	21	52	350	486	717	1203	21	75	1.07	15	3	47	367	11.32
BAvg +++	2018	Rk	Billings	8	1	2	0	0	250	250	250	500	0	50	0.00	0	1	0	0	1.64
Spd +++	2018	Rk	Greeneville	46	11	12	3	12	261	443	543	986	25	74	1.25	1	0	50	283	8.66
Def +++	2018	A	Dayton	96	17	22	3	11	229	321	396	717	12	71	0.46	5	0	45	167	4.56

All-around solid player with instincts and intangibles that play up. Utilizes short, compact swing and stays back well despite big leg lift. Does a good job letting ball travel with an up-the-middle approach. Raw power arrived during spring, continuing into pros. 25-30 HR potential with double digit SB possible.

Isabel,Ibandel — 3 — Cincinnati

EXP MLB DEBUT: 2020 | H/W: 6-4 185 | FUT: Starting 1B | 7E

Bats R Age 23 — 2013 FA (DR)

Skills	Year	Lev	Team	AB	R	H	HR	RBI	Avg	OB	Sig	OPS	bb%	ct%	Eye	SB	CS	x/h%	Iso	RC/G
Pwr ++++	2016	A	Great Lakes	88	17	24	7	15	273	340	591	931	9	53	0.22	1	2	54	318	9.22
BAvg +	2017	A+	Rancho Cuca	444	62	115	28	87	259	320	489	809	8	61	0.23	0	2	39	230	6.06
Spd ++	2018	A+	Rancho Cuca	21	1	5	1	3	238	304	476	781	9	57	0.22	0	0	60	238	6.20
Def ++	2018	A+	Daytona	376	62	97	35	75	258	323	566	889	9	60	0.24	1	1	47	309	7.37

Big-bodied RHH 1B only type led minor leagues in HR despite hitting in pitching friendly Florida State League. Long, sluggish load leads to struggles against advanced velocity and reacting to offspeed pitches. Uses brute strength, leverage and fly ball oriented swing trajectory to sell out for power. Lots of swing-and-miss in profile.

Isbel,Kyle — 8 — Kansas City

EXP MLB DEBUT: 2021 | H/W: 5-11 185 | FUT: Starting OF | 8D

Bats L Age 22 — 2018 (3) UNLV

Skills	Year	Lev	Team	AB	R	H	HR	RBI	Avg	OB	Sig	OPS	bb%	ct%	Eye	SB	CS	x/h%	Iso	RC/G
Pwr +++																				
BAvg +++	2018	NCAA	UNLV	238	59	85	14	56	357	438	643	1080	13	82	0.79	6	3	42	286	9.02
Spd ++++	2018	Rk	Idaho Falls	105	27	40	4	18	381	454	610	1063	12	84	0.82	12	3	38	229	8.79
Def +++	2018	A	Lexington	159	30	46	3	14	289	339	434	773	7	73	0.28	12	3	35	145	5.16

Seasoned collegiate OF proved too advanced for lower minors. Classic lead-off hitter with a patient, up-the-middle approach. Some length in swing but makes up for it with above-average bat speed. Found pull-heavy power stroke using leverage in his swing better; will hit 15-20 HR at maturity. Plus runner with SB instincts.

Jackson,Alex — 2 — Atlanta

EXP MLB DEBUT: 2019 | H/W: 6-2 215 | FUT: Starting C | 7E

Bats R Age 23 — 2014 (1) HS (CA)

Skills	Year	Lev	Team	AB	R	H	HR	RBI	Avg	OB	Sig	OPS	bb%	ct%	Eye	SB	CS	x/h%	Iso	RC/G
	2016	A	Clinton	333	43	81	11	55	243	313	408	722	9	69	0.33	2	1	40	165	4.55
Pwr +++	2017	A+	Florida	257	44	70	14	45	272	307	502	809	5	71	0.18	0	1	44	230	5.42
BAvg +	2017	AA	Mississippi	110	12	28	5	20	255	317	427	744	8	71	0.31	0	0	32	173	4.66
Spd ++	2018	AA	Mississippi	225	27	45	5	24	200	265	329	594	8	65	0.26	0	0	40	129	2.75
Def ++	2018	AAA	Gwinnett	108	15	22	3	17	204	283	426	709	10	61	0.29	0	0	73	222	4.91

Former top prospect struggled after encouraging 2017 as ct% dropped and FB% increased. Patient hitter with pull tendencies. Struggled getting bat head out in front of plate for hard contact. Plus-plus raw power, struggles reaching it. Has become a passable defender after intense work to improve.

Jackson,Drew — 468 — Baltimore

EXP MLB DEBUT: 2019 | H/W: 6-2 175 | FUT: Utility player | 6C

Bats R Age 25 — 2015 (5) Stanford

Skills	Year	Lev	Team	AB	R	H	HR	RBI	Avg	OB	Sig	OPS	bb%	ct%	Eye	SB	CS	x/h%	Iso	RC/G
	2016	A+	Bakersfield	524	87	135	6	47	258	322	345	668	9	80	0.48	16	8	24	88	3.81
Pwr +++	2017	Rk	AZL Dodgers	10	1	2	0	4	200	273	600	873	9	60	0.25	0	0	100	400	8.45
BAvg +	2017	A+	Rancho Cuca	252	48	64	8	30	254	343	429	771	12	73	0.51	14	6	41	175	5.29
Spd ++++	2017	AA	Tulsa	111	22	26	1	10	234	303	324	628	9	75	0.39	7	2	27	90	3.28
Def ++++	2018	AA	Tulsa	342	57	86	15	46	251	339	447	786	12	73	0.48	22	7	42	196	5.40

Plus athlete has impressive raw tools, but contact issues prevent him from reaching potential. Quick bat with above-average power and plus speed give him 20/20 upside. Does draw walks and split time at SS/2B/CF, grooming him for a UT role. Younger brother of former prospect Brett Jackson has a similar high-risk/high-reward potential.

Jackson,Jeremiah — 6 — Los Angeles (A)

EXP MLB DEBUT: 2022 | H/W: 6-0 165 | FUT: Starting MIF | 7C

Bats R Age 19 — 2018 (2) HS (AL)

Skills	Year	Lev	Team	AB	R	H	HR	RBI	Avg	OB	Sig	OPS	bb%	ct%	Eye	SB	CS	x/h%	Iso	RC/G
Pwr ++																				
BAvg ++																				
Spd ++	2018	Rk	AZL Angels	82	13	26	5	14	317	371	598	968	8	70	0.28	6	1	42	280	7.93
Def ++	2018	Rk	Orem	91	13	18	2	9	198	263	396	658	8	63	0.24	4	1	61	198	3.98

Fluid middle infielder with a bat-first profile. Still growing into his wiry frame and expected to add muscle over the next few years. Sound defender with strong arm and instincts, but lacks quick step and likely a future fit for second base. Advanced feel at the plate with good path. Works entire field with line drive barrel work.

Jansen,Danny — 2 — Toronto

EXP MLB DEBUT: 2018 | H/W: 6-2 215 | FUT: Starting C | 8C

Bats R Age 23 — 2013 (16) HS (WI)

Skills	Year	Lev	Team	AB	R	H	HR	RBI	Avg	OB	Sig	OPS	bb%	ct%	Eye	SB	CS	x/h%	Iso	RC/G
	2017	A+	Dunedin	122	19	45	5	18	369	408	541	949	6	89	0.57	0	0	24	172	6.83
Pwr +++	2017	AA	New Hampshire	179	23	52	2	20	291	368	419	787	11	89	1.16	1	0	35	128	5.57
BAvg +++	2017	AAA	Buffalo	67	8	22	3	10	328	423	552	975	14	90	1.57	0	0	36	224	7.77
Spd +	2018	AAA	Buffalo	298	45	82	12	58	275	368	473	842	13	84	0.90	5	1	41	198	6.12
Def +++	2018	MLB	Toronto	81	12	20	3	8	247	322	432	754	10	79	0.53	0	0	45	185	4.89

Offensive-minded backstop went from mid-round pick to one of the best CA prospects in the game. Slight hitch at load, but uses a quick bat and a discerning eye to shoot line drives to all fields. Blasted a career high in HR. Continues to improve on D and receives the ball well with an above-average arm.

Jarrett,Zach — 79 — Baltimore

EXP MLB DEBUT: 2021 | H/W: 6-3 217 | FUT: Reserve OF | 6C

Bats R Age 24 — 2017 (28) UNC Charlotte

Skills	Year	Lev	Team	AB	R	H	HR	RBI	Avg	OB	Sig	OPS	bb%	ct%	Eye	SB	CS	x/h%	Iso	RC/G
Pwr +++																				
BAvg ++	2017	NCAA	UNC Charlotte	237	48	81	13	45	342	388	549	937	7	84	0.49	7	1	27	207	6.75
Spd ++	2017	A-	Aberdeen	139	21	28	2	7	201	250	288	538	6	58	0.15	1	3	29	86	2.00
Def ++	2018	A	Delmarva	501	74	139	14	72	277	332	437	769	8	73	0.30	4	2	33	160	5.08

Physically mature 2017 senior draft sign made strides in first full pro season. Son of NASCAR's Dale Jarrett. Solid, patient approach at plate. Swing has some length to it, exposed to premium velocity. Average power projection at maturity. Game power is pull-dominated. Below-average runner. LF/RF only profile.

Javier,Wander — 6 — Minnesota

EXP MLB DEBUT: 2022 | H/W: 6-1 165 | FUT: Starting SS | 9E

Bats R Age 20 — 2015 FA (DR)

Skills	Year	Lev	Team	AB	R	H	HR	RBI	Avg	OB	Sig	OPS	bb%	ct%	Eye	SB	CS	x/h%	Iso	RC/G
Pwr +++																				
BAvg ++++																				
Spd ++++	2017	Rk	Elizabethton	157	34	47	4	22	299	375	471	846	11	69	0.39	4	3	38	172	6.52
Def ++++	2018	Rk	Did not play - injury																	

Toolsy, athletic SS missed all of 2018 with torn labrum in non-throwing shoulder. Continues to grow into wiry frame. Showed good bat control and ability to find barrel in 2017 debut. Reportedly, has shortened drive and ditched big leg kick in instructs. Power will come as frame fills out. Terrific defender with plus instincts at SS. Plus runner.

Jeffers,Ryan — 2 — Minnesota

EXP MLB DEBUT: 2021 | H/W: 6-4 225 | FUT: Starting C | 7C

Bats R Age 21 — 2018 (2) UNC Wilmington

Skills	Year	Lev	Team	AB	R	H	HR	RBI	Avg	OB	Sig	OPS	bb%	ct%	Eye	SB	CS	x/h%	Iso	RC/G
Pwr +++																				
BAvg +++	2018	NCAA	UNC Wilmgtn	219	53	69	16	59	315	444	635	1079	19	80	1.16	2	1	55	320	9.40
Spd ++	2018	Rk	Elizabethton	102	29	43	3	16	422	516	578	1095	16	84	1.25	0	1	23	157	9.48
Def ++	2018	A	Cedar Rapids	139	19	40	4	17	288	353	446	799	9	78	0.47	0	0	35	158	5.44

Big-bodied, offense-first CA enjoyed successful pro debut. Pull-oriented with solid ct% and bb%, he utilizes quick wrists and strong forearms to get out in front. Frame produces much of his raw power. Adjustments in swing trajectory could bring more. Is a raw defender and still learning the position. High makeup and strong work ethic.

Jenista,Greyson — 9 — Atlanta

EXP MLB DEBUT: 2020 | H/W: 6-4 240 | FUT: Starting OF | 8C

Bats L Age 22
2018 (2) Wichita St
Pwr ++++
BAvg ++
Spd +++
Def +++

Year	Lev	Team	AB	R	H	HR	RBI	Avg	OB	Slg	OPS	bb%	ct%	Eye	SB	CS	x/h%	Iso	RC/G
2018	NCAA	Wichita State	204	54	63	9	38	309	445	475	920	20	80	1.22	12	1	25	167	7.46
2018	Rk	Danville	40	10	10	3	7	250	348	500	848	13	78	0.67	0	1	40	250	6.00
2018	A	Rome	117	20	39	1	23	333	386	453	839	8	85	0.59	4	1	23	120	5.92
2018	A+	Florida	66	3	10	0	4	152	233	227	460	10	77	0.47	0	0	40	76	1.24

Big-bodied, athletic slugger mostly succeeded in pro debut. Incredible athleticism for size. Patient, spray hitter with a feel for the barrel. Swing trajectory geared towards mostly top spin contact. Raw plus-plus power in body. Hit only 13 HR split between college and pro ball. Sneaky SB threat because of instincts and above-average speed.

Jimenez,Anthony — 89 — Seattle

EXP MLB DEBUT: 2020 | H/W: 5-11 165 | FUT: Reserve OF | 6C

Bats R Age 23
2013 FA (VZ)
Pwr ++
BAvg ++
Spd +++
Def +++

Year	Lev	Team	AB	R	H	HR	RBI	Avg	OB	Slg	OPS	bb%	ct%	Eye	SB	CS	x/h%	Iso	RC/G
2016	Rk	AZL Mariners	186	30	58	1	22	312	354	441	794	6	77	0.28	14	6	29	129	5.39
2017	Rk	AZL Mariners	9	1	3	0	1	333	333	667	1000	0	78	0.00	0	0	67	333	8.05
2017	A	Clinton	228	43	68	7	33	298	352	482	835	8	68	0.26	24	10	38	184	6.23
2018	A+	Modesto	385	38	101	6	42	262	302	377	679	5	73	0.21	13	7	29	114	3.78

Athletic, undersized corner OF struggling to break tweener label. Solid, contact-oriented hitter with improving pitch recognition skills. Spray approach but rarely makes hard contact to the opposite field; power exclusively to the pull-side. Below-average potential both in frame and bat. Above-average speed with SB% risk; but could reach double-digits.

Jimenez,Eloy — 7 — Chicago (A)

EXP MLB DEBUT: 2019 | H/W: 6-4 205 | FUT: Starting OF | 9B

Bats R Age 22
2013 FA (DR)
Pwr +++++
BAvg ++++
Spd ++
Def ++

Year	Lev	Team	AB	R	H	HR	RBI	Avg	OB	Slg	OPS	bb%	ct%	Eye	SB	CS	x/h%	Iso	RC/G
2017	A+	Winston-Salem	110	20	38	8	26	345	410	682	1092	10	81	0.57	0	2	53	336	8.97
2017	A+	Myrtle Beach	155	23	42	8	32	271	347	490	837	10	77	0.51	0	0	38	219	5.90
2017	AA	Birmingham	68	11	24	3	7	353	397	559	956	7	76	0.31	1	1	33	206	7.30
2018	AA	Birmingham	205	36	65	10	42	317	372	556	928	8	81	0.46	0	0	42	239	6.90
2018	AAA	Charlotte	211	28	75	12	33	355	396	597	993	6	86	0.47	0	1	35	242	7.36

Strong, muscular OF destroyed upper-level pitching. Advanced feel for barrel. Allows ball to travel deep, trusting hands and bat-to-ball skills to get bat head to ball. Contact rate improved each of throughout 2018. Plus-plus power to all fields. 35+ HR potential. Below-average speed and noodle arm likely limits him to LF long-term.

Jimenez,Leonardo — 46 — Toronto

EXP MLB DEBUT: 2022 | H/W: 6-1 160 | FUT: Starting SS | 7D

Bats R Age 17
2017 FA (PN)
Pwr +
BAvg +++
Spd ++
Def ++++

Year	Lev	Team	AB	R	H	HR	RBI	Avg	OB	Slg	OPS	bb%	ct%	Eye	SB	CS	x/h%	Iso	RC/G
2018	Rk	GCL Blue Jays	132	13	33	0	19	250	331	341	672	11	87	0.94	0	0	30	91	4.24

Short, slender, projectable player has the chops to stick at short and defense will be his ticket to the show. Quick bat with some natural pop. but doesn't use his lower half well and gets out front limiting power. Good strike zone judgment gives him a chance on offense, but there is much work to do and power may never develop.

Johnson,Daniel — 89 — Cleveland

EXP MLB DEBUT: 2020 | H/W: 5-10 175 | FUT: Reserve OF | 7C

Bats L Age 23
2016 (5) New Mexico St
Pwr ++
BAvg ++
4.07 Spd ++++
Def ++

Year	Lev	Team	AB	R	H	HR	RBI	Avg	OB	Slg	OPS	bb%	ct%	Eye	SB	CS	x/h%	Iso	RC/G
2016	A-	Auburn	245	25	65	1	14	265	286	347	633	3	83	0.17	13	3	22	82	3.13
2017	A	Hagerstown	327	61	98	17	52	300	344	529	873	6	79	0.31	12	9	38	229	6.11
2017	A+	Potomac	170	22	50	5	20	294	344	459	803	7	82	0.43	10	2	36	165	5.35
2018	Rk	GCL Nationals	20	3	6	1	4	300	364	450	814	9	90	1.00	1	0	17	150	5.45
2018	AA	Harrisburg	356	48	95	6	31	267	311	410	721	6	75	0.26	21	4	34	143	4.41

Toolkit player with ample power, speed, and plus OF arm, but breaking balls give him fits. Good bat speed from strong forearms/wrists, but overly aggressive at the plate and poor pitch recognition currently caps his profile. Speed an asset in the field and on the bases, but OF routes limit him to a corner; might not be enough bat to start.

Johnson,Osiris — 6 — Miami

EXP MLB DEBUT: 2022 | H/W: 6-0 181 | FUT: Starting SS | 8E

Bats R Age 18
2018 (2) HS (CA)
Pwr +++
BAvg ++
Spd ++++
Def +++

Year	Lev	Team	AB	R	H	HR	RBI	Avg	OB	Slg	OPS	bb%	ct%	Eye	SB	CS	x/h%	Iso	RC/G
2018	Rk	GCL Marlins	103	12	31	1	13	301	327	447	774	4	82	0.21	7	2	35	146	4.93
2018	A	Greensboro	85	4	16	2	6	188	198	294	492	1	60	0.03	0	2	31	106	1.03

Toolsy, quick-twitch SS made pro debut. Aggressive approach with swing-and-miss issues in profile. Plus bat speed pushes hit profile. Struggles with pitch recognition and swing path volatility. Will need to sharpen up. Plus, raw power in frame and swing. Plus-runner w/ SB skill. Mentored by cousin Jimmy Rollins.

Jones,Jahmai — 4 — Los Angeles (A)

EXP MLB DEBUT: 2019 | H/W: 5-11 210 | FUT: Starting 2B | 8C

Bats R Age 21
2015 (2) HS (GA)
Pwr +++
BAvg +++
Spd +++
Def +++

Year	Lev	Team	AB	R	H	HR	RBI	Avg	OB	Slg	OPS	bb%	ct%	Eye	SB	CS	x/h%	Iso	RC/G
2016	A	Burlington	62	8	15	1	10	242	299	306	605	7	79	0.38	1	0	13	65	2.85
2017	A	Burlington	346	54	94	9	30	272	333	425	758	8	82	0.51	18	7	33	153	4.90
2017	A+	Inland Empire	172	32	52	5	17	302	351	488	840	7	75	0.30	9	6	37	186	5.97
2018	A+	Inland Empire	298	47	70	8	35	235	331	383	714	13	79	0.68	13	3	33	148	4.54
2018	AA	Mobile	184	33	45	2	20	245	332	375	707	12	72	0.47	11	1	36	130	4.53

Athletic outfielder-turned-second baseman in 2018 with strong football bloodlines. Saw some hiccups defensively in the move, but pure athleticism, plus speed and instincts should iron that out. Eye at the plate is improving and plays well to his plus bat speed. Power is still developing. Maturing on both sides of the ball.

Jones,Nolan — 5 — Cleveland

EXP MLB DEBUT: 2021 | H/W: 6-3 195 | FUT: Starting 3B | 8C

Bats L Age 20
2016 (2) HS (PA)
Pwr ++++
BAvg ++++
Spd ++
Def ++

Year	Lev	Team	AB	R	H	HR	RBI	Avg	OB	Slg	OPS	bb%	ct%	Eye	SB	CS	x/h%	Iso	RC/G
2016	Rk	AZL Indians	109	10	28	0	9	257	386	339	726	17	55	0.47	3	1	25	83	5.82
2017	A-	Mahoning Val	218	41	69	4	33	317	429	482	911	16	72	0.72	1	0	36	165	7.61
2018	A	Lake County	323	46	90	16	49	279	396	464	861	16	70	0.65	2	1	31	186	6.68
2018	A+	Lynchburg	104	23	31	3	17	298	438	471	910	20	67	0.76	0	0	39	173	7.92

A bat-first left-handed hitting corner infield prospect, so far in his pro career he has hit, and hit for power. He operates with an exaggerated load and occasionally lands heavily into his front side, but has big power when he stays back. Has above-average pitch recognition that result in high walk totals.

Jones,Thomas — 78 — Miami

EXP MLB DEBUT: 2021 | H/W: 6-4 195 | FUT: Starting OF | 7E

Bats R Age 21
2016 (3) HS (SC)
Pwr ++
BAvg ++
Spd ++++
Def ++++

Year	Lev	Team	AB	R	H	HR	RBI	Avg	OB	Slg	OPS	bb%	ct%	Eye	SB	CS	x/h%	Iso	RC/G
2016	Rk	GCL Marlins	64	11	15	0	6	234	347	313	659	15	69	0.55	6	2	27	78	4.03
2017	A-	Batavia	238	31	43	2	21	181	283	282	565	13	61	0.36	7	6	37	101	2.55
2018	A	Greensboro	396	55	88	9	33	222	268	343	612	6	65	0.18	20	8	32	121	2.94

Speedy, athletic OF was exposed a bit in full-season debut. Solid, patient approach. Struggled with long swing and pitch recognition. Solid raw power, completely pull-dominated. Will attack middle-in FB and try to muscle ball over the fence. Plus defender and runner, both carry profile.

Jones,Travis — 359 — Kansas City

EXP MLB DEBUT: 2021 | H/W: 6-4 210 | FUT: Utility player | 6C

Bats R Age 23
2017 (29) Texas
Pwr ++
BAvg +++
Spd ++++
Def +++

Year	Lev	Team	AB	R	H	HR	RBI	Avg	OB	Slg	OPS	bb%	ct%	Eye	SB	CS	x/h%	Iso	RC/G
2017	Rk	Idaho Falls	164	40	55	4	42	335	401	537	938	10	80	0.56	20	3	40	201	7.30
2017	Rk	Burlington	23	3	9	0	4	391	417	522	938	4	87	0.33	0	0	33	130	6.85
2017	Rk	AZL Royals	33	10	16	0	6	485	541	576	1116	11	94	2.00	4	2	13	91	9.21
2018	A	Lexington	228	41	65	5	32	285	335	417	751	7	75	0.30	14	7	29	132	4.76
2018	A+	Wilmington	205	31	61	2	18	298	385	356	741	12	74	0.54	17	5	11	59	4.91

Big-bodied, athletic UT performed well in 2018, split between A-Ball affiliates. Patient approach with solid bat-to-ball skills has struggled to find power stroke due to flat swing trajectory. Plenty of power in frame, not reaching for it. Versatile defender with a solid arm, can play all corners. Aggressive runner with 31 SB in 43 attempts.

Kelenic,Jarred — 8 — Seattle

EXP MLB DEBUT: 2022 | H/W: 6-1 190 | FUT: Starting OF | 9C

Bats L Age 19
2018 (1) HS (WI)
Pwr ++++
BAvg ++++
Spd +++
Def +++

Year	Lev	Team	AB	R	H	HR	RBI	Avg	OB	Slg	OPS	bb%	ct%	Eye	SB	CS	x/h%	Iso	RC/G
2018	Rk	GCL Mets	46	9	19	1	9	413	460	609	1069	8	76	0.36	4	0	26	196	9.06
2018	Rk	Kingsport	174	33	44	5	33	253	337	431	768	11	78	0.56	11	1	39	178	5.20

Just drafted out of HS, he is a promising OF bat. A cross between two recent, successful Mets high picks, Michael Conforto and Brandon Nimmo. Has a simple, sound, compact swing & should fill out and hit for power. Built more like Conforto, with a strong lower half, but, like Nimmo, HS player from cold weather state. Acquired by SEA this off-season.

Kelley, Christian — 2 — Pittsburgh

EXP MLB DEBUT: 2019 **H/W:** 5-11 185 **FUT:** Reserve C **5B**

Bats R   Age 25
2015 (11) Cal Poly Pomona

	Year	Lev	Team	AB	R	H	HR	RBI	Avg	OB	Slg	OPS	bb%	ct%	Eye	SB	CS	x/h%	Iso	RC/G
Pwr +	2015	A-	West Virginia	194	30	45	0	21	232	320	242	562	11	78	0.58	0	0	4	10	2.54
BAvg +	2016	A	West Virginia	259	26	61	2	28	236	303	305	608	9	79	0.45	0	5	23	69	3.05
	2016	A+	Bradenton	31	7	11	0	5	355	394	419	813	6	71	0.22	0	0	18	65	5.75
4.70 Spd +	2017	A+	Bradenton	325	27	79	2	39	243	324	295	620	11	75	0.49	1	6	16	52	3.22
Def ++++	2018	AA	Altoona	311	36	73	8	38	235	292	367	658	7	79	0.39	0	0	32	132	3.56

Plus defensive C who lacks bat to be more than a backup. Lacks size and speed to have any real impact offensively. Will take a walk, but has a hard time driving the ball. Jeff Mathis type.

Kendall, Jeren — 8 — Los Angeles (N)

EXP MLB DEBUT: 2020 **H/W:** 5-10 170 **FUT:** Starting CF **8D**

Bats L   Age 23
2017 (1) Vanderbilt

	Year	Lev	Team	AB	R	H	HR	RBI	Avg	OB	Slg	OPS	bb%	ct%	Eye	SB	CS	x/h%	Iso	RC/G
Pwr +++	2017	NCAA	Vanderbilt	261	59	80	15	53	307	365	556	920	8	72	0.32	20	4	38	249	7.11
BAvg +	2017	Rk	Ogden	22	5	10	1	7	455	455	727	1182	0	86	0.00	4	0	30	273	9.11
Spd +++++	2017	A	Great Lakes	140	21	31	2	18	221	288	400	688	8	70	0.31	5	8	45	179	4.24
Def ++++	2018	A+	Rancho Cuca	438	68	94	12	42	215	298	356	654	11	64	0.33	37	14	37	142	3.74

He has been slow to develop and struggled in the hitter-friendly CAL. Concerns about hit tool cropped up in college and contact issues have carried over. Shows good power when he gets bat to ball, and remains a plus athlete with 20/20 potential and Gold Glove defense. But badly needs a 2019 reboot in 2019.

Kieboom, Carter — 6 — Washington

EXP MLB DEBUT: 2019 **H/W:** 6-2 190 **FUT:** Starting SS **9C**

Bats R   Age 21
2016 (1) HS (GA)

	Year	Lev	Team	AB	R	H	HR	RBI	Avg	OB	Slg	OPS	bb%	ct%	Eye	SB	CS	x/h%	Iso	RC/G
	2017	Rk	GCL Nationals	11	1	5	0	5	455	571	727	1299	21	100		0	0	60	273	12.25
Pwr +++	2017	A-	Auburn	28	4	7	1	4	250	276	393	669	3	93	0.50	1	0	29	143	3.68
BAvg +++	2017	A	Hagerstown	179	36	53	8	26	296	391	497	889	14	78	0.70	2	2	38	201	6.77
4.40 Spd ++	2018	A+	Potomac	245	48	73	11	46	298	388	494	882	13	80	0.72	6	1	36	196	6.60
Def +++	2018	AA	Harrisburg	248	36	65	5	23	262	322	395	717	8	76	0.37	3	1	34	133	4.39

Gained some strength with possibly more to come on his previously lean frame. Hit tool has developed nicely. Bat speed and good pitch recognition lets him wait on pitches that he can drive. Some pull side power now, but uses the whole field when situation warrants. Average runner with great baseball instincts allows entire toolkit to play up.

King, Jose — 6 — Detroit

EXP MLB DEBUT: 2022 **H/W:** 6-0 160 **FUT:** Starting SS **7C**

Bats R   Age 20
2015 FA (DR)

	Year	Lev	Team	AB	R	H	HR	RBI	Avg	OB	Slg	OPS	bb%	ct%	Eye	SB	CS	x/h%	Iso	RC/G
Pwr +	2017	Rk	AZL DBacks	46	7	12	0	9	261	306	348	654	6	57	0.15	2	2	17	87	4.25
BAvg +	2017	Rk	GCL Tigers	112	18	36	0	6	321	356	366	722	5	74	0.21	8	9	11	45	4.32
Spd ++++	2018	Rk	GCL Tigers W	86	20	27	2	12	314	344	477	821	4	76	0.17	5	4	26	163	5.57
Def ++	2018	A-	Connecticut	85	5	18	0	16	212	256	318	573	6	66	0.17	2	0	44	106	2.55

Wiry, quick-twitch shortstop already working as an above-average defender. Light defensive footwork and clean hands with an average arm. Thin frame lacks anything in the way of power with slap-hit approach at the plate. Barrel control is fringy, due to lack of muscle. Near-elite speed makes him a true threat on base.

Kirilloff, Alex — 9 — Minnesota

EXP MLB DEBUT: 2020 **H/W:** 6-1 195 **FUT:** Starting OF **9B**

Bats L   Age 21
2016 (1) HS (PA)

	Year	Lev	Team	AB	R	H	HR	RBI	Avg	OB	Slg	OPS	bb%	ct%	Eye	SB	CS	x/h%	Iso	RC/G
Pwr ++++																				
BAvg +++++	2016	Rk	Elizabethton	216	33	66	7	33	306	339	454	793	5	85	0.34	0	1	26	148	5.02
Spd +++	2018	A	Cedar Rapids	252	36	84	13	56	333	391	607	998	9	81	0.51	1	1	45	274	7.82
Def +++	2018	A+	Fort Myers	260	39	94	7	45	362	394	550	944	5	85	0.36	3	2	35	188	6.90

Proved to be real deal with bat after he lost 2017 season to Tommy John surgery. Short, compact swing is ideal for high contact. Reaches barrel deep in zone, allowing quick wrists and hand/eye skills to spray ball across diamond. Average raw power skills play up due to swing trajectory and leverage in lower half. Instincts play up run tool.

Knizner, Andrew — 2 — St. Louis

EXP MLB DEBUT: 2019 **H/W:** 6-1 190 **FUT:** Starting C **8D**

Bats R   Age 24
2016 (7) North Carolina St

	Year	Lev	Team	AB	R	H	HR	RBI	Avg	OB	Slg	OPS	bb%	ct%	Eye	SB	CS	x/h%	Iso	RC/G
	2016	Rk	Johnson City	185	35	59	6	42	319	388	492	880	10	89	1.00	0	0	32	173	6.44
Pwr +++	2017	A	Peoria	179	18	50	8	29	279	314	480	794	5	88	0.41	1	1	38	201	5.04
BAvg ++	2017	AA	Springfield	182	27	59	4	22	324	372	462	834	7	85	0.52	0	1	29	137	5.72
Spd +	2018	AA	Springfield	281	39	88	7	41	313	365	434	799	8	86	0.58	0	1	23	121	5.30
Def +++	2018	AAA	Memphis	54	3	17	0	4	315	362	407	769	7	85	0.50	0	0	29	93	5.08

Above-average bat speed and strike zone awareness allow him to make consistent, hard contact as he continued to rake in 2018. Has just average power and below average speed. Behind the dish, has shown solid improvement and a strong, accurate arm. Is now the top CA prospect in the system.

Knowles, D'Shawn — 8 — Los Angeles (A)

EXP MLB DEBUT: 2022 **H/W:** 6-0 165 **FUT:** Starting OF **7B**

Bats B   Age 18
2017 FA (BA)

	Year	Lev	Team	AB	R	H	HR	RBI	Avg	OB	Slg	OPS	bb%	ct%	Eye	SB	CS	x/h%	Iso	RC/G
Pwr ++																				
BAvg ++																				
Spd ++++	2018	Rk	AZL Angels	113	19	34	1	14	301	383	381	763	12	76	0.56	7	4	18	80	5.20
Def +++	2018	Rk	Orem	109	27	35	4	15	321	393	550	944	11	65	0.34	2	3	43	229	8.24

Fresh-faced outfielder working all three outfield posts before his 18th birthday. Boasts near plus-plus speed with the defensive feel to work as a primary centerfielder through his first season. Clean swing with projection for added power as he develops physically. Currently works off gap-to-gap, line drive strength with solid plate discipline.

Kramer, Kevin — 4 — Pittsburgh

EXP MLB DEBUT: 2019 **H/W:** 6-0 195 **FUT:** Starting 2B **8C**

Bats L   Age 25
2015 (2) UCLA

	Year	Lev	Team	AB	R	H	HR	RBI	Avg	OB	Slg	OPS	bb%	ct%	Eye	SB	CS	x/h%	Iso	RC/G
	2017	Rk	GCL Pirates	2	0	0	0	1	0	0	0	0	0	50	0.00	0	0	0	0	-7.85
Pwr +++	2017	A	West Virginia	13	1	3	0	2	231	231	231	462	0	85	0.00	1	0	0	0	0.92
BAvg ++++	2017	AA	Altoona	202	31	60	6	27	297	352	500	852	8	75	0.34	7	2	43	203	6.18
4.30 Spd ++	2018	AAA	Indianapolis	476	73	148	15	59	311	362	492	853	7	73	0.30	13	5	36	181	6.19
Def +++	2018	MLB	Pittsburgh	37	5	5	0	4	135	179	135	315	5	46	0.10	0	0	0	0	-1.93

Strong-bodied 2B with a feel for hitting. Capable of hitting for some power, at the expense of BA, or vice versa. Steady defender; though range short for short, he can make routine plays there. Could be good 3B, but best bet is regular 2B or offensive utilityman. Not a threat to steal bases. Poor man's Daniel Murphy.

Larnach, Trevor — 79 — Minnesota

EXP MLB DEBUT: 2020 **H/W:** 6-4 205 **FUT:** Starting OF **8C**

Bats L   Age 22
2018 (1) Oregon St

	Year	Lev	Team	AB	R	H	HR	RBI	Avg	OB	Slg	OPS	bb%	ct%	Eye	SB	CS	x/h%	Iso	RC/G
Pwr ++++																				
BAvg +++	2018	NCAA	Oregon State	256	72	89	19	77	348	454	652	1107	16	74	0.76	4	2	44	305	9.89
Spd +++	2018	Rk	Elizabethton	61	10	19	2	16	311	408	492	900	14	82	0.91	2	0	37	180	6.97
Def +++	2018	A	Cedar Rapids	91	17	27	3	10	297	373	505	878	11	81	0.65	1	0	44	209	6.54

Tall, muscular contact-oriented OF prospect remade swing before 2018 to become collegiate force. Short and compact, it peppers all fields with hard contact. A patient hitter, he adjusts well within AB. Raw plus power showed in college but not in hitter-friendly Appy Lg. 25-30 HR potential, especially selling out to pull-side. Average runner.

Lavigne, Grant — 3 — Colorado

EXP MLB DEBUT: 2022 **H/W:** 6-4 220 **FUT:** Starting 1B **9D**

Bats L   Age 19
2018 (1) HS (NH)

	Year	Lev	Team	AB	R	H	HR	RBI	Avg	OB	Slg	OPS	bb%	ct%	Eye	SB	CS	x/h%	Iso	RC/G
Pwr ++++																				
BAvg +++																				
Spd ++																				
Def +	2018	Rk	Grand Junction	206	45	72	6	38	350	466	519	986	18	81	1.13	12	7	29	170	8.34

One of the top power bats in the draft. Uses massive frame, bat speed, and smooth LH stroke to rocket balls to pull side. Solid approach and strike zone awareness make him more than a masher and debut was impressive with more BB than Ks. Below-average defender and speed limit him to 1B, but has the lefty bat and raw power to make that profile work.

Lee, Braxton — 789 — Miami

EXP MLB DEBUT: 2018 **H/W:** 5-8 165 **FUT:** Reserve OF **6C**

Bats L   Age 25
2014 (12) Mississippi

	Year	Lev	Team	AB	R	H	HR	RBI	Avg	OB	Slg	OPS	bb%	ct%	Eye	SB	CS	x/h%	Iso	RC/G
Pwr +	2017	AA	Jacksonville	214	34	63	1	21	294	396	364	760	14	78	0.75	8	2	21	70	5.33
BAvg ++	2018	A+	Jupiter	24	6	7	0	3	292	370	292	662	11	88	1.00	0	1	0	0	4.01
Spd ++++	2018	AA	Jacksonville	110	16	24	1	7	218	317	300	617	13	83	0.84	3	1	29	82	3.48
Def ++++	2018	AAA	New Orleans	179	24	42	0	9	235	308	291	599	10	79	0.51	4	6	19	56	3.03
	2018	MLB	Miami	17	0	3	0	2	176	222	176	399	6	53	0.13	0	0	0	0	-0.40

Versatile, speedy OF struggled with hard-contact rate at three stops, including MIA. Contact-oriented hitter with patient, spray approach, saw ct% rate, BA and OBP fall throughout 2018. No power whatsoever with swing geared towards ground ball contact. Relies heavily on legs as part of profile, both on bases and in OF.

Lee,Khalil — 8 — Kansas City

EXP MLB DEBUT: 2020 | H/W: 5-10 182 | FUT: Starting OF | 8C

Bats L Age 20
2016 (3) HS (DE)

- Pwr +++
- BAvg +++
- Spd +++
- Def ++++

Year	Lev	Team	AB	R	H	HR	RBI	Avg	OB	Slg	OPS	bb%	ct%	Eye	SB	CS	x/h%	Iso	RC/G
2016	Rk	AZL Royals	182	43	49	6	29	269	381	484	865	15	69	0.58	8	4	43	214	6.99
2017	A	Lexington	451	71	107	17	61	237	333	430	763	13	62	0.38	20	18	44	193	5.60
2018	A+	Wilmington	244	42	66	4	41	270	390	406	796	16	69	0.64	14	3	32	135	6.04
2018	AA	NW Arkansas	102	15	25	2	10	245	319	353	672	10	73	0.39	2	2	28	108	3.83

Lean, athletic OF surged early in High-A and struggled late in Double-A and AFL. Raw hit tool, but quick wrists and a compact swing. Patient hitter with OBP skill. Struggles with spin recognition and making adjustments. Plus raw power, but incredibly pull-oriented in game and BP. Tweener profile risk in corner OF; has above-average speed.

Lewis,Kyle — 8 — Seattle

EXP MLB DEBUT: 2020 | H/W: 6-4 195 | FUT: Starting OF | 8E

Bats R Age 23
2016 (1) Mercer

- Pwr ++++
- BAvg ++
- Spd ++
- Def +++

Year	Lev	Team	AB	R	H	HR	RBI	Avg	OB	Slg	OPS	bb%	ct%	Eye	SB	CS	x/h%	Iso	RC/G
2016	A-	Everett	117	26	35	3	26	299	383	530	913	12	81	0.73	3	0	46	231	7.16
2017	Rk	AZL Mariners	38	9	10	1	7	263	333	447	781	10	63	0.29	1	0	40	184	5.84
2017	A+	Modesto	149	20	38	6	24	255	323	403	726	9	74	0.39	2	1	26	148	4.39
2018	A+	Modesto	196	21	51	5	32	260	300	429	728	5	72	0.20	0	0	45	168	4.48
2018	AA	Arkansas	132	18	29	4	20	220	309	371	680	11	76	0.53	1	0	41	152	3.99

Oft-injured athletic OF hasn't recovered explosiveness since tearing his ACL, medial and lateral meniscuses in his right knee in '16. Despite noise in the load, very quick and compact to the ball. Gets bat head out in front of plate, resulting in hard contact. Significant power in frame and swing. Struggles getting legs under him to power swing.

Lewis,Royce — 6 — Minnesota

EXP MLB DEBUT: 2020 | H/W: 6-1 185 | FUT: Starting SS | 9B

Bats R Age 19
2017 (1) HS (CA)

- Pwr +++
- BAvg +++++
- Spd +++++
- Def +++

Year	Lev	Team	AB	R	H	HR	RBI	Avg	OB	Slg	OPS	bb%	ct%	Eye	SB	CS	x/h%	Iso	RC/G
2017	Rk	GCL Twins	133	38	36	3	17	271	362	414	775	13	87	1.12	15	2	31	143	5.42
2017	A	Cedar Rapids	71	16	21	1	10	296	351	394	745	8	77	0.38	3	1	19	99	4.71
2018	A	Cedar Rapids	295	50	93	9	53	315	367	485	852	8	83	0.49	22	4	34	169	5.94
2018	A+	Fort Myers	188	33	48	5	21	255	324	399	723	9	81	0.54	6	4	29	144	4.48

Athletic infielder has improved tremendously since 2017 draft. Incredible hand/eye coordination, combined with quick reflexes, is driving contact rate. Raw control of barrel, but ball seems to find it. Has become more patient, working counts. Swing trajectory produces solid line-drive loft naturally. Plus-plus run tool but raw SB instincts.

Leyba,Domingo — 4 — Arizona

EXP MLB DEBUT: 2019 | H/W: 5-11 160 | FUT: Utility player | 7C

Bats B Age 23
2012 FA (DR)

- Pwr ++
- BAvg +++
- Spd +++
- Def +++

Year	Lev	Team	AB	R	H	HR	RBI	Avg	OB	Slg	OPS	bb%	ct%	Eye	SB	CS	x/h%	Iso	RC/G
2016	A+	Visalia	340	48	100	6	40	294	350	426	776	8	82	0.47	5	1	32	132	5.12
2016	AA	Mobile	156	21	47	4	20	301	370	436	806	10	86	0.77	4	2	26	135	5.55
2017	A-	Hillsboro	28	4	8	1	6	286	375	429	804	13	93	2.00	0	0	25	143	5.75
2017	AA	Jackson	58	11	16	2	9	276	333	448	782	8	90	0.83	0	0	38	172	5.18
2018	AA	Jackson	320	43	86	5	30	269	341	381	722	10	86	0.76	5	2	28	113	4.62

Athletically strong middle INF on the cusp of big-league callup. Lacks plus tool but has well-rounded skillset headlined by plus ct% ability from switch-hitting setup. Power limited to gaps and has single-digit HR profile. Decent runner who could have sneaky SB impact. Chance to man either SS/2B as his actions and arm are solid-average.

Lin,Tzu-Wei — 6 — Boston

EXP MLB DEBUT: 2017 | H/W: 5-9 155 | FUT: Utility player | 6B

Bats L Age 25
2012 FA (TW)

- Pwr +
- BAvg ++
- 4.10 Spd ++++
- Def ++++

Year	Lev	Team	AB	R	H	HR	RBI	Avg	OB	Slg	OPS	bb%	ct%	Eye	SB	CS	x/h%	Iso	RC/G
2017	AA	Portland	159	31	48	5	19	302	380	491	870	11	83	0.74	8	2	35	189	6.43
2017	AAA	Pawtucket	141	12	32	2	9	227	283	319	602	7	80	0.39	2	4	25	92	2.90
2017	MLB	Boston	56	7	15	0	2	268	369	339	709	14	70	0.53	1	1	13	71	4.71
2018	AAA	Pawtucket	277	33	85	5	25	307	360	448	808	8	77	0.36	3	4	32	141	5.56
2018	MLB	Boston	65	15	16	1	6	246	329	415	744	11	74	0.47	0	1	50	169	5.03

Plus defensive SS who has struggled to be an asset with the bat. Has made some strides but still not likely to ever hit enough to be a regular. Some length to swing and not a lot of natural strength. Red Sox have been moving him to other positions, including CF, the last couple of years, grooming him to be a defense-first utilityman.

Lindsay,Desmond — 78 — New York (N)

EXP MLB DEBUT: 2022 | H/W: 6-0 200 | FUT: Reserve OF | 6D

Bats R Age 22
2015 (2) HS (FL)

- Pwr ++
- BAvg ++
- Spd +++
- Def +++

Year	Lev	Team	AB	R	H	HR	RBI	Avg	OB	Slg	OPS	bb%	ct%	Eye	SB	CS	x/h%	Iso	RC/G
2016	Rk	GCL Mets	10	3	4	0	0	400	600	500	1100	33	50	1.00	0	0	25	100	14.55
2016	A-	Brooklyn	111	18	33	4	17	297	405	450	855	15	77	0.77	3	1	27	153	6.46
2017	A	Columbia	214	40	47	8	30	220	324	388	712	13	64	0.43	4	2	40	168	4.64
2018	Rk	GCL Mets	20	4	6	0	3	300	391	400	791	13	65	0.43	2	0	33	100	6.15
2018	A+	St. Lucie	294	27	64	3	30	218	305	320	625	11	70	0.42	7	7	30	102	3.33

Fallen prospect with some athleticism and tools whose bat has just not come around. Small, strong, injury-prone, Jay Payton type who lacks Payton's plus contact skills. Subpar arm and reads may limit him to LF. Has batspeed, strength and age to still improve some at the plate, but needs to clean up swing and approach.

Liniak,Kingston — 8 — Detroit

EXP MLB DEBUT: 2022 | H/W: 6-2 170 | FUT: Reserve OF | 7C

Bats R Age 19
2018 (4) HS (CA)

- Pwr +
- BAvg +
- Spd +++
- Def ++

Year	Lev	Team	AB	R	H	HR	RBI	Avg	OB	Slg	OPS	bb%	ct%	Eye	SB	CS	x/h%	Iso	RC/G
2018	Rk	GCL Tigers	156	14	35	0	9	224	258	269	527	4	67	0.14	5	4	20	45	1.67
2018	Rk	GCL Tigers W	188	19	44	0	13	234	262	277	538	4	69	0.12	7	4	18	43	1.79
2018	A-	Connecticut	12	1	3	1	2	250	308	500	808	8	58	0.20	1	1	33	250	6.08

Slender outfielder with plenty of projection in his frame. Fluid defensive ability, thanks to pure athleticism. Easy, accurate arm with above-average foot speed. Solid swing-path from the right side with projected strength to come later on. Pitch recognition spotty early on, but instincts beg the prediction this should polish out with more reps.

Listi,Austin — 37 — Philadelphia

EXP MLB DEBUT: 2019 | H/W: 5-11 197 | FUT: Utility player | 7D

Bats R Age 25
2017 (17) Dallas Baptist

- Pwr +++
- BAvg ++
- 4.53 Spd +
- Def ++

Year	Lev	Team	AB	R	H	HR	RBI	Avg	OB	Slg	OPS	bb%	ct%	Eye	SB	CS	x/h%	Iso	RC/G
2017	NCAA	Dallas Baptist	238	62	80	24	55	336	442	735	1177	16	74	0.74	1	1	59	399	10.70
2017	A-	Williamsport	75	14	22	3	17	293	361	480	841	10	79	0.50	3	0	36	187	5.95
2017	A	Lakewood	120	16	29	4	11	242	266	433	699	3	75	0.13	0	0	45	192	3.91
2018	A+	Clearwater	209	37	72	9	45	344	436	560	996	14	80	0.81	0	0	36	215	8.17
2018	AA	Reading	217	26	61	9	39	281	363	447	810	11	76	0.54	0	0	30	166	5.63

Unheralded 2017 draftee has hit at every stop with a grinding mentality and great two-strike approach. Small but strong, hits from a deep crouch, is patient, makes contact and has some power. Strictly a corner IF/OF, has versatility but will need to prove himself at every level. Likely a bench MLB player unless there's another level of game power.

Little,Grant — 78 — San Diego

EXP MLB DEBUT: 2021 | H/W: 6-1 185 | FUT: Starting OF | 7C

Bats R Age 21
2018 (2) Texas Tech

- Pwr ++
- BAvg +++
- Spd +++
- Def +++

Year	Lev	Team	AB	R	H	HR	RBI	Avg	OB	Slg	OPS	bb%	ct%	Eye	SB	CS	x/h%	Iso	RC/G
2018	NCAA	Texas Tech	246	62	91	12	77	370	458	642	1100	14	85	1.05	11	5	44	272	9.34
2018	A-	Tri-City	149	16	39	0	17	262	349	315	665	12	81	0.71	9	2	21	54	4.01

Collegiate OF taken in 2nd round of 2018 draft before signing for below-slot value. Owns well-rounded skillset led by advanced approach and natural ct% ability. Power limited to gaps at present but with more strength could be avg tool. Near-plus runner who could be everyday CF with moderate SB value. High-floor rather than high-upside bat.

Long,Shed — 4 — Cincinnati

EXP MLB DEBUT: 2019 | H/W: 5-10 175 | FUT: Starting 2B | 8D

Bats L Age 23
2013 (12) HS (AL)

- Pwr +++
- BAvg +++
- Spd +++
- Def ++

Year	Lev	Team	AB	R	H	HR	RBI	Avg	OB	Slg	OPS	bb%	ct%	Eye	SB	CS	x/h%	Iso	RC/G
2016	A	Dayton	335	47	94	11	45	281	364	457	821	12	75	0.52	16	3	38	176	5.92
2016	A+	Daytona	143	22	46	4	30	322	366	503	870	7	76	0.29	5	1	30	182	6.31
2017	A+	Daytona	247	37	77	13	36	312	380	543	922	10	74	0.43	6	3	39	231	7.09
2017	AA	Pensacola	141	13	32	3	14	227	319	362	680	12	78	0.61	3	1	34	135	4.10
2018	AA	Pensacola	452	75	118	12	56	261	344	412	755	11	73	0.46	19	6	33	150	5.06

Short-statured and stocky, he continues ascent to full-time role. Makes up for slight hitch in load with quick hands and loose wrists. Sprays the field now, could become pull-dependent later. Swing trajectory geared for hard line drive contact with loft. Power to left and right but rarely to center. Above average speed with 10-15 SB potential.

Longo,Mitch — 789 — Cleveland

EXP MLB DEBUT: 2020 | H/W: 6-0 185 | FUT: Reserve OF | 6B

Bats L Age 24
2016 (14) Ohio

- Pwr +++
- BAvg +++
- 4.15 Spd +++
- Def ++

Year	Lev	Team	AB	R	H	HR	RBI	Avg	OB	Slg	OPS	bb%	ct%	Eye	SB	CS	x/h%	Iso	RC/G
2016	NCAA	Ohio	214	36	77	3	22	360	427	467	894	10	91	1.32	12	5	22	107	6.69
2016	A-	Mahoning Val	137	21	42	1	15	307	345	409	754	6	88	0.47	4	0	26	102	4.78
2017	A	Lake County	202	37	73	4	25	361	427	530	956	10	83	0.66	18	1	33	168	7.49
2017	A+	Lynchburg	16	8	9	0	3	563	650	688	1338	20	88	2.00	2	0	22	125	12.83
2018	A+	Lynchburg	461	73	127	8	52	275	335	410	745	8	79	0.42	18	8	32	134	4.76

Comes right out of the leadoff hitter mold, as a left-handed hitter that can get on-base, run, and generally work tough at-bats. His power mostly translates into game power when he can drop his hands on a low inside fastball, although he is not a dead-pull hitter otherwise. Defense and arm strength limit him to the corner outfield.

Lopez,Nicky — 46 — Kansas City

EXP MLB DEBUT: 2019 | H/W: 5-11 175 | FUT: Starting 2B | 8B

Bats L Age 24	Year	Lev	Team	AB	R	H	HR	RBI	Avg	OB	Slg	OPS	bb%	ct%	Eye	SB	CS	x/h%	Iso	RC/G
2016 (5) Creighton	2016	Rk	Burlington	231	54	65	6	29	281	376	429	805	13	87	1.17	24	4	26	147	5.78
Pwr ++	2017	A+	Wilmington	285	42	84	2	27	295	374	407	781	11	92	1.57	14	8	25	112	5.58
BAvg ++++	2017	AA	NW Arkansas	232	26	60	0	11	259	306	293	600	6	88	0.55	7	4	12	34	3.06
Spd ++++	2018	AA	NW Arkansas	281	42	93	2	27	331	401	416	818	11	92	1.43	9	4	16	85	5.89
Def +++	2018	AAA	Omaha	223	33	62	7	26	278	356	417	773	11	87	0.93	6	2	24	139	5.20

Lean, athletic MIF affects game with plus hit and run tools and tremendous instincts. Contact-oriented hitter with great bat-to-ball skills. Sprays all fields with line drives, though he has below average power potential, as he's completely pull-oriented. Will power up a middle-in FB. Plus runner and double-digit SB threat.

Lowe,Brandon — 47 — Tampa Bay

EXP MLB DEBUT: 2018 | H/W: 6-0 185 | FUT: Utility player | 7B

Bats L Age 24	Year	Lev	Team	AB	R	H	HR	RBI	Avg	OB	Slg	OPS	bb%	ct%	Eye	SB	CS	x/h%	Iso	RC/G
2015 (3) Maryland	2017	A+	Charlotte	315	62	98	9	46	311	401	524	924	13	79	0.72	6	3	47	213	7.34
Pwr +++	2017	AA	Montgomery	95	8	24	2	12	253	268	389	658	2	73	0.08	1	1	33	137	3.33
BAvg +++	2018	AA	Montgomery	199	37	58	8	41	291	397	508	905	15	72	0.64	8	2	45	216	7.31
Spd +++	2018	AAA	Durham	181	36	55	14	35	304	379	613	993	11	74	0.47	0	1	51	309	8.01
Def +++	2018	MLB	Tampa Bay	129	16	30	6	25	233	317	450	767	11	71	0.42	2	1	47	217	5.18

Jack-of-all-Trades UT prospect made it to big leagues during stretch run. Patient, pull hitter who discovered power stroke, striking 28 HR between 3 levels. Dead-red FB hitter, struggles with spin. Heady base runner. Will find AB at 2B, LF & RF.

Lowe,Josh — 8 — Tampa Bay

EXP MLB DEBUT: 2020 | H/W: 6-4 190 | FUT: Starting OF | 8E

Bats L Age 21	Year	Lev	Team	AB	R	H	HR	RBI	Avg	OB	Slg	OPS	bb%	ct%	Eye	SB	CS	x/h%	Iso	RC/G
2016 (1) HS (GA)																				
Pwr +++	2016	Rk	Princeton	80	11	19	3	11	238	371	400	771	18	60	0.53	1	1	26	163	5.91
BAvg ++	2016	Rk	GCL Rays	93	14	24	2	15	258	389	409	798	18	71	0.74	1	1	38	151	6.04
Spd ++++	2017	A	Bowling Green	456	60	122	8	55	268	329	386	715	8	68	0.29	22	8	30	118	4.51
Def +++	2018	A+	Charlotte	399	62	95	6	47	238	318	361	679	11	71	0.40	18	6	36	123	4.07

Athletic, LHH OF prospect struggled with consistent hard contact in High-A. Swing geared towards maximizing pull contact. Struggled cutting off outer half, which caused low BA on balls hit the other way. Patient hitter with history of high BB%. Above-average power potential hasn't materialized yet. Plus runner.

Lowe,Nathaniel — 3 — Tampa Bay

EXP MLB DEBUT: 2019 | H/W: 6-4 230 | FUT: Starting 1B | 8C

Bats L Age 23	Year	Lev	Team	AB	R	H	HR	RBI	Avg	OB	Slg	OPS	bb%	ct%	Eye	SB	CS	x/h%	Iso	RC/G
2016 (13) Mercer	2017	A	Bowling Green	229	34	67	5	35	293	389	415	804	14	77	0.68	0	1	27	122	5.77
Pwr ++++	2017	A+	Charlotte	173	21	43	2	24	249	353	353	706	14	69	0.53	1	1	30	104	4.61
BAvg +++	2018	A+	Charlotte	194	39	69	10	44	356	429	588	1017	11	83	0.76	0	0	36	232	8.11
Spd +	2018	AA	Montgomery	188	36	64	13	42	340	444	606	1050	16	84	1.17	1	1	38	266	8.68
Def ++	2018	AAA	Durham	100	18	26	4	16	260	315	460	775	7	73	0.30	0	0	42	200	5.10

Big-bodied, 1B only prospect closing in on MLB debut. Patient hitter with advanced approach, unafraid of working all fields. Slow to cock hands back to load position, could cause issues with reactions against MLB pitching. Plus power to all-fields close to playing in-game. Slow runner.

Lugo,Dawel — 45 — Detroit

EXP MLB DEBUT: 2018 | H/W: 6-0 188 | FUT: Starting 2B | 7D

Bats R Age 24	Year	Lev	Team	AB	R	H	HR	RBI	Avg	OB	Slg	OPS	bb%	ct%	Eye	SB	CS	x/h%	Iso	RC/G
2011 FA (DR)	2016	AA	Mobile	173	24	53	4	20	306	322	451	773	2	91	0.27	1	1	28	145	4.75
Pwr ++	2017	AA	Jackson	341	40	96	7	43	282	323	428	751	6	85	0.41	1	0	33	147	4.71
BAvg ++	2017	AA	Erie	175	18	47	6	22	269	316	417	733	6	88	0.57	2	1	28	149	4.46
Spd ++	2018	AAA	Toledo	509	56	137	3	59	269	282	350	632	2	87	0.14	12	4	23	81	3.12
Def +++	2018	MLB	Detroit	94	10	20	1	8	213	267	309	576	7	79	0.35	0	0	30	96	2.57

Sturdy infielder who made a seamless defensive transition from third base to second base. Fluid defender with accurate arm and good feet. Despite contact rate, swing is disconnected from lower half, missing out on access to added power. Draws little to no walks and keeps strikeout rate low.

Lund,Brennon — 8 — Los Angeles (A)

EXP MLB DEBUT: 2019 | H/W: 5-11 185 | FUT: Starting OF | 7C

Bats R Age 24	Year	Lev	Team	AB	R	H	HR	RBI	Avg	OB	Slg	OPS	bb%	ct%	Eye	SB	CS	x/h%	Iso	RC/G
2016 (11) Brigham Young	2016	A	Burlington	181	19	49	1	19	271	316	359	675	6	82	0.36	8	1	24	88	3.83
Pwr ++	2017	A	Burlington	173	25	53	2	18	306	391	428	819	12	85	0.92	14	3	25	121	5.95
BAvg +++	2017	A+	Inland Empire	196	26	63	3	23	321	373	423	796	8	79	0.39	5	4	22	102	5.32
Spd +++	2017	AA	Mobile	122	17	35	1	6	287	304	336	640	2	73	0.09	1	2	11	49	3.03
Def ++	2018	AA	Mobile	401	63	106	8	59	264	336	404	740	10	75	0.42	21	5	32	140	4.79

Intriguing outfielder with the repertoire to serve as a solid table-setter in the lineup. Moved quick enough to reach Double-A by his first full season in 2017. Solid barrel control with enough bat speed to build solid contact. Able to draw walks with a decent eye. Enough defensive prowess to serve as an acceptable corner outfield option.

Lutz,Tristen — 79 — Milwaukee

EXP MLB DEBUT: 2020 | H/W: 6-3 210 | FUT: Starting OF | 8C

Bats R Age 20	Year	Lev	Team	AB	R	H	HR	RBI	Avg	OB	Slg	OPS	bb%	ct%	Eye	SB	CS	x/h%	Iso	RC/G
2017 (1) HS (TX)																				
Pwr ++++																				
BAvg +++	2017	Rk	Helena	93	23	31	6	16	333	410	559	969	11	77	0.57	2	4	26	226	7.55
Spd +++	2017	Rk	AZL Brewers	68	12	19	3	11	279	319	559	878	6	69	0.19	1	0	53	279	6.75
Def ++++	2018	A	Wisconsin	444	63	109	13	63	245	316	421	737	9	69	0.33	9	3	45	176	4.85

Tall, strong OF who signed well above slot value in 2017 first round. Production was so-so in full season debut, but packs a punch in his swing and ball jumps off his bat for plus raw power. More "fast" than "quick" bat speed and ct% will require more consistency. Good athlete; could have sneaky SB ability and will likely end up in an OF corner, though could handle CF.

Lux,Gavin — 6 — Los Angeles (N)

EXP MLB DEBUT: 2020 | H/W: 6-2 170 | FUT: Starting SS | 8C

Bats L Age 21	Year	Lev	Team	AB	R	H	HR	RBI	Avg	OB	Slg	OPS	bb%	ct%	Eye	SB	CS	x/h%	Iso	RC/G
2016 (1) HS (WI)	2016	Rk	Ogden	31	7	12	0	3	387	441	484	925	9	74	0.38	1	0	25	97	7.36
Pwr +++	2016	Rk	AZL Dodgers	192	34	53	0	18	276	359	380	740	12	78	0.58	1	0	28	104	5.00
BAvg +++	2017	A	Great Lakes	434	68	106	7	39	244	331	362	692	11	80	0.64	27	10	27	118	4.27
Spd +++	2018	A+	Rancho Cuca	358	64	116	11	48	324	397	520	916	11	81	0.63	11	7	35	196	7.01
Def ++++	2018	AA	Tulsa	105	21	34	4	9	324	403	495	899	12	81	0.70	2	2	26	171	6.75

Breakout campaign, slashing .324/.399/.514 between A+/AA. Quick LH stroke should play as he moves up, and power spike improves his profile. Discerning eye at the plate results in good walk rate and now profiles as a potential 20/20 hitter. Plus defender moves well with a strong arm and should stick at short.

Machado,Carlos — 79 — Houston

EXP MLB DEBUT: 2023 | H/W: 6-2 170 | FUT: Reserve OF | 7D

Bats R Age 20	Year	Lev	Team	AB	R	H	HR	RBI	Avg	OB	Slg	OPS	bb%	ct%	Eye	SB	CS	x/h%	Iso	RC/G
2014 FA (VZ)	2016	Rk	Greeneville	111	12	28	0	8	252	284	261	546	4	81	0.24	4	1	4	9	2.05
Pwr +	2016	Rk	GCL Astros	96	12	30	0	10	313	327	365	691	2	86	0.15	3	5	13	52	3.78
BAvg +++	2017	Rk	Greeneville	29	3	10	0	3	345	367	414	780	3	83	0.20	1	0	20	69	4.90
Spd ++	2017	Rk	GCL Astros	116	18	37	2	14	319	373	474	847	8	85	0.59	5	2	27	155	6.00
Def +++	2018	A-	Tri City	194	25	59	3	28	304	351	412	763	7	87	0.54	5	2	24	108	4.90

Free-swinging outfielder goes up to the plate looking to swing and makes contact most of the time. He's got a smooth swing with solid bat speed but he doesn't generate any loft and as a result limits his power. He's a corner outfielder who is going to need to find some power to fulfill the profile.

Machado,Jonathan — 789 — St. Louis

EXP MLB DEBUT: 2022 | H/W: 5-9 155 | FUT: Starting CF | 7D

Bats L Age 20	Year	Lev	Team	AB	R	H	HR	RBI	Avg	OB	Slg	OPS	bb%	ct%	Eye	SB	CS	x/h%	Iso	RC/G
2016 FA (CU)																				
Pwr +	2017	Rk	GCL Cardinals	124	27	40	2	20	323	364	435	799	6	90	0.62	8	2	25	113	5.29
BAvg +++	2018	Rk	Johnson City	192	30	56	2	21	292	349	375	724	8	79	0.41	9	5	21	83	4.47
Spd +++++	2018	A-	State College	42	2	2	0	2	48	111	48	159	7	64	0.20	0	0	0	0	-3.97
Def ++++	2018	A	Peoria	92	8	17	0	8	185	211	228	439	3	84	0.20	3	2	24	43	0.90

Athletic OF has the best pure speed in the system, but was over-matched in full-season debut and struggled to make consistent contact. Regrouped when moved down to Rookie Ball, but struggled in the NYPL. Small stature and lack of bat speed results in bottom-of-the-scale power and needs to get on base and steal bases to have value.

Maciel,Gabriel — 8 — Minnesota

EXP MLB DEBUT: 2021 | H/W: 5-10 170 | FUT: Starting CF | 7C

Bats B Age 20	Year	Lev	Team	AB	R	H	HR	RBI	Avg	OB	Slg	OPS	bb%	ct%	Eye	SB	CS	x/h%	Iso	RC/G
2016 FA (BR)	2016	Rk	Missoula	79	15	21	0	4	266	310	291	601	6	76	0.26	11	1	10	25	2.75
Pwr +	2016	Rk	AZL DBacks	149	28	43	0	10	289	342	309	650	7	85	0.55	11	4	7	20	3.61
BAvg +++	2017	Rk	Missoula	217	40	70	3	25	323	390	438	828	10	84	0.71	9	8	26	115	5.88
Spd ++++	2018	A	Kane County	279	44	80	1	16	287	356	333	689	10	82	0.60	14	5	14	47	4.16
Def ++++	2018	A	Cedar Rapids	397	60	111	3	23	280	338	348	686	8	82	0.49	16	10	17	68	4.02

Slap-hitting CF with plus speed was acquired in mid-season trade with ARI. Short, compact swing geared towards spraying the field with ground balls and line drives. Works counts and fouls of pitch pitches. Has below-average raw power potential but swing depresses double-digits. Excellent defender in CF and a base-stealer.

Madrigal,Nick

4 | **Chicago (A)** | EXP MLB DEBUT: 2020 | H/W: 5-7 165 | FUT: Starting SS | **9C**

Bats R Age 22
2018 (1) Oregon St

- Pwr ++
- BAvg +++++
- Spd ++++
- Def ++++

Year	Lev	Team	AB	R	H	HR	RBI	Avg	OB	Slg	OPS	bb%	ct%	Eye	SB	CS	x/h%	Iso	RC/G
2018	NCAA	Oregon State	180	42	66	3	34	367	418	511	929	8	96	2.29	15	1	24	144	6.97
2018	Rk	AZL White Sox	13	2	2	0	1	154	214	154	368	7	100		0	1	0	0	1.32
2018	A	Kannapolis	44	9	15	0	6	341	356	409	765	2	100		2	2	20	68	4.92
2018	A+	Winston-Salem	98	14	30	0	9	306	340	347	687	5	95	1.00	6	3	13	41	4.14

Disciplined, contact-oriented LD hitter made easy transition to pro ball. Short in stature, he receives Dustin Pedroia comps but is a better hitter. Barrels pitches to all field via a short, compact swing and rarely chases. Below-average raw power but could surprise with double-digit HRs. A plus runner, though likely tops out at 20 SB or so.

Mahan,Riley

4 | **Miami** | EXP MLB DEBUT: 2020 | H/W: 6-3 185 | FUT: Reserve IF | **6C**

Bats L Age 23
2017 (3) Kentucky

- Pwr ++
- BAvg ++
- Spd +++
- Def +++

Year	Lev	Team	AB	R	H	HR	RBI	Avg	OB	Slg	OPS	bb%	ct%	Eye	SB	CS	x/h%	Iso	RC/G
2017	NCAA	Kentucky	262	58	88	15	67	336	387	618	1006	8	79	0.39	9	3	47	282	7.91
2017	A	Greensboro	27	4	7	1	4	259	259	407	667	0	74	0.00	0	0	29	148	3.19
2018	A+	Jupiter	424	38	106	3	40	250	290	340	630	5	70	0.19	7	2	27	90	3.18

Tall, athletic LH 2B struggled with aggressive High-A assignment. Short, compact swing hampered by bat wrap, which developed early in season. Showed aggressiveness at plate and will expand zone, especially against breaking ball. Doesn't use legs to generate power, which will be below average at maturity. A solid defender at 2B.

Maitan,Kevin

6 | **Los Angeles (A)** | EXP MLB DEBUT: 2021 | H/W: 6-2 190 | FUT: Starting 3B | **9E**

Bats B Age 19
2016 FA (VZ)

- Pwr +++
- BAvg +++
- Spd +++
- Def +++

Year	Lev	Team	AB	R	H	HR	RBI	Avg	OB	Slg	OPS	bb%	ct%	Eye	SB	CS	x/h%	Iso	RC/G
2017	Rk	GCL Braves	35	5	11	0	3	314	351	400	751	5	71	0.20	1	0	27	86	4.89
2017	Rk	Danville	127	10	28	2	15	220	272	323	595	7	69	0.23	1	0	29	102	2.68
2018	Rk	Orem	262	42	65	8	26	248	299	397	696	7	75	0.29	1	2	34	149	3.98

Switch-hitting infielder with raw skill set on both sides of the ball. Some concern surrounding how quickly his frame bulked up. Solid swing path from both sides with eye-catching raw power that should develop with age, although swing-and-miss is still an issue. Good instincts with powerful arm, although move to third base long term is likely.

Marchan,Rafael

2 | **Philadelphia** | EXP MLB DEBUT: 2022 | H/W: 5-9 170 | FUT: Starting C | **8D**

Bats R Age 20
2015 FA (VZ)

- Pwr +++
- BAvg ++++
- Spd ++
- Def ++++

Year	Lev	Team	AB	R	H	HR	RBI	Avg	OB	Slg	OPS	bb%	ct%	Eye	SB	CS	x/h%	Iso	RC/G
2017	Rk	GCL Phillies	84	10	20	0	10	238	273	298	570	5	90	0.50	1	0	25	60	2.77
2018	A-	Williamsport	196	28	59	0	12	301	338	362	700	5	91	0.61	9	6	17	61	4.23

Unique profile: switch-hitting CA with extreme-contact tendencies and projectable pop. Advanced hand/eye coordination, a short swing and an ability to find the barrel. For career, just 26 K in 280 short-season AB. Classic build to stick behind the plate. Rocket arm, good receiver and nabs high marks for pitch-calling and game management. Upside.

Marsh,Brandon

89 | **Los Angeles (A)** | EXP MLB DEBUT: 2020 | H/W: 6-2 190 | FUT: Starting OF | **8C**

Bats L Age 21
2016 (2) HS (GA)

- Pwr +++
- BAvg +++
- Spd +++
- Def +++

Year	Lev	Team	AB	R	H	HR	RBI	Avg	OB	Slg	OPS	bb%	ct%	Eye	SB	CS	x/h%	Iso	RC/G
2016		Did not play																	
2017	Rk	Orem	177	47	62	4	44	350	382	548	930	5	80	0.26	10	2	35	198	6.88
2018	A	Burlington	132	26	39	3	24	295	392	470	862	14	70	0.53	4	0	41	174	6.87
2018	A+	Inland Empire	371	59	95	7	46	256	348	385	733	12	68	0.44	10	4	29	129	4.94

Physically advanced outfielder who excelled in both baseball and football. Polished tools on both sides of the ball. Plus speed, solid routes and a cannon of an arm. Power is expected to develop with advantage of well-proportioned frame. Good swing path with some swing-and-miss to iron out.

Martin,Jason

789 | **Pittsburgh** | EXP MLB DEBUT: 2019 | H/W: 5-10 175 | FUT: Reserve OF | **6C**

Bats L Age 23
2013 (8) HS (CA)

- Pwr +++
- BAvg +++
- 4.20 Spd +++
- Def +++

Year	Lev	Team	AB	R	H	HR	RBI	Avg	OB	Slg	OPS	bb%	ct%	Eye	SB	CS	x/h%	Iso	RC/G
2016	A+	Lancaster	400	74	108	23	75	270	358	533	891	12	73	0.51	20	12	48	263	6.84
2017	A+	Buies Creek	174	34	50	7	29	287	361	494	855	10	76	0.48	9	5	40	207	6.25
2017	AA	Corpus Christi	300	38	82	11	37	273	317	483	800	6	73	0.23	7	6	46	210	5.43
2018	AA	Altoona	255	49	83	9	34	325	392	522	914	10	76	0.46	7	8	33	196	7.03
2018	AAA	Indianapolis	213	20	45	4	21	211	270	319	589	7	76	0.33	5	4	27	108	2.64

Small CF who profiles best as LF or backup OF because of mediocre range and arm in CF. Not as good a hitter as numbers suggest. Second season at that level and some timing issues at plate. Adjustments at higher levels may not come so easy. Can run some but not a good SB threat.

Martin,Mason

3 | **Pittsburgh** | EXP MLB DEBUT: 2023 | H/W: 6-0 201 | FUT: Reserve 1B | **6D**

Bats L Age 19
2017 (17) HS (WA)

- Pwr +++
- BAvg ++
- 4.40 Spd +
- Def ++

Year	Lev	Team	AB	R	H	HR	RBI	Avg	OB	Slg	OPS	bb%	ct%	Eye	SB	CS	x/h%	Iso	RC/G
2017	Rk	GCL Pirates	127	37	39	11	22	307	447	630	1076	20	68	0.78	2	2	49	323	10.03
2018	Rk	Bristol	223	42	52	10	40	233	355	422	776	16	61	0.48	2	2	40	188	5.85
2018	A	West Virginia	150	16	30	4	18	200	286	333	619	11	59	0.29	1	1	40	133	3.35

Had a disastrous 2018, struggling in all aspects of the game, and jeopardizing his prospect status. Bat and body looked slow. Low A pitchers were able to speed him up and make him look bad. Did not handle the adversity well. Lacks athleticism to play anywhere but 1B, which limits his potential.

Martin,Richie

46 | **Baltimore** | EXP MLB DEBUT: 2019 | H/W: 6-0 185 | FUT: Starting SS | **7C**

Bats R Age 24
2015 (1) Florida

- Pwr +
- BAvg +++
- Spd +++
- Def ++++

Year	Lev	Team	AB	R	H	HR	RBI	Avg	OB	Slg	OPS	bb%	ct%	Eye	SB	CS	x/h%	Iso	RC/G
2016	A+	Stockton	330	46	76	3	31	230	306	312	618	10	78	0.49	12	8	25	82	3.22
2016	AA	Midland	15	1	5	0	7	333	444	533	978	17	87	1.50	2	1	40	200	8.35
2017	A+	Stockton	94	16	25	1	6	266	324	383	707	8	78	0.38	1	1	24	117	4.29
2017	AA	Midland	286	43	64	3	27	224	284	315	599	8	80	0.42	12	3	27	91	2.92
2018	AA	Midland	453	68	136	6	42	300	362	439	801	9	81	0.51	25	10	32	139	5.54

Skinny, athletic SS who had offensive breakout in hitter-friendly TL in 2018. Game is centered around playing plus defense at SS and above-avg speed required for moderate SB impact. Owns whip-like bat path that produces solid ct% but lacks leverage for any HR upside. Displays quality plate discipline for OBP ability. Taken by BAL in Rule 5 Draft.

Martinez,Julio Pablo

789 | **Texas** | EXP MLB DEBUT: 2020 | H/W: 5-11 190 | FUT: Starting CF | **8D**

Bats L Age 23
2018 FA (CU)

- Pwr +++
- BAvg +++
- Spd ++++
- Def +++

Year	Lev	Team	AB	R	H	HR	RBI	Avg	OB	Slg	OPS	bb%	ct%	Eye	SB	CS	x/h%	Iso	RC/G
2018	Rk	DSL Rangers	22	10	9	1	3	409	581	682	1262	29	68	1.29	2	3	33	273	13.77
2018	A-	Spokane	234	49	59	8	21	252	347	436	783	13	71	0.49	11	6	37	184	5.54

Toolsy power/speed CFer who came over from Cuba. Speed is more developed that power right now, and should lead to SB early in his career. Though his swing can get long, there's plenty of bat speed that points to pop to come as he makes hard contact. Enough athleticism to stick in CF.

Mateo,Jorge

68 | **Oakland** | EXP MLB DEBUT: 2019 | H/W: 6-0 188 | FUT: Starting CF | **8E**

Bats R Age 23
2012 FA (DR)

- Pwr ++
- BAvg ++
- Spd +++++
- Def ++++

Year	Lev	Team	AB	R	H	HR	RBI	Avg	OB	Slg	OPS	bb%	ct%	Eye	SB	CS	x/h%	Iso	RC/G
2016	A+	Tampa	464	65	119	8	48	256	306	381	687	7	77	0.31	36	15	28	125	3.94
2017	A+	Tampa	275	39	66	4	11	240	282	400	682	5	71	0.20	28	3	42	160	3.97
2017	AA	Trenton	120	26	36	4	26	300	378	525	903	11	73	0.47	11	7	44	225	7.13
2017	AA	Midland	137	25	40	4	20	292	336	518	854	6	76	0.27	13	3	40	226	6.16
2018	AAA	Nashville	470	50	108	3	45	230	275	353	628	6	70	0.21	25	10	33	123	3.25

Wiry athlete with blinding speed yet still unrefined offensive skillset. Is an 80 runner with explosive first step and fluid strides required for elite SB impact. Lacks OBP skills for SB value to flourish and ct% is very shaky; power limited to gaps. Has plus arm and actions for SS and range required for CF. Big overall upside, but also big risk.

Matias,Seuly

9 | **Kansas City** | EXP MLB DEBUT: 2021 | H/W: 6-2 190 | FUT: Starting OF | **9E**

Bats R Age 20
2015 FA (DR)

- Pwr +++++
- BAvg ++
- Spd +++
- Def ++++

Year	Lev	Team	AB	R	H	HR	RBI	Avg	OB	Slg	OPS	bb%	ct%	Eye	SB	CS	x/h%	Iso	RC/G
2016	Rk	AZL Royals	172	32	43	8	29	250	335	477	812	11	58	0.30	2	4	49	227	6.73
2017	Rk	Burlington	222	27	54	7	36	243	294	423	718	7	68	0.22	2	1	43	180	4.48
2018	A	Lexington	338	62	78	31	63	231	282	550	832	7	61	0.18	6	0	58	320	6.26

Powerful, hulking RF put on a power show slugging 31 HR in Single-A. Plus-plus power is loud and completely pull-oriented in games. Quick wrists and strong hands guide plus bat speed. Doesn't have handle of strike zone or pitch recognition, causing ct% issues. An average runner with an incredible arm, profiles in RF.

Matijevic,J.J. — 7 — Houston

EXP MLB DEBUT: 2020 | H/W: 5-11 211 | FUT: Reserve OF | 6B

Bats L | Age 23 | 2017 (2) Arizona

Pwr ++++ | BAvg ++ | Spd ++ | Def +

Year	Lev	Team	AB	R	H	HR	RBI	Avg	OB	Slg	OPS	bb%	ct%	Eye	SB	CS	x/h%	Iso	RC/G
2017	NCAA	Arizona	240	57	92	10	65	383	437	633	1071	9	84	0.61	9	1	43	250	8.64
2017	A-	Tri City	200	34	48	6	27	240	303	400	703	8	70	0.30	11	3	42	160	4.23
2017	A	Quad Cities	24	2	3	1	4	125	160	250	410	4	63	0.11	0	1	33	125	-0.39
2018	A	Quad Cities	48	8	17	3	5	354	446	708	1155	14	79	0.80	3	0	59	354	10.28
2018	A+	Buies Creek	335	58	89	19	57	266	337	513	850	10	69	0.35	10	13	47	248	6.32

Limited to left field as an outfielder due to slow footspeed, he might end up at first base in the long run. He's got a swing built to do damage but he runs into issues making consistent, hard contact. He struggled mightily against left-handers (.186 BA), which forces him into a platoon role at best.

Maton,Nick — 6 — Philadelphia

EXP MLB DEBUT: 2022 | H/W: 6-2 165 | FUT: Utility player | 7C

Bats L | Age 22 | 2017 (7) Eastern Illinois

Pwr +++ | BAvg ++ | 4.34 Spd ++ | Def +++

Year	Lev	Team	AB	R	H	HR	RBI	Avg	OB	Slg	OPS	bb%	ct%	Eye	SB	CS	x/h%	Iso	RC/G
2017	NCAA	Lincoln Land CC	169	60	69	8	46	408	507	722	1229	17	84	1.26	33	2	42	314	11.21
2017	A-	Williamsport	210	34	53	2	13	252	346	333	679	13	78	0.64	10	5	23	81	4.13
2018	A	Lakewood	406	52	104	8	51	256	327	404	731	10	75	0.42	5	3	38	148	4.69

Tools are not loud, but sum of parts creates intrigue. Lean and athletic with great instincts and good arm, makes plays on the run. SS range might be stretched at upper levels, but could morph into UT. Sprays line drives to all fields due to quick hands; recognizes spin and is patient. Sneaky doubles pop could turn into more as he fills out.

Mauricio,Ronny — 6 — New York (N)

EXP MLB DEBUT: 2023 | H/W: 6-3 166 | FUT: Reserve IF | 8D

Bats R | Age 18 | 2017 FA (DR)

Pwr ++ | BAvg ++ | 4.30 Spd ++ | Def +++

Year	Lev	Team	AB	R	H	HR	RBI	Avg	OB	Slg	OPS	bb%	ct%	Eye	SB	CS	x/h%	Iso	RC/G
2018	Rk	GCL Mets	197	26	55	3	31	279	314	421	735	5	84	0.32	1	6	35	142	4.49
2018	Rk	Kingsport	30	6	7	0	4	233	303	333	636	9	70	0.33	1	0	43	100	3.53

Long, athletic Dominican who lacks polish, especially with the bat. Long arms and legs, but this doesn't really help him at the plate. Swing is a long and awkward from both sides. Moves well at SS, but not a smooth runner. Could come into some power with long levered swings. Still very young with upside.

Mazeika,Patrick — 23 — New York (N)

EXP MLB DEBUT: 2020 | H/W: 6-3 210 | FUT: Reserve C | 6D

Bats L | Age 25 | 2015 (8) Stetson

Pwr ++ | BAvg ++ | 4.50 Spd + | Def +

Year	Lev	Team	AB	R	H	HR	RBI	Avg	OB	Slg	OPS	bb%	ct%	Eye	SB	CS	x/h%	Iso	RC/G
2015	Rk	Kingsport	226	44	80	5	48	354	416	540	956	10	88	0.92	1	0	40	186	7.36
2016	A	Columbia	239	34	73	3	35	305	401	402	802	14	84	0.97	2	0	23	96	5.80
2017	A+	St. Lucie	352	45	101	7	50	287	373	406	779	12	85	0.91	2	2	28	119	5.39
2017	AA	Binghamton	21	3	7	0	5	333	391	571	963	9	71	0.33	0	0	71	238	8.32
2018	AA	Binghamton	295	32	68	9	39	231	320	363	683	12	88	1.11	0	0	31	132	4.25

Tall, slow-bodied C who struggles catching and throwing but had hit up until reaching Double-A in 2018. Good walk rate has increased his value, but lacks batpseed to hit enough to be more than a mediocre backup receiver.

McCarthy,Jake — 8 — Arizona

EXP MLB DEBUT: 2021 | H/W: 6-2 195 | FUT: Starting OF | 7C

Bats L | Age 21 | 2018 (1) Virginia

Pwr ++ | BAvg +++ | Spd ++++ | Def +++

Year	Lev	Team	AB	R	H	HR	RBI	Avg	OB	Slg	OPS	bb%	ct%	Eye	SB	CS	x/h%	Iso	RC/G
2018	NCAA	Virginia	82	17	27	0	12	329	402	415	817	11	89	1.11	9	0	26	85	5.92
2018	Rk	AZL DBacks	11	1	3	0	4	273	333	455	788	8	91	1.00	1	0	33	182	5.60
2018	A-	Hillsboro	208	33	60	3	18	288	357	442	799	10	81	0.55	20	8	38	154	5.57

Skinny, athletic OF who signed for just below slot value in 2018 draft's CBA round. Best attribute is his plus speed, which he uses to man a plus CF and pick his spots on the bases for SB value. LH swing is simple, compact and built for high-volume ct% and BA. Power limited to pull-side and likely has fringe HR upside. As a high-pick college OF, he could move quick.

McCarthy,Joe — 7 — Tampa Bay

EXP MLB DEBUT: 2019 | H/W: 6-3 225 | FUT: Starting OF | 7C

Bats L | Age 25 | 2015 (5) Virginia

Pwr +++ | BAvg +++ | Spd +++ | Def ++

Year	Lev	Team	AB	R	H	HR	RBI	Avg	OB	Slg	OPS	bb%	ct%	Eye	SB	CS	x/h%	Iso	RC/G
2016	A+	Charlotte	198	20	56	5	31	283	372	434	806	12	81	0.74	8	3	30	152	5.72
2017	AA	Montgomery	454	76	129	7	56	284	403	434	836	17	79	0.96	20	5	36	150	6.45
2018	Rk	GCL Rays	10	0	1	0	1	100	182	100	282	9	50	0.20	0	0	0	0	-2.71
2018	A+	Charlotte	10	0	0	0	1	0	231	0	231	23	60	0.75	1	0		0	-3.39
2018	AAA	Durham	160	31	43	8	25	269	368	513	880	14	73	0.58	3	1	51	244	6.80

Older brother of ARI prospect Jake McCarthy. Solid hitter with plus OBP skill, he struggled with injuries in 2018. Ended AFL campaign with fractured hand. Big-bodied with some athleticism. Has plus pull power in frame and swing he's yet to reach in-game. Average runner, SB ability plays up due to plus instincts. Defensively challenged in OF.

McClanahan,Chad — 37 — Milwaukee

EXP MLB DEBUT: 2021 | H/W: 6-5 200 | FUT: Starting 1B | 9E

Bats L | Age 21 | 2016 (11) HS (AZ)

Pwr ++++ | BAvg +++ | Spd ++ | Def +++

Year	Lev	Team	AB	R	H	HR	RBI	Avg	OB	Slg	OPS	bb%	ct%	Eye	SB	CS	x/h%	Iso	RC/G
2016	Rk	AZL Brewers	144	22	30	3	14	208	265	333	598	7	69	0.24	1	2	37	125	2.74
2017	Rk	Helena	235	33	55	3	30	234	343	315	658	14	67	0.50	5	5	22	81	3.88
2018	Rk	Helena	183	30	55	8	35	301	382	541	923	12	70	0.44	3	4	45	240	7.53
2018	A	Wisconsin	76	8	13	1	8	171	232	237	469	7	57	0.18	0	0	23	66	0.80

Tall, ultra-lean corner player with some feel to hit and plus raw power. Generates plus bat head speed at contact but swing can get lengthy and struggled vs. quality off-speed in tiny full-season debut. Good athlete, but frame requires projection. Has enough arm for 3B but lack of lateral range suggests the glove, bat will profile better at 1B long-term.

McGuire,Reese — 2 — Toronto

EXP MLB DEBUT: 2018 | H/W: 6-0 181 | FUT: Reserve C | 6B

Bats L | Age 24 | 2013 (1) HS (WA)

Pwr + | BAvg ++ | Spd + | Def ++++

Year	Lev	Team	AB	R	H	HR	RBI	Avg	OB	Slg	OPS	bb%	ct%	Eye	SB	CS	x/h%	Iso	RC/G
2017	Rk	GCL Blue Jays	22	4	9	0	7	409	480	500	980	12	95	3.00	0	1	22	91	7.86
2017	A+	Dunedin	12	1	3	0	1	250	308	333	641	8	83	0.50	0	0	33	83	3.58
2017	AA	New Hampshire	115	19	32	6	20	278	366	496	862	12	83	0.84	2	1	38	217	6.25
2018	AAA	Buffalo	322	31	75	7	37	233	304	339	643	9	76	0.43	3	2	24	106	3.41
2018	MLB	Toronto	31	5	9	2	4	290	333	581	914	6	71	0.22	1	0	56	290	6.96

14th overall pick in 2013 has been slow to develop, but finally made his MLB debut. Below-average bat speed limits power and he now owns a career .344 SLG%. Plus defense is calling card. He blocks and receives well and has been MLB ready for several years. Lack of offensive upside limits him to a backup role.

McKay,Brendan — 3 — Tampa Bay

EXP MLB DEBUT: 2020 | H/W: 6-1 220 | FUT: Starting 1B | 8D

Bats L | Age 23 | 2017 (1) Louisville

Pwr ++++ | BAvg +++ | Spd + | Def +++

Year	Lev	Team	AB	R	H	HR	RBI	Avg	OB	Slg	OPS	bb%	ct%	Eye	SB	CS	x/h%	Iso	RC/G
2017	A-	Hudson Valley	125	16	29	4	22	232	342	376	718	14	74	0.64	2	0	31	144	4.61
2018	Rk	GCL Rays	10	1	0	0	2	0	0	0	0	0	90	0.00	0	0		0	-3.70
2018	A	Bowling Green	63	12	16	1	16	254	484	333	817	31	79	2.15	0	0	19	79	6.82
2018	A+	Charlotte	119	19	25	5	21	210	304	403	707	12	68	0.42	0	0	48	193	4.40

Power-hitting 2-way player much more advanced on mound than at plate. Struggled maintaining hard hit rate and ct% with new swing trajectory geared towards fly ball contact. Displays easy raw plus-plus power in BP but struggles reaching it in games. Uber-patient at plate but has struggled getting beat in, downgrading hit tool upside. Solid 1B.

McKenna,Alex — 8 — Houston

EXP MLB DEBUT: 2021 | H/W: 6-1 195 | FUT: Reserve OF | 7C

Bats R | Age 21 | 2018 (4) Cal Poly

Pwr +++ | BAvg +++ | Spd +++ | Def +++

Year	Lev	Team	AB	R	H	HR	RBI	Avg	OB	Slg	OPS	bb%	ct%	Eye	SB	CS	x/h%	Iso	RC/G
2018	NCAA	Cal Poly	239	51	81	5	31	339	406	506	912	10	84	0.69	6	3	31	167	6.92
2018	A-	Tri City	116	14	38	5	21	328	386	534	920	9	79	0.46	6	5	34	207	6.87
2018	A	Quad Cities	48	5	13	2	7	271	314	458	772	6	67	0.19	0	0	31	188	5.19

The athletic 4th-round OF boasts contact ability thanks to a short swing. He has above-average raw but he limits his power output as a tradeoff for his consistent bat-to-ball skill. His average speed could keep him in CF throughout the minors but is likely to push him to the corners in the future.

McKenna,Ryan — 8 — Baltimore

EXP MLB DEBUT: 2020 | H/W: 5-9 175 | FUT: Starting CF | 8D

Bats R | Age 22 | 2015 (4) HS (NH)

Pwr ++ | BAvg +++ | Spd ++++ | Def ++++

Year	Lev	Team	AB	R	H	HR	RBI	Avg	OB	Slg	OPS	bb%	ct%	Eye	SB	CS	x/h%	Iso	RC/G
2015	Rk	GCL Orioles	34	5	9	0	3	265	375	324	699	15	82	1.00	1	1	11	59	4.64
2016	A-	Aberdeen	220	29	53	1	26	241	310	309	619	9	73	0.37	17	6	23	68	3.16
2017	A	Delmarva	468	62	120	7	42	256	319	380	699	8	73	0.34	20	2	35	124	4.23
2018	A+	Frederick	257	60	97	8	37	377	456	556	1012	13	82	0.82	5	6	29	179	8.26
2018	AA	Bowie	213	35	51	3	16	239	331	338	669	12	74	0.52	4	1	25	99	3.93

Uber-athletic, late-blooming New England OF made strides with hit tool in '18. Short, compact swing w/ spray approach. Improved ct% by staying short to the ball. Plus-plus bunter. Below average power; 10-15 HR at maturity. Plus runner helps CF defense over SB ability. 20 SB potential.

McKinney,Billy

79 | **Toronto** | EXP MLB DEBUT: 2018 | H/W: 6-1 195 | FUT: Reserve OF | **6B**

Bats L Age 24
2013 (1) HS (TX)
Pwr +++
BAvg ++
Spd ++
Def ++

Year	Lev	Team	AB	R	H	HR	RBI	Avg	OB	Slg	OPS	bb%	ct%	Eye	SB	CS	x/h%	Iso	RC/G
2018	AA	Trenton	18	2	4	0	0	222	333	278	611	14	78	0.75	1	1	25	56	3.39
2018	AAA	Scranton/WB	211	27	48	13	32	227	294	498	792	9	73	0.36	0	0	54	270	5.30
2018	AAA	Buffalo	276	37	61	16	40	221	295	486	781	10	74	0.40	0	0	56	264	5.20
2018	MLB	Toronto	119	14	30	6	13	252	315	462	778	8	72	0.33	1	0	43	210	5.12
2018	MLB	NY Yankees	4	0	1	0	0	250	250	250	500	0	75	0.00	0	0	0	0	1.07

Former 1st round pick is with his 4th org and finally made his MLB debut. Solid across-the-board tools, but none that stand out as plus. Quick LH stroke generates solid power and an all-fields approach and willing to take a walk. Struggles with plus velo and breaking balls. Average speed and arm strength make CF a reach. Future is as a 4th OF.

McMillan,Sam

2 | **Detroit** | EXP MLB DEBUT: 2021 | H/W: 5-10 165 | FUT: Starting C | **7D**

Bats R Age 20
2017 (5) HS (FL)
Pwr ++
BAvg +
Spd +
Def ++

Year	Lev	Team	AB	R	H	HR	RBI	Avg	OB	Slg	OPS	bb%	ct%	Eye	SB	CS	x/h%	Iso	RC/G
2017	Rk	GCL Tigers	111	24	32	3	25	288	392	432	825	15	85	1.12	1	1	28	144	6.07
2018	A-	Connecticut	165	16	26	0	8	158	268	206	474	13	72	0.53	7	2	27	48	1.29

Advanced catcher with both bat and glove despite age. Has mature approach at plate and uses quick, compact stroke to put ball in play to all fields. May not have much power projection due to swing path. Has solid defensive tools, highlighted by deft receiving ability. Strong arm is good, but needs to improve throwing accuracy.

Meadows,Parker

8 | **Detroit** | EXP MLB DEBUT: 2022 | H/W: 6-5 185 | FUT: Starting OF | **8E**

Bats L Age 19
2018 (2) HS (GA)
Pwr +
BAvg ++
Spd ++
Def ++

Year	Lev	Team	AB	R	H	HR	RBI	Avg	OB	Slg	OPS	bb%	ct%	Eye	SB	CS	x/h%	Iso	RC/G
2018	Rk	GCL Tigers W	74	16	21	4	8	284	354	500	854	10	66	0.32	3	1	33	216	6.51
2018	A-	Connecticut	19	4	6	0	2	316	381	368	749	10	68	0.33	0	0	17	53	5.11

Younger brother to Austin Meadows with two extra inches to his build and surprising plus speed from his tall frame. Carries plus raw power. Swing is a bit long, but should shorten up as he gets more exposure at the plate. Above-average arm plays well with speed and impressive defensive feel.

Mejia,Francisco

2 | **San Diego** | EXP MLB DEBUT: 2017 | H/W: 5-10 175 | FUT: Starting C | **8B**

Bats B Age 23
2012 FA (DR)
Pwr +++
BAvg ++++
Spd ++
Def ++

Year	Lev	Team	AB	R	H	HR	RBI	Avg	OB	Slg	OPS	bb%	ct%	Eye	SB	CS	x/h%	Iso	RC/G
2017	MLB	Cleveland	13	1	2	0	1	154	214	154	368	7	77	0.33	0	0	0	0	-0.20
2018	AAA	El Paso	122	22	40	7	23	328	364	582	946	5	80	0.28	0	0	40	254	6.93
2018	AAA	Columbus	305	32	85	7	45	279	319	426	745	6	81	0.31	0	0	35	148	4.58
2018	MLB	San Diego	56	6	10	3	8	179	246	375	621	8	66	0.26	0	0	50	196	2.93
2018	MLB	Cleveland	2	0	0	0	0	0	500	0	500	50	100		0	0		0	4.75

Compact, switch-hitting CA acquired via July trade. Possesses good feel to hit via compact, quick stroke; hunts fastballs aggressively. Spray hitter who produces line drive contact from both sides with potentially more power to come in swing. Chance to stay behind dish with strong arm and has improved footwork behind plate. Could move to RF.

Melendez,MJ

2 | **Kansas City** | EXP MLB DEBUT: 2021 | H/W: 6-1 175 | FUT: Starting C | **9E**

Bats L Age 20
2017 (2) HS (AL)
Pwr ++++
BAvg ++
Spd ++
Def ++++

Year	Lev	Team	AB	R	H	HR	RBI	Avg	OB	Slg	OPS	bb%	ct%	Eye	SB	CS	x/h%	Iso	RC/G
2017	Rk	AZL Royals	168	25	44	4	30	262	361	417	777	13	64	0.43	4	2	34	155	5.81
2018	A	Lexington	419	52	105	19	73	251	320	492	812	9	66	0.30	4	6	51	241	6.04

Athletic, all-around CA opened eyes in solid Single-A campaign. A hard-contact machine, but struggled with bat-to-ball, selling out for power with an elongated swing. When swing shortens, he attacks and barrels pitches out in front of plate. Raw plus-plus power in frame, reaching for it in BP and game action. 25-30 HR potential. Thrives at CA.

Mendoza,Evan

5 | **St. Louis** | EXP MLB DEBUT: 2021 | H/W: 6-2 200 | FUT: Starting 3B | **7C**

Bats R Age 22
2017 (11) North Carolina St
Pwr ++
BAvg +++
Spd +++
Def +++

Year	Lev	Team	AB	R	H	HR	RBI	Avg	OB	Slg	OPS	bb%	ct%	Eye	SB	CS	x/h%	Iso	RC/G
2017	A-	State College	162	34	60	3	28	370	427	549	976	9	80	0.48	1	2	33	179	7.77
2017	A	Peoria	74	9	20	1	8	270	289	419	708	3	80	0.13	2	0	40	149	4.05
2018	A+	Palm Beach	149	22	52	3	16	349	386	456	842	6	82	0.33	1	0	19	107	5.70
2018	AA	Springfield	366	36	93	5	26	254	311	339	649	8	79	0.39	1	1	20	85	3.48

Struggled in his draft year at NC State, but has been lights-out as a pro (.300/.353/.415). Quick RH stroke and all-fields approach results in gap power, but other tools are only average or a tick above. Good hands, range, and an above-average arm should allow him to stick at 3B. Needs a stick in power to remain a viable 1st division regular at 3B.

Mendoza,Ramon

45 | **St. Louis** | EXP MLB DEBUT: 2023 | H/W: 5-11 174 | FUT: Starting 3B | **7D**

Bats R Age 18
2018 FA (MX)
Pwr +++
BAvg +++
Spd ++
Def ++

Year	Lev	Team	AB	R	H	HR	RBI	Avg	OB	Slg	OPS	bb%	ct%	Eye	SB	CS	x/h%	Iso	RC/G
2018		Did not play in U.S.																	

Young, athletic 3B has yet to make his state-side debut, but impressed in the DSL, hitting .311/.419/.497. Good bat speed, raw power, and a discerning eye at the plate (22 BB/29 K) gives him the potential to make an impact on offense. Split time at 2B and 3B in the DSL. Should make his U.S. debut in 2019.

Mercado,Oscar

8 | **Cleveland** | EXP MLB DEBUT: 2019 | H/W: 6-2 180 | FUT: Starting CF | **8C**

Bats R Age 24
2013 (2) HS (FL)
Pwr ++
BAvg ++
Spd ++++
Def ++++

Year	Lev	Team	AB	R	H	HR	RBI	Avg	OB	Slg	OPS	bb%	ct%	Eye	SB	CS	x/h%	Iso	RC/G
2015	A	Peoria	472	70	120	4	44	254	289	341	630	5	87	0.38	50	19	25	87	3.29
2016	A+	Palm Beach	442	50	95	0	27	215	286	271	558	9	84	0.62	33	20	25	57	2.64
2017	AA	Springfield	477	76	137	13	46	287	332	428	760	6	77	0.29	38	19	27	140	4.78
2018	AAA	Memphis	382	73	109	8	42	285	347	408	755	9	83	0.56	31	8	28	123	4.87
2018	AAA	Columbus	103	12	26	0	5	252	336	320	657	11	78	0.57	6	4	23	68	3.85

Traded from the Cardinals organization in 2018, his game revolves around speed. The converted infielder has emerged with the bat over the last few years. Has a flat line drive stroke that could allow him to hit at the top of a major league order. He is an excellent defender who has taken well to center field.

Merrell,Kevin

6 | **Oakland** | EXP MLB DEBUT: 2020 | H/W: 6-0 181 | FUT: Starting 2B | **7D**

Bats L Age 23
2017 (1) South Florida
Pwr +
BAvg ++
Spd ++++
Def +++

Year	Lev	Team	AB	R	H	HR	RBI	Avg	OB	Slg	OPS	bb%	ct%	Eye	SB	CS	x/h%	Iso	RC/G
2017	NCAA	South Florida	216	48	83	7	36	384	457	569	1027	12	86	0.94	19	4	27	185	8.29
2017	A-	Vermont	125	27	40	2	9	320	366	424	790	7	82	0.41	10	3	20	104	5.17
2018	Rk	AZL Athletics	10	3	6	0	1	600	636	1000	1636	9	90	1.00	2	1	33	400	15.36
2018	A-	Vermont	16	4	8	0	0	500	579	625	1204	16	81	1.00	0	0	13	125	11.16
2018	A+	Stockton	270	38	72	0	24	267	305	326	631	5	76	0.23	5	4	18	59	3.17

Skinny, athletic SS whose game his predicated off plus-plus speed and ability to make contact. Swing is compact and simple and sprays balls to all fields from left side. Lacks bat speed/strength to create leverage for even average HR output. SS now but footwork and average arm profile him better at 2B.

Miller,Brian

78 | **Miami** | EXP MLB DEBUT: 2019 | H/W: 6-0 177 | FUT: Starting CF | **7C**

Bats L Age 23
2017 (1) North Carolina
Pwr +
BAvg +++
Spd ++++
Def ++++

Year	Lev	Team	AB	R	H	HR	RBI	Avg	OB	Slg	OPS	bb%	ct%	Eye	SB	CS	x/h%	Iso	RC/G
2017	NCAA	North Carolina	271	61	93	7	49	343	424	502	926	12	87	1.09	24	6	28	159	7.15
2017	A	Greensboro	233	42	75	1	28	322	383	416	799	9	85	0.66	21	6	25	94	5.53
2018	A+	Jupiter	256	28	83	0	29	324	359	398	758	5	89	0.52	19	6	19	74	4.84
2018	AA	Jacksonville	262	29	70	0	14	267	314	313	627	6	85	0.46	21	7	14	46	3.32

Quick-moving, athletic OF continues to make contact at a near-elite level. Slashing LHH hitter who doesn't work many walks but sees lots of pitches. A bit undersized and can get overwhelmed with velocity. No power in frame or swing. Relies on ground ball and soft line-drive contact. A plus runner that should produce lots of SB, and can handle CF.

Miller,Ian

78 | **Seattle** | EXP MLB DEBUT: 2019 | H/W: 6-0 175 | FUT: Reserve OF | **6A**

Bats L Age 27
2013 (14) Wagner Coll
Pwr +
BAvg ++
Spd ++++
Def +++

Year	Lev	Team	AB	R	H	HR	RBI	Avg	OB	Slg	OPS	bb%	ct%	Eye	SB	CS	x/h%	Iso	RC/G
2015	AA	Jackson	347	40	88	0	23	254	311	320	631	8	85	0.55	29	13	20	66	3.47
2016	AA	Jackson	430	64	109	0	28	253	324	305	629	9	87	0.83	49	3	14	51	3.61
2017	AA	Arkansas	344	63	112	4	29	326	376	430	807	8	80	0.41	30	4	22	105	5.48
2017	AAA	Tacoma	168	22	45	0	6	268	289	315	604	3	80	0.15	13	1	13	48	2.73
2018	AAA	Tacoma	422	60	110	2	41	261	329	327	656	9	79	0.48	33	9	19	66	3.70

Speedy, spray hitting OF close to MLB debut. Contact-oriented with short, compact swing. Works all fields with swing trajectory geared towards ground ball and line drive contact. Struggles turning on middle-in pitches and can get beat by velocity. Little-to-no power in bat or frame. Single digit HR hitter at maturity.

Miller,Jalen — 4 — San Francisco

EXP MLB DEBUT: 2020 | H/W: 5-10 173 | FUT: Starting 2B | 7C

Bats R Age 22
2015 (3) HS (GA)

Pwr +++ | BAvg +++ | Spd +++ | Def +++

Year	Lev	Team	AB	R	H	HR	RBI	Avg	OB	Sig	OPS	bb%	ct%	Eye	SB	CS	x/h%	Iso	RC/G
2015	Rk	AZL Giants	174	28	38	0	13	218	288	259	547	9	76	0.40	11	2	16	40	2.22
2016	A	Augusta	457	65	102	5	44	223	265	322	587	5	77	0.24	11	5	29	98	2.59
2017	A+	San Jose	431	61	98	6	44	227	279	346	625	7	77	0.31	6	4	36	118	3.16
2018	A+	San Jose	511	73	141	14	62	276	312	434	747	5	76	0.22	11	4	36	159	4.58

Toolsy, athletic 2B took step forward in second High-A stint. Improved in all 3 slash areas while keeping peripheral stats in line. Improved swing mechanics, which aided his positive returns. Using leverage better too—finding power stroke to pull side. Above-average runner and selective on bases; 2B profile.

Miller,Owen — 6 — San Diego

EXP MLB DEBUT: 2020 | H/W: 6-0 190 | FUT: Starting SS | 7C

Bats R Age 22
2018 (3) Illinois St

Pwr +++ | BAvg ++ | Spd +++ | Def +++

Year	Lev	Team	AB	R	H	HR	RBI	Avg	OB	Sig	OPS	bb%	ct%	Eye	SB	CS	x/h%	Iso	RC/G
2018	NCAA	Illinois State	229	45	88	6	35	384	429	537	966	7	90	0.78	8	2	25	153	7.20
2018	A-	Tri-City	191	22	64	2	20	335	383	440	823	7	87	0.63	4	4	20	105	5.66
2018	A	Fort Wayne	107	18	36	2	13	336	360	495	856	4	84	0.24	0	0	36	159	5.80

Collegiate SS drafted in 3rd round who signed for below-slot value. Game predicated on high-volume contact and ability to spray balls to gaps. Does not create leverage in swing necessary for HR impact. Lean, quality athlete; moves well for above-average range at SS and has played some third, but fringe arm could bump him over to 2B.

Miranda,Jose — 45 — Minnesota

EXP MLB DEBUT: 2021 | H/W: 6-2 180 | FUT: Starting 2B | 7C

Bats R Age 20
2016 (2) HS (PR)

Pwr +++ | BAvg ++ | Spd ++ | Def +++

Year	Lev	Team	AB	R	H	HR	RBI	Avg	OB	Sig	OPS	bb%	ct%	Eye	SB	CS	x/h%	Iso	RC/G
2016	Rk	GCL Twins	185	14	42	1	20	227	299	292	591	9	81	0.53	4	5	21	65	2.92
2017	Rk	Elizabethton	223	43	63	11	43	283	331	484	815	7	89	0.67	2	3	33	202	5.38
2018	A	Cedar Rapids	401	52	111	13	72	277	321	434	755	6	87	0.51	0	1	32	157	4.71
2018	A+	Fort Myers	102	9	22	3	10	216	252	353	605	5	89	0.45	0	2	36	137	3.00

Athletic 2B continues to have uptick in HRs while also maintaining high ct%. Quiet setup, slight bat wrap at load. Quick hands unleashes short, compact swing but issues in load prevent bat head from exploding on plus-velocity. Excellent hand/eye and solid plate discipline. Tapping into average pull power. 15-20 HR at projection; no SB potential.

Miroglio,Dominic — 2 — Arizona

EXP MLB DEBUT: 2020 | H/W: 6-0 185 | FUT: Starting C | 7D

Bats R Age 24
2017 (20) UCLA

Pwr ++ | BAvg +++ | Spd ++ | Def +++

Year	Lev	Team	AB	R	H	HR	RBI	Avg	OB	Sig	OPS	bb%	ct%	Eye	SB	CS	x/h%	Iso	RC/G
2017	NCAA	San Francisco	239	30	68	9	40	285	308	473	780	3	88	0.29	4	0	38	188	4.83
2017	Rk	Missoula	142	18	45	1	16	317	378	430	808	9	94	1.75	0	0	31	113	5.76
2018	A+	Visalia	278	41	91	4	42	327	372	460	833	7	85	0.48	5	2	31	133	5.74
2018	AA	Jackson	78	3	18	0	10	231	241	308	548	1	85	0.08	0	1	28	77	2.14

Stocky, medium-framed CA who lacks plus offensive tool but has upside of everyday future backstop. Simple, compact stroke yields above-average contact; shows knowledge of strike zone for BA value. Not the best athlete but is exceptional pitch caller and can handle a big-league staff. Has good release and shows ability to smother balls in dirt.

Mitchell,Calvin — 79 — Pittsburgh

EXP MLB DEBUT: 2022 | H/W: 6-1 200 | FUT: Starting OF | 8D

Bats L Age 20
2017 (2) HS (CA)

Pwr +++ | BAvg ++++ | Spd ++ (4.35) | Def +++

Year	Lev	Team	AB	R	H	HR	RBI	Avg	OB	Sig	OPS	bb%	ct%	Eye	SB	CS	x/h%	Iso	RC/G
2017	Rk	GCL Pirates	159	17	39	2	20	245	344	352	696	13	78	0.69	2	3	33	107	4.41
2018	A	West Virginia	443	55	124	10	65	280	341	427	768	8	75	0.38	4	5	34	147	5.08

Corner OF with a sweet swing. Decent frame but not that powerful or live of body, which limits his upside. Plus feel for the zone and hitting for his age and experience. A little raw on defense but has the time and makeup to improve, but not really a CF option.

Monasterio,Andruw — 6 — Cleveland

EXP MLB DEBUT: 2021 | H/W: 6-0 175 | FUT: Starting MIF | 7C

Bats B Age 21
2014 FA (VZ)

Pwr + | BAvg +++ | Spd +++ | Def ++++

Year	Lev	Team	AB	R	H	HR	RBI	Avg	OB	Sig	OPS	bb%	ct%	Eye	SB	CS	x/h%	Iso	RC/G
2016	A	South Bend	176	25	38	0	11	216	258	256	514	5	81	0.30	7	5	16	40	1.79
2017	A	South Bend	231	42	65	1	23	281	344	368	712	9	84	0.58	7	4	25	87	4.45
2017	A+	Myrtle Beach	87	9	21	0	5	241	305	287	593	8	84	0.57	1	1	19	46	3.00
2018	A+	Potomac	39	6	12	0	5	308	413	359	772	15	85	1.17	2	3	8	51	5.59
2018	A+	Myrtle Beach	369	52	97	3	31	263	354	336	690	12	83	0.81	10	3	20	73	4.34

Twitchy, athletic glove-first IF with actions and hands to handle SS, 2B or 3B. Owns a strong arm and good feet in the field. Makes very good contact with the bat, putting the ball in play, though void of power. Unlikely to project more than 6-8 HR per season. Some speed, but not a burner.

Mondou,Nate — 45 — Oakland

EXP MLB DEBUT: 2020 | H/W: 5-8 190 | FUT: Utility player | 7D

Bats L Age 24
2016 (13) Wake Forest

Pwr ++ | BAvg +++ | Spd +++ | Def +++

Year	Lev	Team	AB	R	H	HR	RBI	Avg	OB	Sig	OPS	bb%	ct%	Eye	SB	CS	x/h%	Iso	RC/G
2016	A-	Vermont	225	27	67	0	24	298	365	364	730	10	84	0.65	6	6	19	67	4.73
2017	A	Beloit	247	31	73	0	32	296	374	385	759	11	83	0.72	8	3	26	89	5.20
2017	A+	Stockton	223	38	62	2	27	278	359	377	735	11	74	0.49	8	5	23	99	4.85
2018	A+	Stockton	344	64	100	8	61	291	353	448	800	9	83	0.57	8	5	33	157	5.46
2018	AA	Midland	165	15	42	0	14	255	332	297	628	10	84	0.73	2	1	17	42	3.54

Shorter, compact 2B who lacks elite tool but has well-rounded skillset. Quick LH stroke lends itself to high-volume ct% and ability to use all fields. Works counts well and knows how to get on base, but struggles to hit LHP. Does not lift ball consistently enough for HR. Average athlete who profiles as UTIL infielder at next level.

Moniak,Mickey — 8 — Philadelphia

EXP MLB DEBUT: 2021 | H/W: 6-2 185 | FUT: Starting OF | 7C

Bats L Age 20
2016 (1) HS (CA)

Pwr ++ | BAvg +++ | Spd ++ | Def +++

Year	Lev	Team	AB	R	H	HR	RBI	Avg	OB	Sig	OPS	bb%	ct%	Eye	SB	CS	x/h%	Iso	RC/G
2016	Rk	GCL Phillies	176	27	50	1	28	284	326	409	735	6	80	0.31	10	4	32	125	4.60
2017	A	Lakewood	466	53	110	5	44	236	279	341	621	6	77	0.26	11	7	30	105	3.06
2018	A+	Clearwater	433	50	117	5	55	270	305	383	689	5	77	0.22	6	5	31	113	3.89

Revived his prospect status with a .817 OPS from July 1 on. Made some mechanical tweaks that allowed him to cover the plate and handle LHP much better. Smaller frame with opportunity to add strength, but will always be hit-over-power and speed seems to be on the decline. Can stick in CF, strong arm, but his bat's utility will be ultimate question.

Montano,Daniel — 9 — Colorado

EXP MLB DEBUT: 2022 | H/W: 6-1 170 | FUT: Starting OF | 7C

Bats L Age 20
2015 FA (VZ)

Pwr +++ | BAvg +++ | Spd +++ | Def +++

Year	Lev	Team	AB	R	H	HR	RBI	Avg	OB	Sig	OPS	bb%	ct%	Eye	SB	CS	x/h%	Iso	RC/G
2017		7 Did not play in the US																	
2018	Rk	DSL Colorado	44	4	8	1	8	182	265	295	561	10	89	1.00	2	0	38	114	2.83
2018	Rk	Grand Junction	240	32	67	4	29	279	337	433	770	8	76	0.37	9	5	36	154	5.15

Raw, toolsy OF finally made his state-side debut. Good strike zone judgment, but has length to his swing and an aggressive approach leads to plenty of swing-and-miss right now. Has the size and speed to develop into an impact player, but still has much work to do and is years away.

Montero,Elehuris — 5 — St. Louis

EXP MLB DEBUT: 2022 | H/W: 6-3 195 | FUT: Starting 3B | 8D

Bats R Age 20
2014 FA (DR)

Pwr +++ | BAvg +++ | Spd ++ | Def ++

Year	Lev	Team	AB	R	H	HR	RBI	Avg	OB	Sig	OPS	bb%	ct%	Eye	SB	CS	x/h%	Iso	RC/G
2017	Rk	GCL Cardinals	173	30	48	5	36	277	359	468	827	11	81	0.67	0	2	46	191	5.95
2018	A	Peoria	382	68	123	15	69	322	376	529	905	8	79	0.41	2	0	37	207	6.68
2018	A+	Palm Beach	98	13	28	1	13	286	320	408	729	5	78	0.23	1	0	36	122	4.42

Polished hitter posted his best season as a pro, slashing a combined .315/.371/.504. Physically strong, with a quick bat and short stroke. Was more aggressive as he hunted for pitchers he could punish, which led to a career-high 16 HR, though bb% headed in the wrong direction. Below-average speed and defense at 3B raise concerns about future position.

Mountcastle,Ryan — 5 — Baltimore

EXP MLB DEBUT: 2019 | H/W: 6-3 195 | FUT: Starting OF | 8C

Bats R Age 22
2015 (1) HS (FL)

Pwr +++ | BAvg +++ | Spd +++ | Def +++

Year	Lev	Team	AB	R	H	HR	RBI	Avg	OB	Sig	OPS	bb%	ct%	Eye	SB	CS	x/h%	Iso	RC/G
2015	A-	Aberdeen	33	2	7	1	5	212	212	303	515	0	70	0.00	0	1	14	91	1.13
2016	A	Delmarva	455	53	128	10	51	281	319	426	745	5	79	0.26	5	4	33	145	4.57
2017	A+	Frederick	360	63	113	15	47	314	340	542	881	4	83	0.23	8	2	45	228	6.05
2017	AA	Bowie	153	18	34	3	15	222	237	366	603	2	77	0.09	0	0	47	144	2.65
2018	AA	Bowie	394	63	117	13	59	297	340	464	805	6	80	0.33	2	0	31	168	5.30

Former High-A batting champion made position transition while continuing to rake at plate. Pure hitter with solid barrel control. Struggled early with some length in swing after fracturing wrist recovery, but made in-season correction. Average power plays up due to barrel rate and swing trajectory. 20-25 HR possible. Arm limits defensive profile to LF or 1B.

Mundell,Brian — 3 — Colorado

EXP MLB DEBUT: 2019 | H/W: 6-3 225 | FUT: Reserve 1B | 7D

Bats R Age 25
2015 (7) Cal Poly
- Pwr +++
- BAvg +++
- Spd +
- Def +

Year	Lev	Team	AB	R	H	HR	RBI	Avg	OB	Slg	OPS	bb%	ct%	Eye	SB	CS	x/h%	Iso	RC/G
2015	A-	Boise	244	35	67	4	36	275	359	410	769	12	82	0.71	7	1	36	135	5.27
2016	A	Asheville	537	94	168	14	83	313	378	503	881	9	85	0.67	7	8	43	190	6.48
2017	A+	Lancaster	264	44	79	12	59	299	381	504	885	12	83	0.80	0	1	37	205	6.54
2017	AA	Hartford	172	30	52	3	19	302	391	424	815	13	85	0.96	1	1	29	122	5.89
2018	AA	Hartford	441	49	116	7	41	263	342	372	714	11	83	0.69	1	3	28	109	4.52

Stocky, muscular 1B-only prospect has a patient approach at the plate as he hunts for pitches he can drive. Short, compact stroke and moderate bat speed generates above-average power, but isn't a true masher. Saw some action in LF, but below-average speed and arm limit him to 1B. Repeat of Double-A didn't go well and at 24 the clock is ticking.

Murphy,Sean — 2 — Oakland

EXP MLB DEBUT: 2019 | H/W: 6-0 194 | FUT: Starting C | 8C

Bats R Age 24
2016 (3) Wright St
- Pwr +++
- BAvg +++
- Spd ++
- Def +++

Year	Lev	Team	AB	R	H	HR	RBI	Avg	OB	Slg	OPS	bb%	ct%	Eye	SB	CS	x/h%	Iso	RC/G
2017	A+	Stockton	165	22	49	9	26	297	341	527	868	6	80	0.33	0	0	41	230	6.00
2017	AA	Midland	191	25	40	4	22	209	288	309	597	10	82	0.62	0	0	28	99	2.98
2018	Rk	AZL Athletics	5	1	1	0	0	200	200	400	600	0	80	0.00	0	0	100	200	2.86
2018	AA	Midland	257	51	74	8	43	288	346	498	844	8	82	0.49	3	0	49	210	5.99
2018	AAA	Nashville	8	2	2	0	0	250	455	250	705	27	75	1.50	0	0	0	0	5.11

Cannon-armed CA who had offensive breakout in AA. Has compact, line-drive oriented swing that yields above-avg ct% and solid BA ability. Lean, strong frame produces mostly gap power now but should materialize into avg HR at next level. Plus-plus arm keeps runners at bay and has improved pitch-calling skills.

Murray,Kyler — 8 — Oakland

EXP MLB DEBUT: 2021 | H/W: 5-11 195 | FUT: Starting OF | 9D

Bats R Age 21
2018 (1) Oklahoma
- Pwr +++
- BAvg +++
- Spd ++++
- Def +++

Year	Lev	Team	AB	R	H	HR	RBI	Avg	OB	Slg	OPS	bb%	ct%	Eye	SB	CS	x/h%	Iso	RC/G
2018		Did not play																	

Dynamic two-sport athlete taken ninth overall in 2018's amateur draft. Chance for average-or-better tools across the board with elite speed, SB upside, and plus defense in CF. Compact frame, strong forearms lend themselves to bat speed and hard contact to all fields. Will need to make contact consistently vs. quality off-speed but has huge overall upside.

Muzziotti,Simon — 8 — Philadelphia

EXP MLB DEBUT: 2022 | H/W: 6-1 175 | FUT: Starting CF | 8E

Bats L Age 20
2016 FA (VZ)
- Pwr +
- BAvg +++
- Spd ++++
- Def +++

Year	Lev	Team	AB	R	H	HR	RBI	Avg	OB	Slg	OPS	bb%	ct%	Eye	SB	CS	x/h%	Iso	RC/G
2017	Rk	GCL Phillies	134	20	36	0	14	269	305	388	693	5	94	0.88	8	3	28	119	4.32
2017	A+	Clearwater	7	2	2	0	0	286	286	286	571	0	71	0.00	1	0	0	0	1.97
2018	Rk	GCL Phillies	22	2	2	0	2	91	167	91	258	8	95	2.00	1	0	0	0	-0.09
2018	A	Lakewood	278	33	73	1	20	263	298	331	629	5	86	0.35	18	4	21	68	3.26

Speedy and lean CF with a promising hit tool. Hands work well, exhibits balance and barrel control. Room for strength, but he's unlikely to develop much power—needs to hit it on the ground and run. Should add some patience to further maximize his plus wheels. Route/reads in CF need work; right now speed makes up for mistakes, which raises his risk.

Naylor,Bo — 2 — Cleveland

EXP MLB DEBUT: 2022 | H/W: 6-0 195 | FUT: Utility player | 8D

Bats L Age 19
2018 (1) HS (ON)
- Pwr +++
- BAvg ++++
- Spd +++
- Def +++

Year	Lev	Team	AB	R	H	HR	RBI	Avg	OB	Slg	OPS	bb%	ct%	Eye	SB	CS	x/h%	Iso	RC/G
2018	Rk	AZL Indians 2	117	17	32	2	17	274	384	402	786	15	76	0.75	5	1	25	128	5.68

A good pure hitter with a smooth left-handed stroke. He has quiet actions at the plate and is hit before power, but should develop some power over time. His ultimate defensive home is to be determined, but he is a good athlete with a strong arm.

Naylor,Josh — 37 — San Diego

EXP MLB DEBUT: 2019 | H/W: 6-0 225 | FUT: Starting 1B | 7B

Bats L Age 21
2015 (1) HS (ON)
- Pwr +++
- BAvg +++
- Spd ++
- Def ++

Year	Lev	Team	AB	R	H	HR	RBI	Avg	OB	Slg	OPS	bb%	ct%	Eye	SB	CS	x/h%	Iso	RC/G
2016	A	Greensboro	342	42	92	9	54	269	313	430	743	6	82	0.35	10	3	38	161	4.58
2016	A+	Lake Elsinore	139	17	35	3	21	252	268	353	620	2	84	0.14	1	1	23	101	2.86
2017	A+	Lake Elsinore	283	41	84	8	45	297	358	452	810	9	83	0.56	7	1	31	155	5.53
2017	AA	San Antonio	156	18	39	2	19	250	320	346	666	9	77	0.44	2	1	28	96	3.79
2018	AA	San Antonio	501	72	149	17	74	297	377	447	824	11	86	0.93	5	5	27	150	5.81

Thick, strong 1B who continues to improve with each step up the ladder. Owns above-average bat-to-ball skills and plus raw power; in-game power is limited as his swing levels out. Has improved vs. LHP and should be good BA source. Lack of athleticism likely limits him to 1B long-term, where he's a fringe defender.

Nelson,James — 5 — Miami

EXP MLB DEBUT: 2020 | H/W: 6-2 180 | FUT: Starting 3B | 7E

Bats R Age 21
2016 (15) Cisco Jr College
- Pwr +++
- BAvg ++
- Spd +++
- Def +++

Year	Lev	Team	AB	R	H	HR	RBI	Avg	OB	Slg	OPS	bb%	ct%	Eye	SB	CS	x/h%	Iso	RC/G
2016	Rk	GCL Marlins	162	26	46	1	24	284	341	364	705	8	81	0.47	7	3	24	80	4.27
2017	A	Greensboro	395	41	122	7	59	309	352	456	807	6	73	0.25	6	2	34	147	5.58
2018	A+	Jupiter	232	27	49	2	28	211	253	280	533	5	72	0.20	1	0	24	69	1.78

Athletic 3B prospect with explosive swing speed struggled through injuries and ineffectiveness in first taste of High-A. Aggressive hitter with solid hand/eye skills. Swing speed pushes profile but swing path will need to improve to take advantage of natural gifts. Average power potential in frame and swing. Average runner, likely long-term 3B.

Neuse,Sheldon — 5 — Oakland

EXP MLB DEBUT: 2019 | H/W: 6-0 175 | FUT: Starting 3B | 7C

Bats R Age 24
2016 (2) Oklahoma
- Pwr +++
- BAvg ++
- Spd ++
- Def +++

Year	Lev	Team	AB	R	H	HR	RBI	Avg	OB	Slg	OPS	bb%	ct%	Eye	SB	CS	x/h%	Iso	RC/G
2016	A-	Auburn	126	16	29	1	11	230	302	341	643	9	79	0.50	2	2	31	111	3.61
2017	A	Hagerstown	292	40	85	9	51	291	347	469	816	8	77	0.38	12	5	36	178	5.62
2017	A+	Stockton	83	21	32	7	22	386	446	675	1120	10	70	0.36	2	0	31	289	9.93
2017	AA	Midland	67	9	25	0	6	373	425	433	857	8	69	0.29	0	0	16	60	6.61
2018	AAA	Nashville	499	48	131	5	55	263	307	357	664	6	66	0.19	4	1	26	94	3.78

Stocky, compact 3B who has well-rounded skillset but lacks elite fantasy tool. Possesses plus raw power and shows ability to use the whole field. Swing is simple and compact but lacks consistent barrel control, leading to fringe ct% skills. Below-average runner and overall athlete. Has plus arm for 3B and will show enough range, footwork to stick.

Neustrom,Robert — 79 — Baltimore

EXP MLB DEBUT: 2021 | H/W: 6-3 200 | FUT: Starting OF | 7D

Bats L Age 22
2018 (5) Iowa
- Pwr +++
- BAvg ++
- Spd +++
- Def ++

Year	Lev	Team	AB	R	H	HR	RBI	Avg	OB	Slg	OPS	bb%	ct%	Eye	SB	CS	x/h%	Iso	RC/G
2018	NCAA	Iowa	212	43	66	11	36	311	384	538	922	11	84	0.74	4	0	39	226	6.88
2018	A-	Aberdeen	228	29	62	4	29	272	311	404	715	5	80	0.29	1	3	34	132	4.22

Powerful, 5th rd 2018 draftee performed well in short-season debut. Contact-oriented hitter despite possessing raw plus power. Solid ct% consistent with college rate but struggled bringing Eye to pro ball. Trouble with velocity. Game HR power to pull-side; 15-22 HR potential with current swing trajectory. His profile is better off selling out for power.

Nevin,Tyler — 53 — Colorado

EXP MLB DEBUT: 2021 | H/W: 6-4 200 | FUT: Starting 1B | 8D

Bats R Age 21
2015 (1) HS (CA)
- Pwr +++
- BAvg +++
- Spd ++
- Def ++

Year	Lev	Team	AB	R	H	HR	RBI	Avg	OB	Slg	OPS	bb%	ct%	Eye	SB	CS	x/h%	Iso	RC/G
2015	Rk	Grand Junction	189	29	50	2	18	265	362	386	749	13	78	0.69	3	7	36	122	5.14
2016	A-	Boise	1	1	1	0	0	1000	1000	2000	3000	0	100		0	0	100	1000	27.71
2017	A-	Boise	30	4	7	1	5	233	233	433	667	0	70	0.00	0	1	57	200	3.44
2017	A	Asheville	298	45	91	7	47	305	363	456	819	8	81	0.48	10	5	31	151	5.65
2018	A+	Lancaster	378	59	124	13	62	328	383	503	886	8	80	0.44	4	3	31	175	6.44

Heady, mature player understands the game with an advanced approach at the plate. Hit tool will carry him far with good barrel awareness and a willingness to shoot lines drives to all fields. Present power is only tick above average despite his large frame, but could add more as he fills out. Solid defender but fringe-average speed and arm.

Newman,Kevin — 6 — Pittsburgh

EXP MLB DEBUT: 2019 | H/W: 6-1 180 | FUT: Starting SS | 8C

Bats R Age 25
2015 (1) Arizona
- Pwr ++
- BAvg ++++
- Spd ++ (4.30)
- Def ++++

Year	Lev	Team	AB	R	H	HR	RBI	Avg	OB	Slg	OPS	bb%	ct%	Eye	SB	CS	x/h%	Iso	RC/G
2016	AA	Altoona	233	41	67	2	28	288	359	378	737	10	90	1.08	6	3	22	90	4.91
2017	AA	Altoona	343	42	89	4	30	259	304	359	663	6	88	0.55	4	2	27	99	3.77
2017	AAA	Indianapolis	166	23	47	0	11	283	312	373	686	4	87	0.32	7	1	28	90	3.94
2018	AAA	Indianapolis	437	74	132	4	35	302	348	407	756	7	89	0.62	28	11	27	105	4.88
2018	MLB	Pittsburgh	91	7	19	0	6	209	242	231	473	4	75	0.17	0	1	11	22	0.98

A probable replacement for Jordy Mercer, he will be a slightly better version. Will hit for a better average, but with the same or less power. A steady defender who is a tough out. Steady and solid, but unspectacular.

Newton,Shervyen — 6 — New York (N)

EXP MLB DEBUT: 2023 | H/W: 6-4 180 | FUT: Starting 1B | 7C

Bats B Age 19
2015 FA (NT)
Pwr ++++
BAvg ++
Spd +++
Def ++

Year	Lev	Team	AB	R	H	HR	RBI	Avg	OB	Slg	OPS	bb%	ct%	Eye	SB	CS	x/h%	Iso	RC/G
2018	Rk	Kingsport	207	50	58	5	41	280	411	449	860	18	59	0.55	4	0	40	169	7.70

One of many athletic SS types the Mets have at the lower levels, he is less likely to stay in the middle of the field, but has more power and bat potential than some of the others. That said, it is all quite raw. He has a long 6-4 frame. Long levers make for a long swing, but there is plus power there, so his bat may play elsewhere.

Nido,Tomas — 2 — New York (N)

EXP MLB DEBUT: 2019 | H/W: 6-0 200 | FUT: Reserve C | 6B

Bats R Age 24
2012 (8) HS (FL)
Pwr +
BAvg +
4.60 Spd +
Def ++++

Year	Lev	Team	AB	R	H	HR	RBI	Avg	OB	Slg	OPS	bb%	ct%	Eye	SB	CS	x/h%	Iso	RC/G
2017	AA	Binghamton	367	41	85	8	60	232	290	354	644	8	83	0.48	0	0	33	123	3.47
2017	MLB	NY Mets	10	0	3	0	3	300	300	400	700	0	80	0.00	0	0	33	100	3.81
2018	AA	Binghamton	215	23	59	5	30	274	297	437	735	3	83	0.19	0	0	41	163	4.34
2018	AAA	Las Vegas	17	3	4	0	1	235	316	353	669	11	88	1.00	0	0	50	118	4.26
2018	MLB	NY Mets	84	10	14	1	9	167	205	238	443	5	68	0.15	0	0	29	71	0.40

Defense-first, probable backup type CA. Like a lot of catchers, is limited by a lack of batspeed. His response has been to take some big cuts with a long swing. Can run into some balls but BA and OBP suffer. A shorter swing will eliminate some of his power. Has defensive skills to stick as a backup.

Noda,Ryan — 379 — Toronto

EXP MLB DEBUT: 2020 | H/W: 6-3 210 | FUT: Starting OF | 7D

Bats L Age 23
2017 (15) Cincinnati
Pwr ++++
BAvg ++
Spd ++
Def +++

Year	Lev	Team	AB	R	H	HR	RBI	Avg	OB	Slg	OPS	bb%	ct%	Eye	SB	CS	x/h%	Iso	RC/G
2017	NCAA	Cincinnati	178	43	42	9	30	236	355	478	833	16	62	0.49	9	2	55	242	6.77
2017	Rk	Bluefield	214	62	78	7	39	364	502	575	1077	22	72	0.98	7	4	36	210	10.23
2018	A	Lansing	403	78	103	20	80	256	414	484	898	21	67	0.81	14	4	47	228	7.65

LH masher is a Three True Outcomes guy. Quick bat and an patient approach as he looks for pitches to crush. When he fires, it is an all-or-nothing approach. That approach results in plenty of swing-and-miss and limits ability to hit for BA, but did draw 109 BB. Average speed and defense limit him to an OF corner, but does have an above-average arm.

Nottingham,Jacob — 2 — Milwaukee

EXP MLB DEBUT: 2019 | H/W: 6-3 200 | FUT: Starting 1B | 7D

Bats R Age 24
2013 (6) HS (CA)
Pwr +++
BAvg ++
Spd ++
Def ++

Year	Lev	Team	AB	R	H	HR	RBI	Avg	OB	Slg	OPS	bb%	ct%	Eye	SB	CS	x/h%	Iso	RC/G
2015	A+	Lancaster	71	14	23	4	14	324	351	606	957	4	86	0.30	0	0	48	282	6.87
2016	AA	Biloxi	415	46	97	11	37	234	284	347	631	7	67	0.21	9	2	26	113	3.13
2017	AA	Biloxi	325	37	68	9	48	209	290	369	659	10	73	0.43	7	3	47	160	3.70
2018	AAA	Col Springs	178	33	50	10	36	281	333	528	861	7	67	0.24	2	1	44	247	6.53
2018	MLB	Milwaukee	20	2	4	0	0	200	333	250	583	17	60	0.50	0	0	25	50	2.93

Strong, big-bodied CA who received his cup of coffee in 2018. Has plus raw power but doesn't translate consistently enough to games with fringe ct% ability. Has improved defensively behind the plate, and will flash a plus arm, but lack of athleticism projects him to move over to 1B long-term.

Nova,Freudis — 6 — Houston

EXP MLB DEBUT: 2023 | H/W: 6-1 180 | FUT: Starting SS | 8D

Bats R Age 19
2016 FA (DR)
Pwr +++
BAvg +++
Spd ++
Def +++

Year	Lev	Team	AB	R	H	HR	RBI	Avg	OB	Slg	OPS	bb%	ct%	Eye	SB	CS	x/h%	Iso	RC/G
2017		Did not play in the US																	
2018	Rk	GCL Astros	146	21	45	6	28	308	336	466	801	4	86	0.29	9	5	22	158	5.00

The athletic SS is just beginning his journey, but all the ingredients are there for something impressive. He isn't a big guy, but showcases above-average raw power on the back of impressive bat speed. He makes a ton of contact—possibly to his detriment. He also flashes enough leather to stick at the six long term.

Nunez,Dom — 2 — Colorado

EXP MLB DEBUT: 2019 | H/W: 6-0 170 | FUT: Reserve C | 6C

Bats L Age 24
2013 (6) HS (CA)
Pwr ++
BAvg +
Spd ++
Def +++

Year	Lev	Team	AB	R	H	HR	RBI	Avg	OB	Slg	OPS	bb%	ct%	Eye	SB	CS	x/h%	Iso	RC/G
2014	Rk	Grand Junction	176	30	55	8	40	313	386	517	903	11	84	0.75	5	7	36	205	6.68
2015	A	Asheville	373	61	105	13	53	282	371	448	819	12	85	0.96	7	7	34	166	5.83
2016	A+	Modesto	390	44	94	10	51	241	326	362	687	11	77	0.54	8	1	27	121	4.07
2017	AA	Hartford	297	37	60	11	28	202	323	354	676	15	72	0.64	7	1	37	152	4.01
2018	AA	Hartford	324	34	72	9	42	222	319	343	662	12	77	0.63	8	6	29	120	3.78

Defensive minded backstop receives the ball well with a strong, accurate arm, but hit tool has not progressed. Makes consistent contact, but struggles to square the ball or generate much pop and had just 21 extra-base hits. Below-average hit tools likely limits him to a backup role.

Ockimey,Josh — 3 — Boston

EXP MLB DEBUT: 2020 | H/W: 6-1 215 | FUT: Starting 1B | 7C

Bats L Age 23
2014 (5) HS (PA)
Pwr ++++
BAvg ++
4.50 Spd +
Def ++

Year	Lev	Team	AB	R	H	HR	RBI	Avg	OB	Slg	OPS	bb%	ct%	Eye	SB	CS	x/h%	Iso	RC/G
2016	A	Greenville	407	60	92	18	62	226	364	425	789	18	68	0.68	3	1	48	199	5.79
2017	A+	Salem	349	56	96	11	63	275	390	438	829	16	68	0.60	1	4	34	163	6.41
2017	AA	Portland	103	12	28	3	11	272	375	427	802	14	68	0.52	0	0	36	155	5.98
2018	AA	Portland	311	43	79	15	56	254	373	473	846	16	64	0.53	0	1	46	219	6.82
2018	AAA	Pawtucket	93	10	20	5	15	215	298	398	696	11	60	0.30	1	0	35	183	4.33

Big, powerful 1B who is a little raw on both sides of the ball. Similar to Josh Bell, but not a switch-hitter. Really struggles against LHP. Plus power is there and will take a walk. Lacks bat-head control that Bell has, but can crush mistakes. 1B only realistic option defensively, and not a plus there. Good makeup guy who will still improve some.

Oliva,Jared — 8 — Pittsburgh

EXP MLB DEBUT: 2021 | H/W: 6-2 181 | FUT: Reserve OF | 7D

Bats R Age 23
2017 (7) Arizona
Pwr ++
BAvg ++
4.25 Spd ++++
Def +++

Year	Lev	Team	AB	R	H	HR	RBI	Avg	OB	Slg	OPS	bb%	ct%	Eye	SB	CS	x/h%	Iso	RC/G
2017	NCAA	Arizona	243	56	78	4	54	321	387	498	885	10	83	0.62	10	3	41	177	6.63
2017	A-	West Virginia	222	30	59	0	17	266	318	374	692	7	74	0.30	15	4	29	108	4.17
2018	A+	Bradenton	396	75	109	9	47	275	342	424	766	9	77	0.44	33	8	34	149	5.08

Toolsy but raw CF with some upside but also some holes in his swing and game. Good size, speed and athleticism, but bat has lagged. Showed some promise and improvement at Hi A in 2018, but old for his level and still a long way to go.

Olivares,Edward — 8 — San Diego

EXP MLB DEBUT: 2020 | H/W: 6-2 186 | FUT: Starting OF | 9E

Bats R Age 23
2014 FA (VZ)
Pwr ++++
BAvg ++
Spd +++
Def +++

Year	Lev	Team	AB	R	H	HR	RBI	Avg	OB	Slg	OPS	bb%	ct%	Eye	SB	CS	x/h%	Iso	RC/G
2015	Rk	GCL Blue Jays	116	21	23	3	10	198	268	362	630	9	77	0.41	14	2	52	164	3.29
2016	Rk	Bluefield	55	8	15	1	6	273	333	418	752	8	78	0.42	1	2	33	145	4.87
2017	A	Lansing	426	82	118	17	65	277	313	500	813	5	81	0.27	18	7	44	223	5.35
2017	A+	Dunedin	68	11	15	0	7	221	303	265	567	11	75	0.47	2	2	13	44	2.56
2018	A+	Lake Elsinore	531	79	147	12	62	277	314	429	744	5	81	0.28	21	8	32	153	4.55

Skinny, wiry athlete with quality all-around skillset and some upside. Long levers create plus bat speed. Peppers gaps and with added strength could be legit HR source. Aggressive at plate but makes contact well enough for power to play. Above-average runner and projects to have moderate SB value. Cannon arm and solid range will help him as CF/RF.

Ornelas,Jonathan — 6 — Texas

EXP MLB DEBUT: 2022 | H/W: 6-0 155 | FUT: Starting 3B | 9E

Bats R Age 18
2018 (3) HS (AZ)
Pwr +++
BAvg +++
Spd ++++
Def +++

Year	Lev	Team	AB	R	H	HR	RBI	Avg	OB	Slg	OPS	bb%	ct%	Eye	SB	CS	x/h%	Iso	RC/G
2018	Rk	AZL Rangers	172	34	52	3	28	302	391	459	850	13	76	0.61	15	5	33	157	6.45

Flew through the AZL with ease with a tantalizing combination of an advanced hit tool, game-awareness skills and quick-twitch athleticism. Has enough barrel awareness and bat speed to project a power surge in the future; very good pitch recognition. Runs well, enough quickness for SS, enough potential bat for 3B. Young, but has a high ceiling.

Ornelas,Tirso — 9 — San Diego

EXP MLB DEBUT: 2021 | H/W: 6-4 180 | FUT: Starting OF | 8D

Bats L Age 19
2016 FA (MX)
Pwr +++
BAvg +++
Spd +++
Def ++

Year	Lev	Team	AB	R	H	HR	RBI	Avg	OB	Slg	OPS	bb%	ct%	Eye	SB	CS	x/h%	Iso	RC/G
2017	Rk	AZL Padres 2	196	46	54	3	26	276	398	408	806	17	69	0.66	0	0	31	133	6.24
2018	A	Fort Wayne	309	45	78	8	40	252	338	392	730	11	78	0.59	5	1	31	139	4.68

Big-bodied OF who burst onto scene as one of MWL's youngest bats in 2018. Employs all-fields approach from left side; has natural feel for the barrel and makes above-average ct%. Owns gap power now but big frame suggests there's more to come. Not the best athlete and won't run much. Likely destined for a corner OF spot.

Ortiz,Jhailyn | 9 | Philadelphia | EXP MLB DEBUT: 2022 | H/W: 6-3 235 | FUT: Starting OF | 9D

Bats R Age 20	Year	Lev	Team	AB	R	H	HR	RBI	Avg	OB	Slg	OPS	bb%	ct%	Eye	SB	CS	x/h%	Iso	RC/G
2015 FA (DR)																				
Pwr ++++																				
BAvg ++	2016	Rk	GCL Phillies	173	29	40	8	27	231	300	434	734	9	69	0.32	8	2	45	202	4.63
4.60 Spd ++	2017	A-	Williamsport	159	27	48	8	30	302	373	560	933	10	70	0.38	5	1	50	258	7.54
Def ++	2018	A	Lakewood	405	51	91	13	47	225	286	375	662	8	63	0.24	2	2	36	151	3.76

Massive and easy all-fields power due to man-child frame, but rest of his game is bare-knuckles raw. Often wildly overswings, chases breaking balls, misses hittable pitches. Maintaining his body will be an issue, moves OK in RF now but likely switches to 1B long-term. Still young, so time to improve, but the trip will be long.

Pache,Cristian | 8 | Atlanta | EXP MLB DEBUT: 2019 | H/W: 6-2 185 | FUT: Starting CF | 8C

Bats R Age 20	Year	Lev	Team	AB	R	H	HR	RBI	Avg	OB	Slg	OPS	bb%	ct%	Eye	SB	CS	x/h%	Iso	RC/G
2015 FA (DR)	2016	Rk	GCL Braves	106	16	30	0	11	283	321	377	699	5	90	0.55	7	3	20	94	4.25
Pwr ++	2016	Rk	Danville	114	12	38	0	10	333	372	404	775	6	89	0.54	4	2	13	70	5.06
BAvg +++	2017	A	Rome	469	60	132	0	42	281	337	343	680	8	78	0.38	32	14	16	62	3.94
Spd ++++	2018	A+	Florida	369	46	105	8	40	285	313	431	743	4	81	0.22	7	6	31	146	4.47
Def +++++	2018	AA	Mississippi	104	10	27	1	7	260	294	337	630	5	73	0.18	0	2	19	77	3.07

Quick-twitch athletic, toolsy OF advanced to Double-A in age-19 season. Quick, compact swing geared towards hard ground ball or topspin heavy line drive contact. Aggressive approach with heavy pull tendencies. Hit first 9 HR of career, mostly turning on fringe pitching. Likely 8 to 15 HR at maturity. Plus runner and the best defensive CF in minors.

Palacios,Josh | 89 | Toronto | EXP MLB DEBUT: 2021 | H/W: 6-1 185 | FUT: Reserve OF | 6C

Bats B Age 23	Year	Lev	Team	AB	R	H	HR	RBI	Avg	OB	Slg	OPS	bb%	ct%	Eye	SB	CS	x/h%	Iso	RC/G
2016 (4) San Jacinto Coll	2016	A-	Vancouver	110	15	39	0	13	355	427	473	900	11	85	0.82	4	2	26	118	6.96
Pwr ++	2016	A	Lansing	38	2	13	0	1	342	359	421	780	3	92	0.33	0	2	23	79	4.93
BAvg +++	2017	A	Lansing	368	65	103	2	39	280	354	361	715	10	79	0.54	12	6	22	82	4.52
Spd +++	2018	A+	Dunedin	507	62	148	8	78	292	352	418	770	8	75	0.38	15	9	29	126	5.14
Def +++	2018	AA	New Hampshire	3	0	0	0	0	0	0	0	0	0	33	0.00	0	0		0	-9.58

Instinctive hitter has a good understanding of the strike zone and held his own at High-A. Was more aggressive at the plate leading to career highs in 2B/HR/RBI, but also made less consistent contact. Good speed with a strong arm, but is stretched in CF and split time in RF where he profiles better. None of his tools stand out as plus.

Palacios,Richard | 4 | Cleveland | EXP MLB DEBUT: 2021 | H/W: 5-10 160 | FUT: Starting 2B | 8C

Bats L Age 21	Year	Lev	Team	AB	R	H	HR	RBI	Avg	OB	Slg	OPS	bb%	ct%	Eye	SB	CS	x/h%	Iso	RC/G
2018 (3) Towson																				
Pwr ++	2018	NCAA	Towson	196	56	59	8	31	301	448	515	963	21	92	3.25	25	1	44	214	8.14
BAvg +++	2018	Rk	AZL Indians	16	4	7	2	6	438	591	875	1466	27	88	3.00	2	0	43	438	14.18
Spd ++++	2018	A-	Mahoning Val	73	12	30	2	17	411	488	589	1077	13	84	0.92	2	1	27	178	9.09
Def +++	2018	A	Lake County	80	10	24	2	7	300	317	425	742	2	84	0.15	3	0	21	125	4.29

Table-setter type of hitter who can run. He hit the ground running in his pro debut, as he continued to hit in his limited sample of 45 games, ending at Low-A. He does not project to hit for much power right now, but is otherwise well-rounded and suited for the 2B.

Paredes,Isaac | 6 | Detroit | EXP MLB DEBUT: 2020 | H/W: 5-11 175 | FUT: Starting MIF | 8C

Bats R Age 20	Year	Lev	Team	AB	R	H	HR	RBI	Avg	OB	Slg	OPS	bb%	ct%	Eye	SB	CS	x/h%	Iso	RC/G
2015 FA (MX)	2016	A	South Bend	12	0	2	0	0	167	167	167	333	0	83	0.00	0	0	0	0	-0.59
Pwr ++	2017	A	West Michigan	115	16	25	4	21	217	297	348	645	10	89	1.00	0	0	28	130	3.70
BAvg ++	2017	A	South Bend	337	49	89	7	49	264	322	401	723	8	84	0.54	2	1	36	136	4.48
Spd +	2018	A+	Lakeland	301	50	78	12	48	259	330	455	785	10	82	0.59	1	0	42	196	5.25
Def ++	2018	AA	Erie	131	20	42	3	22	321	407	458	865	13	83	0.86	1	0	29	137	6.46

Athletic shortstop with ability to defend beyond his years. Already nearing his physical development max with a rock-solid, compact frame and broad shoulders. Accurate arm with good footwork despite size. Works the entire field with advanced ability to barrel the ball. Impressive plate discipline.

Park,Hoy Jun | 46 | New York (A) | EXP MLB DEBUT: 2020 | H/W: 6-1 175 | FUT: Reserve IF | 6C

Bats L Age 22	Year	Lev	Team	AB	R	H	HR	RBI	Avg	OB	Slg	OPS	bb%	ct%	Eye	SB	CS	x/h%	Iso	RC/G
2014 FA (KR)																				
Pwr ++	2016	A	Charleston (Sc)	435	60	98	2	34	225	329	329	657	13	72	0.56	32	3	30	103	3.94
BAvg ++	2017	A	Charleston (Sc)	324	53	85	6	34	262	342	367	709	11	81	0.62	18	7	20	105	4.40
Spd ++++	2017	A+	Tampa	94	20	20	1	5	213	308	330	638	12	85	0.93	7	0	40	117	3.81
Def +++	2018	A+	Tampa	341	46	88	6	34	258	381	349	730	17	80	0.99	18	5	19	91	4.97

Lean LHH MIF brings patient approach and speed to the table. Improved BB%, close to an elite skill, and ct% maintained career norms. Cleaned up swing path, attacking baseball better. Below-average pull power potential despite limited strength. 10 HR potential. Plus runner with solid SB%. Soft hand defender with a fringe-average arm at SS.

Patterson,Jordan | 39 | Colorado | EXP MLB DEBUT: 2016 | H/W: 6-4 200 | FUT: Reserve OF | 7C

Bats L Age 27	Year	Lev	Team	AB	R	H	HR	RBI	Avg	OB	Slg	OPS	bb%	ct%	Eye	SB	CS	x/h%	Iso	RC/G
2013 (4) South Alabama	2015	AA	New Britain	185	26	53	7	32	286	327	503	829	6	77	0.26	9	4	49	216	5.66
Pwr +++	2016	AAA	Albuquerque	427	75	125	14	61	293	363	480	843	10	72	0.40	10	0	36	187	6.22
BAvg ++	2016	MLB	Colorado	18	1	8	0	2	444	474	500	974	5	94	1.00	0	1	13	56	7.14
Spd ++	2017	AAA	Albuquerque	484	78	137	26	92	283	333	539	872	7	74	0.28	3	5	47	256	6.34
Def +++	2018	AAA	Albuquerque	413	77	112	26	76	271	338	525	864	9	69	0.33	6	2	46	254	6.45

Continues to put up impressive numbers, but hasn't seen the majors since 2016. Smooth LH stroke and above-average bat speed and slugged 52 HR over two seasons. Swing can get long, resulting in contact issues, but does plenty of damage on balls in play. Fringe speed hurts his profile in Coors, but does have a strong arm from days as a reliever.

Pelletier,Ben | 7 | Philadelphia | EXP MLB DEBUT: 2023 | H/W: 6-2 190 | FUT: Starting OF | 7D

Bats R Age 20	Year	Lev	Team	AB	R	H	HR	RBI	Avg	OB	Slg	OPS	bb%	ct%	Eye	SB	CS	x/h%	Iso	RC/G
2015 (34) HS (QC)																				
Pwr ++++																				
BAvg ++	2016	Rk	GCL Phillies	83	14	18	0	5	217	261	265	526	6	70	0.20	1	0	17	48	1.73
Spd +	2017	Rk	GCL Phillies	171	21	57	3	26	333	363	474	837	4	82	0.27	1	0	30	140	5.63
Def ++	2018	A-	Williamsport	256	29	71	9	45	277	320	480	800	6	75	0.25	1	1	42	203	5.35

Good sized, late-round 2015 pick from Canada still getting his reps in. Swing is built for loft and is powerful, but can get a bit long. Can be overly patient, and there's some swing and miss that he'll need to clean up going forward. Very little speed to speak of, which will keep him in an outfield corner. He will be a slow mover for now.

Pena,Jeremy | 6 | Houston | EXP MLB DEBUT: 2021 | H/W: 6-0 175 | FUT: Reserve SS | 7C

Bats R Age 21	Year	Lev	Team	AB	R	H	HR	RBI	Avg	OB	Slg	OPS	bb%	ct%	Eye	SB	CS	x/h%	Iso	RC/G
2018 (3) Maine																				
Pwr ++																				
BAvg ++																				
Spd ++++	2018	NCAA	Maine	211	50	65	5	28	308	387	469	856	11	80	0.64	10	0	29	161	6.32
Def ++++	2018	A-	Tri City	136	22	34	1	10	250	338	309	646	12	86	0.95	3	0	18	59	3.85

A defensive virtuoso, Pena boasts a strong arm complemented by above-average range. He's likely to accrue most of his value going forward due to his above-average speed and playing time based on his defense. His offense is otherwise not fantasy noteworthy.

Pentecost,Max | 2 | Toronto | EXP MLB DEBUT: 2019 | H/W: 6-2 191 | FUT: Starting C | 7D

Bats R Age 26	Year	Lev	Team	AB	R	H	HR	RBI	Avg	OB	Slg	OPS	bb%	ct%	Eye	SB	CS	x/h%	Iso	RC/G
2014 (1) Kennesaw St	2016	A	Lansing	239	36	75	7	34	314	369	490	859	8	79	0.41	4	2	33	176	6.15
Pwr +++	2016	A+	Dunedin	49	6	12	3	7	245	288	469	758	6	65	0.18	1	1	42	224	4.91
BAvg ++	2017	Rk	GCL Blue Jays	2	0	0	0	0	0	0	0	0	0	100		0	0		0	-2.66
Spd ++	2017	A+	Dunedin	286	34	79	9	54	276	330	434	764	7	78	0.37	0	1	32	157	4.87
Def +++	2018	AA	New Hampshire	344	40	87	10	52	253	284	401	685	4	74	0.17	1	0	33	148	3.73

Athletic backstop was finally healthy, but put up pedestrian numbers at AA. Quick RH stroke with average to above power, but comes open on follow-through and is pull-heavy. Moves well behind the plate with a strong arm despite two shoulder injuries. Doesn't chase out of the zone, but struggles to square up the ball on a consistent basis.

Perdomo,Geraldo | 6 | Arizona | EXP MLB DEBUT: 2022 | H/W: 6-2 184 | FUT: Starting SS | 8E

Bats R Age 19	Year	Lev	Team	AB	R	H	HR	RBI	Avg	OB	Slg	OPS	bb%	ct%	Eye	SB	CS	x/h%	Iso	RC/G
2016 FA (DR)																				
Pwr ++																				
BAvg +++	2018	Rk	Missoula	22	3	10	0	2	455	586	545	1132	24	82	1.75	1	1	10	91	10.84
Spd +++	2018	Rk	AZL DBacks	86	20	27	1	8	314	410	442	852	14	80	0.82	14	1	26	128	6.49
Def ++++	2018	A-	Hillsboro	103	20	31	3	14	301	405	456	861	15	78	0.78	9	4	26	155	6.57

Lean, wiry middle infielder who played on three levels in 2018. Combines good plate discipline skills with smooth LH stroke that projects for future BA returns. Very good athlete who shows quick first step necessary for solid SB impact. Will need to add strength to skinny frame, but should have range and actions required to man SS at next level.

Pereira,Everson

8 | **New York (A)** | EXP MLB DEBUT: 2022 | H/W: 6-0 191 | FUT: Starting CF | **9E**

Bats R Age 17
2017 FA (VZ)

- Pwr +++
- BAvg +++
- Spd ++++
- Def ++++

Year	Lev	Team	AB	R	H	HR	RBI	Avg	OB	Slg	OPS	bb%	ct%	Eye	SB	CS	x/h%	Iso	RC/G
2018	Rk	Pulaski	167	21	44	3	26	263	324	389	713	8	64	0.25	3	2	30	126	4.66

Athletic, toolsy OF made pro debut and held own in aggressive Appy League assignment. Quick, unrefined swing. It's short and compact but he struggles incorporating lower half. Raw plus power in frame. Will need to tighten up lower half to reach power potential. Plus runner who didn't run enough in debut. Potential plus-plus defender in CF.

Perez,Delvin

6 | **St. Louis** | EXP MLB DEBUT: 2021 | H/W: 6-3 165 | FUT: Starting SS | **7D**

Bats R Age 20
2016 (1) HS (PR)

- Pwr ++
- BAvg ++
- Spd ++++
- Def ++++

Year	Lev	Team	AB	R	H	HR	RBI	Avg	OB	Slg	OPS	bb%	ct%	Eye	SB	CS	x/h%	Iso	RC/G
2016	Rk	GCL Cardinals	163	19	48	0	19	294	343	393	735	7	83	0.43	12	1	25	98	4.67
2017	Rk	Johnson City	76	7	14	0	4	184	295	224	519	14	82	0.86	3	4	14	39	2.28
2017	Rk	GCL Cardinals	42	7	10	0	5	238	319	357	676	11	76	0.50	2	1	30	119	4.15
2018	A-	State College	239	22	51	1	21	213	296	272	568	10	77	0.52	8	6	18	59	2.60

He looked like a steal when he fell to the Cardinals at #23 in the 2016 draft, but he no longer looks like a sure thing. Average bat speed and raw strength leave him over-matched at the plate and he now has a punch-less slash line of .237/.320/.310 in 520 AB. He still shows above-average tools on defense, but otherwise there is nothing going on.

Perez,Joe

5 | **Houston** | EXP MLB DEBUT: 2023 | H/W: 6-3 210 | FUT: Starting 3B | **8D**

Bats R Age 19
2017 (2) HS (FL)

- Pwr ++++
- BAvg ++
- Spd +
- Def ++

Year	Lev	Team	AB	R	H	HR	RBI	Avg	OB	Slg	OPS	bb%	ct%	Eye	SB	CS	x/h%	Iso	RC/G
2018	Rk	GCL Astros	11	1	4	0	0	364	500	364	864	21	91	3.00	1	0	0	0	7.16

Tommy John surgery caused him to miss much of the 2018 season. Many clubs liked him on the mound where he threw in the mid-to-upper 90s but the Astros like him at the dish. He displays plus power potential and flashes the ability to hit for average, though some scouts question how much he'll hit. He's not rangy but his plus-plus arm compensates.

Perez,Wenceel

6 | **Detroit** | EXP MLB DEBUT: 2022 | H/W: 5-11 170 | FUT: Starting SS | **7B**

Bats B Age 19
2016 FA (DR)

- Pwr +
- BAvg ++
- Spd ++
- Def ++

Year	Lev	Team	AB	R	H	HR	RBI	Avg	OB	Slg	OPS	bb%	ct%	Eye	SB	CS	x/h%	Iso	RC/G
2018	Rk	GCL Tigers W	81	20	31	2	14	383	462	543	1006	13	83	0.86	2	1	29	160	8.22
2018	A-	Connecticut	82	8	20	1	8	244	287	305	592	6	85	0.42	7	3	15	61	2.80
2018	A	West Michigan	68	8	21	0	9	309	329	441	770	3	88	0.25	4	1	29	132	4.89

Still a teenager, has a feel on both sides of the ball well beyond his years. Raw profile with improving footwork and arm accuracy. His quick-twitch instinct gets the better of him at times. Needs to pace himself better. Able to barrel the ball with an exceptional eye and ability to draw walks. Power should escalate as he continues to fill out.

Perez,Yanio

35 | **Texas** | EXP MLB DEBUT: 2021 | H/W: 6-2 205 | FUT: Reserve OF | **7C**

Bats R Age 23
2016 FA (CU)

- Pwr +++
- BAvg +
- 4.50 Spd +++
- Def ++

Year	Lev	Team	AB	R	H	HR	RBI	Avg	OB	Slg	OPS	bb%	ct%	Eye	SB	CS	x/h%	Iso	RC/G
2017	A	Hickory	180	27	58	9	30	322	384	533	917	9	81	0.53	3	0	33	211	6.76
2017	A+	Down East	281	31	71	5	36	253	302	370	672	7	77	0.30	3	1	30	117	3.73
2018	Rk	AZL Rangers	10	0	2	0	1	200	333	200	533	17	50	0.40	0	0	0	0	2.21
2018	A+	Down East	163	12	36	4	18	221	278	313	591	7	75	0.32	0	1	19	92	2.57
2018	AA	Frisco	44	8	10	0	5	227	333	250	583	14	66	0.47	0	0	10	23	2.77

Knee injury sidetracked beginning of 2018 and was never able to shake off the rust. Has shown better plate control in the past, but failed to make much hard contact and prospect status backed up after a big-money bonus from Cuba in 2016. Good frame with some power projection, but limited to IF/OF corner spots.

Perkins,Blake

78 | **Kansas City** | EXP MLB DEBUT: 2020 | H/W: 6-1 165 | FUT: Reserve OF | **6B**

Bats R Age 22
2015 (2) HS (AZ)

- Pwr +
- BAvg ++
- Spd ++++
- Def ++++

Year	Lev	Team	AB	R	H	HR	RBI	Avg	OB	Slg	OPS	bb%	ct%	Eye	SB	CS	x/h%	Iso	RC/G
2016	A-	Auburn	209	31	49	1	16	234	316	282	599	11	81	0.64	10	3	14	48	3.08
2016	A	Hagerstown	25	4	5	0	2	200	333	200	533	17	76	0.83	0	1	0	0	2.31
2017	A	Hagerstown	482	105	123	8	48	255	352	378	730	13	76	0.61	31	8	32	122	4.82
2018	A+	Wilmington	485	87	115	3	39	237	359	305	664	16	72	0.69	29	9	23	68	4.06
2018	A+	Potomac	252	39	59	1	21	234	344	290	633	14	73	0.63	12	5	20	56	3.57

Switch-hitting, athletic OF was acquired in mid-season trade from WAS. Slap hitter, learning to switch hit, relies heavily on legs to beat out ground balls. Struggles getting bat head around on velocity and with pitch recognition. Swing plane flat, doesn't generate loft, depressing power potential. Plus runner and a future SB threat.

Peters,DJ

89 | **Los Angeles (N)** | EXP MLB DEBUT: 2019 | H/W: 6-5 210 | FUT: Starting OF | **8D**

Bats R Age 23
2016 (4) Cal St Fullerton

- Pwr ++++
- BAvg ++
- Spd +++
- Def +++

Year	Lev	Team	AB	R	H	HR	RBI	Avg	OB	Slg	OPS	bb%	ct%	Eye	SB	CS	x/h%	Iso	RC/G
2016	Rk	Ogden	262	63	92	13	48	351	428	615	1042	12	75	0.53	5	3	43	263	8.88
2017	A+	Rancho Cuca	504	91	139	27	82	276	357	514	871	11	63	0.34	3	3	44	238	7.18
2018	AA	Tulsa	491	79	116	29	60	236	300	473	773	8	61	0.23	1	2	47	236	5.57

Huge, athletic OF has the best raw power in the system and blasted a career-high in HR. Aggressive approach and long levers result in tons of swing-and-miss and limits hit tool. Has above-average speed and covers ground well in CF, but doesn't translate on the bases. Long-term, profiles better in RF due to a plus arm.

Peterson,Dustin

5 | **Detroit** | EXP MLB DEBUT: 2019 | H/W: 6-2 185 | FUT: Reserve OF | **6B**

Bats R Age 24
2013 (2) HS (AZ)

- Pwr +
- BAvg +
- Spd +
- Def +

Year	Lev	Team	AB	R	H	HR	RBI	Avg	OB	Slg	OPS	bb%	ct%	Eye	SB	CS	x/h%	Iso	RC/G
2016	AA	Mississippi	524	65	148	12	88	282	339	431	770	8	81	0.45	4	1	35	149	5.04
2017	AAA	Gwinnett	314	35	78	1	30	248	308	318	626	8	75	0.35	1	2	24	70	3.24
2018	AAA	Gwinnett	406	46	109	11	55	268	319	406	725	7	76	0.31	3	0	31	138	4.37
2018	MLB	Detroit	2	0	0	0	0	0	0	0	0	0	50	0.00	0	0		0	-7.85
2018	MLB	Atlanta	2	0	0	0	0	0	0	0	0	0	50	0.00	0	0		0	-7.85

Infielder-turned-outfielder after two seasons at third base. Younger brother to Mariners' first-round pick D.J. Peterson, he thrives off athleticism to complement average profile across the board. Contact rate needs improvement with rate of power that should play at least above-average down the road.

Peterson,Kort

79 | **Kansas City** | EXP MLB DEBUT: 2021 | H/W: 6-1 195 | FUT: Reserve OF | **6C**

Bats L Age 24
2016 (23) UCLA

- Pwr +++
- BAvg ++
- Spd +++
- Def +++

Year	Lev	Team	AB	R	H	HR	RBI	Avg	OB	Slg	OPS	bb%	ct%	Eye	SB	CS	x/h%	Iso	RC/G
2016	Rk	Burlington	176	39	61	5	35	347	404	545	950	9	78	0.45	7	2	34	199	7.41
2017	A	Lexington	193	24	56	1	19	290	348	389	736	8	72	0.31	5	3	27	98	4.78
2017	A+	Wilmington	39	7	13	1	1	333	366	590	956	5	79	0.25	0	0	46	256	7.32
2018	A+	Wilmington	219	34	64	8	33	292	343	498	841	7	73	0.29	5	1	42	205	6.03
2018	AA	NW Arkansas	166	24	38	7	27	229	281	440	721	7	63	0.20	6	3	47	211	4.68

Older, under-the-radar prospect earned mid-season promotion to Double-A and struggled mightily. A late-bloomer, found power stroke without significant ct% dip. Average power likely at maturity. Hit tool has swing-and-miss risk. Beaten up in zone and by higher velocities. An average runner and defender, likely a tweener profile in COF.

Polo,Tito

78 | **Chicago (A)** | EXP MLB DEBUT: 2019 | H/W: 5-11 180 | FUT: Reserve OF | **6B**

Bats R Age 24
2012 FA (CB)

- Pwr ++
- BAvg ++
- Spd ++++
- Def +++

Year	Lev	Team	AB	R	H	HR	RBI	Avg	OB	Slg	OPS	bb%	ct%	Eye	SB	CS	x/h%	Iso	RC/G
2017	A+	Tampa	233	42	66	4	20	283	329	429	759	6	73	0.26	19	5	30	146	4.94
2017	AA	Trenton	55	14	21	1	17	382	443	545	988	10	85	0.75	7	1	29	164	7.79
2017	AA	Birmingham	72	10	20	0	7	278	325	389	714	6	79	0.33	7	3	30	111	4.40
2018	Rk	AZL White Sox	22	7	7	3	7	318	444	727	1172	19	82	1.25	5	1	43	409	10.01
2018	AA	Birmingham	163	22	40	1	8	245	297	337	635	7	79	0.35	15	4	25	92	3.34

Speedy OF struggled with injuries in 2018. Aggressive hitter with an innate ability to foul of 2-strike pitches. Struggles getting swing started and with swing path inconsistencies. Gap oriented power to take advantage of legs. Below-average HR power, and completely pull-oriented. A plus-runner, could steal 30 plus if given significant playing time.

Pompey,Tristan

789 | **Miami** | EXP MLB DEBUT: 2020 | H/W: 6-4 195 | FUT: Starting OF | **8E**

Bats B Age 22
2018 (3) Kentucky

- Pwr ++
- BAvg +++
- Spd ++++
- Def +++

Year	Lev	Team	AB	R	H	HR	RBI	Avg	OB	Slg	OPS	bb%	ct%	Eye	SB	CS	x/h%	Iso	RC/G
2018	NCAA	Kentucky	185	41	62	7	39	335	436	557	993	15	75	0.70	10	3	44	222	8.47
2018	Rk	GCL Marlins	12	1	3	0	1	250	400	250	650	20	67	0.75	1	1	0	0	3.96
2018	A	Greensboro	86	12	27	2	9	314	422	430	852	16	74	0.73	5	3	22	116	6.56
2018	A+	Jupiter	86	13	25	1	13	291	384	384	768	13	76	0.62	4	1	24	93	5.33

Brother of Dalton Pompey. Athletic pick quickly moved through lower minors in pro debut. Showed advanced plate skills from both sides of plate, including high contact rate. Swing is geared towards top-heavy line-drive contact. However, strength in frame suggest some power potential untapped. Plus runner. Stole 10 bases.

Potts,Hudson

5 | San Diego | EXP MLB DEBUT: 2020 | H/W: 6-2 180 | FUT: Starting 3B | 8D

Bats R Age 20
2016 (1) HS (TX)
Pwr ++++
BAvg +++
Spd ++
Def +++

Year	Lev	Team	AB	R	H	HR	RBI	Avg	OB	Slg	OPS	bb%	ct%	Eye	SB	CS	x/h%	Iso	RC/G
2016	Rk	AZL Padres	183	35	54	1	21	295	328	399	727	5	81	0.26	8	4	28	104	4.39
2016	A-	Tri-City	60	7	14	0	6	233	333	267	600	13	78	0.69	2	1	7	33	3.16
2017	A	Fort Wayne	491	67	124	20	69	253	286	438	724	4	71	0.16	0	1	38	185	4.27
2018	A+	Lake Elsinore	406	66	114	17	58	281	341	498	838	8	72	0.33	3	1	46	217	6.04
2018	AA	San Antonio	78	5	12	2	5	154	250	231	481	11	58	0.30	1	0	17	77	0.87

Tall, strong 3B who led CAL in x/h% as a mere 19-year-old. Produces big-time loft in swing and has plus raw power to all fields. Downside is an over-aggressive approach in which contact can be hard to come by consistently, though bb% shot up last season. Owns plus arm required for 3B and will flash above-average range. Decent athlete, but not an SB source.

Pratto,Nick

3 | Kansas City | EXP MLB DEBUT: 2021 | H/W: 6-1 195 | FUT: Starting 1B | 8C

Bats L Age 20
2017 (1) HS (CA)
Pwr +++
BAvg +++
Spd +++
Def ++++

Year	Lev	Team	AB	R	H	HR	RBI	Avg	OB	Slg	OPS	bb%	ct%	Eye	SB	CS	x/h%	Iso	RC/G
2017	Rk	AZL Royals	198	25	49	4	34	247	329	414	743	11	71	0.41	10	4	45	167	5.01
2018	A	Lexington	485	79	136	14	62	280	342	443	785	8	69	0.30	22	5	36	163	5.46

Top HS hitter from 2017 draft has struggled with plummeting ct% since becoming pro. Long, looping swing attributes to big K totals. Shortened up late and produced better results. Uses leverage well with gap-to-gap approach. Plus raw power potential but below average production for 1B. Below average runner despite SB totals.

Pujols,Jose

9 | Philadelphia | EXP MLB DEBUT: 2020 | H/W: 6-3 175 | FUT: Starting OF | 7D

Bats R Age 23
2012 FA (DR)
Pwr ++++
BAvg ++
Spd ++
Def ++

Year	Lev	Team	AB	R	H	HR	RBI	Avg	OB	Slg	OPS	bb%	ct%	Eye	SB	CS	x/h%	Iso	RC/G
2016	A	Lakewood	498	67	120	24	82	241	303	440	742	8	64	0.25	5	3	40	199	4.91
2017	A+	Clearwater	325	24	63	8	29	194	247	305	552	7	54	0.15	2	2	30	111	2.36
2018	A+	Clearwater	352	56	106	18	58	301	361	523	884	9	64	0.26	1	1	36	222	7.15
2018	AA	Reading	89	11	24	4	18	270	369	427	796	14	61	0.40	2	2	25	157	6.10

Adjusting his hand position and a more balanced swing led to a High-A breakout for the slugger, restoring his prospect status. Bat speed, strong wrists and improved plate patience are the pluses. RF-quality defense with strong arm. But still struggles with contact enough that a full-time MLB role is a shaky proposition.

Quinn,Heath

79 | San Francisco | EXP MLB DEBUT: 2020 | H/W: 6-2 190 | FUT: Starting OF | 7C

Bats R Age 23
2016 (3) Samford
Pwr +++
BAvg +++
Spd +++
Def +++

Year	Lev	Team	AB	R	H	HR	RBI	Avg	OB	Slg	OPS	bb%	ct%	Eye	SB	CS	x/h%	Iso	RC/G
2016	Rk	AZL Giants	5	4	3	0	0	600	714	800	1514	29	80	2.00	0	0	33	200	16.58
2016	A-	Salem-Keizer	205	37	69	9	34	337	411	571	982	11	76	0.52	3	0	42	234	8.01
2016	A+	San Jose	17	2	6	0	0	353	421	412	833	11	59	0.29	0	0	17	59	7.15
2017	A+	San Jose	272	24	62	10	29	228	281	371	652	7	68	0.23	0	0	31	143	3.38
2018	A+	San Jose	357	53	107	14	51	300	373	485	858	11	73	0.43	4	1	36	185	6.38

Athletic OF returned from injury-marred season to produce eye-opening year. Short, compact swing, but ct% drop associated with continued struggle against breaking pitches. Average-raw power to gaps and pull-side but swing is oriented towards line-drive contact with top-spin profile. Average runner, not a threat on bases.

Quiroz,Esteban

4 | Boston | EXP MLB DEBUT: 2020 | H/W: 5-7 175 | FUT: Reserve IF | 6D

Bats L Age 27
2018 FA (MX)
Pwr ++
BAvg ++++
4.50 Spd +
Def ++

Year	Lev	Team	AB	R	H	HR	RBI	Avg	OB	Slg	OPS	bb%	ct%	Eye	SB	CS	x/h%	Iso	RC/G
2018	Rk	GCL Red Sox	19	3	4	0	7	211	400	316	716	24	84	2.00	0	0	25	105	5.42
2018	AA	Portland	87	19	26	7	24	299	390	598	988	13	78	0.68	1	1	46	299	7.83

Stocky, unathletic INF brought in from Mexican League who has a feel to hit. 2B but lack of range and agility make it hard for his high OBP bat to find a chance to play. Best bet is to be a Lenny Harris type PH or bat off the bench, but a a hard guy to carry on a MLB roster. Bat not good enough to be a quality DH option.

Raleigh,Cal

2 | Seattle | EXP MLB DEBUT: 2021 | H/W: 6-3 205 | FUT: Starting C | 8D

Bats B Age 22
2018 (3) Florida St
Pwr +++
BAvg +++
Spd ++
Def +++

Year	Lev	Team	AB	R	H	HR	RBI	Avg	OB	Slg	OPS	bb%	ct%	Eye	SB	CS	x/h%	Iso	RC/G
2018	NCAA	Florida State	230	44	75	13	54	326	448	583	1031	18	81	1.19	2	1	43	257	8.76
2018	A-	Everett	146	25	42	8	29	288	366	534	900	11	80	0.62	1	1	45	247	6.70

Strong bodied, switch-hitting CA prospect has chance with glove and bat. Power-oriented hitter with solid ct% and patient approach. From LH side, extreme pull hitter. From RH side, gap-to-gap approach. Above-average raw power. 20-25 HR at projection likely. Defensively sound, manages pitching staff well.

Raley,Luke

379 | Minnesota | EXP MLB DEBUT: 2019 | H/W: 6-3 220 | FUT: Starting OF | 7C

Bats L Age 24
2016 (7) Lake Erie College
Pwr +++
BAvg ++
Spd +++
Def +++

Year	Lev	Team	AB	R	H	HR	RBI	Avg	OB	Slg	OPS	bb%	ct%	Eye	SB	CS	x/h%	Iso	RC/G
2016	A	Great Lakes	200	24	49	2	17	245	298	370	668	7	77	0.32	4	4	35	125	3.77
2017	A+	Rancho Cuca	478	102	141	14	62	295	353	473	826	8	74	0.35	9	1	33	178	5.86
2018	AA	Tulsa	386	65	106	17	53	275	317	477	794	6	73	0.23	3	0	37	202	5.24
2018	AA	Chattanooga	98	15	27	3	16	276	355	449	804	11	67	0.38	1	0	30	173	5.92

Strong, muscular OF continues to rake in the upper minors. Acquired mid-season in trade with LA, hit 20 HRs overall, showcasing plus power to all fields. Struggles with contact brought on by poor 2-strike approach and pitch recognition issues. Average runner with above-average instincts. Profiles best in LF.

Ramirez,Tyler

789 | Oakland | EXP MLB DEBUT: 2019 | H/W: 5-9 197 | FUT: Starting OF | 7D

Bats L Age 24
2016 (7) North Carolina
Pwr ++
BAvg +++
Spd +++
Def +++

Year	Lev	Team	AB	R	H	HR	RBI	Avg	OB	Slg	OPS	bb%	ct%	Eye	SB	CS	x/h%	Iso	RC/G
2016	Rk	AZL Athletics	28	5	8	0	8	286	310	536	846	3	64	0.10	1	0	63	250	7.01
2016	A-	Vermont	150	22	33	2	15	220	308	327	634	11	74	0.49	5	0	33	107	3.45
2017	A+	Stockton	279	51	84	7	39	301	398	434	832	14	71	0.56	5	2	25	133	6.28
2017	AA	Midland	208	29	64	4	24	308	390	428	818	12	75	0.53	3	3	25	120	5.93
2018	AA	Midland	512	73	147	10	79	287	364	430	794	11	71	0.42	5	4	33	143	5.68

Shorter, slender OF who shows modest pop and on-base ability. Smooth LH stroke lends itself to average ct% skills and he shows ability to use the whole field consistently. Power is limited to gaps but peppers them consistently; hits LHP well. Aggressive approach but owns above-average bb% in each step as a pro. Average athlete likely limited to LF/RF.

Ramos,Heliot

8 | San Francisco | EXP MLB DEBUT: 2021 | H/W: 6-1 188 | FUT: Starting CF | 9E

Bats R Age 19
2017 (1) HS (PR)
Pwr ++++
BAvg ++
Spd ++++
Def +++

Year	Lev	Team	AB	R	H	HR	RBI	Avg	OB	Slg	OPS	bb%	ct%	Eye	SB	CS	x/h%	Iso	RC/G
2017	Rk	AZL Giants	138	33	48	6	27	348	392	645	1037	7	65	0.21	10	2	48	297	9.53
2018	A	Augusta	485	61	119	11	52	245	296	396	692	7	72	0.26	8	7	36	151	4.04

Muscular, quick-twitch CF with plus power potential made strides with hit tool despite statistical struggle. Shortened up an unbalanced, mechanically awkward swing and it became more controllable as season wore on. Aggressive approach, attacking anything close. Plus power is real and shows up in games; barrel rate will need to improve to reach it.

Ramos,Jefrey

7 | Atlanta | EXP MLB DEBUT: 2021 | H/W: 6-1 185 | FUT: Reserve OF | 6C

Bats R Age 20
2016 FA (DR)
Pwr +++
BAvg ++
Spd ++
Def ++

Year	Lev	Team	AB	R	H	HR	RBI	Avg	OB	Slg	OPS	bb%	ct%	Eye	SB	CS	x/h%	Iso	RC/G
2017	Rk	GCL Braves	117	22	38	6	30	325	368	556	924	6	77	0.30	1	0	37	231	6.82
2017	Rk	Danville	72	7	20	1	8	278	307	403	709	4	79	0.20	0	0	35	125	4.09
2018	A	Rome	469	57	115	16	69	245	286	424	711	5	81	0.30	2	0	40	179	4.12

Thick, aggressive OF was up and down in full season debut. LF only profile with plus raw power potential. Has solid bat/ball skills but swing struggles getting out in front of plate. Aggressive hitter, will try to jump on first FB over plate. Over-the-fence power completely pull-dominant. A below-average run tool.

Ramos,Roberto

3 | Colorado | EXP MLB DEBUT: 2020 | H/W: 6-4 220 | FUT: Reserve 1B | 7D

Bats L Age 24
2014 (16) College of the Canyons
Pwr +++
BAvg ++
Spd +
Def ++

Year	Lev	Team	AB	R	H	HR	RBI	Avg	OB	Slg	OPS	bb%	ct%	Eye	SB	CS	x/h%	Iso	RC/G
2016	Rk	Grand Junction	57	12	23	5	23	404	424	789	1213	3	77	0.15	3	1	48	386	10.23
2016	A+	Modesto	78	7	18	2	9	231	318	397	716	11	67	0.38	0	0	50	167	4.69
2017	A+	Lancaster	478	72	142	13	68	297	353	444	796	8	74	0.33	3	2	30	146	5.40
2018	A+	Lancaster	214	44	65	17	43	304	394	640	1034	13	70	0.49	3	1	54	336	9.03
2018	AA	Hartford	199	26	46	15	34	231	320	503	823	12	62	0.35	2	1	52	271	6.22

Thick-bodied masher has plus raw power from the LH side. Drives fastballs and mistakes to the pull side, but swing can get long and strikeout rate at Double-A raises concerns. Solid defender with soft hands and good instincts, but lack of athleticism and range limit him to 1B.

Randolph,Corneilus

7 | Philadelphia | EXP MLB DEBUT: 2020 | H/W: 5-11 205 | FUT: Reserve OF | 7E

Bats L Age 21	Year	Lev	Team	AB	R	H	HR	RBI	Avg	OB	Sig	OPS	bb%	ct%	Eye	SB	CS	x/h%	Iso	RC/G
2015 (1) HS (GA)	2015	Rk	GCL Phillies	172	35	52	1	24	302	412	442	854	16	81	1.00	7	5	37	140	6.68
Pwr +++	2016	Rk	GCL Phillies	12	1	1	0	0	83	214	83	298	14	75	0.67	0	0	0	0	-1.03
BAvg +++	2016	A	Lakewood	241	33	66	2	27	274	345	357	701	10	76	0.46	5	4	23	83	4.29
4.37 Spd +	2017	A+	Clearwater	440	47	110	13	55	250	333	402	736	11	72	0.44	7	3	33	152	4.77
Def ++	2018	AA	Reading	410	52	99	5	40	241	321	322	643	10	78	0.52	3	3	23	80	3.53

Star is dimming on former 10th overall pick. Natural inside-out swing takes pitches the other way; had trouble turning on balls in first shot at AA. Will take a walk but can be too passive and let hittable pitches go by. Smaller sized with thick lower half and a poor arm, so limited to LF. Still young, but void of power, this is a 4th OF profile.

Ray,Corey

8 | Milwaukee | EXP MLB DEBUT: 2019 | H/W: 5-11 185 | FUT: Starting OF | 9E

Bats L Age 24	Year	Lev	Team	AB	R	H	HR	RBI	Avg	OB	Sig	OPS	bb%	ct%	Eye	SB	CS	x/h%	Iso	RC/G
2016 (1) Louisville	2016	NCAA	Louisville	268	55	83	15	60	310	391	545	936	12	85	0.88	44	0	39	235	7.10
Pwr +++	2016	A	Wisconsin	12	2	1	0	0	83	267	83	350	20	67	0.75	1	1	0	0	-0.79
BAvg ++	2016	A+	Brevard County	231	24	57	5	17	247	307	385	692	8	77	0.37	9	5	35	139	4.05
Spd ++++	2017	A+	Carolina	449	56	107	7	48	238	312	367	679	10	65	0.31	24	10	37	129	4.17
Def ++++	2018	AA	Biloxi	532	86	128	27	75	241	318	479	797	10	67	0.34	37	7	52	239	5.72

Premium athlete whose tools finally culminated in breakout 2018 campaign in AA. Tapped into power with more fly balls and pull-side juice; will be HR threat. Exceptional runner who has tools for elite SB output at next level. Still sorting out contact issues which cap his upside. Patrols OF well, but poor arm means LF is where he lands.

Read,Raudy

2 | Washington | EXP MLB DEBUT: 2017 | H/W: 6-0 170 | FUT: Starting C | 7C

Bats R Age 25	Year	Lev	Team	AB	R	H	HR	RBI	Avg	OB	Sig	OPS	bb%	ct%	Eye	SB	CS	x/h%	Iso	RC/G
2011 FA (DR)	2016	A+	Potomac	386	54	101	9	51	262	317	415	731	7	86	0.58	6	3	40	153	4.58
Pwr +++	2017	AA	Harrisburg	411	44	109	17	61	265	311	455	765	6	81	0.34	2	0	39	190	4.78
BAvg +++	2017	MLB	Washington	11	1	3	0	0	273	273	273	545	0	73	0.00	0	0	0	0	1.63
Spd +	2018	AA	Harrisburg	147	14	42	3	24	286	335	435	771	7	80	0.37	0	0	33	150	5.01
Def +++	2018	AAA	Syracuse	50	2	13	0	2	260	275	300	575	2	84	0.13	0	0	15	40	2.39

Suspended for 80 games for PEDs in the pre-season, he couldn't hold power gains from 2017 upon his return. Although he continues to make good contact and at his best has short, compact swing, consistency has been a problem. A strong arm is his best defensive attribute; shortcomings with the glove is what's holding him back.

Reed,Buddy

78 | San Diego | EXP MLB DEBUT: 2020 | H/W: 6-4 185 | FUT: Starting OF | 8D

Bats B Age 23	Year	Lev	Team	AB	R	H	HR	RBI	Avg	OB	Sig	OPS	bb%	ct%	Eye	SB	CS	x/h%	Iso	RC/G
2016 (2) Florida	2016	NCAA	Florida	256	57	67	4	32	262	359	395	754	13	76	0.63	24	0	30	133	5.18
Pwr +++	2016	A-	Tri-City	205	31	52	0	13	254	326	337	663	10	74	0.42	15	5	25	83	3.86
BAvg ++	2017	A	Fort Wayne	316	48	74	6	35	234	286	396	682	7	69	0.24	12	8	42	161	4.02
Spd +++++	2018	A+	Lake Elsinore	315	54	102	12	47	324	372	549	921	7	73	0.29	33	7	39	225	7.11
Def ++++	2018	AA	San Antonio	179	21	32	1	15	179	230	235	465	6	65	0.19	18	3	25	56	0.77

Long, wiry athlete who had full breakout in hitter-friendly CAL. Possesses elite speed and acceleration for impact SB at next level; reads ball well off bat and has plus range/arm for CF. Struggles making consistent ct% and can be over-aggressive at plate. Creates natural loft in swing and has some HR upside if he can make more contact.

Rengifo,Luis

4 | Los Angeles (A) | EXP MLB DEBUT: 2020 | H/W: 5-10 165 | FUT: Starting MIF | 7B

Bats B Age 22	Year	Lev	Team	AB	R	H	HR	RBI	Avg	OB	Sig	OPS	bb%	ct%	Eye	SB	CS	x/h%	Iso	RC/G
2013 FA (VZ)	2017	A	Clinton	400	65	100	11	44	250	307	413	720	8	80	0.41	29	14	39	163	4.38
Pwr +	2017	A	Bowling Green	96	14	24	1	8	250	308	333	641	8	82	0.47	5	3	21	83	3.46
BAvg ++	2018	A+	Inland Empire	161	36	52	2	16	323	420	466	886	14	86	1.23	22	8	31	143	6.92
Spd ++	2018	AA	Mobile	151	37	46	2	21	305	397	477	873	13	85	1.05	13	2	37	172	6.73
Def ++	2018	AAA	Salt Lake	190	36	52	3	27	274	358	421	779	12	84	0.81	6	6	33	147	5.44

Exciting switch-hitting middle infielder who took a big step forward in 2018. Shows steady contact from both sides, complemented by solid plate discipline. Power should tick up a few notches, but he'll find more success with line drive contact. Well-balanced defensive profile with experience in INF and OF. Good fit at short for now.

Reyes,Pablo

578 | Pittsburgh | EXP MLB DEBUT: 2019 | H/W: 5-10 150 | FUT: Utility player | 7C

Bats R Age 25	Year	Lev	Team	AB	R	H	HR	RBI	Avg	OB	Sig	OPS	bb%	ct%	Eye	SB	CS	x/h%	Iso	RC/G
2012 FA (DR)	2016	A+	Bradenton	306	41	81	5	45	265	344	386	730	11	85	0.79	13	8	32	121	4.76
Pwr ++	2017	AA	Altoona	420	62	115	10	50	274	352	410	762	11	83	0.73	21	14	30	136	5.09
BAvg +++	2018	AA	Altoona	45	3	11	0	5	244	306	311	617	8	89	0.80	3	0	27	67	3.47
4.30 Spd +++	2018	AAA	Indianapolis	356	52	103	8	36	289	341	435	777	7	80	0.39	13	7	31	146	5.07
Def +++	2018	MLB	Pittsburgh	58	9	17	3	7	293	349	483	832	8	81	0.45	0	1	29	190	5.59

Small, toolsy INF/OF type. Can handle himself all over the field. Some length to swing but gets away with it some because of good all-field approach and selectivity. Some power here, but can get him in trouble when gets away from all-field approach. Might be exposed as every day player against RHP, but could hold own defensively every day.

Reynolds,Bryan

Pittsburgh | EXP MLB DEBUT: 2020 | H/W: 6-2 195 | FUT: Reserve OF | 6B

Bats B Age 24	Year	Lev	Team	AB	R	H	HR	RBI	Avg	OB	Sig	OPS	bb%	ct%	Eye	SB	CS	x/h%	Iso	RC/G
2016 (2) Vanderbilt	2016	NCAA	Vanderbilt	224	59	74	13	57	330	451	603	1053	18	74	0.84	8	5	43	272	9.36
Pwr +++	2016	A-	Salem-Keizer	154	28	48	5	30	312	358	500	858	7	73	0.27	2	0	38	188	6.21
BAvg +++	2016	A	Augusta	63	11	20	1	8	317	348	444	793	5	68	0.15	1	0	30	127	5.49
4.20 Spd +++	2017	A+	San Jose	491	72	153	10	63	312	360	462	822	7	78	0.35	5	3	29	151	5.67
Def +++	2018	AA	Altoona	331	56	100	7	46	302	382	438	820	11	78	0.59	4	4	28	136	5.89

Rangy, solid-bodied CF who is a solid, all-around switch-hitter and athlete. However, is something of a tweener: Defense in CF is not good enough to be a regular and bat not good enough to be an be an everyday corner OF. Some length to his swing from both sides limits him, but capable of being at least a tough out. Good eye and patience.

Riley,Austin

5 | Atlanta | EXP MLB DEBUT: 2019 | H/W: 6-2 230 | FUT: Starting 3B | 8B

Bats R Age 22	Year	Lev	Team	AB	R	H	HR	RBI	Avg	OB	Sig	OPS	bb%	ct%	Eye	SB	CS	x/h%	Iso	RC/G
2015 (1) HS (MS)	2017	A+	Florida	306	43	77	12	47	252	304	408	712	7	76	0.31	0	2	30	157	4.13
Pwr ++++	2017	AA	Mississippi	178	28	56	8	27	315	384	511	895	10	72	0.40	2	0	32	197	6.86
BAvg +++	2018	Rk	GCL Braves	18	3	5	1	3	278	381	611	992	14	67	0.50	0	0	80	333	8.97
Spd ++	2018	AA	Mississippi	99	17	33	6	20	333	383	677	1060	7	72	0.29	0	0	58	343	9.15
Def +++	2018	AAA	Gwinnett	291	41	82	12	47	282	341	464	805	8	67	0.27	1	0	35	182	5.72

Powerful, strong-bodied 3B is on the cusp of his MLB debut. Has continued to lean up physique, quieting some bad body comps. Advanced approach. Worked on being more aggressive early in the count. Compact swing geared towards fly ball contact. Plus power is no longer just pull-oriented; 25-30 HR at maturity. Average defender with a strong arm at 3B.

Rincon,Carlos

789 | Los Angeles (N) | EXP MLB DEBUT: 2021 | H/W: 6-3 190 | FUT: Starting OF | 8E

Bats R Age 21	Year	Lev	Team	AB	R	H	HR	RBI	Avg	OB	Sig	OPS	bb%	ct%	Eye	SB	CS	x/h%	Iso	RC/G
2015 FA (DR)	2016	Rk	AZL Dodgers	103	13	31	7	23	301	314	621	936	2	71	0.07	0	2	52	320	7.08
Pwr ++++	2017	Rk	Ogden	51	8	14	3	13	275	288	529	818	2	69	0.06	0	0	50	255	5.54
BAvg +	2017	A	Great Lakes	334	41	66	18	48	198	268	404	672	9	57	0.22	6	1	48	207	4.15
Spd +++	2018	A	Great Lakes	288	28	65	7	33	226	322	358	680	12	68	0.45	5	1	34	132	4.10
Def +++	2018	A+	Rancho Cuca	110	36	36	15	35	327	413	818	1231	13	72	0.52	0	1	67	491	11.29

Athletic OF struggled to get on track at Low-A, but took off when moved up to the CAL. Plus raw power and all-or-nothing approach resulted in career-high 22 HR, but also 69% ct% and a.323 BABIP. Does draw walks, but needs to quiet his approach to have success. Average speed with enough arm for RF. High-risk/high-reward.

Rios,Edwin

3 | Los Angeles (N) | EXP MLB DEBUT: 2019 | H/W: 6-3 170 | FUT: Starting 1B | 7D

Bats L Age 24	Year	Lev	Team	AB	R	H	HR	RBI	Avg	OB	Sig	OPS	bb%	ct%	Eye	SB	CS	x/h%	Iso	RC/G
2015 (6) Florida Int'l	2016	A+	Rancho Cuca	177	37	65	16	46	367	395	712	1106	4	80	0.23	0	0	43	345	8.65
Pwr ++++	2016	AA	Tulsa	122	14	31	5	17	254	300	434	734	6	75	0.26	0	0	39	180	4.42
BAvg ++	2017	AA	Tulsa	306	47	97	15	62	317	353	533	886	5	77	0.25	1	1	37	216	6.24
Spd +	2017	AAA	Oklahoma City	169	23	50	9	29	296	364	533	896	10	75	0.43	0	1	44	237	6.71
Def +	2018	AAA	Oklahoma City	309	45	94	10	55	304	352	482	835	7	64	0.21	0	1	37	178	6.40

Massive hitter has above-average all-fields power, but an aggressive all-or-nothing approach and needs to make more contact. Does have good eye-hand coordination. Bottom of the scale runner and defender limits him to 1B or DH and he has to mash to stay relevant. So far, so good.

Rivas,Leonardo

6 | Los Angeles (A) | EXP MLB DEBUT: 2021 | H/W: 5-10 150 | FUT: Starting MIF | 7C

Bats B Age 21	Year	Lev	Team	AB	R	H	HR	RBI	Avg	OB	Sig	OPS	bb%	ct%	Eye	SB	CS	x/h%	Iso	RC/G
2014 FA (VZ)	2016	Rk	AZL Angels	91	22	23	1	4	253	364	341	705	15	82	1.00	6	3	26	88	4.66
Pwr +	2017	Rk	Orem	137	37	41	2	29	299	455	445	900	22	84	1.77	11	0	29	146	7.57
BAvg ++	2017	A	Burlington	90	24	24	0	7	267	400	322	722	18	76	0.91	8	1	21	56	5.03
Spd +++	2018	Rk	AZL Angels	8	2	2	1	3	250	250	750	1000	0	75	0.00	0	0	100	500	7.40
Def ++	2018	A	Burlington	454	62	106	4	34	233	353	326	679	16	70	0.61	16	10	25	93	4.28

Compact switch-hitting shortstop with a fluid work both at the plate and in the field. Able to work counts and draw walks with good plate discipline. Plus speed adds to his value as a stealing threat. Small frame not likely to generate much power. Light footwork and solid range should keep him as a sound middle infield asset.

Rivera,Emmanuel | 5 | Kansas City

EXP MLB DEBUT: 2020 | H/W: 6-2 195 | FUT: Reserve IF | 6C

Bats R Age 22
2015 (19) Univ Interamericana

- Pwr +++
- BAvg ++
- Spd ++
- Def ++

Year	Lev	Team	AB	R	H	HR	RBI	Avg	OB	Slg	OPS	bb%	ct%	Eye	SB	CS	x/h%	Iso	RC/G
2016	Rk	Burlington	217	25	54	2	27	249	315	373	688	9	80	0.48	7	3	35	124	4.16
2017	A	Lexington	464	60	144	12	72	310	354	468	821	6	81	0.36	8	10	31	157	5.53
2018	Rk	AZL Royals	26	4	5	0	2	192	222	269	491	4	77	0.17	0	0	20	77	1.38
2018	A+	Wilmington	375	45	105	6	61	280	332	427	758	7	84	0.49	3	2	35	147	4.91

Under-the-radar IF with solid ct% adjusted well to High-A. Physically mature, projects to CIF, despite lacking quickness or below-average reactions. Lots of length in swing and doesn't get to power potential in game, which is 100% pull-oriented when it shows up. Has chance if he can shorten swing.

Rivera,Laz | 46 | Chicago (A)

EXP MLB DEBUT: 2020 | H/W: 6-0 180 | FUT: Reserve IF | 6C

Bats R Age 24
2017 (28) Miami

- Pwr ++
- BAvg ++
- Spd +++
- Def +++

Year	Lev	Team	AB	R	H	HR	RBI	Avg	OB	Slg	OPS	bb%	ct%	Eye	SB	CS	x/h%	Iso	RC/G
2017	NCAA	U of Tampa	200	46	71	4	32	355	377	475	852	3	92	0.41	6	1	20	120	5.65
2017	Rk	AZL White Sox	186	37	55	2	24	296	325	446	771	4	86	0.31	3	4	35	151	4.92
2018	A	Kannapolis	237	42	82	6	24	346	362	502	864	2	80	0.13	7	3	28	156	5.83
2018	A+	Winston-Salem	225	38	63	7	37	280	302	458	760	3	80	0.16	10	7	38	178	4.59

Older, lower minor SS prospect struggled in Arizona Fall League assignment. Contact-oriented hitter, relying on bat-to-ball skills to make solid contact. Struggles chasing, resulting in weak contact. Compact swing geared towards gap power. Tops out at 10 HR power. Versatile defender, could be useful utility IF. Makes most of average run tool.

Rizzo,Joe | 5 | Seattle

EXP MLB DEBUT: 2020 | H/W: 5-9 194 | FUT: Reserve IF | 6C

Bats L Age 21
2016 (2) HS (NJ)

- Pwr ++
- BAvg ++
- Spd ++
- Def ++

Year	Lev	Team	AB	R	H	HR	RBI	Avg	OB	Slg	OPS	bb%	ct%	Eye	SB	CS	x/h%	Iso	RC/G
2016	Rk	AZL Mariners	148	21	43	2	21	291	364	392	756	10	76	0.47	2	1	23	101	5.02
2017	A	Clinton	410	47	104	7	50	254	353	346	699	13	72	0.56	3	1	23	93	4.38
2017	A+	Modesto	20	1	4	0	1	200	238	300	538	5	60	0.13	0	0	25	100	2.12
2018	A+	Modesto	461	46	111	4	55	241	301	321	622	8	77	0.37	6	1	24	80	3.17

Former 2nd rd pick has struggled offensively in three professional seasons. A patient hitter with a spray approach, struggles with hard contact rate. Raw above-average power has yet to show up in games. Doesn't use leverage in swing or lower half, depressing power potential. Defensively, not suited for regular work at any position. Below-average runner.

Robert,Luis | 8 | Chicago (A)

EXP MLB DEBUT: 2020 | H/W: 6-3 185 | FUT: Starting CF | 9E

Bats R Age 21
2017 FA (CU)

- Pwr ++++
- BAvg ++
- Spd ++++
- Def ++++

Year	Lev	Team	AB	R	H	HR	RBI	Avg	OB	Slg	OPS	bb%	ct%	Eye	SB	CS	x/h%	Iso	RC/G
2017		Did not play in the US																	
2018	Rk	AZL White Sox	18	5	7	0	2	389	389	611	1000	0	83	0.00	3	0	43	222	7.50
2018	A	Kannapolis	45	5	13	0	4	289	347	400	747	8	73	0.33	4	2	31	111	4.98
2018	A+	Winston-Salem	123	21	30	0	11	244	290	309	599	6	70	0.22	8	2	23	65	2.80

Muscular, athletic OF has a tool shed full of toys. Features plus bat speed and has improved his swing mechanics but struggles mightily with pitch recognition. Raw power is plus-plus, run tool is plus, so 20/20 seasons early on isn't far fetched. Should stick in CF to start, but may grow out of position later in career. Impact potential.

Robinson,Errol | 46 | Los Angeles (N)

EXP MLB DEBUT: 2020 | H/W: 5-11 170 | FUT: Utility player | 6C

Bats R Age 24
2016 (6) Mississippi

- Pwr +
- BAvg ++
- Spd ++++
- Def ++++

Year	Lev	Team	AB	R	H	HR	RBI	Avg	OB	Slg	OPS	bb%	ct%	Eye	SB	CS	x/h%	Iso	RC/G
2016	Rk	Ogden	220	40	62	2	26	282	333	395	729	7	81	0.40	18	2	32	114	4.55
2017	A	Great Lakes	77	13	19	3	13	247	301	455	756	7	73	0.29	6	1	47	208	4.87
2017	A+	Rancho Cuca	70	13	20	2	8	286	333	514	848	7	76	0.29	5	1	45	229	6.12
2017	AA	Tulsa	227	35	62	2	14	273	355	352	708	11	78	0.58	11	3	19	79	4.45
2018	AA	Tulsa	433	53	107	10	50	247	306	353	660	8	76	0.36	18	9	23	106	3.55

High-energy, glove first middle infielder struggled with the bat at Double-A. Plus range and good instincts with enough arm to stick at short and split time at 2B in 2018. Above-average to plus runner profiles as a top of the order hitter. Lack of bat speed and raw strength limit power upside and likely limit him to a utility role.

Robinson,Kristian | 8 | Arizona

EXP MLB DEBUT: 2022 | H/W: 6-3 190 | FUT: Starting OF | 8E

Bats R Age 18
2017 FA (BA)

- Pwr +++
- BAvg +++
- Spd ++++
- Def +++

Year	Lev	Team	AB	R	H	HR	RBI	Avg	OB	Slg	OPS	bb%	ct%	Eye	SB	CS	x/h%	Iso	RC/G
2018	Rk	AZL DBacks	162	35	44	4	31	272	337	414	751	9	72	0.35	7	5	34	142	4.92
2018	Rk	Missoula	60	13	18	3	10	300	408	467	875	15	65	0.52	5	3	22	167	7.10

Strong, high-waisted OF with raw tools a'plenty. Possesses quick-twitch athleticism that manifests in plus bat speed and raw power for future HR impact. Solid approach for age and shows quality bat-to-ball skills. Plus runner who can get down the line and projects to have SB value. Owns plus arm and range for either LF/RF.

Robles,Victor | 8 | Washington

EXP MLB DEBUT: 2017 | H/W: 6-0 185 | FUT: Starting CF | 9A

Bats R Age 21
2013 FA (DR)

- Pwr +++
- BAvg ++++
- Spd +++++
- Def ++++

Year	Lev	Team	AB	R	H	HR	RBI	Avg	OB	Slg	OPS	bb%	ct%	Eye	SB	CS	x/h%	Iso	RC/G
2017	MLB	Washington	24	2	6	0	4	250	250	458	708	0	75	0.00	0	1	50	208	4.24
2018	Rk	GCL Nationals	18	7	6	0	1	333	520	389	909	28	78	1.75	4	1	17	56	8.13
2018	A-	Auburn	16	0	3	0	3	188	235	188	423	6	88	0.50	1	0	0	0	0.98
2018	AAA	Syracuse	158	25	44	2	10	278	352	386	738	10	84	0.69	14	6	27	108	4.82
2018	MLB	Washington	59	8	17	3	10	288	333	525	859	6	80	0.33	3	2	41	237	5.94

Thumb injury derailed what was to be his breakout rookie MLB season. Came back with same insane bat speed, elite run tool, and outstanding CF defense as ever. Still growing into his power, but a chance for early-career monster BA/SB numbers. But the type of player who could go 20+ HR/30 SB in his peak seasons.

Robson,Jacob | 789 | Detroit

EXP MLB DEBUT: 2019 | H/W: 5-10 175 | FUT: Reserve OF | 7C

Bats L Age 24
2016 (8) Mississippi St

- Pwr ++
- BAvg ++
- Spd +++
- Def +

Year	Lev	Team	AB	R	H	HR	RBI	Avg	OB	Slg	OPS	bb%	ct%	Eye	SB	CS	x/h%	Iso	RC/G
2016	A-	Connecticut	76	14	25	1	6	329	440	461	900	16	74	0.75	1	2	28	132	7.42
2017	A	West Michigan	228	38	75	1	27	329	409	395	804	12	74	0.53	5	9	16	66	5.82
2017	A+	Lakeland	224	27	62	2	18	277	344	388	733	9	74	0.39	16	9	27	112	4.75
2018	AA	Erie	262	46	75	7	32	286	379	450	829	13	70	0.50	11	4	35	164	6.28
2018	AAA	Toledo	220	36	67	4	15	305	370	427	798	9	72	0.37	7	6	27	123	5.62

Outfielder with ability to make tools look bigger than they are through gritty style of play. Compact frame will prevent him from producing much power, but has improved in plate discipline and maximizes ability to use the whole field. Above-average runner with sub-par arm, complemented by solid defensive instincts.

Rocchio,Bryan | 6 | Cleveland

EXP MLB DEBUT: 2023 | H/W: 5-10 150 | FUT: Starting SS | 8D

Bats S Age 18
2018 FA (VZ)

- Pwr ++
- BAvg ++++
- Spd ++++
- Def ++++

Year	Lev	Team	AB	R	H	HR	RBI	Avg	OB	Slg	OPS	bb%	ct%	Eye	SB	CS	x/h%	Iso	RC/G
2018		Did not play																	

A very polished player for his age, both at the plate and in the field. With the bat, he has a disciplined approach and a contact-oriented swing that should allow him to post high OBPs. In the field he has good hands and instincts that give him a good chance to stay at SS.

Rodgers,Brendan | 645 | Colorado

EXP MLB DEBUT: 2019 | H/W: 6-0 180 | FUT: Starting SS | 9C

Bats R Age 22
2015 (1) HS (FL)

- Pwr ++++
- BAvg ++++
- Spd +++
- Def +++

Year	Lev	Team	AB	R	H	HR	RBI	Avg	OB	Slg	OPS	bb%	ct%	Eye	SB	CS	x/h%	Iso	RC/G
2016	A	Asheville	442	73	124	19	73	281	333	480	813	7	78	0.36	6	3	40	199	5.46
2017	A+	Lancaster	222	44	86	12	47	387	404	671	1075	3	84	0.17	2	1	42	284	8.17
2017	AA	Hartford	150	20	39	6	17	260	297	413	711	5	76	0.22	0	2	28	153	3.99
2018	AA	Hartford	357	49	98	17	62	275	331	493	824	8	79	0.39	12	3	43	218	5.60
2018	AAA	Albuquerque	69	5	16	0	5	232	243	290	533	1	77	0.06	0	0	25	58	1.73

Top-shelf prospect has exciting raw tools, but can't stay healthy. Solid campaign at AA was derailed by a hamstring injury that limited him to 19 G at AAA. Plus hit tool and power and split time between SS, 2B, 3B. Overly aggressive at the plate, but bat-to-ball skills are good and BA could tick up if he becomes more selective.

Rodriguez,Alfredo | 6 | Cincinnati

EXP MLB DEBUT: 2020 | H/W: 6-0 190 | FUT: Reserve SS | 6C

Bats R Age 24
2016 FA (CU)

- Pwr +
- BAvg ++
- Spd +++
- Def ++++

Year	Lev	Team	AB	R	H	HR	RBI	Avg	OB	Slg	OPS	bb%	ct%	Eye	SB	CS	x/h%	Iso	RC/G
2017		Did not play in the US																	
2017	A+	Daytona	483	52	122	2	36	253	289	294	583	5	84	0.32	11	9	13	41	2.63
2018	Rk	AZL Reds	20	3	5	0	3	250	286	400	686	5	85	0.33	0	0	60	150	4.08
2018	A+	Daytona	111	12	23	2	12	207	261	324	585	7	80	0.36	4	0	35	117	2.68
2018	AA	Pensacola	26	4	5	0	0	192	250	192	442	7	73	0.29	0	0	0	0	0.60

Defensively sound, Cuban import continues to struggle with bat as he made it up to Double-A in 2018. Lots of moving parts in swing takes awhile to get going. Solid hand/eye lends self to high ct%. Struggles getting bat head quick enough to hit position, resulting in lots of soft contact. Power is limited. An average runner on his best days.

Rodriguez, Carlos — 8 — Milwaukee

EXP MLB DEBUT: 2022 H/W: 5-10 150 FUT: Starting OF **9E**

Bats L Age 18
2017 FA (VZ)

	Pwr	++
	BAvg	+++
	Spd	++++
	Def	++++

Year	Lev	Team	AB	R	H	HR	RBI	Avg	OB	Slg	OPS	bb%	ct%	Eye	SB	CS	x/h%	Iso	RC/G
2018	Rk	AZL Brewers	20	4	7	0	1	350	409	350	759	9	95	2.00	2	1	0	0	5.16
2018	Rk	DSL Brewers	217	38	70	2	32	323	344	419	763	3	91	0.37	12	8	23	97	4.74

Toolsy Venezuelan OF with chance for impact in several categories. Makes easy contact from the left side with smooth, level stroke through the zone. Chance for more raw power as he fills out this thin frame. Is a plus runner who should have moderate SB impact and ability to play an above-average CF everyday.

Rodriguez, Johnathan — 789 — Cleveland

EXP MLB DEBUT: 2023 H/W: 6-3 180 FUT: Starting OF **8E**

Bats B Age 19
2017 (3) HS (PR)

	Pwr	++++
	BAvg	++
	Spd	+++
	Def	+++

Year	Lev	Team	AB	R	H	HR	RBI	Avg	OB	Slg	OPS	bb%	ct%	Eye	SB	CS	x/h%	Iso	RC/G
2017	Rk	AZL Indians	96	13	24	0	11	250	385	333	718	18	76	0.91	0	1	25	83	5.00
2018	Rk	AZL Indians	187	36	55	1	22	294	368	406	775	11	76	0.50	8	3	27	112	5.38

A raw toolsy outfielder, his calling card is his power potential. To date it is still more raw strength than game power. Encouragingly for someone of his profile he has shown a decent approach at the plate in two short seasons so far. Strong arm, projects as a right fielder.

Rodriguez, Julio — 9 — Seattle

EXP MLB DEBUT: 2021 H/W: 6-3 180 FUT: Starting OF **9E**

Bats R Age 18
2018 FA (DR)

	Pwr	++++
	BAvg	+++
	Spd	+++
	Def	+++

Year	Lev	Team	AB	R	H	HR	RBI	Avg	OB	Slg	OPS	bb%	ct%	Eye	SB	CS	x/h%	Iso	RC/G
2017		Did not play in the US																	
2018	Rk	DSL Mariners	219	50	69	5	36	315	398	525	923	12	82	0.75	10	0	39	210	7.26

Toolsy, power-hitting 2017 international prospect had big season in pro debut. Tantalizing power potential with solid bat-to-ball skills. Above-average hit tool plays up due to advanced patience at plate. Raw plus-plus power potential. Can grow into significant power in frame. RF profile with arm.

Roederer, Cole — 8 — Chicago (N)

EXP MLB DEBUT: 2022 H/W: 6-0 175 FUT: Starting CF **8D**

Bats L Age 19
2018 (2) HS (CA)

	Pwr	+++
	BAvg	+++
	Spd	+++
	Def	+++

Year	Lev	Team	AB	R	H	HR	RBI	Avg	OB	Slg	OPS	bb%	ct%	Eye	SB	CS	x/h%	Iso	RC/G
2018	Rk	AZL Cubs 2	142	30	39	5	24	275	356	465	821	11	74	0.49	13	4	33	190	5.92

Advanced prep hitter fell out of round one due to shoulder injury. Above-average tools across the board highlighted by an advanced hit tool and the potential for 20 HR power. Shows good bat speed and barrels balls consistently. Above-average speed plays well and should allow him to stick in CF. Underrated prospect who fared well in his pro debut.

Rogers, Jake — 2 — Detroit

EXP MLB DEBUT: 2020 H/W: 6-2 185 FUT: Starting C **8D**

Bats R Age 23
2016 (3) Tulane

	Pwr	++
	BAvg	+
	Spd	+
	Def	+++

Year	Lev	Team	AB	R	H	HR	RBI	Avg	OB	Slg	OPS	bb%	ct%	Eye	SB	CS	x/h%	Iso	RC/G
2016	A	Quad Cities	72	7	15	1	4	208	288	319	607	10	65	0.32	1	0	33	111	3.05
2017	A	Quad Cities	102	17	26	6	15	255	315	520	835	8	73	0.32	1	0	54	265	5.90
2017	A+	Lakeland	7	0	1	0	0	143	250	143	393	13	71	0.50	0	0	0	0	0.02
2017	A+	Buies Creek	313	43	83	12	55	265	356	457	813	12	77	0.61	13	8	40	192	5.77
2018	AA	Erie	352	57	77	17	56	219	300	412	712	10	68	0.37	7	1	43	193	4.36

The top defensive catcher in his 2016 draft class, he has come as advertised behind the plate. Filled defensive need for Detroit's farm with accurate arm and advanced receiving and framing skills. Flashed power at the plate, but hit tool still lags behind. Can use all fields with good swing path, but lacks contact.

Rooker, Brent — 37 — Minnesota

EXP MLB DEBUT: 2019 H/W: 6-3 210 FUT: Starting OF **8C**

Bats R Age 24
2017 (1) Mississippi St

	Pwr	++++
	BAvg	++
	Spd	++
	Def	+

Year	Lev	Team	AB	R	H	HR	RBI	Avg	OB	Slg	OPS	bb%	ct%	Eye	SB	CS	x/h%	Iso	RC/G
2017	NCAA	Mississippi St	248	60	96	23	82	387	486	810	1297	16	77	0.83	18	5	58	423	12.28
2017	Rk	Elizabethton	85	19	24	7	17	282	365	588	953	11	75	0.52	2	2	50	306	7.39
2017	A+	Fort Myers	143	23	40	11	35	280	352	552	905	10	67	0.34	0	0	43	273	7.08
2018	AA	Chattanooga	503	72	128	22	79	254	329	465	794	10	70	0.37	6	1	45	211	5.56

A slugger who is close to physical projection, he made the jump to Double-A. Swing mechanics geared towards fly-ball contact; shows plus in-game power, but is mostly pull-oriented. Can get beat by hard stuff up; breakers down and away. Not much of a runner but always hustling. He's a liability defensively, especially at 1B.

Rortvedt, Ben — 2 — Minnesota

EXP MLB DEBUT: 2021 H/W: 5-10 190 FUT: Starting C **7C**

Bats L Age 21
2016 (2) HS (WI)

	Pwr	++
	BAvg	+++
	Spd	++
	Def	++++

Year	Lev	Team	AB	R	H	HR	RBI	Avg	OB	Slg	OPS	bb%	ct%	Eye	SB	CS	x/h%	Iso	RC/G
2016	Rk	GCL Twins	59	3	12	0	3	203	266	254	520	8	86	0.63	0	0	25	51	2.23
2016	Rk	Elizabethton	40	2	10	0	7	250	333	250	583	11	95	2.50	0	0	0	0	3.46
2017	A	Cedar Rapids	308	33	69	4	30	224	276	315	591	7	81	0.37	1	0	29	91	2.75
2018	A	Cedar Rapids	145	14	40	1	16	276	323	386	709	6	76	0.29	1	0	30	110	4.28
2018	A+	Fort Myers	172	20	43	4	27	250	332	372	704	11	83	0.72	0	0	28	122	4.37

Defensive-oriented CA made strides offensively in 2018. Short, compact LH swing geared towards line drive contact. Spray hitter who works counts, XBHs mostly to CF and LF. Completely pull-heavy below-average HR power. Around 10 HRs at projection. Likely MLB CA; hit tool will determine role.

Rosario, Eguy — 4 — San Diego

EXP MLB DEBUT: 2020 H/W: 5-9 150 FUT: Utility player **7D**

Bats R Age 19
2015 FA (DR)

	Pwr	++
	BAvg	++
	Spd	+++
	Def	+++

Year	Lev	Team	AB	R	H	HR	RBI	Avg	OB	Slg	OPS	bb%	ct%	Eye	SB	CS	x/h%	Iso	RC/G
2017	Rk	AZL Padres 2	206	36	58	1	33	282	357	422	779	10	79	0.56	16	7	34	141	5.45
2017	A	Fort Wayne	180	15	37	0	13	206	285	278	563	10	72	0.39	17	5	30	72	2.47
2018	A+	Lake Elsinore	457	60	109	9	45	239	297	363	660	8	74	0.32	9	8	35	125	3.61
2018	AA	San Antonio	11	2	2	0	2	182	308	182	490	15	55	0.40	1	0	0	0	1.23

Strong, compact INF who was one of the youngest hitters in the CAL. Employs a short, compact stroke that produces GB/LD contact to all fields. Aggressive at plate and attacks fastballs; will need to shore up ct% vs. quality off-speed. Has bulked up and projects to be fringe runner. Solid glove for 2B and just enough arm for 3B.

Rosario, Jeisson — 8 — San Diego

EXP MLB DEBUT: 2020 H/W: 6-1 175 FUT: Starting OF **8C**

Bats L Age 19
2016 FA (DR)

	Pwr	++
	BAvg	++++
	Spd	+++
	Def	+++

Year	Lev	Team	AB	R	H	HR	RBI	Avg	OB	Slg	OPS	bb%	ct%	Eye	SB	CS	x/h%	Iso	RC/G
2017	Rk	AZL Padres	187	31	56	1	24	299	405	369	774	15	81	0.92	8	6	20	70	5.53
2018	A	Fort Wayne	436	79	118	3	34	271	367	353	720	13	75	0.61	18	12	21	83	4.72

Athletic, pure-hitting OF who is well rounded in all facets of the game. Has selective approach and hunts pitches he can drive. Smooth, level LH stroke lends itself to above-average ct% in all four quadrants of zone. Hands are quiet and doesn't get ideal separation for raw power; potentially more as he muscles up. Plus defender in CF with a strong arm.

Ruiz, Esteury — 4 — San Diego

EXP MLB DEBUT: 2021 H/W: 6-0 150 FUT: Starting OF **9E**

Bats R Age 20
2015 FA (DR)

	Pwr	+++
	BAvg	++
	Spd	++++
	Def	+++

Year	Lev	Team	AB	R	H	HR	RBI	Avg	OB	Slg	OPS	bb%	ct%	Eye	SB	CS	x/h%	Iso	RC/G
2017	Rk	AZL Padres	120	23	36	1	16	300	349	475	824	7	72	0.26	17	6	42	175	6.07
2017	Rk	AZL Royals	86	12	36	3	23	419	444	779	1224	4	77	0.20	4	5	53	360	10.94
2018	A	Fort Wayne	439	63	111	9	53	253	312	403	716	8	68	0.27	49	11	33	150	4.47

Lean, ultra-athletic IF who flaunted power/speed potential in MWL. Combines plus bat speed with natural loft for plus raw power. Employs deep hand load and swing has some effort to it, leading to subpar ct% and poor pitch recognition. Aggressive baserunner who busts down the line and is fluid runner underway; will be SB source as everyday player.

Ruiz, Keibert — 2 — Los Angeles (N)

EXP MLB DEBUT: 2020 H/W: 6-0 165 FUT: Starting C **8B**

Bats B Age 20
2014 FA (VZ)

	Pwr	++
	BAvg	+++
	Spd	++
	Def	++

Year	Lev	Team	AB	R	H	HR	RBI	Avg	OB	Slg	OPS	bb%	ct%	Eye	SB	CS	x/h%	Iso	RC/G
2016	Rk	Ogden	189	28	67	2	33	354	393	503	896	6	88	0.52	0	0	33	148	6.45
2016	Rk	AZL Dodgers	33	5	16	0	15	485	528	667	1194	8	88	0.75	0	0	31	182	10.14
2017	A	Great Lakes	227	34	72	2	24	317	367	423	790	7	87	0.60	0	0	26	106	5.30
2017	A+	Rancho Cuca	149	24	47	6	27	315	346	497	843	4	85	0.30	0	0	30	181	5.56
2018	AA	Tulsa	377	44	101	12	47	268	315	401	716	6	91	0.79	0	1	26	133	4.35

Switch-hitting backstop put up solid numbers at AA and now owns a career .309/.357/.441 slash line. Good plate discipline and line-drive approach should result in BA, but limits power upside. Smooth actions behind the plate with good receiving and framing skills and a strong, accurate arm. Has all the tools to be an impact backstop.

Rutherford, Blake — 9 — Chicago (A)

EXP MLB DEBUT: 2020 | H/W: 6-3 195 | FUT: Starting OF | 8C
Bats L | Age 21 | 2016 (1) HS (CA)
Pwr +++ | BAvg +++ | Spd +++ | Def +++

Year	Lev	Team	AB	R	H	HR	RBI	Avg	OB	Slg	OPS	bb%	ct%	Eye	SB	CS	x/h%	Iso	RC/G
2016	Rk	Pulaski	89	13	34	2	9	382	439	618	1057	9	73	0.38	0	2	38	236	9.27
2017	A	Charleston (Sc)	274	41	77	2	30	281	341	391	732	8	80	0.45	9	4	31	109	4.66
2017	A	Kannapolis	122	11	26	0	5	213	289	254	543	10	83	0.62	1	0	19	41	2.43
2018	A+	Winston-Salem	447	67	131	7	78	293	343	436	779	7	80	0.38	15	8	31	143	5.15

Divisive contact-oriented OF prospect had his best offensive season in 2018. Short, compact swing finds the barrel with ease. Wrists are quick enough to allow pitches to travel deep. Plus raw power in BP; in games, will occasionally sell out to his pull side. Likely 15-20 HR at projection if swing can generate more loft. 5-10 SB potential.

Sananta, Cristian — 35 — Los Angeles (N)

EXP MLB DEBUT: 2021 | H/W: 6-2 175 | FUT: Starting 3B | 7C
Bats R | Age 22 | 2013 FA (DR)
Pwr +++ | BAvg ++ | Spd ++ | Def +++

Year	Lev	Team	AB	R	H	HR	RBI	Avg	OB	Slg	OPS	bb%	ct%	Eye	SB	CS	x/h%	Iso	RC/G
2016	Rk	AZL Dodgers	172	26	44	8	24	256	277	453	730	3	73	0.11	0	1	36	198	4.20
2017	Rk	Ogden	41	18	22	5	16	537	596	1000	1596	13	85	1.00	0	0	36	463	14.74
2017	A	Great Lakes	174	18	56	5	25	322	341	460	801	3	76	0.12	0	1	25	138	5.08
2018	A+	Rancho Cuca	548	75	150	24	109	274	299	447	746	4	74	0.14	2	2	31	173	4.40

Offensive-minded player had a solid campaign, including career high in HR. Aggressive approach as he hunts for balls he can crush results in contact issues. Hands start high with a lot of motion and swing is all or nothing, but ball jumps when he does make contact. Moves well on D with good hands and a plus arm to stick at 3B.

Sanchez, Ali — 2 — New York (N)

EXP MLB DEBUT: 2022 | H/W: 6-0 175 | FUT: Reserve C | 6C
Bats R | Age 22 | 2013 FA (VZ)
Pwr ++ | BAvg ++ | Spd + (4.60) | Def +++

Year	Lev	Team	AB	R	H	HR	RBI	Avg	OB	Slg	OPS	bb%	ct%	Eye	SB	CS	x/h%	Iso	RC/G
2015	Rk	GCL Mets	162	20	45	0	17	278	328	315	642	7	84	0.46	2	0	13	37	3.48
2016	A-	Brooklyn	171	15	37	0	11	216	260	275	535	6	85	0.38	2	0	27	58	2.21
2017	A	Columbia	182	20	42	1	15	231	282	264	546	7	86	0.50	2	3	10	33	2.34
2018	A	Columbia	193	26	50	4	22	259	296	389	684	5	88	0.43	1	1	32	130	3.91
2018	A+	St. Lucie	135	11	37	2	16	274	300	385	685	4	89	0.33	1	1	30	111	3.86

Slow-bodied CA who knows how to play the game but is limited by a lack of life in his bat and body. Some length to his natural inside-out swing, but does show a feel for using the whole field, so may be able to become a tough enough out to be a backup. Defense is solid, even though does not have the quickest feet.

Sanchez, Jesus — 9 — Tampa Bay

EXP MLB DEBUT: 2020 | H/W: 6-3 210 | FUT: Starting OF | 8B
Bats L | Age 21 | 2014 FA (DR)
Pwr +++ | BAvg +++ | Spd +++ | Def +++

Year	Lev	Team	AB	R	H	HR	RBI	Avg	OB	Slg	OPS	bb%	ct%	Eye	SB	CS	x/h%	Iso	RC/G
2016	Rk	Princeton	49	8	17	3	8	347	385	612	997	6	76	0.25	1	0	41	265	7.76
2016	Rk	GCL Rays	164	25	53	4	31	323	347	530	878	4	81	0.19	1	0	34	207	6.15
2017	A	Bowling Green	475	81	145	15	82	305	349	478	827	6	81	0.35	7	2	33	173	5.59
2018	A+	Charlotte	359	56	108	10	64	301	329	462	791	4	80	0.21	6	3	33	162	5.03
2018	AA	Montgomery	98	14	21	1	11	214	294	327	620	10	79	0.52	1	1	43	112	3.31

Muscular, athletic OF with above-average tools across the board. Aggressive hitter with super quick wrists and strong forearms. Struggles expanding the zone, especially against spin. Plus bat-to-ball skills allow bat to find barrel, even on otherwise unhittable pitches. Plus raw power, likely above-average at projection. Profiles in RF.

Sanchez, Jose — 6 — Washington

EXP MLB DEBUT: 2023 | H/W: 5-11 155 | FUT: Starting SS | 7D
Bats R | Age 18 | 2016 FA (VZ)
Pwr + | BAvg ++ | Spd ++ | Def ++++

Year	Lev	Team	AB	R	H	HR	RBI	Avg	OB	Slg	OPS	bb%	ct%	Eye	SB	CS	x/h%	Iso	RC/G
2017	Rk	GCL Nationals	158	22	33	1	20	209	273	247	520	8	84	0.54	0	2	12	38	2.04
2018	A-	Auburn	209	20	48	0	23	230	309	282	591	10	73	0.43	1	0	21	53	2.86

Smooth on defense and good around the bag, he has shortstop actions. Small frame but not tiny; has more feel for contact than expected from a teenager. Good approach with pitch recognition and good bat control; will take walks and has a line drive swing. Power is limited due to lack of strength currently. Quick, but not a base-stealer.

Sanchez, Lolo — 8 — Pittsburgh

EXP MLB DEBUT: 2022 | H/W: 6-0 150 | FUT: Reserve OF | 6D
Bats R | Age 19 | 2015 FA (DR)
Pwr + | BAvg ++ | Spd ++++ (4.15) | Def +++

Year	Lev	Team	AB	R	H	HR	RBI	Avg	OB	Slg	OPS	bb%	ct%	Eye	SB	CS	x/h%	Iso	RC/G
2017	Rk	GCL Pirates	204	42	58	4	20	284	351	417	768	9	91	1.11	14	7	29	132	5.20
2018	A	West Virginia	378	57	92	4	34	243	317	328	645	10	81	0.57	30	13	25	85	3.61

Small CF who had a disappointing season with the bat at Low A. Should be called "Low load" because his low hand position to start his swing was a big part of his problem. Should be able to solve that some, but the bat will probably never be enough for him to be a regular. Should run and field well enough to have MLB backup value down the line.

Sanquintin, Junior — 6 — Cleveland

EXP MLB DEBUT: 2023 | H/W: 6-0 182 | FUT: Starting MIF | 7E
Bats B | Age 17 | 2018 FA (DR)
Pwr +++ | BAvg +++ | Spd +++ | Def ++

Year	Lev	Team
2018		Did not play in U.S.

Switch-hitting middle infielder with an aggressive, but controlled stroke from both sides of the plate. Employs a big leg kick that allows him to transfer his weight well in his swing and allows for a plus power projection. Can be overaggressive at times, but that is very common at his age.

Santana, Luis — 4 — New York (N)

EXP MLB DEBUT: 2022 | H/W: 5-9 165 | FUT: Starting 2B | 7D
Bats R | Age 19 | 2016 FA (DR)
Pwr ++ | BAvg +++ | Spd ++ | Def ++

Year	Lev	Team	AB	R	H	HR	RBI	Avg	OB	Slg	OPS	bb%	ct%	Eye	SB	CS	x/h%	Iso	RC/G
2018	Rk	Kingsport	204	34	71	3	35	348	424	471	895	12	89	1.17	8	3	24	123	6.75

Think a shorter Dilson Herrera here, or dream and it's Jose Altuve. Stocky 2B who can hit and hit for power some, but other tools are limited. Has torn it up at the lowest levels, but has yet to play full-season baseball. Remains to be seen if his huge, sometimes off balance swing can play at higher levels, but has shown a good eye so far.

Schales, Brian — 45 — Minnesota

EXP MLB DEBUT: 2019 | H/W: 6-1 185 | FUT: Reserve IF | 6C
Bats R | Age 23 | 2014 (4) HS (CA)
Pwr ++ | BAvg ++ | Spd +++ | Def +++

Year	Lev	Team	AB	R	H	HR	RBI	Avg	OB	Slg	OPS	bb%	ct%	Eye	SB	CS	x/h%	Iso	RC/G
2014	Rk	GCL Marlins	173	24	42	1	23	243	307	306	613	8	84	0.57	2	5	21	64	3.22
2015	A	Greensboro	443	59	115	4	45	260	318	348	666	8	83	0.50	3	2	24	88	3.80
2016	A+	Jupiter	371	38	72	0	16	194	273	224	496	10	79	0.52	3	1	14	30	1.70
2017	A+	Jupiter	367	41	92	6	42	251	323	351	674	10	74	0.41	0	4	24	101	3.88
2018	AA	Jacksonville	422	52	109	10	49	258	347	403	749	12	74	0.53	4	2	36	145	5.00

Contact-oriented IF acquired in off-season trade with MIA. Had best season as pro in Double-A. Patient hitter, understands zone. Average swing speed and with line-drive plane. Gap-to-gap approach has become pull-dominant, leading to career high 10 HR. Below average hit and power projection. Works at 2B and 3B, could add OF. Super-utility type ceiling.

Schnell, Nick — 89 — Tampa Bay

EXP MLB DEBUT: 2022 | H/W: 6-3 180 | FUT: Starting CF | 8E
Bats L | Age 19 | 2018 (1) HS (IN)
Pwr +++ | BAvg +++ | Spd ++++ | Def ++++

Year	Lev	Team	AB	R	H	HR	RBI	Avg	OB	Slg	OPS	bb%	ct%	Eye	SB	CS	x/h%	Iso	RC/G
2018	Rk	GCL Rays	67	8	16	1	4	239	370	373	744	17	66	0.61	2	6	38	134	5.40

Toolsy, athletic OF emerged on prep scene after strong spring, leading to first round selection. Scouts fell in love with patient, all-fields approach. Does great job finding barrel with FB but struggles with spin and off-speed stuff. Body should grow into power. However, doesn't do well incorporating lower half. Plus run and defensive tools.

Schrock, Max — 4 — St. Louis

EXP MLB DEBUT: 2019 | H/W: 5-8 173 | FUT: Starting 2B | 7C
Bats L | Age 24 | 2015 (13) South Carolina
Pwr + | BAvg ++++ | Spd ++ | Def ++

Year	Lev	Team	AB	R	H	HR	RBI	Avg	OB	Slg	OPS	bb%	ct%	Eye	SB	CS	x/h%	Iso	RC/G
2016	A+	Stockton	9	0	1	0	0	111	111	111	222	0	100		0	0	0	0	-0.55
2016	A+	Potomac	232	30	79	5	29	341	365	453	818	4	91	0.41	7	2	20	112	5.28
2016	AA	Midland	23	3	9	0	3	391	391	435	826	0	100		1	1	11	43	5.26
2017	AA	Midland	417	55	134	7	46	321	373	422	795	8	90	0.81	4	2	20	101	5.33
2018	AAA	Memphis	417	41	104	4	42	249	290	331	621	5	91	0.67	10	5	25	82	3.37

Struggled in his Cards debut. Has some of the best bat-to-ball skills in the system and gets surprising pop from his small frame but is more of a gap-to-gap hitter and has just 21 career HR. Average range and a below-average arm limit him to 2B, but he is a career .305 hitter. Needs to draw more walks to compensate for the lack of power and speed.

Scott,Connor | 8 | Miami | EXP MLB DEBUT: 2022 | H/W: 6-4 180 | FUT: Starting CF | 9E

Bats L Age 19 — 2018 (1) HS (FL)
- Pwr +++
- BAvg +++
- Spd ++++
- Def ++++

Year	Lev	Team	AB	R	H	HR	RBI	Avg	OB	Slg	OPS	bb%	ct%	Eye	SB	CS	x/h%	Iso	RC/G
2018	Rk	GCL Marlins	103	15	23	0	8	223	316	311	627	12	72	0.48	8	5	22	87	3.47
2018	A	Greensboro	76	4	16	1	5	211	302	276	579	12	64	0.37	1	3	19	66	2.58

Speedy, athletic OF with a premium frame to add muscle and bulk. Advanced, patient approach with a solid swing plane and plus bat speed. Struggled against breaking pitches in pro debut. Raw plus power potential in swing and in frame, as he ads muscle. Speedy runner with raw instincts. Pitching is a fallback option if hit tools don't develop.

Seigler,Anthony | 2 | New York (A) | EXP MLB DEBUT: 2022 | H/W: 6-0 200 | FUT: Starting C | 8C

Bats B Age 19 — 2018 (1) HS (GA)
- Pwr +++
- BAvg +++
- Spd +++
- Def +++

Year	Lev	Team	AB	R	H	HR	RBI	Avg	OB	Slg	OPS	bb%	ct%	Eye	SB	CS	x/h%	Iso	RC/G
2018	Rk	Pulaski	43	4	9	0	5	209	333	233	566	16	88	1.60	0	0	11	23	3.25
2018	Rk	GCL Yankees W	36	7	12	1	4	333	429	472	901	14	81	0.86	0	0	25	139	6.99

Athletic, ambidextrous CA who is super athletic for position. Played all over as amateur, including as a switch-pitcher. Switch-hitter at the plate with advanced approach. Great ct% and bb% returns in debut. More explosive hitter from LH side, where he reaches average power.

Seise,Chris | 6 | Texas | EXP MLB DEBUT: 2022 | H/W: 6-2 175 | FUT: Starting SS | 8D

Bats R Age 20 — 2017 (1) HS (FL)
- Pwr +++
- BAvg +++
- Spd +++
- Def +++

Year	Lev	Team	AB	R	H	HR	RBI	Avg	OB	Slg	OPS	bb%	ct%	Eye	SB	CS	x/h%	Iso	RC/G
2017	Rk	AZL Rangers	116	23	39	3	27	336	384	509	893	7	74	0.30	5	0	28	172	6.71
2017	A-	Spokane	99	10	22	0	9	222	252	273	525	4	70	0.13	1	1	18	51	1.65
2018		Did not play - injury																	

Missed the entire 2018 due to right shoulder surgery, but should be ready for 2019. Athletic with quick actions, showed an advanced all-around game hit highlighted by and advanced hit tool. Some raw power, runs well, should stick at SS, though he'll need to prove himself again after the year off.

Senzel,Nick | 45 | Cincinnati | EXP MLB DEBUT: 2019 | H/W: 6-1 205 | FUT: Starting 3B | 9B

Bats R Age 23 — 2016 (1) Tennessee
- Pwr ++++
- BAvg ++++
- Spd +++
- Def ++++

Year	Lev	Team	AB	R	H	HR	RBI	Avg	OB	Slg	OPS	bb%	ct%	Eye	SB	CS	x/h%	Iso	RC/G
2016	Rk	Billings	33	3	5	0	4	152	282	182	464	15	85	1.20	3	0	20	30	1.84
2016	A	Dayton	210	38	69	7	36	329	417	567	984	13	77	0.65	15	7	48	238	8.22
2017	A+	Daytona	246	41	75	4	31	305	364	476	840	9	78	0.43	9	2	43	171	6.07
2017	AA	Pensacola	209	40	71	10	34	340	413	560	973	11	79	0.60	5	4	35	220	7.66
2018	AAA	Louisville	171	23	53	6	25	310	379	509	888	10	77	0.49	8	2	38	199	6.66

Athletic RH 3B has dealt with various injuries over past couple seasons. Does a little bit of everything at the plate. Short, compact swing generates hard contact to all fields with loft. 25-30 HR potential at maturity. A heady runner, gets most out of average run tool. 10-15 SB potential. Versatile defender with plus potential at 3B; also dabbled in OF in fall instructional league.

Severino,Yunior | 46 | Minnesota | EXP MLB DEBUT: 2022 | H/W: 6-1 180 | FUT: Starting 2B | 8E

Bats B Age 19 — 2016 FA (DR)
- Pwr ++++
- BAvg ++
- Spd ++
- Def +++

Year	Lev	Team	AB	R	H	HR	RBI	Avg	OB	Slg	OPS	bb%	ct%	Eye	SB	CS	x/h%	Iso	RC/G
2017	Rk	GCL Braves	189	27	54	3	27	286	341	444	786	8	68	0.26	0	1	41	159	5.64
2018	Rk	Elizabethton	198	32	52	8	28	263	321	424	745	8	74	0.33	0	1	31	162	4.62

Quick-twitch, toolsy switch-hitting 2B was picked up by MIN after ATL scouting scandal. Statistically, better from LH side, even with a pronounced hitch in load. Hitting mechanics and strength better from RH side. Lots of power in profile, still adding strength to his body. Fits best at 2B defensively. Not a base stealing threat.

Seymour,Anfernee | 9 | Miami | EXP MLB DEBUT: 2020 | H/W: 5-11 165 | FUT: Reserve OF | 6C

Bats R Age 23 — 2014 (7) HS (BM)
- Pwr +
- BAvg ++
- Spd +++++
- Def +++

Year	Lev	Team	AB	R	H	HR	RBI	Avg	OB	Slg	OPS	bb%	ct%	Eye	SB	CS	x/h%	Iso	RC/G
2017	A	Rome	108	17	31	0	6	287	330	352	682	6	80	0.32	8	3	19	65	3.90
2017	A+	Florida	307	45	86	1	18	280	340	358	699	8	71	0.31	17	17	21	78	4.28
2018	A+	Jupiter	288	34	74	3	30	257	303	389	692	6	74	0.25	20	7	35	132	4.08
2018	A+	Florida	87	7	17	0	6	195	247	287	535	6	68	0.21	4	2	41	92	1.97
2018	AA	Jacksonville	51	6	13	1	5	255	333	392	725	11	82	0.67	4	1	38	137	4.66

Speedy, athletic OF was acquired after outright release from ATL. Patient, switch-hitter with a spray, punch-and-Judy approach to better utilize plus-plus run tool. Little-to-no power in profile or swing. Will occasionally power up on middle-in FB. Has improved base-runner reads. 24 for 32 in SB attempts. Not afraid to press the action.

Shaw,Chris | 37 | San Francisco | EXP MLB DEBUT: 2018 | H/W: 6-3 229 | FUT: Starting OF | 7C

Bats L Age 25 — 2015 (1) Boston College
- Pwr ++++
- BAvg ++
- Spd +
- Def ++

Year	Lev	Team	AB	R	H	HR	RBI	Avg	OB	Slg	OPS	bb%	ct%	Eye	SB	CS	x/h%	Iso	RC/G
2016	AA	Richmond	232	26	57	5	30	246	306	414	719	8	76	0.36	0	0	44	168	4.46
2017	AA	Richmond	133	16	40	6	29	301	384	511	895	12	80	0.69	0	0	40	211	6.73
2017	AAA	Sacramento	336	42	97	18	50	289	329	530	858	6	68	0.19	0	0	45	241	6.32
2018	AAA	Sacramento	394	55	102	24	65	259	296	505	801	5	63	0.15	0	0	46	246	5.73
2018	MLB	SF Giants	54	2	10	1	7	185	279	278	556	11	57	0.30	1	0	30	93	2.33

Defensively-limited, power-hitting LF made MLB debut but ct% and bb% continues to dip. Sells out to power and struggles with breaking ball recognition. Pull-oriented on ground, will spray balls in the air. Big power in bat and frame. Has reached it but mostly pull-driven. Bad footwork at 1B and struggles in LF. Poor foot speed.

Sheets,Gavin | 3 | Chicago (A) | EXP MLB DEBUT: 2020 | H/W: 6-4 215 | FUT: Starting 1B | 7D

Bats L Age 22 — 2017 (2) Wake Forest
- Pwr +++
- BAvg +++
- Spd +
- Def +++

Year	Lev	Team	AB	R	H	HR	RBI	Avg	OB	Slg	OPS	bb%	ct%	Eye	SB	CS	x/h%	Iso	RC/G
2017	NCAA	Wake Forest	240	57	76	21	84	317	427	629	1056	16	85	1.24	1	0	42	313	8.65
2017	Rk	AZL White Sox	12	3	6	1	3	500	600	917	1517	20	100		0	0	50	417	13.90
2017	A	Kannapolis	192	16	51	3	25	266	335	365	699	9	82	0.59	0	0	25	99	4.25
2018	A+	Winston-Salem	437	58	128	6	61	293	368	407	775	11	81	0.64	1	0	28	114	5.29

1B-only prospect with solid hit and OBP skills has struggled to bring BP power to game. All-fields approach with line-drive stroke. Lives in deep counts, frustrating pitchers. Raw power in frame and BP. Struggles creating loft, depressing power. A base-clogger. Son of former OF Larry Sheets.

Short,Zack | 456 | Chicago (N) | EXP MLB DEBUT: 2019 | H/W: 5-9 155 | FUT: Utility player | 7C

Bats R Age 23 — 2016 (17) Sacred Heart
- Pwr +++
- BAvg ++
- Spd ++
- Def +++

Year	Lev	Team	AB	R	H	HR	RBI	Avg	OB	Slg	OPS	bb%	ct%	Eye	SB	CS	x/h%	Iso	RC/G
2016	Rk	AZL Cubs	44	12	14	0	8	318	483	386	869	24	80	1.56	5	1	21	68	7.36
2016	A-	Eugene	127	22	30	1	23	236	394	323	717	21	81	1.38	10	5	27	87	5.10
2017	A	South Bend	236	50	56	7	26	237	379	424	803	19	77	1.00	15	5	48	186	6.02
2017	A+	Myrtle Beach	232	34	61	6	21	263	371	414	785	15	78	0.80	3	5	33	151	5.58
2018	AA	Tennessee	436	68	99	17	59	227	349	417	767	16	69	0.60	8	3	47	190	5.43

Undersized athlete generates surprising bat speed and blasted a career best 17 HR at AA. Advanced understanding of strike zone and ability to make consistent, hard contact are best tools. Quickness, good hands, and versatility give him added value and profiles as a utility player with some pop down the road. Owns a career .380 OB%.

Siani,Mike | 8 | Cincinnati | EXP MLB DEBUT: 2022 | H/W: 6-1 180 | FUT: Starting CF | 8E

Bats L Age 19 — 2018 (4) HS (PA)
- Pwr ++
- BAvg +++
- Spd ++++
- Def ++++

Year	Lev	Team	AB	R	H	HR	RBI	Avg	OB	Slg	OPS	bb%	ct%	Eye	SB	CS	x/h%	Iso	RC/G
2018	Rk	Greeneville	184	24	53	2	13	288	345	386	731	8	81	0.46	6	4	21	98	4.58

Athletic, contact-hitting CF with 5-tool potential. Scrappy and instinctful, scouts rated his defense as potential plus-plus at maturity. A spray hitter, uses speed to grind out hits and cause havoc on bases. Power potential present, but swing trajectory built more for slap, not loft. Some doubt raw power ever reaches potential.

Siri,Jose | 8 | Cincinnati | EXP MLB DEBUT: 2020 | H/W: 6-2 175 | FUT: Starting OF | 8E

Bats R Age 23 — 2012 FA (DR)
- Pwr +++
- BAvg ++
- Spd ++++
- Def +++

Year	Lev	Team	AB	R	H	HR	RBI	Avg	OB	Slg	OPS	bb%	ct%	Eye	SB	CS	x/h%	Iso	RC/G
2016	Rk	Billings	241	52	77	10	35	320	341	560	902	3	73	0.12	17	4	39	241	6.66
2016	A	Dayton	83	5	12	0	3	145	165	181	345	2	59	0.06	3	2	25	36	-1.22
2017	A	Dayton	498	92	146	24	76	293	337	530	867	6	74	0.25	46	12	40	237	6.24
2018	A+	Daytona	119	15	31	1	9	261	285	395	680	3	73	0.13	9	1	39	134	3.80
2018	AA	Pensacola	253	42	58	12	34	229	296	474	770	9	64	0.26	14	5	50	245	5.48

Athletic, wiry OF whose contact rate declined significantly against Double-A competition. Swing mechanics fairly simple and trajectory geared for flyball contact. Struggles with a hitch in his load and inability to lay off off-speed pitches. Mostly pull power, but creates enough loft to get to power the other way. Does, though, have 20-SB potential.

Smith,Kevin — 56 — Toronto

EXP MLB DEBUT: 2022 | H/W: 6-0 172 | FUT: Starting SS | 8D

Bats R Age 22 — 2017 (4) Maryland

Pwr +++ | BAvg +++ | Spd +++ | Def +++

Year	Lev	Team	AB	R	H	HR	RBI	Avg	OB	Slg	OPS	bb%	ct%	Eye	SB	CS	x/h%	Iso	RC/G
2017	NCAA	Maryland	194	38	52	13	48	268	317	552	869	7	75	0.29	4	0	50	284	6.14
2017	Rk	Bluefield	262	43	71	8	43	271	313	466	779	6	73	0.23	9	0	48	195	5.15
2018	A	Lansing	183	36	65	7	44	355	410	639	1049	9	82	0.52	12	1	52	284	8.55
2018	A+	Dunedin	340	57	93	18	49	274	320	468	787	6	74	0.26	17	5	30	194	5.04

Hard nosed player used a revamped swing to launch a monster season. Short, powerful stroke and aggressive approach led to .302 BA with 25 HR/29 SB. Speed is just a tick above-average, but he picks his spots well. Solid range, arm, and instincts should allow him to stick at SS. Does have some swing-and-miss, but upside is legit.

Smith,Pavin — 3 — Arizona

EXP MLB DEBUT: 2020 | H/W: 6-2 210 | FUT: Starting 1B | 7B

Bats L Age 23 — 2017 (1) Virginia

Pwr ++ | BAvg ++++ | Spd ++ | Def +++

Year	Lev	Team	AB	R	H	HR	RBI	Avg	OB	Slg	OPS	bb%	ct%	Eye	SB	CS	x/h%	Iso	RC/G
2017	NCAA	Virginia	228	53	78	13	77	342	436	570	1006	14	95	3.17	2	0	32	228	8.05
2017	A-	Hillsboro	195	34	62	0	27	318	401	415	816	12	88	1.13	2	1	27	97	6.01
2018	A+	Visalia	439	63	112	11	54	255	341	392	733	11	85	0.88	3	2	33	137	4.79

Former collegiate standout 1B whose pro game is centered around high-volume contact and plate discipline. Smooth LH stroke lends itself to natural bat-to-skills and ability to spray balls to all fields. Works counts well and knows how to walk. Lacks leverage in swing for impact HR but will have average power output. Capable defender at 1B.

Smith,Will — 25 — Los Angeles (N)

EXP MLB DEBUT: 2019 | H/W: 6-0 178 | FUT: Starting C | 8D

Bats R Age 24 — 2016 (1) Louisville

Pwr +++ | BAvg ++ | Spd +++ | Def ++++

Year	Lev	Team	AB	R	H	HR	RBI	Avg	OB	Slg	OPS	bb%	ct%	Eye	SB	CS	x/h%	Iso	RC/G
2016	A+	Rancho Cuca	97	13	21	2	12	216	315	320	635	13	68	0.45	1	0	29	103	3.43
2017	A+	Rancho Cuca	250	38	58	11	43	232	331	448	779	13	72	0.52	6	2	50	216	5.42
2017	AA	Tulsa	1	0	0	0	0	0	0	0	0	0	0	0.00	1	0		0	
2018	AA	Tulsa	265	48	70	19	53	264	352	532	884	12	72	0.48	4	0	47	268	6.66
2018	AAA	Oklahoma City	87	9	12	1	6	138	202	218	421	7	57	0.19	1	0	42	80	0.03

Strong-bodied, athletic catcher has above-average raw power with a career-high HR at AA, but cratered when moved up to AAA. Aggressive approach at the plate does lead to swing-and-miss and a career .236 BA. Moves well behind the with a strong arm and quick release and nailed 38% of runners. Best defender in the system.

Solak,Nick — 478 — Tampa Bay

EXP MLB DEBUT: 2019 | H/W: 5-11 163 | FUT: Utility player | 7C

Bats R Age 24 — 2016 (2) Louisville

Pwr ++ | BAvg +++ | Spd ++++ | Def +++

Year	Lev	Team	AB	R	H	HR	RBI	Avg	OB	Slg	OPS	bb%	ct%	Eye	SB	CS	x/h%	Iso	RC/G
2016	NCAA	Louisville	165	49	62	5	29	376	466	564	1030	15	87	1.27	9	0	32	188	8.54
2016	A-	Staten Island	240	48	77	3	25	321	396	421	817	11	84	0.77	8	0	22	100	5.82
2017	A+	Tampa	346	56	104	10	44	301	393	460	853	13	78	0.70	13	4	30	159	6.38
2017	AA	Trenton	119	16	34	2	9	286	341	429	770	8	80	0.42	1	1	35	143	5.07
2018	AA	Montgomery	478	91	135	19	76	282	372	450	822	12	77	0.61	21	6	29	167	5.85

Speedy, Jack-of-all-trades prospect had solid Rays organization debut. Lean physique with surprising strength. Patient approach plays up pull-dominated approach. Struggles getting bat head out in front against higher velocities. Took advantage of short porch in LF for his HR total; likely closer to 10-15 HR at maturity. Plus runner.

Sosa,Edmundo — 456 — St. Louis

EXP MLB DEBUT: 2018 | H/W: 5-11 170 | FUT: Utility player | 6B

Bats R Age 23 — 2012 FA (PN)

Pwr + | BAvg +++ | Spd +++ | Def ++++

Year	Lev	Team	AB	R	H	HR	RBI	Avg	OB	Slg	OPS	bb%	ct%	Eye	SB	CS	x/h%	Iso	RC/G
2017	A+	Palm Beach	193	25	55	0	14	285	327	347	674	6	82	0.35	3	0	20	62	3.80
2017	AA	Springfield	4	0	0	0	0	0	200	0	200	20	100		0	0		0	0.30
2018	AA	Springfield	261	34	72	7	32	276	300	429	729	3	80	0.17	1	2	35	153	4.23
2018	AAA	Memphis	191	31	50	5	27	262	309	408	717	6	78	0.31	5	2	36	147	4.26
2018	MLB	St. Louis	2	1	0	0	0	0	333	0	333	33	50	1.00	0	0		0	-2.91

Slick fielding SS missed two months of action with a broken hamate bone. Quick bat and good contact skills but an aggressive approach and very little power limit his offensive upside, as shown by his career .361 SLG%. Moves well at short, but average arm saw him splitting time at 2B when he returned to action.

Soto,Carlos — 2 — St. Louis

EXP MLB DEBUT: 2023 | H/W: 6-2 220 | FUT: Starting C | 7D

Bats L Age 19 — 2016 FA (MX)

Pwr +++ | BAvg +++ | Spd ++ | Def ++

Year	Lev	Team	AB	R	H	HR	RBI	Avg	OB	Slg	OPS	bb%	ct%	Eye	SB	CS	x/h%	Iso	RC/G
2017	Rk	GCL Cardinals	113	11	27	0	12	239	306	257	563	9	82	0.55	0	0	7	18	2.57
2018	Rk	GCL Cardinals	40	7	8	3	10	200	289	475	764	11	78	0.56	0	0	63	275	4.85
2018	Rk	Johnson City	98	14	27	2	23	276	377	408	785	14	73	0.62	0	1	33	133	5.63

Big bodied international FA held his own in state-side debut. Uses slight leg kick to start swing with good balance and above-average bat speed. Shows above-average raw power, but will need to work hard on conditioning to stick behind the plate. Solid catch and throw skills, but below-average agility could move him to RF where he shows a plus arm.

Soto,Isael — 79 — Miami

EXP MLB DEBUT: 2021 | H/W: 6-0 190 | FUT: Starting OF | 7E

Bats L Age 22 — 2013 FA (DR)

Pwr ++++ | BAvg + | Spd ++ | Def +++

Year	Lev	Team	AB	R	H	HR	RBI	Avg	OB	Slg	OPS	bb%	ct%	Eye	SB	CS	x/h%	Iso	RC/G
2015	A-	Batavia	21	1	2	0	0	95	136	95	232	5	52	0.10	0	0	0	0	-3.48
2015	A	Greensboro	64	2	8	0	1	125	164	141	305	4	58	0.11	0	0	13	16	-1.96
2016	A	Greensboro	401	51	99	9	38	247	320	399	719	10	71	0.37	3	0	38	152	4.56
2017	A	Did not play - injured																	
2018	A	Greensboro	339	47	78	15	69	230	296	440	736	9	71	0.33	2	3	49	209	4.64

Quick-twitch, toolsy OF had woeful season returning from a broken foot and torn meniscus. Meniscus injury sapped physical tools. Still, peripheral stats support more left in tank. Continued patient approach and didn't lose ct% despite lacking explosiveness in lower half. Swing path change located additional power. Speed gone; below-average runner.

Soto,Livan — 6 — Los Angeles (A)

EXP MLB DEBUT: 2021 | H/W: 6-0 160 | FUT: Starting SS | 7B

Bats R Age 18 — 2016 FA (VZ)

Pwr + | BAvg ++ | Spd ++ | Def +++

Year	Lev	Team	AB	R	H	HR	RBI	Avg	OB	Slg	OPS	bb%	ct%	Eye	SB	CS	x/h%	Iso	RC/G
2017	Rk	GCL Braves	173	24	39	0	14	225	330	254	584	14	85	1.04	7	3	13	29	3.20
2018	Rk	Orem	172	31	50	0	11	291	378	349	726	12	86	1.00	9	3	20	58	4.89

Thin-framed shortstop acquired by the Angels through penalty implemented against the Braves. Little in the way of power, but body projects to add muscle and power should result in fringe-average. Has a sound swing path with strong instincts in managing the strike zone. Shines defensively with above-average speed and a plus arm.

Spanberger,Chad — 3 — Toronto

EXP MLB DEBUT: 2020 | H/W: 6-2 225 | FUT: Reserve 1B | 6B

Bats L Age 23 — 2017 (6) Arkansas

Pwr ++++ | BAvg ++ | Spd ++ | Def +

Year	Lev	Team	AB	R	H	HR	RBI	Avg	OB	Slg	OPS	bb%	ct%	Eye	SB	CS	x/h%	Iso	RC/G
2017	NCAA	Arkansas	239	54	73	20	67	305	374	619	993	10	73	0.40	2	0	47	314	7.97
2017	Rk	Grand Junction	235	49	69	19	51	294	366	617	983	10	70	0.38	2	0	52	323	8.11
2018	A	Lansing	36	6	10	2	6	278	297	500	797	3	83	0.17	1	0	30	222	4.87
2018	A	Asheville	349	65	110	22	75	315	352	579	931	5	77	0.24	16	4	41	264	6.82
2018	A+	Dunedin	78	8	18	3	9	231	348	372	720	15	78	0.82	0	0	28	141	4.61

Tall, physically mature player is a natural-born masher and came over as part of the S. Oh deal. Quick LH bat and raw strength led to a career-high 27 HR and an .893 OPS. Runs well for his size and swiped 17 bases, but below-average defense limits him to 1B. Struggles vs. LHP could limit him to a platoon role, but the bat should play.

Spillane,Bren — 39 — Cincinnati

EXP MLB DEBUT: 2021 | H/W: 6-4 210 | FUT: Starting 1B | 7D

Bats R Age 22 — 2018 (3) Illinois

Pwr ++++ | BAvg ++ | Spd ++ | Def ++

Year	Lev	Team	AB	R	H	HR	RBI	Avg	OB	Slg	OPS	bb%	ct%	Eye	SB	CS	x/h%	Iso	RC/G
2018	NCAA	Illinois	175	57	68	23	60	389	493	903	1396	17	67	0.63	16	0	62	514	14.63
2018	Rk	Billings	148	28	35	5	22	236	365	439	804	17	49	0.39	2	2	49	203	7.95

Slugging 1B/OF college junior slugged his way to 3rd round selection. Incredible length in swing causing a good share of swing and miss issues. Big power in frame and in swing trajectory. Uses leverage well to elevate fly balls, mostly from CF to the gaps. Big power only if he can make enough contact, which isn't likely. Below average runner.

Stafford,Deon — 2 — Pittsburgh

EXP MLB DEBUT: 2023 | H/W: 6-0 202 | FUT: Reserve C | 5B

Bats R Age 23 — 2017 (5) Saint Joseph's

Pwr ++ | BAvg ++ | 4.50 Spd + | Def +++

Year	Lev	Team	AB	R	H	HR	RBI	Avg	OB	Slg	OPS	bb%	ct%	Eye	SB	CS	x/h%	Iso	RC/G
2017	NCAA	Saint Joseph's	146	35	42	8	22	288	447	521	967	22	81	1.50	3	1	40	233	8.18
2017	A-	West Virginia	182	22	51	4	28	280	335	418	753	8	71	0.28	3	1	31	137	4.92
2018	A	West Virginia	344	60	87	11	49	253	309	433	742	8	71	0.28	0	3	40	180	4.75

Energectic, strong-bodied C who won't hit enough to be a regular. Defense should be good with time once improves accuracy of throws, and will buy him time to see if the bat can surprise.

Stallings,Jacob — 2 — Pittsburgh
EXP MLB DEBUT: 2016 | H/W: 6-5 200 | FUT: Reserve C | 6C

Bats R Age 29 | 2012 (7) North Carolina | Pwr + | BAvg ++ | 4.60 Spd + | Def ++++

Year	Lev	Team	AB	R	H	HR	RBI	Avg	OB	Slg	OPS	bb%	ct%	Eye	SB	CS	x/h%	Iso	RC/G
2016	MLB	Pittsburgh	15	0	6	0	2	400	400	467	867	0	73	0.00	1	0	17	67	5.96
2017	AAA	Indianapolis	216	35	65	4	38	301	352	431	782	7	86	0.57	1	2	31	130	5.16
2017	MLB	Pittsburgh	14	3	5	0	3	357	438	500	938	13	86	1.00	0	0	40	143	7.51
2018	AAA	Indianapolis	256	37	73	3	40	285	325	414	739	6	80	0.29	1	2	36	129	4.57
2018	MLB	Pittsburgh	37	2	8	0	5	216	275	216	491	8	76	0.33	0	0	0	0	1.35

The second coming of Chris Stewart. Has improved with bat enough that he probably won't kill your BA. But he cheats so much just to make solid contact that power and OBP are not coming. Plus defense, including top-notch arm, will get him ML backup time for a long time.

Stephenson,Tyler — 2 — Cincinnati
EXP MLB DEBUT: 2020 | H/W: 6-4 225 | FUT: Starting C | 8E

Bats R Age 22 | 2015 (1) HS (GA) | Pwr +++ | BAvg ++ | Spd + | Def +++

Year	Lev	Team	AB	R	H	HR	RBI	Avg	OB	Slg	OPS	bb%	ct%	Eye	SB	CS	x/h%	Iso	RC/G
2015	Rk	Billings	194	28	52	1	16	268	343	361	703	10	78	0.52	0	2	31	93	4.39
2016	Rk	AZL Reds	20	4	5	1	2	250	318	450	768	9	65	0.29	0	0	40	200	5.27
2016	A	Dayton	139	17	30	3	16	216	278	324	602	8	68	0.27	0	0	27	108	2.79
2017	A	Dayton	295	39	82	6	50	278	372	414	785	13	80	0.76	2	1	34	136	5.52
2018	A+	Daytona	388	60	97	11	59	250	328	392	720	10	75	0.46	1	0	33	142	4.48

Sturdy CA prospect with a solid offensive profile, made strides early with hard contact before faltering late. Has plus, all-fields power and simple swing mechanics geared for line-drive contact with loft, but relies too much on upper body strength. Swing can get stiff, and he struggles against premium velocity. No speed.

Stewart,Christin — 7 — Detroit
EXP MLB DEBUT: 2018 | H/W: 6-0 215 | FUT: Starting OF | 7B

Bats L Age 25 | 2015 (1) Tennessee | Pwr +++ | BAvg ++ | Spd + | Def +

Year	Lev	Team	AB	R	H	HR	RBI	Avg	OB	Slg	OPS	bb%	ct%	Eye	SB	CS	x/h%	Iso	RC/G
2017	AA	Erie	485	67	124	28	86	256	333	501	834	10	72	0.41	3	0	48	245	5.99
2018	Rk	GCL Tigers W	9	2	2	2	3	222	300	889	1189	10	100		0	0	100	667	8.94
2018	Rk	GCL Tigers	5	1	1	1	1	200	333	800	1133	17	100		0	0	100	600	8.92
2018	AAA	Toledo	444	69	117	23	77	264	360	480	840	13	76	0.62	0	0	40	216	6.10
2018	MLB	Detroit	60	7	16	2	10	267	371	417	788	14	78	0.77	0	0	25	150	5.53

Bat-first outfielder with the most impressive raw power in the organization. Early struggle with strikeouts, but his ct% has improved though is still below average. Works off pure power at the plate with an improving eye and ability to work counts. Sub-par left fielder who profiles as a future DH.

Stewart,DJ — 79 — Baltimore
EXP MLB DEBUT: 2018 | H/W: 6-0 215 | FUT: Reserve OF | 6B

Bats L Age 25 | 2015 (1) Florida St | Pwr ++ | BAvg ++ | Spd +++ | Def ++

Year	Lev	Team	AB	R	H	HR	RBI	Avg	OB	Slg	OPS	bb%	ct%	Eye	SB	CS	x/h%	Iso	RC/G
2016	A	Delmarva	213	27	49	4	25	230	357	352	709	16	73	0.72	16	6	35	122	4.67
2016	A+	Frederick	201	41	56	6	30	279	388	448	836	15	77	0.78	10	3	36	169	6.28
2017	AA	Bowie	457	80	127	21	79	278	368	481	849	12	81	0.75	20	4	39	204	6.15
2018	AAA	Norfolk	421	59	99	12	55	235	322	387	709	11	76	0.52	11	4	38	152	4.40
2018	MLB	Baltimore	40	8	10	3	10	250	318	550	868	9	70	0.33	2	1	60	300	6.42

Big-bodied, former 1st round pick made solid MLB debut. A patient hitter, struggles with consistent hard contact due to swing speed and elongation of swing. Raw-plus power hasn't translated to game due to struggles getting bat around on balls to drive. Will struggle against velocity. A solid runner. 10-15 SB potential contingent on playing time.

Stokes Jr.,Troy — 79 — Milwaukee
EXP MLB DEBUT: 2019 | H/W: 5-8 182 | FUT: Starting OF | 7B

Bats R Age 23 | 2014 (4) HS (MD) | Pwr +++ | BAvg ++ | Spd +++ | Def +++

Year	Lev	Team	AB	R	H	HR	RBI	Avg	OB	Slg	OPS	bb%	ct%	Eye	SB	CS	x/h%	Iso	RC/G
2015	Rk	Helena	226	51	61	5	27	270	363	407	770	13	78	0.66	26	6	31	137	5.30
2016	A	Wisconsin	314	50	84	4	29	268	343	395	738	10	80	0.58	20	4	33	127	4.83
2017	A+	Carolina	364	60	91	14	56	250	336	445	781	11	79	0.61	21	9	42	195	5.30
2017	AA	Biloxi	135	19	34	6	18	252	331	452	783	11	75	0.47	9	3	44	200	5.28
2018	AA	Biloxi	467	74	109	19	58	233	327	430	757	12	69	0.44	19	2	44	197	5.17

Shorter, athletic OF who narrowly missed 20/20 season in AA. Swing packs a punch with loads of pull-side power and fly balls. Aggressive hitter who will swing over top of quality RH SL/CB, but will also take his walks in bunches. Plus runner who projects to bring SB value to table. Fringe arm limits him to LF/CF but can cover ground in the OF.

Stowers,Josh — 8 — Seattle
EXP MLB DEBUT: 2021 | H/W: 6-0 205 | FUT: Starting OF | 8D

Bats R Age 22 | 2018 (2) Louisville | Pwr +++ | BAvg +++ | Spd ++++ | Def +++

Year	Lev	Team	AB	R	H	HR	RBI	Avg	OB	Slg	OPS	bb%	ct%	Eye	SB	CS	x/h%	Iso	RC/G
2018	NCAA	Louisville	220	72	74	9	60	336	463	559	1022	19	83	1.41	36	0	36	223	8.78
2018	A-	Everett	200	32	52	5	28	260	376	410	786	16	72	0.65	20	4	38	150	5.72

Athletic, muscular OF received high marks for approach and game planning in first pro season. Physically maturing, body may outgrow CF. Patient approach with some spray in swing despite mostly pull results. Power in body and swing. Currently, only to pull-side. Struggles a bit with a bat wrap, reacting to pitches. Plus runner with SB smarts.

Straw,Myles — 789 — Houston
EXP MLB DEBUT: 2018 | H/W: 5-10 180 | FUT: Reserve OF | 5A

Bats R Age 24 | 2015 (12) StJohns River St Coll | Pwr + | BAvg +++ | Spd +++++ | Def ++++

Year	Lev	Team	AB	R	H	HR	RBI	Avg	OB	Slg	OPS	bb%	ct%	Eye	SB	CS	x/h%	Iso	RC/G
2017	A+	Buies Creek	437	81	129	1	41	295	412	373	785	17	84	1.24	36	9	19	78	5.84
2017	AA	Corpus Christi	46	9	11	0	3	239	340	239	579	13	80	0.78	2	0	0	0	2.91
2018	AA	Corpus Christi	251	47	82	1	17	327	409	390	800	12	83	0.83	35	6	13	64	5.70
2018	AAA	Fresno	265	48	68	0	14	257	350	317	667	13	77	0.63	35	3	19	60	4.03
2018	MLB	Houston	9	4	3	1	1	333	400	667	1067	10	100		2	0	33	333	8.10

The speedy OF could use some route-refinement, but has the wheels to outrun his mistakes. Straw has an inside-out swing and consistently goes to the opposite field, limiting any potential power. He's got a reserve outfield profile but could be a fantasy asset if he stumbles into playing time thanks to his high-end speed.

Stubbs,Garrett — 2 — Houston
EXP MLB DEBUT: 2019 | H/W: 5-9 150 | FUT: Reserve C | 7C

Bats L Age 25 | 2015 (8) USC | Pwr ++ | BAvg +++ | Spd +++ | Def ++++

Year	Lev	Team	AB	R	H	HR	RBI	Avg	OB	Slg	OPS	bb%	ct%	Eye	SB	CS	x/h%	Iso	RC/G
2016	A+	Lancaster	206	35	60	6	38	291	379	442	820	12	82	0.78	10	3	32	150	5.86
2016	AA	Corpus Christi	120	23	39	4	16	325	396	517	912	10	91	1.27	5	0	36	192	6.85
2017	AA	Corpus Christi	263	36	62	4	25	236	319	331	649	11	83	0.73	8	0	27	95	3.74
2017	AAA	Fresno	77	11	17	0	12	221	318	286	604	13	81	0.73	3	0	29	65	3.29
2018	AAA	Fresno	297	60	92	4	38	310	383	455	837	11	82	0.66	6	0	32	145	6.09

The small-framed catcher saw a return to form in 2018. He's at his best when he isn't gearing up for power, but rather using his short swing to spray line drives. He's a terrific pitch framer who faces doubts about whether he can hold up for a full season at catcher. He's the new Austin Barnes.

Suarez,Kervin — 48 — Boston
EXP MLB DEBUT: 2022 | H/W: 5-11 165 | FUT: Utility player | 6D

Bats B Age 20 | 2015 FA (VZ) | Pwr + | BAvg ++ | 4.10 Spd +++ | Def ++

Year	Lev	Team	AB	R	H	HR	RBI	Avg	OB	Slg	OPS	bb%	ct%	Eye	SB	CS	x/h%	Iso	RC/G
2017	Rk	GCL Red Sox	190	33	52	2	13	274	333	363	696	8	75	0.36	11	1	23	89	4.14
2017	A-	Lowell	8	1	2	0	0	250	400	250	650	20	75	1.00	0	0	0	0	4.03
2018	A	Greenville	470	71	110	7	39	234	276	340	616	5	62	0.15	25	6	28	106	3.13

Decent little athlete and switch hitter, who probably has too far to come on both sides of the ball and the plate. Moved to CF some in 2018 and that looks like a better fit than 2B. That said, bat unlikely to come enough. Hurt by big swings and poor balance from left and right.

Swaggerty,Travis — 789 — Pittsburgh
EXP MLB DEBUT: 2022 | H/W: 5-11 180 | FUT: Starting OF | 8D

Bats L Age 21 | 2018 (1) South Alabama | Pwr ++++ | BAvg +++ | Spd +++ | Def +++

Year	Lev	Team	AB	R	H	HR	RBI	Avg	OB	Slg	OPS	bb%	ct%	Eye	SB	CS	x/h%	Iso	RC/G
2018	NCAA	South Alabama	213	57	63	13	38	296	438	526	964	20	82	1.42	9	5	37	230	7.94
2018	A-	West Virginia	139	22	40	4	15	288	357	453	810	10	71	0.38	9	3	35	165	5.80
2018	A	West Virginia	62	6	8	1	5	129	217	226	443	10	71	0.39	0	0	38	97	0.66

Stout body; a LHH who they hope will hit for big power as corner OF. Showed some pop but struggled to hit for average and command the zone, especially when advanced to full-season low A in 2018. Will take a walk and has a touch of speed.

Tatis Jr.,Fernando — 6 — San Diego
EXP MLB DEBUT: 2019 | H/W: 6-3 185 | FUT: Starting SS | 9C

Bats R Age 20 | 2015 FA (DR) | Pwr ++++ | BAvg +++ | Spd +++ | Def ++++

Year	Lev	Team	AB	R	H	HR	RBI	Avg	OB	Slg	OPS	bb%	ct%	Eye	SB	CS	x/h%	Iso	RC/G
2016	Rk	AZL Padres	176	35	48	4	20	273	312	426	738	5	75	0.23	14	2	38	153	4.54
2016	A-	Tri-City	44	4	12	0	5	273	319	455	774	6	70	0.23	1	1	50	182	5.50
2017	A	Fort Wayne	431	78	121	21	69	281	387	520	907	15	71	0.60	29	15	45	239	7.33
2017	AA	San Antonio	55	6	14	1	6	255	281	327	608	4	69	0.12	3	0	14	73	2.64
2018	AA	San Antonio	353	77	101	16	43	286	347	507	854	9	69	0.30	16	5	42	221	6.40

Dominican SS who tore up AA in 2018 and already has established power/speed ability. Long, lean levers generate quality bat speed required for plus raw power to pull-side. Aggressive hitter with some swing-and-miss tendencies that could cap his HR production early on. Gifted athlete with smooth actions and plus arm for either SS or 3B.

Taveras,Leody | 8 | Texas | EXP MLB DEBUT: 2021 | H/W: 6-1 170 | FUT: Starting CF | 9D

Bats B Age 20	Year	Lev	Team	AB	R	H	HR	RBI	Avg	OB	Slg	OPS	bb%	ct%	Eye	SB	CS	x/h%	Iso	RC/G
2015 FA (DR)																				
Pwr ++	2016	Rk	AZL Rangers	144	22	40	1	15	278	329	382	711	7	83	0.46	11	4	25	104	4.35
BAvg ++	2016	A-	Spokane	123	14	28	0	9	228	275	293	567	6	79	0.31	3	1	25	65	2.47
4.22 Spd +++	2017	A	Hickory	522	73	130	8	50	249	311	360	671	8	82	0.51	20	6	27	111	3.87
Def ++++	2018	A+	Down East	521	65	128	5	48	246	313	332	645	9	82	0.53	19	11	22	86	3.58

Much was expected of him by this point, and though he remains the best defensive OFer in the system, his bat has yet to develop. He still flashes the power and sweet swing in BP, and knows balls from strikes, but he's struggled with poor quality of contact, especially in 2018. Has the impact tools, but needs to turn them into production.

Taylor,Logan | 57 | Seattle | EXP MLB DEBUT: 2020 | H/W: 6-1 200 | FUT: Utility player | 6B

Bats R Age 25	Year	Lev	Team	AB	R	H	HR	RBI	Avg	OB	Slg	OPS	bb%	ct%	Eye	SB	CS	x/h%	Iso	RC/G
2015 (12) Texas A&M	2017	A+	Modesto	316	37	76	8	59	241	294	418	712	7	66	0.22	4	4	49	177	4.53
Pwr ++	2017	AAA	Tacoma	11	1	2	1	3	182	182	455	636	0	82	0.00	0	1	50	273	2.62
BAvg +++	2018	A+	Modesto	127	18	37	3	22	291	396	449	845	15	65	0.50	4	1	35	157	6.86
Spd +++	2018	AA	Arkansas	226	24	61	7	31	270	329	412	741	8	70	0.30	0	0	28	142	4.71
Def ++	2018	AAA	Tacoma	4	2	2	0	0	500	500	500	1000	0	50	0.00	0	0	0	0	11.13

Solid, UT type player with no distinctive carrying tool to maximize ABs. A solid hitter with a patient approach, struggles a bit against velocity and making contact. Stocky frame, generating some power potential. 10-15 HR with playing time at projection. An average runner, doesn't translate to SB. Versatile, solid at 4 positions.

Taylor,Samad | 4 | Toronto | EXP MLB DEBUT: 2021 | H/W: 5-10 160 | FUT: Starting 2B | 6B

Bats B Age 20	Year	Lev	Team	AB	R	H	HR	RBI	Avg	OB	Slg	OPS	bb%	ct%	Eye	SB	CS	x/h%	Iso	RC/G
2016 (10) HS (CA)	2016	Rk	AZL Indians	116	25	34	1	14	293	354	397	751	9	79	0.46	6	2	24	103	4.89
Pwr ++	2017	Rk	Bluefield	16	1	4	0	3	250	368	250	618	16	63	0.50	1	0	0	0	3.38
BAvg ++	2017	A-	Vancouver	68	7	20	2	8	294	342	426	769	7	74	0.28	2	2	25	132	4.94
Spd ++++	2017	A-	Mahoning Val	120	18	36	4	19	300	328	467	795	4	80	0.21	4	2	31	167	5.03
Def ++++	2018	A	Lansing	460	67	105	9	53	228	313	387	700	11	78	0.58	44	16	46	159	4.37

Small, wiry, athlete moved from SS to 2B where he has good range, a strong arm, and good footwork around the bag. Has plus speed and swiped a career-best 44 SB. Gets surprising pop from his slender frame but is more gap than over the fence. Willing to draw walks, but looked over-matched at Low-A and may need to repeat.

Tebow,Tim | 7 | New York (N) | EXP MLB DEBUT: 2019 | H/W: 6-4 245 | FUT: Reserve OF | 6E

Bats L Age 31	Year	Lev	Team	AB	R	H	HR	RBI	Avg	OB	Slg	OPS	bb%	ct%	Eye	SB	CS	x/h%	Iso	RC/G
FA Florida																				
Pwr ++++																				
BAvg +	2017	A	Columbia	214	29	47	3	23	220	298	336	635	10	68	0.35	0	1	38	117	3.45
4.40 Spd +	2017	A+	St. Lucie	216	21	50	5	29	231	294	356	650	8	74	0.33	2	1	32	125	3.46
Def +	2018	AA	Binghamton	271	32	74	6	36	273	328	399	726	8	62	0.21	1	0	28	125	4.90

Not really a prospect, of course, but appears destined to get there because of his football fame. Plus raw power his only real baseball tool, but it is legit. To his credit, improved his swing and made some strides making contact in AA in 2018. A liability in LF. Below average arm, misreads a ton of fly balls and takes poor routes.

Tejeda,Anderson | 6 | Texas | EXP MLB DEBUT: 2021 | H/W: 5-11 160 | FUT: Starting SS | 8C

Bats L Age 20	Year	Lev	Team	AB	R	H	HR	RBI	Avg	OB	Slg	OPS	bb%	ct%	Eye	SB	CS	x/h%	Iso	RC/G
2014 FA (DR)																				
Pwr ++++	2016	Rk	AZL Rangers	133	22	39	1	21	293	333	496	830	6	73	0.22	1	0	49	203	6.09
BAvg ++	2016	A-	Spokane	94	15	26	8	19	277	313	553	866	5	65	0.15	1	0	35	277	6.39
Spd +++	2017	A	Hickory	401	68	99	8	53	247	309	411	720	8	67	0.27	10	7	41	165	4.70
Def +++	2018	A+	Down East	467	76	121	19	74	259	329	439	768	9	70	0.35	11	4	34	180	5.16

His raw power found its way into games in 2018, as he took a big step forward with the bat. His contact rate improved slightly, though there are still issues with pitch recognition and expanding the zone. Also provides some speed, and made improvements on defense—footwork, hands—that will keep him at SS. Has rocket arm.

Tellez,Rowdy | 3 | Toronto | EXP MLB DEBUT: 2018 | H/W: 6-4 220 | FUT: Starting 1B | 7C

Bats L Age 24	Year	Lev	Team	AB	R	H	HR	RBI	Avg	OB	Slg	OPS	bb%	ct%	Eye	SB	CS	x/h%	Iso	RC/G
2013 (30) HS (CA)																				
Pwr +++	2016	AA	New Hampshire	438	71	130	23	81	297	385	530	915	13	79	0.68	4	3	42	233	7.01
BAvg +++	2017	AAA	Buffalo	445	45	99	6	56	222	297	333	629	10	79	0.50	6	1	36	110	3.38
Spd +	2018	AAA	Buffalo	393	43	106	13	50	270	337	425	762	9	81	0.54	7	4	33	155	4.93
Def +	2018	MLB	Toronto	70	10	22	4	14	314	333	614	948	3	70	0.10	0	0	59	300	7.42

Big, thick-bodied hitter has above-average raw power, but isn't just a masher and had an impressive MLB debut. Plus bat speed and a disciplined approach at the plate results in consistent hard contact. Should continue to hit for power and average as he moves up. Bottom of the scale runner limits him to 1B.

Terry,Curtis | 3 | Texas | EXP MLB DEBUT: 2022 | H/W: 6-2 230 | FUT: Reserve 1B | 7D

Bats R Age 22	Year	Lev	Team	AB	R	H	HR	RBI	Avg	OB	Slg	OPS	bb%	ct%	Eye	SB	CS	x/h%	Iso	RC/G
2015 (13) HS (GA)	2015	Rk	AZL Rangers	127	17	33	1	24	260	314	394	708	7	74	0.30	2	0	42	134	4.37
Pwr ++++	2016	Rk	AZL Rangers	141	20	43	4	23	305	347	525	871	6	79	0.30	0	0	51	220	6.28
BAvg ++	2016	A-	Spokane	31	4	6	1	3	194	194	323	516	0	52	0.00	0	0	33	129	1.81
Spd +	2017	A-	Spokane	229	26	59	12	30	258	280	467	747	3	74	0.12	3	0	41	210	4.38
Def +	2018	A-	Spokane	246	51	83	15	60	337	414	606	1019	12	74	0.50	1	1	41	268	8.50

The short-season Northwest Lg MVP, he has plenty of power and improved his walk rate, but little else to his game. Is confined to first base defensively and is a bottom of the scale runner. As a R/R first baseman, he'll need to continue to hit.

Thaiss,Matt | 3 | Los Angeles (A) | EXP MLB DEBUT: 2019 | H/W: 5-11 197 | FUT: Starting 1B | 8D

Bats L Age 23	Year	Lev	Team	AB	R	H	HR	RBI	Avg	OB	Slg	OPS	bb%	ct%	Eye	SB	CS	x/h%	Iso	RC/G
2016 (1) Virginia	2016	A	Burlington	199	24	55	4	31	276	348	427	776	10	86	0.79	1	0	35	151	5.28
Pwr ++	2017	A+	Inland Empire	336	46	89	8	48	265	343	399	742	11	82	0.68	4	3	28	134	4.82
BAvg +++	2017	AA	Mobile	178	29	52	1	25	292	414	388	802	17	72	0.74	4	3	29	96	6.14
Spd ++	2018	AA	Mobile	157	24	45	6	25	287	353	490	843	9	78	0.46	2	1	40	204	6.01
Def ++	2018	AAA	Salt Lake	368	54	102	10	51	277	328	457	785	7	82	0.41	6	3	39	179	5.17

Disciplined infielder with a natural feel at the plate. Advanced barrel-to-ball skills through a solid swing path and ability to work the whole field. Impressive eye against opposing pitching with keen feel for drawing walks. Serviceable presence at first, although tools can be fringy overall.

Thomas,Alek | 8 | Arizona | EXP MLB DEBUT: 2022 | H/W: 5-11 175 | FUT: Starting OF | 8E

Bats L Age 18	Year	Lev	Team	AB	R	H	HR	RBI	Avg	OB	Slg	OPS	bb%	ct%	Eye	SB	CS	x/h%	Iso	RC/G
2018 (2) HS (IL)																				
Pwr ++																				
BAvg +++																				
4.25 Spd ++++	2018	Rk	Missoula	123	26	42	2	17	341	396	496	891	8	85	0.58	4	3	33	154	6.55
Def +++	2018	Rk	AZL DBacks	123	24	40	0	10	325	390	431	821	10	85	0.72	8	2	20	106	5.88

Shorter, athletic OF with well-rounded skillset headlined by plus speed. Plays quality CF with above-average range and arm required to stick there. Has some bat speed and keeps things compact through swing, leading to quality ct%. Works counts well and will have OBP value. With added strength could have average HR value with SB upside.

Thompson,Bubba | 789 | Texas | EXP MLB DEBUT: 2022 | H/W: 6-2 180 | FUT: Starting CF | 9D

Bats R Age 20	Year	Lev	Team	AB	R	H	HR	RBI	Avg	OB	Slg	OPS	bb%	ct%	Eye	SB	CS	x/h%	Iso	RC/G
2017 (1) HS (AL)																				
Pwr +++																				
BAvg +++																				
Spd ++++	2017	Rk	AZL Rangers	113	23	29	3	12	257	294	434	728	5	75	0.21	5	5	41	177	4.40
Def +++	2018	A	Hickory	332	52	96	8	42	289	335	446	781	6	69	0.22	32	7	32	157	5.37

Developed athlete, but raw baseball player, which made his full-season debut all the more impressive. Excellent bat speed, some present raw power, with more on the way; will need to make better contact to actualize it. But has enough quickness to be a base stealer. On defense, speed makes up for questionable reads/routes. Should stick in CF.

Thompson,David | 5 | New York (N) | EXP MLB DEBUT: 2020 | H/W: 6-1 180 | FUT: Reserve 3B | 6D

Bats R Age 25	Year	Lev	Team	AB	R	H	HR	RBI	Avg	OB	Slg	OPS	bb%	ct%	Eye	SB	CS	x/h%	Iso	RC/G
2015 (4) Miami	2016	A	Columbia	228	45	67	5	58	294	335	474	808	6	79	0.29	3	0	43	180	5.47
Pwr +++	2016	A+	St. Lucie	204	29	54	6	37	265	315	412	727	7	80	0.37	3	0	33	147	4.37
BAvg ++	2017	AA	Binghamton	476	62	125	16	68	263	320	429	748	8	81	0.43	8	6	37	166	4.69
4.60 Spd +	2018	A-	Brooklyn	12	1	2	0	1	167	231	250	481	8	83	0.50	0	0	50	83	1.68
Def +++	2018	AAA	Las Vegas	66	10	17	1	5	258	300	379	679	6	70	0.20	2	2	35	121	3.87

Solid-bodied 3B who lacks life in bat to be consistent offensive threat at ML level. Capable of hitting mistakes out and making routine plays at 3B, but lacks athleticism to help at other positions. Getting up there in age. Hard to see more improvement coming.

Thompson-Williams,Dom — 8 — Seattle — EXP MLB DEBUT: 2020 — H/W: 6-0 190 — FUT: Starting OF — 7C

Bats L Age 23 · 2016 (5) South Carolina · Pwr +++ · BAvg ++ · Spd +++ · Def +++

Year	Lev	Team	AB	R	H	HR	RBI	Avg	OB	Slg	OPS	bb%	ct%	Eye	SB	CS	x/h%	Iso	RC/G
2017	A-	Staten Island	141	17	39	3	22	277	358	390	749	11	79	0.60	7	6	26	113	4.91
2017	A	Charleston (Sc)	80	6	15	0	6	188	270	213	482	10	81	0.60	2	2	13	25	1.62
2018	A	Charleston (Sc)	37	7	14	5	9	378	410	811	1221	5	81	0.29	3	2	43	432	9.80
2018	A+	Tampa	331	56	96	17	65	290	351	517	867	9	71	0.33	17	7	39	227	6.42

Muscular, athletic CF prospect had best season as pro. Hit 22 HR despite low FB%. Regression likely. Patient approach, with pull tendencies on ground balls. Sprays line drives and fly balls across diamond. Above-average power plays to all fields. Also above-average runner with heady instincts. 20-for-29 in SB attempts.

Toro-Hernandez,Abraham — 5 — Houston — EXP MLB DEBUT: 2020 — H/W: 6-0 190 — FUT: Starting 3B — 7D

Bats B Age 22 · 2016 (5) Seminole St Coll · Pwr +++ · BAvg ++++ · Spd + · Def +

Year	Lev	Team	AB	R	H	HR	RBI	Avg	OB	Slg	OPS	bb%	ct%	Eye	SB	CS	x/h%	Iso	RC/G
2016	Rk	Greeneville	177	20	45	0	19	254	294	322	616	5	82	0.32	2	1	20	68	3.10
2017	A-	Tri City	104	20	30	6	16	288	398	529	927	15	80	0.90	1	3	43	240	7.27
2017	A	Quad Cities	134	25	28	9	17	209	316	463	779	14	78	0.70	2	0	50	254	5.20
2018	A+	Buies Creek	296	54	76	14	56	257	355	473	828	13	79	0.73	5	1	46	216	5.95
2018	AA	Corpus Christi	178	16	41	2	22	230	297	371	668	9	74	0.37	3	3	46	140	3.89

Switch-hitting 3B with a thick lower half. Natural feel for the barrel from both sides of the plate. Hit over power profile. Advanced approach allows him to pick his spots to get long and add loft. Below-average speed and an average arm conspire to make him a fringe-average 3B. Could move off in the long-term.

Torres,Christopher — 4 — Miami — EXP MLB DEBUT: 2021 — H/W: 5-11 170 — FUT: Starting SS — 7E

Bats B Age 21 · 2014 FA (DR) · Pwr ++ · BAvg ++ · Spd ++++ · Def ++++

Year	Lev	Team	AB	R	H	HR	RBI	Avg	OB	Slg	OPS	bb%	ct%	Eye	SB	CS	x/h%	Iso	RC/G
2017	Rk	AZL Mariners	9	1	2	0	1	222	417	667	1083	25	44	0.60	1	0	100	444	16.15
2017	A-	Everett	193	44	46	6	22	238	326	435	761	11	67	0.39	13	3	43	197	5.37
2018	Rk	GCL Marlins	6	1	0	0	0	0	143	0	143	14	83	1.00	0	0		0	-2.27
2018	A-	Batavia	23	6	8	1	4	348	444	609	1053	15	78	0.80	0	1	38	261	9.09
2018	A	Greensboro	88	20	22	1	6	250	394	307	701	19	66	0.70	3	1	9	57	4.70

Oft-injured, athletic switch-hitting MIF struggled with leg injuries early before making full-season debut. Advanced approach despite some contact issues. Quick hands struggled getting going out of load. Stocky body with some power in frame. Could reach average power with a few tweaks and better contact. Plus runner and a capable defender at SS, though played 2B mostly.

Trammell,Taylor — 78 — Cincinnati — EXP MLB DEBUT: 2020 — H/W: 6-2 194 — FUT: Starting OF — 9C

Bats L Age 21 · 2016 (1) HS (GA) · Pwr +++ · BAvg ++++ · Spd ++++ · Def ++++

Year	Lev	Team	AB	R	H	HR	RBI	Avg	OB	Slg	OPS	bb%	ct%	Eye	SB	CS	x/h%	Iso	RC/G
2016	Rk	Billings	228	39	69	2	34	303	367	421	788	9	75	0.40	24	7	25	118	5.47
2017	A	Dayton	491	80	138	13	77	281	372	450	822	13	75	0.58	41	12	34	169	6.03
2018	A+	Daytona	397	71	110	8	41	277	369	406	775	13	74	0.55	25	10	28	128	5.41

Toolsy, athletic OF continues ascent to big leagues. Continued to improve on patience and staying within zone. Contact-oriented with some spray ability. Best driving ball to the gaps. Raw plus power hasn't materialized in games due to leverage issues; may never reach power potential. But a 30-SB threat, and arm fits best in LF.

Travis,Sam — 37 — Boston — EXP MLB DEBUT: 2017 — H/W: 6-0 195 — FUT: Reserve 1B — 7D

Bats R Age 25 · 2014 (2) Indiana · Pwr +++ · BAvg +++ · 4.50 Spd + · Def +++

Year	Lev	Team	AB	R	H	HR	RBI	Avg	OB	Slg	OPS	bb%	ct%	Eye	SB	CS	x/h%	Iso	RC/G
2016	AAA	Pawtucket	173	26	47	6	29	272	330	434	763	8	77	0.38	1	0	34	162	4.88
2017	AAA	Pawtucket	304	40	82	6	24	270	349	375	724	11	81	0.65	6	2	24	105	4.59
2017	MLB	Boston	76	13	20	0	1	263	317	342	659	7	70	0.26	1	0	30	79	3.73
2018	AAA	Pawtucket	361	35	93	8	43	258	313	360	673	7	75	0.33	1	2	23	102	3.70
2018	MLB	Boston	36	5	8	1	7	222	263	389	652	5	72	0.20	0	0	50	167	3.41

1B who lacks versatility, athleticism and thump to break through as a regular. Tried to go for more power in 2018, but BA and OBP suffered. Tried some OF, but not a great option there because of lack of speed. Best best is to be platoon/bench option, but rhh 1B can be hard to carry on roster. Probably headed back to AAA.

Trevino,Jose — 2 — Texas — EXP MLB DEBUT: 2018 — H/W: 5-11 211 — FUT: Reserve C — 7D

Bats R Age 26 · 2014 (6) Oral Roberts · Pwr ++ · BAvg ++ · Spd + · Def ++++

Year	Lev	Team	AB	R	H	HR	RBI	Avg	OB	Slg	OPS	bb%	ct%	Eye	SB	CS	x/h%	Iso	RC/G
2015	A	Hickory	424	62	111	14	63	262	292	415	707	4	86	0.30	1	4	32	153	4.00
2016	A+	High Desert	433	67	131	9	68	303	342	434	776	6	89	0.53	2	1	30	132	4.99
2017	AA	Frisco	402	39	97	7	42	241	276	323	599	5	89	0.43	1	2	20	82	2.92
2018	AA	Frisco	184	18	43	3	16	234	284	332	616	7	85	0.48	0	1	26	98	3.15
2018	MLB	Texas	8	0	2	0	3	250	250	250	500	0	88	0.00	0	0	0	0	1.47

A defensive stalwart with classic catcher's size and skills, his strides with the bat have stalled the past two seasons at AA. Still makes very good contact and has some pop, but 2018 quad and shoulder injuries dimmed his year. Defense will get him to majors, bat will determine whether it's as a starter or reserve.

Tucker,Cole — 6 — Pittsburgh — EXP MLB DEBUT: 2020 — H/W: 6-3 185 — FUT: Starting SS — 8D

Bats B Age 22 · 2014 (1) HS (AZ) · Pwr +++ · BAvg +++ · 4.20 Spd +++ · Def +++

Year	Lev	Team	AB	R	H	HR	RBI	Avg	OB	Slg	OPS	bb%	ct%	Eye	SB	CS	x/h%	Iso	RC/G
2016	A	West Virginia	61	9	16	1	2	262	308	443	750	6	85	0.44	1	1	44	180	4.82
2016	A+	Bradenton	269	36	64	1	25	238	312	301	613	10	77	0.47	5	6	22	63	3.16
2017	A+	Bradenton	277	46	79	4	32	285	363	426	789	11	75	0.49	36	12	32	141	5.58
2017	AA	Altoona	167	25	43	2	18	257	340	377	718	11	81	0.68	11	3	26	120	4.63
2018	AA	Altoona	517	77	134	5	44	259	330	356	686	10	80	0.53	35	12	25	97	4.12

Long-limbed player who is still finding his way. Defense should be solid if unspectacular and allow time for his bat to come. Swing from both sides is OK, but has never found consistency. Shows power in BP. Not a plus runner but plus feel for SB. Great makeup and feel for game. Floor is the next Donald Kelly; ceiling is Chipper Jones lite.

Tucker,Kyle — 789 — Houston — EXP MLB DEBUT: 2018 — H/W: 6-4 190 — FUT: Starting OF — 9B

Bats L Age 22 · 2015 (1) HS (FL) · Pwr ++++ · BAvg ++++ · Spd +++ · Def +++

Year	Lev	Team	AB	R	H	HR	RBI	Avg	OB	Slg	OPS	bb%	ct%	Eye	SB	CS	x/h%	Iso	RC/G
2016	A+	Lancaster	59	13	20	3	13	339	435	661	1096	14	90	1.67	1	3	55	322	9.25
2017	A+	Buies Creek	177	31	51	9	43	288	373	554	927	12	75	0.53	13	5	49	266	7.34
2017	AA	Corpus Christi	287	39	76	16	47	265	317	512	829	7	78	0.34	8	4	50	247	5.63
2018	AAA	Fresno	407	86	135	24	93	332	402	590	992	11	79	0.57	20	4	40	258	7.83
2018	MLB	Houston	64	10	9	0	4	141	214	203	417	9	80	0.46	1	1	33	63	0.74

Lanky, high-waisted OF continued to flash ability to impact multiple categories but struggled in his major-league debut. One of the smoother swings in the minors produces easy power and he gets on base enough to put his speed to use. Should see more of the majors in short order.

Turang,Brice — 6 — Milwaukee — EXP MLB DEBUT: 2022 — H/W: 6-1 165 — FUT: Starting 2B — 9E

Bats L Age 19 · 2018 (1) HS (CA) · Pwr +++ · BAvg +++ · Spd ++++ · Def +++

Year	Lev	Team	AB	R	H	HR	RBI	Avg	OB	Slg	OPS	bb%	ct%	Eye	SB	CS	x/h%	Iso	RC/G
2018	Rk	AZL Brewers	47	11	15	0	7	319	429	362	790	16	87	1.50	8	1	13	43	5.89
2018	Rk	Helena	112	26	30	1	11	268	388	348	736	16	75	0.79	6	1	20	80	5.08

First-round pick who had quality pro debut in rookie/short-season ball. Lanky, thin frame produces good bat speed and flat path through zone for line-drive contact. Knows strike zone well and power should come. Plus runner with good instincts on the basepaths for future SB impact. Plays quality SS now but ideal move could be 2B as he fills out.

Urena,Jhoan — 79 — New York (N) — EXP MLB DEBUT: 2020 — H/W: 6-1 200 — FUT: Reserve OF — 6D

Bats B Age 24 · 2011 FA (DR) · Pwr +++ · BAvg ++ · 4.40 Spd + · Def ++

Year	Lev	Team	AB	R	H	HR	RBI	Avg	OB	Slg	OPS	bb%	ct%	Eye	SB	CS	x/h%	Iso	RC/G
2015	A+	St. Lucie	210	15	45	0	18	214	253	267	520	5	81	0.28	2	0	18	52	1.86
2016	A+	St. Lucie	383	52	86	9	53	225	301	350	651	10	80	0.56	0	1	33	125	3.62
2017	A+	St. Lucie	458	72	129	11	62	282	365	437	802	12	75	0.53	17	3	36	155	5.70
2017	AAA	Las Vegas	44	5	10	3	8	227	292	477	769	8	64	0.25	1	0	40	250	5.24
2018	AA	Binghamton	421	47	110	14	63	261	324	418	742	8	73	0.35	2	4	33	157	4.68

Hefty corner OF who can show some pop from either side of the plate, but won't hit enough to overcome lack of defense and versatility. Too pull oriented from both sides. Doesn't cover plate or lay off bad pitches consistently enough.

Urias,Luis — 4 — San Diego — EXP MLB DEBUT: 2018 — H/W: 5-9 160 — FUT: Starting 2B — 8B

Bats R Age 21 · 2013 FA (MX) · Pwr ++ · BAvg ++++ · Spd +++ · Def +++

Year	Lev	Team	AB	R	H	HR	RBI	Avg	OB	Slg	OPS	bb%	ct%	Eye	SB	CS	x/h%	Iso	RC/G
2016	A+	Lake Elsinore	466	71	154	5	52	330	383	440	823	8	92	1.11	7	13	23	109	5.77
2016	AAA	El Paso	9	6	4	1	3	444	643	778	1421	36	89	5.00	1	0	25	333	14.29
2017	AA	San Antonio	442	77	131	3	38	296	390	380	770	13	85	1.05	7	5	21	84	5.44
2018	AAA	El Paso	450	83	133	8	45	296	387	447	834	13	76	0.61	2	1	34	151	6.24
2018	MLB	San Diego	48	5	10	2	5	208	255	354	609	6	79	0.30	1	0	30	146	2.74

Shorter, athletic 2B who made MLB debut in August. Employs high-contact approach with natural bat-to-ball skills; creates low line-drive trajectories and hard GBs to all fields for BA impact. Barrel control and disciplined approach should lend themselves to average power at maturity. Very good defender at second and has enough arm for SS if needed.

Urias, Ramon — 4 — St. Louis

Bats R Age 24
2018 FA (MX)
EXP MLB DEBUT: 2019 H/W: 5-10 150 FUT: Utility player **7C**

Pwr ++
BAvg +++
Spd ++
Def ++

Year	Lev	Team	AB	R	H	HR	RBI	Avg	OB	Slg	OPS	bb%	ct%	Eye	SB	CS	x/h%	Iso	RC/G
2018	AA	Springfield	168	28	56	8	27	333	398	589	987	10	83	0.62	1	2	48	256	7.71
2018	AAA	Memphis	142	20	37	5	17	261	291	430	720	4	80	0.21	0	0	38	169	4.12

Mexican League standout was signed in Jan and had an impressive debut, hitting .300/.356/.516 between AA/AAA. Quick, balanced RH stroke and plus bat to ball result in average power and skills should carry over as he moves up. Moves well with good hands and a strong arm on D and split time between 2B, SS, and 3B. Older brother of Padres Luis Urias.

Uselton, Conner — 789 — Pittsburgh

Bats R Age 20
2017 (2) HS (OK)
EXP MLB DEBUT: 2024 H/W: 6-3 190 FUT: Reserve OF **7D**

Pwr +++
BAvg +++
Spd ++
Def +++

Year	Lev	Team	AB	R	H	HR	RBI	Avg	OB	Slg	OPS	bb%	ct%	Eye	SB	CS	x/h%	Iso	RC/G
2017	Rk	GCL Pirates	7	0	3	0	1	429	429	571	1000	0	86	0.00	0	0	33	143	7.25
2018	Rk	Bristol	160	15	36	0	14	225	279	250	529	7	81	0.39	0	2	8	25	2.01

Toolsy, high pick RF with a good frame but bat and power have not come in his limited pro AB so far. Still young and has time, but concern has to be there.

Valbuena, Luvin — 2 — Arizona

Bats R Age 19
2015 FA (VZ)
EXP MLB DEBUT: 2023 H/W: 5-9 165 FUT: Starting C **7E**

Pwr ++
BAvg ++
Spd ++
Def ++++

Year	Lev	Team	AB	R	H	HR	RBI	Avg	OB	Slg	OPS	bb%	ct%	Eye	SB	CS	x/h%	Iso	RC/G
2018	Rk	AZL DBacks	60	7	15	0	7	250	297	267	564	6	80	0.33	1	0	7	17	2.36

Shorter, lean CA whose glove and arm stood out in AZL. Possesses quick release and plus arm necessary to hold running game at big-league level. Blocks balls well and should make gains with framing in near future. Offensive upside limited with compact stroke and lack of raw power, but his glove and arm alone will give him value moving forward.

Valera, George — 8 — Cleveland

Bats L Age 18
2018 FA (DR)
EXP MLB DEBUT: 2023 H/W: 5-10 160 FUT: Starting OF **9D**

Pwr +++
BAvg ++++
Spd +++
Def ++

Year	Lev	Team	AB	R	H	HR	RBI	Avg	OB	Slg	OPS	bb%	ct%	Eye	SB	CS	x/h%	Iso	RC/G
2018	Rk	AZL Indians 2	18	4	6	1	6	333	429	556	984	14	83	1.00	1	1	33	222	7.85

Has a beautiful, whippy left-handed stroke that is mechanically similar to Robinson Cano in how he slowly rocks back and how his hands load. He has a good approach to hitting and should develop power over time. He will be limited to the corner outfield and is a below average runner.

Vallot, Chase — 2 — Kansas City

Bats R Age 22
2014 (1) HS (LA)
EXP MLB DEBUT: 2021 H/W: 6-0 215 FUT: Reserve C **6D**

Pwr ++++
BAvg +
Spd +
Def ++

Year	Lev	Team	AB	R	H	HR	RBI	Avg	OB	Slg	OPS	bb%	ct%	Eye	SB	CS	x/h%	Iso	RC/G
2016	Rk	AZL Royals	30	5	4	2	2	133	212	367	579	9	53	0.21	0	0	75	233	2.62
2016	A	Lexington	272	37	67	13	44	246	341	463	804	13	57	0.33	0	0	49	217	6.67
2017	A+	Wilmington	281	34	65	12	37	231	374	438	812	19	55	0.50	0	0	52	206	7.10
2018	Rk	Idaho Falls	145	23	38	7	28	262	327	510	837	9	51	0.20	0	0	58	248	8.13
2018	A+	Wilmington	148	19	16	7	24	108	263	277	540	17	46	0.39	0	0	69	169	2.17

Strong-body offensive-first CA struggled with bat in 2nd shot at High-A, ending up back in rookie-ball. Struggled with injuries past 2 seasons. Three True Outcomes player with little hit tool. Swing was sluggish, contributing to big dip in ct%. Plus-plus raw power. Contact struggles depress power impact. Not a runner and a below-average defender.

Vargas, Yerdel — 46 — Oakland

Bats R Age 19
2016 FA (DR)
EXP MLB DEBUT: 2021 H/W: 6-1 170 FUT: Starting 2B **7D**

Pwr ++
BAvg +++
Spd +++
Def ++

Year	Lev	Team	AB	R	H	HR	RBI	Avg	OB	Slg	OPS	bb%	ct%	Eye	SB	CS	x/h%	Iso	RC/G
2017	Rk	DSL Athletics	52	6	9	0	6	173	173	173	346	0	71	0.00	1	0	0	0	-1.04
2017	Rk	AZL Athletics	144	13	30	0	13	208	240	306	546	4	75	0.17	3	4	33	97	2.09
2018	Rk	AZL Athletics	61	15	11	9	4	180	333	705	1038	19	67	0.70	3	1	109	525	9.02

Ultra-lean, athletic SS who signed for $1.5 million as July 2 signee in 2016. Chance for average HR impact given plus bat speed and projectable build that he will add strength to. Contact will require work as he struggles to barrel up off-speed in the low minors. Shows good approach and identifies spin well out of hand. SS now; profiles better at 3B.

Varsho, Daulton — 2 — Arizona

Bats L Age 22
2017 (2) Wisconsin-Milwau
EXP MLB DEBUT: 2020 H/W: 5-10 190 FUT: Starting C **8C**

Pwr +++
BAvg +++
Spd +++
Def +++

Year	Lev	Team	AB	R	H	HR	RBI	Avg	OB	Slg	OPS	bb%	ct%	Eye	SB	CS	x/h%	Iso	RC/G
2017	NCAA	UW Milwaukee	199	47	72	11	39	362	482	643	1125	19	80	1.18	10	0	39	281	10.09
2017	A-	Hillsboro	193	36	60	7	39	311	367	534	900	8	84	0.57	7	2	43	223	6.59
2018	Rk	AZL DBacks	12	4	6	1	1	500	500	1083	1583	0	92	0.00	0	0	67	583	13.38
2018	A+	Visalia	304	44	87	11	44	286	350	451	801	9	77	0.42	19	3	29	164	5.42

Thick, strong CA with surprising athleticism and a chance to stick behind the plate. Muscles balls to pull-side with plus bat speed and hard LD stroke. Displays ability to make above-average contact; works counts well; identifies spin out of hand easily. Good athlete who smothers balls in dirt well behind plate; lacks plus arm and may end up in LF.

Vavra, Terrin — 6 — Colorado

Bats L Age 21
2018 (3) Minnesota
EXP MLB DEBUT: 2021 H/W: 6-0 180 FUT: Starting 2B **7C**

Pwr +++
BAvg +++
Spd ++
Def ++

Year	Lev	Team	AB	R	H	HR	RBI	Avg	OB	Slg	OPS	bb%	ct%	Eye	SB	CS	x/h%	Iso	RC/G
2018	NCAA	Minnesota	223	55	86	10	59	386	458	614	1073	12	90	1.36	8	1	31	229	8.70
2018	A-	Boise	169	22	51	4	26	302	395	467	862	13	76	0.65	9	1	31	166	6.60

Polished collegiate player has an advanced understanding of the strike zone and makes consistent, hard contact. Line drive approach limits present power, but does have raw strength and barrel awareness, so should hit 15-20 HR down the road. Smart defender with plus instincts, but limited range arm strength and will likely move off SS.

Velazquez, Nelson — 79 — Chicago (N)

Bats R Age 20
2017 (5) HS (PR)
EXP MLB DEBUT: 2021 H/W: 6-0 190 FUT: Starting OF **8D**

Pwr ++++
BAvg ++
Spd +++
Def +++

Year	Lev	Team	AB	R	H	HR	RBI	Avg	OB	Slg	OPS	bb%	ct%	Eye	SB	CS	x/h%	Iso	RC/G
2017	Rk	AZL Cubs	110	26	26	8	17	236	328	536	864	12	65	0.38	5	2	58	300	6.83
2018	A-	Eugene	264	35	66	11	33	250	310	458	768	8	69	0.28	12	4	47	208	5.15
2018	A	South Bend	112	6	21	0	7	188	235	196	432	6	62	0.16	3	0	5	9	0.17

Toolsy, athletic OF has plus bat speed and projects to have above-average power if he can make enough contact. Doesn't chase out of the zone, but too often swings for the fences. Above-average speed and solid arm allow him to play all three OF slots. Raw, but lots of upside.

Verdugo, Alex — 789 — Los Angeles (N)

Bats L Age 22
2014 (2) HS (AZ)
EXP MLB DEBUT: 2017 H/W: 6-0 200 FUT: Starting OF **8A**

Pwr +++
BAvg ++++
Spd ++
Def ++++

Year	Lev	Team	AB	R	H	HR	RBI	Avg	OB	Slg	OPS	bb%	ct%	Eye	SB	CS	x/h%	Iso	RC/G
2016	AA	Tulsa	477	58	130	13	63	273	334	407	741	8	86	0.66	2	6	28	134	4.69
2017	AAA	Oklahoma City	433	67	136	6	62	314	388	436	824	11	88	1.04	9	3	27	122	5.93
2017	MLB	LA Dodgers	23	1	4	1	1	174	240	304	544	8	83	0.50	0	1	25	130	2.11
2018	AAA	Oklahoma City	343	44	113	10	44	329	390	472	862	9	86	0.72	8	2	26	143	6.13
2018	MLB	LA Dodgers	77	11	20	1	4	260	329	377	706	9	82	0.57	0	0	35	117	4.38

Continues to make adjustments at the plate and shows a willingness to use all fields. Plus bat speed and a discerning eye give him tools to hit for BA. Power development is the only thing keeping him from being an overall Top 10 prospect. Played all 3 OF spots where he shows good range and a plus arm. Just needs to find PT.

Vientos, Mark — 5 — New York (N)

Bats R Age 19
2017 (2) HS (FL)
EXP MLB DEBUT: 2022 H/W: 6-4 185 FUT: Reserve IF **7D**

Pwr +++
BAvg +++
4.50 Spd +
Def +++

Year	Lev	Team	AB	R	H	HR	RBI	Avg	OB	Slg	OPS	bb%	ct%	Eye	SB	CS	x/h%	Iso	RC/G
2017	Rk	GCL Mets	174	22	45	4	24	259	314	397	710	7	76	0.33	0	2	36	138	4.25
2017	Rk	Kingsport	17	1	5	0	2	294	333	412	745	6	76	0.25	0	0	40	118	4.77
2018	Rk	Kingsport	223	32	64	11	52	287	388	489	877	14	81	0.86	1	0	36	202	6.58

The second coming of Wilmer Flores. Like Flores, has been billed as a future SS who can hit and maybe hit for power. But, he is knock-kneed, and, like Flores, his slow feet will keep him from playing a middle infield position, and maybe even 3B. Bat has promise, despite some length to swing, but probably not enough to make him a corner regular.

Vierling,Matt

7 | Philadelphia | EXP MLB DEBUT: 2021 | H/W: 6-3 205 | FUT: Starting OF | 7C

Bats R Age 22
2018 (5) Notre Dame
Pwr ++
BAvg +++
4.45 Spd +++
Def ++

Year	Lev	Team	AB	R	H	HR	RBI	Avg	OB	Slg	OPS	bb%	ct%	Eye	SB	CS	x/h%	Iso	RC/G
2018	NCAA	Notre Dame	210	38	65	10	43	310	396	505	901	13	87	1.07	5	0	29	195	6.73
2018	A-	Williamsport	50	8	21	1	6	420	453	580	1033	6	96	1.50	2	1	24	160	7.81
2018	A	Lakewood	184	24	54	6	25	293	330	473	803	5	79	0.26	5	5	39	179	5.24

Athletic and broad-shouldered, he got his pro career off to a quick start. He has a feel to hit and some power, though using the whole field for hard line drives is his natural inclination. He hustles, will steal an occasional base or two, has played all three OF positions. Will likely settle as a LFer, where the bat will need to stand out.

Vilade,Ryan

6 | Colorado | EXP MLB DEBUT: 2021 | H/W: 6-2 190 | FUT: Starting 2B | 8D

Bats R Age 20
2017 (2) HS (TX)
Pwr ++++
BAvg +++
Spd ++
Def +++

Year	Lev	Team	AB	R	H	HR	RBI	Avg	OB	Slg	OPS	bb%	ct%	Eye	SB	CS	x/h%	Iso	RC/G
2017	Rk	Grand Junction	117	23	36	5	21	308	438	496	933	19	74	0.87	5	5	28	188	7.78
2018	A	Asheville	457	77	125	5	44	274	344	368	711	10	79	0.51	17	13	23	94	4.42

Heady, athletic player has a solid understanding of the strike zone and barrels line drives to all fields. Uses slight toe-tap as a timing mechanism and can get out front, sapping power. Slight uppercut swing generates good attack angle. Does have good bat speed and should develop at least average power. Lack of quickness makes move off SS likely.

Wade,LaMonte

789 | Minnesota | EXP MLB DEBUT: 2019 | H/W: 6-1 180 | FUT: Starting OF | 7D

Bats L Age 25
2015 (9) Maryland
Pwr ++
BAvg +++
Spd +++
Def +++

Year	Lev	Team	AB	R	H	HR	RBI	Avg	OB	Slg	OPS	bb%	ct%	Eye	SB	CS	x/h%	Iso	RC/G
2016	A	Cedar Rapids	207	32	58	4	27	280	406	396	803	18	87	1.63	5	3	22	116	6.05
2016	A+	Fort Myers	110	17	35	4	24	318	375	518	893	8	85	0.59	1	1	37	200	6.48
2017	AA	Chattanooga	424	74	124	7	67	292	400	408	808	15	83	1.07	9	2	26	116	5.95
2018	AA	Chattanooga	171	30	51	7	27	298	391	444	835	13	88	1.30	5	2	20	146	6.02
2018	AAA	Rochester	253	24	58	4	21	229	330	336	666	13	79	0.70	5	1	28	107	3.98

Well-rounded, athletic OF struggled in 1st taste of Triple-A. Line drive hitter with short-stroke, works counts and takes walks. Contact rate fell almost 10% due to late-season struggles. Becoming more pull-oriented to attempt to reach power potential. Swing trajectory creates loads of top spin, depressing loft. Defensively sound, average runner.

Walker,Steele

8 | Chicago (A) | EXP MLB DEBUT: 2021 | H/W: 5-11 190 | FUT: Starting OF | 8D

Bats L Age 22
2018 (2) Oklahoma
Pwr ++++
BAvg +++
Spd +++
Def ++

Year	Lev	Team	AB	R	H	HR	RBI	Avg	OB	Slg	OPS	bb%	ct%	Eye	SB	CS	x/h%	Iso	RC/G
2018	NCAA	Oklahoma	216	48	76	13	53	352	433	606	1040	13	78	0.65	7	3	37	255	8.62
2018	Rk	Great Falls	34	4	7	2	4	206	229	412	640	3	79	0.14	1	1	43	206	2.94
2018	Rk	AZL White Sox	11	0	5	0	0	455	500	455	955	8	91	1.00	0	0	0	0	7.12
2018	A	Kannapolis	113	13	21	3	17	186	240	310	549	7	74	0.28	5	1	38	124	2.03

Strong, athletic OF struggled in professional debut. Quick wrists, strong forearms with a swing geared for fly ball contact. Some swing-and-miss against higher velocity. Raw plus power will mature, potentially to 25-30 HR. Will outgrow CF; profiles best in RF. A heady base-runner, he has 10-15 SB potential.

Wall,Forrest

8 | Toronto | EXP MLB DEBUT: 2020 | H/W: 6-0 176 | FUT: Starting CF | 7D

Bats L Age 23
2014 (1) HS (FL)
Pwr ++
BAvg ++
Spd ++++
Def +++

Year	Lev	Team	AB	R	H	HR	RBI	Avg	OB	Slg	OPS	bb%	ct%	Eye	SB	CS	x/h%	Iso	RC/G
2016	A+	Modesto	459	57	121	6	56	264	324	355	679	8	79	0.42	22	11	21	92	3.90
2017	A+	Lancaster	87	17	26	3	16	299	365	471	836	9	82	0.56	5	3	31	172	5.86
2018	A+	Lancaster	203	43	62	3	19	305	376	453	829	10	77	0.49	20	8	31	148	6.03
2018	AA	New Hampshire	299	46	70	7	25	234	304	368	672	9	71	0.34	18	6	33	134	3.84
2018	AA	Hartford	170	27	35	6	12	206	278	359	637	9	75	0.40	8	3	37	153	3.27

Acquired in the S. Oh deal, he transitioned from 2B to CF with mixed results. Plus runner with moderate pop posted career highs in SB and HR, but ct% headed in the wrong direction. Below-average arm made even 2B a reach. Does have interesting tools and if he can make more contact could develop into an A. Eaton-type with 20/20 potential.

Walton,Donnie

4 | Seattle | EXP MLB DEBUT: 2020 | H/W: 5-9 165 | FUT: Reserve 2B | 6B

Bats L Age 24
2016 (5) Oklahoma St
Pwr +
BAvg +++
Spd +++
Def +++

Year	Lev	Team	AB	R	H	HR	RBI	Avg	OB	Slg	OPS	bb%	ct%	Eye	SB	CS	x/h%	Iso	RC/G
2016	A-	Everett	178	43	50	5	23	281	360	421	781	11	87	0.92	6	0	28	140	5.33
2017	Rk	AZL Mariners	16	2	5	2	5	313	353	688	1040	6	100		2	0	40	375	7.46
2017	A+	Modesto	242	37	65	2	24	269	342	368	710	10	80	0.55	6	6	29	99	4.45
2018	A+	Modesto	217	35	67	3	19	309	393	433	826	12	83	0.81	8	3	27	124	6.02
2018	AA	Arkansas	208	22	49	1	22	236	306	327	633	9	84	0.62	3	1	33	91	3.55

Contact-oriented 2B continues to display a solid hit tool. Gave up switch-hitting due to struggles as RHH. Now, exclusively hitting LHH, takes advantage of spray approach. Struggled in Double-A pulling ball on ground. Not much of power in swing. Doesn't incorporate leverage in legs for power either. Average runner. Likely limited to reserve role.

Ward,Drew

35 | Washington | EXP MLB DEBUT: 2019 | H/W: 6-3 215 | FUT: Reserve IF | 6A

Bats L Age 24
2013 (3) HS (OK)
Pwr +++
BAvg ++
Spd +
Def ++

Year	Lev	Team	AB	R	H	HR	RBI	Avg	OB	Slg	OPS	bb%	ct%	Eye	SB	CS	x/h%	Iso	RC/G
2016	A+	Potomac	230	36	64	11	32	278	371	491	863	13	70	0.49	0	1	42	213	6.65
2016	AA	Harrisburg	178	19	39	3	24	219	305	309	614	11	71	0.43	0	1	26	90	3.08
2017	AA	Harrisburg	413	47	97	10	53	235	325	356	681	12	68	0.42	0	0	31	121	4.07
2018	AA	Harrisburg	320	59	83	13	56	259	368	456	824	15	70	0.58	1	1	40	197	6.18
2018	AAA	Syracuse	54	5	10	0	2	185	279	222	501	11	63	0.35	0	1	20	37	1.45

Though has idea size for corner IF and still runs into some HR, bat has stalled at Double-A. Good pitch recognition, but lots of swing and miss and not enough power to compensate. Can play either COR IF position, but not enough athleticism for the OF. Nor enough sting in his bat.

Ward,Je'Von

7 | Milwaukee | EXP MLB DEBUT: 2021 | H/W: 6-5 190 | FUT: Starting OF | 8D

Bats L Age 19
2017 (12) HS (CA)
Pwr ++
BAvg +++
Spd ++++
Def +++

Year	Lev	Team	AB	R	H	HR	RBI	Avg	OB	Slg	OPS	bb%	ct%	Eye	SB	CS	x/h%	Iso	RC/G
2017	Rk	AZL Brewers	123	15	34	0	15	276	326	325	651	7	68	0.23	2	7	18	49	3.55
2018	Rk	Helena	238	40	73	2	21	307	389	403	792	12	76	0.56	13	5	23	97	5.63

Lanky, premium athlete with promising tools. Plus runner who gets down the line and should be valuable SB source even as he fills out physically. Lacks power now but shows feel for barrel and utilizes opposite field well. Recognizes spin and will take his walks. Still a project, but has some upside.

Ward,Taylor

5 | Los Angeles (A) | EXP MLB DEBUT: 2018 | H/W: 6-2 190 | FUT: Starting 3B | 7D

Bats R Age 25
2015 (1) Fresno St
Pwr ++
BAvg ++
Spd ++
Def ++

Year	Lev	Team	AB	R	H	HR	RBI	Avg	OB	Slg	OPS	bb%	ct%	Eye	SB	CS	x/h%	Iso	RC/G
2017	A+	Inland Empire	207	32	50	6	30	242	351	391	743	14	79	0.81	0	0	36	150	4.99
2017	AA	Mobile	119	14	34	3	19	286	397	387	784	16	86	1.29	0	0	18	101	5.61
2018	AA	Mobile	148	26	51	6	25	345	452	520	972	16	78	0.88	8	1	27	176	8.05
2018	AAA	Salt Lake	227	42	80	8	35	352	441	537	979	14	73	0.59	10	2	33	185	8.24
2018	MLB	LA Angels	135	14	24	6	15	178	229	333	563	6	67	0.20	2	0	38	156	2.02

Newly-appointed third baseman after spending first three seasons behind the plate. Debuted at the hot corner in Double-A and the new assignment stuck up through his major league debut. Changed to be average defender at the corner post. Has serviceable bat-to-ball skills. Eye at the plate needs polish.

Warmoth,Logan

6 | Toronto | EXP MLB DEBUT: 2020 | H/W: 6-0 184 | FUT: Starting SS | 6B

Bats R Age 23
2017 (1) North Carolina
Pwr +
BAvg +++
Spd +++
Def +++

Year	Lev	Team	AB	R	H	HR	RBI	Avg	OB	Slg	OPS	bb%	ct%	Eye	SB	CS	x/h%	Iso	RC/G
2017	NCAA	North Carolina	271	60	91	10	49	336	398	554	951	9	83	0.60	18	3	37	218	7.30
2017	Rk	GCL Blue Jays	21	2	5	1	3	238	273	381	654	5	90	0.50	1	0	20	143	3.42
2017	A-	Vancouver	160	18	49	1	20	306	335	419	754	4	79	0.21	5	2	29	113	4.70
2018	Rk	GCL Blue Jays	11	4	3	0	0	273	385	273	657	15	64	0.50	0	0	0	0	3.98
2018	A+	Dunedin	282	31	70	1	28	248	321	319	640	10	76	0.43	9	0	23	71	3.50

Former 1st round pick looked over-matched with High-A assignment though was limited by injuries. Solid across-the-board tools, but none stand out as plus. Slow lower half cuts into raw power, but should put up better numbers in 2019. Solid defender with good speed, soft hands, and enough arm to stick at short.

Waters,Drew

8 | Atlanta | EXP MLB DEBUT: 2021 | H/W: 6-2 185 | FUT: Starting CF | 8C

Bats B Age 20
2017 (2) HS (GA)
Pwr +++
BAvg +++
Spd ++++
Def ++++

Year	Lev	Team	AB	R	H	HR	RBI	Avg	OB	Slg	OPS	bb%	ct%	Eye	SB	CS	x/h%	Iso	RC/G
2017	Rk	Danville	149	20	38	2	14	255	327	383	710	10	60	0.27	4	2	37	128	4.92
2017	Rk	GCL Braves	49	13	17	2	10	347	429	571	1000	13	78	0.64	2	1	35	224	8.25
2018	A	Rome	337	58	102	9	36	303	344	513	857	6	79	0.29	20	5	46	211	6.09
2018	A+	Florida	123	14	33	0	3	268	313	374	687	6	73	0.24	3	0	30	106	4.06

Athletic, switch-hitting OF improved significantly in first full season. Lean, athletic build. Smaller than teammates, still packs solid punch. Better from LH side than RH. Swing is unconventional but gets job done with solid barrel control. Raw, plus power in frame. Likely average HR power at projection. Plus runner with good instincts.

Welker,Colton — 5 — Colorado

EXP MLB DEBUT: 2021 | H/W: 6-0 205 | FUT: Starting 3B | 8B

Bats R Age 21 — 2016 (4) HS (FL)
Pwr +++ | BAvg ++++ | Spd ++ | Def +++

Year	Lev	Team	AB	R	H	HR	RBI	Avg	OB	Sig	OPS	bb%	ct%	Eye	SB	CS	x/h%	Iso	RC/G
2016	Rk	Grand Junction	210	38	69	5	36	329	368	490	858	6	87	0.46	6	4	32	162	5.93
2017	A	Asheville	254	32	89	6	33	350	393	500	893	7	83	0.43	5	7	28	150	6.40
2018	A+	Lancaster	454	74	151	13	82	333	389	489	878	8	77	0.41	5	1	30	156	6.43

Advanced hitting prospect continues to refine his game and showed an uptick in power. Some of the best barrel awareness in the system, and led the CAL with a .333 BA. Got more loft from his swing and now profiles as an impact hitter. Plus defender at 3B with an above-average arm and soft hands.

Walls,Taylor — 6 — Tampa Bay

EXP MLB DEBUT: 2021 | H/W: 5-10 180 | FUT: Utility player | 7C

Bats B Age 22 — 2017 (3) Florida St
Pwr ++ | BAvg +++ | Spd +++ | Def +++

Year	Lev	Team	AB	R	H	HR	RBI	Avg	OB	Sig	OPS	bb%	ct%	Eye	SB	CS	x/h%	Iso	RC/G
2017	NCAA	Florida State	260	82	71	8	47	273	422	423	845	20	83	1.49	10	2	28	150	6.63
2017	A-	Hudson Valley	164	22	35	1	21	213	332	287	618	15	68	0.55	5	4	29	73	3.36
2018	A	Bowling Green	467	87	142	6	57	304	390	428	819	12	83	0.83	31	12	28	124	5.95

Switch-hitting, athletic SS with chance to develop into solid utility player made significance strides against pro pitching. Contact-oriented approach from both sides. Quicker bat from RH side with much more power potential. Made adjustments with hands from LH side, shortening swing and taking hands through the ball. Plus runner.

Whatley,Matt — 2 — Texas

EXP MLB DEBUT: 2021 | H/W: 5-10 190 | FUT: Starting C | 7D

Bats R Age 23 — 2017 (3) Oral Roberts
Pwr ++ | BAvg ++ | Spd ++ | Def +++

Year	Lev	Team	AB	R	H	HR	RBI	Avg	OB	Sig	OPS	bb%	ct%	Eye	SB	CS	x/h%	Iso	RC/G
2017	NCAA	Oral Roberts	212	45	64	11	49	302	435	509	945	19	81	1.22	10	1	34	208	7.70
2017	Rk	AZL Rangers	17	5	6	0	3	353	421	471	892	11	82	0.67	0	1	17	118	6.83
2017	A-	Spokane	149	23	43	6	25	289	358	450	807	10	81	0.57	3	4	28	161	5.45
2018	A	Hickory	19	3	4	1	1	211	286	368	654	10	63	0.29	0	0	25	158	3.47
2018	A+	Down East	143	11	25	2	13	175	239	280	518	8	66	0.25	1	1	36	105	1.64

Known for his defense including strong arm, he was aggressively assigned to Hi-A and his bat failed miserably. Prior to 2018, made good contact, controlled the plate well, and showed some gap power. Most of those attributes disappeared in 2018. Young enough to re-set, but needs to take some steps forward.

White,Eli — 46 — Texas

EXP MLB DEBUT: 2019 | H/W: 6-2 175 | FUT: Starting MIF | 7B

Bats R Age 24 — 2016 (11) Clemson
Pwr +++ | BAvg +++ | Spd +++ | Def +++

Year	Lev	Team	AB	R	H	HR	RBI	Avg	OB	Sig	OPS	bb%	ct%	Eye	SB	CS	x/h%	Iso	RC/G
2016	NCAA	Clemson	250	57	68	4	30	272	370	380	750	13	76	0.66	24	6	26	108	5.10
2016	Rk	AZL Athletics	3	0	0	0	0	0	0	0	0	0	100		0	0		0	-2.66
2016	A-	Vermont	233	31	65	2	25	279	351	361	712	10	72	0.40	12	3	22	82	4.47
2017	A+	Stockton	448	71	121	4	36	270	331	395	726	8	73	0.34	12	5	35	125	4.66
2018	AA	Midland	504	81	154	9	55	306	382	450	832	11	77	0.53	18	9	31	145	6.07

Slender, athletic MIF prospect who impressed in AA and in AFL campaign. Compact, level stroke yields above-average contact and line-drive trajectories. Works counts and reads spin out of hand. Gap power at present but could produce avg HR totals as he adds strength. Good athlete capable of manning multiple INF positions and stealing bases.

White,Evan — 3 — Seattle

EXP MLB DEBUT: 2020 | H/W: 6-3 200 | FUT: Starting 1B | 8C

Bats R Age 22 — 2017 (1) Kentucky
Pwr +++ | BAvg +++ | Spd +++ | Def ++++

Year	Lev	Team	AB	R	H	HR	RBI	Avg	OB	Sig	OPS	bb%	ct%	Eye	SB	CS	x/h%	Iso	RC/G
2017	NCAA	Kentucky	212	48	79	10	41	373	439	637	1076	11	85	0.81	5	2	44	264	8.77
2017	A-	Everett	47	6	13	3	12	277	358	532	890	11	87	1.00	1	1	38	255	6.49
2018	A+	Modesto	476	72	144	11	66	303	371	458	829	10	78	0.50	4	3	31	155	5.92
2018	AAA	Tacoma	18	0	4	0	0	222	222	333	556	0	72	0.00	0	0	50	111	2.05

Athletic, RHH 1B showcases advanced hitting aptitude. Hit-over-power currently drives profile. Contact-oriented hitter with patient, spray approach. Above-average raw power has yet to show up in games. May limit overall projection at 1B. Plus defender; could be in consideration for a few Gold Gloves.

Whitley,Garrett — 789 — Tampa Bay

EXP MLB DEBUT: 2020 | H/W: 6-1 195 | FUT: Starting OF | 8E

Bats R Age 22 — 2015 (1) HS (NY)
Pwr +++ | BAvg ++ | Spd ++++ | Def ++++

Year	Lev	Team	AB	R	H	HR	RBI	Avg	OB	Sig	OPS	bb%	ct%	Eye	SB	CS	x/h%	Iso	RC/G
2015	Rk	GCL Rays	96	12	18	3	13	188	304	365	668	14	74	0.64	5	4	50	177	3.97
2015	A-	Hudson Valley	42	3	6	0	4	143	234	190	425	11	71	0.42	3	1	17	48	0.51
2016	A-	Hudson Valley	256	38	68	1	31	266	343	379	722	10	71	0.40	21	5	29	113	4.77
2017	A	Bowling Green	358	65	89	13	61	249	352	430	782	14	66	0.47	21	4	39	182	5.71
2018		Did not play - injury																	

Athletic OF who missed entire season after tearing his is right shoulder labrum diving for ball in spring training. When healthy, offers premium bat speed and a patient approach. Struggles with swing path and breaking ball recognition. There's raw plus power in bat and frame. Likely, 20-25 HR hitter at projection. Plus runner with solid SB%.

Wiel,Zander — 37 — Minnesota

EXP MLB DEBUT: 2019 | H/W: 6-3 215 | FUT: Reserve OF | 6C

Bats R Age 26 — 2015 (12) Vanderbilt
Pwr ++ | BAvg ++ | Spd +++ | Def ++

Year	Lev	Team	AB	R	H	HR	RBI	Avg	OB	Sig	OPS	bb%	ct%	Eye	SB	CS	x/h%	Iso	RC/G
2015	Rk	Elizabethton	36	5	7	1	8	194	326	333	659	16	64	0.54	0	0	43	139	3.92
2016	A	Cedar Rapids	501	75	130	19	86	259	333	459	792	10	75	0.44	7	1	42	200	5.42
2017	A+	Fort Myers	452	59	113	13	67	250	340	429	770	12	77	0.60	8	2	43	179	5.27
2018	AA	Chattanooga	386	53	120	7	58	311	376	446	821	9	79	0.49	8	4	30	135	5.79
2018	AAA	Rochester	51	5	10	3	7	196	241	412	653	6	75	0.23	1	0	40	216	3.21

Overachieving former 12th rd pick has advanced to Triple-A in 4th pro season. Average swing speed, swing geared towards low line drive contact. Tweener profile in LF. Average power, completely pull-oriented, and an average runner. Struggles on reads in OF; solid defender at 1B.

Toffey,Will — 5 — New York (N)

EXP MLB DEBUT: 2020 | H/W: 6-2 195 | FUT: Starting 3B | 7C

Bats L Age 24 — 2017 (4) Vanderbilt
Pwr +++ | BAvg +++ | 4.40 Spd + | Def +++

Year	Lev	Team	AB	R	H	HR	RBI	Avg	OB	Sig	OPS	bb%	ct%	Eye	SB	CS	x/h%	Iso	RC/G
2017	NCAA	Vanderbilt	206	55	73	12	64	354	476	602	1078	19	85	1.60	5	4	36	248	9.28
2017	A-	Vermont	209	38	55	1	22	263	377	349	726	15	78	0.84	2	2	25	86	4.95
2018	A+	Stockton	164	17	40	5	32	244	358	384	742	15	70	0.59	0	0	33	140	5.01
2018	AA	Binghamton	134	23	34	4	19	254	390	433	823	18	73	0.83	2	0	47	179	6.32

Not the livest body, but a strong player with a good eye at the plate and a feel for the game. Doesn't do it pretty at 3B but should be able to hold his own there. Not the livest bat, but patient and makes good adjustments. Can get in trouble when tries to hit for too much power, but can hit mistakes out. Plus arm. Not a runner.

Willems,Jonathan — 4 — Cincinnati

EXP MLB DEBUT: 2022 | H/W: 5-11 180 | FUT: Starting 3B | 8E

Bats R Age 20 — 2015 FA (CC)
Pwr +++ | BAvg +++ | Spd +++ | Def +++

Year	Lev	Team	AB	R	H	HR	RBI	Avg	OB	Sig	OPS	bb%	ct%	Eye	SB	CS	x/h%	Iso	RC/G
2017	Rk	AZL Reds	64	7	15	0	4	234	258	281	539	3	70	0.11	7	2	20	47	1.79
2018	Rk	Greeneville	217	30	57	8	39	263	286	470	756	3	75	0.13	0	2	44	207	4.63
2018	Rk	Billings	19	3	4	0	0	211	250	211	461	5	84	0.33	0	1	0	0	1.19

Projectable IF prospect with incredibly raw skill set, including above-average power potential. Has shortened up his swing but still struggles with contact due to poor pitch recognition. Raw plus power began showing up in game. 20-25 HR potential. Struggles with footwork defensively, putting 2B role in doubt. Ceiling potential equals Juan Uribe.

Williams,Justin — 9 — St. Louis

EXP MLB DEBUT: 2018 | H/W: 6-2 215 | FUT: Starting OF | 7B

Bats L Age 23 — 2013 (2) HS (LA)
Pwr +++ | BAvg +++ | Spd ++ | Def ++

Year	Lev	Team	AB	R	H	HR	RBI	Avg	OB	Sig	OPS	bb%	ct%	Eye	SB	CS	x/h%	Iso	RC/G
2016	AA	Montgomery	148	20	37	6	28	250	275	446	720	3	80	0.17	0	1	41	196	4.08
2017	AA	Montgomery	366	53	110	14	72	301	365	489	854	9	81	0.54	6	2	35	189	6.06
2018	AAA	Memphis	69	8	15	3	11	217	270	391	662	7	75	0.29	0	1	40	174	3.45
2018	AAA	Durham	356	41	92	8	46	258	307	376	683	7	77	0.31	4	3	28	118	3.82
2018	MLB	Tampa Bay	1	0	0	0	0	0	0	0	0	0	100		0	0		0	-2.66

Solid, all-around player came over as part of the Tommy Pham deal. Uses a short, compact stroke and is starting to tap into his above-average to plus raw power. Struggled after being traded, with a more aggressive approach at the plate, but long-term the skills remain intriguing. Solid defender with enough arm to stick in RF.

Williams,Nonie — 8 — Los Angeles (A)

EXP MLB DEBUT: 2021 | H/W: 6-2 195 | FUT: Starting OF | 7B

Bats R Age 20 — 2016 (3) HS (KS)
Pwr ++ | BAvg ++ | Spd +++ | Def ++

Year	Lev	Team	AB	R	H	HR	RBI	Avg	OB	Sig	OPS	bb%	ct%	Eye	SB	CS	x/h%	Iso	RC/G
2016	Rk	AZL Angels	156	23	38	0	11	244	280	282	563	5	74	0.20	8	3	13	38	2.21
2017	Rk	AZL Angels	168	22	37	1	15	220	280	280	560	8	68	0.26	11	3	16	60	2.24
2018	Rk	Orem	161	27	31	2	24	193	257	342	599	8	69	0.28	1	1	48	149	2.93

Former switch-hitter now working from the right side of the plate. Good resume of tools with progressing raw power able to find gaps. Above-average speed works well enough to grab some bags. Pitch recognition from right-handed swing is improving. Spent all of 2018 in the OF (previously was at 2B) and instincts and plus arm should work there long term.

Wilson,D.J.
8 | Chicago (N) | EXP MLB DEBUT: 2020 | H/W: 5-8 177 | FUT: Reserve OF | 7D

Bats L Age 22 / 2015 (4) HS (OH)	Year	Lev	Team	AB	R	H	HR	RBI	Avg	OB	Slg	OPS	bb%	ct%	Eye	SB	CS	x/h%	Iso	RC/G
Pwr ++	2015	Rk	AZL Cubs	79	12	21	0	6	266	318	354	672	7	81	0.40	5	1	24	89	3.89
BAvg ++	2016	A-	Eugene	245	37	63	3	29	257	313	371	685	8	77	0.36	21	8	32	114	3.98
Spd +++	2017	Rk	AZL Cubs	8	5	4	3	5	500	600	1750	2350	20	88	2.00	1	0	100	1250	22.87
Def +++	2017	A	South Bend	310	56	71	9	45	229	303	419	723	10	71	0.37	15	7	46	190	4.61
	2018	A+	Myrtle Beach	237	27	52	1	13	219	312	287	599	12	70	0.45	10	6	23	68	2.99

Toolsy OF has yet to find his groove as a pro but has plus raw tools. Solid understanding of the strike zone, plus bat speed, and contact-oriented approach undermined by high-leg kick and limited in-game power. Approach at the plate needs to be revamped to reach potential. Plus speed and defense could be his ticket to the majors.

Wilson,Izzy
789 | Atlanta | EXP MLB DEBUT: 2020 | H/W: 6-3 185 | FUT: Starting OF | 7E

Bats Age 21 / 2014 FA (NT)	Year	Lev	Team	AB	R	H	HR	RBI	Avg	OB	Slg	OPS	bb%	ct%	Eye	SB	CS	x/h%	Iso	RC/G
Pwr ++++	2016	Rk	Danville	130	19	25	2	12	192	271	315	586	10	61	0.27	6	2	44	123	2.83
BAvg +	2017	Rk	Danville	68	11	17	4	12	250	338	544	882	12	74	0.50	2	0	53	294	6.72
Spd ++++	2017	A	Rome	168	28	44	2	20	262	333	351	685	10	69	0.35	9	3	18	89	4.10
Def +++	2018	A	Rome	223	38	51	6	25	229	315	372	687	11	65	0.36	11	4	35	143	4.22
	2018	A+	Florida	135	16	29	2	10	215	289	311	600	9	68	0.33	5	1	28	96	2.85

Quick-twitch, athletic OF continues to struggle with hit tool. 5-tool athlete with average or better raw tool shed. Patient approach with compact, uppercut swing. Biggest issue is swing path inconsistencies. Raw plus power, completely to pull-side. Plus runner with solid SB%. Is a terrific drag bunter.

Wilson,Marcus
8 | Arizona | EXP MLB DEBUT: 2020 | H/W: 6-3 175 | FUT: Starting OF | 7D

Bats R Age 22 / 2014 (2) HS (CA)	Year	Lev	Team	AB	R	H	HR	RBI	Avg	OB	Slg	OPS	bb%	ct%	Eye	SB	CS	x/h%	Iso	RC/G
Pwr ++	2015	Rk	Missoula	213	42	55	1	22	258	358	338	696	13	71	0.54	7	4	25	80	4.45
BAvg ++	2016	A-	Hillsboro	136	24	34	0	15	250	414	316	730	22	71	0.95	18	3	21	66	5.31
Spd ++++	2016	A	Kane County	99	11	25	1	5	253	339	384	723	12	68	0.41	7	2	40	131	4.88
Def +++	2017	A	Kane County	383	56	113	9	54	295	384	446	830	13	77	0.61	15	7	31	151	6.10
	2018	A+	Visalia	447	60	105	10	48	235	303	369	673	9	68	0.31	16	6	36	134	3.89

Wiry, athletic OF who tapped into power in hitter-friendly CAL in 2018. Has good bat speed with slight uppercut to swing and fringe power works mostly to pull side. Has become more aggressive as pro and overall contact ability and OBP value has deteriorated. Good first step and plus runner underway. Profiles well at either LF/CF/RF with solid range

Wiseman,Rhett
79 | Washington | EXP MLB DEBUT: 2020 | H/W: 5-11 187 | FUT: Reserve OF | 7D

Bats L Age 24 / 2015 (3) Vanderbilt	Year	Lev	Team	AB	R	H	HR	RBI	Avg	OB	Slg	OPS	bb%	ct%	Eye	SB	CS	x/h%	Iso	RC/G
Pwr +++	2015	NCAA	Vanderbilt	290	70	92	15	49	317	400	566	966	12	75	0.55	12	2	41	248	7.82
BAvg ++	2015	A-	Auburn	210	25	52	5	35	248	307	376	683	8	75	0.35	6	2	33	129	3.89
4.51 Spd ++	2016	A	Hagerstown	478	71	122	13	75	255	315	410	725	8	78	0.40	19	10	35	155	4.46
Def ++	2017	A+	Potomac	432	55	99	13	55	229	285	391	677	7	78	0.35	2	4	39	162	3.78
	2018	A+	Potomac	407	65	103	21	63	253	353	484	837	13	70	0.52	8	2	47	231	6.27

Medium-build OF who opened up his swing in 2018 with expected results. Finished with career-high in HR and Slg, but pitchers found holes and he struck out at an elevated rate. Features a discerning eye and can chip in a few SB. Has a RF arm and ability to cover ground, but no one standout tool.

Wong,Connor
2 | Los Angeles (N) | EXP MLB DEBUT: 2020 | H/W: 5-10 170 | FUT: Starting C | 6C

Bats R Age 22 / 2017 (3) Houston	Year	Lev	Team	AB	R	H	HR	RBI	Avg	OB	Slg	OPS	bb%	ct%	Eye	SB	CS	x/h%	Iso	RC/G
Pwr +++	2017	NCAA	Houston	265	61	76	12	36	287	361	494	856	10	82	0.63	26	4	37	208	6.13
BAvg ++	2017	Rk	AZL Dodgers	1	0	0	0	0	0	0	0	0	0	0	0.00	0	0		0	
Spd +++	2017	A	Great Lakes	97	19	27	5	18	278	327	495	822	7	73	0.27	1	1	41	216	5.61
Def +++	2018	A+	Rancho Cuca	383	64	103	19	60	269	335	480	815	9	64	0.28	6	2	40	211	6.09

Offensive-oriented CA was moved from SS when drafted. Plus bat speed and an aggressive approach at the plate results in above-average power, but also contact issues. A work in progress behind the dish. He moves well, but is still working on blocking balls. Average arm gives and a high baseball IQ gives him a chance to stick at the position.

Wong,Kean
47 | Tampa Bay | EXP MLB DEBUT: 2019 | H/W: 5-11 190 | FUT: Utility player | 6B

Bats L Age 23 / 2013 (4) HS (HI)	Year	Lev	Team	AB	R	H	HR	RBI	Avg	OB	Slg	OPS	bb%	ct%	Eye	SB	CS	x/h%	Iso	RC/G
Pwr ++	2015	A+	Charlotte	394	46	108	1	36	274	324	332	656	7	84	0.45	15	6	17	58	3.65
BAvg +++	2016	AA	Montgomery	446	52	123	5	56	276	323	368	691	6	84	0.43	10	10	24	92	4.02
Spd +++	2017	AA	Montgomery	45	5	10	0	4	222	271	244	515	6	80	0.33	3	0	10	22	1.78
Def +++	2017	AAA	Durham	377	44	100	5	44	265	326	361	687	8	79	0.44	14	9	26	95	4.01
	2018	AAA	Durham	451	65	127	9	50	282	340	406	746	8	75	0.36	7	3	28	124	4.76

Brother of Kolten Wong. Undervalued, solid athletic IF continues to outshine hit tool limitations. Had best season as pro in Triple-A employing slap approach from LH box. Powered up for career high in power, utilizing pull-field. Has lost a step since pro debut but still above-average runner. Passable defender in LF, 2B & 3B.

Yerzy,Andy
2 | Arizona | EXP MLB DEBUT: 2021 | H/W: 6-3 215 | FUT: Starting C | 8E

Bats L Age 20 / 2016 (2) HS (ON)	Year	Lev	Team	AB	R	H	HR	RBI	Avg	OB	Slg	OPS	bb%	ct%	Eye	SB	CS	x/h%	Iso	RC/G
Pwr +++	2016	Rk	AZL DBacks	102	5	20	1	15	196	226	255	481	4	78	0.18	0	0	20	59	1.16
BAvg +++	2016	Rk	Missoula	60	2	15	0	1	250	250	283	533	0	73	0.00	0	1	13	33	1.56
Spd +	2017	Rk	Missoula	225	36	67	13	45	298	365	524	890	10	80	0.53	0	0	37	227	6.43
Def ++	2018	A-	Hillsboro	239	30	71	8	34	297	371	452	823	10	72	0.42	0	0	28	155	5.91

Bat-first CA who has yet to make full-season debut but shows offensive promise. Possesses plus bat speed and good pull-side power as LHH. Short load and compact stroke yields solid-average contact ability, and displays ability to work counts well. Defense remains question mark and will need to work on blocking skills and throwing accuracy.

Ynfante,Wadye
8 | St. Louis | EXP MLB DEBUT: 2021 | H/W: 6-0 160 | FUT: Starting OF | 8E

Bats R Age 21 / 2014 FA (DR)	Year	Lev	Team	AB	R	H	HR	RBI	Avg	OB	Slg	OPS	bb%	ct%	Eye	SB	CS	x/h%	Iso	RC/G
Pwr ++																				
BAvg ++	2016	Rk	GCL Cardinals	17	1	1	0	0	59	111	59	170	6	76	0.25	0	1	0	0	-2.82
Spd ++++	2017	Rk	Johnson City	167	27	50	7	23	299	364	491	855	9	69	0.33	11	3	36	192	6.40
Def +++	2018	A-	State College	253	33	54	4	25	213	274	328	602	8	60	0.21	10	5	37	115	3.05

Projectable OF scuffled in short-season ball and at 21 needs to show more to remain a prospect. Moves well in the OF with good range and a decent arm. Sprays line drives to all fields with plus bat speed and good raw power, but overly aggressive approach resulted in abysmal ct% rate. Plus speed but needs to get on base to have value.

Yrizarri,Yeyson
6 | Chicago (A) | EXP MLB DEBUT: 2020 | H/W: 6-0 175 | FUT: Utility player | 6C

Bats R Age 22 / 2013 FA (VZ)	Year	Lev	Team	AB	R	H	HR	RBI	Avg	OB	Slg	OPS	bb%	ct%	Eye	SB	CS	x/h%	Iso	RC/G
Pwr ++	2016	A	Hickory	450	53	121	7	53	269	283	389	672	2	80	0.10	20	15	31	120	3.49
BAvg ++	2017	A	Hickory	269	22	71	5	30	264	277	390	668	2	82	0.10	5	4	32	126	3.43
Spd ++++	2017	A+	Winston-Salem	112	12	33	1	11	295	307	330	637	2	81	0.10	1	4	6	36	2.95
Def ++++	2017	A+	Down East	29	5	6	2	7	207	233	483	716	3	72	0.13	0	0	67	276	4.01
	2018	A+	Winston-Salem	372	44	92	6	46	247	282	363	645	5	80	0.24	16	7	32	116	3.31

Speedy, unrefined MIF struggles with consistent hard contact. Contact approach, but too agressive. Hand/eye skills are plus, however, no understanding of strike zone. Below-average power, completely to pull side. Speed burner getting better picking SB opportunities. Doesn't hit enough to start. Could be nice utility player.

Zagunis,Mark
79 | Chicago (N) | EXP MLB DEBUT: 2017 | H/W: 6-0 195 | FUT: Reserve OF | 7C

Bats R Age 26 / 2014 (3) Virginia Tech	Year	Lev	Team	AB	R	H	HR	RBI	Avg	OB	Slg	OPS	bb%	ct%	Eye	SB	CS	x/h%	Iso	RC/G
Pwr ++	2016	AAA	Iowa	179	31	49	6	25	274	353	486	839	11	77	0.52	4	0	45	212	6.14
BAvg ++++	2017	AAA	Iowa	330	59	88	13	55	267	395	455	850	18	72	0.75	4	3	40	188	6.62
Spd ++	2017	MLB	Chi Cubs	14	0	0	0	1	0	222	0	222	22	57	0.67	2	0		0	-3.82
Def ++	2018	AAA	Iowa	371	63	101	7	40	272	388	375	762	16	73	0.69	11	1	24	102	5.37
	2018	MLB	Chi Cubs	5	0	2	0	1	400	500	600	1100	17	80	1.00	0	0	50	200	10.07

Has a professional approach at the plate and career .400 OB%. Injuries have stalled his development and a shoulder injury clouds his future. Other tools are fringe at best and needs a change of scenery, but he can hit and get on base. Could be a solid 4th OF.

Zavala,Seby
2 | Chicago (A) | EXP MLB DEBUT: 2019 | H/W: 6-0 175 | FUT: Starting C | 7C

Bats R Age 25 / 2015 (12) San Diego St	Year	Lev	Team	AB	R	H	HR	RBI	Avg	OB	Slg	OPS	bb%	ct%	Eye	SB	CS	x/h%	Iso	RC/G
Pwr +++	2016	A	Kannapolis	360	40	91	7	49	253	319	381	700	9	70	0.32	1	1	32	128	4.26
BAvg ++	2017	A	Kannapolis	185	32	48	13	34	259	308	514	822	7	72	0.25	0	0	44	254	5.53
Spd +	2017	A+	Winston-Salem	202	31	61	8	38	302	376	485	861	11	74	0.46	1	0	34	183	6.36
Def +++	2018	AA	Birmingham	199	32	54	11	31	271	358	472	831	12	67	0.42	0	0	33	201	6.14
	2018	AAA	Charlotte	181	18	44	2	20	243	267	359	626	3	76	0.14	0	2	39	116	3.02

Stocky CA struggled after Triple-A promotion. Offense has outperformed his skills as a pro. Compact swing with a middle-in approach. Works the zone. Swing speed not optimal against higher velocities. Average power completely to pull-side; 15-20 HR potential. Sells out to power for periods of time. Defense has improved. Will stick at CA.

Pitchers are classified as Starters (SP) or Relievers (RP).

THROWS: Handedness — right (RH) or left (LH).

AGE: Pitcher's age, as of April 1, 2019.

DRAFTED: The year, round, and school that the pitcher performed at as an amateur if drafted, or the year and country where the player was signed from, if a free agent.

EXP MLB DEBUT: The year a player is expected to debut in the major leagues.

H/W: The player's height and weight.

FUT: The role that the pitcher is expected to have for the majority of his major league career, not necessarily his greatest upside.

PITCHES: Each pitch that a pitcher throws is graded and designated with a "+", indicating the quality of the pitch, taking into context the pitcher's age and level pitched. Pitches are graded for their velocity, movement, and command. An average pitch will receive three "+" marks. If known, a pitcher's velocity for each pitch is indicated.

FB	fastball
CB	curveball
SP	split-fingered fastball
SL	slider
CU	change-up
CT	cut-fastball
KC	knuckle-curve
KB	knuckle-ball
SC	screwball
SU	slurve

PLAYER STAT LINES: Pitchers receive statistics for the last five teams that they played for (if applicable), including college and the major leagues.

TEAM DESIGNATIONS: Each team that the pitcher performed for during a given year is included.

LEVEL DESIGNATIONS: The level for each team a player performed is included. "AAA" means Triple-A, "AA" means Double-A, "A+" means high Class-A, "A-" means low Class-A and "Rk" means rookie level.

SABERMETRIC CATEGORIES: Descriptions of all the sabermetric categories appear in the glossary.

CAPSULE COMMENTARIES: For each pitcher, a brief analysis of their skills/statistics, and their future potential is provided.

ELIGIBILITY: Eligibility for inclusion is the standard for which Major League Baseball adheres to; 50 innings pitched or 45 days on the 25-man roster, not including the month of September.

POTENTIAL RATINGS: The Potential Ratings are a two-part system in which a player is assigned a number rating based on his upside potential (1-10) and a letter rating based on the probability of reaching that potential (A-E).

Potential

10:	Hall of Famer	5:	MLB reserve
9:	Elite player	4:	Top minor leaguer
8:	Solid regular	3:	Average minor leaguer
7:	Average regular	2:	Minor league reserve
6:	Platoon player	1:	Minor league roster filler

Probability Rating

A: 90% probability of reaching potential
B: 70% probability of reaching potential
C: 50% probability of reaching potential
D: 30% probability of reaching potential
E: 10% probability of reaching potential

FASTBALL: Scouts grade a fastball in terms of both velocity and movement. Movement of a pitch is purely subjective, but one can always watch the hitter to see how he reacts to a pitch or if he swings and misses. Pitchers throw four types of fastballs with varying movement. A two-seam fastball is often referred to as a sinker. A four-seam fastball appears to maintain its plane at high velocities. A cutter can move in different directions and is caused by the pitcher both cutting-off his extension out front and by varying the grip. A split-fingered fastball (forkball) is thrown with the fingers spread apart against the seams and demonstrates violent downward movement. Velocity is often graded on the 20-80 scale and is indicated by the chart below.

Scout Grade	Velocity (mph)
80	96+
70	94-95
60	92-93
50 (avg)	89-91
40	87-88
30	85-86
20	82-84

PITCHER RELEASE TIMES: The speed (in seconds) that a pitcher releases a pitch from the stretch is extremely important in terms of halting the running game and establishing good pitching mechanics. Pitchers are timed from the movement of the front leg until the baseball reaches the catcher's mitt. The phrases "slow to the plate" or "quick to the plate" may appear in the capsule commentary box.

1.0-1.2	+
1.3-1.4	MLB average
1.5+	–

Abbott,Cory
SP | **Chicago (N)** | EXP MLB DEBUT: 2020 | H/W: 6-1 210 | FUT: #4 starter | **7D**

Thrws R Age 23
2017 (2) Loyola Marymount
- 91-93 FB ++
- 86-88 SL +++
- 80-82 CB ++
- 84-85 CU ++

Year	Lev	Team	W	L	Sv	IP	K	ERA	WHIP	BF/G	OBA	H%	S%	xERA	Ctl	Dom	Cmd	hr/9	BPV
2017	NCAA	Loyola Mrymt	11	2	0	98	130	1.74	0.91	24.4	181	28	81	1.31	2.6	11.9	4.6	0.3	163
2017	A-	Eugene	0	0	0	14	18	3.86	1.21	11.3	262	38	69	3.43	1.9	11.6	6.0	0.6	174
2018	A	South Bend	4	1	0	47	57	2.48	1.02	20.1	209	28	81	2.56	2.5	10.9	4.4	1.0	147
2018	A+	Myrtle Beach	4	5	0	67	74	2.54	1.26	21.1	237	33	80	3.03	3.5	9.9	2.8	0.4	102

Late developing RHP continues to impress, despite average stuff. FB sits at 91-93 but plays up due to ability to locate to both sides of the plate. Solid secondary offerings; plus SL is a swing-and-miss pitch, also sports a power CB and improved CU. Pounds the zone and owns a career 2.65 ERA and a 10.3 Dom, but still profiles as back-end starter.

Abreu,Albert
SP | **New York (A)** | EXP MLB DEBUT: 2020 | H/W: 6-2 175 | FUT: #3 starter | **8C**

Thrws R Age 23
2014 FA (DR)
- 95-98 FB ++++
- 83-85 CB +++
- 85-87 CU ++++

Year	Lev	Team	W	L	Sv	IP	K	ERA	WHIP	BF/G	OBA	H%	S%	xERA	Ctl	Dom	Cmd	hr/9	BPV
2017	A+	Tampa	1	3	0	34	31	4.22	1.41	16.0	255	32	70	3.76	4.0	8.2	2.1	0.5	58
2018	Rk	GCL Yankees W	0	3	0	5	5	23.40	3.20	10.0	498	61	19	12.64	3.6	9.0	2.5	0.0	83
2018	Rk	GCL Yankees	0	1	0	2	2	18.00	2.00	9.6	415	52	0	7.49	0.0	9.0		0.0	180
2018	A+	Tampa	4	3	0	62	65	4.20	1.33	19.9	235	29	73	4.03	4.2	9.4	2.2	1.3	74
2018	AA	Trenton	0	0	0	5	4	0.00	0.20	15.1	0	0	100		1.8	7.2	4.0	0.0	99

Lean, athletic high-upside RHP has struggled with injury bug in 2017-18. Elastic 3/4s, slightly cross-armed delivery with plus arm speed. Features three pitches. FB gets on hitters with late run. Throws hard CB with solid shape and break. Replicates FB arm-speed with late-fading CU; potentially a plus pitch at projection.

Abreu,Bryan
RP | **Houston** | EXP MLB DEBUT: 2022 | H/W: 6-1 175 | FUT: Setup reliever | **8D**

Thrws R Age 21
2013 FA (DR)
- 94-97 FB ++++
- 85-87 SL +++
- 83-85 CB +++
- 88-89 CU ++

Year	Lev	Team	W	L	Sv	IP	K	ERA	WHIP	BF/G	OBA	H%	S%	xERA	Ctl	Dom	Cmd	hr/9	BPV
2016	Rk	Greeneville	0	1	0	5		12.35	2.16	8.5	294	42	36	5.68	8.8	10.6	1.2	0.0	-30
2016	Rk	GCL Astros	2	4	0	33	35	3.81	1.45	14.1	261	36	71	3.44	4.1	9.5	2.3	0.0	79
2017	Rk	Greeneville	1	3	0	29	40	8.04	1.72	16.5	261	37	52	5.24	6.5	12.4	1.9	1.2	65
2018	A-	Tri City	2	0	0	16	22	1.13	1.06	15.5	196	28	100	2.67	3.4	12.4	3.7	1.1	150
2018	A	Quad Cities	4	1	3	38	68	1.65	1.02	14.6	170	34	86	1.63	4.0	16.1	4.0	0.5	199

Shortish right-hander with an explosive fastball, a slider that flashes above-average, and a 12-to-6 curve with elite spin. The fastball sits mid-to-upper 90s and occasionally shows late, arm-side break. The slider is thrown confidently and has late break, darting in under the hands of right-handed batters or used away as a chase pitch.

Acevedo,Domingo
SP | **New York (A)** | EXP MLB DEBUT: 2019 | H/W: 6-7 242 | FUT: Setup reliever | **7B**

Thrws R Age 24
2013 FA (DR)
- 94-96 FB ++++
- 85-88 SL +++
- 84-85 CU +

Year	Lev	Team	W	L	Sv	IP	K	ERA	WHIP	BF/G	OBA	H%	S%	xERA	Ctl	Dom	Cmd	hr/9	BPV
2017	A+	Tampa	0	4	0	41	52	4.60	1.41	24.8	297	41	70	4.87	2.0	11.4	5.8	1.1	170
2017	AA	Trenton	5	1	0	79	82	2.39	1.04	21.8	226	29	82	2.79	1.9	9.3	4.8	0.9	134
2017	AAA	Scranton/WB	1	1	0	12	8	4.46	1.65	27.1	260	31	70	3.97	6.0	6.0	1.0	0.0	-36
2018	A-	Staten Island	0	0	0	4	3	4.29	1.43	8.9	297	36	67	3.93	2.1	6.4	3.0	0.0	76
2018	AA	Trenton	3	3	0	64	52	2.94	1.11	18.0	220	27	74	2.45	2.8	7.3	2.6	0.4	74

Tall, big-bodied with arm-heavy delivery struggled with bicep injury during 2nd half of season. Unorthodox, high-3/4s slot with stiffness, likely works best as RP. Mid-90s FB has late life and can reach high-90s in spurts. SL has tightened up with late darting action. No feel for CU.

Adams,Chance
SP | **New York (A)** | EXP MLB DEBUT: 2018 | H/W: 6-0 205 | FUT: Setup reliever | **7C**

Thrws R Age 24
2015 (5) Dallas Baptist
- 91-94 FB +++
- 84-86 SL +++
- 76-79 CB +++
- 84-85 CU ++

Year	Lev	Team	W	L	Sv	IP	K	ERA	WHIP	BF/G	OBA	H%	S%	xERA	Ctl	Dom	Cmd	hr/9	BPV
2016	AA	Trenton	8	1	0	69	71	2.08	0.85	19.5	152	19	80	1.24	3.1	9.2	3.0	0.7	100
2017	AA	Trenton	4	0	0	35	32	1.03	1.09	22.8	189	24	94	2.11	3.9	8.2	2.1	0.5	62
2017	AAA	Scranton/WB	11	5	0	115	103	2.89	1.08	21.4	200	25	76	2.39	3.4	8.1	2.4	0.7	72
2018	AAA	Scranton/WB	4	5	0	113	113	4.78	1.41	17.7	241	29	69	4.26	4.6	9.0	1.9	1.3	55
2018	MLB	NY Yankees	0	1	0	7	4	7.50	1.67	10.8	283	23	67	7.86	5.0	5.0	1.0	3.8	-27

Physically-mature RHP made MLB debut despite control and velocity issues. Struggles repeating 3/4s cross-fire delivery. Lost velocity on 4-seam FB, which negated effectiveness despite late running action. Improved shape of 11-to-5 CB, becoming 2nd best pitch. Sharp SL misses barrels but not bat. Repeats FB delivery but CU suffers from flatness.

Adams,Spencer
SP | **Chicago (A)** | EXP MLB DEBUT: 2019 | H/W: 6-3 171 | FUT: #5 SP/swingman | **6B**

Thrws R Age 22
2014 (2) HS (GA)
- 90-93 FB ++
- 81-84 SL +++
- 75-77 CB ++
- 82-85 CU +++

Year	Lev	Team	W	L	Sv	IP	K	ERA	WHIP	BF/G	OBA	H%	S%	xERA	Ctl	Dom	Cmd	hr/9	BPV
2016	A+	Winston-Salem	8	7	0	107	74	4.03	1.32	24.6	284	33	69	4.01	1.8	6.2	3.5	0.6	82
2016	AA	Birmingham	2	5	0	55	26	3.92	1.25	24.9	275	31	67	3.49	1.6	4.2	2.6	0.3	50
2017	AA	Birmingham	7	15	0	152	113	4.43	1.39	24.6	285	32	71	4.70	2.4	6.7	2.8	1.1	74
2018	AA	Birmingham	3	6	0	68	53	4.62	1.47	22.5	294	33	72	5.21	2.6	7.0	2.7	1.3	73
2018	AAA	Charlotte	4	7	0	90	42	3.20	1.33	24.9	244	25	80	3.90	3.8	4.2	1.1	1.0	-9

Lean, athletic former 2nd round pick had solid season. Easy, 3/4s cross-fire delivery. Four-pitch pitcher. 2-seam FB sits low 90s with solid, arm-side run. Commands well down but hurt when left up in zone. SL is best secondary offering, featuring 2-plane break that generates soft contact. CB has never progressed beyond a fringe pitch. CU has deceptive late fade.

Adcock,Brett
RP | **Houston** | EXP MLB DEBUT: 2019 | H/W: 6-0 215 | FUT: Middle reliever | **7B**

Thrws L Age 23
2016 (4) Michigan
- 90-92 FB ++
- 78-82 CB ++++
- 82-83 CU +++

Year	Lev	Team	W	L	Sv	IP	K	ERA	WHIP	BF/G	OBA	H%	S%	xERA	Ctl	Dom	Cmd	hr/9	BPV
2016	A-	Tri City	0	0	0	4	6	6.59	1.22	5.5	206	35	40	2.11	4.4	13.2	3.0	0.0	137
2017	A	Quad Cities	1	0	0	23	37	1.16	0.95	17.5	187	35	86	1.19	2.7	14.4	5.3	0.0	203
2017	A+	Buies Creek	4	4	1	84	80	4.71	1.31	17.3	248	31	65	3.82	3.4	8.6	2.5	1.0	80
2018	A+	Buies Creek	5	3	1	67	67	2.55	1.01	16.1	145	20	73	1.09	4.8	9.0	1.9	0.1	49
2018	AA	Corpus Christi	4	2	0	38	28	3.53	1.47	18.2	240	29	76	3.66	5.2	6.6	1.3	0.5	-3

The stout southpaw beat up on younger competition to open the season and then found the Texas League a little tougher. A pedestrian fastball belies a hard, 12-to-6 downer curve that he uses to miss bats. The change-up consistency has improved and it is an average offering, but his lack of control will likely push him to the bullpen.

Adon,Melvin
SP | **San Francisco** | EXP MLB DEBUT: 2019 | H/W: 6-3 195 | FUT: Setup reliever | **7C**

Thrws R Age 24
2015 FA (DR)
- 95-98 FB ++++
- 86-89 SL +++
- 86-88 CU ++

Year	Lev	Team	W	L	Sv	IP	K	ERA	WHIP	BF/G	OBA	H%	S%	xERA	Ctl	Dom	Cmd	hr/9	BPV
2016	A-	Salem-Keizer	5	5	0	67	55	5.50	1.77	22.0	310	38	67	5.37	4.6	7.4	1.6	0.4	28
2017	A	Augusta	3	11	0	99	89	4.36	1.46	18.5	282	36	69	4.21	3.2	8.1	2.5	0.5	78
2018	Rk	AZL Giants O	0	1	0	4	8	8.57	2.86	11.9	432	70	67	9.95	6.4	17.1	2.7	0.0	153
2018	A+	San Jose	2	5	0	77	71	4.90	1.50	20.9	274	34	67	4.41	4.0	8.3	2.1	0.7	60

Big-bodied, physical RHP worked out of pen successfully in AFL stint. 3/4s delivery with fair extension. As a starter, throws heavy 2-seam FB with solid run, but struggles commanding it due to delivery flaws. Pitch plays up as RP. SL has solid two-plane break but can suffer from slurvy shape. CU is a workable pitch to LHH in limited bursts.

Agrazal,Dario
SP | **Pittsburgh** | EXP MLB DEBUT: 2020 | H/W: 6-3 190 | FUT: Middle reliever | **7D**

Thrws R Age 24
2012 FA (PN)
- 88-92 FB ++
- 83-85 SL ++++
- 81-84 CU ++

Year	Lev	Team	W	L	Sv	IP	K	ERA	WHIP	BF/G	OBA	H%	S%	xERA	Ctl	Dom	Cmd	hr/9	BPV
2016	A	West Virginia	8	12	0	150	88	4.20	1.27	22.7	290	32	70	4.46	1.1	5.3	4.9	1.1	84
2017	A+	Bradenton	5	3	0	80	63	2.92	1.04	22.1	244	30	72	2.61	1.1	7.1	6.3	0.4	115
2017	AA	Altoona	0	1	0	4	2	4.50	1.25	16.3	210	24	60	2.33	4.5	4.5	1.0	0.0	-23
2018	A+	Bradenton	0	0	0	8	4	0.00	0.38	12.8	117	14	100		0.0	4.5		0.0	99
2018	AA	Altoona	5	6	0	85	52	4.01	1.22	23.0	275	30	69	3.98	1.4	5.5	4.0	1.0	80

Big, strong slider master who sometimes falls in love with the pitch too much. It's good and he commands it well, but it's not great. Does not command or use his FB well enough. CU not a plus either, so struggles with LHH. Starter who needs to move to pen where maybe his FB will play up. Best bet is right-on-right reliever, playing off the slider.

Aiken,Brady
SP | **Cleveland** | EXP MLB DEBUT: 2022 | H/W: 6-4 205 | FUT: #4 starter | **8E**

Thrws L Age 22
2016 (1) IMG Academy
- 86-92 FB +++
- 75-80 CB +++
- 82-83 CU +++

Year	Lev	Team	W	L	Sv	IP	K	ERA	WHIP	BF/G	OBA	H%	S%	xERA	Ctl	Dom	Cmd	hr/9	BPV
2016	Rk	AZL Indians	0	4	0	24	35	7.13	1.88	12.5	321	49	59	5.72	4.9	13.1	2.7	0.4	123
2016	A-	Mahoning Vall	2	1	0	22	22	4.48	1.27	18.1	243	30	68	3.88	3.3	9.0	2.8	1.2	91
2017	A	Lake County	5	13	0	132	89	4.77	1.78	22.5	265	30	74	5.12	6.9	6.1	0.9	0.8	-59

When we last saw him pitch in 2017 his stuff was far from the stuff he had when he was drafted #1 overall by the Astros in 2014. The 2019 season could be a crossroads for Aiken, as he needs to be healthy and regain some of the lost zip on his fastball to remain in the realm of prospecthood.

Akin,Keegan
SP | **Baltimore** | EXP MLB DEBUT: 2019 | H/W: 6-0 225 | FUT: #4 starter | **7B**

Thrws L Age 24
2016 (2) Western Michigan
- 91-94 FB ++++
- 81-83 SL +++
- 76-78 CB ++
- 80-81 CU +++

Year	Lev	Team	W	L	Sv	IP	K	ERA	WHIP	BF/G	OBA	H%	S%	xERA	Ctl	Dom	Cmd	hr/9	BPV
2016	NCAA	W Michigan	7	4	0	109	133	1.82	0.94	24.1	190	29	79	1.31	2.5	11.0	4.4	0.1	149
2016	A-	Aberdeen	0	1	0	26	29	1.04	0.85	10.6	170	25	86	0.79	2.4	10.0	4.1	0.0	133
2017	A+	Frederick	7	8	0	100	111	4.14	1.35	19.9	240	31	72	3.91	4.1	10.0	2.4	1.1	86
2018	AA	Bowie	14	7	0	137	142	3.28	1.25	22.4	228	29	78	3.49	3.8	9.3	2.4	1.0	83

Short, big-bodied advanced pitcher is knocking on door of MLB debut. Improved repeatable, deceptive cross-armed 3/4s delivery to get more out of pitches. Everything played up. 2-seam FB has solid arm-side run. Commands to both sides of plate. Best secondary is tight SL with 2-plane movement. CU is third pitch with solid fade and feel.

Albertos,Jose

Name	Pos	Team	EXP MLB DEBUT	H/W	FUT	Rating
Albertos,Jose	SP	Chicago (N)	2020	6-1 185	Setup reliever	9E

Thrws R	Age 20
2016 FA (MX)	
94-96 FB	++++
75-78 CB	++
CU	++++

Year	Lev	Team	W	L	Sv	IP	K	ERA	WHIP	BF/G	OBA	H%	S%	xERA	Ctl	Dom	Cmd	hr/9	BPV
2016	Rk	AZL Cubs	0	0	0	4	7	0.00	0.50	13.3	81	19	100		2.3	15.8	7.0	0.0	241
2017	Rk	AZL Cubs	0	0	0	8	6	4.44	1.11	15.9	208	26	56	1.93	3.3	6.7	2.0	0.0	48
2017	A-	Eugene	2	1	0	34	42	2.89	1.11	16.8	199	31	71	1.78	3.7	11.1	3.0	0.0	117
2018	A-	Eugene	0	4	0	17	21	12.11	3.04	9.1	283	41	56	7.73	17.4	11.1	0.6	0.0	-252
2018	A	South Bend	0	5	0	13	17	18.69	3.77	9.5	317	45	46	10.73	22.2	11.8	0.5	0.7	-368

Strong-armed RHP has plus velocity, but mechanics fell apart. FB sits at 94-97 with good late sink, but could not find a consistent release point. FB was up in the zone; then spiked his breaking ball. CB has some potential but lacks depth and consistency and a CU that flashes plus give him the tools to be a #2 starter, but that seems unlikely now.

Alcala,Jorge

Name	Pos	Team	EXP MLB DEBUT	H/W	FUT	Rating
Alcala,Jorge	SP	Minnesota	2019	6-3 180	#3 starter	8E

Thrws R	Age 23
2015 FA (DR)	
92-97 FB	++++
82-83 SL	++
76-79 CB	++++
85-87 CU	+

Year	Lev	Team	W	L	Sv	IP	K	ERA	WHIP	BF/G	OBA	H%	S%	xERA	Ctl	Dom	Cmd	hr/9	BPV
2017	A	Quad Cities	2	0	0	31	35	2.03	0.90	19.2	155	20	84	1.59	3.5	10.2	2.9	0.9	107
2017	A+	Buies Creek	5	6	0	78	60	3.46	1.13	19.3	200	23	72	2.63	3.8	6.9	1.8	0.8	40
2018	A+	Buies Creek	1	4	2	38	45	3.06	1.13	15.1	188	27	73	2.14	4.2	10.6	2.5	0.5	94
2018	AA	Corpus Christi	2	3	1	40	37	3.58	1.32	18.5	241	31	71	3.06	3.8	8.3	2.2	0.2	64
2018	AA	Chattanooga	0	4	0	20	22	5.85	1.85	18.7	290	36	73	6.54	6.3	9.9	1.6	1.8	26

Hard-throwing, thin RHP acquired in mid-season trade with HOU. Lots of red flags. Skinny build not conducive for added bulk. High 3/4s slot features short arm circle and violent sudden stop. Has four pitches, including 2-seam FB with solid arm-side bore, but lacks command. Best secondary is 12-to-6 power CB with violent break. SL, CU need work.

Alcantara,Sandy

Name	Pos	Team	EXP MLB DEBUT	H/W	FUT	Rating
Alcantara,Sandy	SP	Miami	2017	6-4 170	#2 starter	9E

Thrws R	Age 23
2014 FA (DR)	
93-97 FB	++++
84-87 SL	++++
82-83 CB	++
88-91 CU	++++

Year	Lev	Team	W	L	Sv	IP	K	ERA	WHIP	BF/G	OBA	H%	S%	xERA	Ctl	Dom	Cmd	hr/9	BPV
2017	AA	Springfield	7	5	0	125		4.32	1.43	21.3	262	31	72	4.29	3.9	7.6	2.0	0.9	50
2017	MLB	St. Louis	0	0	0	8	10	4.44	1.85	4.7	283	35	85	6.82	6.7	11.1	1.7	2.2	38
2018	A+	Jupiter	0	0	0	11	8	4.05	1.35	15.4	242	30	67	2.96	4.1	6.5	1.6	0.0	25
2018	AAA	New Orleans	6	3	0	115	88	3.91	1.26	24.7	248	29	70	3.53	3.0	6.9	2.3	0.8	62
2018	MLB	Miami	2	3	0	34	30	3.44	1.41	24.0	207	25	78	3.41	6.1	7.9	1.3	0.8	-3

Explosive, lean RHP was solid during MLB stint in 2018. Athletic, 3/4 delivery with plus-plus arm speed, but struggles to corral arsenal. Throws 2-seam and 4-seam FB, both with late run and a high whiff%. Late-fading CU mimics FB arm speed with great separation. SL has solid 2-plane movement. CB is loopy and not effective.

Alexy,A.J.

Name	Pos	Team	EXP MLB DEBUT	H/W	FUT	Rating
Alexy,A.J.	SP	Texas	2021	6-4 195	#3 starter	8C

Thrws R	Age 20
2016 (11) HS (PA)	
92-94 FB	+++
75-79 CB	++++
82-83 CU	++

Year	Lev	Team	W	L	Sv	IP	K	ERA	WHIP	BF/G	OBA	H%	S%	xERA	Ctl	Dom	Cmd	hr/9	BPV
2016	Rk	AZL Dodgers	1	0	0	13	12	4.77	1.52	8.2	314	37	72	5.67	2.0	8.2	4.0	1.4	110
2017	A	Hickory	1	1	0	20	27	3.12	1.39	17.0	186	25	84	3.57	6.7	12.0	1.8	1.3	54
2017	A	Great Lakes	2	6	0	73	86	3.69	1.13	15.2	182	26	66	2.00	4.5	10.6	2.3	0.4	86
2018	A	Hickory	6	8	0	108	138	3.58	1.31	20.3	226	34	72	2.98	4.3	11.5	2.7	0.4	108

Smoothed out delivery and added strength, and more velocity followed. FB has some life, but command of it could still improve. Possesses a hammer curveball with downer action, and his change-up, while still needing reps, has flashed average. Was second in SAL k/9 and has a sturdy, starter's frame.

Allard,Kolby

Name	Pos	Team	EXP MLB DEBUT	H/W	FUT	Rating
Allard,Kolby	SP	Atlanta	2018	6-1 175	#4 starter	7B

Thrws L	Age 21
2015 (1) HS (CA)	
88-91 FB	+++
71-75 CB	+++
79-81 CU	++++

Year	Lev	Team	W	L	Sv	IP	K	ERA	WHIP	BF/G	OBA	H%	S%	xERA	Ctl	Dom	Cmd	hr/9	BPV
2016	Rk	Danville	3	0	0	27	33	1.33	0.85	19.9	191	29	83	1.02	1.7	11.0	6.6	0.0	170
2016	A	Rome	5	3	0	60	62	3.74	1.23	22.1	242	31	71	3.33	3.0	9.3	3.1	0.7	104
2017	AA	Mississippi	8	11	0	150	129	3.18	1.27	22.7	257	31	77	3.57	2.7	7.7	2.9	0.7	84
2018	AAA	Gwinnett	6	4	0	112	89	2.73	1.21	23.8	244	30	78	3.08	2.7	7.1	2.6	0.5	73
2018	MLB	Atlanta	1	1	0	8	3	12.38	2.88	15.2	457	45	60	13.92	4.5	3.4	0.8	3.4	-43

Pitchability LHP with solid MiLB track record continues to lose velocity on FB. Easy, repeatable 3/4s delivery with limited extension. 3-pitch pitcher; rides 4-seam FB up, setting up hitters for secondaries. 1-to-7 CB hasn't profiled as previously projected, struggles to get swings and misses. Out pitch is late fading CU. Good separation from FB.

Allen,Logan

Name	Pos	Team	EXP MLB DEBUT	H/W	FUT	Rating
Allen,Logan	SP	San Diego	2019	6-3 200	#4 starter	8B

Thrws L	Age 21
2015 (8) HS (FL)	
91-94 FB	+++
84-88 SL	+++
82-83 CU	++++

Year	Lev	Team	W	L	Sv	IP	K	ERA	WHIP	BF/G	OBA	H%	S%	xERA	Ctl	Dom	Cmd	hr/9	BPV
2017	A	Fort Wayne	5	4	0	68	85	2.11	1.10	20.5	203	31	80	1.93	3.4	11.2	3.3	0.1	127
2017	A+	Lake Elsinore	2	5	0	56	57	4.00	1.39	21.5	275	36	70	3.77	2.9	9.1	3.2	0.3	104
2018	AA	San Antonio	10	6	0	121	125	2.75	1.05	23.4	207	27	75	2.22	2.8	9.3	3.3	0.5	109
2018	AAA	El Paso	4	0	0	27	26	1.65	1.25	22.1	215	25	97	3.59	4.3	8.6	2.0	1.3	57

Strong, durable LHP who posted 9.1 Dom in nearly 150 IP in upper minors in 2018. Features a low-90s fastball that plays up with late life from 3/4 arm slot. Repeats arm speed & delivery well for deception on CU that flashes plus at next level; SL works as passable third pitch. Not a prolific strike thrower, but has pitchability and mixes things up.

Almonte,Yency

Name	Pos	Team	EXP MLB DEBUT	H/W	FUT	Rating
Almonte,Yency	RP	Colorado	2018	6-3 185	Setup reliever	7C

Thrws R	Age 24
2012 (17) HS (FL)	
93-96 FB	++++
85-87 SL	+++
83-85 CU	++

Year	Lev	Team	W	L	Sv	IP	K	ERA	WHIP	BF/G	OBA	H%	S%	xERA	Ctl	Dom	Cmd	hr/9	BPV
2016	AA	Hartford	3	1	0	30	22	3.00	1.27	24.5	206	22	82	3.43	4.8	6.6	1.4	1.2	7
2017	AA	Hartford	5	3	0	76	71	2.01	1.17	21.7	213	27	85	2.56	3.7	8.4	2.3	0.5	70
2017	AAA	Albuquerque	3	1	0	35	22	4.89	1.77	20.1	293	31	78	6.44	5.4	5.7	1.0	1.8	-26
2018	AAA	Albuquerque	3	5	1	43	34	5.63	1.34	10.0	265	29	62	4.81	2.9	7.1	2.4	1.7	67
2018	MLB	Colorado	0	0	0	14	14	1.90	1.34	4.2	273	35	89	3.91	2.5	8.9	3.5	0.6	109

Live-armed hurler logged 14 impressive MLB innings after scuffling at AAA. Best offering is a plus mid-90s sinker that tops out at 98 mph. Mixes in an above-average hard SL and an improved CU. Two stints on the DL with arm fatigue raise concerns about durability and the move to relief seems permanent.

Alvarez,Yadier

Name	Pos	Team	EXP MLB DEBUT	H/W	FUT	Rating
Alvarez,Yadier	SP	Los Angeles (N)	2019	6-3 175	Closer	9E

Thrws R	Age 23
2015 FA (CU)	
95-98 FB	+++++
86-88 SL	++++
87-90 CU	++

Year	Lev	Team	W	L	Sv	IP	K	ERA	WHIP	BF/G	OBA	H%	S%	xERA	Ctl	Dom	Cmd	hr/9	BPV
2016	A	Great Lakes	3	2	0	39	55	2.30	1.07	16.9	219	35	78	2.13	2.5	12.7	5.0	0.2	178
2017	A+	Rancho Cuca	2	4	1	59	61	5.33	1.46	18.0	268	35	61	3.97	3.8	9.3	2.4	0.5	82
2017	AA	Tulsa	2	2	0	33	36	3.55	1.64	21.0	238	33	77	3.85	6.8	9.8	1.4	0.3	11
2018	Rk	AZL Dodgers	0	0	0	7	10	1.29	0.86	12.9	202	34	83	1.16	1.3	12.9	10.0	0.0	215
2018	AA	Tulsa	1	2	1	48	52	4.68	1.66	12.7	214	30	71	3.72	8.0	9.7	1.2	0.4	-24

FB tops out at 101 mph with good late life. Backs up the heater with a potential plus mid-80s power SL, while CU remains inconsistent and below average. Struggled to repeat mechanics and find the strike zone. Would not be surprising to seem him moved to a relief role full-time.

Alzolay,Adbert

Name	Pos	Team	EXP MLB DEBUT	H/W	FUT	Rating
Alzolay,Adbert	SP	Chicago (N)	2019	6-0 179	#2 starter	9D

Thrws R	Age 24
2013 FA (VZ)	
92-95 FB	++++
80-83 CB	+++
85-88 CU	++

Year	Lev	Team	W	L	Sv	IP	K	ERA	WHIP	BF/G	OBA	H%	S%	xERA	Ctl	Dom	Cmd	hr/9	BPV
2015	A-	Eugene	6	2	0	53	49	2.04	0.83	16.1	163	19	82	1.49	2.5	8.3	3.3	0.8	99
2016	A	South Bend	9	4	0	120	81	4.35	1.22	22.1	260	30	64	3.52	2.1	6.1	2.9	0.7	71
2017	A+	Myrtle Beach	7	1	0	81	78	2.99	1.07	21.1	221	27	76	2.80	2.4	8.6	3.5	0.9	108
2017	AA	Tennessee	0	3	0	32	30	3.07	1.21	18.5	229	31	72	2.42	3.4	8.4	2.5	0.0	78
2018	AAA	Iowa	2	4	0	39	27	4.82	1.43	20.8	280	32	67	4.54	3.0	6.2	2.1	0.9	49

Hard-thrower logged only 8 starts before being shut down with a strained lat. Ball comes out of his hand easy; FB sits at 92-95 and touches 98. Above-average CB and improving CU give him a three-pitch mix. Needs to find a consistent release point and doesn't miss as many bats as he should. Look for a rebound in 2019.

Anderson,Drew

Name	Pos	Team	EXP MLB DEBUT	H/W	FUT	Rating
Anderson,Drew	SP	Philadelphia	2017	6-3 185	Middle reliever	7D

Thrws R	Age 25
2012 (21) HS (NV)	
90-94 FB	+++
74-75 CB	+++
83-85 CU	++
82-84 SL	+

Year	Lev	Team	W	L	Sv	IP	K	ERA	WHIP	BF/G	OBA	H%	S%	xERA	Ctl	Dom	Cmd	hr/9	BPV
2017	AA	Reading	9	4	0	107	86	3.61	1.13	20.2	211	24	72	3.03	3.4	7.2	2.2	1.1	57
2017	AAA	Lehigh Valley	0	0	0	6	7	1.45	1.13	24.5	222	28	100	3.48	2.9	10.2	3.5	1.5	123
2017	MLB	Philadelphia	0	0	0	2	2	25.71	3.33	6.5	503	60	14	13.13	4.3	8.6	2.0	0.0	57
2018	AAA	Lehigh Valley	9	4	0	104	84	3.89	1.16	21.8	238	27	71	3.56	2.5	7.3	2.9	1.2	81
2018	MLB	Philadelphia	0	1	0	12	11	5.16	1.56	10.7	331	42	63	4.77	1.5	8.1	5.5	0.0	124

Four-pitch starter with a biting slow curve for his best offspeed, but who hasn't gotten enough swings and misses at the upper levels with any of his offerings. Uses his good size for downhill plane, but no one consistent out pitch, and though his control improved, it needs to be more polished for the majors.

Anderson,Ian

Name	Pos	Team	EXP MLB DEBUT	H/W	FUT	Rating
Anderson,Ian	SP	Atlanta	2019	6-3 170	#1 starter	9C

Thrws R	Age 20
2016 (1) HS (NY)	
91-95 FB	++++
76-79 CB	++++
84-86 CU	++++

Year	Lev	Team	W	L	Sv	IP	K	ERA	WHIP	BF/G	OBA	H%	S%	xERA	Ctl	Dom	Cmd	hr/9	BPV
2016	Rk	GCL Braves	1	0	0	18	18	0.00	1.00	13.8	216	30	100	1.73	2.0	9.0	4.5	0.0	126
2016	Rk	Danville	0	2	0	21	18	3.82	1.27	17.4	241	30	69	3.14	3.4	7.6	2.3	0.4	64
2017	A	Rome	4	5	0	83	101	3.14	1.35	17.3	228	34	74	2.73	4.7	11.0	2.3	0.2	89
2018	A+	Florida	2	6	0	100	118	2.52	1.13	19.8	206	30	77	2.08	3.6	10.6	3.0	0.2	112
2018	AA	Mississippi	2	1	0	19	24	2.36	1.20	19.2	206	32	78	2.10	4.2	11.3	2.7	0.0	107

Hard-throwing athletic former 1st round pick took big step in development behind added strength and improved control of FB. 3-pitch pitcher, all plus potential. 2-seam FB has solid arm-side run and plus sink. Consistency of 12-to-6 CB took big step forward, now with solid shape and plus break. Maintains FB arm speed with late-fading CU.

Anderson,Shaun

SP | San Francisco | EXP MLB DEBUT: 2019 | H/W: 6-4 235 | FUT: #4 starter | 7B

Thrws R Age 24
2016 (3) Florida

Velo	Pitch	Grade
92-94	FB	+++
83-86	SL	++++
84-86	CU	+++

Year	Lev	Team	W	L	Sv	IP	K	ERA	WHIP	BF/G	OBA	H%	S%	xERA	Ctl	Dom	Cmd	hr/9	BPV
2017	A	Greenville	3	0	0	38	37	2.59	1.07	21.2	218	28	77	2.38	2.6	8.7	3.4	0.5	105
2017	A+	San Jose	3	3	0	25	22	3.57	0.91	15.7	211	27	59	1.79	1.4	7.9	5.5	0.4	121
2017	A+	Salem	3	3	0	58	48	4.02	1.22	21.4	244	29	69	3.52	2.8	7.4	2.7	0.9	76
2018	AA	Richmond	6	5	0	94	93	3.45	1.22	22.4	260	33	75	3.66	2.1	8.9	4.2	0.9	121
2018	AAA	Sacramento	2	2	0	47	34	4.20	1.25	24.0	265	30	69	3.93	2.1	6.5	3.1	1.0	78

Physically mature pitcher got first taste of Triple-A after strong Double-A season. Upright 3/4s straight-on delivery. Picked up velocity with 2-seam FB but lost some of the arm-side action. Tightened up SL, which caused Dom jump; now a two-plane breaker. Found better command of average CU, maintaining FB arm speed.

Anderson,Tanner

SP | Pittsburgh | EXP MLB DEBUT: 2019 | H/W: 6-3 190 | FUT: Middle reliever | 6C

Thrws R Age 25
2015 (20) Harvard

Velo	Pitch	Grade
91-94	FB	+++
83-85	SL	++
81-84	CU	+++

Year	Lev	Team	W	L	Sv	IP	K	ERA	WHIP	BF/G	OBA	H%	S%	xERA	Ctl	Dom	Cmd	hr/9	BPV
2016	A	West Virginia	2	2	0	47	33	3.44	1.06	9.6	218	27	64	1.93	2.5	6.3	2.5	0.0	64
2016	A+	Bradenton	1	1	1	40	17	3.81	1.44	10.1	302	33	73	4.48	2.0	3.8	1.9	0.4	32
2017	AA	Altoona	10	8	0	133	97	3.38	1.25	18.1	263	32	73	3.38	2.2	6.6	2.9	0.4	76
2018	AAA	Indianapolis	3	2	6	61	49	2.65	1.31	6.5	274	34	79	3.56	2.2	7.2	3.3	0.3	88
2018	MLB	Pittsburgh	1	0	0	11	6	6.49	2.07	9.1	324	36	68	6.75	6.5	4.9	0.8	0.8	-70

Hi-kick righty who has some deception and feel to go along with a solid sinker. Lacks good breaker to put away RHH. Throws strikes but lacks plus command to be consistent quality help at MLB level.

Aquino,Stiward

RP | Los Angeles (A) | EXP MLB DEBUT: 2022 | H/W: 6-6 170 | FUT: #4 starter | 8E

Thrws R Age 19
2016 FA (DR)

Velo	Pitch	Grade
92-96	FB	+++
	CB	+++
	CU	++

Year	Lev	Team	W	L	Sv	IP	K	ERA	WHIP	BF/G	OBA	H%	S%	xERA	Ctl	Dom	Cmd	hr/9	BPV
2017	Rk	AZL Angels	1	0	0	5	2	1.73	1.73	11.8	254	28	89	4.11	6.9	3.5	0.5	0.0	-107
2018		Did not pitch - injury																	

Lanky teenage starter working his way back in hopes of being the latest Tommy John success story. The injury cost him the 2018 season. Prior, took a nice step forward in velocity, now tipping 96 mph on his fastball. Shows impressive body control for his size, with strong spin rate through his plus curve, followed up by developing change-up.

Armenteros,Rogelio

SP | Houston | EXP MLB DEBUT: 2019 | H/W: 6-1 215 | FUT: #5 SP/swingman | 7C

Thrws R Age 24
2015 FA (CU)

Velo	Pitch	Grade
90-94	FB	+++
80-82	CU	++++
73-78	CB	++
84-86	SL	++

Year	Lev	Team	W	L	Sv	IP	K	ERA	WHIP	BF/G	OBA	H%	S%	xERA	Ctl	Dom	Cmd	hr/9	BPV
2016	A+	Lancaster	6	4	1	90	107	4.20	1.38	19.9	255	33	74	4.38	3.7	10.7	2.9	1.3	111
2016	AA	Corpus Christi	2	0	0	18	13	1.99	1.16	24.0	250	30	85	3.05	2.0	6.5	3.3	0.5	81
2017	AA	Corpus Christi	2	3	1	65	74	1.94	1.04	18.0	211	30	83	2.15	2.6	10.2	3.9	0.4	131
2017	AAA	Fresno	8	1	0	58	72	2.17	1.05	22.5	204	29	84	2.41	2.9	11.2	3.8	0.8	139
2018	AAA	Fresno	8	1	1	118	134	3.74	1.31	22.1	242	31	76	3.88	3.7	10.2	2.8	1.1	103

Solidly built right-hander with an over-the-top delivery. He utilizes a four-pitch mix led by a low-90s two-seam fastball with movement that can tick up a bit more when he goes with a four-seamer. His change-up has good velo separation and flashes plus. The breaking balls are fringy at present but important if he wants to remain in the rotation.

Ashby,Aaron

SP | Milwaukee | EXP MLB DEBUT: 2021 | H/W: 6-1 170 | FUT: #4 starter | 8D

Thrws L Age 20
2018 (4) Crowder College

Velo	Pitch	Grade
91-94	FB	+++
71-74	CB	++++
79-82	SL	+++
	CU	++

Year	Lev	Team	W	L	Sv	IP	K	ERA	WHIP	BF/G	OBA	H%	S%	xERA	Ctl	Dom	Cmd	hr/9	BPV
2018	NCAA	Crowder Col	11	2	1	74	156	2.30	1.19	19.8	177	45	80	1.87	5.2	18.9	3.6	0.2	218
2018	Rk	Helena	1	2	1	20	19	6.27	1.29	13.8	241	28	52	4.04	3.6	8.5	2.4	1.3	74
2018	A	Wisconsin	1	1	0	37	47	2.18	1.32	21.9	277	40	83	3.53	2.2	11.4	5.2	0.2	164

Lean, athletic, mid-sized SP who posted big-time Dom in pro debut. Uses funky delivery and timing for whiffs despite not overpowering stuff. FB sits 91-94 and complements with downer CB in low 70s. Blends in hard SL as pace-changer and CU is fringe pitch. More control than command, but plus CB gives him legit out-pitch to work with.

Ashcraft,Braxton

SP | Pittsburgh | EXP MLB DEBUT: 2023 | H/W: 6-5 195 | FUT: #3 starter | 9D

Thrws R Age 19
2018 (2) HS (TX)

Velo	Pitch	Grade
90-95	FB	++++
80-84	SL	++++
82-84	CU	+++

Year	Lev	Team	W	L	Sv	IP	K	ERA	WHIP	BF/G	OBA	H%	S%	xERA	Ctl	Dom	Cmd	hr/9	BPV
2018	Rk	GCL Pirates	0	1	0	17	12	4.71	1.22	13.9	248	28	63	3.70	2.6	6.3	2.4	1.0	60

An athletic second round pick out of HS in 2018, he barely pitched as a pro, but he shows big upside. Pretty similar in build and stuff to Chris Archer. Slurve SL looks like it can be a plus pitch. Falls off to 1B some, but arm action and delivery are pretty clean. Still a long way away.

Assad,Javier

SP | Chicago (N) | EXP MLB DEBUT: 2022 | H/W: 6-1 200 | FUT: #4 starter | 7D

Thrws R Age 21
2016 FA (MX)

Velo	Pitch	Grade
88-92	FB	++
80-82	SL	++
80-83	CU	++

Year	Lev	Team	W	L	Sv	IP	K	ERA	WHIP	BF/G	OBA	H%	S%	xERA	Ctl	Dom	Cmd	hr/9	BPV
2016	Rk	AZL Cubs	2	2	1	37	42	2.90	1.40	15.7	271	38	78	3.66	3.1	10.2	3.2	0.2	116
2017	A-	Eugene	5	6	0	66	72	4.23	1.36	21.2	270	37	67	3.60	2.9	9.8	3.4	0.3	117
2018	A	South Bend	5	7	0	106	89	4.41	1.46	19.7	293	36	69	4.42	2.6	7.5	2.9	0.5	83

Stocky RHP comes after hitters from a high 3/4 arm slot. Average FB sits at 88-92, but plays up due to downhill tilt and late sinking action. SL keeps hitters honest, but lacks late life and deception. Steady drop in Dom is not surprising and limits future upside. Not athletic and lack of projection limits him to a back-end starter or relief role.

Avila,Pedro

SP | San Diego | EXP MLB DEBUT: 2020 | H/W: 5-11 170 | FUT: #4 starter | 8C

Thrws R Age 22
2015 FA (VZ)

Velo	Pitch	Grade
90-94	FB	+++
74-76	CB	+++
82-84	CU	++++

Year	Lev	Team	W	L	Sv	IP	K	ERA	WHIP	BF/G	OBA	H%	S%	xERA	Ctl	Dom	Cmd	hr/9	BPV
2016	A	Hagerstown	7	7	0	93	92	3.48	1.33	19.3	247	31	77	3.87	3.7	8.9	2.4	1.0	79
2017	A	Fort Wayne	7	1	0	85	117	3.06	1.04	23.5	235	37	70	2.34	1.6	12.4	7.8	0.3	198
2017	A+	Lake Elsinore	1	4	0	43	53	5.01	1.58	19.0	291	41	67	4.57	3.8	11.1	2.9	0.4	116
2018	A+	Lake Elsinore	7	9	1	130	142	4.29	1.46	23.2	270	36	70	4.10	3.7	9.8	2.6	0.6	94

Stout, athletic RH who led CAL in Dom. Possesses advanced feel for off-speed including plus CU with fade and drop for whiffs. CB also flashes plus at times but has better feel for CU. Hums in the low-90s with late sinking action to FB and shows lateral command of it. Repeats arm slot and delivery well; should have plus Cmd. A name to watch.

Bachlor,Tyler

RP | New York (N) | EXP MLB DEBUT: 2018 | H/W: 6-0 220 | FUT: Setup reliever | 7D

Thrws R Age 25
2013 (11) So Georgia St Coll

Velo	Pitch	Grade
95-97	FB	++++
83-85	CB	++

Year	Lev	Team	W	L	Sv	IP	K	ERA	WHIP	BF/G	OBA	H%	S%	xERA	Ctl	Dom	Cmd	hr/9	BPV
2016	A+	St. Lucie	0	1	0	5	5	5.29	1.18	5.1	218	30	50	2.19	3.5	8.8	2.5	0.0	82
2017	A+	St. Lucie	2	2	10	35	61	4.89	1.54	4.5	251	46	66	3.71	5.4	15.7	2.9	0.3	155
2017	AA	Binghamton	1	0	3	14	23	0.00	0.77	4.3	149	29	100	0.35	2.5	14.6	5.8	0.0	212
2018	AA	Binghamton	0	3	7	24	30	2.63	1.08	4.7	171	24	79	2.10	4.5	11.3	2.5	0.8	99
2018	MLB	NY Mets	0	3	0	32	25	4.22	1.19	5.3	224	23	72	3.90	3.4	7.0	2.1	1.7	53

Athletic but raw and inexperienced reliever who has a plus FB but is still searching for a quality offspeed to go with it. CB is more of a slurve and is often flat and up in zone. Reached major leagues in 2018 despite a lack of experience because of his velocity but probably needs to go back to minors to improve his command and his arsenal.

Baez,Joan

SP | Washington | EXP MLB DEBUT: 2020 | H/W: 6-3 190 | FUT: Middle reliever | 7E

Thrws R Age 24
2014 FA (DR)

Velo	Pitch	Grade
92-95	FB	+++
77-79	CB	++
85-87	CU	++

Year	Lev	Team	W	L	Sv	IP	K	ERA	WHIP	BF/G	OBA	H%	S%	xERA	Ctl	Dom	Cmd	hr/9	BPV
2015	A	Hagerstown	0	1	0	10	6	11.58	1.88	15.8	313	35	33	6.17	5.3	5.3	1.0	0.9	-30
2016	A	Hagerstown	9	7	0	125	119	3.95	1.47	19.9	254	33	72	3.73	4.6	8.6	1.9	0.4	48
2017	Rk	GCL Nationals	2	0	0	18	23	1.49	0.77	16.3	150	24	79	0.38	2.5	11.4	4.6	0.0	157
2017	A+	Potomac	4	8	0	79	65	3.87	1.65	20.8	223	28	76	3.77	7.5	7.4	1.0	0.3	-52
2018	A+	Potomac	9	9	0	123	101	3.80	1.41	20.8	231	28	74	3.56	5.0	7.4	1.5	0.7	15

Above average fastball with late life, but controlling it has been a problem. Made some small strides later in the season, but will need to refine more. Curve is best secondary with long break and could be workable with more polish. Change-up is far behind, and what makes it more likely he ends up in relief where he can air out the FB.

Baez,Michel

SP | San Diego | EXP MLB DEBUT: 2020 | H/W: 6-8 220 | FUT: #3 starter | 9D

Thrws R Age 23
2016 FA (CU)

Velo	Pitch	Grade
93-96	FB	++++
81-83	SL	++++
77-79	CB	+++
83-86	CU	+++

Year	Lev	Team	W	L	Sv	IP	K	ERA	WHIP	BF/G	OBA	H%	S%	xERA	Ctl	Dom	Cmd	hr/9	BPV
2017	Rk	AZL Padres	1	0	0	5	7	3.60	0.80	18.1	124	12	67	1.87	3.6	12.6	3.5	1.8	148
2017	A	Fort Wayne	6	2	0	58	82	2.47	0.84	21.3	200	29	80	2.26	1.2	12.7	10.3	1.2	213
2018	A+	Lake Elsinore	4	7	0	86	92	2.92	1.23	20.5	231	31	77	2.97	3.4	9.6	2.8	0.5	98
2018	AA	San Antonio	0	3	0	18	21	7.46	1.88	21.3	301	37	63	6.96	6.0	10.4	1.8	2.0	45

Tall, big-armed RH who broke through in just his second pro season. Gets downhill plane on mid-90s FB that will touch 99 mph on occasion with little effort. SL flashes plus two-plane bend for whiffs and CU also projects to be above-average. May never have average command, but repeats delivery well for size and is a decent athlete. Big upside.

Baez,Sandy — RP — Detroit

EXP MLB DEBUT: 2018 | H/W: 6-2 180 | FUT: Middle reliever | 7C

Thrws R Age 25		Year	Lev	Team	W	L	Sv	IP	K	ERA	WHIP	BF/G	OBA	H%	S%	xERA	Ctl	Dom	Cmd	hr/9	BPV
2012 FA (DR)		2016	A	West Michigan	7	9	0	113	88	3.82	1.35	22.5	282	34	72	4.03	2.2	7.0	3.1	0.6	84
92-98 FB	+++	2017	A+	Lakeland	6	7	0	88	92	3.88	1.27	21.2	261	34	70	3.66	2.4	9.4	3.8	0.7	121
81-85 SL	+++	2017	AA	Erie	0	1	0	10	13	4.50	1.40	21.1	242	28	82	5.57	4.5	11.7	2.6	2.7	107
83-86 CU	+	2018	AA	Erie	1	9	1	103	86	5.67	1.55	13.7	281	32	67	5.55	4.0	7.5	1.9	1.7	45
		2018	MLB	Detroit	0	0	0	14	10	5.11	1.49	6.8	232	25	68	4.38	5.7	6.4	1.1	1.3	-22

Bullish starter-turned-reliever who made his major league debut in 2018 with flashes of improved command after lingering struggle. High-heat fastball intensifies later into his outings with improved slider that still begs for consistency. Needs to locate to access full value.

Bahr,Jason — SP — Texas

EXP MLB DEBUT: 2022 | H/W: 6-5 200 | FUT: #5 SP/swingman | 7D

Thrws R Age 24		Year	Lev	Team	W	L	Sv	IP	K	ERA	WHIP	BF/G	OBA	H%	S%	xERA	Ctl	Dom	Cmd	hr/9	BPV
2017 (5) Central Florida		2017	NCAA	Central Florida	0	2	1	60	98	2.99	0.95	9.4	198	33	74	2.31	2.2	14.7	6.5	1.0	221
91-94 FB	+++	2017	A-	Salem-Keizer	3	2	0	33	36	3.55	1.27	10.4	250	35	69	2.83	3.0	9.8	3.3	0.0	114
73-75 CB	++	2018	A	Augusta	6	4	0	68	88	2.77	1.07	20.4	213	31	76	2.46	2.8	11.6	4.2	0.7	152
80-83 SL	++	2018	A+	San Jose	2	0	0	16	15	1.69	0.88	19.7	210	23	100	2.93	1.1	8.4	7.5	1.7	140
81-83 CU	+	2018	A+	Down East	2	4	0	35	32	5.88	1.53	19.2	297	36	62	5.14	3.1	8.2	2.7	1.0	82

Has a starter's build and throws four pitches, but overall package is a bit light. Still needs to improve spotting his FB; both breaking pitches flash average but are inconsistent, and CU currently just a show-me offering. Delivery a bit stiff, but without a reliable offspeed pitch, reliever is the likely outcome.

Bailey,Brandon — SP — Houston

EXP MLB DEBUT: 2020 | H/W: 5-9 180 | FUT: #5 SP/swingman | 6B

Thrws R Age 24		Year	Lev	Team	W	L	Sv	IP	K	ERA	WHIP	BF/G	OBA	H%	S%	xERA	Ctl	Dom	Cmd	hr/9	BPV
2016 (6) Gonzaga		2016	A-	Vermont	3	1	0	38		3.08	0.92	14.2	195	28	65	1.49	2.1	9.9	4.7	0.2	140
89-93 FB	++	2017	A	Beloit	1	1	0	57	73	2.68	1.07	14.8	199	29	77	2.27	3.3	11.5	3.5	0.6	136
82-83 CU	+++	2017	A+	Stockton	2	1	1	34	47	4.24	1.12	14.9	226	33	65	3.10	2.6	12.4	4.7	1.1	170
75-76 CB	+++	2018	A+	Buies Creek	5	8	0	97	113	2.50	1.15	19.3	201	28	80	2.44	4.0	10.5	2.6	0.6	99
		2018	AA	Corpus Christi	1	0	1	24	23	4.09	1.24	19.6	235	26	76	4.32	3.3	8.6	2.6	1.9	82

Undersized and lacking in dazzling stuff, but he continues to make it work. As an elder statesman at 24 in A-ball, he baffled hitters with his advanced straight change-up that tunnels effectively off his fastball. His curve is major-league quality, with two-plane break.

Banda,Anthony — SP — Tampa Bay

EXP MLB DEBUT: 2017 | H/W: 6-3 175 | FUT: Setup reliever | 7C

Thrws L Age 25		Year	Lev	Team	W	L	Sv	IP	K	ERA	WHIP	BF/G	OBA	H%	S%	xERA	Ctl	Dom	Cmd	hr/9	BPV
2012 (10) San Jacinto Coll		2016	AAA	Reno	4	4	0	73	68	3.69	1.37	23.6	261	33	74	3.93	3.3	8.4	2.5	0.7	79
93-96 FB	++++	2017	AAA	Reno	8	7	0	122	116	5.39	1.44	23.6	267	33	64	4.54	3.8	8.6	2.3	1.1	70
82-84 CB	++	2017	MLB	Arizona	2	3	0	25	25	6.07	1.43	13.4	268	35	54	3.82	3.6	8.9	2.5	0.4	82
87-88 CU	+++	2018	AAA	Durham	4	3	0	42	49	3.64	1.45	22.4	266	37	76	4.11	3.9	10.5	2.7	0.6	103
		2018	MLB	Tampa Bay	1	0	0	14	10	3.80	1.06	18.3	231	27	64	2.67	1.9	6.3	3.3	0.6	81

Hard-throwing LHP pitched well in brief second MLB stint before season was cut short due to Tommy John surgery. 3/4s, slight cross-fire delivery with solid extension and effort. Three pitches, featuring a four-seam FB with late-tailing run. Throws slurvy CB, which profiles like a SL. It's a below-average offering. Late-fading, above-average CU is best secondary.

Baumann,Michael — SP — Baltimore

EXP MLB DEBUT: 2020 | H/W: 6-4 200 | FUT: Setup reliever | 7D

Thrws R Age 23		Year	Lev	Team	W	L	Sv	IP	K	ERA	WHIP	BF/G	OBA	H%	S%	xERA	Ctl	Dom	Cmd	hr/9	BPV
2017 (3) Jacksonville		2017	NCAA	Jacksonville	5	3	0	87	97	3.10	1.21	25.0	222	29	77	3.08	3.6	10.0	2.8	0.8	101
91-94 FB	++++	2017	Rk	GCL Orioles	0	0	0	1	2	0.00	2.00	4.8	415	71	100	7.40	0.0	18.0		0.0	342
76-80 SL	++	2017	A-	Aberdeen	4	2	0	41	41	1.31	1.07	16.0	177	23	90	1.86	4.2	9.0	2.2	0.4	67
86-88 CU	++	2018	A	Delmarva	5	0	0	38	47	1.42	0.95	20.5	177	28	83	1.11	3.1	11.1	3.6	0.0	135
		2018	A+	Frederick	8	5	0	92	59	3.90	1.32	22.5	240	27	73	3.69	3.9	5.8	1.5	0.9	16

Physically strong RHP close to physical maturity advanced to High-A in second pro season. Jerky, 3/4s delivery with limited extension. 3-pitch pitcher. Workhorse pitch is 4-seam FB with little-to-no run. SL is slurvy with inconsistent movement depending on tightness. Solid deception in delivery for CU but suffers from same movement issues as FB.

Baz,Shane — SP — Tampa Bay

EXP MLB DEBUT: 2021 | H/W: 6-3 190 | FUT: #2 starter | 9E

Thrws R Age 19		Year	Lev	Team	W	L	Sv	IP	K	ERA	WHIP	BF/G	OBA	H%	S%	xERA	Ctl	Dom	Cmd	hr/9	BPV
2017 (1) HS (TX)																					
92-96 FB	++++																				
87-89 CT	+++	2017	Rk	GCL Pirates	0	3	0	23	19	3.88	1.72	10.5	284	34	79	5.21	5.4	7.4	1.4	0.8	4
82-85 SL	+++	2018	Rk	Bristol	4	3	0	45	54	3.99	1.51	19.5	261	37	73	3.95	4.6	10.8	2.3	0.4	88
84-86 CU	+++	2018	Rk	Princeton	4	5	0	52	59	4.49	1.63	19.3	276	38	72	4.58	5.0	10.2	2.0	0.5	66

Athletic, hard-throwing RHP acquired in mid-season trade with PIT. Spent second year in short-season ball, mostly refining delivery. 3/4s online delivery with some effort and limited extension. Stays tall in delivery. Four-pitch arsenal projects average-or-better across the board. FB has solid run and terrific plane. SL & CB movement blend together.

Beck,Tristan — SP — Atlanta

EXP MLB DEBUT: 2021 | H/W: 6-4 165 | FUT: #4 starter | 7C

Thrws R Age 22		Year	Lev	Team	W	L	Sv	IP	K	ERA	WHIP	BF/G	OBA	H%	S%	xERA	Ctl	Dom	Cmd	hr/9	BPV
2018 (4) Stanford																					
90-94 FB	+++																				
74-80 CB	+++																				
80-84 CU	+++	2018	NCAA	Stanford	8	4	0	90	73	2.99	1.22	24.3	237	29	77	3.12	3.1	7.3	2.4	0.6	66
		2018	Rk	GCL Braves	0	0	0	4	7	0.00	1.43	5.9	252	45	100	3.21	4.3	15.0	3.5	0.0	172

Saw his draft prospect capital fall due to a delayed recovery from Tommy John surgery. 3/4s, cross-armed delivery with moderate arm-torque; pre-surgery stuff hasn't returned. FB velocity was hovering around 90 late in college season. CB & SL has morphed into slurvy hybrid, lacking shape and finish. Feel for late-fading CU is coming back.

Beede,Tyler — SP — San Francisco

EXP MLB DEBUT: 2018 | H/W: 6-4 200 | FUT: #4 starter | 7C

Thrws R Age 25		Year	Lev	Team	W	L	Sv	IP	K	ERA	WHIP	BF/G	OBA	H%	S%	xERA	Ctl	Dom	Cmd	hr/9	BPV
2014 (1) Vanderbilt		2017	AAA	Sacramento	6	7	0	109	83	4.79	1.47	24.6	282	32	70	4.89	3.2	6.9	2.1	1.2	54
91-93 FB	+++	2018	Rk	AZL Giants O	0	0	0	1	2	0.00	0.00	2.8	0	0			0.0	18.0		0.0	342
87-88 CT	+++	2018	A+	San Jose	0	0	0	5	4	1.80	0.80	18.1	66	9	75		5.4	7.2	1.3	0.0	2
77-80 CB	+++	2018	AAA	Sacramento	4	9	0	74	75	7.05	1.86	10.5	282	35	63	5.92	6.8	9.1	1.3	1.2	-2
80-82 CU	+++	2018	MLB	SF Giants	0	1	0	7	9	8.75	2.36	18.7	307	44	59	6.39	10.0	11.3	1.1	0.0	-50

Tall, strong SP had woeful season split between Triple-A and MLB. Suffered from sudden poor control but stuff still played well when in zone. Workhorse is heavy 2-seam FB with solid movement that is hard to elevate. CT keeps hitters honest off FB. CB is big 12-to-6 breaker with great shape. CU mimics FB arm speed and movement profile.

Beras,Jario — SP — Texas

EXP MLB DEBUT: 2020 | H/W: 6-6 195 | FUT: Setup reliever | 8D

Thrws R Age 23		Year	Lev	Team	W	L	Sv	IP	K	ERA	WHIP	BF/G	OBA	H%	S%	xERA	Ctl	Dom	Cmd	hr/9	BPV
2012 FA (DR)																					
94-95 FB	++++																				
84-87 SL	+++	2017	A	Hickory	0	0	0	1	0	0.00	0.00	2.8	0	0			0.0	0.0		0.0	18
		2017	A+	Down East	0	1	0	13	14	5.50	1.53	3.3	229	28	67	4.50	6.2	9.6	1.6	1.4	24
		2018	A+	Down East	3	2	3	54	75	4.33	1.13	5.6	187	29	61	2.30	4.3	12.5	2.9	0.7	126

Converted OF has arm strength in spades, sitting mid-90s with a developing slider. Spent season working on mechanics and battling his tendency to fly open in his delivery. As such, command still needs work. More reps necessary.

Bielak,Brandon — SP — Houston

EXP MLB DEBUT: 2020 | H/W: 6-1 193 | FUT: #4 starter | 7B

Thrws R Age 23		Year	Lev	Team	W	L	Sv	IP	K	ERA	WHIP	BF/G	OBA	H%	S%	xERA	Ctl	Dom	Cmd	hr/9	BPV
2017 (11) Notre Dame		2017	NCAA	Notre Dame	2	6	0	73	75	5.55	1.67	21.9	282	37	65	4.76	5.1	9.2	1.8	0.5	48
91-94 FB	+++	2017	Rk	GCL Astros	1	0	0	4	5	0.00	0.98	7.8	206	31	100	1.52	2.2	11.0	5.0	0.0	156
84-85 SL	+++	2017	A-	Tri City	1	1	1	29	37	0.93	0.76	13.0	180	29	86	0.66	1.2	11.4	9.3	0.0	191
83-85 CU	++	2018	A+	Buies Creek	5	3	2	55	74	2.12	1.11	15.5	220	34	81	2.32	2.8	12.1	4.4	0.3	160
81-82 CB	++++	2018	AA	Corpus Christi	2	5	0	61	57	2.36	1.21	22.4	232	29	83	3.01	3.2	8.4	2.6	0.6	82

The former-11th rounder has flown through the minors on the back of a funky delivery and some funky stuff. He's got an above-average curveball with plus-plus spin rates, a good spin rates on his slider too. The fastball isn't elite in velocity but, you guessed it, has plus spin. Scouts are split on whether he's a starter or not long-term.

Bishop,Cameron — SP — Baltimore

EXP MLB DEBUT: 2021 | H/W: 6-4 215 | FUT: #5 SP/swingman | 6C

Thrws L Age 23		Year	Lev	Team	W	L	Sv	IP	K	ERA	WHIP	BF/G	OBA	H%	S%	xERA	Ctl	Dom	Cmd	hr/9	BPV
2017 (26) California-Irvin																					
89-92 FB	+++																				
80-83 SL	++	2017	Rk	GCL Orioles	0	0	0	3	1	0.00	0.33	9.5	106	12	100		0.0	3.0		0.0	72
73-76 CB	++	2017	A-	Aberdeen	1	1	0	34	38	0.79	1.05	16.6	172	25	94	1.58	4.2	10.0	2.4	0.3	84
80-83 CU	++	2018	A	Delmarva	9	7	0	125	99	2.95	1.01	21.8	233	29	70	2.32	1.4	7.1	5.0	0.4	107

Tall, command/control LHP with decent shot at ceiling. Stays tall in delivery throwing from a 3/4s slot. Doesn't use height well creating extension. 4-pitch pitcher. Has control of 2-seam FB with solid arm-side run. Struggles with effectiveness of secondaries. Has best chance of developing CU. Has fading action and deceptive off FB.

Black,Ray
RP | **San Francisco** | EXP MLB DEBUT: 2018 | H/W: 6-4 220 | FUT: Closer | **8E**

Thrws R Age 28 — 2011 (7) Pittsburgh

Velo	Pitch	Grade
96-99	FB	+++++
84-88	SL	++++
80-81	CB	++

Year	Lev	Team	W	L	Sv	IP	K	ERA	WHIP	BF/G	OBA	H%	S%	xERA	Ctl	Dom	Cmd	hr/9	BPV
2017	Rk	AZL Giants	0	0	0	2	7	4.29	2.38	3.6	252	217	80	5.46	12.9	30.0	2.3	0.0	211
2018	AA	Richmond	0	0	4	10	20	0.90	0.80	3.6	124	33	88	0.13	3.6	18.0	5.0	0.0	245
2018	AAA	Sacramento	3	0	1	25	46	3.21	0.91	3.6	174	34	67	1.62	2.9	16.4	5.8	0.7	237
2018	MLB	SF Giants	2	2	0	23	33	6.23	1.17	3.5	207	29	48	3.47	3.9	12.9	3.3	1.6	144

Strong-armed, mauling reliever enjoyed first healthy season as pro. Results up and made MLB debut. Improved control has allowed for FB movement to play up. Throws high-octane 4-seam FB with electrifying late movement. Throws SL from identical plane as FB. Tightened up pitch, creating a later start to vertical break. Closer mentality.

Blackham,Matt
RP | **New York (N)** | EXP MLB DEBUT: 2020 | H/W: 5-11 150 | FUT: Setup reliever | **7D**

Thrws R Age 26 — 2014 (29) Mid Tennessee St

Velo	Pitch	Grade
92-95	FB	++++
81-83	CB	++++
81-82	CU	++

Year	Lev	Team	W	L	Sv	IP	K	ERA	WHIP	BF/G	OBA	H%	S%	xERA	Ctl	Dom	Cmd	hr/9	BPV
2014	Rk	Kingsport	2	0	0	19	25	1.42	1.00	6.6	157	22	94	1.92	4.3	11.8	2.8	0.9	116
2015	A-	Brooklyn	2	2	0	30	42	3.87	1.23	20.4	227	37	65	2.39	3.6	12.5	3.5	0.0	147
2017	A	Columbia	4	2	8	56	82	1.44	1.00	5.4	189	33	84	1.36	3.0	13.1	4.3	0.0	172
2018	A+	St. Lucie	4	1	2	23	29	1.94	1.03	5.3	144	22	83	1.35	5.0	11.3	2.2	0.4	84
2018	AA	Binghamton	1	2	0	26	36	3.45	1.34	4.9	197	30	76	2.96	5.9	12.4	2.1	0.7	83

Athletic reliever who put himself in the mix with a good 2018 season. Features a plus FB and a knuckle CB which is nasty at times, but inconsistent. Has some deception too, with compact arm action. Command and control are the concerns, as his walk rate was particularly bad once promoted to Double-A.

Blewett,Scott
SP | **Kansas City** | EXP MLB DEBUT: 2019 | H/W: 6-6 210 | FUT: #5 SP/swingman | **6C**

Thrws R Age 22 — 2014 (2) HS (NY)

Velo	Pitch	Grade
90-93	FB	+++
75-78	CB	+++
83-84	CU	+
82-84	SL	++

Year	Lev	Team	W	L	Sv	IP	K	ERA	WHIP	BF/G	OBA	H%	S%	xERA	Ctl	Dom	Cmd	hr/9	BPV
2014	Rk	Burlington	1	2	0	28		4.82	1.50	15.1	255	32	69	4.38	4.8	9.3	1.9	1.0	56
2015	A	Lexington	3	5	0	81	60	5.22	1.38	18.9	278	33	61	4.15	2.7	6.7	2.5	0.7	66
2016	A	Lexington	8	11	0	129	121	4.32	1.46	22.1	275	34	71	4.33	3.6	8.4	2.4	0.7	74
2017	A+	Wilmington	7	10	0	152	129	4.08	1.35	23.5	263	31	72	4.11	3.1	7.6	2.5	0.9	72
2018	AA	NW Arkansas	8	6	0	148	100	4.80	1.44	24.3	282	32	67	4.42	3.0	6.1	2.0	0.7	47

Big-bodied, long RH workhorse SP struggled to take step forward in development. Deliberate, high 3/4s delivery with long arm progression. Doesn't take advantage of height in delivery. 2-seam FB with solid arm-side bore. 12-to-6 CB has solid depth and break. SL is slurvy and ineffective. Struggles mechanically with CU, causing ineffectiveness.

Bostick,Akeem
SP | **Houston** | EXP MLB DEBUT: 2019 | H/W: 6-4 180 | FUT: Middle reliever | **5A**

Thrws R Age 23 — 2013 (2) HS (SC)

Velo	Pitch	Grade
90-92	FB	++
75-77	CB	+++
85-87	SL	+++

Year	Lev	Team	W	L	Sv	IP	K	ERA	WHIP	BF/G	OBA	H%	S%	xERA	Ctl	Dom	Cmd	hr/9	BPV
2016	A+	Lancaster	5	3	0	68	48	5.01	1.77	22.4	291	33	73	5.58	5.5	6.3	1.1	0.9	-18
2017	A+	Buies Creek	2	1	0	19	16	1.88	0.84	17.5	157	21	75	0.66	2.8	7.5	2.7	0.0	77
2017	AA	Corpus Christi	6	6	0	80	58	4.61	1.46	19.0	300	35	69	4.80	2.2	6.5	2.9	0.8	75
2018	AA	Corpus Christi	2	5	3	93	97	3.48	1.29	18.2	245	32	74	3.45	3.4	9.4	2.8	0.7	96
2018	AAA	Fresno	0	0	0	5	8	7.20	1.40	21.1	262	40	50	4.96	3.6	14.4	4.0	1.8	180

The lanky right-hander is somehow still just 23 years old and continues to attack hitters with a pedestrian fastball and a solid curveball. The new wrinkle is the slide piece, introduced in 2017 and refined in 2018, often sneaking under the bats of opposing hitters with small, but late bite.

Bowden,Ben
RP | **Colorado** | EXP MLB DEBUT: 2019 | H/W: 6-4 220 | FUT: Setup reliever | **7C**

Thrws L Age 24 — 2016 (2) Vanderbilt

Velo	Pitch	Grade
90-93	FB	+++
80-83	SL	++
	CU	+++

Year	Lev	Team	W	L	Sv	IP	K	ERA	WHIP	BF/G	OBA	H%	S%	xERA	Ctl	Dom	Cmd	hr/9	BPV
2016	NCAA	Vanderbilt	2	1	10	48	65	3.55	1.29	8.2	261	39	73	3.52	2.6	12.1	4.6	0.6	166
2016	A	Asheville	0	1	0	23	29	3.10	1.64	4.0	260	38	81	4.24	5.8	11.3	1.9	0.4	63
2017		Did not pitch - injury																	
2018	A	Asheville	3	0	0	15	25	3.58	1.46	4.3	285	46	80	4.86	3.0	14.9	5.0	1.2	206
2018	A+	Lancaster	4	2	0	36	53	4.23	1.38	4.5	255	37	75	4.55	3.7	13.2	3.5	1.5	154

Lefty reliever missed all of 2017 with a bulging disk in his back and survived an extended stint in the CAL in 2018. FB velocity was in the 90-93 range most of 2018. CU and SL make him tough vs LHB and his Dom should play as he moves up. Injuries and struggles vs RHB will keep him in a relief role.

Bradley,Taj
SP | **Tampa Bay** | EXP MLB DEBUT: 2023 | H/W: 6-2 190 | FUT: #3 starter | **8E**

Thrws R Age 18 — 2018 (5) HS (GA)

Velo	Pitch	Grade
91-94	FB	++++
72-75	CB	+++
85-87	CU	++

Year	Lev	Team	W	L	Sv	IP	K	ERA	WHIP	BF/G	OBA	H%	S%	xERA	Ctl	Dom	Cmd	hr/9	BPV
2018	Rk	GCL Rays	1	4	0	23	24	5.09	1.65	10.3	286	38	68	4.67	4.7	9.4	2.0	0.4	60

Athletic, pop-up draft arm signed for overslot deal with TAM. High 3/4s online delivery with natural downward plane and great extension despite rawness. 2-seam FB has average arm-side bore and can miss bats up. CB has good depth with solid command. Raw feel for pitching. Physically mature and muscular for age.

Braymer,Ben
SP | **Washington** | EXP MLB DEBUT: 2020 | H/W: 6-2 195 | FUT: Middle reliever | **7C**

Thrws L Age 24 — 2016 (18) Auburn

Velo	Pitch	Grade
92-94	FB	++
79-81	CB	+++
83-85	CU	++

Year	Lev	Team	W	L	Sv	IP	K	ERA	WHIP	BF/G	OBA	H%	S%	xERA	Ctl	Dom	Cmd	hr/9	BPV
2016	Rk	GCL Nationals	0	2	0	19	24	4.22	1.35	10.0	194	30	65	2.33	6.1	11.3	1.8	0.0	56
2017	A-	Auburn	2	0	0	27	39	2.32	1.36	19.0	238	38	83	3.18	4.3	12.9	3.0	0.3	134
2017	A	Hagerstown	3	2	0	37	37	5.32	1.45	22.7	305	39	63	4.76	1.9	9.0	4.6	0.7	127
2018	A	Hagerstown	3	0	0	25	25	1.79	0.91	13.4	202	26	86	2.01	1.8	8.9	5.0	0.7	131
2018	A+	Potomac	6	3	2	89	93	2.43	1.15	16.8	225	30	80	2.58	2.9	9.4	3.2	0.4	108

Solidly built, gets some deception from closed front shoulder, crossfire delivery and high slot. Curveball is best pitch, with lots of depth and break. Fastball a tick below average, though he controls it fairly well. Change-up is far away; enough that this is probably a L/L reliever profile.

Brigham,Jeff
SP | **Miami** | EXP MLB DEBUT: 2018 | H/W: 6-0 200 | FUT: Middle reliever | **6B**

Thrws R Age 27 — 2014 (4) Washington

Velo	Pitch	Grade
91-94	FB	+++
79-81	SL	+++
86-87	CU	++

Year	Lev	Team	W	L	Sv	IP	K	ERA	WHIP	BF/G	OBA	H%	S%	xERA	Ctl	Dom	Cmd	hr/9	BPV
2017	A+	Jupiter	4	2	0	59	53	2.90	1.17	21.4	228	29	75	2.59	3.1	8.1	2.7	0.3	81
2018	Rk	GCL Marlins	1	0	0	5	5	0.00	0.40	16.1	124	18	100		0.0	9.0		0.0	180
2018	AA	Jacksonville	4	1	0	38	41	1.18	0.95	20.5	201	28	89	1.63	2.1	9.7	4.6	0.2	135
2018	AAA	New Orleans	5	2	0	52	48	3.45	1.27	23.7	265	32	78	4.18	2.2	8.3	3.7	1.2	107
2018	MLB	Miami	0	4	0	16	12	6.15	1.80	18.6	261	30	67	5.39	7.3	6.7	0.9	1.1	-57

Under-sized, 3/4s RHP made MLB debut in 2018. Utilizes drop and drive, cross-armed delivery. 3 pitch pitcher. Has late giddy-up on 4-seam FB that keeps the ball off of barrels. Best secondary pitch is 11-to-5 SL with solid break that he commands well. Shows CU but isn't enough to keep LHH off FB.

Brown,Zack
SP | **Milwaukee** | EXP MLB DEBUT: 2019 | H/W: 6-1 180 | FUT: #4 starter | **7B**

Thrws R Age 24 — 2016 (5) Kentucky

Velo	Pitch	Grade
91-93	FB	+++
76-78	CB	++++
84-86	CU	+++

Year	Lev	Team	W	L	Sv	IP	K	ERA	WHIP	BF/G	OBA	H%	S%	xERA	Ctl	Dom	Cmd	hr/9	BPV
2016	A	Wisconsin	1	2	1	33	29	3.00	1.03	14.1	238	29	74	2.85	1.4	7.9	5.8	0.8	124
2017	A	Wisconsin	4	5	0	85	84	3.39	1.32	19.5	246	31	76	3.59	3.6	8.9	2.5	0.7	81
2017	A+	Carolina	3	0	0	25	23	2.16	1.04	24.1	254	33	80	2.66	0.7	8.3	11.5	0.4	148
2018	Rk	AZL Brewers	0	0	0	2	3	0.00	2.00	9.6	347	53	100	6.12	4.5	13.5	3.0	0.0	140
2018	AA	Biloxi	9	1	0	125	116	2.44	1.05	22.0	212	27	79	2.34	2.6	8.3	3.2	0.6	98

High-effort SP who led SL in ERA with quality Dom/Cmd marks. FB maxes out at 95 and will sit in low-90s with varied action. Shows feel for above-average CB and CU will also flash plus action and deception. Athletic frame and is likely maxed out physically. Command has improved and keeps ball on the ground frequently. Competes on the mound.

Brubaker,JT
SP | **Pittsburgh** | EXP MLB DEBUT: 2020 | H/W: 6-3 170 | FUT: #5 SP/swingman | **7D**

Thrws R Age 25 — 2015 (6) Akron

Velo	Pitch	Grade
90-95	FB	+++
78-81	CB	++
85-87	SL	++
87-89	CU	+++

Year	Lev	Team	W	L	Sv	IP	K	ERA	WHIP	BF/G	OBA	H%	S%	xERA	Ctl	Dom	Cmd	hr/9	BPV
2016	A	West Virginia	4	5	0	62	77	3.48	1.29	21.2	243	32	79	4.00	3.5	11.2	3.2	1.3	125
2016		A+	2	6	0	67	43	5.36	1.47	20.6	289	33	63	4.68	2.9	5.8	2.0	0.8	42
2017	AA	Altoona	7	6	0	129	109	4.46	1.51	21.5	292	36	70	4.63	3.1	7.6	2.4	0.6	70
2018	AA	Altoona	2	2	0	35	35	1.80	1.06	22.6	227	31	83	2.25	2.1	9.0	4.4	0.3	124
2018	AAA	Indianapolis	8	4	0	119	96	3.10	1.32	22.4	265	32	77	3.68	2.7	7.3	2.7	0.5	75

Tall command righty who uses decent FB well but lacks out pitch or strikeout pitch. Has struggled to find consistent breaking ball over the last couple of years. CU is solid but not a separator. Competes and knows how to pitch. Stuff may play up in shorter roles, but still would be far from overpowering.

Bubic,Kris
SP | **Kansas City** | EXP MLB DEBUT: 2021 | H/W: 6-3 220 | FUT: #4 starter | **7C**

Thrws L Age 21 — 2018 (1) Stanford

Velo	Pitch	Grade
90-92	FB	+++
76-79	CB	+++
79-82	CU	++++

Year	Lev	Team	W	L	Sv	IP	K	ERA	WHIP	BF/G	OBA	H%	S%	xERA	Ctl	Dom	Cmd	hr/9	BPV
2018	NCAA	Stanford	8	1	0	86	101	2.62	1.07	22.3	198	28	77	2.16	3.3	10.6	3.2	0.5	118
2018	Rk	Idaho Falls	2	3	0	38	53	4.03	1.50	16.4	262	40	73	3.98	4.5	12.6	2.8	0.5	122

Command/control LHP made pro debut with consistent, straight-on 3/4s delivery with deception. Uses three pitches. Two-seam FB is heavy with solid arm-side bore. 1-to-7 CB has average depth and movement. Best pitch is late-fading CU with FB arm speed. High floor, #4-#5 starter.

Bukauskas,J.B. — SP — Houston

EXP MLB DEBUT: 2020 | H/W: 5-11 200 | FUT: Setup reliever | 8C

Thrws R Age 22 — 2017 (1) North Carolina

Velo	Pitch	Grade
93-97	FB	++++
84-89	SL	++++
90-92	CU	++

Year	Lev	Team	W	L	Sv	IP	K	ERA	WHIP	BF/G	OBA	H%	S%	xERA	Ctl	Dom	Cmd	hr/9	BPV
2018	Rk	GCL Astros	0	0	0	1	2	15.00	4.17	8.4	596	78	60	18.64	0.0	15.0		0.0	288
2018	A-	Tri City	0	0	0	8	9	0.00	1.23	10.9	259	37	100	2.86	2.2	10.0	4.5	0.0	138
2018	A	Quad Cities	1	2	0	15	21	4.20	1.47	16.1	262	41	68	3.46	4.2	12.6	3.0	0.0	131
2018	A+	Buies Creek	3	0	0	28	31	1.61	0.93	21.0	141	20	84	1.01	4.2	10.0	2.4	0.3	85
2018	AA	Corpus Christi	0	0	0	6	8	0.00	0.50	19.9	56	10	100		3.0	12.0	4.0	0.0	153

A bulging disc in his back sidelined the short right-hander for a couple months. He was highly effective across five levels, when healthy, dazzling batters with an upper-90s fastball and flashing a nasty, biting slider. His height and frame conspire to put him in the bullpen, but he might fit the multi-inning bullpen ace role that has emerged.

Burdi,Nick — SP — Pittsburgh

EXP MLB DEBUT: 2019 | H/W: 6-5 215 | FUT: Setup reliever | 8D

Thrws R Age 26 — 2014 (2) Louisville

Velo	Pitch	Grade
94-97	FB	++++
84-86	SL	+++

Year	Lev	Team	W	L	Sv	IP	K	ERA	WHIP	BF/G	OBA	H%	S%	xERA	Ctl	Dom	Cmd	hr/9	BPV
2017	AA	Chattanooga	2	0	1	17	20	0.53	0.76	4.4	158	22	100	0.95	2.1	10.6	5.0	0.5	151
2018	A+	Bradenton	0	0	0	2	6	4.50	0.50	3.3	151	0		3.78	0.0	27.0		4.5	504
2018	AA	Altoona	0	0	0	4	3	6.75	2.00	6.4	347	42	63	6.19	4.5	6.8	1.5	0.0	18
2018	AAA	Indianapolis	0	2	0	5	5	5.40	2.60	5.4	390	50	77	8.47	7.2	9.0	1.3	0.0	-14
2018	MLB	Pittsburgh	0	0	0	1	2	24.55	4.55	4.1	492	64	50	23.45	16.4	16.4	1.0	8.2	-129

Raw power arm the Pirates ended up with in the Rule 5 draft after the Twins left him unprotected. Then they waited on as he recovered from Tommy John surgery for most of 2018. Power FB/SL arsenal. Wild and ineffective in very limited innings at four levels last year.

Burdi,Zack — RP — Chicago (A)

EXP MLB DEBUT: 2019 | H/W: 6-3 195 | FUT: Closer | 9E

Thrws R Age 24 — 2016 (1) Louisville

Velo	Pitch	Grade
97-99	FB	+++++
88-91	SL	++++
87-88	CU	+++

Year	Lev	Team	W	L	Sv	IP	K	ERA	WHIP	BF/G	OBA	H%	S%	xERA	Ctl	Dom	Cmd	hr/9	BPV
2016	A+	Winston-Salem	0	0	0	5		5.40	1.20	5.0	299	33	60	5.06	0.0	7.2		1.8	148
2016	AA	Birmingham	0	0	0	16	24	3.94	1.00	5.1	134	19	64	1.83	5.1	13.5	2.7	1.1	124
2016	AAA	Charlotte	1	0	1	16	22	2.25	1.25	7.2	166	28	80	1.75	6.2	12.4	2.0	0.0	74
2017	AAA	Charlotte	0	4	7	33	51	4.08	1.42	4.8	243	40	71	3.59	4.6	13.9	3.0	0.5	143
2018	Rk	AZL White Sox	0	1	0	6	7	2.95	1.48	3.7	225	33	78	3.02	5.9	10.3	1.8	0.0	45

Hard-throwing RHP has suffered Tommy John surgery setbacks. Velocity hasn't come back; sat low-to-mid 90s during AFL. Still, a legitimate 3-pitch RP: 2-seam FB with plus arm-side break and downward sink; 2-plane SL that was down a tick but still profiles as plus; late-fading CU that plays well off the FB. Health is main concern.

Burke,Brock — SP — Texas

EXP MLB DEBUT: 2020 | H/W: 6-2 170 | FUT: #5 SP/swingman | 6C

Thrws L Age 22 — 2014 (3) HS (CO)

Velo	Pitch	Grade
92-95	FB	++++
82-84	SL	+++
85-86	CU	++

Year	Lev	Team	W	L	Sv	IP	K	ERA	WHIP	BF/G	OBA	H%	S%	xERA	Ctl	Dom	Cmd	hr/9	BPV
2016	A-	Hudson Valley	3	3	0	61	61	3.39	1.34	19.5	236	32	73	2.97	4.3	9.0	2.1	0.1	64
2017	A	Bowling Green	6	0	0	57	59	1.10	1.00	21.8	187	27	88	1.37	3.2	9.3	3.0	0.0	100
2017	A+	Charlotte	5	6	0	66	49	4.64	1.38	21.3	287	33	67	4.42	2.2	6.7	3.1	0.8	79
2018	A+	Charlotte	3	5	0	82	87	3.84	1.40	21.6	269	36	72	3.83	3.3	9.5	2.9	0.4	101
2018	AA	Montgomery	6	1	0	55	71	1.96	0.96	23.2	201	30	80	1.72	2.3	11.6	5.1	0.3	165

Lean, high 3/4s LHP had great Double-A run to close out season. Dom and Cmd improved with no remarkable difference between levels. Three-pitch pitcher. Plus velocity with 4-seam FB. Fairly straight, most overpower to get swings-and-misses. SL plays up due to late sweepy movement. Above-average pitch at projection. CU is inconsistent. Came over in Profar trade.

Burr,Ryan — RP — Chicago (A)

EXP MLB DEBUT: 2018 | H/W: 6-4 210 | FUT: Setup reliever | 7C

Thrws R Age 24 — 2015 (5) Arizona St

Velo	Pitch	Grade
93-97	FB	++++
88-90	CT	+++
81-84	SL	++
84-85	CU	++

Year	Lev	Team	W	L	Sv	IP	K	ERA	WHIP	BF/G	OBA	H%	S%	xERA	Ctl	Dom	Cmd	hr/9	BPV
2017	A+	Winston-Salem	0	0	1	8	13	0.00	1.23	5.5	180	34	100	1.84	5.6	14.4	2.6	0.0	128
2017	A+	Visalia	1	0	1	25	29	0.72	0.76	5.3	156	24	89	0.42	2.2	10.4	4.8	0.0	148
2018	AA	Birmingham	4	2	2	43	43	2.72	1.23	5.8	198	26	80	2.69	4.8	9.0	1.9	0.6	50
2018	AAA	Charlotte	0	1	0	8	8	1.11	0.74	4.1	149	21	83	0.32	2.2	8.9	4.0	0.0	118
2018	MLB	Chi White Sox	0	0	0	9	6	7.83	1.96	5.5	316	31	67	8.32	5.9	5.9	1.0	2.9	-35

Physically mature, powerful over-the-top RHP made MLB debut. Solid delivery, achieves significant extension, playing up arsenal. Varieties between 2-seam FB with solid arm-side run and natural sink and CT with late action. Fair command on both pitches. Best secondary is above-average SL. 2-plane break, struggles with consistency. Has feel for CU.

Burrows,Beau — SP — Detroit

EXP MLB DEBUT: 2019 | H/W: 6-2 200 | FUT: #4 starter | 8C

Thrws R Age 22 — 2015 (1) HS (TX)

Velo	Pitch	Grade
92-97	FB	++++
76-79	CB	+++
84-86	SL	++
	CU	+

Year	Lev	Team	W	L	Sv	IP	K	ERA	WHIP	BF/G	OBA	H%	S%	xERA	Ctl	Dom	Cmd	hr/9	BPV
2015	Rk	GCL Tigers	1	0	0	28	33	1.61	1.04	10.8	186	28	83	1.44	3.5	10.6	3.0	0.0	113
2016	A	West Michigan	6	4	0	97	67	3.15	1.21	18.6	241	29	72	2.76	2.8	6.2	2.2	0.2	55
2017	A+	Lakeland	4	3	0	58	62	1.24	0.96	20.0	215	29	91	2.05	1.7	9.6	5.6	0.5	145
2017	AA	Erie	6	4	0	76	75	4.73	1.47	21.8	269	35	67	4.16	3.9	8.9	2.3	0.6	72
2018	AA	Erie	10	9	0	134	127	4.10	1.36	21.5	250	31	71	3.82	3.8	8.5	2.3	0.8	70

Sturdy starter with an ability to overpower hitters on his fastball alone. Tapped into plus-plus velocity in 2018, complemented by a bullish ability to pound the zone. Command has gradually improved from early struggles, but remains a project to continue working on. Four-pitch mix will play well higher up, as long as locating improves.

Burrows,Thomas — RP — Atlanta

EXP MLB DEBUT: 2019 | H/W: 6-1 220 | FUT: Middle reliever | 6C

Thrws L Age 24 — 2016 (4) Alabama

Velo	Pitch	Grade
89-91	FB	+++
78-81	SL	+++

Year	Lev	Team	W	L	Sv	IP	K	ERA	WHIP	BF/G	OBA	H%	S%	xERA	Ctl	Dom	Cmd	hr/9	BPV
2016	A-	Everett	0	1	6	24		2.60	1.40	5.1	252	41	82	3.51	4.1	13.8	3.4	0.4	155
2017	A	Rome	3	5	3	66	92	2.18	1.10	6.8	205	33	79	1.94	3.4	12.5	3.7	0.1	151
2018	A	Rome	0	0	1	2	4	0.00	0.00	5.6	0	0			0.0	18.0		0.0	342
2018	A+	Florida	6	2	4	46	55	1.36	1.47	6.8	226	34	90	3.02	5.8	10.7	1.8	0.0	53
2018	AA	Mississippi	0	0	6	19	27	1.42	0.84	4.6	157	27	81	0.62	2.8	12.8	4.5	0.0	171

3/4s LHP with solid deception and two above-average pitches, marched on to Double-A. Unorthodox delivery. Hides ball until last second, so FB gets on hitters quickly despite limited extension. 2-seam FB plays up due to late timing of moderate arm-side run and sink in progression. Can adjust grip on SL to achieve sharp or sweep break.

Cabrera,Edward — SP — Miami

EXP MLB DEBUT: 2021 | H/W: 6-4 175 | FUT: #3 starter | 8D

Thrws R Age 20 — 2016 FA (DR)

Velo	Pitch	Grade
93-95	FB	++++
79-82	CB	+++
88-91	CU	+++

Year	Lev	Team	W	L	Sv	IP	K	ERA	WHIP	BF/G	OBA	H%	S%	xERA	Ctl	Dom	Cmd	hr/9	BPV
2016	Rk	GCL Marlins	2	6	0	47	28	4.21	1.36	17.9	289	34	67	3.84	1.9	5.4	2.8	0.2	63
2017	A-	Batavia	1	3	0	35	32	5.37	1.42	11.5	297	38	59	4.14	2.0	8.2	4.0	0.3	110
2018	A	Greensboro	4	8	0	100	93	4.23	1.47	19.5	271	33	74	4.56	3.8	8.4	2.2	1.0	67

Lean, hard-throwing RHP made strides with secondaries, especially CU. Athletic 3/4s delivery with plus arm speed. Achieves solid extension within delivery. Heavy 2-seam FB with plus arm-side run. Can reach for premium velocity. Throws hard CB with solid break, but will need refinement. Late-fading CU profile improved as season wore on.

Cabrera,Genesis — SP — St. Louis

EXP MLB DEBUT: 2019 | H/W: 6-0 155 | FUT: #3 starter | 8D

Thrws L Age 22 — 2014 FA (DR)

Velo	Pitch	Grade
92-95	FB	++++
84-86	SL	++
87-88	CU	

Year	Lev	Team	W	L	Sv	IP	K	ERA	WHIP	BF/G	OBA	H%	S%	xERA	Ctl	Dom	Cmd	hr/9	BPV
2017	A+	Charlotte	4	5	0	69	60	2.86	1.01	20.4	187	24	72	1.79	3.3	7.8	2.4	0.4	71
2017	AA	Montgomery	5	4	0	64	51	3.64	1.59	23.6	293	35	79	5.05	3.8	7.1	1.9	0.8	44
2018	AA	Springfield	1	3	0	24	21	4.83	1.53	21.0	260	31	71	4.69	4.8	7.8	1.6	1.1	28
2018	AA	Montgomery	7	6	0	113	124	4.13	1.30	22.2	220	29	70	3.34	4.5	9.9	2.2	0.9	73
2018	AAA	Memphis	0	0	0	2	3	0.00	0.50	6.6	0	0	100		4.5	13.5	3.0	0.0	140

Strong-armed hurler came over in the Tommy Pham deal and has seen an uptick in velocity. FB now sits at 92-95, topping out at 97 mph. Above-average power SL gives him a solid 1-2 punch and mixes in a occasional below-average CU. Control can be an issue, but .218 BAA and 9.5 Dom on the year show the potential.

Canning,Griffin — SP — Los Angeles (A)

EXP MLB DEBUT: 2019 | H/W: 6-3 175 | FUT: #3 starter | 8D

Thrws R Age 22 — 2017 (2) UCLA

Velo	Pitch	Grade
91-95	FB	+++
79-81	CB	++
81-84	SL	+++
	CU	+++

Year	Lev	Team	W	L	Sv	IP	K	ERA	WHIP	BF/G	OBA	H%	S%	xERA	Ctl	Dom	Cmd	hr/9	BPV
2017	NCAA	UCLA	7	4	0	119	140	2.34	1.05	27.1	217	31	79	2.27	2.4	10.6	4.4	0.5	143
2018	A+	Inland Empire	0	0	0	8	12	0.00	0.85	15.1	147	26	100	0.54	3.3	13.2	4.0	0.0	166
2018	AA	Mobile	1	0	0	45	49	1.99	1.02	17.3	175	24	82	1.66	3.8	9.8	2.6	0.4	91
2018	AAA	Salt Lake	3	3	0	59	64	5.49	1.53	19.7	290	38	64	4.90	3.4	9.8	2.9	0.9	103

Well-proportioned starter fresh off his first full year, after being shut down following the draft in 2017 as a health precaution. Legitimate four-pitch mix has developed as advertised with deception fastball playing off plus change-up, average curve and slider. All pitches thrown for strikes through repeatable delivery.

Carlson,Sam — SP — Seattle

EXP MLB DEBUT: 2022 | H/W: 6-3 193 | FUT: #3 starter | 8E

Thrws R Age 20 — 2017 (2) HS (MN)

Velo	Pitch	Grade
90-94	FB	+++
81-82	SL	+++
	CU	++

Year	Lev	Team	W	L	Sv	IP	K	ERA	WHIP	BF/G	OBA	H%	S%	xERA	Ctl	Dom	Cmd	hr/9	BPV
2017	Rk	AZL Mariners	0	0	0	3	3	3.00	1.33	6.2	321	42	75	4.04	0.0	9.0		0.0	180
2018		Did not pitch - injury																	

Cold-weather HS RHP has only thrown 3 IP in 2 professional season due to arm injuries, including Tommy John surgery. Terrific athlete with a good frame to add muscle to. Two-seam FB is heavy with solid arm-side run. SL features above-average 2-plane movement. Has feel for CU with athleticism likely playing up the pitch. Needs pitching reps.

Carrillo,Gerardo — SP — Los Angeles (N)

EXP MLB DEBUT: 2021 | H/W: 6-0 154 | FUT: #4 starter | 7D

Thrws R Age 20
2017 FA (MX)

- 93-97 FB +++
- CB +++
- CU +++

Year	Lev	Team	W	L	Sv	IP	K	ERA	WHIP	BF/G	OBA	H%	S%	xERA	Ctl	Dom	Cmd	hr/9	BPV
2018	Rk	AZL Dodgers	2	0	1	11	13	0.82	0.73	9.8	162	25	88	0.40	1.6	10.6	6.5	0.0	165
2018	A	Great Lakes	2	1	0	49	37	1.65	1.02	20.9	202	24	87	2.15	2.8	6.8	2.5	0.6	66

Short pitcher has quick arm action and surprising velocity. FB sits at 93-95 with good late sink and tops at 97. CB flashes as above-average and CU as potentially plus. Limited hits and he works effectively down in the zone. Gave up just 3 HR in 60 IP. Able to work backwards, getting ahead of hitters, enabling FB to play up.

Carroll,Cody — RP — Baltimore

EXP MLB DEBUT: 2018 | H/W: 6-5 200 | FUT: Setup reliever | 7C

Thrws R Age 26
2015 (22) Southern Miss

- 95-98 FB ++++
- 82-85 SL ++++
- 86-88 SP ++

Year	Lev	Team	W	L	Sv	IP	K	ERA	WHIP	BF/G	OBA	H%	S%	xERA	Ctl	Dom	Cmd	hr/9	BPV
2017	A+	Tampa	1	0	2	20	30	2.25	0.90	5.7	151	25	76	1.11	3.6	13.5	3.8	0.5	164
2017	AA	Trenton	2	5	5	47	59	2.68	1.23	7.3	213	30	81	2.97	4.2	11.3	2.7	0.8	107
2018	AAA	Scranton/WB	3	0	9	41	55	2.40	1.09	5.0	189	31	76	1.60	3.9	12.0	3.1	0.0	128
2018	AAA	Norfolk	4	0	9	46	58	2.73	1.15	4.9	193	30	74	1.80	4.3	11.3	2.6	0.0	106
2018	MLB	Baltimore	0	2	0	17	16	9.00	2.00	5.5	305	32	61	8.45	6.9	8.5	1.2	3.2	-15

Hard-throwing, physical RHP made MLB debut after mid-season trade with NYY. 3/4s cross-armed delivery with some effort. 3-pitch pitcher. High-octane FB has late run and is hard to square up when on. Struggles to control FB due to unbalanced delivery. SL is sharp with tight 2-plane movement. CU is a show-me pitch to keep LHH off FB.

Castellani,Ryan — SP — Colorado

EXP MLB DEBUT: 2019 | H/W: 6-4 195 | FUT: #3 starter | 8D

Thrws R Age 23
2014 (2) HS (AZ)

- 92-95 FB ++++
- 84-86 SL +++
- 84-86 CU ++

Year	Lev	Team	W	L	Sv	IP	K	ERA	WHIP	BF/G	OBA	H%	S%	xERA	Ctl	Dom	Cmd	hr/9	BPV
2014	A-	Tri-City	1	2	0	37		3.65	1.19	14.8	251	29	69	3.13	2.2	6.1	2.8	0.5	68
2015	A	Asheville	2	7	0	113	94	4.46	1.44	17.8	296	36	68	4.31	2.3	7.5	3.2	0.4	90
2016	A+	Modesto	7	8	0	167	142	3.82	1.23	26.1	249	31	68	3.14	2.7	7.6	2.8	0.4	83
2017	AA	Hartford	9	12	0	157	132	4.81	1.34	24.2	269	32	65	4.14	2.7	7.6	2.8	0.9	81
2018	AA	Hartford	7	9	0	134	91	5.50	1.53	22.4	263	29	65	4.64	4.7	6.1	1.3	1.0	1

Big, hard-throwing RHP struggled mightily with control, but has some of the best raw stuff in the system. FB sits at 92-95, topping out at 97 with good arm-side run and sink, but command was off all year. Rough mechanics add deception, but proved difficult to repeat. SL and CU flash plus, but remain inconsistent.

Castillo,Jesus — SP — Los Angeles (A)

EXP MLB DEBUT: 2019 | H/W: 6-2 165 | FUT: #4 starter | 7C

Thrws R Age 23
2011 FA (VZ)

- 89-93 FB +++
- 77-79 CB ++
- 81-83 CU ++

Year	Lev	Team	W	L	Sv	IP	K	ERA	WHIP	BF/G	OBA	H%	S%	xERA	Ctl	Dom	Cmd	hr/9	BPV
2016	A	Burlington	3	2	0	29	23	2.47	1.37	20.4	286	35	82	3.90	2.2	7.1	3.3	0.3	87
2017	A	Burlington	1	1	0	19	22	2.37	0.79	17.1	195	28	71	1.38	0.9	10.4	11.0	0.5	180
2017	A+	Inland Empire	8	3	0	82	74	3.62	1.27	21.0	271	32	78	4.47	2.0	8.1	4.1	1.4	111
2017	AA	Mobile	0	2	0	23	22	3.10	1.42	19.7	292	37	81	4.55	2.3	8.5	3.7	0.8	109
2018	AA	Mobile	9	5	0	98	60	4.95	1.30	19.3	260	29	61	3.69	2.8	5.5	1.9	0.6	40

Efficient starter with repeatable delivery and deceptive pitch mix. Thrives on deception and movement, as evidenced through the late sink of his low-90s fastball. Change-up and curve should both develop above-average, but change-up appears to be progressing more quickly.

Castro,Anthony — SP — Detroit

EXP MLB DEBUT: 2021 | H/W: 6-2 180 | FUT: #5 SP/swingman | 7B

Thrws R Age 23
2011 FA (VZ)

- 92-97 FB ++
- 79-82 CB ++
- SU ++
- 85-87 CU +

Year	Lev	Team	W	L	Sv	IP	K	ERA	WHIP	BF/G	OBA	H%	S%	xERA	Ctl	Dom	Cmd	hr/9	BPV
2016	Rk	GCL Tigers	3	3	0	50	54	4.30	1.35	19.1	269	37	65	3.30	2.9	9.7	3.4	0.0	115
2017	A	West Michigan	10	6	0	108	95	2.50	1.17	20.5	230	29	79	2.64	2.9	7.9	2.7	0.3	82
2018	A+	Lakeland	9	4	0	116	101	2.94	1.33	21.9	255	31	80	3.65	3.3	7.8	2.3	0.6	69
2018	AA	Erie	0	0	0	10	4	8.10	2.00	16.1	221	22	58	5.20	10.8	3.6	0.3	0.9	-209

A lean Tommy John success story, he isn't just stronger, he's adding velocity: 2-3 ticks to his above-average fastball in 2018, along with more confidence behind his entire offspeed set. Improvements to curveball shape and bottom-dwelling sinker. Does well attacking the strike zone, with good work on the corners and added deception.

Cate,Tim — SP — Washington

EXP MLB DEBUT: 2022 | H/W: 6-0 185 | FUT: #4 starter | 7C

Thrws L Age 21
2018 (2) Connecticut

- 88-92 FB ++
- 78-80 CB +++
- 80-82 CU ++

Year	Lev	Team	W	L	Sv	IP	K	ERA	WHIP	BF/G	OBA	H%	S%	xERA	Ctl	Dom	Cmd	hr/9	BPV
2018	NCAA	Connecticut	5	4	0	52	67	2.93	1.32	19.7	254	37	78	3.31	3.3	11.6	3.5	0.3	137
2018	A-	Auburn	2	3	0	31	26	4.65	1.42	14.6	280	35	65	3.92	2.9	7.5	2.6	0.3	75
2018	A	Hagerstown	0	3	0	21	19	5.57	1.38	22.1	280	32	64	5.15	2.6	8.1	3.2	1.7	95

Small, narrow framed pitcher was one of best collegiate southpaws in 2018. Curveball artist, with a big downer break and tight rotation for his best pitch. Fastball on the short side (88-92) and is straight and without much movement. Change-up has some medium action and he shows some feel, but not a lot of separation from FB. Compact delivery.

Cease,Dylan — SP — Chicago (A)

EXP MLB DEBUT: 2020 | H/W: 6-1 175 | FUT: #2 starter | 9E

Thrws R Age 23
2014 (6) HS (GA)

- 95-98 FB +++++
- 83-86 SL ++
- 74-78 CB ++++
- 84-87 CU ++

Year	Lev	Team	W	L	Sv	IP	K	ERA	WHIP	BF/G	OBA	H%	S%	xERA	Ctl	Dom	Cmd	hr/9	BPV
2016	A-	Eugene	2	0	0	44	66	2.24	1.18	14.7	178	31	80	1.87	5.1	13.4	2.6	0.2	122
2017	A	South Bend	1	2	0	51	74	2.81	1.27	16.1	213	34	78	2.65	4.6	13.0	2.8	0.4	129
2017	A	Kannapolis	0	8	0	41	52	3.93	1.29	18.8	232	35	67	2.82	3.9	11.4	2.9	0.2	116
2018	A+	Winston-Salem	9	2	0	71	82	2.91	1.12	21.6	206	28	76	2.49	3.5	10.4	2.9	0.6	109
2018	AA	Birmingham	3	0	0	52	78	1.73	1.00	19.9	170	28	86	1.63	3.8	13.5	3.5	0.5	158

Hard-throwing, high 3/4 slot RHP enjoyed dominant 3-month run to close the season. Easy, on-line delivery with good extension. Mid-to-high 90s FB with natural sink and little horizontal movement. 12-to-6 CB has great shape and violent break; plus-plus potential. SL is a new wrinkle, working out kinks. CU flashes average arm-side fade.

Civale,Aaron — SP — Cleveland

EXP MLB DEBUT: 2019 | H/W: 6-1 210 | FUT: #5 SP/swingman | 7B

Thrws R Age 23
2016 (3) Northeastern

- 89-93 FB +++
- 82-85 SL +++
- 78-82 CB ++
- CU ++

Year	Lev	Team	W	L	Sv	IP	K	ERA	WHIP	BF/G	OBA	H%	S%	xERA	Ctl	Dom	Cmd	hr/9	BPV
2016	NCAA	Northeastern	9	3	0	114	121	1.74	0.93	28.5	220	29	85	2.11	1.2	9.5	8.1	0.6	158
2016	A-	Mahoning Vall	0	2	0	37	28	1.69	0.83	10.5	180	23	77	0.90	1.9	6.8	3.5	0.0	88
2017	A	Lake County	2	4	0	57	53	4.58	1.21	23.0	285	37	60	3.47	0.8	8.4	10.6	0.3	147
2017	A+	Lynchburg	11	2	0	107	88	2.60	0.98	24.0	241	28	79	2.87	0.8	7.4	9.8	0.9	131
2018	AA	Akron	5	7	0	106	78	3.90	1.28	20.7	278	32	73	4.23	1.8	6.6	3.7	1.0	89

Polished arm who has moved quickly since being drafted. He has pinpoint control and an above average SL, but the rest of his arsenal is mediocre. Needs to throw strikes to be successful, but each year that he is able to consistently do so as he approaches the majors increases his chances for success at the MLB level.

Clarke,Taylor — SP — Arizona

EXP MLB DEBUT: 2019 | H/W: 6-4 195 | FUT: #4 starter | 7C

Thrws R Age 25
2015 (3) Towson

- 91-94 FB ++++
- 79-83 SL +++
- 76-77 CB +
- 82-85 CU ++

Year	Lev	Team	W	L	Sv	IP	K	ERA	WHIP	BF/G	OBA	H%	S%	xERA	Ctl	Dom	Cmd	hr/9	BPV
2016	A+	Visalia	1	1	0	23	22	2.74	1.13	22.7	227	27	83	3.29	2.7	8.6	3.1	1.2	99
2016	AA	Mobile	8	6	0	97	72	3.61	1.23	23.2	265	31	73	3.76	1.9	6.7	3.4	0.8	86
2017	AA	Jackson	9	7	0	111	107	2.92	1.20	21.3	231	30	77	2.94	3.2	8.7	2.7	0.6	89
2017	AAA	Reno	3	2	0	33	31	4.88	1.27	22.6	236	25	71	4.69	3.5	8.4	2.4	2.2	74
2018	AAA	Reno	13	8	0	152	125	4.03	1.27	23.0	258	31	69	3.63	2.6	7.4	2.8	0.7	81

Tall, high-slot RH who spent all of 2018 in hitter-friendly PCL. Features low-90s FB with boring arm-side action that he shows good command of. CU/SL are both average offerings; still developing feel for CB. Low effort and athleticism in delivery allow for above-average command. Lack of plus pitch limits overall upside but has look of back-end SP.

Clifton,Trevor — SP — Chicago (N)

EXP MLB DEBUT: 2019 | H/W: 6-4 170 | FUT: #4 starter | 7C

Thrws R Age 23
2013 (12) HS (TN)

- 91-94 FB +++
- 74-76 CB ++
- 82-83 CU ++

Year	Lev	Team	W	L	Sv	IP	K	ERA	WHIP	BF/G	OBA	H%	S%	xERA	Ctl	Dom	Cmd	hr/9	BPV
2015	A	South Bend	8	10	0	108	103	3.99	1.28	19.3	230	29	69	3.14	3.9	8.6	2.2	0.6	67
2016	A+	Myrtle Beach	7	7	0	119	129	2.72	1.16	20.6	224	31	76	2.50	3.1	9.8	3.1	0.3	110
2017	AA	Tennessee	5	8	0	100	86	5.21	1.57	20.9	284	35	66	4.75	4.0	7.7	1.9	0.7	48
2018	AA	Tennessee	3	4	0	56	45	2.88	1.14	18.5	206	27	72	1.96	3.7	7.2	2.0	0.0	48
2018	AAA	Iowa	4	3	0	69	56	3.91	1.36	20.6	250	29	74	4.06	3.8	7.3	1.9	1.0	47

Raw stuff and funky mechanics suggests a back-end or relief role. Quick delivery and herky-jerky mechanics leads to some deception. Short arm action from a low 3/4 arm slot allows his 91-94 mph FB to play up. CB, CT, and CU all show average potential, but lack consistency. Career 3.8 Ctl and 8.4 Dom leaves little margin for error.

Clouse,Corbin — RP — Atlanta

EXP MLB DEBUT: 2019 | H/W: 6-1 225 | FUT: Middle reliever | 6C

Thrws L Age 23
2016 (27) Davenport

- 92-94 FB +++
- 81-82 SL +++
- 84-85 CU +++

Year	Lev	Team	W	L	Sv	IP	K	ERA	WHIP	BF/G	OBA	H%	S%	xERA	Ctl	Dom	Cmd	hr/9	BPV
2016	A	Rome	4	0	4	23	37	1.55	1.12	6.1	166	30	88	1.76	5.0	14.4	2.8	0.4	140
2017	A+	Florida	2	0	2	35	46	2.31	1.49	6.0	239	37	83	3.21	5.4	11.8	2.2	0.0	85
2017	AA	Mississippi	3	4	1	22	26	2.86	1.55	6.0	253	35	84	4.32	5.3	10.6	2.0	0.8	66
2018	AA	Mississippi	5	2	4	49	65	1.84	1.20	5.2	216	34	83	2.20	3.9	11.9	3.1	0.0	129
2018	AAA	Gwinnett	1	0	0	16	18	2.25	1.00	8.7	210	31	75	1.64	2.3	10.1	4.5	0.0	140

Stocky LHP ironed out delivery in the 2nd half to post solid returns, split between Double-A & Triple-A. Pitchability type, relies heavily on mixing pitches in and out. 3/4s delivery with effort, struggles at times following through. 3-pitch, pitcher, all average or better offerings. Relies on throwing each from same plane, causing deception.

Coleman,Dylan

SP | San Diego | EXP MLB DEBUT: 2021 | H/W: 6-6 215 | FUT: Setup reliever | 8D

Thrws R Age 22
2018 (4) Missouri St

Velo	Pitch	Grade
92-94	FB	+++
84-86	SL	+++
78-80	CB	+++
	CU	++

Year	Lev	Team	W	L	Sv	IP	K	ERA	WHIP	BF/G	OBA	H%	S%	xERA	Ctl	Dom	Cmd	hr/9	BPV
2018	NCAA	Missouri State	10	2	0	102	129	3.79	1.30	24.8	204	30	71	2.90	5.2	11.4	2.2	0.6	82
2018	A-	Tri-City	0	0	1	6	7	3.00	1.33	5.0	262	38	75	3.14	3.0	10.5	3.5	0.0	126
2018	A	Fort Wayne	1	2	3	16	22	3.33	1.42	5.3	235	37	74	2.98	5.0	12.2	2.4	0.0	103

Tall, athletic RH who started in college but made pro debut from the 'pen. Can bring mid-90s heat when he's on and blend in flashes of a plus SL for whiffs. CB and CU are a work in progress but he may not need them if he's destined for setup relief. Command is spotty at present but as a natural ability to miss barrels.

Conlon,PJ

SP | New York (N) | EXP MLB DEBUT: 2019 | H/W: 6-0 175 | FUT: Middle reliever | 6D

Thrws L Age 25
2015 (13) San Diego

Velo	Pitch	Grade
86-89	FB	+
74-76	CB	++
77-79	CU	+++

Year	Lev	Team	W	L	Sv	IP	K	ERA	WHIP	BF/G	OBA	H%	S%	xERA	Ctl	Dom	Cmd	hr/9	BPV
2017	AA	Binghamton	8	9	1	136	108	3.38	1.24	19.7	253	30	76	3.68	2.5	7.1	2.8	0.9	79
2018	AAA	Las Vegas	4	9	0	114	82	6.55	1.63	22.1	314	35	62	6.18	3.1	6.5	2.1	1.6	51
2018	MLB	NY Mets	0	0	0	7	5	8.75	2.36	12.4	425	46	67	11.00	2.5	6.3	2.5	2.5	63

Soft-tossing lefty who had an unusual year, going from a prospect who made his MLB debut, to a guy who may not have big league value any more after posting awful numbers in Triple-A, although it was at Las Vegas. FB is short, and he lacks plus command to overcome it. Does not have the plus breaking ball he would need to be a quality reliever. Needs reboot.

Contreras,Roansy

SP | New York (A) | EXP MLB DEBUT: 2021 | H/W: 6-0 175 | FUT: #3 starter | 8D

Thrws R Age 19
2017 FA (DR)

Velo	Pitch	Grade
93-95	FB	++++
82-84	CB	++++
86-87	CU	++

Year	Lev	Team	W	L	Sv	IP	K	ERA	WHIP	BF/G	OBA	H%	S%	xERA	Ctl	Dom	Cmd	hr/9	BPV
2017	Rk	GCL Yankees	4	1	0	31	17	4.33	1.51	16.9	285	32	71	4.50	3.5	4.9	1.4	0.6	13
2018	A-	Staten Island	0	0	0	28	32	1.28	0.85	20.7	159	23	87	0.98	2.9	10.2	3.6	0.3	124
2018	A	Charleston (Sc)	0	2	0	34	28	3.42	1.20	19.6	231	27	76	3.42	3.2	7.4	2.3	1.1	65

Athletic, undersized RHP saw stuff and velocity tick up in big development year. High-3/4s online delivery. Three-pitch pitcher. 2-seam FB has solid arm-side run and downward action. Plays up due to advanced command. 12-to-6 CB has solid depth but inconsistent movement. Still, flashes plus potential. Lacks consistent feel of CU.

Corry,Seth

SP | San Francisco | EXP MLB DEBUT: 2021 | H/W: 6-2 195 | FUT: #4 starter | 7D

Thrws L Age 20
2017 (3) HS (UT)

Velo	Pitch	Grade
89-92	FB	+++
76-79	CB	+++
81-83	CU	+++

Year	Lev	Team	W	L	Sv	IP	K	ERA	WHIP	BF/G	OBA	H%	S%	xERA	Ctl	Dom	Cmd	hr/9	BPV
2017	Rk	AZL Giants	0	2	0	24	21	5.60	1.49	8.0	171	22	60	2.81	8.2	7.8	1.0	0.4	-63
2018	Rk	AZL Giants O	3	1	0	38	42	2.61	1.45	18.0	262	36	81	3.66	4.0	9.9	2.5	0.2	88
2018	A-	Salem-Keizer	1	2	0	19	17	5.63	1.51	16.6	205	26	61	3.33	7.0	8.0	1.1	0.5	-28

Former 3rd round pick with three average-or-better pitches struggles with control and high pitch counts. High 3/4s delivery, mostly straight-on to plate. 2-seam FB has solid arm-side run and natural sink. 1-to-6 CB is best pitch, with solid shape and strong movement. CU took step ahead in 2018, now repeats FB arm speed with some solid late fade.

Cox,Austin

SP | Kansas City | EXP MLB DEBUT: 2021 | H/W: 6-3 205 | FUT: #5 SP/swingman | 6C

Thrws L Age 22
2018 (5) Mercer

Velo	Pitch	Grade
89-92	FB	+++
81-83	SL	++
74-77	CB	+++
80-83	CU	++

Year	Lev	Team	W	L	Sv	IP	K	ERA	WHIP	BF/G	OBA	H%	S%	xERA	Ctl	Dom	Cmd	hr/9	BPV
2018	NCAA	Mercer	7	4	0	87	124	4.54	1.63	22.8	287	44	72	4.71	4.4	12.8	2.9	0.5	129
2018	Rk	Burlington	1	1	0	33	51	3.81	1.33	15.3	237	40	70	3.02	4.1	13.9	3.4	0.3	157

Long, herky-jerky LHP made pro debut in Appy League. Cross-armed 3/4s delivery with lots of moving parts, creating deception. Four pitches including 2-seam FB as moderate arm-side run at a favorable hitter's plane. 1-to-7 CB is best secondary offering with solid depth and break. SL blends closely with CB; slurvy. Struggles with feel of CU.

Crawford,Cutter

SP | Boston | EXP MLB DEBUT: 2021 | H/W: 6-1 192 | FUT: Middle reliever | 6D

Thrws R Age 23
2017 (16) Florida Gulf Coast

Velo	Pitch	Grade
89-94	FB	+++
74-80	CB	++
84-86	CU	++

Year	Lev	Team	W	L	Sv	IP	K	ERA	WHIP	BF/G	OBA	H%	S%	xERA	Ctl	Dom	Cmd	hr/9	BPV
2017	A-	Lowell	0	0	0	1	2	0.00	2.00	4.8	262	55	100	4.75	9.0	18.0	2.0	0.0	99
2018	A	Greenville	5	4	0	112	120	2.97	1.23	21.6	248	33	77	3.15	2.7	9.6	3.5	0.5	118
2018	A+	Salem	2	3	0	31	37	4.34	1.35	21.6	242	36	64	2.92	4.1	10.7	2.6	0.0	101

Had success as a starter at Low-A in 2018, but less once got to High-A. No plus pitches and lacks plus feel or command to make it play, especially as a starter. Not helped by an arm action that is very trackable. Best bet is to see if stuff plays up out of pen.

Crawford,Leo

SP | Los Angeles (N) | EXP MLB DEBUT: 2021 | H/W: 6-0 180 | FUT: #5 SP/swingman | 6C

Thrws L Age 22
2015 FA (NI)

Velo	Pitch	Grade
90-92	FB	+++
	CB	++
	CU	+

Year	Lev	Team	W	L	Sv	IP	K	ERA	WHIP	BF/G	OBA	H%	S%	xERA	Ctl	Dom	Cmd	hr/9	BPV
2016	A	Great Lakes	4	1	0	28	24	2.23	1.10	18.4	217	25	86	2.89	2.9	7.7	2.7	1.0	78
2017	A	Great Lakes	7	10	0	135	97	4.60	1.34	22.5	260	30	66	3.93	3.1	6.5	2.1	0.8	50
2018	A	Great Lakes	0	5	0	47	33	4.02	1.23	13.6	282	33	66	3.57	1.1	6.3	5.5	0.4	101
2018	A+	Rancho Cuca	8	0	0	68	61	2.78	1.15	20.8	235	30	76	2.71	2.5	8.1	3.2	0.4	95
2018	AAA	Oklahoma City	0	1	0	0	0		30.00	3.3	780	0	0	183.98		0.0	0.0	90.0	-4842

Short LHP had a solid bounce-back season between A/A+. Uses a high leg kick to drive home a good low-90 fastball and has the arm strength for more velocity. Also mixes in a CB and a rudimentary CU. Will need High-A Dom to continue to enhance chances of success.

Crouse,Hans

SP | Texas | EXP MLB DEBUT: 2022 | H/W: 6-5 190 | FUT: #2 starter | 9D

Thrws R Age 20
2017 (2) HS (CA)

Velo	Pitch	Grade
93-97	FB	++++
83-86	SL	+++
88-91	CU	++

Year	Lev	Team	W	L	Sv	IP	K	ERA	WHIP	BF/G	OBA	H%	S%	xERA	Ctl	Dom	Cmd	hr/9	BPV
2017	Rk	AZL Rangers	0	0	0	20	30	0.45	0.70	7.0	110	19	100	0.21	3.2	13.5	4.3	0.5	176
2018	A-	Spokane	5	1	0	38	47	2.37	0.95	17.9	189	28	76	1.70	2.6	11.1	4.3	0.5	148
2018	A	Hickory	0	2	0	16	15	2.78	1.60	14.3	283	36	84	4.66	4.4	8.3	1.9	0.6	48

Brings the goods with 1-2 punch of mid-90s fastball that he can both locate and miss bats with and slider that has a chance to end up as plus also. Change-up is stuill developing. Throws strikes despite herky-jerky delivery. Prototypical power pitcher's build; could be a quick riser.

Crowe,Wil

SP | Washington | EXP MLB DEBUT: 2021 | H/W: 6-3 230 | FUT: #4 starter | 7C

Thrws R Age 24
2017 (2) South Carolina

Velo	Pitch	Grade
91-93	FB	+++
82-85	SL	+++
84-86	CU	++

Year	Lev	Team	W	L	Sv	IP	K	ERA	WHIP	BF/G	OBA	H%	S%	xERA	Ctl	Dom	Cmd	hr/9	BPV
2017	Rk	GCL Nationals	0	0	0	3	2	5.63	1.25	6.5	250	30	50	2.81	2.8	5.6	2.0	0.0	43
2017	A-	Auburn	0	0	0	20	15	2.67	1.04	11.1	240	26	83	3.41	1.3	6.7	5.0	1.3	102
2018	A-	Auburn	0	0	0	3	1	0.00	1.33	12.5	191	21	100	2.33	6.0	3.0	0.5	0.0	-90
2018	A+	Potomac	11	0	0	87	78	2.69	1.16	21.6	224	28	79	2.83	3.1	8.1	2.6	0.6	79
2018	AA	Harrisburg	0	5	0	26	15	6.21	1.80	24.1	296	32	67	6.17	5.5	5.2	0.9	1.4	-38

Relies on sinker/slider/change-up mix—none is overpowering, but gets by on pitchability and changing speeds. Some effort to his delivery; limited athleticism but throws strikes. Slider his best pitch, with long late break at its best.

Davidson,Tucker

SP | Atlanta | EXP MLB DEBUT: 2020 | H/W: 6-2 215 | FUT: Middle reliever | 6C

Thrws L Age 23
2016 (19) Midland College

Velo	Pitch	Grade
92-95	FB	+++
76-78	CB	++
82-85	CU	+++

Year	Lev	Team	W	L	Sv	IP	K	ERA	WHIP	BF/G	OBA	H%	S%	xERA	Ctl	Dom	Cmd	hr/9	BPV
2016	Rk	GCL Braves	0	3	0	29	32	1.54	1.23	10.8	280	38	89	3.44	1.2	9.9	8.0	0.3	162
2017	A	Rome	5	4	2	103	101	2.62	1.22	13.5	248	33	79	3.02	2.6	8.8	3.4	0.3	106
2018	A+	Florida	7	10	0	118	99	4.19	1.51	21.3	265	33	71	4.01	4.4	7.5	1.7	0.4	34

Big-bodied, hard-throwing LHP struggled with control in High-A debut. Uses cross-armed high-3/4s delivery. Best pitch is 2-seam FB; been up in high 90s in shorter outings with solid arm-side run and natural sink. Lacks feel for 1-to-7 CB, struggling to get on top of pitch. CU has profiled in past as best secondary, but struggled to match FB delivery.

De La Cruz,Jassell

SP | Atlanta | EXP MLB DEBUT: 2021 | H/W: 6-1 175 | FUT: #4 starter | 7E

Thrws R Age 21
2015 FA (DR)

Velo	Pitch	Grade
91-95	FB	++++
87-91	SL	+++
84-87	CU	++

Year	Lev	Team	W	L	Sv	IP	K	ERA	WHIP	BF/G	OBA	H%	S%	xERA	Ctl	Dom	Cmd	hr/9	BPV
2016	Rk	GCL Braves	2	0	0	15	12	0.00	0.33	7.9	86	12	100		0.6	7.2	12.0	0.0	131
2017	Rk	Danville	0	2	0	23	19	5.43	1.55	14.5	276	34	63	4.29	4.3	7.4	1.7	0.4	35
2017	Rk	GCL Braves	2	1	0	19	17	1.89	1.05	18.4	195	25	84	2.06	3.3	8.1	2.4	0.5	73
2018	A	Rome	3	4	0	69	65	4.83	1.43	19.6	250	31	67	4.00	4.4	8.5	1.9	0.8	51

Hard-throwing, athletic RHP had an up-and-down season in Single-A. Unrefined, cross-armed 3/4s delivery with effort. 3-pitch pitcher. Struggles commanding 2-seam FB w/ solid run to arm-side. SL has sharp 2-plane break from FB slot; hard to pick up out of hand. Overthrows CU trying to match FB arm speed. Flat movement.

De La Cruz,Oscar | SP | Chicago (N) | EXP MLB DEBUT: 2019 | H/W: 6-4 200 | FUT: #4 starter | 7C

Thrws R Age 24	Year	Lev	Team	W	L	Sv	IP	K	ERA	WHIP	BF/G	OBA	H%	S%	xERA	Ctl	Dom	Cmd	hr/9	BPV
2012 FA (DR)	2016	A-	Eugene	0	0	0	8	14	1.11	0.86	14.9	180	31	100	1.94	2.2	15.6	7.0	1.1	238
92-95 FB +++	2016	A	South Bend	1	2	0	27	35	3.31	1.10	17.8	223	35	67	2.04	2.6	11.6	4.4	0.0	155
76-78 CB +++	2017	Rk	AZL Cubs	0	0	0	2	1	0.00	0.00	5.6	0	0			0.0	4.5		0.0	99
CU ++	2017	A+	Myrtle Beach	4	3	0	54	47	3.49	1.25	18.4	265	32	76	3.94	2.2	7.8	3.6	1.0	100
	2018	AA	Tennessee	6	7	0	77	73	5.25	1.39	20.3	259	32	63	4.14	3.6	8.5	2.4	0.9	74

Another rough season for once highly regarded hurler. Struggled in 16 starts and received an 80-game suspension for a banned substance. Stuff can be electric and is highlighted by a plus 92-95 mph FB with good late life and a plus power 11-to-6 CB. CU shows potential. Power pitching frame and mentality, but a move to relief seems likely.

De Los Santos,Enyel | SP | Philadelphia | EXP MLB DEBUT: 2018 | H/W: 6-3 170 | FUT: Middle reliever | 7B

Thrws R Age 23	Year	Lev	Team	W	L	Sv	IP	K	ERA	WHIP	BF/G	OBA	H%	S%	xERA	Ctl	Dom	Cmd	hr/9	BPV
2015 FA (DR)	2016	A	Fort Wayne	3	2	0	52	45	2.93	1.00	18.1	205	26	70	1.92	2.4	7.8	3.2	0.3	92
92-96 FB ++++	2016	A+	Lake Elsinore	5	3	0	68	52	4.36	1.38	19.1	267	30	73	4.74	3.2	6.9	2.2	1.5	56
85-89 CU +++	2017	AA	San Antonio	10	6	0	150	138	3.78	1.19	23.2	236	29	69	3.15	2.9	8.3	2.9	0.7	89
80-84 SL +	2018	AAA	Lehigh Valley	10	5	0	126	110	2.64	1.16	22.9	226	27	81	3.08	3.1	7.8	2.6	0.9	76
	2018	MLB	Philadelphia	1	0	0	19	15	4.74	1.42	11.5	262	31	68	4.29	3.8	7.1	1.9	0.9	44

Had excellent year as SP in Triple-A after coming over in Freddy Galvis trade. Low-90s FB and a power CU are the main attractions; gets soft contact at his best. Tall with room for more strength, looks like a starter, but hasn't found reliable breaking ball yet and control is not pristine. Could end up in relief.

De Paula,Juan | SP | San Francisco | EXP MLB DEBUT: 2022 | H/W: 6-3 165 | FUT: #4 starter | 7D

Thrws R Age 21	Year	Lev	Team	W	L	Sv	IP	K	ERA	WHIP	BF/G	OBA	H%	S%	xERA	Ctl	Dom	Cmd	hr/9	BPV
2014 FA (DR)																				
90-94 FB ++++	2016	Rk	AZL Mariners	1	2	0	41		3.07	1.27	15.2	262	38	76	3.38	2.4	11.6	4.8	0.4	162
74-78 CB +++	2017	A-	Staten Island	5	5	0	62	53	2.90	1.08	20.2	194	26	70	1.67	3.6	7.7	2.1	0.0	59
81-84 CU ++	2018	A-	Staten Island	2	2	0	47	46	1.72	1.30	19.4	209	28	87	2.56	5.0	8.8	1.8	0.2	42
	2018	A	Augusta	0	1	0	5	9	1.80	0.60	17.1	124	16	100	1.33	1.8	16.2	9.0	1.8	261

Athletic, raw hurler acquired in mid-season trade with NYY. Athletic 3/4s delivery with some elasticity in arm. Could achieve greater extension to take advantage of lower half strength. Hard low-to-mid 90s FB with late tail. Raw CB has solid shape when finished pitch. Has a feel for CU.

Dease,Ryan | SP | Texas | EXP MLB DEBUT: 2023 | H/W: 6-3 175 | FUT: #4 starter | 7D

Thrws R Age 19	Year	Lev	Team	W	L	Sv	IP	K	ERA	WHIP	BF/G	OBA	H%	S%	xERA	Ctl	Dom	Cmd	hr/9	BPV
2017 (4) HS (FL)																				
90-93 FB +++																				
80-82 SL ++	2017	Rk	AZL Rangers	3	1	0	22	19	2.05	0.91	7.5	225	27	83	2.38	0.8	7.8	9.5	0.8	136
CU ++	2018	A-	Spokane	5	4	0	55	39	5.38	1.63	20.5	337	38	70	6.45	1.8	6.4	3.5	1.5	84
	2018	A	Hickory	1	0	0	5	3	0.00	1.00	19.1	262	31	100	2.35	0.0	5.4		0.0	115

Pitchability righthander who has an idea on the mound, but stuff currently a bit short. Some life his fastball and he changes speeds effectively from a high slot, but too many mistake pitches led to rough 2018. Gets swings and misses on potentially plus CU. Has a projectable frame that could benefit from some added strength.

Deetz,Dean | RP | Houston | EXP MLB DEBUT: 2018 | H/W: 6-1 190 | FUT: Middle reliever | 7B

Thrws R Age 25	Year	Lev	Team	W	L	Sv	IP	K	ERA	WHIP	BF/G	OBA	H%	S%	xERA	Ctl	Dom	Cmd	hr/9	BPV
2014 (11) NE Oklahoma A&M	2017	AAA	Fresno	3	4	0	45	55	6.40	1.93	12.6	266	36	67	5.65	8.2	11.0	1.3	1.0	-5
94-96 FB ++++	2018	A	Quad Cities	0	0	0	3	7	3.00	2.67	5.5	262	67	88	6.40	15.0	21.0	1.4	0.0	-9
83-85 CB +++++	2018	AA	Corpus Christi	0	0	0	3	6	0.00	0.63	3.7	181	40	100	0.30	0.0	16.9		0.0	322
	2018	AAA	Fresno	2	0	0	34	50	0.79	1.18	6.5	187	31	95	2.03	4.8	13.2	2.8	0.3	128
	2018	MLB	Houston	0	0	0	3	3	5.81	1.61	3.4	314	34	75	7.36	2.9	8.7	3.0	2.9	96

Opening the season serving an 80-game suspension is a tough start. Finishing it having reached the majors softens the blow a bit. A fireballing righty who was actually tougher on lefties than righties in the minors in 2018, it's a reversal from previous years. His potentially plus-plus curveball helps neutralize southpaws.

Del Rosario,Yefri | SP | Kansas City | EXP MLB DEBUT: 2021 | H/W: 6-2 180 | FUT: #3 starter | 8D

Thrws R Age 19	Year	Lev	Team	W	L	Sv	IP	K	ERA	WHIP	BF/G	OBA	H%	S%	xERA	Ctl	Dom	Cmd	hr/9	BPV
2016 FA (DR)																				
92-95 FB ++++																				
78-80 CB ++++																				
86-87 CU +++	2017	Rk	GCL Braves	1	1	0	32	29	3.93	1.46	12.5	290	37	72	4.16	2.8	8.1	2.9	0.3	89
	2018	A	Lexington	6	5	0	79	72	3.19	1.24	21.4	236	28	80	3.66	3.3	8.2	2.5	1.1	76

Projectable RHP teenager has raw, high 3/4s power delivery. Two types of FB, both effective. Two-seamer is workhorse with solid arm-side action; four-seamer misses bats. 11-to-5 CB with solid movement; potential plus at projection. Aggressive with CU despite inconsistency; also has above-average potential.

Denaburg,Mason | SP | Washington | EXP MLB DEBUT: 2022 | H/W: 6-4 195 | FUT: #3 starter | 8D

Thrws R Age 19	Year	Lev	Team	W	L	Sv	IP	K	ERA	WHIP	BF/G	OBA	H%	S%	xERA	Ctl	Dom	Cmd	hr/9	BPV
2018 (1) HS (FL)																				
90-94 FB +++																				
78-80 CB +++																				
CU ++																				
	2018		Did not pitch - injury																	

Broad-shouldered and athletic, he comes from a semi-windup and stays tall, then gets good extension out front, delivering his 90-94 fastball. Has some life to it, and gets on hitters quickly. Adds a potentially plus CB with sharp break, and change-up is a distant third pitch. He missed time his senior year with tendinitis and slipped in the draft.

Diaz,Jhonathan | SP | Boston | EXP MLB DEBUT: 2021 | H/W: 6-0 170 | FUT: #5 SP/swingman | 6D

Thrws L Age 22	Year	Lev	Team	W	L	Sv	IP	K	ERA	WHIP	BF/G	OBA	H%	S%	xERA	Ctl	Dom	Cmd	hr/9	BPV
2014 FA (VZ)																				
89-91 FB +++	2016	Rk	GCL Red Sox	4	4	0	60	57	2.85	1.17	18.4	235	31	75	2.67	2.7	8.6	3.2	0.3	99
73-75 CB ++	2017	A	Greenville	6	6	0	88	80	4.59	1.46	21.0	289	37	67	4.26	2.9	8.2	2.9	0.4	88
80-82 CU +++	2018	A	Greenville	11	8	0	153	147	3.00	1.06	22.8	222	29	71	2.28	2.3	8.6	3.8	0.4	112
	2018	A+	Salem	0	1	0	4	4	6.59	2.20	20.6	377	44	75	9.27	4.4	8.8	2.0	2.2	58

Lefty signed out of Venezuela who has held his own as a starter at the lower levels by keeping the ball on the ground. Lacks size and stuff, so remains to be seen how he will fair at higher levels.

Diaz,Yennsy | SP | Toronto | EXP MLB DEBUT: 2021 | H/W: 6-1 160 | FUT: Setup reliever | 6C

Thrws R Age 22	Year	Lev	Team	W	L	Sv	IP	K	ERA	WHIP	BF/G	OBA	H%	S%	xERA	Ctl	Dom	Cmd	hr/9	BPV
2014 FA (DR)																				
92-94 FB +++	2016	Rk	Bluefield	4	6	0	56	48	5.79	1.54	20.3	272	31	65	5.18	4.3	7.7	1.8	1.4	40
76-78 CB +++	2017	A	Lansing	5	2	0	77	82	4.79	1.45	20.6	246	31	70	4.35	4.8	9.6	2.0	1.2	61
86-88 CU +	2018	A	Lansing	5	1	0	47	42	2.10	1.00	20.0	142	16	84	1.61	4.8	8.0	1.7	0.8	33
	2018	A+	Dunedin	5	4	0	99	83	3.54	1.20	22.2	245	30	70	3.04	2.5	7.5	3.0	0.5	85

Short, athletic hurler had a breakout campaign. FB sits at 92-94, topping at 96 with good late life up in the zone. Backs up the FB with an above-average but inconsistent CB that has slurvy action, and mixes in a fringe CU that lacks separation. Lack of a viable 3rd offering likely limits in to a relief role down the road.

Dibrell,Tony | SP | New York (N) | EXP MLB DEBUT: 2020 | H/W: 6-3 220 | FUT: Middle reliever | 6D

Thrws R Age 23	Year	Lev	Team	W	L	Sv	IP	K	ERA	WHIP	BF/G	OBA	H%	S%	xERA	Ctl	Dom	Cmd	hr/9	BPV
2017 (4) Kennesaw St																				
86-90 FB ++																				
72-75 CB +++	2017	NCAA	Kennesaw St	7	4	0	95	103	2.46	1.22	27.5	223	30	83	2.97	3.7	9.7	2.6	0.7	94
79-81 SL +++	2017	A-	Brooklyn	1	1	0	19	28	5.16	1.41	6.8	260	36	70	5.03	3.8	13.1	3.5	1.9	153
78-81 CU +++	2018	A	Columbia	7	6	0	131	147	3.50	1.27	23.3	233	31	74	3.24	3.7	10.1	2.7	0.7	100

Offspeed specialist who has had success at lower levels, but FB velo and FB command too short to have significant value. CB, SL and CU are all pretty effective, although none are nasty. Chance to help out of bullpen if FB plays up in that role.

Diehl,Phillip | RP | New York (A) | EXP MLB DEBUT: 2019 | H/W: 6-3 170 | FUT: Middle reliever | 6B

Thrws L Age 24	Year	Lev	Team	W	L	Sv	IP	K	ERA	WHIP	BF/G	OBA	H%	S%	xERA	Ctl	Dom	Cmd	hr/9	BPV
2016 (27) Evansville																				
91-94 FB +++	2016	A-	Staten Island	1	0	0	2	3	0.00	0.50	6.6	151	27	100		0.0	13.5		0.0	261
81-83 SL +++	2017	A	Charleston (Sc)	9	3	2	85	101	3.17	1.20	12.2	241	34	73	2.91	2.7	10.7	3.9	0.4	136
	2018	A+	Tampa	2	2	3	48	79	3.17	1.02	7.4	214	38	68	2.03	2.2	14.8	6.6	0.4	223
	2018	AA	Trenton	0	1	1	26	29	1.37	1.11	7.3	196	26	93	2.39	3.8	10.0	2.6	0.7	95

Lean, deceptive LHP is poised to make 2019 MLB debut. 3/4s, cross-fire delivery with effort and solid extension. Ball explodes on hitters despite average velocity. Commands FB to both sides of the plate. Changes angles well on above-average SL. More situational LH upside potential than anything.

Diplan,Marcos — SP — Milwaukee

EXP MLB DEBUT: 2019 | H/W: 6-0 160 | FUT: Setup reliever | 9E

Thrws R Age 22 — 2016 FA (DR)

- 92-95 FB ++++
- 79-82 SL ++++
- 83-85 CU ++

Year	Lev	Team	W	L	Sv	IP	K	ERA	WHIP	BF/G	OBA	H%	S%	xERA	Ctl	Dom	Cmd	hr/9	BPV
2016	A	Wisconsin	6	2	1	70	89	1.80	1.16	16.4	199	30	86	2.25	4.1	11.4	2.8	0.4	113
2016	A+	Brevard County	1	2	0	43	40	5.01	1.51	18.7	279	35	67	4.63	3.8	8.4	2.2	0.8	67
2017	A+	Carolina	7	8	0	125	119	5.25	1.57	21.2	263	33	67	4.52	5.1	8.6	1.7	0.8	34
2018	A+	Carolina	3	2	0	61	60	3.54	1.57	20.6	252	33	77	4.04	5.6	8.8	1.6	0.4	26
2018	AA	Biloxi	2	6	0	57	57	4.58	1.65	21.2	265	33	74	4.89	5.7	9.0	1.6	0.9	27

Smallish, strong-armed RH who had inconsistent AA debut. FB will touch 97 mph and sit around 94 with late life. Misses barrels regularly with plus vertical SL. CU flashes good fade but doesn't use enough in games. Lack of balance and high-effort delivery leads to BBs and hard contact up in zone. High upside, high risk arm.

Dodson,Tanner — SP — Tampa Bay

EXP MLB DEBUT: 2021 | H/W: 6-1 170 | FUT: Setup reliever | 7C

Thrws R Age 21 — 2018 (2) California

- 93-96 FB ++++
- 88-91 SL +++
- 79-83 CB +++
- CU ++

Year	Lev	Team	W	L	Sv	IP	K	ERA	WHIP	BF/G	OBA	H%	S%	xERA	Ctl	Dom	Cmd	hr/9	BPV
2018	NCAA	California	2	1	11	40	35	2.48	1.08	8.2	242	30	80	2.88	1.6	7.9	5.0	0.7	117
2018	A-	Hudson Valley	1	0	1	25	25	1.44	0.68	9.7	145	21	76	0.13	1.8	9.0	5.0	0.0	131

Hard-throwing 2-way player most scouts prefer working out of 'pen. Athletic, 3/4s cross-fire delivery with great extension. 4-pitch pitcher with solid secondary offerings. 2-seam FB sits mid-90s with arm-side run and some sink. Throws sharp SL with late vertical drop. 11-to-5 CB has good shape and average movement. CU is workable, keeps LHH honest.

Doval,Camilo — RP — San Francisco

EXP MLB DEBUT: 2020 | H/W: 6-2 185 | FUT: Setup reliever | 7C

Thrws R Age 21 — 2016 FA (DR)

- 94-97 FB ++++
- 85-87 SL +++
- 88-90 CT +++

Year	Lev	Team	W	L	Sv	IP	K	ERA	WHIP	BF/G	OBA	H%	S%	xERA	Ctl	Dom	Cmd	hr/9	BPV
2017	Rk	AZL Giants	1	2	1	32	51	3.93	1.12	7.4	203	37	61	1.82	3.6	14.3	3.9	0.0	177
2018	A	Augusta	0	3	11	53	78	3.06	1.26	4.9	211	35	75	2.61	4.6	13.2	2.9	0.3	133

Elastic, hard-throwing RH RP dominated Single-A competition. High, side-arm slot with effort. Three pitches; added velo to 2-seam FB with natural arm-side movement. Throws both CT and SL. CT has late cutting action. SL is more of sweeping variety with solid 2-plane break. Struggles with control and inconsistent release points.

Doyle,Tommy — RP — Colorado

EXP MLB DEBUT: 2020 | H/W: 6-6 215 | FUT: Setup reliever | 7B

Thrws R Age 22 — 2017 (2) Virginia

- 94-97 FB ++++
- 83-87 SL +++
- 85-88 CU +

Year	Lev	Team	W	L	Sv	IP	K	ERA	WHIP	BF/G	OBA	H%	S%	xERA	Ctl	Dom	Cmd	hr/9	BPV
2017	NCAA	Virginia	3	1	14	33	38	1.90	1.14	5.7	230	32	86	2.76	2.7	10.3	3.8	0.5	130
2017	Rk	Grand Junction	3	3	3	21	18	5.14	1.86	4.9	329	40	73	6.31	4.3	7.7	1.8	0.9	41
2018	A	Asheville	7	6	18	58	66	2.32	1.10	4.4	241	34	79	2.57	1.9	10.2	5.5	0.3	152

Large-bodied collegiate reliever scuffled in pro debut, but was much better in full-season action. Uses huge frame to get downhill tilt on 94-97 mph FB with good late life. SL can be plus at times with two-plane action, but CU is below-average and seldom used. Has the size and stuff to be a high leverage MLB reliever.

Duggar,Robert — SP — Miami

EXP MLB DEBUT: 2019 | H/W: 6-2 185 | FUT: Middle reliever | 6C

Thrws R Age 23 — 2016 (18) Texas Tech

- 89-92 FB +++
- 78-82 SL +++
- 83 CU ++

Year	Lev	Team	W	L	Sv	IP	K	ERA	WHIP	BF/G	OBA	H%	S%	xERA	Ctl	Dom	Cmd	hr/9	BPV
2016	AAA	Tacoma	0	0	0	4	4	6.75	1.25	8.1	307	41	40	3.61	0.0	9.0		0.0	180
2017	A	Clinton	4	1	2	72	69	2.00	0.99	12.5	213	28	82	2.13	2.0	8.6	4.3	0.5	119
2017	A+	Modesto	2	5	0	45	47	3.98	1.44	21.4	278	36	74	4.39	3.2	9.4	2.9	0.8	100
2018	A+	Jupiter	3	1	0	41	34	2.41	1.14	23.3	257	32	80	3.03	1.5	7.4	4.9	0.4	111
2018	AA	Jacksonville	7	6	0	109	107	3.79	1.25	24.6	245	30	73	3.72	3.0	8.8	3.0	1.1	97

Lean, athletic RHP with RP upside. Struggles repeating 3/4s crossfire delivery with effort. 3-pitch pitcher. 2-seam FB clearly best offering with above-average arm-side movement but struggles commanding pitch due to delivery issues. Solid SL with good depth is likely average pitch at projection. CU is a fairly flat.

Dunn,Justin — SP — Seattle

EXP MLB DEBUT: 2020 | H/W: 6-1 170 | FUT: #3 starter | 8B

Thrws R Age 23 — 2016 (1) Boston College

- 92-95 FB ++++
- 78-80 CB +++
- 80-84 SL ++++
- 85-87 CU +++

Year	Lev	Team	W	L	Sv	IP	K	ERA	WHIP	BF/G	OBA	H%	S%	xERA	Ctl	Dom	Cmd	hr/9	BPV
2016	NCAA	Boston College	4	2	2	65	72	2.07	1.07	14.1	220	30	82	2.34	2.5	9.9	4.0	0.4	130
2016	A-	Brooklyn	1	1	0	30	35	1.50	1.17	10.9	228	33	88	2.56	3.0	10.5	3.5	0.3	126
2017	A+	St. Lucie	5	6	0	95	75	5.02	1.57	20.9	274	33	67	4.37	4.5	7.1	1.6	0.5	23
2018	A+	St. Lucie	2	3	0	45	51	2.39	1.28	20.6	252	35	82	3.26	3.0	10.2	3.4	0.4	120
2018	AA	Binghamton	6	5	0	89	105	4.24	1.37	24.9	253	35	70	3.76	3.7	10.6	2.8	0.7	108

Rare starter who was a college reliever. Drafted first by the Mets and traded to the Mariners after the 2018 season. A plus athlete who has made good strides becoming more of a pitcher, and now has a good mixture. CB and SL blend at times, but SL has a chance to be plus pitch. FB is plus. CU is improving. Could always go back to pen and thrive.

Dunning,Dane — SP — Chicago (A)

EXP MLB DEBUT: 2019 | H/W: 6-3 190 | FUT: #3 starter | 8B

Thrws R Age 24 — 2016 (1) Florida

- 90-93 FB ++++
- 83-86 SL ++++
- 78-80 CB +++
- 82-83 CU +++

Year	Lev	Team	W	L	Sv	IP	K	ERA	WHIP	BF/G	OBA	H%	S%	xERA	Ctl	Dom	Cmd	hr/9	BPV
2016	A-	Auburn	3	2	0	33	29	2.17	0.99	18.1	217	28	78	1.99	1.9	7.9	4.1	0.3	108
2017	A	Kannapolis	2	0	0	26	33	0.35	0.58	22.1	151	24	93		0.7	11.4	16.5	0.0	205
2017	A+	Winston-Salem	6	8	0	118	135	3.51	1.27	21.9	255	33	77	3.97	2.7	10.3	3.8	1.1	129
2018	A+	Winston-Salem	1	1	0	24	31	2.61	0.95	22.7	227	33	76	2.42	1.1	11.6	10.3	0.7	196
2018	AA	Birmingham	5	2	0	62	69	2.76	1.29	23.2	246	35	76	2.82	3.3	10.0	3.0	0.0	108

Solid, 3/4s RHP continued ascent towards big leagues with successful Double-A season. Repeatable, easy delivery. 4-pitch pitcher. Workhorse is a sinker with drop-off-the-table break. Tight, 2-plane breaking SL is best secondary. Reintroduced 11-to-5 CB, which has fringe depth but solid late break. Has refined CU. It's an above-average pitch at projection.

Dunshee,Parker — SP — Oakland

EXP MLB DEBUT: 2019 | H/W: 6-1 210 | FUT: #5 SP/swingman | 7B

Thrws R Age 24 — 2017 (7) Wake Forest

- 90-92 FB +++
- 84-85 SL +++
- 79-82 CB ++
- 82-84 CU +++

Year	Lev	Team	W	L	Sv	IP	K	ERA	WHIP	BF/G	OBA	H%	S%	xERA	Ctl	Dom	Cmd	hr/9	BPV
2017	NCAA	Wake Forest	9	1	0	103	111	3.92	1.24	24.6	252	33	71	3.68	2.6	9.7	3.7	1.0	122
2017	Rk	AZL Athletics	0	0	0	2	3	13.50	2.50	10.6	470	60	50	14.26	0.0	13.5		4.5	261
2017	A-	Vermont	1	0	0	38	45	0.00	0.60	10.9	123	19	100		1.9	10.6	5.6	0.0	158
2018	A+	Stockton	6	2	0	70	82	2.70	1.11	23.0	236	32	80	3.09	2.2	10.5	4.8	0.9	149
2018	AA	Midland	7	4	0	80	81	2.02	0.91	24.9	207	27	81	1.91	1.6	9.1	5.8	0.6	139

Athletic, medium-framed RH who replicated success well after bump to AA mid-year. Pounds the zone and shows command of four average pitches. FB is 90-92 mph with some sink and blends in effective fading CU to LHH. SL works better than CB but both will be useable. Good athlete; repeats 3/4 slot well; low effort in delivery. High-floor arm.

Duplantier,Jon — SP — Arizona

EXP MLB DEBUT: 2019 | H/W: 6-4 210 | FUT: #2 starter | 9C

Thrws R Age 24 — 2016 (3) Rice

- 92-96 FB ++++
- 85-87 SL ++++
- 77-81 CB +++
- 84-86 CU +++

Year	Lev	Team	W	L	Sv	IP	K	ERA	WHIP	BF/G	OBA	H%	S%	xERA	Ctl	Dom	Cmd	hr/9	BPV
2016	A-	Hillsboro	0	0	0	1	3	0.00	2.00	4.8	0	0	100	2.00	18.0	27.0	1.5	0.0	18
2017	A	Kane County	6	1	0	72	78	1.25	0.83	20.3	181	25	89	1.35	1.9	9.7	5.2	0.5	143
2017	A+	Visalia	6	2	0	63	87	1.57	1.16	20.9	205	33	87	2.22	3.9	12.4	3.2	0.3	137
2018	Rk	AZL DBacks	0	0	0	7	9	1.29	1.00	13.4	202	32	86	1.53	2.6	11.6	4.5	0.0	157
2018	AA	Jackson	5	1	0	67	68	2.69	1.19	19.2	216	28	79	2.71	3.8	9.1	2.4	0.5	81

Tall, physical athlete with swing-and-miss stuff and four quality pitches. FB hums in mid-90s and will touch 98 mph with heavy arm-side movement for GBs. Owns power SL with late action. CU gets tumble and fade and will be above-average at next level. Long arm action in back limits overall command and has been source of elbow injuries in past.

Duran,Jhoan — SP — Minnesota

EXP MLB DEBUT: 2021 | H/W: 6-5 175 | FUT: #3 starter | 8D

Thrws R Age 21 — 2015 FA (DR)

- 95-98 FB ++++
- 92-94 SP ++++
- 79-81 SL +++
- 85-88 CU ++

Year	Lev	Team	W	L	Sv	IP	K	ERA	WHIP	BF/G	OBA	H%	S%	xERA	Ctl	Dom	Cmd	hr/9	BPV
2016	Rk	AZL DBacks	1	2	0	20	13	5.85	1.45	21.4	299	35	57	4.43	2.3	5.9	2.6	0.5	63
2017	Rk	AZL DBacks	0	2	0	11	13	7.30	2.07	18.1	378	51	61	6.89	3.2	10.5	3.3	0.0	120
2017	A-	Hillsboro	6	3	0	51	36	4.24	1.20	18.6	234	27	66	3.30	3.0	6.4	2.1	0.9	51
2018	A	Kane County	5	4	0	64	71	4.77	1.51	18.5	276	36	69	4.58	3.9	10.0	2.5	0.8	91
2018	A	Cedar Rapids	7	5	0	100	115	3.77	1.26	19.5	237	32	71	3.30	3.4	10.3	3.0	0.7	112

Tall, hard-throwing RHP acquired in mid-season trade with ARI. Lean build with room to grow; comes from a 3/4s slot. Workhorse is high-90s 4-seam FB with late action that misses bats in all quadrants of zone. Splitter has tumble like a CU and is hard to elevate. SL lacks tightness and consistent 2-plane break but projects average. CU needs work.

DuRapau,Montana — RP — Pittsburgh

EXP MLB DEBUT: 2019 | H/W: 5-10 175 | FUT: Setup reliever | 7C

Thrws R Age 27 — 2014 (32) Bethune-Cookman

- 91-94 FB +++
- 86-88 CT ++++
- 82-85 SL +++

Year	Lev	Team	W	L	Sv	IP	K	ERA	WHIP	BF/G	OBA	H%	S%	xERA	Ctl	Dom	Cmd	hr/9	BPV
2016	AA	Altoona	3	3	22	49	51	3.67	1.26	4.0	237	30	75	3.68	3.5	9.3	2.7	1.1	92
2017	AA	Altoona	2	2	14	36	39	1.50	1.16	5.3	216	31	86	2.12	3.5	9.7	2.8	0.0	99
2017	AAA	Indianapolis	1	0	1	16	23	3.33	0.80	3.9	133	18	64	1.32	3.3	12.8	3.8	1.1	158
2018	AA	Altoona	0	1	2	9	13	2.97	0.77	4.1	214	32	67	2.01	0.0	12.9		1.0	249
2018	AAA	Indianapolis	1	1	0	21	25	6.40	1.47	8.2	261	32	62	5.47	4.3	10.7	2.5	2.1	95

Small, over-achieving cut FB specialist who does not lack guts or confidence. Has plus command of a plus cutter. Usés it a lot, getting in on both LHH and RHH. Commands FB well enough to set it up. Solid SL works to change speeds some. Lives up in zone a lot, so HR may be a problem.

Eastman,Colton

SP | Philadelphia | EXP MLB DEBUT: 2022 | H/W: 6-3 185 | FUT: #4 starter | 7C

Thrws R Age 22			Year	Lev	Team	W	L	Sv	IP	K	ERA	WHIP	BF/G	OBA	H%	S%	xERA	Ctl	Dom	Cmd	hr/9	BPV
2018 (4) Cal St Fullerton																						
88-91	FB	++																				
	CB	+++																				
	CU	++	2018	NCAA	Cal St Fullerton	10	4	0	117	124	2.38	1.00	26.3	212	29	77	2.10	2.2	9.5	4.4	0.5	131
			2018	A-	Williamsport	0	2	0	18	23	3.00	1.39	9.5	262	38	79	3.74	3.5	11.5	3.3	0.5	131

Like many of his Cal St Fullerton brethren, thrives on pitchability over stuff. FB a bit short, but can locate it and sets up a high-spin CB with a big break and above average potential. CU features some deception but is inconsistent. Will likely top out as a back-end starter unless arsenal develops further.

Eckelman,Matt

RP | Pittsburgh | EXP MLB DEBUT: 2020 | H/W: 6-4 220 | FUT: Middle reliever | 7E

Thrws R Age 25			Year	Lev	Team	W	L	Sv	IP	K	ERA	WHIP	BF/G	OBA	H%	S%	xERA	Ctl	Dom	Cmd	hr/9	BPV
2016 (21) Saint Louis			2016	NCAA	Saint Louis	9	4	0	101	81	3.12	1.21	27.1	246	29	77	3.40	2.6	7.2	2.8	0.8	78
91-95	FB	+++	2016	Rk	Bristol	5	3	0	62	55	2.76	0.97	18.1	226	27	76	2.59	1.3	8.0	6.1	0.9	126
82-94	CB	+++	2017	A	West Virginia	5	6	1	72	63	4.63	1.36	8.1	262	32	67	4.06	3.3	7.9	2.4	0.9	72
88-90	CU	+++	2018	A+	Bradenton	4	0	6	23	27	2.33	1.16	5.4	225	31	84	2.96	3.1	10.5	3.4	0.8	123
	SP		2018	AA	Altoona	1	1	11	24	17	1.86	1.36	4.4	209	25	88	2.93	5.6	6.3	1.1	0.4	-19

Huge, hefty reliever with decent stuff but command and consistency lacking. His poor conditioning is most likely a contributing factor, as it limits his ability to repeat his delivery. Could be a surprise if would get those issues in check.

Elledge,Seth

RP | St. Louis | EXP MLB DEBUT: 2020 | H/W: 6-2 238 | FUT: Middle reliever | 6A

Thrws R Age 22			Year	Lev	Team	W	L	Sv	IP	K	ERA	WHIP	BF/G	OBA	H%	S%	xERA	Ctl	Dom	Cmd	hr/9	BPV
2017 (4) Dallas Baptist			2017	NCAA	Dallas Baptist	2	1	13	31		2.60	1.22	5.7	222	33	81	2.87	3.8	12.2	3.2	0.6	135
93-95	FB	++++	2017	A-	Everett	0	0	0	4	7	4.50	1.00	3.8	151	32	50	0.92	4.5	15.8	3.5	0.0	180
80-83	SL	++	2017	A	Clinton	3	0	5	21	35	3.00	0.95	5.3	191	35	68	1.65	2.6	15.0	5.8	0.4	219
	CU	+	2018	A+	Modesto	5	1	9	38	54	1.18	0.87	4.5	143	24	88	0.76	3.5	12.8	3.6	0.2	152
			2018	AA	Springfield	3	1	4	16	20	4.44	1.17	5.0	222	28	69	3.77	3.3	11.1	3.3	1.7	128

Righty reliever come over as part of the Sam Tuivailala deal. Traditional sinker/slider reliever with plus FB velo. Heater sits at 93-95, topping at 97 mph with good late sink and run. Slider has good late break, but at times acts more like a cutter. Stiff, non-athletic mechanics results in fringe command and limit him to a middle relief role.

Englert,Mason

SP | Texas | EXP MLB DEBUT: 2024 | H/W: 6-4 205 | FUT: #3 starter | 8D

Thrws R Age 19			Year	Lev	Team	W	L	Sv	IP	K	ERA	WHIP	BF/G	OBA	H%	S%	xERA	Ctl	Dom	Cmd	hr/9	BPV
2018 (4) HS (TX)																						
91-95	FB	+++																				
82-84	SL	+++																				
75-77	CB	++																				
82-86	CU	+	2018		Did not pitch																	

Big and strong with a starter's frame, he throws with some effort but adds deception and early signs indicate he has good control. Evaluators split on whether CB or SL is his best secondary, but he has a feel for spin, and his CU has shown flashes. Still needs to work on repeating his delivery. Will get first shot at pro hitters in 2019.

English,William

RP | Los Angeles (A) | EXP MLB DEBUT: 2023 | H/W: 6-2 185 | FUT: Middle reliever | 7D

Thrws R Age 18			Year	Lev	Team	W	L	Sv	IP	K	ERA	WHIP	BF/G	OBA	H%	S%	xERA	Ctl	Dom	Cmd	hr/9	BPV
2018 (5) HS (MI)																						
91-95	FB	+++																				
	CB	+																				
	CU	++																				
			2018		Did not pitch																	

Two-way standout from Detroit, Michigan who received the Angels blessing to continue working on both sides of the ball. Already sizable at 17, he's projected to add velocity to a plus arm as he matures. Curve and change-up project to surface as average offerings. Boasts plus speed in the field, but current strength points to the mound.

Enlow,Blayne

SP | Minnesota | EXP MLB DEBUT: 2022 | H/W: 6-3 170 | FUT: #3 starter | 8D

Thrws R Age 20			Year	Lev	Team	W	L	Sv	IP	K	ERA	WHIP	BF/G	OBA	H%	S%	xERA	Ctl	Dom	Cmd	hr/9	BPV
2017 (3) HS (LA)																						
90-95	FB	++++																				
80-84	CB	++++																				
86-89	CU	+++	2017	Rk	GCL Twins	3	0	0	20	19	1.34	0.70	11.8	150	19	85	0.64	1.8	8.5	4.8	0.4	123
			2018	A	Cedar Rapids	3	5	1	94	71	3.26	1.37	19.7	262	32	76	3.64	3.4	6.8	2.0	0.4	50

Athletic RHP made full-season debut. Raw cross-fire delivery should become refined and repeatable with reps. Has natural deception due to high 3/4s arm slot. Features a 2-seam FB w/ sight arm-side run and natural sink. Power CB is best pitch; a 12-to-6 breaker with average depth and violent break. CU inconsistent, though flashes late fade.

Escobar,Luis

SP | Pittsburgh | EXP MLB DEBUT: 2020 | H/W: 6-1 155 | FUT: Middle reliever | 7B

Thrws R Age 22			Year	Lev	Team	W	L	Sv	IP	K	ERA	WHIP	BF/G	OBA	H%	S%	xERA	Ctl	Dom	Cmd	hr/9	BPV
2013 FA (CB)			2015	A-	West Virginia	0	0	0	6	5	5.90	1.80	14.1	289	36	64	4.75	5.9	7.4	1.3	0.0	-9
91-95	FB	+++	2016	A-	West Virginia	6	5	0	67	61	2.95	1.16	17.8	209	26	76	2.55	3.8	8.2	2.2	0.5	64
77-79	CB	++	2017	A	West Virginia	10	7	0	131	168	3.84	1.20	20.3	208	30	68	2.67	4.1	11.5	2.8	0.6	114
83-85	SL	+++	2018	A+	Bradenton	7	6	0	92	85	4.00	1.24	22.0	226	28	70	3.28	3.7	8.3	2.2	0.9	67
79-81	CU	+++	2018	AA	Altoona	4	0	0	35	25	4.60	1.45	21.5	232	26	70	4.04	5.4	6.4	1.2	1.0	-12

Big, powerful starter who tends to overthrow even though has plenty of stuff. Inconsistent delivery and line to plate costs him command and feel. FB, SL and CU can all be good pitches when stays within self, which is rare. CU is deceptive but not a real feel pitch, which limits ability to start. Move to pen may help him trust his stuff.

Espinoza,Anderson

SP | San Diego | EXP MLB DEBUT: 2020 | H/W: 6-0 160 | FUT: #2 starter | 9E

Thrws R Age 21			Year	Lev	Team	W	L	Sv	IP	K	ERA	WHIP	BF/G	OBA	H%	S%	xERA	Ctl	Dom	Cmd	hr/9	BPV
2014 FA (VZ)			2015	A	Greenville	0	1	0	3	4	11.61	1.94	14.7	314	46	33	5.42	5.8	11.6	2.0	0.0	70
94-97	FB	++++	2016	A	Greenville	5	8	0	76	72	4.38	1.37	18.7	264	35	66	3.51	3.2	8.5	2.7	0.2	85
74-77	CB	++++	2016	A	Fort Wayne	1	3	0	32	28	4.77	1.43	17.1	296	37	64	4.17	2.2	7.9	3.5	0.3	99
80-82	CU	++++	2017		Did not play - injury																	
			2018		Did not play - injury																	

Former heralded SP missed second straight year with injuries. When on, he'll touch 99 and sit mid-90s from a smaller, athletic frame with relative ease. Locates hammer 12-to-6 CB down in zone for GBs; fading CU is weapon vs. LHH. Potential for three plus offerings and #2 SP upside if things come together post Tommy John surgery, but that's a big "if."

Estrada,Jeremiah

SP | Chicago (N) | EXP MLB DEBUT: 2023 | H/W: 6-1 180 | FUT: #3 starter | 8D

Thrws R Age 20			Year	Lev	Team	W	L	Sv	IP	K	ERA	WHIP	BF/G	OBA	H%	S%	xERA	Ctl	Dom	Cmd	hr/9	BPV
2017 (6) HS (CA)																						
88-93	FB	++																				
74-76	CB	++																				
	CU	+++																				
			2017	Rk	AZL Cubs	0	0	0	6	6	1.48	1.80	7.1	225	31	91	3.86	8.9	8.9	1.0	0.0	-62

Projectable RHP saw limited action in pro debut before being shut down. Features a lively 88-93 mph FB that tops at 96. FB has good late life, but lacks feels and command. CB has good late bite, but is not located well. CU is best pitch at present and flashes as plus. With good health and improved command he could emerge as a back-end starter.

Eusebio,Breiling

SP | Colorado | EXP MLB DEBUT: 2021 | H/W: 6-1 175 | FUT: #4 starter | 7D

Thrws L Age 22			Year	Lev	Team	W	L	Sv	IP	K	ERA	WHIP	BF/G	OBA	H%	S%	xERA	Ctl	Dom	Cmd	hr/9	BPV
2014 FA (DR)																						
91-95	FB	+++	2016	A-	Boise	2	5	0	63	42	5.28	1.71	22.0	305	35	70	5.57	4.3	6.0	1.4	0.9	10
75-78	CB	++	2017	A-	Boise	3	0	0	17	22	1.59	0.82	20.6	173	28	79	0.75	2.1	11.6	5.5	0.0	170
81-83	CU	+++	2017	A	Asheville	3	3	0	40	31	4.49	1.50	21.6	280	33	70	4.48	3.6	7.0	1.9	0.7	46
			2018	A	Asheville	0	1	0	9	11	4.95	1.65	13.6	319	43	71	5.71	3.0	10.9	3.7	1.0	134

Slender lefty logged just 9.1 IP before hitting the DL with Tommy John surgery. Should be back in action by mid-2019. Prior, featured an above-average 91-95 heater with good late sink. Mixes in above-average CB and CU that shows plus potential. Repeating mechanics and throwing strikes are areas of need and won't be helped by the long layoff.

Eveld,Tommy

RP | Miami | EXP MLB DEBUT: 2019 | H/W: 6-5 194 | FUT: Closer | 8D

Thrws R Age 25			Year	Lev	Team	W	L	Sv	IP	K	ERA	WHIP	BF/G	OBA	H%	S%	xERA	Ctl	Dom	Cmd	hr/9	BPV
2016 (9) South Florida			2017	A	Kane County	1	0	14	27	33	0.33	0.66	4.3	115	19	94		2.6	10.9	4.1	0.0	143
93-96	FB	++++	2017	A+	Visalia	0	5	2	22	26	5.73	1.50	5.0	262	37	59	3.94	4.5	10.6	2.4	0.4	88
87-89	SL	++++	2018	A+	Visalia	2	2	12	36	42	1.25	1.00	4.3	222	32	89	2.01	1.7	10.5	6.0	0.2	159
88-90	CU	++	2018	AA	Jacksonville	2	1	4	14	19	0.64	0.79	3.9	151	25	91	0.42	2.6	12.2	4.8	0.0	168
78-81	CB	++	2018	AA	Jackson	1	0	1	4	5	0.00	0.49	4.5	80	13	100		2.2	11.0	5.0	0.0	156

Hard-throwing RP took unorthodox root to pro ball. Former college football player, brings football mentality to mound. Attacks hitters with 2 plus pitches, a 93-96 FB with late run and a hard, tight SL with two-plane break. Also shows a 11-to-5 CB and a straight CU. Closer mentality, will thrive in role.

Faedo,Alex — SP — Detroit

EXP MLB DEBUT: 2020 | H/W: 6-4 220 | FUT: #4 starter | 8D

Thrws R Age 23
2017 (1) Florida

Velo	Pitch	Grade
89-93	FB	+++
81-84	SL	+++
	CU	++

Year	Lev	Team	W	L	Sv	IP	K	ERA	WHIP	BF/G	OBA	H%	S%	xERA	Ctl	Dom	Cmd	hr/9	BPV
2017	NCAA	Florida	9	2	1	123	157	2.26	1.11	24.2	215	32	80	2.24	3.1	11.5	3.7	0.3	142
2018	A+	Lakeland	2	4	0	61	51	3.10	1.02	19.5	222	28	69	2.26	1.9	7.5	3.9	0.4	102
2018	AA	Erie	3	6	0	60	59	4.95	1.27	20.4	242	26	70	4.84	3.3	8.9	2.7	2.3	88

Dominant SEC hurler who sat out the 2017 season after signing out of Florida. Profile failed to live up to expectations, specifically his slider, which stood out in college but backed up in the pros. Fastball lost 3-4 mph and arsenal as a whole lost the expected bite. Only one year in, notable improvements are needed for 2019.

Feliz,Ignacio — SP — San Diego

EXP MLB DEBUT: 2023 | H/W: 6-1 180 | FUT: #4 starter | 8D

Thrws R Age 19
2017 FA (DR)

Velo	Pitch	Grade
88-92	FB	++
84-87	CT	++++
	CB	++++

Year	Lev	Team	W	L	Sv	IP	K	ERA	WHIP	BF/G	OBA	H%	S%	xERA	Ctl	Dom	Cmd	hr/9	BPV
2018	Rk	AZL Indians 2	4	2	0	34	36	2.12	0.97	18.4	193	28	76	1.38	2.6	9.5	3.6	0.0	118
2018	Rk	AZL Indians	5	3	0	45	54	3.00	1.07	17.5	211	32	69	1.82	2.8	10.8	3.9	0.0	137

A rare projection arm of this ilk where the excitement largely comes from his off-speed pitches as opposed to a big FB. FB has room to grow into average, and has natural cut on it that makes it workable. He also throws a true CT that could be an above average pitch as well as the ability to spin a CB with 12-to-6 movement.

Feltman,Durbin — RP — Boston

EXP MLB DEBUT: 2019 | H/W: 6-0 205 | FUT: Setup reliever | 7C

Thrws R Age 21
2018 (3) TCU

Velo	Pitch	Grade
93-97	FB	++++
83-87	SL	++++

Year	Lev	Team	W	L	Sv	IP	K	ERA	WHIP	BF/G	OBA	H%	S%	xERA	Ctl	Dom	Cmd	hr/9	BPV
2018	A-	Lowell	0	0	0	4	7	0.00	0.00	2.8	0	0			0.0	15.8		0.0	302
2018	A	Greenville	0	1	3	7	14	2.57	1.00	3.8	233	51	71	1.85	1.3	18.0	14.0	0.0	307
2018	A+	Salem	1	0	1	12	15	2.23	1.32	4.6	260	39	81	3.08	3.0	11.2	3.8	0.0	138

Just drafted in 2018 as a reliever who could come quickly, he had great success at three levels, although in limited innings. He is a stocky righty with a high effort delivery, who features a plus FB and SL.

Fernandez,Junior — RP — St. Louis

EXP MLB DEBUT: 2019 | H/W: 6-1 180 | FUT: Closer | 8E

Thrws R Age 22
2014 FA (DR)

Velo	Pitch	Grade
94-98	FB	+++++
85-88	SL	+
78-81	CU	++

Year	Lev	Team	W	L	Sv	IP	K	ERA	WHIP	BF/G	OBA	H%	S%	xERA	Ctl	Dom	Cmd	hr/9	BPV
2016	A	Peoria	6	5	0	78	63	3.34	1.34	23.2	244	30	75	3.28	3.9	7.3	1.9	0.3	43
2016	A+	Palm Beach	2	2	0	43	25	5.42	1.57	19.0	283	31	66	4.88	4.2	5.2	1.3	0.8	-1
2017	A+	Palm Beach	5	3	0	90	58	3.70	1.34	23.4	244	28	72	3.44	3.9	5.8	1.5	0.5	17
2018	A+	Palm Beach	1	0	3	9	7	0.00	1.20	4.6	258	32	100	2.77	2.0	6.8	3.5	0.0	88
2018	AA	Springfield	0	0	0	21	17	5.14	1.67	5.9	243	30	68	4.16	6.9	7.3	1.1	0.4	-36

Athletic hurler continues to be plagued by injuries. Was shut down in 2017 with a strained biceps and was on the DL again in 2018. At best, can dominate with a plus mid-90s FB that tops at 99 with late movement. SL has sharp late break, but needs refinement. CU flashes as plus and gives him a chance to dominate if he can fix control issues.

Ferrell,Riley — RP — Miami

EXP MLB DEBUT: 2019 | H/W: 6-2 200 | FUT: Middle reliever | 7B

Thrws R Age 25
2015 (3) Texas Christian

Velo	Pitch	Grade
94-97	FB	++++
84-87	SL	++++

Year	Lev	Team	W	L	Sv	IP	K	ERA	WHIP	BF/G	OBA	H%	S%	xERA	Ctl	Dom	Cmd	hr/9	BPV
2016	A+	Lancaster	0	1	4	10	14	1.80	1.10	4.9	242	36	90	3.11	1.8	12.6	7.0	0.9	196
2017	A+	Buies Creek	0	0	2	2	5	0.00	0.00	2.8	0	0			0.0	22.5		0.0	423
2017	AA	Corpus Christi	2	2	4	52	55	3.81	1.25	5.9	258	35	68	3.21	2.4	9.5	3.9	0.3	124
2018	AA	Corpus Christi	2	2	7	23	33	1.94	1.38	4.6	176	29	87	2.54	7.0	12.8	1.8	0.4	60
2018	AAA	Fresno	2	1	2	28	34	6.75	1.79	5.9	301	40	63	6.05	5.1	10.9	2.1	1.3	76

The well-built reliever continues to pump in plus, high-spin fastballs in the upper-90s and devastating sliders. He also continues to miss the zone with regularity. Was taken in Rule 5 Draft by the Marlins.

Festa,Matthew — RP — Seattle

EXP MLB DEBUT: 2018 | H/W: 6-1 190 | FUT: Setup reliever | 7C

Thrws R Age 26
2016 (7) East Stroudsburg

Velo	Pitch	Grade
91-94	FB	+++
86-88	SL	+++
78-82	CB	++

Year	Lev	Team	W	L	Sv	IP	K	ERA	WHIP	BF/G	OBA	H%	S%	xERA	Ctl	Dom	Cmd	hr/9	BPV
2016	NCAA	East Stroudsburg	11	2	0	88	105	2.35	1.06	26.2	225	33	78	2.25	2.1	10.7	5.0	0.3	153
2016	A-	Everett	6	2	0	60	58	3.74	1.23	17.4	261	34	69	3.32	2.1	8.7	4.1	0.4	118
2017	A+	Modesto	4	2	6	69	99	3.25	1.16	6.6	238	36	75	3.21	2.5	12.9	5.2	0.9	183
2018	AA	Arkansas	5	2	20	49	67	2.76	1.27	4.5	266	38	84	4.04	2.2	12.3	5.6	1.1	180
2018	MLB	Seattle	0	0	0	8	4	2.22	1.85	4.7	363	41	87	6.11	2.2	4.4	2.0	0.0	38

Solid RHP made it to MLB in 2018 after being a 2016 senior sign. Easy, straight-on, 3/4s delivery with big leg kick. 3-pitch pitcher. Has control of 2-seam FB with solid arm-side run. Struggles commanding to arm-side. SL has two-plane break but needs to tighten up to be effective in big leagues. Shows CU; solid arm-side run without fade.

Fisher,Braydon — SP — Los Angeles (N)

EXP MLB DEBUT: 2022 | H/W: 6-4 180 | FUT: #4 starter | 7D

Thrws R Age 18
2018 (4) HS (TX)

Velo	Pitch	Grade
92-95	FB	++++
80-83	SL	+++
	CU	+

Year	Lev	Team	W	L	Sv	IP	K	ERA	WHIP	BF/G	OBA	H%	S%	xERA	Ctl	Dom	Cmd	hr/9	BPV
2018	Rk	AZL Dodgers	1	2	0	22	19	2.05	1.36	8.4	253	31	89	3.89	3.7	7.8	2.1	0.8	59

Projectable hurler saw spike in velocity. FB now sits at 92-95 with room for more. Slow worker is not overly athletic and jerks his head towards 1B on release. Front-side mechanics need to be refined, but has the arm-strength to make an impact. Low-80s SL is above-average, but CU lacks consistency. Nice upside, but lots of work to do.

Flexen,Chris — SP — New York (N)

EXP MLB DEBUT: 2017 | H/W: 6-3 215 | FUT: Middle reliever | 7D

Thrws R Age 24
2012 (14) HS (CA)

Velo	Pitch	Grade
91-94	FB	+++
77-83	CB	+++
81-84	CU	++
87-89	CT	+++

Year	Lev	Team	W	L	Sv	IP	K	ERA	WHIP	BF/G	OBA	H%	S%	xERA	Ctl	Dom	Cmd	hr/9	BPV
2017	A+	St. Lucie	0	0	0	12	13	2.21	1.23	16.5	259	34	86	3.54	2.2	9.6	4.3	0.7	131
2017	AA	Binghamton	6	1	0	48	50	1.68	0.73	24.4	171	22	84	1.21	1.3	9.3	7.1	0.7	151
2017	MLB	NY Mets	3	6	0	48	36	7.88	2.02	16.6	314	34	64	7.62	6.6	6.8	1.0	2.1	-38
2018	AAA	Las Vegas	6	7	0	92	78	4.40	1.52	22.2	296	35	74	5.15	3.0	7.6	2.5	1.1	73
2018	MLB	NY Mets	0	2	0	6	3	13.28	3.28	9.3	449	46	61	14.32	8.9	4.4	0.5	3.0	-141

Hefty starter with some idea of how to pitch and mix but whose stuff plays pretty fringy as a starter, but would probably play up out of bullpen. Similar to Joe Biagini. Throws both CB and SL but neither are consistent. Maybe would be better off choosing one. Cutter has some potential.

Florentino,Juan — SP — Boston

EXP MLB DEBUT: 2021 | H/W: 5-10 182 | FUT: Middle reliever | 6D

Thrws R Age 22
2015 FA (DR)

Velo	Pitch	Grade
89-93	FB	+++
80-84	CB	+++
82-85	CU	+++

Year	Lev	Team	W	L	Sv	IP	K	ERA	WHIP	BF/G	OBA	H%	S%	xERA	Ctl	Dom	Cmd	hr/9	BPV
2017	A-	Lowell	1	2	5	18	25	0.99	0.88	5.6	214	33	93	1.83	1.0	12.4	12.5	0.5	214
2017	A	Greenville	0	0	3	17	18	2.12	1.29	7.0	273	38	82	3.21	2.1	9.5	4.5	0.0	132
2018	A	Greenville	5	5	2	54	52	5.66	1.39	6.9	282	33	63	5.15	2.5	8.7	3.5	1.7	106

A total sleeper, he is a stocky righty with good feel for a solid 3-pitch mix. Poor man's Fernando Rodney. Plus feel for his breaking ball. CU is deceptive and has diving action, so capable of being a swing-and-miss pitch. Lacks good plane to the plate and was hurt by a poor fielding team in Low A. Could surprise.

Flores,Bernardo — SP — Chicago (A)

EXP MLB DEBUT: 2020 | H/W: 6-4 170 | FUT: #5 SP/swingman | 6C

Thrws L Age 23
2016 (7) USC

Velo	Pitch	Grade
89-93	FB	+++
82-83	SL	++
75-76	CB	+++
82-84	CU	+++

Year	Lev	Team	W	L	Sv	IP	K	ERA	WHIP	BF/G	OBA	H%	S%	xERA	Ctl	Dom	Cmd	hr/9	BPV
2016	Rk	AZL White Sox	0	1	0	6	7	1.50	0.67	7.0	191	29	75	0.58	0.0	10.5		0.0	207
2017	A	Kannapolis	8	4	0	78	70	3.00	1.10	21.9	249	31	74	2.95	1.5	8.1	5.4	0.6	123
2017	A+	Winston-Salem	2	3	0	40	33	4.26	1.55	19.5	275	32	75	4.95	4.3	7.4	1.7	1.1	36
2018	A+	Winston-Salem	5	4	0	77	58	2.56	1.19	25.8	256	30	80	3.29	2.0	6.8	3.4	0.6	86
2018	AA	Birmingham	3	5	0	78	47	2.77	1.19	24.1	264	30	78	3.40	1.6	5.4	3.4	0.6	72

Command/control LHP pitched well. Repeatable, 3/4s, cross-fire delivery with average extension. Spots 2-seam FB well to arm-side. Solid movement, below average velocity. No deception. Best secondary is late-fading CU. Above-average pitch with swing-and-miss. 11-to-5 CB has depth and solid break. Eye-level changer. SL is below-average pitch.

Florez,Santiago — SP — Pittsburgh

EXP MLB DEBUT: 2023 | H/W: 6-5 222 | FUT: #3 starter | 8E

Thrws R Age 18
2016 FA (CB)

Velo	Pitch	Grade
92-94	FB	+++
74-76	CB	++
81-83	CU	++

Year	Lev	Team	W	L	Sv	IP	K	ERA	WHIP	BF/G	OBA	H%	S%	xERA	Ctl	Dom	Cmd	hr/9	BPV
2018	Rk	GCL Pirates	5	2	0	43	35	4.18	1.39	18.2	233	30	67	2.94	4.8	7.3	1.5	0.0	20

A lower-level arm to watch due to imposing size, youth and a FB that improved up to 96 mph by the end of the GCL season. Battled start-to-start consistency and both secondary pitches are below average. Gets good extension, but needs to work on control and get more reps. Time is on his side.

Foley,Jason — RP — Detroit

EXP MLB DEBUT: 2021 | H/W: 6-4 200 | FUT: Closer | 8D

Thrws R Age 23
2016 Sacred Heart

Velo	Pitch	Grade
94-98	FB	++++
83-87	SL	+
	CU	++

Year	Lev	Team	W	L	Sv	IP	K	ERA	WHIP	BF/G	OBA	H%	S%	xERA	Ctl	Dom	Cmd	hr/9	BPV
2016	Rk	GCL Tigers	0	0	1	1	1	0.00	1.00	3.8	262	35	100	2.32	0.0	9.0		0.0	180
2016	A-	Connecticut	0	0	0	6	6	4.43	2.13	6.0	259	35	77	5.12	10.3	8.9	0.9	0.0	-102
2017	A	West Michigan	3	1	5	29	36	1.55	0.86	5.9	197	30	80	1.12	1.6	11.2	7.2	0.0	177
2017	A+	Lakeland	0	2	1	7	5	6.34	1.41	5.0	285	32	56	4.90	2.5	6.3	2.5	1.3	64
2018		Did not pitch - injury																	

Flame-throwing closer who came out of nowhere with late-blooming triple-digit velocity. Dominated the Midwest League with a jump to High-A in 2017 before falling victim to Tommy John surgery. Fastball is an overpowering piece with late tailing action. Slider and changeup showed flashes of consistency, with the slider as the more reliable.

Franklin,Austin — SP — Tampa Bay

EXP MLB DEBUT: 2021 | H/W: 6-3 215 | FUT: Middle reliever | 6C

Thrws R Age 21
2016 (3) HS (FL)

Velo	Pitch	Grade
91-93	FB	+++
75-78	CB	+++
	CU	++

Year	Lev	Team	W	L	Sv	IP	K	ERA	WHIP	BF/G	OBA	H%	S%	xERA	Ctl	Dom	Cmd	hr/9	BPV
2016	Rk	GCL Rays	1	2	1	43	40	2.71	1.07	15.2	198	27	72	1.68	3.3	8.4	2.5	0.0	78
2017	A-	Hudson Valley	4	2	0	69	71	2.21	1.19	21.3	207	28	83	2.58	4.0	9.2	2.3	0.5	75
2018	A	Bowling Green	6	5	0	82	65	3.62	1.32	21.2	250	30	74	3.59	3.4	7.1	2.1	0.7	55

Physically mature with command concerns turned in solid 2018 season in Single-A. High 3/4s, online delivery with solid extension. 2-seam FB has some natural sink with RP plane. 12-to-6 CB could miss bats if he can get on top of pitch consistently enough. Rarely throws CU. Profile will push to RP role.

Funkhouser,Kyle — SP — Detroit

EXP MLB DEBUT: 2019 | H/W: 6-2 218 | FUT: #4 starter | 8D

Thrws R Age 25
2015 (1) Louisville

Velo	Pitch	Grade
91-96	FB	+++
82-85	SL	+++
78-82	CB	++
82-84	CU	++

Year	Lev	Team	W	L	Sv	IP	K	ERA	WHIP	BF/G	OBA	H%	S%	xERA	Ctl	Dom	Cmd	hr/9	BPV
2016	A-	Connecticut	0	2	0	37		2.67	1.13	11.3	245	32	74	2.43	1.9	8.2	4.3	0.0	114
2017	A	West Michigan	4	1	0	31	49	3.18	1.38	18.7	255	41	80	3.95	3.8	14.2	3.8	0.9	172
2017	A+	Lakeland	1	1	0	31	34	1.74	0.93	23.3	208	29	82	1.72	1.7	9.8	5.7	0.3	148
2018	AA	Erie	4	5	0	89	89	3.74	1.43	22.2	260	33	77	4.31	3.9	9.0	2.3	1.0	74
2018	AAA	Toledo	0	2	0	8	7	6.59	2.20	20.6	257	33	67	5.28	11.0	7.7	0.7	0.0	-140

Imposing, solidly-built starter overcame an elbow strain from 2017 to power his way to Triple-A in 2018. Plus fastball boasts late life low in the zone, and he mixes in an above-average hard slider and a curve with good shape. Change-up lacks confidence, but should end up as above-average offering. Will have to overcome late-season ankle injury.

Gaddis,Will — SP — Colorado

EXP MLB DEBUT: 2021 | H/W: 6-2 200 | FUT: #5 SP/swingman | 6C

Thrws R Age 23
2017 (3) Furman

Velo	Pitch	Grade
88-93	FB	+++
85-87	CT	++
71-73	CB	++
76-78	CU	++

Year	Lev	Team	W	L	Sv	IP	K	ERA	WHIP	BF/G	OBA	H%	S%	xERA	Ctl	Dom	Cmd	hr/9	BPV
2017	NCAA	Furman	9	3	1	105	89	1.89	0.92	23.1	215	27	82	1.93	1.4	7.6	5.6	0.4	118
2017	Rk	Grand Junction	3	1	0	44	26	5.71	1.66	17.9	347	38	67	6.47	1.4	5.3	3.7	1.2	75
2018	A	Asheville	6	6	0	121	82	5.05	1.41	22.3	289	33	65	4.68	2.4	6.1	2.6	1.0	63

Stocky RHP has a solid four-pitch mix and pounds the strike zone, but lacks plus velocity or a true swing-and-miss offering. FB sits at 88-92 with a bit of late arm-side run. Shows good feel for his CU, which is his best offering and mixes in a CB and CT. Back-end strike thrower lacks upside and move to relief seems likely.

Gallardo,Richard — SP — Chicago (N)

EXP MLB DEBUT: 2023 | H/W: 6-1 187 | FUT: #3 starter | 8D

Thrws R Age 16
2018 FA (CU)

Velo	Pitch	Grade
89-93	FB	+++
70-75	CB	+++
	CU	++

Year	Lev	Team	W	L	Sv	IP	K	ERA	WHIP	BF/G	OBA	H%	S%	xERA	Ctl	Dom	Cmd	hr/9	BPV
2018		Did not pitch in U.S.																	

Projectable hurler signed for $1 million in July. Already featured an above-average to plus FB that sits at 90-93, topping at 97 mph. Backs up the heater with a potentially plus late breaking 70-75 mph CB and a usable CU. FB has good late sink and arm-side run when down in the zone and the CB is swing-and-miss. Very raw, but upside is exciting.

Gallen,Zac — SP — Miami

EXP MLB DEBUT: 2019 | H/W: 6-0 170 | FUT: #5 SP/swingman | 6B

Thrws R Age 23
2016 (3) North Carolina

Velo	Pitch	Grade
90-92	FB	+++
87-88	CT	+++
74-77	CB	++
82-84	CU	+++

Year	Lev	Team	W	L	Sv	IP	K	ERA	WHIP	BF/G	OBA	H%	S%	xERA	Ctl	Dom	Cmd	hr/9	BPV
2016	Rk	GCL Cardinals	0	0	1	9	15	1.96	0.76	5.5	212	39	71	1.02	0.0	14.7		0.0	282
2017	A+	Palm Beach	5	2	0	55	56	1.63	0.98	23.3	220	30	83	1.87	1.6	9.1	5.6	0.2	138
2017	AA	Springfield	4	5	0	71	42	3.80	1.34	22.7	275	30	75	4.33	2.4	5.3	2.2	1.0	49
2017	AAA	Memphis	1	1	0	20	23	3.56	1.19	20.2	240	32	73	3.33	2.7	10.2	3.8	0.9	130
2018	AAA	New Orleans	8	9	0	133	136	3.65	1.47	22.9	283	36	78	4.69	3.2	9.2	2.8	0.9	96

Solid, RHP with average pitch profile struggled with base runners in Triple-A debut. Cross-armed, 3/4s delivery with unorthodox timing pause in windup. Fourpitches, but no one pitch outshines the rest. 2-seam FB has solid run with late sink profile. CT changes eye levels and misses barrels. 11-to-5 CB has slurvy movement. CU is an average pitch.

Garcia,Bryan — RP — Detroit

EXP MLB DEBUT: 2020 | H/W: 6-1 195 | FUT: Middle reliever | 8D

Thrws R Age 23
2016 (6) Miami

Velo	Pitch	Grade
94-96	FB	+++
84-88	SL	+++
	CU	++

Year	Lev	Team	W	L	Sv	IP	K	ERA	WHIP	BF/G	OBA	H%	S%	xERA	Ctl	Dom	Cmd	hr/9	BPV
2017	A	West Michigan	1	2	9	14	27	3.19	1.13	4.0	232	48	69	2.18	2.6	17.2	6.8	0.0	259
2017	A+	Lakeland	2	0	0	8	15	0.00	1.10	4.6	232	46	100	2.10	2.2	16.5	7.5	0.0	255
2017	AA	Erie	1	1	8	18	24	0.99	0.82	3.9	120	18	93	0.67	4.0	11.9	3.0	0.5	125
2017	AAA	Toledo	1	0	0	13	12	4.12	1.37	3.9	213	27	71	3.28	5.5	8.2	1.5	0.7	18
2018		Did not pitch - injury																	

A fast-tracking reliever prior to undergoing Tommy John surgery in 2018. Aggressively attacks and challenges hitters on both sides of the plate. Strong ability to throw strikes with a mix of power slider and a late-sinking fastball. Successful rehab will give good preview of future timeline.

Garcia,Delvi — SP — New York (A)

EXP MLB DEBUT: 2020 | H/W: 5-9 140 | FUT: Closer | 8C

Thrws R Age 19
2016 FA (DR)

Velo	Pitch	Grade
90-93	FB	+++
79-83	CB	+++++
84-85	CU	+++

Year	Lev	Team	W	L	Sv	IP	K	ERA	WHIP	BF/G	OBA	H%	S%	xERA	Ctl	Dom	Cmd	hr/9	BPV
2017	Rk	Pulaski	2	1	0	28	43	4.50	1.29	19.2	226	36	67	3.42	4.2	13.8	3.3	1.0	154
2017	Rk	GCL Yankees	3	0	0	16	24	3.33	0.80	14.7	165	22	70	2.16	2.2	13.3	6.0	1.7	198
2018	A	Charleston (Sc)	2	4	0	40	63	3.81	1.02	19.3	215	34	67	2.76	2.2	14.1	6.3	1.1	211
2018	A+	Tampa	2	0	0	28	35	1.28	0.96	21.2	193	30	85	1.33	2.6	11.2	4.4	0.0	151
2018	AA	Trenton	1	0	0	5	7	0.00	0.40	16.1	0	0	100		3.6	12.6	3.5	0.0	148

Small-statured, athletic RHP has developed into a quality SP prospect despite delivery concerns. Max-effort, cross-fire delivery with plus arm speed. 3-pitch pitcher dominated across 3 levels. Low-90s FB has slight run but is deceptive out of hand. 12-to-6 CB has great shape and terrific break. Plus-plus offering. Developing CU has average potential.

Garcia,Rico — SP — Colorado

EXP MLB DEBUT: 2020 | H/W: 5-11 190 | FUT: #5 SP/swingman | 7C

Thrws R Age 25
2016 (30) Hawaii Pacific

Velo	Pitch	Grade
92-95	FB	+++
72-78	CB	+++
81-84	CU	++

Year	Lev	Team	W	L	Sv	IP	K	ERA	WHIP	BF/G	OBA	H%	S%	xERA	Ctl	Dom	Cmd	hr/9	BPV
2016	A-	Boise	0	4	0	35	35	6.41	1.91	10.4	336	43	64	5.97	4.4	9.0	2.1	0.3	62
2017	A-	Boise	0	4	0	41	35	3.95	1.49	22.1	302	37	73	4.55	2.4	7.7	3.2	0.4	91
2017	A	Asheville	2	2	0	28	30	2.57	1.21	14.1	255	34	81	3.36	2.3	9.6	4.3	0.6	131
2018	A+	Lancaster	7	7	0	100	101	3.42	1.21	25.2	260	32	76	3.83	2.0	9.1	4.6	1.1	128
2018	AA	Hartford	6	2	0	67	61	2.28	1.10	23.9	222	26	86	3.08	2.7	8.2	3.1	1.1	93

Uptick in FB velocity fueled a breakout in 2018. Heater now sits at 92-95 mph with good late life. Improved CB gives him a second above-average offering and CU flash plus, but will need to improve in order to neutralize LHB. Small frame could limit effectiveness, but high 3/4 arm slot results in good late action and plenty off swings-and-misses.

Garcia,Rony — SP — New York (A)

EXP MLB DEBUT: 2021 | H/W: 6-3 200 | FUT: #5 SP/swingman | 6C

Thrws R Age 21
2016 FA (DR)

Velo	Pitch	Grade
91-93	FB	+++
80-85	SL	+++
87-88	CU	+++

Year	Lev	Team	W	L	Sv	IP	K	ERA	WHIP	BF/G	OBA	H%	S%	xERA	Ctl	Dom	Cmd	hr/9	BPV
2017	Rk	Pulaski	0	0	0	11	11	4.05	1.17	22.2	260	33	67	3.49	1.6	8.9	5.5	0.8	135
2017	A	Charleston (Sc)	2	3	0	64	45	2.25	1.05	22.5	223	27	80	2.35	2.1	6.3	3.0	0.4	75
2018	A	Charleston (Sc)	3	4	0	71	62	4.18	1.21	20.4	267	33	65	3.53	1.6	7.9	4.8	0.6	115
2018	A+	Tampa	1	5	0	48	45	4.50	1.29	21.9	258	33	63	3.35	2.8	8.4	3.0	0.4	94

Big-bodied, strong RHP stuff picked up in solid 2018 season. Repeatable, cookie-cutter 3/4s delivery. 4-seam FB is workhorse pitch. Commands well with solid late run up. SL lacks consistent shape but best when tightened up for sharp action. CU has shot of becoming above-average offering with solid fade and delivery deception.

Garrett,Braxton — SP — Miami

EXP MLB DEBUT: 2021 | H/W: 6-3 190 | FUT: #3 starter | 8E

Thrws L Age 21
2016 (1) HS (AL)

Velo	Pitch	Grade
90-92	FB	+++
75-79	CB	++++
83-84	CU	+++

Year	Lev	Team	W	L	Sv	IP	K	ERA	WHIP	BF/G	OBA	H%	S%	xERA	Ctl	Dom	Cmd	hr/9	BPV
2016		Did not pitch																	
2017	A	Greensboro	1	0	0	15	16	2.98	1.26	15.4	234	27	88	4.27	3.6	9.5	2.7	1.8	93

Pitchability LHP has been relegated to 15.1 IP due to arm injuries, including 2017 Tommy John surgery. Utilizes repeatable, 3/4s delivery with some deception. Three pitches; has advanced control of FB with late run. Best pitch is 11-5 CB from FB arm s lot. Late breaking, hard to pick up spin. Has feel for above-average CU, which plays up due to athleticism.

Garza, Justin — SP — Cleveland

Thrws R | Age 25 | 2015 (8) Cal St Fullerton
EXP MLB DEBUT: 2021 | H/W: 5-10 160 | FUT: #5 SP/swingman | 6C

- 91-95 FB +++
- 83-87 SL ++
- 84-85 CU ++

Year	Lev	Team	W	L	Sv	IP	K	ERA	WHIP	BF/G	OBA	H%	S%	xERA	Ctl	Dom	Cmd	hr/9	BPV
2016	Rk	AZL Indians	0	2	0	9	9	7.00	2.11	7.4	321	42	63	6.00	7.0	9.0	1.3	0.0	-9
2017	A	Lake County	4	6	3	95	86	5.86	1.50	15.8	265	32	62	4.71	4.3	8.1	1.9	1.1	47
2018	A-	Mahoning Vall	0	0	0	7	7	0.00	0.29	10.9	92	14	100		0.0	9.0	0.0		180
2018	A+	Lynchburg	5	6	0	68	69	3.71	1.15	16.9	226	29	68	2.84	2.9	9.1	3.1	0.7	104

Pitches primarily with a slightly above average fastball with life. Can pitch up in the zone effectively with the FB and use it to generate swings and misses. SL is inconsistent, and ranges from a far below average pitch to an average pitch. He shows a slightly below average CU, but rarely uses it. Flyball pitcher with an ability to miss bats.

Gatto, Joe — SP — Los Angeles (A)

Thrws R | Age 23 | 2014 (2) HS (NJ)
EXP MLB DEBUT: 2020 | H/W: 6-3 204 | FUT: #4 starter | 7C

- 91-94 FB +++
- 78-81 CB +++
- 81-84 CU ++

Year	Lev	Team	W	L	Sv	IP	K	ERA	WHIP	BF/G	OBA	H%	S%	xERA	Ctl	Dom	Cmd	hr/9	BPV
2016	A	Burlington	3	8	0	64	54	7.03	1.89	20.1	328	40	61	6.23	4.6	7.6	1.6	0.7	29
2017	A	Burlington	5	7	0	96	78	3.47	1.40	19.3	249	31	74	3.36	4.2	7.3	1.7	0.2	36
2017	A+	Inland Empire	2	1	1	32	23	3.36	1.40	22.6	255	31	75	3.53	3.9	6.4	1.6	0.3	28
2018	A+	Inland Empire	5	2	0	43	51	4.18	1.42	20.3	261	37	69	3.73	3.6	10.6	2.8	0.4	108
2018	AA	Mobile	3	4	0	76	49	5.79	1.59	21.0	283	32	64	5.02	4.3	5.8	1.4	0.9	7

Homegrown right-handed starter with consistently improving profile. Two-seam fastball delivered with good downhill plane. Curveball already above-average and able to miss bats regularly. Change-up has lagged and development depends on how hard he'll work to gain more confidence in delivering it. Lacking solid third pitch option.

Geoff, Hartlieb — RP — Pittsburgh

Thrws R | Age 25 | 2016 (29) Lindenwood
EXP MLB DEBUT: 2020 | H/W: 6-6 210 | FUT: Middle reliever | 7C

- 92-98 FB ++++
- 84-88 SL +++
- 84-85 CU ++

Year	Lev	Team	W	L	Sv	IP	K	ERA	WHIP	BF/G	OBA	H%	S%	xERA	Ctl	Dom	Cmd	hr/9	BPV
2016	NCAA	Lindenwood U	2	7	0	65		7.62	1.72	22.7	299	36	52	4.95	4.7	6.8	1.4	0.3	13
2016	Rk	Bristol	1	1	1	26	28	4.48	1.34	6.8	261	34	69	4.13	3.1	9.7	3.1	1.0	108
2017	A	West Virginia	1	2	6	32	26	0.84	0.87	5.9	195	24	93	1.43	1.7	7.3	4.3	0.3	104
2017	A+	Bradenton	1	4	3	31	36	3.48	1.23	6.6	249	34	74	3.52	2.6	10.5	4.0	0.9	136
2018	AA	Altoona	8	2	10	58	56	3.25	1.38	5.2	255	33	77	3.61	3.7	8.7	2.3	0.5	74

Power sinker/SL reliever. Similar to Jared Hughes, but with better stuff. Like Hughes, has had to come a long way in terms of repeating his delivery and commanding his pitches, partly because he is not a great athlete. That said, how power sinker can be nasty. Gets a ton of ground balls. The SL can be good against RHH. Lacks good weapons for LHH.

Gerber, Joey — RP — Seattle

Thrws R | Age 21 | 2018 (8) Illinois
EXP MLB DEBUT: 2020 | H/W: 6-4 215 | FUT: Setup reliever | 7D

- 93-96 FB ++++
- 82-85 SL ++++

Year	Lev	Team	W	L	Sv	IP	K	ERA	WHIP	BF/G	OBA	H%	S%	xERA	Ctl	Dom	Cmd	hr/9	BPV
2018	NCAA	Illinois	1	1	14	28	45	3.19	1.13	4.5	185	33	71	1.94	4.5	14.4	3.2	0.3	156
2018	A-	Everett	1	0	6	14	21	1.93	1.07	4.2	186	33	80	1.50	3.9	13.5	3.5	0.0	157
2018	A	Clinton	0	0	2	11	22	2.41	1.25	5.1	222	48	79	2.34	4.0	17.7	4.4	0.0	228

High-floor RP-only prospect made professional debut in 2018. 3/4s max-effort delivery. 2-pitch pitcher, both presently plus offerings. FB has solid late-run, missing bats throughout the zone. Sharp, tight 2-plane SL is well commanded in and out of zone. Mixes pitches well for age/level.

German, Frank — SP — New York (A)

Thrws R | Age 21 | 2018 (4) North Florida
EXP MLB DEBUT: 2021 | H/W: 6-2 180 | FUT: #5 SP/swingman | 6C

- 92-95 FB ++++
- 81-83 SU ++
- CU +++

Year	Lev	Team	W	L	Sv	IP	K	ERA	WHIP	BF/G	OBA	H%	S%	xERA	Ctl	Dom	Cmd	hr/9	BPV
2018	NCAA	North Florida	8	3	0	91	108	1.58	0.83	23.8	194	28	83	1.40	1.4	10.7	7.7	0.4	173
2018	Rk	GCL Yankees W	0	0	0	2	3	0.00	0.00	5.6	0	0			0.0	13.5		0.0	261
2018	A-	Staten Island	1	3	1	28	38	2.24	1.00	10.7	217	35	75	1.70	1.9	12.2	6.3	0.0	185

Pitchability RHP catapulted self into 5th rd of 2018 draft made pro debut. Lean pitcher, sold out for velocity in limited pro action. 3/4s cross-fire delivery with effort and a long arm progression. FB ticked up as a pro, sitting in the mid-to-high 90s during shorter appearances. Throws slurve, which will need to tighten up. CU has solid late fade.

Gil, Luis — SP — New York (A)

Thrws R | Age 20 | 2015 FA (DR)
EXP MLB DEBUT: 2022 | H/W: 6-1 160 | FUT: #3 starter | 8E

- 91-95 FB ++++
- 79-82 CB +++
- CU +

Year	Lev	Team	W	L	Sv	IP	K	ERA	WHIP	BF/G	OBA	H%	S%	xERA	Ctl	Dom	Cmd	hr/9	BPV
2018	Rk	Pulaski	2	1	0	39	58	1.38	1.18	15.6	160	28	89	1.70	5.8	13.4	2.3	0.2	103
2018	A-	Staten Island	0	2	0	6	10	5.81	2.74	17.2	386	57	81	10.07	8.7	14.5	1.7	1.5	44

Lean, hard-throwing RHP acquired in early-season trade with MIN. Easy 3/4s delivery with plus extension despite rawness of delivery. 3-pitch pitcher. 4-seam FB has solid, late run, plus-plus at maturity. Throws a slurvy CB, which will need to be refined moving forward. Has struggled with feel for CU but athleticism gives hope for development.

Gilbert, Logan — SP — Seattle

Thrws R | Age 21 | 2018 (1) Stetson
EXP MLB DEBUT: 2020 | H/W: 6-6 225 | FUT: #3 starter | 8C

- 90-95 FB ++++
- 77-82 SL ++++
- 71-75 CB ++
- 81 CU +++

Year	Lev	Team
2018		Did not play - illness

Athletic, well-rounded RHP missed his pro debut with mononucleosis. Repeatable 3/4s delivery with high leg kick and plus arm speed. Lean build, should put on nice muscle. 5-pitch pitcher. 2-seam FB with solid arm-side run and sink created by plane. Mixes CT. SL is best pitch with plus-plus sharp, 2-plane break. CB & CU round out arsenal.

Gingery, Steven — SP — St. Louis

Thrws L | Age 21 | 2018 (4) Texas Tech
EXP MLB DEBUT: 2021 | H/W: 6-1 210 | FUT: #4 starter | 7D

- 88-92 FB ++
- 72-75 CU ++++
- 78-81 CB ++

Year	Lev	Team
2018		Did not pitch - injury

Had TJS prior to the draft and will be sidelined until 2020. Prior to the injury showed a plus CU with good fade and sink. Fringe FB sits at 88-92 but also has good late sink with above-average command. FB/CU combo from LH side is good enough that he should move quickly once he returns to action.

Goddard, Jackson — SP — Arizona

Thrws R | Age 22 | 2018 (3) Kansas
EXP MLB DEBUT: 2020 | H/W: 6-3 220 | FUT: #4 starter | 8D

- 92-94 FB +++
- 81-83 SL +++
- 82-84 CU +++

Year	Lev	Team	W	L	Sv	IP	K	ERA	WHIP	BF/G	OBA	H%	S%	xERA	Ctl	Dom	Cmd	hr/9	BPV
2018	NCAA	Kansas	5	1	0	52	60	4.14	1.46	22.3	246	35	69	3.40	4.8	10.3	2.1	0.2	74
2018	Rk	AZL DBacks	0	0	0	1	0	0.00	0.00	2.8	0	0			0.0	0.0		0.0	18
2018	A-	Hillsboro	1	3	0	28	27	4.18	1.11	8.5	194	26	60	2.04	3.9	8.7	2.3	0.3	70

Tall, physical RH who has a chance to have three average-or-better pitches. FB sits in the low 90s but can reach 96 mph with late life up in the zone. SL works as primary secondary pitch and will be weapon vs. RHH; CU requires more refinement. Command is spotty and will need to work on pounding strike zone to realize potential.

Gohara, Luiz — SP — Atlanta

Thrws L | Age 22 | 2013 FA (BR)
EXP MLB DEBUT: 2017 | H/W: 6-3 210 | FUT: #3 starter | 8D

- 91-95 FB ++++
- 80-84 SL ++++
- 88-91 CU ++

Year	Lev	Team	W	L	Sv	IP	K	ERA	WHIP	BF/G	OBA	H%	S%	xERA	Ctl	Dom	Cmd	hr/9	BPV
2017	AAA	Gwinnett	2	2	0	35	48	3.33	1.34	20.9	238	35	79	3.79	4.1	12.3	3.0	1.0	129
2017	MLB	Atlanta	1	3	0	29	31	4.95	1.37	24.4	281	37	63	4.10	2.5	9.6	3.9	0.6	124
2018	AA	Mississippi	0	1	0	3	4	2.90	2.58	16.7	364	51	88	7.90	8.7	11.6	1.3	0.0	-8
2018	AAA	Gwinnett	3	4	0	54	55	4.98	1.27	18.5	261	32	65	4.40	2.5	9.1	3.7	1.5	115
2018	MLB	Atlanta	0	1	1	19	18	6.09	1.25	8.7	228	26	52	3.83	3.8	8.4	2.3	1.4	69

Husky, hard-throwing LHP struggled through injury-marred season. Reportedly leaned up in off-season but body may always be a struggle to maintain. Lost 2 mph and effectiveness of movement on FB in 2018. Best pitch still remained SL. Adjusts grips to through both sharp and sweeping varieties. Telegraphed and loss feel for CU.

Gonsalves, Stephen — SP — Minnesota

Thrws L | Age 24 | 2013 (4) HS (CA)
EXP MLB DEBUT: 2018 | H/W: 6-5 190 | FUT: #5 SP/swingman | 6A

- 87-91 FB ++
- 82-85 SL ++
- 70-74 CB +++
- 79-82 CU +++

Year	Lev	Team	W	L	Sv	IP	K	ERA	WHIP	BF/G	OBA	H%	S%	xERA	Ctl	Dom	Cmd	hr/9	BPV
2017	AA	Chattanooga	8	3	0	87	96	2.69	1.03	22.4	214	29	77	2.46	2.4	9.9	4.2	0.7	132
2017	AAA	Rochester	1	2	0	22	22	5.68	1.58	19.5	301	36	68	5.87	3.2	8.9	2.8	1.6	91
2018	AA	Chattanooga	3	0	0	20	25	1.79	1.00	19.4	163	22	89	2.05	4.5	11.2	2.5	0.9	99
2018	AAA	Rochester	9	3	0	100	95	2.97	1.20	21.2	187	24	76	2.40	4.9	8.5	1.7	0.5	38
2018	MLB	Minnesota	2	2	0	24	16	6.69	2.07	16.9	291	33	67	6.15	8.2	6.0	0.7	0.7	-96

Kitchen-sink throwing LHP lost velocity and stuff but still made MLB debut. Upright pitching motion with high 3/4s slot. Throws four pitches; best is a 12-to-6 CB with solid depth and late break. Struggles commanding FB and CU at times. SL is fringe-average offering.

Gonsolin,Tony — SP — Los Angeles (N)

EXP MLB DEBUT: 2019 | H/W: 6-2 180 | FUT: #3 starter | 8D

Thrws R Age 24 — 2016 (9) St. Mary's Coll of CA

	Year	Lev	Team	W	L	Sv	IP	K	ERA	WHIP	BF/G	OBA	H%	S%	xERA	Ctl	Dom	Cmd	hr/9	BPV
93-97 FB ++++	2017	A	Great Lakes	0	1	1	8	12	3.38	1.00	10.2	262	36	83	4.39	0.0	13.5		2.3	261
92-94 SP ++++	2017	A+	Rancho Cuca	7	5	5	62	73	3.92	1.27	6.5	259	35	70	3.63	2.6	10.6	4.1	0.7	138
84-86 CB +++	2018	A+	Rancho Cuca	4	2	0	83	106	2.70	1.18	19.6	235	34	78	2.89	2.8	11.5	4.1	0.5	148
SL ++	2018	AA	Tulsa	6	0	0	44	49	2.45	1.09	19.2	205	28	80	2.37	3.3	10.0	3.1	0.6	110

Late developing RHP had a breakout campaign. Uptick in FB velocity fueled the rise and the pitch now sits at 93-97, topping at 100 mph. Mid-80 splitter is second plus offering and CB/SL give him a solid four-pitch mix. Quick, high 3/4 arm slot adds deception and FB/SP allow him to dominate. Needs to prove 2018 was no fluke, but the stuff is filthy.

Gonzalez,Luis — SP — Baltimore

EXP MLB DEBUT: 2020 | H/W: 6-2 170 | FUT: #5 SP/swingman | 6C

Thrws L Age 27 — 2010 FA (DR)

	Year	Lev	Team	W	L	Sv	IP	K	ERA	WHIP	BF/G	OBA	H%	S%	xERA	Ctl	Dom	Cmd	hr/9	BPV
	2015	A+	Frederick	6	11	0	117	91	6.91	1.95	21.5	338	39	64	6.83	4.5	7.0	1.5	1.0	21
92-94 FB ++++	2016	A+	Frederick	1	2	2	31	43	3.17	0.93	9.0	193	27	72	2.32	2.3	12.4	5.4	1.2	179
84-85 SL ++	2017	A+	Frederick	6	2	5	62	75	2.47	1.02	6.6	182	27	77	1.76	3.5	10.9	3.1	0.4	120
78-82 CB ++	2018	AA	Bowie	2	1	7	45	58	2.19	0.93	6.1	180	26	82	1.85	2.8	11.5	4.1	0.8	151
82-84 CU ++	2018	AAA	Norfolk	0	2	2	25	27	5.04	1.72	8.1	305	41	69	5.10	4.3	9.7	2.3	0.4	76

Late-blooming LHP worked way into organization's plan eight years after pro debut. 3/4s cross-armed delivery with effort. Four pitches, but struggles with inconsistent release point and overall control. 2-seam FB has solid arm-side run and plus natural sink. Secondaries lack the promise. All three are workable options. RP risk given age/command.

Gonzalez,Merandy — SP — Miami

EXP MLB DEBUT: 2018 | H/W: 6-1 175 | FUT: Middle reliever | 6B

Thrws R Age 23 — 2013 FA (DR)

	Year	Lev	Team	W	L	Sv	IP	K	ERA	WHIP	BF/G	OBA	H%	S%	xERA	Ctl	Dom	Cmd	hr/9	BPV
	2017	A	Columbia	8	1	0	69		1.56	0.91	23.5	204	27	85	1.72	1.7	8.5	5.0	0.4	125
93-96 FB +++	2017	A+	St. Lucie	4	2	0	36	24	2.24	1.14	23.8	245	29	80	2.69	2.0	6.0	3.0	0.2	72
75-77 CB +++	2017	A+	Jupiter	1	0	1	24	14	1.12	0.95	18.2	209	25	87	1.57	1.9	5.2	2.8	0.0	62
83-84 CU ++	2018	AA	Jacksonville	3	6	0	73	47	4.32	1.38	21.9	248	28	70	3.94	4.1	5.8	1.4	0.9	12
91-93 CT +	2018	MLB	Miami	2	1	0	22	19	5.73	1.77	12.6	333	39	71	6.90	3.3	7.8	2.4	1.6	70

Undersized max-effort RHP made MLB debut. Slight build with little physical projection. Taxes arm for velocity. Three-pitch pitcher. Has solid control of mid-90s four-seam FB with little-to-no movement. Developed CT to keep hitters off FB. CB is best pitch. Above-average offering at projection. CU is a show pitch to LHH.

Gore,MacKenzie — SP — San Diego

EXP MLB DEBUT: 2020 | H/W: 6-3 180 | FUT: #1 starter | 9C

Thrws L Age 20 — 2017 (1) HS (NC)

	Year	Lev	Team	W	L	Sv	IP	K	ERA	WHIP	BF/G	OBA	H%	S%	xERA	Ctl	Dom	Cmd	hr/9	BPV
92-94 FB ++++																				
78-80 CB ++++																				
84-86 SL +++	2017	Rk	AZL Padres	0	1	0	21	34	1.28	1.00	11.5	190	35	86	1.35	3.0	14.5	4.9	0.0	198
78-82 CU +++	2018	A	Fort Wayne	2	5	0	60	74	4.49	1.31	15.5	264	37	66	3.82	2.7	11.1	4.1	0.7	144

Tall, lean LH with front-line SP look and potential for four above-average pitches. Uses big leg kick and has moving parts in delivery, but shows advanced command of 92-94 mph FB and complements with plus downer CB. Still ironing out CU, but shows feel of it along with useable SL. Innings were controlled in 2018; will likely be turned loose now.

Gowdy,Kevin — SP — Philadelphia

EXP MLB DEBUT: 2022 | H/W: 6-4 170 | FUT: #3 starter | 8E

Thrws R Age 21 — 2016 (2) HS (CA)

	Year	Lev	Team	W	L	Sv	IP	K	ERA	WHIP	BF/G	OBA	H%	S%	xERA	Ctl	Dom	Cmd	hr/9	BPV
91-94 FB +++																				
86-88 SL +++	2016	Rk	GCL Phillies	0	1	0	9	9	4.00	1.22	9.1	262	35	64	2.88	2.0	9.0	4.5	0.0	126
83-84 CU ++	2017		Did not pitch - injury																	
	2018		Did not pitch - injury																	

Back on the mound in 2018 fall instructional league following Tommy John surgery, he showed the FB/SL mix that excited observers from his prep days. Uses a full windup, has balanced delivery with good extension, sports a projectable frame and is still young. Will be a slow burn, but ingredients in place if health cooperates.

Graterol,Brusdar — SP — Minnesota

EXP MLB DEBUT: 2020 | H/W: 6-1 180 | FUT: #2 starter | 9C

Thrws R Age 20 — 2014 FA (VZ)

	Year	Lev	Team	W	L	Sv	IP	K	ERA	WHIP	BF/G	OBA	H%	S%	xERA	Ctl	Dom	Cmd	hr/9	BPV
95-98 FB ++++	2017	Rk	GCL Twins	2	0	0	19	21	1.41	0.73	13.6	157	21	85	0.81	1.9	9.9	5.3	0.5	145
82-86 SL ++++	2017	Rk	Elizabethton	2	1	0	20	24	4.01	1.24	16.4	219	31	67	2.76	4.0	10.7	2.7	0.4	102
87-90 CU +++	2018	A	Cedar Rapids	3	2	0	41	51	2.19	0.95	19.4	206	29	81	2.07	2.0	11.2	5.7	0.7	166
	2018	A+	Fort Myers	5	2	0	60	56	3.14	1.30	22.5	258	34	73	3.01	2.8	8.4	2.9	0.0	92

Powerful pitcher increased prospect momentum during successful 2018 campaign. 2-seam FB sits mid-to-high 90s with solid arm-side run and ability to miss bats up. SL is best secondary; is a tight, 2-plane breaker. CU has solid fading action but struggles maintaining FB arm-speed. Has toyed with CB; could use to change eye levels.

Gray,Josiah — SP — Los Angeles (N)

EXP MLB DEBUT: 2021 | H/W: 6-1 190 | FUT: Setup reliever | 7E

Thrws R Age 21 — 2018 (2) Le Moyne College

	Year	Lev	Team	W	L	Sv	IP	K	ERA	WHIP	BF/G	OBA	H%	S%	xERA	Ctl	Dom	Cmd	hr/9	BPV
92-94 FB ++++																				
81-83 SL +++																				
85-88 CU +																				
	2018	Rk	Greeneville	2	2	0	52	59	2.59	0.88	16.1	165	24	69	0.99	2.9	10.2	3.5	0.2	122

Athletic RHP is a three-pitch pitcher relying on hard-breaking 2-seam FB with late bore and sink to attack hitters. Sinker-like with a FB spin rate, should gain velocity later. SL has potential to be a swing-and-miss offering with sharp 2-plane break. CU far behind; delivery concerns also pushing RP projection. Traded to Dodgers in Puig/Kemp deal.

Green,Nick — SP — Arizona

EXP MLB DEBUT: 2020 | H/W: 6-1 165 | FUT: #5 SP/swingman | 6B

Thrws R Age 24 — 2014 (7) Indian Hills CC

	Year	Lev	Team	W	L	Sv	IP	K	ERA	WHIP	BF/G	OBA	H%	S%	xERA	Ctl	Dom	Cmd	hr/9	BPV
90-94 FB +++	2016	A	Charleston (Sc)	3	0	0	17	14	1.06	0.94	21.3	213	28	88	1.56	1.6	7.4	4.7	0.0	109
79-83 CB +++	2017	A	Charleston (Sc)	8	9	0	126	112	4.50	1.35	20.2	269	34	66	3.78	2.8	8.0	2.9	0.5	87
CU ++	2018	A+	Tampa	7	5	0	115	93	3.28	1.40	24.3	243	30	76	3.45	4.5	7.3	1.6	0.4	29
	2018	AA	Trenton	1	2	0	17	9	3.68	1.11	22.4	199	20	71	2.84	3.7	4.7	1.3	1.1	4

Undersized RHP limits hard contact with barrel missing arsenal. Repeatable, high 3/4s delivery with some cross-fire action. Three-pitch pitcher. Heavy 2-seam FB is workhorse, inducing lots of soft, ground ball contact. 12-to-6 CB has solid shape but inconsistent break. Above-average potential. Solid fade with CU with solid separation off FB. Rule 5 pick of the DBacks.

Greene,Conner — RP — Kansas City

EXP MLB DEBUT: 2019 | H/W: 6-3 165 | FUT: Setup reliever | 6C

Thrws R Age 24 — 2013 (7) HS (CA)

	Year	Lev	Team	W	L	Sv	IP	K	ERA	WHIP	BF/G	OBA	H%	S%	xERA	Ctl	Dom	Cmd	hr/9	BPV
	2016	A+	Dunedin	4	4	0	77	51	2.91	1.45	22.0	254	29	81	3.92	4.4	5.9	1.3	0.6	5
94-97 FB ++++	2016	AA	New Hampshire	6	5	0	68	48	4.22	1.32	23.5	229	26	68	3.33	4.4	6.3	1.5	0.7	14
CB +	2017	AA	New Hampshire	5	10	0	132	92	5.31	1.69	23.0	274	32	67	4.72	5.7	6.3	1.1	0.5	-22
CU +	2018	AA	Springfield	4	3	0	48	43	4.48	1.56	19.2	240	31	69	3.61	6.0	8.0	1.3	0.2	1
	2018	AAA	Memphis	0	2	0	39	26	3.68	1.64	6.0	230	27	77	3.97	7.1	6.0	0.8	0.5	-67

Plus FB sits at 94-97 topping out at 99 mph with late sink and arm-side run. Can be overly reliant on the FB and secondary offerings (CB and CU) lag behind. Unorthodox upright delivery adds some deception, but below-average command limits effectiveness.

Greene,Hunter — SP — Cincinnati

EXP MLB DEBUT: 2021 | H/W: 6-3 195 | FUT: #1 starter | 9C

Thrws R Age 19 — 2017 (1) HS (CA)

	Year	Lev	Team	W	L	Sv	IP	K	ERA	WHIP	BF/G	OBA	H%	S%	xERA	Ctl	Dom	Cmd	hr/9	BPV
97-100 FB +++++																				
83-85 SL ++++																				
90-92 CU ++++	2017	Rk	Billings	0	1	0	4	6	13.17	2.20	6.9	409	59	33	7.81	2.2	13.2	6.0	0.0	196
	2018	A	Dayton	3	7	0	68	89	4.49	1.31	15.6	256	37	66	3.72	3.0	11.8	3.9	0.8	148

Electric, athletic RHP made full-season debut. Struggled early, came on late before an elbow strain ended his season. Features easy, prime velocity—straight, but he keeps hitters from squaring it up by creating great extension with lower half and by changing eye levels. Both secondaries flash plus. SL has two-plane movement and CU fades well.

Groome,Jason — SP — Boston

EXP MLB DEBUT: 2023 | H/W: 6-5 200 | FUT: #2 starter | 9C

Thrws L Age 20 — 2016 (1) HS (NJ)

	Year	Lev	Team	W	L	Sv	IP	K	ERA	WHIP	BF/G	OBA	H%	S%	xERA	Ctl	Dom	Cmd	hr/9	BPV
	2016	Rk	GCL Red Sox	0	0	0	4	8	2.25	0.75	7.1	210	48	67	0.93	0.0	18.0		0.0	342
92-96 FB ++++	2016	A-	Lowell	0	0	0	2	2	4.09	1.82	10.2	0	0	75	1.73	16.4	8.2	0.5	0.0	-277
80-84 CB ++++	2017	A-	Lowell	0	2	0	11	14	1.64	0.91	13.7	139	23	80	0.61	4.1	11.5	2.8	0.0	114
82-85 CU +++	2017	A	Greenville	3	7	0	44	58	6.73	1.56	17.6	261	36	57	4.85	5.1	11.8	2.3	1.2	93
	2018		Did not pitch - injury																	

The first round pick in 2016 missed the entire 2018 season after having Tommy John surgery in May. Talent is not an issue for the big lefty, but he has had trouble staying healthy. There were also some off-field makeup issues which caused him to drop to 12th in the draft. When healthy he has an easy, clean delivery, a plus FB and CB, and ace potential.

Grove,Michael — SP — Los Angeles (N)

EXP MLB DEBUT: 2022 | H/W: 6-3 200 | FUT: #3 starter | 8D

Thrws R Age 22 — 2018 (2) West Virginia

Velo	Pitch	Grade
92-96	FB	+++
85-87	SL	++++
	CU	+

Year	Lev	Team	W	L	Sv	IP	K	ERA	WHIP	BF/G	OBA	H%	S%	xERA	Ctl	Dom	Cmd	hr/9	BPV
2018		Did not pitch - injury																	

Signed for $1.3M despite missing all of 2018 with Tommy John surgery. Before it, he pounded the zone with an above-average 92-96 mph FB that has good arm-side run, a plus power SL, and a fringe CU. Simple, repeatable mechanics and a quick delivery bode well for long-term development, but will need to prove he is 100% healthy.

Gutierrez,Vladimir — SP — Cincinnati

EXP MLB DEBUT: 2019 | H/W: 6-0 190 | FUT: #4 starter | 7C

Thrws R Age 23 — 2016 FA (CU)

Velo	Pitch	Grade
90-94	FB	+++
76-82	CB	+++
81-83	CU	+++

Year	Lev	Team	W	L	Sv	IP	K	ERA	WHIP	BF/G	OBA	H%	S%	xERA	Ctl	Dom	Cmd	hr/9	BPV
2017	A+	Daytona	7	8	0	103	94	4.46	1.23	22.0	271	33	65	3.86	1.7	8.2	4.9	0.9	121
2018	AA	Pensacola	9	10	0	147	145	4.35	1.20	21.9	251	31	67	3.72	2.3	8.9	3.8	1.1	115

Slim, athletic hurler's underlying metrics were better than his 2018 outcome. A three-pitch pitcher, he lacks a plus offering. Relies on command and consistent plane to achieve swing and misses with FB. Two-seamer hits spots, and not afraid to elevate, especially against RHH. 12-to-6 CB is refined and his CU flashes average.

Guzman,Jorge — SP — Miami

EXP MLB DEBUT: 2020 | H/W: 6-2 182 | FUT: Closer | 8D

Thrws R Age 23 — 2015 FA (DR)

Velo	Pitch	Grade
97-99	FB	+++++
84-85	CB	++++
86-89	CU	+

Year	Lev	Team	W	L	Sv	IP	K	ERA	WHIP	BF/G	OBA	H%	S%	xERA	Ctl	Dom	Cmd	hr/9	BPV
2016	Rk	Greeneville	2	3	0	22	29	4.86	1.44	15.8	285	42	65	4.12	2.8	11.8	4.1	0.4	153
2016	Rk	GCL Astros	1	1	0	17	25	3.16	0.82	8.9	77	15	57	-0.22	5.3	13.2	2.5	0.0	113
2017	A-	Staten Island	5	3	0	66	88	2.31	1.04	19.7	215	32	80	2.29	2.4	12.0	4.9	0.5	167
2018	A+	Jupiter	0	9	0	96	101	4.03	1.54	19.9	237	31	74	3.96	6.0	9.5	1.6	0.7	26

Big-bodied, over-powering RHP struggled with control in High-A debut. Rough, high-3/4s delivery with stiffness. 3-pitch pitcher. Easy, premium velocity. 4-seam FB has sneaky late run but struggles to control pitch. 11-to-5 CB has solid depth and sharp bite but lacks consistency. Does not have a feel for his CU. Profiles works best in pen.

Hall,DL — SP — Baltimore

EXP MLB DEBUT: 2021 | H/W: 6-0 180 | FUT: #2 starter | 9D

Thrws L Age 20 — 2017 (1) HS (GA)

Velo	Pitch	Grade
92-95	FB	++++
74-79	CB	+++
80-83	CU	++++

Year	Lev	Team	W	L	Sv	IP	K	ERA	WHIP	BF/G	OBA	H%	S%	xERA	Ctl	Dom	Cmd	hr/9	BPV
2017	Rk	GCL Orioles	0	0	0	10	12	7.13	1.98	9.7	260	35	63	5.58	8.9	10.7	1.2	0.9	-30
2018	A	Delmarva	2	7	0	94	100	2.10	1.17	17.1	204	27	85	2.54	4.0	9.6	2.4	0.6	82

Athletic, former 1st round pick took off in 2018. 3/4s delivery that incorporates great extension. 3-pitch pitcher. 2-seam FB features solid arm-side run and natural drop. Slurvy 2-to-7 CB has solid shape and late life. CU becoming primary secondary. Late-fading, deceptive. Athleticism plays pitch up.

Hamilton,Ian — RP — Chicago (A)

EXP MLB DEBUT: 2018 | H/W: 6-0 195 | FUT: Closer | 8D

Thrws R Age 23 — 2016 (11) Washington St

Velo	Pitch	Grade
95-98	FB	++++
88-90	SL	+++++
88-89	CU	++

Year	Lev	Team	W	L	Sv	IP	K	ERA	WHIP	BF/G	OBA	H%	S%	xERA	Ctl	Dom	Cmd	hr/9	BPV
2017	A+	Winston-Salem	3	3	6	52	52	1.72	0.79	6.3	183	25	78	0.96	1.4	9.0	6.5	0.2	142
2017	AA	Birmingham	1	3	1	19	22	5.21	1.79	6.3	327	45	68	5.27	3.8	10.4	2.8	0.0	103
2018	AA	Birmingham	2	1	12	25	34	1.79	1.27	4.9	220	35	84	2.44	4.3	12.2	2.8	0.0	121
2018	AAA	Charlotte	1	1	10	26	28	1.72	0.84	4.3	197	26	85	1.74	1.4	9.7	7.0	0.7	155
2018	MLB	Chicago (A)	1	2	0	8	5	4.50	1.00	3.1	210	19	67	3.80	2.3	5.6	2.5	2.3	59

Hard-throwing, physically mature RHP made MLB debut. Cross-fire, 3/4s delivery. 3-pitch pitcher. Relies heavily on 4-seam FB/SL mix to dominate hitters. FB sits mid-to-high 90s with minimal, but late action and misses barrels. SL is devastating, tight 2-plane out pitch. Keeps LHH of FB by utilizing fringe CU to change up looks. Bulldog mentality.

Hanhold,Eric — RP — New York (N)

EXP MLB DEBUT: 2018 | H/W: 6-4 190 | FUT: Middle reliever | 6D

Thrws R Age 25 — 2015 (6) Florida

Velo	Pitch	Grade
93-97	FB	++++
87-89	SL	+++
88-90	CU	++

Year	Lev	Team	W	L	Sv	IP	K	ERA	WHIP	BF/G	OBA	H%	S%	xERA	Ctl	Dom	Cmd	hr/9	BPV
2018	Rk	GCL Mets	0	0	0	1	3	0.00	0.00	2.8	0	0			0.0	27.0		0.0	504
2018	A-	Brooklyn	0	0	0	4	2	0.00	0.25	4.1	81	10	100		0.0	4.5		0.0	99
2018	AA	Binghamton	3	1	8	25	32	2.87	1.20	5.9	229	34	76	2.69	3.2	11.5	3.6	0.4	137
2018	AAA	Las Vegas	2	2	0	19	20	7.11	1.68	6.1	318	42	55	5.32	3.3	9.5	2.9	0.5	99
2018	MLB	NY Mets	0	0	0	2	2	8.57	2.38	3.6	403	50	60	8.20	4.3	8.6	2.0	0.0	57

Tall late-bloomer who pitched himself to the majors in 2018, but did not fare well there in a limited look. Awkward and inconsistent with his delivery, he relies on velocity and plane. Command and control will always be concerns. Probably would need to come up with a nasty secondary pitch to have any real relevance.

Hanifee,Brenan — SP — Baltimore

EXP MLB DEBUT: 2020 | H/W: 6-4 185 | FUT: #4 starter | 7D

Thrws R Age 20 — 2016 (4) HS (VA)

Velo	Pitch	Grade
89-92	FB	+++
81-84	SL	++
82-83	CU	+++

Year	Lev	Team	W	L	Sv	IP	K	ERA	WHIP	BF/G	OBA	H%	S%	xERA	Ctl	Dom	Cmd	hr/9	BPV
2017	A-	Aberdeen	7	3	0	68	44	2.77	1.13	22.4	253	30	75	2.80	1.6	5.8	3.7	0.3	80
2018	A	Delmarva	8	6	0	132	85	2.86	1.08	22.4	244	28	75	2.81	1.5	5.8	3.9	0.5	82

Projectable, big-bodied athlete transitioned successfully to pro ball. Lean physique with lots of room to grow. Struggles repeating high 3/4s cross-armed delivery. 3-pitch pitcher. 2-seam FB has solid arm-side run with heaviness down in zone. SL breaks on one-plane with limited shape. CU has average potential.

Hankins,Ethan — SP — Cleveland

EXP MLB DEBUT: 2021 | H/W: 6-6 200 | FUT: #2 starter | 9E

Thrws R Age 18 — 2018 (1) HS (GA)

Velo	Pitch	Grade
92-98	FB	+++++
86-88	CU	+++
78-81	CB	++
	SL	++

Year	Lev	Team	W	L	Sv	IP	K	ERA	WHIP	BF/G	OBA	H%	S%	xERA	Ctl	Dom	Cmd	hr/9	BPV
2018		Did not pitch																	

Has dealt with shoulder ailments, but when healthy features an easy plus FB with plus movement that can generate swings and misses. He operates with three off-speed pitches, a CB, SL and CU that all have potential to be average or better. CU is currently ahead of the breaking balls.

Hansen,Alec — SP — Chicago (A)

EXP MLB DEBUT: 2020 | H/W: 6-7 215 | FUT: #3 starter | 8E

Thrws R Age 24 — 2016 (2) Oklahoma

Velo	Pitch	Grade
92-94	FB	++++
79-83	SL	++
83-86	CB	++
83-85	CU	+

Year	Lev	Team	W	L	Sv	IP	K	ERA	WHIP	BF/G	OBA	H%	S%	xERA	Ctl	Dom	Cmd	hr/9	BPV
2017	A	Kannapolis	7	3	0	72	92	2.49	1.11	21.8	219	33	78	2.36	2.9	11.5	4.0	0.4	147
2017	A+	Winston-Salem	4	5	0	58	82	2.94	1.15	21.0	204	31	77	2.66	3.9	12.7	3.3	0.8	142
2017	AA	Birmingham	0	0	0	10	17	4.46	1.78	23.2	345	57	72	5.51	2.7	15.1	5.7	0.0	218
2018	A+	Winston-Salem	0	1	0	15	20	5.92	2.04	14.8	246	38	68	4.70	10.1	11.8	1.2	0.0	-41
2018	AA	Birmingham	0	4	0	35	35	6.65	2.05	19.0	232	30	67	5.28	10.7	8.9	0.8	0.8	-111

Tall RHP struggles repeating delivery resulting in poor command. High 3/4s, slight cross-fire delivery with good extension. Struggles rushing upper half through pitch progression. Riding FB with downward plane created by height. Movement is late. Struggles consistently snapping off quality SL & CB. SL is straight and hittable, with zero deception.

Hanson,Nick — SP — Cincinnati

EXP MLB DEBUT: 2021 | H/W: 6-5 210 | FUT: #3 starter | 8E

Thrws R Age 20 — 2016 (3) HS (MN)

Velo	Pitch	Grade
91-94	FB	++++
79-83	CB	+++
	CU	++

Year	Lev	Team	W	L	Sv	IP	K	ERA	WHIP	BF/G	OBA	H%	S%	xERA	Ctl	Dom	Cmd	hr/9	BPV
2016	Rk	AZL Reds	0	2	0	16	15	9.44	2.47	10.7	354	44	59	7.99	8.3	8.3	1.0	0.6	-57
2017		Did not pitch - injury																	
2018	Rk	AZL Reds	0	1	0	4	2	4.50	1.00	5.1	210	24	50	1.70	2.3	4.5	2.0	0.0	38

Made late-season return to mound after missing all of 2017 and most of 2018 after Tommy John surgery. Velocity returned after layoff with more possible as he continues to grow into large frame. Secondaries both raw. CB said to be best of the bunch, albeit a bit slurvy at times. Has feel for CU but struggled with consistency before injury.

Harris,Hogan — SP — Oakland

EXP MLB DEBUT: 2021 | H/W: 6-3 230 | FUT: #4 starter | 8D

Thrws L Age 22 — 2018 (3) LA-Lafayette

Velo	Pitch	Grade
91-94	FB	+++
79-83	CB	++++
	SL	+++
	CU	++

Year	Lev	Team	W	L	Sv	IP	K	ERA	WHIP	BF/G	OBA	H%	S%	xERA	Ctl	Dom	Cmd	hr/9	BPV
2018		Did not pitch																	

Crafty, deceptive LH drafted in 3rd round of 2018's amateur draft. Will mix arm angles but mostly operate from 3/4 slot with major crossfire in delivery. FB sits 91-94 and complements it with above-average CB with 1-to-7 action. SL/CU are fringe third offerings right now. Good athlete who should develop avg command as he tightens up his delivery.

Hartman,Ryan — SP — Houston
EXP MLB DEBUT: 2019 | H/W: 6-3 200 | FUT: Middle reliever | 6B

Thrws L Age 24	Year	Lev	Team	W	L	Sv	IP	K	ERA	WHIP	BF/G	OBA	H%	S%	xERA	Ctl	Dom	Cmd	hr/9	BPV
2016 (9) Cypress College																				
89-92 FB +++	2016	A-	Tri City	2	0	0	45	48	2.39	1.08	12.6	248	32	82	3.08	1.4	9.6	6.9	0.8	152
74-77 CB ++	2017	A	Quad Cities	3	1	1	39	37	2.76	1.17	17.4	224	28	81	3.13	3.2	8.5	2.6	0.9	84
83-85 CU +	2017	A+	Buies Creek	2	6	1	69	53	4.17	1.25	17.5	256	29	69	3.86	2.5	6.9	2.8	1.0	76
	2018	AA	Corpus Christi	11	4	0	120	143	2.70	1.08	18.8	235	32	79	2.92	1.9	10.7	5.5	0.8	158

It doesn't really make sense. The stuff doesn't pop off the page in any way shape or form and yet he posted a 30% strikeout rate in 120 AA innings. His fastball sits in the low-90s and he offers a fringy breaking ball, and a passable change-up. He'll cut the fastball and he can put it where he wants, rarely issuing a free pass.

Harvey,Hunter — SP — Baltimore
EXP MLB DEBUT: 2019 | H/W: 6-3 175 | FUT: #3 starter | 8E

Thrws R Age 24	Year	Lev	Team	W	L	Sv	IP	K	ERA	WHIP	BF/G	OBA	H%	S%	xERA	Ctl	Dom	Cmd	hr/9	BPV
2013 (1) HS (NC)	2016	A-	Aberdeen	0	1	0	7	7	3.75	2.08	11.8	307	40	80	5.71	7.5	8.8	1.2	0.0	-27
93-96 FB ++++	2017	Rk	GCL Orioles	0	0	0	5	6	0.00	1.20	6.7	299	43	100	3.33	0.0	10.8		0.0	212
78-82 CB ++++	2017	A-	Aberdeen	0	0	0	5	10	0.00	0.80	9.1	66	20	100		5.4	18.0	3.3	0.0	196
85-87 CU ++	2017	A	Delmarva	0	1	0	8	14	2.20	0.85	10.0	147	30	71	0.52	3.3	15.4	4.7	0.0	206
	2018	AA	Bowie	1	2	0	32	30	5.61	1.40	15.1	285	35	60	4.45	2.5	8.4	3.3	0.8	101

Oft-injured former Top 100 prospect struggled with shoulder injury, derailing season. 3/4s delivery with effort; gets great extension. Shiny tools still there despite injury history. High-powered FB jumps on hitters with late run. 11-to-5 CB has great shape, good depth and plus break. CU lags due to limited usage.

Hatch,Thomas — SP — Chicago (N)
EXP MLB DEBUT: 2019 | H/W: 6-1 190 | FUT: #5 SP/swingman | 7D

Thrws R Age 24	Year	Lev	Team	W	L	Sv	IP	K	ERA	WHIP	BF/G	OBA	H%	S%	xERA	Ctl	Dom	Cmd	hr/9	BPV
2016 (3) Oklahoma St																				
89-94 FB ++																				
84-87 SL ++																				
78-83 CU ++	2017	A+	Myrtle Beach	5	11	0	124	126	4.06	1.42	20.2	265	36	69	3.54	3.6	9.1	2.5	0.1	85
	2018	AA	Tennessee	8	6	0	143	117	3.83	1.31	22.8	239	28	74	3.76	3.8	7.4	1.9	1.0	47

FB sits at 90-94 with good late sink and 4-seamer tops out at 96 mph. 3/4 arm slot gives SL above-average action and CU has solid average potential. Elbow injury in college is a thing of the past and he logged a career-high IP. Deliberate worker continues to struggle finding the strike zone and a move to middle relief seems likely.

Hearn,Taylor — SP — Texas
EXP MLB DEBUT: 2019 | H/W: 6-5 190 | FUT: #3 starter | 8C

Thrws L Age 24	Year	Lev	Team	W	L	Sv	IP	K	ERA	WHIP	BF/G	OBA	H%	S%	xERA	Ctl	Dom	Cmd	hr/9	BPV
2015 (5) San Jacinto Coll	2016	A	Hagerstown	1	0	0	22	31	3.24	1.44	11.8	285	41	83	4.87	2.8	12.6	4.4	1.2	168
92-96 FB ++++	2017	Rk	GCL Pirates	0	0	0	2	3	0.00	0.00	5.6	0	0			0.0	13.5		0.0	261
81-84 SL +++	2017	A+	Bradenton	4	6	0	87	106	4.13	1.17	19.3	209	29	66	2.83	3.8	11.0	2.9	0.8	112
84-85 CU +++	2018	AA	Frisco	1	2	0	25	33	5.04	1.52	21.7	291	39	73	5.71	3.2	11.9	3.7	1.8	144
	2018	AA	Altoona	3	6	0	104	107	3.12	1.09	21.4	204	27	72	2.28	3.3	9.3	2.8	0.5	96

Long, lean southpaw with clean, easy delivery that projects to plus command. Long arm action, but has the athleticism to compensate and ability to tweak mechanics going forward. Elite arm strength and great extension plays up the FB; secondaries a bit raw but ingredients are in place. Likely to be a high-strikeout guy.

Heatherly,Jacob — SP — Cincinnati
EXP MLB DEBUT: 2021 | H/W: 6-1 210 | FUT: #3 starter | 8E

Thrws L Age 20	Year	Lev	Team	W	L	Sv	IP	K	ERA	WHIP	BF/G	OBA	H%	S%	xERA	Ctl	Dom	Cmd	hr/9	BPV
2017 (3) HS (AL)																				
91-93 FB ++++																				
75-78 CB +++	2017	Rk	AZL Reds	2	1	0	30	26	2.98	1.39	14.1	234	28	82	3.78	4.8	7.7	1.6	0.9	29
82-84 CU +++	2017	Rk	Billings	0	1	0	9	5	12.00	2.33	15.5	401	45	43	8.08	4.0	5.0	1.3	0.0	0
	2018	Rk	Greeneville	1	5	0	38	49	5.89	1.94	16.5	240	35	69	5.02	9.4	11.5	1.2	0.7	-29

Physically mature, stocky LHP cleaned up mechanics in successful Appy League stint. Three-pitch pitcher; uses two FB, which both flash above-average movement and have deceptive velocity. Achieves extension in delivery and has deception with his arm slot. CB and CU both project as above-average or better offerings.

Helsley,Ryan — SP — St. Louis
EXP MLB DEBUT: 2019 | H/W: 6-2 205 | FUT: #3 starter | 8D

Thrws R Age 24	Year	Lev	Team	W	L	Sv	IP	K	ERA	WHIP	BF/G	OBA	H%	S%	xERA	Ctl	Dom	Cmd	hr/9	BPV
2015 (5) Northeastern St	2017	AA	Springfield	3	1	0	33	41	2.71	1.20	22.3	211	29	83	3.17	4.1	11.1	2.7	1.1	108
93-96 FB ++++	2017	AAA	Memphis	0	0	0	5	5	3.60	2.00	24.1	332	43	80	5.90	5.4	9.0	1.7	0.0	34
80-81 CB ++++	2018	Rk	GCL Cardinals	0	0	0	2	4	0.00	1.82	10.2	139	31	100	2.86	12.3	16.4	1.3	0.0	-19
87-89 CT ++	2018	AA	Springfield	3	2	0	41	44	4.39	1.22	23.7	206	26	67	3.18	4.4	9.7	2.2	1.1	73
CU ++	2018	AAA	Memphis	2	1	0	26	34	3.78	1.03	20.2	196	29	64	2.18	3.1	11.7	3.8	0.7	145

Continues steady climb toward the majors, but was shut down in June with shoulder fatigue. FB sits at 93-96 and tops out at 98 mph. Power CB has good late bite. CU and CT also flash plus and were more consistent in 2018, giving him four above-average offerings. Control and command are the last hurdles and will determine his long-term upside.

Hendrix,Ryan — RP — Cincinnati
EXP MLB DEBUT: 2020 | H/W: 6-3 185 | FUT: Setup reliever | 7C

Thrws R Age 24	Year	Lev	Team	W	L	Sv	IP	K	ERA	WHIP	BF/G	OBA	H%	S%	xERA	Ctl	Dom	Cmd	hr/9	BPV
2016 (5) Texas A&M	2016	Rk	Billings	0	0	0	8	5	5.49	1.95	6.5	322	38	69	5.65	5.5	5.5	1.0	0.0	-31
95-97 FB ++++	2016	A	Dayton	3	1	0	26	31	3.09	1.11	6.9	221	33	69	2.04	2.7	10.6	3.9	0.0	135
83-86 CB ++++	2017	A	Dayton	4	1	6	34	61	2.38	0.85	5.4	165	33	74	1.19	2.6	16.1	6.1	0.5	237
	2017	A+	Daytona	1	4	2	27	27	3.64	1.76	5.2	274	33	84	5.66	6.3	8.9	1.4	1.3	9
	2018	A+	Daytona	4	4	12	51	79	1.76	1.25	4.7	209	36	87	2.56	4.6	13.9	3.0	0.4	145

Hard-throwing, sturdy RH relief-only prospect had successful run in the Florida State League. A two-pitch pitcher, primarily FB, which sits mid-90s with heavy sink and ellicits swings and misses. Power CB took huge step forward as the season grew on. Consistent, 11-to-5 hard downward sink. Is able to change eye levels. Two plus pitches at maturity.

Henteges,Sam — SP — Cleveland
EXP MLB DEBUT: 2021 | H/W: 6-6 235 | FUT: #4 starter | 8C

Thrws L Age 22	Year	Lev	Team	W	L	Sv	IP	K	ERA	WHIP	BF/G	OBA	H%	S%	xERA	Ctl	Dom	Cmd	hr/9	BPV
2014 (4) HS (MN)																				
89-93 FB +++	2016	A	Lake County	2	4	0	60	73	6.14	1.66	19.2	295	40	64	5.58	4.3	10.9	2.5	1.2	98
75-79 CB +++	2017	Rk	AZL Indians	0	3	0	13	18	4.85	1.46	9.3	304	43	71	5.36	2.1	12.5	6.0	1.4	186
83-84 CU ++	2017	A-	Mahoning Vall	0	1	0	17	23	2.09	0.99	13.1	93	14	81	0.86	6.3	12.0	1.9	0.5	65
SL ++	2018	A+	Lynchburg	6	6	0	118	122	3.28	1.41	21.7	255	34	76	3.55	4.0	9.3	2.3	0.3	76

Uses his height to create plane and the FB plays up. For a pitcher of his size, he has a clean, simple delivery that allows for plus fastball command up and around the zone. CB shows most promise of offspeed pitches. Has shown feel for the CU in the past, and will need it to reach his potential as a starter.

Henzman,Lincoln — SP — Chicago (A)
EXP MLB DEBUT: 2020 | H/W: 6-2 194 | FUT: #4 starter | 7C

Thrws R Age 23	Year	Lev	Team	W	L	Sv	IP	K	ERA	WHIP	BF/G	OBA	H%	S%	xERA	Ctl	Dom	Cmd	hr/9	BPV
2017 (4) Louisville																				
91-94 FB +++	2017	NCAA	Louisville	3	0	16	37	37	1.69	0.86	5.1	173	23	83	1.33	2.4	9.0	3.7	0.5	114
87-89 CT +++	2017	Rk	Great Falls	0	3	0	27	16	4.00	1.33	11.2	262	31	67	3.19	3.0	5.3	1.8	0.0	33
82-83 CU +++	2018	A	Kannapolis	6	3	0	72	60	2.24	1.05	21.5	250	30	82	2.89	1.0	7.5	7.5	0.6	126
	2018	A+	Winston-Salem	0	1	0	34	20	2.63	1.29	10.0	261	30	79	3.31	2.6	5.3	2.0	0.3	42

Former collegiate RP having success as full-time starter. Low-effort, cross-fire 3/4s delivery. Three-pitch pitcher. 2-seam FB has solid arm-side run and slight sink. Commands FB well to arm-side but struggles away from body. CT survives with late run; mimics 1-plane SL at times. CU is solid, with some fade. Needs true breaker to reach projection.

Herget,Jimmy — RP — Cincinnati
EXP MLB DEBUT: 2019 | H/W: 6-3 155 | FUT: Middle reliever | 6B

Thrws R Age 25	Year	Lev	Team	W	L	Sv	IP	K	ERA	WHIP	BF/G	OBA	H%	S%	xERA	Ctl	Dom	Cmd	hr/9	BPV
2015 (6) South Florida	2015	Rk	Billings	3	0	15	25	26	3.23	1.08	4.1	184	25	69	1.88	3.9	9.3	2.4	0.4	79
93-96 FB ++++	2016	A+	Daytona	4	4	24	60	83	1.79	1.15	4.8	217	34	86	2.49	3.3	12.4	3.8	0.4	153
75-82 SL +++	2017	AA	Pensacola	1	3	16	29	44	2.77	1.16	4.8	211	35	76	2.32	3.7	13.6	3.7	0.3	162
80-81 CU +	2017	AAA	Louisville	3	1	9	32	28	3.08	1.21	4.6	249	29	80	3.75	2.5	7.9	3.1	1.1	91
	2018	AAA	Louisville	1	3	0	59	65	3.50	1.35	4.9	261	35	76	3.90	3.2	9.9	3.1	0.8	110

Tall, lean RHP with unorthodox low 3/4s-to-sidearm delivery is knocking on big league door. Primarily two-pitch pitcher but throws a show me CU. 2-seam FB has natural arm-side run with some sink. Hard to pick up from RHH. SL is a sharp two-plane breaking pitch on its best days but struggles on other achieving vertical bite. R-on-R reliever ceiling.

Hernandez,Carlos — SP — Kansas City
EXP MLB DEBUT: 2021 | H/W: 6-4 175 | FUT: #3 starter | 8D

Thrws R Age 22	Year	Lev	Team	W	L	Sv	IP	K	ERA	WHIP	BF/G	OBA	H%	S%	xERA	Ctl	Dom	Cmd	hr/9	BPV
2016 FA (VZ)																				
91-95 FB ++++																				
82-83 SL +++																				
84-86 CU +++	2017	Rk	Burlington	1	4	0	62	62	5.51	1.47	22.2	268	34	62	4.39	3.9	9.0	2.3	0.9	74
	2018	A	Lexington	6	5	0	79	82	3.30	1.19	21.1	241	31	75	3.26	2.6	9.3	3.6	0.8	115

Sturdy, hard-throwing RHP had successful Single-A debut cut short by injury. Easy, cross-fire 3/4s delivery. Gets solid extension, which plays up velocity. Two-seam FB with late arm-side bore. SL flashes quality two-plane movement. CU took step from non-existent to somewhat interesting; at best, it's an average pitch.

Hernandez,Darwinzon — RP — Boston

EXP MLB DEBUT: 2020 | H/W: 6-2 180 | FUT: Setup reliever | 7C

Thrws L Age 22 — 2014 FA (VZ)

Velo	Pitch	Grade
93-97	FB	++++
74-78	CB	++++
81-86	SL	++++
89-91	CU	++

Year	Lev	Team	W	L	Sv	IP	K	ERA	WHIP	BF/G	OBA	H%	S%	xERA	Ctl	Dom	Cmd	hr/9	BPV
2016	A-	Lowell	3	5	0	48	58	4.12	1.56	15.0	223	33	72	3.38	6.7	10.9	1.6	0.2	31
2017	A	Greenville	4	5	0	103	116	4.02	1.30	18.5	226	31	70	3.25	4.3	10.1	2.4	0.7	85
2018	A+	Salem	9	5	0	101	124	3.56	1.39	18.5	219	33	72	2.80	5.3	11.0	2.1	0.1	73
2018	AA	Portland	0	0	0	6	10	3.00	2.00	5.8	262	46	83	4.78	9.0	15.0	1.7	0.0	45

The sturdy lefty who always had a plus arm put it together once moved to the pen midway through the season, and then kept the nastiness once promoted to AA. Has a plus FB and both of breaking balls can be plus at times too. Control has been a problem and still can be at times. Tends to rush and overthrow. When he throws strikes he is tough to hit.

Hernandez,Jonathan — SP — Texas

EXP MLB DEBUT: 2020 | H/W: 6-2 150 | FUT: #3 starter | 8C

Thrws R Age 22 — 2013 FA (TN)

Velo	Pitch	Grade
93-96	FB	+++
86-88	SL	++++
82-85	CU	+++
77-79	CB	++

Year	Lev	Team	W	L	Sv	IP	K	ERA	WHIP	BF/G	OBA	H%	S%	xERA	Ctl	Dom	Cmd	hr/9	BPV
2016	A	Hickory	10	9	0	116	85	4.57	1.37	20.3	251	28	69	4.15	3.8	6.6	1.7	1.1	34
2017	A	Hickory	2	5	0	46	46	4.88	1.48	22.0	297	37	68	4.94	2.5	9.0	3.5	1.0	111
2017	A+	Down East	3	6	0	65	64	3.46	1.49	20.0	264	35	76	3.85	4.3	8.8	2.1	0.3	62
2018	A+	Down East	4	2	0	57	77	2.21	0.95	21.5	187	27	83	2.10	2.7	12.1	4.5	0.9	164
2018	AA	Frisco	4	4	0	64	57	4.92	1.47	22.9	243	30	67	4.05	5.1	8.0	1.6	0.8	26

Stuff ticked up across the board and led to early success. Complements hard FB with armside run with three good secondaries, led by plus swing-and-miss SL with excellent tilt. Sells CU well, and has usable CB. Bit of crossfire delivery that affects FB command that will determine his ceiling. But four usable pitches.

Hernandez,Wilkel — SP — Detroit

EXP MLB DEBUT: 2021 | H/W: 6-3 160 | FUT: #4 starter | 8D

Thrws R Age 19 — 2016 FA (VZ)

Velo	Pitch	Grade
90-95	FB	+++
78-82	CB	+++
	CU	++

Year	Lev	Team	W	L	Sv	IP	K	ERA	WHIP	BF/G	OBA	H%	S%	xERA	Ctl	Dom	Cmd	hr/9	BPV
2017	Rk	Orem	1	0	0	3		3.00	1.33	12.5	191	24	75	2.30	6.0	6.0	1.0	0.0	-36
2017	Rk	AZL Angels	3	1	0	41	42	2.63	1.05	14.4	166	23	74	1.47	4.4	9.2	2.1	0.2	65
2018	A-	Connecticut	0	2	0	5	11	8.65	1.92	12.3	290	52	63	8.20	6.9	19.0	2.8	3.5	174
2018	A	West Michigan	2	5	0	42	34	4.71	1.33	17.4	252	30	65	3.85	3.4	7.3	2.1	0.9	57

Projectable and wiry, his frame is far from filled out, but he's likely to add muscle over the next few years. Making improvements to his delivery, but still inconsistent. Building confidence in throwing his change-up and showing good movement to both his fastball and curve. A raw skill set, but progressing enough to keep an eye on.

Herrera,Carlos — RP — Milwaukee

EXP MLB DEBUT: 2021 | H/W: 6-2 150 | FUT: Middle reliever | 7C

Thrws R Age 21 — 2015 FA (DR)

Velo	Pitch	Grade
90-92	FB	+++
	CB	+++
	CU	++

Year	Lev	Team	W	L	Sv	IP	K	ERA	WHIP	BF/G	OBA	H%	S%	xERA	Ctl	Dom	Cmd	hr/9	BPV
2016	Rk	AZL Brewers	3	6	0	50	49	4.50	1.28	14.6	269	34	65	3.81	2.2	8.8	4.1	0.7	118
2017	Rk	Helena	2	0	0	21	26	4.29	1.00	20.1	213	25	69	3.68	2.1	11.1	5.2	2.1	161
2017	A	Wisconsin	3	2	0	38	26	3.79	1.08	16.5	183	20	68	2.45	4.0	6.2	1.5	0.9	20
2018	A	Wisconsin	3	6	1	85	60	5.49	1.68	13.7	283	33	66	4.85	5.1	6.3	1.3	0.5	-5

Lean, athletic Dominican RH whose K-rate plummeted in first taste of full-season ball. Works from low 3/4 slot and operates around 90-92 mph with average FB; works a tick above that as RP. Maintains arm speed on avg CU; CB has chance to be above-avg pitch. Effort in delivery suggests RP role will be permanent.

Hill,Brigham — SP — Washington

EXP MLB DEBUT: 2021 | H/W: 6-0 175 | FUT: Middle reliever | 7D

Thrws R Age 23 — 2017 (5) Texas A&M

Velo	Pitch	Grade
90-91	FB	++
79-82	CU	+++
	CB	++

Year	Lev	Team	W	L	Sv	IP	K	ERA	WHIP	BF/G	OBA	H%	S%	xERA	Ctl	Dom	Cmd	hr/9	BPV
2017	NCAA	Texas A&M	8	3	0	100	111	3.15	1.19	23.6	238	33	74	2.89	2.8	10.0	3.6	0.5	122
2017	A-	Auburn	0	1	0	13	9	2.73	1.14	13.1	244	30	73	2.45	2.0	6.1	3.0	0.0	73
2017	A	Hagerstown	0	1	0	29	30	6.16	1.58	21.4	332	41	62	5.99	1.5	9.2	6.0	1.2	143
2018	Rk	GCL Nationals	0	2	0	6	5	4.50	2.00	14.5	321	40	75	5.74	6.0	7.5	1.3	0.0	-9
2018	A	Hagerstown	4	3	0	49	35	3.11	1.30	20.3	249	31	73	2.93	3.3	6.4	1.9	0.0	44

The fastball/change-up duo has only had inconsistent success so far; strikeouts from his collegiate days are way down. His CB is a distant third pitch, but something he needs for his arsenal to work. Short of stature with little projection left, he'll look to High-A to make more strides but it looks like a non-impact reliever profile at best.

Hillman,Juan — SP — Cleveland

EXP MLB DEBUT: 2022 | H/W: 6-2 183 | FUT: #5 SP/swingman | 7E

Thrws L Age 21 — 2015 (1) HS (FL)

Velo	Pitch	Grade
88-93	FB	++
79-81	CB	+++
	CU	+++

Year	Lev	Team	W	L	Sv	IP	K	ERA	WHIP	BF/G	OBA	H%	S%	xERA	Ctl	Dom	Cmd	hr/9	BPV
2015	Rk	AZL Indians	0	2	0	24	20	4.13	1.29	12.3	278	35	65	3.29	1.9	7.5	4.0	0.0	102
2016	A-	Mahoning Vall	3	4	0	63	47	4.43	1.43	17.8	271	32	69	4.22	3.4	6.7	2.0	0.7	46
2017	A	Lake County	7	10	0	137	101	6.10	1.50	22.8	290	32	61	5.36	3.1	6.6	2.1	1.4	52
2018	A	Lake County	6	12	0	128	110	5.20	1.50	21.3	279	35	64	4.29	3.7	7.7	2.1	0.5	58

A young athletic lefty, but at some point we need to see performance. For two straight years he has been roughed up in A ball. He possesses a slightly below average fastball that gets hit hard and a slightly above average curveball and change-up. He throws enough strikes to succeed, but needs to figure out how to avoid hard contact.

Hinsz,Gage — SP — Pittsburgh

EXP MLB DEBUT: 2022 | H/W: 6-4 210 | FUT: #5 SP/swingman | 6C

Thrws R Age 22 — 2014 (11) HS (MT)

Velo	Pitch	Grade
91-94	FB	+++
77-79	CB	++
82-85	CU	++

Year	Lev	Team	W	L	Sv	IP	K	ERA	WHIP	BF/G	OBA	H%	S%	xERA	Ctl	Dom	Cmd	hr/9	BPV
2014	Rk	GCL Pirates	0	0	0	8	7	3.38	1.50	11.5	262	34	75	3.59	4.5	7.9	1.8	0.0	38
2015	Rk	Bristol	3	4	0	38	24	3.79	1.58	16.7	257	30	75	3.96	5.4	5.7	1.0	0.2	-27
2016	A	West Virginia	6	8	0	93	67	3.67	1.27	22.4	262	30	73	3.74	2.4	6.5	2.7	0.8	69
2017	A+	Bradenton	5	5	0	94	52	5.64	1.52	20.4	297	33	63	4.97	3.0	5.0	1.7	0.9	27

Command righty who lacks the plus feel or deception to make fringy stuff play. Lacks an out pitch. The ability to throw strikes as well as mix-and-match should earn him promotions and a chance to pitch at higher levels. Low ceiling, however.

Hjelle,Sean — SP — San Francisco

EXP MLB DEBUT: 2020 | H/W: 6-11 200 | FUT: #3 starter | 8E

Thrws R Age 21 — 2018 (2) Kentucky

Velo	Pitch	Grade
92-94	FB	++++
80-83	CB	+++
85-86	CU	+++

Year	Lev	Team	W	L	Sv	IP	K	ERA	WHIP	BF/G	OBA	H%	S%	xERA	Ctl	Dom	Cmd	hr/9	BPV
2018	NCAA	Kentucky	7	5	0	99	91	3.45	1.10	25.9	237	30	68	2.68	2.0	8.3	4.1	0.5	113
2018	A-	Salem-Keizer	0	0	0	21	22	5.12	1.33	7.3	287	35	67	5.10	1.7	9.4	5.5	1.7	141

Tall, lanky RHP offers finish over stuff with outside shot as #3 starter. Repeatable, high 3/4s cross-armed delivery with below average extension compared to height. 3-pitch pitcher. Workhorse pitch is 2-seam FB with solid bore. Commands pitch to both sides of plate well. Best secondary offering is 12-to-6 CB and has consistent average CU.

Holmes,Clay — SP — Pittsburgh

EXP MLB DEBUT: 2018 | H/W: 6-5 230 | FUT: Middle reliever | 7C

Thrws R Age 26 — 2011 (9) HS (AL)

Velo	Pitch	Grade
93-97	FB	++++
81-84	CB	+++
87-89	CT	++
81-88	CU	++

Year	Lev	Team	W	L	Sv	IP	K	ERA	WHIP	BF/G	OBA	H%	S%	xERA	Ctl	Dom	Cmd	hr/9	BPV
2016	AA	Altoona	10	9	0	136	101	4.23	1.48	22.5	264	31	72	4.22	4.2	6.7	1.6	0.7	24
2017	AAA	Indianapolis	10	5	0	112	99	3.37	1.38	18.9	233	30	75	3.21	4.7	7.9	1.7	0.3	33
2018	A+	Bradenton	0	0	0	6	8	1.50	0.67	20.9	191	31	75	0.56	0.0	12.0		0.0	234
2018	AAA	Indianapolis	8	3	0	95	100	3.41	1.41	18.3	260	35	75	3.67	3.8	9.5	2.5	0.4	86
2018	MLB	Pittsburgh	1	3	0	26	21	6.90	2.03	11.5	290	35	65	5.97	7.9	7.2	0.9	0.7	-66

Huge, wide-hipped AAA starter whose stuff plays better out of pen. Has made great strides repeating his delivery and throwing more strikes, but still command and feel a little short. Great plane helps his stuff, but lack of movement hurts his FB. Struggled to find consistent offspeed to get strikeouts and set up his FB better.

Holmes,Grant — SP — Oakland

EXP MLB DEBUT: 2020 | H/W: 6-1 215 | FUT: #4 starter | 8D

Thrws R Age 23 — 2014 (1) HS (SC)

Velo	Pitch	Grade
92-94	FB	++++
79-83	CB	+++
84-86	CU	++

Year	Lev	Team	W	L	Sv	IP	K	ERA	WHIP	BF/G	OBA	H%	S%	xERA	Ctl	Dom	Cmd	hr/9	BPV
2015	A	Great Lakes	6	4	0	103	117	3.14	1.36	17.9	228	32	78	3.26	4.7	10.2	2.2	0.5	75
2016	A+	Stockton	3	3	0	28	24	7.02	1.91	22.3	356	42	64	7.32	3.2	7.7	2.4	1.3	70
2016	A+	Rancho Cuca	8	4	1	105	100	4.02	1.39	22.1	258	33	71	3.73	3.7	8.6	2.3	0.5	73
2017	AA	Midland	11	12	0	148	150	4.50	1.42	21.6	263	33	70	4.24	3.7	9.1	2.5	0.9	82
2018	A+	Stockton	0	0	0	6	8	4.50	1.00	11.5	191	25	60	2.81	3.0	12.0	4.0	1.5	153

Strong, aggressive RH who missed most of 2018 with shoulder issues that could be worse than originally thought. Pumped a mid-90s fastball previously with sinking action but poor command. Feel for 12-to-6 CB that will flash plus at times. CU has been work in progress but should be useable third pitch. Showed solid SwK floor but a lot hinges on health.

Honeywell,Brent — SP — Tampa Bay

EXP MLB DEBUT: 2019 | H/W: 6-2 180 | FUT: #1 starter | 9C

Thrws R Age 24 — 2014 (2) Walters St CC

Velo	Pitch	Grade
92-96	FB	++++
87-88	SL	+++
81-84	CU	++++
75-79	SU	++++

Year	Lev	Team	W	L	Sv	IP	K	ERA	WHIP	BF/G	OBA	H%	S%	xERA	Ctl	Dom	Cmd	hr/9	BPV
2015	A+	Charlotte	5	2	0	65	53	3.46	1.11	21.3	237	30	67	2.53	2.1	7.3	3.5	0.3	94
2016	A+	Charlotte	4	1	0	56	64	2.41	0.96	21.2	214	29	80	2.35	1.8	10.3	5.8	0.8	155
2016	AA	Montgomery	3	2	0	59	53	2.28	1.10	23.2	234	29	82	2.78	2.1	8.1	3.8	0.6	106
2017	AA	Montgomery	1	1	0	13	20	2.08	0.62	22.3	98	15	71	0.11	2.8	13.8	5.0	0.7	192
2017	AAA	Durham	12	8	0	123	152	3.65	1.31	21.2	272	38	74	3.97	2.3	11.1	4.9	0.8	157

Five-pitch pitcher was poised for MLB debut before missing entire season with Tommy John surgery. Sits low-to-mid 90s with 2-seam FB; solid arm-side run and advanced command. Best known for plus-plus SC but don't sleep on plus CU. It's a plus pitch with swing-and-miss movement. SL is above-average offering and CB used mostly to change eye levels.

Houck,Tanner | SP | Boston | EXP MLB DEBUT: 2021 | H/W: 6-5 215 | FUT: Middle reliever | 6B

Thrws R Age 22	Year	Lev	Team	W	L	Sv	IP	K	ERA	WHIP	BF/G	OBA	H%	S%	xERA	Ctl	Dom	Cmd	hr/9	BPV
2017 (1) Missouri																				
90-95 FB ++++																				
83-87 SL +++	2017	NCAA	Missouri	4	7	0	94	95	3.34	1.08	26.3	227	30	69	2.52	2.3	9.1	4.0	0.5	119
88-90 CT +++	2017	A-	Lowell	0	3	0	22	25	3.67	1.31	9.1	252	36	69	2.96	3.3	10.2	3.1	0.0	113
82-85 CU ++	2018	A+	Salem	7	11	0	119	111	4.24	1.43	22.0	247	31	72	3.98	4.5	8.4	1.9	0.8	47

Athletic righty was the victim of some mechanical changes early in his pro career, but went back to his old lower slot and found himself again midway through the 2018 season. FB, SL combo can be quite nasty against RHH from the low slot. The concern is how much feel and command he has to get LHH out.

Houser,Adrian | RP | Milwaukee | EXP MLB DEBUT: 2019 | H/W: 6-4 205 | FUT: Middle reliever | 7B

Thrws R Age 26	Year	Lev	Team	W	L	Sv	IP	K	ERA	WHIP	BF/G	OBA	H%	S%	xERA	Ctl	Dom	Cmd	hr/9	BPV
2011 (2) HS (OK)																				
93-96 FB ++++	2017	A	Wisconsin	1	0	0	9	11	1.00	0.56	10.1	165	26	80		0.0	11.0		0.0	216
78-81 CB ++++	2018	AA	Biloxi	0	1	0	26	30	4.81	1.41	13.9	289	38	68	4.69	2.4	10.3	4.3	1.0	139
86-88 CU ++	2018	AAA	COL Springs	2	3	0	52	37	5.19	1.62	17.7	310	35	69	5.58	3.1	6.4	2.1	1.0	49
	2018	MLB	Milwaukee	0	0	0	13	8	3.41	1.52	8.2	259	31	75	3.61	4.8	5.5	1.1	0.0	-13

Strong, physical RH who relies heavily on power FB/CB mix. Will run FB up to 97 mph with late sink for ground balls in bunches; curve has legit swing-and-miss ability with downer 11-to-5 action. Missed time in previous two seasons post-Tommy John surgery. Likely headed for middle relief as a solid ground-ball type arm.

Houston,Zac | RP | Detroit | EXP MLB DEBUT: 2019 | H/W: 6-5 234 | FUT: Setup reliever | 7B

Thrws R Age 24	Year	Lev	Team	W	L	Sv	IP	K	ERA	WHIP	BF/G	OBA	H%	S%	xERA	Ctl	Dom	Cmd	hr/9	BPV
2016 (11) Mississippi St	2016	A	West Michigan	1	0	4	19		0.47	0.89	5.5	85	17	94	0.01	5.6	14.1	2.5	0.0	119
93-97 FB +++	2017	A	West Michigan	0	0	2	46	71	2.54	1.00	7.3	156	28	73	1.17	4.3	13.9	3.2	0.2	152
74-76 CB +++	2017	A+	Lakeland	0	1	4	11	20	0.80	0.98	5.3	87	21	91	0.26	6.4	16.1	2.5	0.0	134
79-84 SP ++	2018	AA	Erie	1	1	0	17	25	2.63	0.99	5.0	142	23	75	1.34	4.7	13.2	2.8	0.5	127
	2018	AAA	Toledo	0	1	10	38	55	1.18	0.95	4.3	157	26	91	1.33	3.8	13.0	3.4	0.5	150

Broad-shouldered, intimidating reliever. Has showed improvement to command and control, in addition to adding a splitter in 2018. Big velo fastball that attacks opposing hitters. Big frame adds natural downhill motion and sink. Good improvement to mixing in offspeed pieces and handled International League hitters with little issue.

Howard,Brian | SP | Oakland | EXP MLB DEBUT: 2019 | H/W: 6-9 205 | FUT: #4 starter | 8D

Thrws R Age 23	Year	Lev	Team	W	L	Sv	IP	K	ERA	WHIP	BF/G	OBA	H%	S%	xERA	Ctl	Dom	Cmd	hr/9	BPV
2017 (8) Texas Christian																				
88-92 FB +++	2017	NCAA	Texas Christian	12	3	0	105	113	3.77	1.15	22.0	225	30	67	2.70	3.0	9.7	3.2	0.5	111
84-86 CT +++	2017	A-	Vermont	2	1	1	31	29	1.16	0.74	10.1	201	27	83	0.89	0.3	8.4	29.0	0.0	161
77-79 CB +++	2018	A+	Stockton	7	3	0	72	77	2.38	0.93	22.5	207	26	83	2.49	1.8	9.6	5.5	1.1	144
CU ++	2018	AA	Midland	4	4	0	67	63	3.49	1.31	23.1	256	31	77	3.90	3.1	8.5	2.7	0.9	87

Towering RHP who flashed durability and Dom upside in full-season debut. Big frame produces average low-90s FB that plays up with great extension toward plate. Blends in average mid-80s CT and CB with improving CU. Low-effort delivery from 3/4 slot required for solid Cmd ratios. Induces GBs at high rate with solid SwK ability.

Howard,Sam | SP | Colorado | EXP MLB DEBUT: 2018 | H/W: 6-3 170 | FUT: #4 starter | 7C

Thrws L Age 26	Year	Lev	Team	W	L	Sv	IP	K	ERA	WHIP	BF/G	OBA	H%	S%	xERA	Ctl	Dom	Cmd	hr/9	BPV
2014 (3) Georgia Southern	2016	AA	Hartford	5	6	0	90	67	4.00	1.56	24.7	308	35	78	5.47	2.8	6.7	2.4	1.1	63
91-94 FB ++++	2017	AA	Hartford	1	4	0	46	40	2.34	0.89	19.0	193	22	81	2.10	2.0	7.8	4.0	1.0	106
80-83 SL ++	2017	AAA	Albuquerque	4	4	0	81	64	3.89	1.42	22.9	264	32	73	4.05	3.7	7.1	1.9	0.7	47
CU +++	2018	AAA	Albuquerque	3	8	0	96	80	5.06	1.46	19.6	281	33	68	4.91	3.2	7.5	2.4	1.2	67
	2018	MLB	Colorado	0	0	0	4	1	2.25	2.00	4.8	307	33	88	5.57	6.8	2.3	0.3	0.0	-124

Finesse lefty struggled for most of the season, but did make his MLB debut. Average 90-93 mph sinking FB with arm-side run is his best weapon and does have good late action. SL is average and circle change can be plus at times, but lacks consistency. Not overpowering, but a consistent strike thrower with good deception and plenty of GB outs.

Howard,Spencer | SP | Philadelphia | EXP MLB DEBUT: 2020 | H/W: 6-3 200 | FUT: #3 starter | 8C

Thrws R Age 22	Year	Lev	Team	W	L	Sv	IP	K	ERA	WHIP	BF/G	OBA	H%	S%	xERA	Ctl	Dom	Cmd	hr/9	BPV
2017 (2) Cal Poly																				
93-97 FB ++++																				
85-90 SL ++++	2017	NCAA	Cal Poly	8	1	1	87	97	1.96	1.09	20.1	226	31	85	2.65	2.4	10.0	4.2	0.6	134
79-83 CU +++	2017	A-	Williamsport	1	1	0	28	40	4.48	1.42	13.2	217	36	65	2.77	5.8	12.8	2.2	0.0	93
76-78 CB ++	2018	A	Lakewood	9	8	0	112	147	3.78	1.26	19.9	242	36	70	3.13	3.2	11.8	3.7	0.5	144

Classic SP build with a clean delivery; he got stronger as the season went on and was holding mid-90s deep into games. Elevates a lively FB for swings/misses; hard SL has depth and plus potential. Big velo difference for CU, and even drops in CB for strikes. Release point can waver, which affects control. But mixes and moves.

Hudson,Bryan | SP | Chicago (N) | EXP MLB DEBUT: 2020 | H/W: 6-8 220 | FUT: #5 SP/swingman | 7D

Thrws L Age 21	Year	Lev	Team	W	L	Sv	IP	K	ERA	WHIP	BF/G	OBA	H%	S%	xERA	Ctl	Dom	Cmd	hr/9	BPV
2015 (3) HS (IL)																				
89-92 FB ++	2015	Rk	AZL Cubs	0	0	0	6	5	2.90	1.29	5.1	255	32	75	2.98	2.9	7.3	2.5	0.0	70
75-78 CB ++	2016	A-	Eugene	5	4	0	58	41	5.10	1.67	20.1	254	30	69	4.50	6.3	6.3	1.0	0.6	-39
78-80 CU +	2017	A	South Bend	9	3	0	124	81	3.92	1.45	22.1	268	30	74	4.25	3.8	5.9	1.6	0.7	22
	2018	A+	Myrtle Beach	6	11	0	113	78	4.70	1.42	20.8	242	29	65	3.43	4.6	6.2	1.3	0.3	5

Tall lefty uses his size to pitch downhill causing hitters to beat his FB into the ground; gave up just 4 HR in 113 IP. Inability to repeat mechanics and find the strike zone remain his downfall. CB flashes above-average but lacks consistent spin and depth and CU is below-average. A move to relief seems likely in the near future.

Hudson,Dakota | SP | St. Louis | EXP MLB DEBUT: 2018 | H/W: 6-4 185 | FUT: #3 starter | 8B

Thrws R Age 24	Year	Lev	Team	W	L	Sv	IP	K	ERA	WHIP	BF/G	OBA	H%	S%	xERA	Ctl	Dom	Cmd	hr/9	BPV
2016 (1) Mississippi St	2016	A+	Palm Beach	1	1	3	9	10	0.99	1.43	4.8	190	28	92	2.48	6.9	9.9	1.4	0.0	9
93-95 FB ++++	2017	AA	Springfield	9	4	0	114	77	2.53	1.27	25.9	257	30	81	3.33	2.7	6.1	2.3	0.4	55
87-91 SL +++	2017	AAA	Memphis	1	1	0	38	19	4.48	1.34	22.7	250	28	65	3.49	3.5	4.5	1.3	0.5	3
75-78 CB +++	2018	AAA	Memphis	13	3	0	111	87	2.51	1.30	24.1	254	32	79	3.08	3.1	7.0	2.3	0.1	62
80-82 CU ++	2018	MLB	St. Louis	4	1	0	27	19	2.66	1.37	4.4	199	25	78	2.47	6.0	6.3	1.1	0.0	-30

Strong-armed hurler had another dominant season and impressed in MLB debut. Doesn't blow hitters away despite a plus mid-90s heater and instead relies on late sink to induce weak contact. SL is second plus offering and CU continues to improve and average CB round out the arsenal. Could see a spike in Dom as he settles in.

Humphreys,Jordan | SP | New York (N) | EXP MLB DEBUT: 2021 | H/W: 6-1 190 | FUT: #4 starter | 8D

Thrws R Age 22	Year	Lev	Team	W	L	Sv	IP	K	ERA	WHIP	BF/G	OBA	H%	S%	xERA	Ctl	Dom	Cmd	hr/9	BPV
2015 (18) HS (FL)	2016	Rk	Kingsport	3	5	0	69	76	3.78	1.16	22.9	250	34	66	2.91	2.0	9.9	5.1	0.4	143
91-94 FB +++	2016	A-	Brooklyn	0	1	0	6	9	1.50	1.33	24.9	293	47	88	3.55	1.5	13.5	9.0	0.0	221
76-78 CB +++	2017	A	Columbia	10	1	0	69	80	1.43	0.72	22.3	174	25	81	0.76	1.2	10.4	8.9	0.3	174
83-85 SL ++	2017	A+	St. Lucie	0	0	0	11	3	4.09	1.82	25.5	354	36	79	6.66	2.5	2.5	1.0	0.8	-4
82-85 CU +++	2018		Did not pitch - injury																	

Had promising beginning to his pro career before being sidelined by Tommy John surgery at the end of the 2017 season. Missed 2018 but should be ready for Hi-A to start 2019. Sturdy, wide body with solid stuff and a simple delivery, he has done a good job avoiding walks at the lower levels. We will see how well his good command plays as he moves up.

Humphreys,Reid | RP | Colorado | EXP MLB DEBUT: 2019 | H/W: 6-1 201 | FUT: Closer | 8C

Thrws R Age 24	Year	Lev	Team	W	L	Sv	IP	K	ERA	WHIP	BF/G	OBA	H%	S%	xERA	Ctl	Dom	Cmd	hr/9	BPV
2016 (7) Mississippi St																				
95-99 FB ++++	2016	Rk	Grand Junction	1	0	0	10	9	3.56	1.58	4.9	279	36	75	4.03	4.5	8.0	1.8	0.0	42
88-91 CT +++	2017	A	Asheville	1	3	13	45	47	2.59	0.84	3.8	201	26	71	1.70	1.2	9.4	7.8	0.6	154
83-85 SL ++	2018	A+	Lancaster	2	0	22	34	51	1.85	1.03	3.7	186	32	82	1.64	3.4	13.5	3.9	0.3	168
CU ++	2018	AA	Hartford	0	1	4	5	7	3.46	1.92	3.5	170	28	80	3.49	12.1	12.1	1.0	0.0	-91

Converted to relief and had a breakout season, notching 26 saves in 28 attempts. Attacks hitters with a plus 95-99 mph 4-seam FB that gets on hitters quickly and allows him to dominate. Mixes in a plus CT, SL, and fringe CU. Control comes and goes, but gave up just 1 HR in 40 IP and has the stuff to close in the majors.

Irvin,Cole | SP | Philadelphia | EXP MLB DEBUT: 2019 | H/W: 6-4 180 | FUT: #5 SP/swingman | 7A

Thrws L Age 25	Year	Lev	Team	W	L	Sv	IP	K	ERA	WHIP	BF/G	OBA	H%	S%	xERA	Ctl	Dom	Cmd	hr/9	BPV
2016 (5) Oregon	2016	NCAA	Oregon	6	4	0	105	93	3.17	1.11	24.3	254	31	74	3.24	1.4	8.0	5.8	0.8	124
88-90 FB ++	2016	A-	Williamsport	5	1	0	45	37	1.99	0.97	17.1	220	27	81	2.10	1.6	7.4	4.6	0.4	108
85-88 CT +++	2017	A+	Clearwater	4	6	0	67	52	2.55	1.22	22.6	265	33	79	3.19	1.9	7.0	3.7	0.3	93
82-83 CU ++	2017	AA	Reading	5	3	0	84	66	4.07	1.14	25.6	233	26	69	3.52	2.6	7.1	2.8	1.3	76
73-76 CB ++	2018	AAA	Lehigh Valley	14	4	0	161	131	2.57	1.06	24.0	229	28	78	2.62	2.0	7.3	3.7	0.6	97

Simple mechanics with a bit of crossfire, he's around the zone and can manipulate. Only the CT is a MLB-average pitch; also throws a more traditional low-80s SL with more depth. Commandable array of offerings allows him to pitch backwards and keep hitters off balance, but no real "finisher." Durable, pitch-to-contact ground baller.

Irvin,Jake — SP — Washington

EXP MLB DEBUT: 2022 | H/W: 6-4 190 | FUT: #4 starter | 8D

Thrws R Age 22 — 2018 (4) Oklahoma

- 91-94 FB +++
- 81-84 SL ++
- CU ++

Year	Lev	Team	W	L	Sv	IP	K	ERA	WHIP	BF/G	OBA	H%	S%	xERA	Ctl	Dom	Cmd	hr/9	BPV
2018	NCAA	Oklahoma	6	2	0	95	115	3.41	1.08	23.2	219	30	73	2.93	2.7	10.9	4.1	1.0	142
2018	Rk	GCL Nationals	1	0	0	12	9	1.48	1.07	6.8	225	28	85	2.03	2.2	6.6	3.0	0.0	78
2018	A-	Auburn	0	0	0	8	6	2.25	1.25	8.1	210	27	80	2.30	4.5	6.8	1.5	0.0	18

A strong body and a clean, effortless arm action and delivery are the starting points. Fastball is in the low-90s that he commands well, slider has a short, cutter-like break and he has a feel for the change-up, but it's still a work in progress. Had a big strikeout rate in college, but it's less likely to transfer to the pros.

Ivey,Tyler — SP — Houston

EXP MLB DEBUT: 2020 | H/W: 6-4 200 | FUT: Middle reliever | 6B

Thrws R Age 22 — 2017 (3) Grayson CC

- 91-95 FB +++
- 75-78 CB ++++
- 81-83 CU ++
- 84-87 SL ++

Year	Lev	Team	W	L	Sv	IP	K	ERA	WHIP	BF/G	OBA	H%	S%	xERA	Ctl	Dom	Cmd	hr/9	BPV
2017	NCAA	Grayson CC	9	0	0	78	122	2.08	1.13	25.7	214	38	80	2.08	3.2	14.1	4.4	0.1	184
2017	Rk	GCL Astros	0	0	0	2	3	0.00	1.50	8.6	151	27	100	2.20	9.0	13.5	1.5	0.0	18
2017	A-	Tri City	0	3	0	36	41	5.98	1.47	14.1	287	39	57	4.31	3.0	10.2	3.4	0.5	121
2018	A	Quad Cities	1	3	2	41	53	3.50	1.07	17.8	237	35	67	2.54	1.7	11.6	6.6	0.4	179
2018	A+	Buies Creek	3	3	1	70	82	2.70	1.01	17.9	202	29	74	1.93	2.7	10.5	3.9	0.4	135

Ideal pitcher's frame. Mechanics feature significant effort, including head whack. Can run his heater up to 95 and complements it with a 12-to-6 curve. While both the change-up and slider are presently below-average, the change-up projects to average over time. His delivery presents challenges due to its herk-and-jerk, pace, and length in the back.

James,Josh — SP — Houston

EXP MLB DEBUT: 2018 | H/W: 6-3 200 | FUT: #3 starter | 9E

Thrws R Age 26 — 2014 (34) W Oklahoma St Coll

- 96-98 FB +++++
- 87-89 SL ++++
- 86-88 CU ++

Year	Lev	Team	W	L	Sv	IP	K	ERA	WHIP	BF/G	OBA	H%	S%	xERA	Ctl	Dom	Cmd	hr/9	BPV
2016	A+	Lancaster	9	5	1	110		4.82	1.45	20.5	279	37	68	4.53	3.3	9.9	3.0	0.9	108
2017	AA	Corpus Christi	4	8	3	76	72	4.38	1.46	15.5	269	35	67	3.70	3.8	8.5	2.3	0.1	69
2018	AA	Corpus Christi	0	0	1	21	38	2.55	1.27	14.5	221	42	81	2.81	4.2	16.1	3.8	0.4	194
2018	AAA	Fresno	6	4	0	92	133	3.42	1.10	21.2	193	30	71	2.38	3.8	13.0	3.4	0.8	149
2018	MLB	Houston	2	0	0	23	29	2.35	0.96	14.5	188	25	84	2.36	2.7	11.3	4.1	1.2	148

He burst onto the scene with an electric fastball that reached into the triple digits and a slider that consistently missed bats. Much of his value will depend on whether he sticks as a starter in the long-term. If he does, he can operate as a high-whiff mid-rotation arm. If he ends up in the bullpen he has the stuff to close.

Jarvis,Justin — SP — Milwaukee

EXP MLB DEBUT: 2022 | H/W: 6-2 168 | FUT: #4 starter | 8D

Thrws R Age 19 — 2018 (5) HS (NC)

- 88-92 FB +++
- 75-77 CB +++
- 83-84 CU +++

Year	Lev	Team	W	L	Sv	IP	K	ERA	WHIP	BF/G	OBA	H%	S%	xERA	Ctl	Dom	Cmd	hr/9	BPV
2018	Rk	AZL Brewers	1	2	0	19	18	6.63	1.47	8.2	309	38	54	5.10	1.9	8.5	4.5	0.9	120

Fifth-round pick who made pro debut in AZL this summer. Rail-thin build with room for added strength to lower half. Anywhere from 88-92 mph with FB; lacks life from high slot and hittable up in zone. CB has 12-to-6 shape and flashes above-average depth but backs up on him too much; CU is firm and inconsistent. A long-term project, but some upside.

Javier,Cristian — SP — Houston

EXP MLB DEBUT: 2021 | H/W: 6-1 170 | FUT: #5 SP/swingman | 7D

Thrws R Age 22 — 2015 FA (DR)

- 90-92 FB ++
- 78-81 SL +++
- 86-87 CU +++
- 71-74 CB ++

Year	Lev	Team	W	L	Sv	IP	K	ERA	WHIP	BF/G	OBA	H%	S%	xERA	Ctl	Dom	Cmd	hr/9	BPV
2017	A-	Tri City	0	0	0	16	24	2.78	1.23	16.4	194	34	75	2.01	5.0	13.3	2.7	0.0	123
2017	A	Quad Cities	2	0	1	37	47	2.42	1.08	18.1	192	28	81	2.29	3.6	11.4	3.1	0.7	125
2017	A+	Buies Creek	1	0	0	5	9	0.00	0.96	9.8	120	26	100	0.52	5.2	15.6	3.0	0.0	158
2018	A	Quad Cities	2	2	1	49	80	1.83	1.04	17.2	168	30	85	1.73	4.2	14.7	3.5	0.5	168
2018	A+	Buies Creek	5	4	0	60	66	3.44	1.18	17.2	206	27	74	2.89	4.0	9.9	2.4	0.9	87

Crafty righty isn't a typical pitcher profile, but it applies here. He doesn't boast a plus offering, but he misses the fat parts of bats and has shown steady improvement in his change-up, which is now an average pitch. He's got feel on the mound and it should get him to the majors, but expect him to miss fewer bats in the upper minors.

Jax,Griffin — SP — Minnesota

EXP MLB DEBUT: 2020 | H/W: 6-1 190 | FUT: #4 starter | 7D

Thrws R Age 24 — 2016 (3) Air Force

- 90-93 FB +++
- 83-86 SL ++
- 83-84 CU +++

Year	Lev	Team	W	L	Sv	IP	K	ERA	WHIP	BF/G	OBA	H%	S%	xERA	Ctl	Dom	Cmd	hr/9	BPV
2016	NCAA	Air Force	9	2	0	105	90	2.06	1.08	27.4	241	30	82	2.58	1.7	7.7	4.5	0.3	110
2016	Rk	Elizabethton	0	1	0	8	8	4.39	1.95	9.8	393	46	86	8.98	1.1	8.8	8.0	2.2	146
2017	Rk	Elizabethton	0	1	0	4	7	4.29	1.43	17.8	336	51	80	6.49	0.0	15.0		2.1	288
2017	A	Cedar Rapids	2	1	0	26	13	2.41	1.00	24.9	205	23	76	1.95	2.4	4.5	1.9	0.3	34
2018	A+	Fort Myers	3	4	0	87	66	3.72	1.24	23.6	274	33	69	3.41	1.5	6.8	4.4	0.3	99

Athletic, 3/4s RHP has missed development time due to Air Force commitment. 3-pitch pitcher with clean delivery. Workhorse is 2-seam FB with moderate arm-side break. Sticks in lower quadrant, commanded well to both sides of plate. CU is late fading variety. Plays up due to ability to repeat FB delivery and arm-speed. SL lacks deceptive plane.

Jay,Tyler — RP — Minnesota

EXP MLB DEBUT: 2019 | H/W: 6-1 170 | FUT: Middle reliever | 6B

Thrws L Age 24 — 2015 (1) Illinois

- 90-93 FB +++
- 82-84 SL +++
- 76-78 CB ++
- 81-83 CU ++

Year	Lev	Team	W	L	Sv	IP	K	ERA	WHIP	BF/G	OBA	H%	S%	xERA	Ctl	Dom	Cmd	hr/9	BPV
2016	AA	Chattanooga	0	0	0	14	9	5.79	1.29	11.5	248	27	56	4.09	3.2	5.8	1.8	1.3	35
2017	Rk	GCL Twins	0	0	0	3	7	5.63	2.19	5.3	399	71	83	10.17	2.8	19.7	7.0	2.8	296
2017	A+	Fort Myers	3	0	0	6	10	1.50	0.67	7.0	191	37	75	0.53	0.0	15.0		0.0	288
2017	AA	Chattanooga	0	0	0	2	2	4.50	2.00	4.8	151	0	100	7.74	13.5	9.0	0.7	4.5	-185
2018	AA	Chattanooga	4	5	2	59	49	4.26	1.59	6.9	307	36	76	5.48	3.0	7.4	2.5	1.1	70

Former 1st round pick has struggled with injuries and ineffectiveness since debut. 4-pitch pitcher, even in relief. Struggles commanding 2-seam FB, especially to inside to RHH. Solid movement in lower quadrant of zone. Best pitch is a borderline-plus low 80s SL with sweep. Loopy CB and CU with minimal fade round out arsenal.

Jefferies,Daulton — SP — Oakland

EXP MLB DEBUT: 2020 | H/W: 6-0 165 | FUT: #4 starter | 8D

Thrws R Age 23 — 2016 (1) California

- 90-93 FB +++
- 80-82 SL +++
- 82-84 CU ++++

Year	Lev	Team	W	L	Sv	IP	K	ERA	WHIP	BF/G	OBA	H%	S%	xERA	Ctl	Dom	Cmd	hr/9	BPV
2016	NCAA	California	7	0	0	50	53	1.08	0.84	22.9	194	25	95	1.73	1.4	9.5	6.6	0.7	151
2016	Rk	AZL Athletics	0	0	0	11	17	2.43	1.17	8.9	260	43	77	2.67	1.6	13.8	8.5	0.0	222
2017	A+	Stockton	0	0	0	7	6	2.57	1.14	13.9	262	34	75	2.69	1.3	7.7	6.0	0.0	122
2018	Rk	AZL Athletics	0	0	0	2	5	0.00	0.50	6.6	151	61	100		0.0	22.5		0.0	423

Lean, athletic RH who has missed significant time post Tommy John surgery in three pro seasons. Owns plus command of three above-average pitches including low-90s FB that he manipulates. Replicates arm speed and delivery well on plus fading CU for whiffs and owns solid-average two-plane SL. Will need to add strength to frame if he remains an SP.

Jennings,Steven — SP — Pittsburgh

EXP MLB DEBUT: 2023 | H/W: 6-2 180 | FUT: #5 SP/swingman | 7C

Thrws R Age 20 — 2017 (2) HS (TN)

- 90-92 FB +++
- 75-77 CB +++
- 84-86 SL ++
- 83-84 CU +++

Year	Lev	Team	W	L	Sv	IP	K	ERA	WHIP	BF/G	OBA	H%	S%	xERA	Ctl	Dom	Cmd	hr/9	BPV
2017	Rk	GCL Pirates	0	2	0	26	13	4.14	1.57	11.5	296	32	74	4.95	3.4	4.5	1.3	0.7	6
2018	Rk	Bristol	3	4	0	65	53	4.84	1.46	21.4	270	33	67	4.26	3.7	7.3	2.0	0.7	49

Drafted in the secound round in 2017 out of HS, he is still a long way away. Results at the low levels of pro ball have been uninspiring, but he is still young, athletic and projectable. Conventional four-pitch mix, but concern that none are plus. Good plane to upright delivery but gets across body some. Patience is needed here.

Jewell,Jake — RP — Los Angeles (A)

EXP MLB DEBUT: 2018 | H/W: 6-3 220 | FUT: Middle reliever | 7C

Thrws R Age 25 — 2014 (5) NE Oklahoma A&M

- 91-96 FB +++
- 83-86 SL +++
- 75-77 CU ++

Year	Lev	Team	W	L	Sv	IP	K	ERA	WHIP	BF/G	OBA	H%	S%	xERA	Ctl	Dom	Cmd	hr/9	BPV
2017	A+	Inland Empire	0	1	0	16	15	2.25	0.88	19.7	196	25	77	1.70	1.7	8.4	5.0	0.6	124
2017	AA	Mobile	7	8	0	124	81	4.86	1.43	22.0	280	31	67	4.62	3.0	5.9	2.0	1.0	43
2018	AA	Mobile	1	0	2	13	11	2.08	1.31	7.7	290	35	88	4.16	1.4	7.6	5.5	0.7	118
2018	AAA	Salt Lake	2	4	3	25	24	3.60	1.60	5.8	246	31	79	4.30	6.1	8.6	1.4	0.7	8
2018	MLB	LA Angels	0	1	0	2	1	9.00	1.50	2.9	262	30	33	3.62	4.5	4.5	1.0	0.0	-23

Durable starter-turned-reliever who impressed the Angels enough to earn his MLB debut in 2018. Moved to full time relief in 2018, working a sound pitch mix that can lack consistency on occasion. Four-seam fastball has reached 97 mph in front of slider that has flashed plus. Needing third pitch and command improvement.

Johnson,Tyler — RP — Chicago (A)

EXP MLB DEBUT: 2020 | H/W: 6-2 180 | FUT: Middle reliever | 6C

Thrws R Age 23 — 2017 (5) South Carolina

- 93-97 FB ++++
- 82-85 SL +++
- CU ++

Year	Lev	Team	W	L	Sv	IP	K	ERA	WHIP	BF/G	OBA	H%	S%	xERA	Ctl	Dom	Cmd	hr/9	BPV
2017	NCAA	South Carolina	1	2	10	26	40	2.41	1.34	5.7	214	37	80	2.51	5.2	13.8	2.7	0.0	127
2017	Rk	Great Falls	1	1	0	10	16	0.90	1.40	5.3	199	36	93	2.47	6.3	14.4	2.3	0.0	107
2017	A	Kannapolis	0	0	2	15	21	5.92	2.04	5.3	307	46	68	5.56	7.1	12.4	1.8	0.0	50
2018	A	Kannapolis	5	0	7	27	46	1.33	0.96	5.1	174	33	88	1.39	3.3	15.3	4.6	0.3	204
2018	A+	Winston-Salem	4	0	7	31	43	1.45	0.81	5.4	179	29	83	1.04	1.7	12.5	7.2	0.3	196

Hard-throwing, 3/4s RHP dominated lower minors in relief. Moderate-effort, cross-fire deliver with average extension. Mid-90s FB is thrown at a hitter-friendly plane with little-to-no movement. SL has 2-plane break. Will need to tighten up to keep hitters off FB. CU used to keep LHH off FB.

Johnston,Kyle — SP — Washington

EXP MLB DEBUT: 2022 | H/W: 6-0 202 | FUT: #5 SP/swingman | 7C

Thrws R Age 22
2017 (6) Texas

Velo	Pitch	Grade
92-94	FB	+++
82-84	SL	++
85-87	CU	+

Year	Lev	Team	W	L	Sv	IP	K	ERA	WHIP	BF/G	OBA	H%	S%	xERA	Ctl	Dom	Cmd	hr/9	BPV
2017	NCAA	Texas	3	2	2	73	52	3.57	1.40	18.1	234	29	72	3.09	4.8	6.4	1.3	0.1	4
2017	Rk	GCL Nationals	0	0	0	2	1	0.00	1.00	7.6	0	0	100		9.0	4.5	0.5	0.0	-144
2017	A-	Auburn	0	2	0	44	32	3.46	1.45	13.5	248	30	76	3.66	4.7	6.5	1.4	0.4	9
2018	A	Hagerstown	2	3	2	55	59	3.43	1.36	12.8	243	33	75	3.43	4.1	9.6	2.4	0.5	81
2018	A+	Potomac	5	2	0	47	37	4.97	1.46	20.2	236	28	66	3.88	5.4	7.1	1.3	0.8	1

Thickish build with strong lower half, his delivery employs lots of moving parts. This adds to deception but seem to adversely affect control. Can touch 95 early, but velo fades through his start. His SL flashes some sharpness, so does have a two-pitch reliever fallback. If CU develops, and/or control improves, could be a back-end starter.

Jones,Connor — SP — St. Louis

EXP MLB DEBUT: 2019 | H/W: 6-2 200 | FUT: #4 starter | 7D

Thrws R Age 24
2016 (2) Virginia

Velo	Pitch	Grade
90-93	FB	+++
80-83	SL	+++
	CB	+
	CU	++

Year	Lev	Team	W	L	Sv	IP	K	ERA	WHIP	BF/G	OBA	H%	S%	xERA	Ctl	Dom	Cmd	hr/9	BPV
2016	A-	State College	0	0	1	10	8	4.41	1.67	6.5	343	42	71	5.26	1.8	7.1	4.0	0.0	97
2017	A+	Palm Beach	8	5	1	113	76	3.98	1.49	20.3	273	33	72	3.98	3.9	6.0	1.6	0.2	22
2017	AA	Springfield	1	0	0	6	2	2.90	1.45	26.5	255	24	88	4.79	4.4	2.9	0.7	1.5	-47
2018	AA	Springfield	5	5	0	94	66	3.82	1.56	18.8	265	32	75	4.16	4.9	6.3	1.3	0.4	0
2018	AAA	Memphis	1	0	0	15	16	6.56	2.25	19.1	320	42	70	6.89	8.3	9.5	1.1	0.6	-36

Stocky, back-end starter uses a plus low-90s FB that has nasty late sink to get hitters to beat the ball into the ground (69% GB rate). Slurvy SL gets some swing and misses, but lacks shape and depth and CU and CB are solid average. Lacks a true out pitch and struggles with control led to a combined .272 OppBA and a 1.65 WHIP.

Kaprielian,James — SP — Oakland

EXP MLB DEBUT: 2020 | H/W: 6-3 190 | FUT: Setup reliever | 9E

Thrws R Age 25
2015 (1) UCLA

Velo	Pitch	Grade
94-97	FB	++++
84-86	SL	++++
79-82	CB	+++
86-88	CU	++++

Year	Lev	Team	W	L	Sv	IP	K	ERA	WHIP	BF/G	OBA	H%	S%	xERA	Ctl	Dom	Cmd	hr/9	BPV
2015	Rk	GCL Yankees 2	0	0	0	2	2	12.86	1.90	5.0	252	34	25	4.47	8.6	8.6	1.0	0.0	-59
2015	A-	Staten Island	0	1	0	9	12	2.00	1.11	11.8	240	37	80	2.27	2.0	12.0	6.0	0.0	180
2016	A+	Tampa	2	1	0	18	22	1.50	0.61	20.6	136	20	80	0.31	1.5	11.0	7.3	0.5	176
2017		Did not pitch - injury																	
2018		Did not pitch - injury																	

Athletic, strong RH who hasn't pitched since 2016 AFL due to various arm injuries. Will flash three potential plus offerings when he's on, including explosive mid-90s FB, tight SL, plus fading CU along with useable CB. Pounds zone efficiently and projects to have average command. Big-time upside arm who could be ultimately destined for the bullpen.

Kasowski,Marshall — RP — Los Angeles (N)

EXP MLB DEBUT: 2019 | H/W: 6-3 220 | FUT: Setup reliever | 7B

Thrws R Age 24
2017 (13) Houston

Velo	Pitch	Grade
93-97	FB	++++
73-75	CB	++
	CU	+

Year	Lev	Team	W	L	Sv	IP	K	ERA	WHIP	BF/G	OBA	H%	S%	xERA	Ctl	Dom	Cmd	hr/9	BPV
2017	Rk	AZL Dodgers	0	0	0	5	9	0.00	0.78	4.6	65	16	100		5.3	15.9	3.0	0.0	161
2017	A	Great Lakes	1	1	0	6	6	6.00	3.17	7.2	371	45	83	10.96	13.5	9.0	0.7	1.5	-185
2018	A	Great Lakes	0	1	0	28	49	2.57	1.11	7.3	141	29	77	1.40	5.8	15.8	2.7	0.3	145
2018	A+	Rancho Cuca	2	0	4	23	44	1.16	0.91	5.4	133	30	90	0.85	4.3	17.1	4.0	0.4	210
2018	AA	Tulsa	0	0	1	13	18	2.77	1.23	5.3	160	21	86	2.94	6.2	12.5	2.0	1.4	74

Late developing lefty reliever absolutely dominated at three levels. Plus, plus FB sits at 92-97 mph. High spin rate and over-the-top delivery allows FB to hold its plane and provides solid deception. Mixes in fringe 12-to-6 CB and a below-average CU. Limited opposing batters to a .136 OppBA.

Kay,Anthony — SP — New York (N)

EXP MLB DEBUT: 2020 | H/W: 6-0 218 | FUT: Setup reliever | 8D

Thrws L Age 24
2016 (1) Connecticut

Velo	Pitch	Grade
90-95	FB	+++
74-77	CB	+++
79-83	CU	++

Year	Lev	Team	W	L	Sv	IP	K	ERA	WHIP	BF/G	OBA	H%	S%	xERA	Ctl	Dom	Cmd	hr/9	BPV
2017		Did not pitch - injury																	
2018	A	Columbia	4	4	0	69	78	4.56	1.37	22.3	273	36	67	4.13	2.9	10.2	3.5	0.8	123
2018	A+	St. Lucie	3	7	0	53	45	3.90	1.47	22.8	254	32	71	3.56	4.6	7.6	1.7	0.2	32

Aggressive lefty who has succeeded some as a starter at lower levels but may have to move to the pen to find MLB success. More of a power guy than a finesse guy. Really loves to pitch in with FB. CB shows some potential but is inconsistent. CU is firm and deceptive at times, but not a feel pitch. Stuff and demeanor should play well in relief role.

Keller,Mitch — SP — Pittsburgh

EXP MLB DEBUT: 2019 | H/W: 6-3 195 | FUT: #3 starter | 8B

Thrws R Age 23
2014 (2) HS (IA)

Velo	Pitch	Grade
92-96	FB	++++
80-82	CB	+++
86-89	CU	++

Year	Lev	Team	W	L	Sv	IP	K	ERA	WHIP	BF/G	OBA	H%	S%	xERA	Ctl	Dom	Cmd	hr/9	BPV
2017	A+	Bradenton	6	3	0	77	64	3.15	1.00	19.6	208	25	69	2.18	2.3	7.5	3.2	0.6	89
2017	AA	Altoona	2	2	0	34	45	3.16	1.05	22.1	206	31	71	2.20	2.9	11.8	4.1	0.5	153
2018	A+	Bradenton	0	0	0	4	2	2.25	2.00	19.3	383	43	88	6.87	2.3	4.5	2.0	0.0	38
2018	AA	Altoona	9	2	0	86	76	2.72	1.12	24.2	209	26	79	2.63	3.3	8.0	2.4	0.7	71
2018	AAA	Indianapolis	3	2	0	52	57	4.84	1.55	22.8	287	38	68	4.54	3.8	9.8	2.6	0.5	93

Tall machine of a pitcher; can pound zone from a plus plane with hard FB. Commands it well to both sides, but lacks movement. CB more of a hard slurve—can be nasty but it's not a great feel pitch. CU hard and deceptive but also not a feel pitch. Struggles to throw offspeed when behind in the count. Tough and competitive; durable.

Kelly,Levi — SP — Arizona

EXP MLB DEBUT: 2022 | H/W: 6-2 205 | FUT: #4 starter | 7C

Thrws R Age 19
2018 (8) HS (FL)

Velo	Pitch	Grade
92-94	FB	+++
	SL	+++
	CU	++

Year	Lev	Team	W	L	Sv	IP	K	ERA	WHIP	BF/G	OBA	H%	S%	xERA	Ctl	Dom	Cmd	hr/9	BPV
2018	Rk	AZL DBacks	0	0	0	6	6	0.00	0.83	5.5	151	22	100	0.57	3.0	9.0	3.0	0.0	99

Athletic, medium-framed RHP who signed for above-slot value in eighth round last summer. FB sits in low-90s and will touch 95 mph with moderate arm-side movement. Shows some feel for vertical SL that projects as average pitch. Will need to throw CU more in pro ranks to remain SP. Room to add some velo as he adds mass to leaner frame.

Kent,Matt — SP — Boston

EXP MLB DEBUT: 2019 | H/W: 6-0 180 | FUT: #4 starter | 7C

Thrws L Age 26
2015 (13) Texas A&M

Velo	Pitch	Grade
85-89	FB	++
75-78	CB	+++
78-82	SL	+++
80-82	CU	++++

Year	Lev	Team	W	L	Sv	IP	K	ERA	WHIP	BF/G	OBA	H%	S%	xERA	Ctl	Dom	Cmd	hr/9	BPV
2016	A	Greenville	0	0	0	12	5	1.50	1.08	23.4	210	24	85	1.91	3.0	3.8	1.3	0.0	5
2016	A+	Salem	10	7	0	156	120	3.69	1.31	24.8	280	34	70	3.58	1.9	6.9	3.6	0.2	91
2017	A+	Salem	7	7	0	164	142	4.23	1.37	24.5	287	35	69	4.22	2.1	7.8	3.7	0.7	102
2018	AA	Portland	11	8	0	143	123	3.58	1.24	21.5	262	32	73	3.71	2.2	7.7	3.5	0.8	98
2018	AAA	Pawtucket	0	0	0	5	6	7.06	1.57	22.4	327	46	50	4.72	1.8	10.6	6.0	0.0	161

Overachieving lefty. Resembles Tom Milone but has a better arsenal and better command. Actually throws as many as seven pitches, including an occasional 60-mph eephus, from a couple of different slots. But does it consistently well. Smart and competitive, he basically is doing all he can to make his limited physical skills play.

Kilkenny,Mitchell — SP — Colorado

EXP MLB DEBUT: 2022 | H/W: 6-5 210 | FUT: #4 starter | 7D

Thrws R Age 22
2018 (2) Texas A&M

Velo	Pitch	Grade
91-94	FB	++
	SL	++
	CU	++

Year	Lev	Team	W	L	Sv	IP	K	ERA	WHIP	BF/G	OBA	H%	S%	xERA	Ctl	Dom	Cmd	hr/9	BPV
2018		Did not pitch - injury																	

Hard-throwing collegiate RHP had Tommy Jphn surgery in May 2018 and will have to wait until 2020 to make his pro debut. Prior to the injury he had an SEC-best 2.20 ERA. FB sits at 91-94 and is backed by an average hard SL and CU that shows late sink and fade. Profiles as a back-end starter once healthy, but it will be a long road to the majors.

Kilome,Franklyn — SP — New York (N)

EXP MLB DEBUT: 2021 | H/W: 6-6 175 | FUT: Setup reliever | 7C

Thrws R Age 23
2014 FA (DR)

Velo	Pitch	Grade
92-96	FB	++++
92-86	SL	+++
82-85	CU	++

Year	Lev	Team	W	L	Sv	IP	K	ERA	WHIP	BF/G	OBA	H%	S%	xERA	Ctl	Dom	Cmd	hr/9	BPV
2016	A	Lakewood	5	8	0	114	130	3.86	1.43	21.1	260	36	73	3.80	3.9	10.2	2.6	0.5	96
2017	A+	Clearwater	6	4	0	97	83	2.60	1.37	21.4	260	32	82	3.67	3.4	7.7	2.2	0.5	64
2017	AA	Reading	1	3	0	29	20	3.70	1.37	24.5	233	27	74	3.47	4.6	6.2	1.3	0.6	4
2018	AA	Reading	4	6	0	102	83	4.24	1.44	22.9	250	30	71	3.87	4.5	7.3	1.6	0.6	28
2018	AA	Binghamton	4	9	0	140	125	4.18	1.34	22.4	243	30	69	3.55	3.9	8.0	2.0	0.6	57

Acquired from the Phillies at mid-season, the long righty has always had potential, but underwent Tommy John surgery, so will probably be out until 2020. Groomed to start, he has always lacked plus feel for his offspeed, and has struggled to find something consistent to go with his easy, plus FB. Part of his problem is an awkward arm action.

King,Michael — SP — New York (A)

EXP MLB DEBUT: 2019 | H/W: 6-3 204 | FUT: #4 starter | 7A

Thrws R Age 23
2016 (12) Boston College

Velo	Pitch	Grade
91-94	FB	++++
87-88	CT	+++
81-83	SL	++
82-85	CU	+++

Year	Lev	Team	W	L	Sv	IP	K	ERA	WHIP	BF/G	OBA	H%	S%	xERA	Ctl	Dom	Cmd	hr/9	BPV
2016	A	Greensboro	0	0	0	4	2	0.00	1.22	16.6	257	29	100	2.85	2.2	4.4	2.0	0.0	38
2017	A	Greensboro	11	9	0	149	106	3.14	1.09	22.4	251	29	74	3.21	1.3	6.4	5.0	0.8	99
2018	A+	Tampa	1	3	0	40	45	1.80	1.07	22.3	226	32	83	2.23	2.2	10.1	4.5	0.2	139
2018	AA	Trenton	6	2	0	82	76	2.09	0.95	25.8	219	28	80	2.06	1.4	8.3	5.8	0.4	130
2018	AAA	Scranton/WB	4	0	0	39	31	1.15	0.67	22.7	154	18	91	0.85	1.4	7.2	5.2	0.7	109

Physically mature, command/control RHP is knocking on MLB door. Easy, repeatable 3/4s cross-armed delivery utilizes his solid base. Best pitch is 2-seam FB with plus movement and command. Mixes above-average CT in to deviate off FB. SL lacks quality movement but deceptive due to plane. Fading CU average pitch.

Kline,Branden
RP | **Baltimore** | EXP MLB DEBUT: 2019 | H/W: 6-3 185 | FUT: Setup reliever | **7C**

Thrws R Age 27
2012 (2) Virginia

Velo	Pitch	Grade
95-98	FB	++++
85-87	SL	+++

Year	Lev	Team	W	L	Sv	IP	K	ERA	WHIP	BF/G	OBA	H%	S%	xERA	Ctl	Dom	Cmd	hr/9	BPV
2015	AA	Bowie	3	3	0	39	27	3.68	1.38	20.5	241	27	76	3.89	4.4	6.2	1.4	0.9	12
2016		Did not pitch - injury																	
2017		Did not pitch - injury																	
2018	A+	Frederick	1	0	2	20	23	1.34	1.14	6.7	260	37	87	2.63	1.3	10.2	7.7	0.0	166
2018	AA	Bowie	4	4	15	45	48	1.80	1.04	5.4	201	27	86	2.22	3.0	9.6	3.2	0.6	110

Athletic RHP made successful transition to pen after 2 year absence due to elbow injury. Achieves solid extension utilizing 3/4s crossfire delivery. Limits hard contact while increasing Dom out of pen. Ditched CU in relief. Now 2-pitch pitcher: 2-seam FB overpowers with solid arm-side run, SL is firmer with tight 2-plane break.

Kloffenstein,Adam
SP | **Toronto** | EXP MLB DEBUT: 2023 | H/W: 6-5 243 | FUT: #3 starter | **7D**

Thrws R Age 18
2018 (3) HS (TX)

Velo	Pitch	Grade
88-93	FB	+++
80-83	SL	++
76-78	CB	++
80-83	CU	+++

Year	Lev	Team	W	L	Sv	IP	K	ERA	WHIP	BF/G	OBA	H%	S%	xERA	Ctl	Dom	Cmd	hr/9	BPV

Tall, sturdy hurler logged just 2 IP in his pro debut due to heavy use in HS. Solid 4-pitch mix highlighted by plus low-90s FB that has good late sink and tops at 96 mph. CU flashes as plus with good late fade and sink and SL and CB are both above-average. If CU and SL continue to improve he has the size to be a workhorse mid-rotation starter.

Knight,Blaine
SP | **Baltimore** | EXP MLB DEBUT: 2021 | H/W: 6-3 165 | FUT: #3 starter | **8C**

Thrws R Age 22
2018 (3) Arkansas

Velo	Pitch	Grade
90-95	FB	++++
81-84	SL	++++
72-76	CB	++
80-82	CU	+++

Year	Lev	Team	W	L	Sv	IP	K	ERA	WHIP	BF/G	OBA	H%	S%	xERA	Ctl	Dom	Cmd	hr/9	BPV
2018	NCAA	Arkansas	14	0	0	112	102	2.81	1.08	23.0	233	27	83	3.50	2.0	8.2	4.1	1.4	111
2018	A-	Aberdeen	0	1	0	10	8	2.67	1.58	11.1	313	37	87	5.41	2.7	7.1	2.7	0.9	74

Lean, athletic power RH with repeatable 3/4s delivery and good extension. Velocity product of arm speed and lower half. Four-pitch pitcher. Commands 2-seam FB with solid bore to both sides. SL potentially best pitch with tight, two-plane break. CB slurvy, lacks finish. Has feel for CU with late fade, also lacks finish.

Kopech,Michael
SP | **Chicago (A)** | EXP MLB DEBUT: 2018 | H/W: 6-3 195 | FUT: #1 starter | **9C**

Thrws R Age 22
2014 (1) HS (TX)

Velo	Pitch	Grade
95-98	FB	+++++
87-90	SL	++++
81-83	CB	++
88-91	CU	+++

Year	Lev	Team	W	L	Sv	IP	K	ERA	WHIP	BF/G	OBA	H%	S%	xERA	Ctl	Dom	Cmd	hr/9	BPV
2016	A+	Salem	4	1	0	52	82	2.25	1.04	18.2	146	27	77	1.14	5.0	14.2	2.8	0.2	138
2017	AA	Birmingham	8	7	0	119	155	2.87	1.15	21.5	187	28	76	2.15	4.5	11.7	2.6	0.5	106
2017	AAA	Charlotte	1	1	0	15	17	3.00	1.33	20.8	262	37	75	3.14	3.0	10.2	3.4	0.0	121
2018	AAA	Charlotte	7	7	0	126	170	3.71	1.28	21.5	221	33	72	3.06	4.3	12.1	2.8	0.6	121
2018	MLB	Chi White Sox	1	1	0	14	15	5.11	1.56	15.4	335	39	78	7.23	1.3	9.6	7.5	2.6	156

Hard-throwing, athletic 3/4 slot RHP who made four MLB starts before Tommy John surgery. Backed off FB velocity and improved command in process. FB still explosive; tight spinning SL is best secondary with 2-plane movement and late bite. Fading CU continues to improve, likely an above-average offering. Added CB to change eye levels of hitters.

Kowar,Jackson
SP | **Kansas City** | EXP MLB DEBUT: 2020 | H/W: 6-4 170 | FUT: #3 starter | **8D**

Thrws R Age 22
2018 (1) Florida

Velo	Pitch	Grade
92-94	FB	++++
74-78	CB	++
84-85	CU	++++

Year	Lev	Team	W	L	Sv	IP	K	ERA	WHIP	BF/G	OBA	H%	S%	xERA	Ctl	Dom	Cmd	hr/9	BPV
2018	NCAA	Florida	10	5	0	112	115	3.05	1.28	25.6	242	31	79	3.52	3.5	9.2	2.7	0.8	91
2018	A	Lexington	0	1	0	26	22	3.45	1.19	11.6	205	25	72	2.73	4.1	7.6	1.8	0.7	43

Long, lean RHP made successful pro debut. Easy, cross-armed 3/4s delivery with ideal physical frame to grow. Commands heavy two-seam FB with arm-side bore well, making it hard to elevate. CU is a plus offering with late fading action and velocity separation that mimicks FB delivery. Lack of a quality breaking ball hurts the package.

Kranick,Max
SP | **Pittsburgh** | EXP MLB DEBUT: 2021 | H/W: 6-3 175 | FUT: Middle reliever | **6C**

Thrws R Age 21
2016 (11) HS (PA)

Velo	Pitch	Grade
89-92	FB	+++
74-80	CB	++
80-82	CU	+++

Year	Lev	Team	W	L	Sv	IP	K	ERA	WHIP	BF/G	OBA	H%	S%	xERA	Ctl	Dom	Cmd	hr/9	BPV
2016	Rk	GCL Pirates	1	2	0	33	21	2.45	1.06	14.3	249	29	76	2.58	1.1	5.7	5.3	0.3	91
2017	Rk	GCL Pirates	0	0	0	12	9	0.00	1.31	16.8	259	32	100	3.08	3.0	6.6	2.3	0.0	58
2017	Rk	Bristol	1	0	0	11	9	2.41	1.07	21.8	240	28	82	2.98	1.6	7.2	4.5	0.8	105
2018	A	West Virginia	4	5	1	78	77	3.81	1.15	18.2	247	31	69	3.26	2.1	8.9	4.3	0.8	122

Deceptive strike-thrower with mediocre stuff. Best bet would be to go to bullpen and see if stuff plays up. Hides ball some with compact arm action. CB is a bit of soft slurve. Avoided walks at Low A, but will need do more, show more in the future.

Kremer,Dean
SP | **Baltimore** | EXP MLB DEBUT: 2019 | H/W: 6-2 185 | FUT: #4 starter | **7C**

Thrws R Age 23
2016 (14) San Joaquin Delta Coll

Velo	Pitch	Grade
88-91	FB	+++
72-77	CB	+++
80-82	CU	+++

Year	Lev	Team	W	L	Sv	IP	K	ERA	WHIP	BF/G	OBA	H%	S%	xERA	Ctl	Dom	Cmd	hr/9	BPV
2017	A+	Rancho Cuca	1	4	3	80	96	5.18	1.50	10.5	276	38	65	4.39	3.8	10.8	2.8	0.7	109
2018	A+	Rancho Cuca	5	3	0	79	114	3.30	1.18	19.7	231	36	74	3.07	3.0	13.0	4.4	0.8	172
2018	AA	Tulsa	1	0	0	7	11	0.00	0.86	25.7	132	26	100	0.39	3.9	14.1	3.7	0.0	168
2018	AA	Bowie	4	2	0	45	53	2.59	1.22	22.8	230	32	81	3.00	3.4	10.6	3.1	0.6	117

Long, athletic RHP acquired in mid-season trade from LA. Repeatable 3/4s, cross-armed delivery with solid extension, utilizing height. Solid, unspectacular profile. Solid 2-seam FB. Commands well to corners but a bit wild in zone. Average CB and CU play up due to solid command. High K% likely unsustainable in MLB due to stuff limitations.

Kyle,Cody
SP | **Texas** | EXP MLB DEBUT: 2020 | H/W: 6-7 245 | FUT: #4 starter | **8E**

Thrws R Age 24
2016 (6) Kentucky

Velo	Pitch	Grade
92-96	FB	++++
80-82	CB	+++
82-83	SL	++
83-85	CU	++

Year	Lev	Team	W	L	Sv	IP	K	ERA	WHIP	BF/G	OBA	H%	S%	xERA	Ctl	Dom	Cmd	hr/9	BPV
2016	NCAA	Kentucky	6	2	0	83	75	3.36	1.30	24.5	250	32	73	3.22	3.2	8.1	2.5	0.3	76
2016	A-	Spokane	2	5	0	47	53	5.16	1.46	16.8	297	39	65	4.70	2.5	10.1	4.1	0.8	133
2017	A	Hickory	6	6	0	95	101	2.84	1.16	21.0	223	30	75	2.55	3.1	9.6	3.1	0.4	106
2017	A+	Down East	3	0	0	30	35	2.09	1.16	24.0	227	33	80	2.24	3.0	10.4	3.5	0.0	125
2018	Rk	AZL Rangers	0	0	0	5	9	0.00	0.60	8.6	124	28	100		1.8	16.2	9.0	0.0	261

Lost 2018 to Tommy John surgery just as he was nearing the high minors. Huge frame built for innings and power; with health, commands a plus FB down in the zone as his best pitch. CB has most promise of secondaries. Still a starter's package, but will be eased back and has additional risk attached.

Lacy,Rollie
SP | **Tampa Bay** | EXP MLB DEBUT: 2020 | H/W: 6-3 185 | FUT: #5 SP/swingman | **7C**

Thrws R Age 23
2017 (11) Creighton

Velo	Pitch	Grade
89-91	FB	+++
80-82	SL	+++
81-84	CU	++

Year	Lev	Team	W	L	Sv	IP	K	ERA	WHIP	BF/G	OBA	H%	S%	xERA	Ctl	Dom	Cmd	hr/9	BPV
2017	Rk	AZL Cubs	1	1	1	19	17	0.94	0.78	8.6	194	24	93	1.36	0.9	8.0	8.5	0.5	136
2017	A-	Eugene	0	2	1	9	10	5.87	1.41	13.0	298	41	54	3.87	2.0	9.8	5.0	0.0	141
2018	A	South Bend	4	1	0	71	84	2.03	1.04	17.2	212	30	82	2.12	2.5	10.6	4.2	0.4	141
2018	A+	Myrtle Beach	1	1	0	9	10	5.93	1.65	20.3	300	36	69	6.35	4.0	9.9	2.5	2.0	89
2018	A+	Down East	2	3	0	37	37	4.84	1.45	19.9	261	33	67	4.12	4.1	9.0	2.2	0.7	68

Deceptive delivery, good control and ability to sequence gives him a chance at an MLB future. Fastball velo is a bit short, but relies on plus movement and spotting it down in the zone to get GB outs. With a slender frame, he gets by on pitchability and smarts. Double-A will be a good test.

Lakins,Travis
RP | **Boston** | EXP MLB DEBUT: 2019 | H/W: 6-1 175 | FUT: Setup reliever | **6B**

Thrws R Age 24
2015 (6) Ohio St

Velo	Pitch	Grade
90-96	FB	++++
78-81	CB	++++
84-85	SL	+++
87-89	CT	+++

Year	Lev	Team	W	L	Sv	IP	K	ERA	WHIP	BF/G	OBA	H%	S%	xERA	Ctl	Dom	Cmd	hr/9	BPV
2016	A+	Salem	6	3	0	91	79	5.93	1.62	21.2	302	37	63	5.20	3.6	7.8	2.2	0.8	63
2017	A+	Salem	5	0	0	38	43	2.61	1.18	21.7	230	32	79	2.79	3.1	10.2	3.3	0.5	118
2017	AA	Portland	0	4	0	30	19	6.28	1.83	17.5	286	33	64	5.34	6.3	5.7	0.9	0.6	-49
2018	AA	Portland	2	2	1	38	42	2.61	1.05	5.7	201	27	78	2.34	3.1	9.9	3.2	0.7	114
2018	AAA	Pawtucket	1	0	2	16	15	1.68	0.99	6.1	195	27	81	1.46	2.8	8.4	3.0	0.0	93

Because he has broken his arm twice while pitching, the Sox moved him to the pen, where his stuff played way up, and he moved himself into MLB consideration. Command has always been a concern, but is less so out of the pen and with all the weapons he has. FB, SL, CB and cutter, are all tough to square up.

Lambert,Jimmy
SP | **Chicago (A)** | EXP MLB DEBUT: 2019 | H/W: 6-1 160 | FUT: #5 SP/swingman | **6B**

Thrws R Age 24
2016 (5) Fresno St

Velo	Pitch	Grade
91-93	FB	++
80-82	SL	++
74-77	CB	++
80-82	CU	++++

Year	Lev	Team	W	L	Sv	IP	K	ERA	WHIP	BF/G	OBA	H%	S%	xERA	Ctl	Dom	Cmd	hr/9	BPV
2016	A	Kannapolis	0	5	0	29	30	5.86	1.71	12.0	321	41	65	5.58	3.4	9.2	2.7	0.6	93
2017	A	Kannapolis	7	2	0	74	43	2.19	1.19	24.7	270	31	80	3.05	1.3	5.2	3.9	0.1	76
2017	A+	Winston-Salem	5	4	0	76	59	5.45	1.51	23.5	286	33	66	5.09	3.4	7.0	2.0	1.2	51
2018	A+	Winston-Salem	5	7	0	70	80	3.97	1.11	21.2	224	31	64	2.69	2.7	10.3	3.8	0.6	130
2018	AA	Birmingham	3	1	0	25	30	2.88	1.04	19.3	221	31	75	2.54	2.2	10.8	5.0	0.7	154

Lean, athletic RHP made it to Double-A before injury ended season early. Max-effort, High 3/4s delivery with limited extension snd no deception. 4-pitch pitcher, relies on pitchability over stuff. Low-90s FB is flat, lacking favorable plane. Both breaking balls are below-average offerings. Best pitch is late fading CU; his lone swing-and-miss pitch.

Lambert,Peter — SP — Colorado

EXP MLB DEBUT: 2019 | H/W: 6-2 185 | FUT: #3 starter | 8C

Thrws R Age 21 — 2015 (2) HS (CA)

Velo	Pitch	Grade
92-95	FB	+++
73-75	CB	+++
82-84	CU	++++
	SL	++

Year	Lev	Team	W	L	Sv	IP	K	ERA	WHIP	BF/G	OBA	H%	S%	xERA	Ctl	Dom	Cmd	hr/9	BPV
2015	Rk	Grand Junction	0	4	0	31	26	3.47	1.29	16.0	248	30	76	3.69	3.2	7.5	2.4	0.9	67
2016	A	Asheville	5	8	0	126	108	3.93	1.25	19.7	260	32	68	3.42	2.4	7.7	3.3	0.5	93
2017	A+	Lancaster	9	8	0	142	131	4.18	1.25	22.2	268	32	70	4.10	1.9	8.3	4.4	1.1	116
2018	AA	Hartford	8	2	0	92	75	2.25	1.00	23.5	235	29	80	2.53	1.2	7.3	6.3	0.6	118
2018	AAA	Albuquerque	2	5	0	55	31	5.06	1.58	22.0	317	35	68	5.40	2.5	5.1	2.1	0.8	43

Has a polished 4-pitch mix that is geared towards inducing weak contact. FB sits at 92-95, topping out at 96 with good late sink and run. Low-80s CB has good depth and late break. Plus CU is best offering with good late fade. Cmd is among the best in the system and fixed issue with long-ball. Doesn't blow you away, but knows how to pitch.

Lange,Alex — SP — Chicago (N)

EXP MLB DEBUT: 2020 | H/W: 6-3 198 | FUT: #3 starter | 7B

Thrws R Age 23 — 2017 (1) Louisiana St

Velo	Pitch	Grade
90-93	FB	+++
80-83	CB	++++
82-85	CU	++

Year	Lev	Team	W	L	Sv	IP	K	ERA	WHIP	BF/G	OBA	H%	S%	xERA	Ctl	Dom	Cmd	hr/9	BPV
2017	NCAA	LSU	10	5	0	124	150	2.97	1.24	26.5	232	32	78	3.20	3.5	10.9	3.1	0.7	120
2017	A-	Eugene	0	1	0	9	13	4.95	1.32	9.4	260	42	58	3.05	3.0	12.9	4.3	0.0	169
2018	A+	Myrtle Beach	6	8	0	120	101	3.75	1.18	20.9	235	29	68	2.86	2.8	7.6	2.7	0.4	77

Has the frame and stuff to develop into a mid-rotation innings-eater. Comes after hitters with an average 90-93 mph FB that he locates to both sides. Plus power curve is his best offering and showed an improved change-up in 2018. Pounds the strike zone, issuing just 38 free passes in his full-season debut, but doesn't miss a ton of bats.

Lara,Janser — SP — Kansas City

EXP MLB DEBUT: 2021 | H/W: 6-0 170 | FUT: #3 starter | 8E

Thrws R Age 22 — 2016 FA (DR)

Velo	Pitch	Grade
92-94	FB	++++
78-81	SL	+++
82-83	CU	++

Year	Lev	Team	W	L	Sv	IP	K	ERA	WHIP	BF/G	OBA	H%	S%	xERA	Ctl	Dom	Cmd	hr/9	BPV
2017	Rk	Idaho Falls	4	2	0	52	57	4.15	1.54	18.9	258	32	78	4.90	5.0	9.8	2.0	1.4	60
2018	Rk	AZL Royals	0	1	0	1	1	9.00	2.00	4.8	415	52	50	7.49	0.0	9.0		0.0	180
2018	Rk	Burlington	0	0	0	4	5	10.98	2.93	11.8	438	58	58	10.32	6.6	11.0	1.7	0.0	38
2018	A	Lexington	4	3	1	66	75	3.41	1.24	11.7	225	31	74	3.07	3.8	10.2	2.7	0.7	99

Hard-throwing RHP struggled with injury and ineffectiveness early to mount a solid run as a RP late. Short-statured, cross-fire 3/4s delivery. 3-pitch pitcher. 2-seam FB has solid arm-side run but struggles with command. Slurvy SL has sharp bite and projects as average offering. Feel for CU with moderate fading action.

Lawrence,Justin — RP — Colorado

EXP MLB DEBUT: 2019 | H/W: 6-4 220 | FUT: Setup reliever | 7B

Thrws R Age 24 — 2015 (12) Jacksonville

Velo	Pitch	Grade
94-98	FB	++++
80-83	SL	++
	CU	++

Year	Lev	Team	W	L	Sv	IP	K	ERA	WHIP	BF/G	OBA	H%	S%	xERA	Ctl	Dom	Cmd	hr/9	BPV
2015	A-	Boise	0	3	0	19	15	8.05	1.89	5.6	282	32	58	6.20	7.1	7.1	1.0	1.4	-46
2016	A-	Boise	2	1	8	28	40	2.23	1.17	4.9	253	41	79	2.59	1.9	12.8	6.7	0.0	196
2016	A	Asheville	2	5	0	36	23	7.23	1.72	6.3	320	36	57	5.97	3.5	5.7	1.6	1.0	27
2017	A	Asheville	0	2	6	16	20	1.68	0.87	3.7	180	26	85	1.48	2.2	11.2	5.0	0.6	159
2018	A+	Lancaster	0	2	11	54	62	2.66	1.16	3.9	191	27	77	2.14	4.5	10.3	2.3	0.3	82

Rare side-arm hurler with plus velocity. Fastball sits in the mid-90s topping out at 98 mph with good late sink and deception. SL and CU keep hitters honest and off-balance, but FB is the main weapon and neutralizes RHP. Could be in the majors by late 2019.

Lawson,Reggie — SP — San Diego

EXP MLB DEBUT: 2020 | H/W: 6-4 200 | FUT: #4 starter | 8D

Thrws R Age 21 — 2016 (2) HS (CA)

Velo	Pitch	Grade
91-93	FB	++++
75-78	CB	+++
86-88	CU	++

Year	Lev	Team	W	L	Sv	IP	K	ERA	WHIP	BF/G	OBA	H%	S%	xERA	Ctl	Dom	Cmd	hr/9	BPV
2016	Rk	AZL Padres	0	0	0	8	7	8.78	1.83	7.6	342	43	47	5.65	3.3	7.7	2.3	0.0	67
2017	A	Fort Wayne	4	6	0	73	89	5.30	1.37	18.0	240	33	62	3.86	4.3	11.0	2.5	1.0	99
2018	A+	Lake Elsinore	8	5	0	117	117	4.69	1.55	21.3	283	36	71	4.78	3.9	9.0	2.3	0.8	74

Tall, athletic RH who struggles to command FB but has fairly low-effort delivery on 91-93 mph heater with late cutting action. Flashes hammer CB that could be weapon at next level. CU remains so-so but should develop into avg third pitch. Chance for more velo with added strength.

Lemons,Caden — SP — Milwaukee

EXP MLB DEBUT: 2021 | H/W: 6-6 175 | FUT: #3 starter | 9E

Thrws R Age 20 — 2017 (2) HS (AL)

Velo	Pitch	Grade
88-92	FB	+++
79-81	SL	+++
	CU	++

Year	Lev	Team	W	L	Sv	IP	K	ERA	WHIP	BF/G	OBA	H%	S%	xERA	Ctl	Dom	Cmd	hr/9	BPV
2017	Rk	AZL Brewers	0	1	0	2	1	8.18	0.91	2.7	244	16	0	5.74	0.0	4.1		4.1	92
2018	Rk	AZL Brewers	0	0	0	13	11	1.38	0.92	9.7	160	21	83	0.91	3.5	7.6	2.2	0.0	62
2018	Rk	Helena	1	2	0	18	17	6.43	1.92	17.3	336	41	67	6.71	4.5	8.4	1.9	1.0	49

Long, lean, athletic RH topped out at 97 mph as prep arm but operated in low-90s with an average SL in AZL. CU remains very raw, but he is a good athlete and should develop feel for it. Struggles to repeat mechanics and arm slot; may have command issues down the road. High-upside arm if things come together.

Liberatore,Matthew — SP — Tampa Bay

EXP MLB DEBUT: 2022 | H/W: 6-5 200 | FUT: #2 starter | 9E

Thrws L Age 19 — 2018 (1) HS (AZ)

Velo	Pitch	Grade
91-95	FB	++++
83-86	SL	++
74-77	CB	++++
83-86	CU	++++

Year	Lev	Team	W	L	Sv	IP	K	ERA	WHIP	BF/G	OBA	H%	S%	xERA	Ctl	Dom	Cmd	hr/9	BPV
2018	Rk	Princeton	1	0	0	5	5	3.60	1.40	21.1	262	35	71	3.32	3.6	9.0	2.5	0.0	83
2018	Rk	GCL Rays	1	2	0	27	32	0.99	0.99	13.0	173	26	89	1.19	3.6	10.6	2.9	0.0	110

Athletic, prep LHP brings 3 advanced pitches and pitchability to the table. High 3/4s delivery, repeatable with solid extension and good downward plane. 2-seam FB has solid arm-side run. Could add a few MPHs with additional strength. 12-to-6 CB has great shape and tremendous depth. Advance feel for CU with solid fade. SL lags behind rest of package.

Linares,Resly — SP — Tampa Bay

EXP MLB DEBUT: 2021 | H/W: 6-2 165 | FUT: #4 starter | 7C

Thrws L Age 21 — 2015 FA (DR)

Velo	Pitch	Grade
87-91	FB	+++
73-77	CB	+++
79-82	CU	+++

Year	Lev	Team	W	L	Sv	IP	K	ERA	WHIP	BF/G	OBA	H%	S%	xERA	Ctl	Dom	Cmd	hr/9	BPV
2016	Rk	Princeton	2	3	0	32	30	5.34	1.50	17.3	307	36	69	5.83	2.3	8.4	3.8	1.7	109
2017	A-	Hudson Valley	3	3	0	61	60	2.36	0.97	17.8	173	23	75	1.42	3.4	8.8	2.6	0.3	86
2018	A	Bowling Green	7	3	0	84	97	3.21	1.12	19.5	225	31	73	2.72	2.7	10.4	3.9	0.6	133

Tall, paper thin command/control LHP has used deceptive arm angles to wreck lower level hitters. Stays tall in cross-fire delivery altering slows from 3/4s to low 3/4s. 2-seam FB arm-side movement profile increases at the lower slot. Slow CB is more like slurve and can profile as SL too. Maintains great arm speed with late-fading CU.

Lindow,Ethan — SP — Philadelphia

EXP MLB DEBUT: 2022 | H/W: 6-4 185 | FUT: #5 SP/swingman | 7C

Thrws L Age 20 — 2017 (5) HS (GA)

Velo	Pitch	Grade
88-91	FB	++
72-74	CB	+++
80-83	CU	++
80-82	SL	++

Year	Lev	Team	W	L	Sv	IP	K	ERA	WHIP	BF/G	OBA	H%	S%	xERA	Ctl	Dom	Cmd	hr/9	BPV
2017	Rk	GCL Phillies	2	2	0	27	34	4.63	1.40	14.3	253	36	67	3.80	4.0	11.3	2.8	0.7	113
2018	A-	Williamsport	3	2	0	70	63	2.19	1.10	21.1	227	29	80	2.36	2.4	8.1	3.3	0.3	98

Tall lefty improved his control in short-season and added a slider to his FB/CB/CU mix. Velocity and movement on his CU also improved. Has an advanced feel for mixing up his arsenal, but lacks one go-to out pitch. Not a lot of projection left; needs a separator offering to go along with his advanced pitchability.

Little,Brendon — SP — Chicago (N)

EXP MLB DEBUT: 2021 | H/W: 6-1 195 | FUT: #4 starter | 7C

Thrws L Age 22 — 2017 (1) North Carolina

Velo	Pitch	Grade
91-94	FB	+++
75-77	CB	+++
80-83	CU	+

Year	Lev	Team	W	L	Sv	IP	K	ERA	WHIP	BF/G	OBA	H%	S%	xERA	Ctl	Dom	Cmd	hr/9	BPV
2017	A-	Eugene	0	2	0	16	12	9.50	1.86	12.6	316	36	46	6.37	5.0	6.7	1.3	1.1	3
2018	A	South Bend	5	11	0	101	90	5.16	1.47	19.7	271	33	65	4.32	3.8	8.0	2.1	0.7	59

Struggled in his full-season debut. FB sits at 91-94 mph, topping out at 96 with good late life and sink. Is backed up by an above-average 12-to-6 CB. CU remains inconsistent but shows promise. Inconsistent mechanics resulted in struggles with command. Size, stuff, and unrefined CU suggest a future move to relief.

Littell,Zack — SP — Minnesota

EXP MLB DEBUT: 2018 | H/W: 6-3 190 | FUT: #5 SP/swingman | 6B

Thrws R Age 23 — 2013 (11) HS (NC)

Velo	Pitch	Grade
89-93	FB	+++
85-88	SL	++
74-76	CB	+++
84-86	CU	++

Year	Lev	Team	W	L	Sv	IP	K	ERA	WHIP	BF/G	OBA	H%	S%	xERA	Ctl	Dom	Cmd	hr/9	BPV
2017	AA	Trenton	5	0	0	44	52	2.05	1.02	24.2	230	32	83	2.51	1.6	10.6	6.5	0.6	165
2017	AA	Chattanooga	5	0	0	41	33	2.84	1.24	23.9	221	28	76	2.61	3.9	7.2	1.8	0.2	42
2018	AA	Chattanooga	0	3	0	23	32	5.87	1.52	20.0	302	43	63	5.28	2.7	12.5	4.6	1.2	169
2018	AAA	Rochester	6	6	0	106	98	3.57	1.32	23.1	251	32	73	3.38	3.4	8.3	2.5	0.4	76
2018	MLB	Minnesota	0	2	0	20	14	6.27	1.79	11.6	306	34	67	6.25	4.9	6.3	1.3	1.3	-2

Command/control RHP made MLB debut. Close to physical projection. 5-pitch pitcher, mostly fringe-to-average offerings. Workhorse is 4-seam FB but will also throw true SU. Both have average presentation. Best breaking ball is 11-to-5 CB, which is only pitch with swing-and-miss potential. SL & CU round out repertoire. Needs to improve command to survive.

Llovera,Mauricio | RP | Philadelphia | EXP MLB DEBUT: 2020 | H/W: 5-11 200 | FUT: Setup reliever | 8D

Thrws R Age 22
2015 FA (VZ)

Velo	Pitch	Grade
94-98	FB	++++
83-85	SL	+++
84-87	CU	++

Year	Lev	Team	W	L	Sv	IP	K	ERA	WHIP	BF/G	OBA	H%	S%	xERA	Ctl	Dom	Cmd	hr/9	BPV
2016	Rk	GCL Phillies	7	1	0	53	56	1.87	0.96	18.2	207	29	78	1.51	2.0	9.5	4.7	0.0	134
2017	A	Lakewood	2	4	0	86	94	3.35	1.33	11.9	250	35	73	3.17	3.5	9.8	2.8	0.2	102
2018	A+	Clearwater	8	7	0	121	137	3.72	1.11	20.7	227	30	70	3.09	2.5	10.2	4.0	1.0	133

Short, stout right-hander with present strength but little projection left. Mechanics are a bit crude, but arm action is clean and delivers a heavy, mid-90s FB and flashes a 2-plane, potentially plus SL. Also has enough confidence in mid-80s CU. Control, command still work in progress; some say he'll be a RP who could be fast-tracked to majors.

Loaisiga,Jonathan | SP | New York (A) | EXP MLB DEBUT: 2018 | H/W: 5-11 165 | FUT: #2 starter | 9D

Thrws R Age 24
2013 FA (NI)

Velo	Pitch	Grade
94-97	FB	++++
83-86	SL	++++
86-89	CU	++++

Year	Lev	Team	W	L	Sv	IP	K	ERA	WHIP	BF/G	OBA	H%	S%	xERA	Ctl	Dom	Cmd	hr/9	BPV
2018	Rk	GCL Yankees W	0	0	0	1	1	0.00	1.67	5.4	228	30	100	3.57	7.5	7.5	1.0	0.0	-50
2018	A+	Tampa	3	0	0	20	26	1.35	1.00	19.1	252	38	85	2.16	0.5	11.7	26.0	0.0	216
2018	AA	Trenton	3	1	0	34	40	3.96	1.26	15.5	278	36	76	4.67	1.6	10.6	6.7	1.6	165
2018	MLB	NY Yankees	2	0	0	24	33	5.21	1.57	11.8	276	39	69	4.97	4.5	12.3	2.8	1.1	118

Hard-throwing RHP emerged after several seasons plagued by arm injuries and got to majors in 2018. 4-pitch pitcher with easy, repeatable delivery. High-octane FB has limited movement profile. CB has bled into SL shape, with sharp 2-plane movement profile. Late fading CU took step forward, eliciting swings and misses.

Lopez,Yoan | RP | Arizona | EXP MLB DEBUT: 2018 | H/W: 6-3 185 | FUT: Setup reliever | 8B

Thrws R Age 26
2015 FA (CU)

Velo	Pitch	Grade
94-97	FB	++++
84-86	SL	++++

Year	Lev	Team	W	L	Sv	IP	K	ERA	WHIP	BF/G	OBA	H%	S%	xERA	Ctl	Dom	Cmd	hr/9	BPV
2016	AA	Mobile	4	7	0	62		5.52	1.60	19.6	277	29	69	5.44	4.6	5.2	1.1	1.5	-13
2017	Rk	AZL DBacks	0	0	1	1	3	0.00	1.00	3.8	0	0	100		9.0	27.0	3.0	0.0	261
2017	A+	Visalia	2	0	4	30	56	0.89	0.83	5.5	158	32	96	1.12	2.7	16.7	6.2	0.6	246
2017	AA	Jackson	2	6	12	61	87	2.94	1.05	5.3	180	28	73	1.94	3.8	12.8	3.3	0.6	145
2018	MLB	Arizona	0	0	0	9	11	3.00	0.89	3.3	216	26	83	3.31	1.0	11.0	11.0	2.0	189

Athletic, high-waisted RP who made MLB debut from the bullpen in September. Features explosive mid-90s four seam FB that will touch 99 mph and power mid-80s SL that misses bats regularly. Has taken big steps forward with Cmd as he has transitioned to the bullpen. Could have enough stuff to thrive in closer-type role soon.

Lovelady,Richard | RP | Kansas City | EXP MLB DEBUT: 2019 | H/W: 6-0 170 | FUT: Setup reliever | 7C

Thrws L Age 23
2016 (10) Kennesaw St

Velo	Pitch	Grade
93-96	FB	++++
85-87	SL	++++

Year	Lev	Team	W	L	Sv	IP	K	ERA	WHIP	BF/G	OBA	H%	S%	xERA	Ctl	Dom	Cmd	hr/9	BPV
2016	Rk	Idaho Falls	0	1	6	14	16	1.90	1.20	4.4	200	29	82	2.02	4.4	10.1	2.3	0.0	81
2016	Rk	AZL Royals	2	0	3	10	14	1.78	0.59	4.3	123	22	67		1.8	12.5	7.0	0.0	194
2017	A+	Wilmington	1	0	7	33	41	1.09	0.66	5.5	162	26	82	0.24	1.1	11.1	10.3	0.0	189
2017	AA	NW Arkansas	3	2	3	33	36	2.18	1.24	6.4	231	32	83	2.76	3.5	9.8	2.8	0.3	99
2018	AAA	Omaha	3	3	9	73	71	2.47	1.01	6.1	205	27	76	1.97	2.6	8.8	3.4	0.4	106

Deceptive, short-statured LH RP close to MLB debut. Utilizes low arm-slot to create deception in delivery. 2-pitch pitcher, both plus potential pitches out of pen. 2-seam FB has plus arm-side bore and gets on hitters quickly. Sweeping SL has solid 2-plane break. LOOGY floor with setup upside. With health, a potentially long-tenured MLB pitcher.

Lowther,Zac | SP | Baltimore | EXP MLB DEBUT: 2020 | H/W: 6-2 230 | FUT: #5 SP/swingman | 6C

Thrws L Age 22
2017 (2) Xavier

Velo	Pitch	Grade
87-90	FB	++
79-83	SL	++
72-76	CB	+++
82-84	CU	+++

Year	Lev	Team	W	L	Sv	IP	K	ERA	WHIP	BF/G	OBA	H%	S%	xERA	Ctl	Dom	Cmd	hr/9	BPV
2017	A-	Aberdeen	2	2	0	54	75	1.66	0.85	16.5	187	30	80	1.12	1.8	12.5	6.8	0.2	193
2018	A	Delmarva	3	1	0	31	51	1.16	0.68	18.1	121	22	89	0.36	2.6	14.8	5.7	0.6	214
2018	A+	Frederick	5	3	0	92	100	2.54	1.08	21.2	222	30	79	2.55	2.5	9.8	3.8	0.6	125

Thick, 3/4s deceptive LHP enjoyed Dom success against younger competition. Easy cross-armed delivery. Hides ball well within XL frame and has advanced command. Features four pitches: FB has solid action to both sides of plate. 1-to-7 CB has good depth and decent break. Has feel for CU, doesn't utilize. SL is one-plane breaker.

Luciano,Elvis | SP | Toronto | EXP MLB DEBUT: 2021 | H/W: 6-2 184 | FUT: #3 starter | 8E

Thrws R Age 19
2016 FA (DR)

Velo	Pitch	Grade
90-94	FB	++++
80-82	SL	+++
85-87	CU	++

Year	Lev	Team	W	L	Sv	IP	K	ERA	WHIP	BF/G	OBA	H%	S%	xERA	Ctl	Dom	Cmd	hr/9	BPV
2017	Rk	Missoula	0	0	0	2	2	0.00	0.00	5.6	0	0			0.0	9.0		0.0	180
2017	Rk	AZL DBacks	1	0	1	16	9	2.80	1.18	16.1	261	31	74	2.79	1.7	5.0	3.0	0.0	63
2018	Rk	Burlington	3	5	0	56	56	4.66	1.34	21.2	258	33	65	3.73	3.2	9.0	2.8	0.6	93
2018	Rk	Idaho Falls	2	0	0	11	14	0.00	0.82	20.0	162	26	100	0.63	2.5	11.5	4.7	0.0	158

Sturdy, projectable RHP acquired as Rule 5 selection from KC. Cross-fire, high 3/4s delivery with some effort. Heavy two-seam FB with solid arm-side bore is go-to pitch. Slurvy CB has potential with improved depth to become above-average offering. Has a feel for average CU but struggles with consistency. Workhorse starter body.

Luzardo,Jesus | SP | Oakland | EXP MLB DEBUT: 2019 | H/W: 5-11 209 | FUT: #2 starter | 9C

Thrws L Age 21
2016 (3) HS (FL)

Velo	Pitch	Grade
92-95	FB	++++
78-80	CB	+++
	CU	++++

Year	Lev	Team	W	L	Sv	IP	K	ERA	WHIP	BF/G	OBA	H%	S%	xERA	Ctl	Dom	Cmd	hr/9	BPV
2017	Rk	AZL Athletics	0	1	0	11	13	1.61	0.89	10.4	222	33	80	1.51	0.8	10.4	13.0	0.0	184
2017	A-	Vermont	1	0	0	18	20	2.00	0.89	13.4	191	26	80	1.61	2.0	10.0	5.0	0.5	144
2018	A+	Stockton	2	1	0	14	25	1.27	0.77	17.0	130	29	82	0.15	3.2	15.8	5.0	0.0	218
2018	AA	Midland	7	3	0	78	86	2.30	0.97	18.5	208	28	79	2.09	2.1	9.9	4.8	0.6	140
2018	AAA	Nashville	1	1	0	16	18	7.31	2.00	19.3	357	46	63	7.37	3.9	10.1	2.6	1.1	94

Advanced LH who scooted up three levels in 2018 and looks almost ready to contribute. Projects to have three above-average pitches in low/mid-90s sinking FB that he can command well and plus CU with fade. Sequences CB well to get outs and has good feel for spin. Moderate effort in delivery but repeats 3/4 slot well and is good athlete. Big-upside arm.

Lynch,Daniel | SP | Kansas City | EXP MLB DEBUT: 2020 | H/W: 6-4 175 | FUT: #2 starter | 9E

Thrws L Age 22
2018 (1) Virginia

Velo	Pitch	Grade
91-94	FB	++++
82-87	SL	++++
84-86	CU	+++

Year	Lev	Team	W	L	Sv	IP	K	ERA	WHIP	BF/G	OBA	H%	S%	xERA	Ctl	Dom	Cmd	hr/9	BPV
2018	NCAA	Virginia	4	4	0	88	105	3.98	1.25	27.6	257	34	72	3.91	2.4	10.7	4.4	1.1	145
2018	Rk	Burlington	0	0	0	11	14	1.62	0.99	14.1	223	34	82	1.77	1.6	11.4	7.0	0.0	179
2018	A	Lexington	5	1	0	40	47	1.58	1.03	17.1	237	34	85	2.24	1.4	10.6	7.8	0.2	172

Late-blooming, long 3/4s LHP propelled himself into 1st round. Clean, low-effort delivery with room to grow; added velocity over last 2 years. Has advanced command of two-seam FB with solid arm-side bore. Throws two types of SL, both effective breakers; sweeper projects as plus. Solid fade on CU. Above-average potential.

MacGregor,Travis | SP | Pittsburgh | EXP MLB DEBUT: 2023 | H/W: 6-3 180 | FUT: #4 starter | 7D

Thrws R Age 21
2016 (2) HS (FL)

Velo	Pitch	Grade
89-93	FB	+++
80-83	CB	++
82-83	CU	+++

Year	Lev	Team	W	L	Sv	IP	K	ERA	WHIP	BF/G	OBA	H%	S%	xERA	Ctl	Dom	Cmd	hr/9	BPV
2016	Rk	GCL Pirates	1	1	0	31	19	3.17	1.25	14.1	248	29	74	3.06	2.9	5.5	1.9	0.3	39
2017	Rk	Bristol	1	4	0	41	32	7.88	1.97	16.4	345	41	58	6.68	4.4	7.0	1.6	0.7	26
2018	Rk	GCL Pirates	0	0	0	7	6	2.57	1.00	13.4	233	27	83	3.16	1.3	7.7	6.0	1.3	122
2018	A	West Virginia	1	4	0	63	74	3.28	1.25	17.1	246	33	78	3.65	3.0	10.5	3.5	1.0	127

Rangy, former second round pick who throws from a high slot with a clean and compact delivery. Overall stuff is nothing special but he has a chance to have plus command. Posted good numbers at Low A before experiencing some arm problems and eventually undergoing Tommy John surgery in Sept. Will miss all of 2019.

Madison,Ben | SP | San Francisco | EXP MLB DEBUT: 2022 | H/W: 6-3 205 | FUT: #4 starter | 7D

Thrws R Age 21
2018 (9) Central Baptist Coll

Velo	Pitch	Grade
91-94	FB	++++
82-83	SL	+++
	CU	++

Year	Lev	Team	W	L	Sv	IP	K	ERA	WHIP	BF/G	OBA	H%	S%	xERA	Ctl	Dom	Cmd	hr/9	BPV
2018	NCAA	Central Baptist Coll	6	6	0	96	172	2.71	1.21	24.2	181	36	78	2.12	5.2	16.1	3.1	0.4	166
2018	Rk	AZL Giants O	0	0	0	16	23	3.38	1.44	7.6	237	39	74	3.05	5.1	12.9	2.6	0.0	114

Physically strong, athletic RHP has had trouble staying out of trouble in past. Rededicated life, stayed on field in college. Built like NFL athlete. Was up to 97 with late-running FB in spring. Heavy GB and swing-and-miss tendencies. SL effective breaker; above-average at maturity. Has a feel for CU but rarely uses. Will need to improve to start.

Manning,Matt | SP | Detroit | EXP MLB DEBUT: 2020 | H/W: 6-3 185 | FUT: #3 starter | 8B

Thrws R Age 21
2016 (1) HS (CA)

Velo	Pitch	Grade
92-97	FB	++++
74-76	CB	+++
82-85	CU	+++

Year	Lev	Team	W	L	Sv	IP	K	ERA	WHIP	BF/G	OBA	H%	S%	xERA	Ctl	Dom	Cmd	hr/9	BPV
2017	A-	Connecticut	2	2	0	33	36	1.90	1.24	14.9	224	32	83	2.42	3.8	9.8	2.6	0.0	91
2017	A	West Michigan	2	0	0	17	26	5.76	1.45	14.7	224	38	56	2.92	5.8	13.6	2.4	0.0	107
2018	A	West Michigan	3	3	0	55	76	3.42	1.36	21.0	232	36	75	3.25	4.6	12.4	2.7	0.5	118
2018	A+	Lakeland	4	4	0	51	65	2.99	1.00	21.7	182	26	72	1.96	3.3	11.4	3.4	0.7	134
2018	AA	Erie	0	1	0	10	13	4.41	1.47	21.9	277	41	67	3.68	3.5	11.5	3.3	0.0	129

Athletic, mid-rotation starter poised to be an MLB impact arm. Works long arms and legs to produce impressive extension towards attacking the strike zone. Curve is a developing out-pitch and ahead of above-average changeup. Fastball is a lively easy plus offering that plays well off his offspeed mix.

Maples,Dillon — RP — Chicago (N)
EXP MLB DEBUT: 2017 | H/W: 6-2 195 | FUT: Closer | 7B

Thrws R Age 26
2011 (14) HS (NC)
95-98 FB +++++
85-88 SL +++
75-78 CU ++

Year	Lev	Team	W	L	Sv	IP	K	ERA	WHIP	BF/G	OBA	H%	S%	xERA	Ctl	Dom	Cmd	hr/9	BPV
2017	AA	Tennessee	1	1	6	13	28	3.41	1.67	4.2	228	54	77	3.45	7.5	19.1	2.5	0.0	159
2017	AAA	Iowa	1	2	4	18	28	1.99	1.27	4.4	190	32	86	2.52	5.5	13.9	2.5	0.5	121
2017	MLB	Chi Cubs	0	0	0	5	11	10.59	2.35	4.4	294	64	50	6.09	10.6	19.4	1.8	0.0	82
2018	AAA	Iowa	2	3	10	38	75	2.83	1.60	4.1	170	39	82	2.83	9.2	17.7	1.9	0.2	88
2018	MLB	Chi Cubs	1	0	0	5	9	12.35	2.35	2.9	327	48	50	9.96	8.8	15.9	1.8	3.5	66

Power reliever had mixed results. Plus velo and three-pitch mix gives him the stuff to dominate and he whiffed a ton at AAA, but inability to find the strike zone is problematic. Comes after hitters with a plus 94-98 mph FB that tops at 100 mph with good run and sink. Mixes in a plus high-80 SL and a usable 12-to-6 CB. Has yet to take the next step.

Marinan,James — SP — Cincinnati
EXP MLB DEBUT: 2021 | H/W: 6-5 210 | FUT: #4 starter | 7D

Thrws R Age 20
2017 (4) HS (FL)
91-94 FB ++++
75-79 CB +++
83-85 CU ++

Year	Lev	Team	W	L	Sv	IP	K	ERA	WHIP	BF/G	OBA	H%	S%	xERA	Ctl	Dom	Cmd	hr/9	BPV
2017	Rk	AZL Dodgers	2	0	0	17	14	1.59	1.65	8.4	226	29	89	3.49	7.4	7.4	1.0	0.0	-49
2018	Rk	AZL Dodgers	0	0	0	10	11	0.88	1.47	14.6	277	38	93	3.70	3.5	9.7	2.8	0.0	97
2018	Rk	Billings	3	2	0	43	39	3.98	1.58	17.2	288	37	73	4.36	4.0	8.2	2.1	0.2	58

Strong, physical RHP acquired in mid-season deal from LA. Low-to-mid 90s 2-seam FB gets plenty of whiffs due to heavy sink and late arm-side run. His best secondary is a high-70s CB, which slurvy shape. Add velocity, it could become a SL. Flashes a solid CU. Will need to improve pitch to start long term. Competitive streak plays up pitches.

Marks,Wyatt — SP — Oakland
EXP MLB DEBUT: 2020 | H/W: 6-3 196 | FUT: #4 starter | 7C

Thrws R Age 23
2017 (13) Louisiana-Laf
90-92 FB +++
79-83 CB +++
CU ++

Year	Lev	Team	W	L	Sv	IP	K	ERA	WHIP	BF/G	OBA	H%	S%	xERA	Ctl	Dom	Cmd	hr/9	BPV
2017	NCAA	Louisiana-Laf	2	1	7	59		2.28	0.91	7.4	148	26	81	1.54	3.8	15.2	4.0	0.9	189
2017	Rk	AZL Athletics	0	0	0	5	7	0.00	1.00	9.6	175	30	100	1.22	3.6	12.6	3.5	0.0	148
2017	A-	Vermont	3	0	0	37	49	2.68	1.11	13.2	217	28	88	3.58	2.9	11.9	4.1	1.7	154
2018	A	Beloit	5	6	0	106	127	3.23	1.18	21.2	231	32	74	2.99	3.0	10.8	3.6	0.7	132
2018	A+	Stockton	2	0	0	27	32	3.64	1.43	23.1	231	30	80	4.23	5.3	10.6	2.0	1.3	66

Strong, athletic RHP who features solid but not flashy three-pitch mix. FB will touch 94 mph and sit 90-92 with flashes of above-average lateral command. Spins a hammer CB in low-80s that has makings of future 'out' pitch. CU requires work and lacks movement to miss bats. Control will come and go but has the look of a future back-end SP.

Marquez,Brailyn — SP — Chicago (N)
EXP MLB DEBUT: 2022 | H/W: 6-4 185 | FUT: #3 starter | 9D

Thrws L Age 20
2015 FA (DR)
94-95 FB ++++
83-85 CB ++
82-84 CU ++

Year	Lev	Team	W	L	Sv	IP	K	ERA	WHIP	BF/G	OBA	H%	S%	xERA	Ctl	Dom	Cmd	hr/9	BPV
2017	Rk	AZL Cubs	2	1	0	44	52	5.52	1.41	16.9	287	39	59	4.27	2.5	10.6	4.3	0.6	143
2018	A-	Eugene	1	4	0	47	52	3.24	1.27	19.3	257	34	78	3.82	2.7	9.9	3.7	1.0	124
2018	A	South Bend	0	0	0	7	7	2.57	1.29	14.4	262	35	78	3.04	2.6	9.0	3.5	0.0	111

Breakout prospect showed across-the-board gains. FB velo jumped from low-90s to 94-95 mph, topping at 98 with good late life. CU has good deception and late sink vs. RHB. Slurvy breaking ball rounds out the arsenal. Tall, athletic frame gives him the tools to start in the majors, but consistency and improved command will be key to his development.

Marte,Jose — SP — San Francisco
EXP MLB DEBUT: 2021 | H/W: 6-3 180 | FUT: Setup reliever | 7C

Thrws R Age 22
2016 FA (DR)
92-95 FB ++++
82-84 CB +++
83-88 CU +

Year	Lev	Team	W	L	Sv	IP	K	ERA	WHIP	BF/G	OBA	H%	S%	xERA	Ctl	Dom	Cmd	hr/9	BPV
2017	Rk	AZL Giants	0	0	0	1	2	0.00	0.00	2.8	0	0			0.0	18.0		0.0	342
2017	A-	Salem-Keizer	2	5	0	54	42	5.33	1.76	17.7	286	35	68	4.91	5.7	7.0	1.2	0.3	-9
2018	A	Augusta	7	7	0	118	112	4.72	1.50	20.4	276	35	69	4.49	3.8	8.5	2.2	0.8	69

Athletic, hard-throwing RHP elevated his prospect status with solid Single-A season. Older for level but with two solid pitching tools. Touched high 90s early with late-boring 2-seam FB. 11-to-5 CB has a a solid spin profile but struggles with execution. Has no feel for CU. Better suited for splitter than CU.

Martin,Corbin — SP — Houston
EXP MLB DEBUT: 2021 | H/W: 6-2 190 | FUT: #3 starter | 8C

Thrws R Age 23
2017 (2) Texas A&M
93-96 FB ++++
84-86 SL +++
79-82 CB +++
87-88 CU ++

Year	Lev	Team	W	L	Sv	IP	K	ERA	WHIP	BF/G	OBA	H%	S%	xERA	Ctl	Dom	Cmd	hr/9	BPV
2017	NCAA	Texas A&M	7	4	0	87	95	3.82	1.46	15.5	266	36	74	4.00	3.9	9.8	2.5	0.5	89
2017	Rk	GCL Astros	0	0	0	5	5	0.00	0.20	7.6	0	0	100		1.8	9.0	5.0	0.0	131
2017	A-	Tri City	0	1	1	27	38	2.65	1.03	13.1	207	33	74	1.96	2.6	12.6	4.8	0.3	173
2018	A+	Buies Creek	2	0	1	19	26	0.00	0.58	16.1	69	13	100		3.3	12.3	3.7	0.0	150
2018	AA	Corpus Christi	7	2	0	103	96	2.97	1.09	19.2	224	28	74	2.63	2.4	8.4	3.4	0.6	103

The solidly-built right-hander has flown through the professional ranks on the back of an advanced four-pitch mix. The headliner is the mid-90s fastball which he locates consistently. His breaking balls vary on which is better depending on the day and both can flash above-average, with vertical break. His fading change-up lags but could approach average.

Martinez,Nolan — SP — New York (A)
EXP MLB DEBUT: 2021 | H/W: 6-2 165 | FUT: #4 starter | 7D

Thrws R Age 20
2016 (3) HS (CA)
90-92 FB +++
76-79 CB +++
83-86 SL ++

Year	Lev	Team	W	L	Sv	IP	K	ERA	WHIP	BF/G	OBA	H%	S%	xERA	Ctl	Dom	Cmd	hr/9	BPV
2017	Rk	Pulaski	0	0	0	4	2	0.00	0.50	13.3	151	18	100		0.0	4.5		0.0	99
2017	Rk	GCL Yankees	0	0	0	9	12	0.98	0.98	7.0	188	30	89	1.31	2.9	11.7	4.0	0.0	150
2018	A-	Staten Island	4	0	0	36	26	1.24	0.88	16.8	171	21	87	1.17	2.7	6.5	2.4	0.2	61
2018	A	Charleston (Sc)	0	4	0	25	15	6.48	1.52	21.7	254	28	56	4.23	5.0	5.4	1.1	0.7	-21

Lean, command/control RHP continues to limit base runners despite not having swing-and-miss stuff. Utilizes repeatable, 3/4s cross-fire delivery with solid extension. 3 pitch pitcher. Late-moving FB doesn't miss bats but avoids barrels, contributing to low hard-hit rate. 11-to-5 CB has solid shape and break. Above-average pitch at projection. Has feel for CU.

Mata,Bryan — SP — Boston
EXP MLB DEBUT: 2022 | H/W: 6-3 160 | FUT: Middle reliever | 6C

Thrws R Age 19
2016 FA (VZ)
89-93 FB +++
76-78 CB +++
84-86 CU +++

Year	Lev	Team	W	L	Sv	IP	K	ERA	WHIP	BF/G	OBA	H%	S%	xERA	Ctl	Dom	Cmd	hr/9	BPV
2017	A	Greenville	5	6	0	77	74	3.74	1.31	18.7	257	33	70	3.36	3.0	8.6	2.8	0.4	92
2018	A+	Salem	6	3	0	72	61	3.50	1.61	18.8	222	29	77	3.47	7.3	7.6	1.1	0.1	-41

Had a disastrous 2018 season at Hi-A, walking a ton of guys. Has potential for decent three-pitch mix with his FB, CB and CU, but all were inconsistent. Stuff can play very flat and up in the zone. Still very young so has a chance to regroup. But command and control will have to go from bad to plus.

Matuella,Michael — SP — Texas
EXP MLB DEBUT: 2020 | H/W: 6-6 220 | FUT: Setup reliever | 8D

Thrws R Age 24
2015 (3) Duke
95-97 FB ++++
84-86 SL +++
89-92 CU ++

Year	Lev	Team	W	L	Sv	IP	K	ERA	WHIP	BF/G	OBA	H%	S%	xERA	Ctl	Dom	Cmd	hr/9	BPV
2015		Did not play in minors																	
2016	A-	Spokane	0	0	0	3	1	0.00	1.00	11.5	106	12	100	0.61	6.0	3.0	0.5	0.0	-90
2017	A	Hickory	4	6	0	75	60	4.20	1.48	15.4	294	35	72	4.68	2.8	7.2	2.6	0.7	73
2018	A+	Down East	3	5	2	51	44	8.28	1.72	11.6	317	35	54	6.96	3.7	7.7	2.1	2.1	58

Once a promising top-tier SP prospect, health issues have dimmed his potential. Was moved to bullpen mid-2018, and given durability concerns, likely to stay here. FB has elite velocity but only average movement and fringy command; SL is average but needs polish to work consistently in MLB. Delivery has effort and he struggles to repeat.

May,Dustin — SP — Los Angeles (N)
EXP MLB DEBUT: 2020 | H/W: 6-6 180 | FUT: #2 starter | 9D

Thrws R Age 21
2016 (3) HS (TX)
93-97 FB ++++
80-83 CB +++
84-87 CU ++
CT +

Year	Lev	Team	W	L	Sv	IP	K	ERA	WHIP	BF/G	OBA	H%	S%	xERA	Ctl	Dom	Cmd	hr/9	BPV
2016	Rk	AZL Dodgers	0	1	1	30	34	3.89	1.36	12.6	304	42	68	3.82	1.2	10.2	8.5	0.0	169
2017	A	Great Lakes	9	6	0	123	113	3.88	1.20	21.5	259	33	68	3.32	1.9	8.3	4.3	0.6	115
2017	A+	Rancho Cuca	0	0	0	11	15	0.82	0.64	19.0	162	27	86	0.16	0.8	12.3	15.0	0.0	217
2018	A+	Rancho Cuca	7	3	0	98	94	3.30	1.10	22.6	248	31	73	3.16	1.6	8.6	5.5	0.8	131
2018	AA	Tulsa	2	2	0	34	28	3.70	1.14	22.5	219	28	64	2.14	3.2	7.4	2.3	0.0	66

Huge RH hurler has the best stuff in the system and had a breakout in 2018. FB up a tick from when drafted and now sits at 93-97 mph with plus late sink and run. Ditched his SL for an above-average power CB. CT and fringe CU round out his four-pitch mix. FB is bread and butter and mixes an aggressive approach with plus control to dominate.

McClanahan,Shane — SP — Tampa Bay
EXP MLB DEBUT: 2021 | H/W: 6-1 165 | FUT: #3 starter | 8C

Thrws L Age 21
2018 (1) South Florida
93-97 FB ++++
81-84 SL +++
84-86 CU +++

Year	Lev	Team	W	L	Sv	IP	K	ERA	WHIP	BF/G	OBA	H%	S%	xERA	Ctl	Dom	Cmd	hr/9	BPV
2018	NCAA	South Florida	5	6	0	76	120	3.43	1.30	22.4	192	33	74	2.59	5.7	14.2	2.5	0.5	120
2018	Rk	Princeton	0	0	0	4	7	0.00	0.75	7.1	151	32	100	0.29	2.3	15.8	7.0	0.0	241
2018	Rk	GCL Rays	0	0	0	3	6	0.00	0.33	4.7	106	29	100		0.0	18.0		0.0	342

Lean, over-powering LHP made pro debut after compensation round selection. With low 3/4s online delivery, he achieves plus-plus arm speed, albeit with significant effort. FB sits in upper 90s with late, plus-plus run. CU is over SL right now, both could be plus with consistency. Durability and control concerns could push profile to pen.

McCreery,Adam — RP — Los Angeles (N)
EXP MLB DEBUT: 2018 | H/W: 6-8 219 | FUT: Middle reliever | 6C

Thrws L Age 26
2014 (22) Arizona St
90-94 FB +++
79-82 CT ++++

Year	Lev	Team	W	L	Sv	IP	K	ERA	WHIP	BF/G	OBA	H%	S%	xERA	Ctl	Dom	Cmd	hr/9	BPV
2017	A	Rome	2	0	2	31	47	2.88	1.31	6.4	228	39	76	2.62	4.3	13.6	3.1	0.0	145
2017	A+	Florida	1	1	5	30	43	2.68	1.46	7.2	198	32	81	2.90	6.9	12.8	1.9	0.3	64
2018	AA	Mississippi	2	5	2	47	61	3.83	1.72	6.3	266	40	76	4.35	6.3	11.7	1.8	0.2	58
2018	AAA	Gwinnett	0	0	0	7	10	2.50	0.97	3.4	129	23	71	0.66	5.0	12.5	2.5	0.0	108
2018	MLB	Atlanta	0	0	0	1	2	18.00	4.00	6.8	587	83	50	17.75	0.0	18.0		0.0	342

Big-bodied, lurch-like LHP made MLB debut last season. Cross-armed 3/4s delivery with limited extension. Doesn't use height well enough for premium velocity. 2-pitch pitcher. 2-seam FB has solid arm-side run with downward plane a result of delivery. CT is workhorse and best pitch with late movement. Has always produced high Dom but has messy Ctl.

McKay,Brendan — SP — Tampa Bay
EXP MLB DEBUT: 2019 | H/W: 6-1 220 | FUT: #2 starter | 9C

Thrws L Age 23
2017 (1) Louisville
91-95 FB ++++
87-89 CT ++++
76-80 CB ++++
83-86 CU +++

Year	Lev	Team	W	L	Sv	IP	K	ERA	WHIP	BF/G	OBA	H%	S%	xERA	Ctl	Dom	Cmd	hr/9	BPV
2017	NCAA	Louisville	11	3	0	109	146	2.56	1.03	24.7	200	31	76	1.96	2.9	12.1	4.2	0.4	157
2017	A-	Hudson Valley	1	0	0	20	21	1.80	0.75	11.9	151	17	92	1.62	2.3	9.5	4.2	1.4	127
2018	Rk	GCL Rays	0	0	0	6	9	1.50	0.50	10.0	106	20	67		1.5	13.5	9.0	0.0	221
2018	A	Bowling Green	2	0	0	24	40	1.12	0.41	13.0	105	20	78		0.7	14.9	20.0	0.4	266
2018	A+	Charlotte	3	2	0	47	54	3.24	1.19	17.2	253	35	72	3.01	2.1	10.3	4.9	0.4	147

Two-way player who is pitch over hit. Repeatable, easy high-3/4s delivery. Four advanced pitches: 2-seam FB with advanced command and arm-side bore that lives in lower half of zone. Added CT as pro, already plus as he manipulates grip to change movement. Good 1-to-7 CB with bat missing break. CU is average offering presently.

McKay,David — RP — Seattle
EXP MLB DEBUT: 2019 | H/W: 6-3 200 | FUT: Setup reliever | 7C

Thrws R Age 24
2016 (14) Florida Atlantic
91-94 FB +++
78-82 CB +++

Year	Lev	Team	W	L	Sv	IP	K	ERA	WHIP	BF/G	OBA	H%	S%	xERA	Ctl	Dom	Cmd	hr/9	BPV
2017	Rk	Idaho Falls	6	5	0	79		6.49	1.54	24.6	318	37	60	5.93	2.1	7.7	3.8	1.5	102
2017	A	Lexington	0	0	0	9	11	13.70	2.61	8.3	423	50	50	12.86	4.9	10.8	2.2	3.9	80
2018	A+	Modesto	1	1	0	7	14	3.75	1.67	5.4	351	64	75	5.31	1.3	17.5	14.0	0.0	299
2018	AA	Arkansas	5	1	1	50	71	2.51	1.14	5.7	203	32	80	2.37	3.8	12.7	3.4	0.5	145
2018	AAA	Tacoma	0	0	0	1	0	0.00	0.00	2.8	0	0			0.0	0.0		0.0	18

RP-only type continues to use deception over stuff to fuel high Dom. Hides ball until last possible moment in 3/4s delivery; two pitch pitcher. 2-seam FB has late, above-average arm-side bore. Can adjust SL to create either sharp or sweeping break, although not a swing-and-miss offering. Close to big league ready.

McKenzie,Triston — SP — Cleveland
EXP MLB DEBUT: 2020 | H/W: 6-5 165 | FUT: #3 starter | 8C

Thrws R Age 21
2015 (1) HS (FL)
92-96 FB +++
79-83 CB ++++
84-86 CU ++

Year	Lev	Team	W	L	Sv	IP	K	ERA	WHIP	BF/G	OBA	H%	S%	xERA	Ctl	Dom	Cmd	hr/9	BPV
2016	A-	Mahoning Vall	4	3	0	49	55	0.55	0.96	20.6	183	26	98	1.56	2.9	10.1	3.4	0.4	120
2016	A	Lake County	2	2	0	34	49	3.18	0.97	21.5	220	35	68	2.15	1.6	13.0	8.2	0.5	209
2017	A+	Lynchburg	12	6	0	143	186	3.46	1.05	22.1	207	30	70	2.53	2.8	11.7	4.1	0.9	152
2018	AA	Akron	7	4	0	90	87	2.69	1.01	21.6	199	25	77	2.29	2.8	8.7	3.1	0.8	99

One of the top pitching prospects in the game, he faced the AA hurdle and passed the test with flying colors. Has a compact, athletic delivery that he repeats well, which has allowed him to avoid some of the growing pains that pitchers of his height often go through. The arsenal is FB/CB/CU; could stand to improve his stamina.

McRae,Alex — SP — Pittsburgh
EXP MLB DEBUT: 2020 | H/W: 6-3 185 | FUT: Middle reliever | 7E

Thrws R Age 26
2014 (10) Jacksonville
93-96 FB +++
78-81 CB ++
85-87 SL +++
87-89 CU ++

Year	Lev	Team	W	L	Sv	IP	K	ERA	WHIP	BF/G	OBA	H%	S%	xERA	Ctl	Dom	Cmd	hr/9	BPV
2016	A+	Bradenton	3	4	0	67	35	2.69	1.18	22.3	247	27	79	3.12	2.3	4.7	2.1	0.5	41
2016	AA	Altoona	8	6	0	88	67	4.80	1.58	24.2	315	37	70	5.25	2.6	6.8	2.7	0.7	72
2017	AA	Altoona	10	5	0	149	89	3.62	1.38	23.2	288	33	74	4.19	2.2	5.4	2.5	0.5	56
2018	AAA	Indianapolis	3	10	1	117	104	4.77	1.57	19.8	289	36	70	4.80	3.8	8.0	2.1	0.7	58
2018	MLB	Pittsburgh	0	1	0	6	5	5.90	2.13	15.1	317	40	69	6.01	7.4	7.4	1.0	0.0	-48

Current starter who has never been able to make decent stuff play. Lacks command and and a go-to pitch. Doesn't succeed in keeping hitters honest and off FB. Unless stuff plays up out of pen not likely to have much future MLB value.

McWilliams,Sam — SP — Kansas City
EXP MLB DEBUT: 2019 | H/W: 6-7 190 | FUT: Middle reliever | 6C

Thrws R Age 23
2014 (8) HS (TN)
92-95 FB ++++
85-87 SL +++
84-85 CU +

Year	Lev	Team	W	L	Sv	IP	K	ERA	WHIP	BF/G	OBA	H%	S%	xERA	Ctl	Dom	Cmd	hr/9	BPV
2016	A	Kane County	3	6	0	74	43	4.00	1.40	20.9	291	33	71	4.24	2.2	5.2	2.4	0.5	53
2017	A	Kane County	11	6	0	133	98	2.84	1.08	20.7	230	28	73	2.43	2.1	6.6	3.2	0.3	81
2018	A+	Visalia	1	1	0	25	32	2.14	1.03	19.4	220	33	80	2.16	2.1	11.4	5.3	0.4	166
2018	A+	Charlotte	0	1	0	11	7	4.02	1.43	15.9	292	35	69	3.86	2.4	5.6	2.3	0.0	54
2018	AA	Montgomery	6	7	0	100	94	5.03	1.51	22.8	282	34	69	4.99	3.6	8.5	2.4	1.2	73

Tall, lean hard-throwing RHP snathced up by KC in Rule 5 draft. Jerky 3/4s online delivery with moderate effort. Struggles maintaining mechanics, likely pushes profile to pen. Three-pitch pitcher. FB explodes with late run. Struggles with slot for SL but could be above-average pitch at maturity. CU is too firm to be a workable pitch.

Medeiros,Kodi — SP — Chicago (A)
EXP MLB DEBUT: 2019 | H/W: 6-2 180 | FUT: #5 SP/swingman | 6B

Thrws L Age 22
2014 (1) HS (HI)
88-91 FB ++
81-83 SL +++
82-83 CU +++

Year	Lev	Team	W	L	Sv	IP	K	ERA	WHIP	BF/G	OBA	H%	S%	xERA	Ctl	Dom	Cmd	hr/9	BPV
2015	A	Wisconsin	4	5	1	93	94	4.45	1.28	15.3	231	32	61	2.61	3.9	9.1	2.4	0.0	77
2016	A+	Brevard County	4	12	0	85	64	5.93	1.94	17.6	299	36	68	5.64	6.7	6.8	1.0	0.4	-40
2017	A+	Carolina	8	9	1	128	121	4.99	1.31	19.6	241	31	60	3.30	3.7	8.5	2.3	0.5	70
2018	AA	Birmingham	7	7	0	137	141	3.61	1.37	21.3	238	31	76	3.73	4.4	9.2	2.1	0.9	66
2018	AA	Biloxi	7	5	0	103	107	3.14	1.31	21.3	236	31	79	3.49	3.9	9.3	2.4	0.8	80

Former hard-throwing LHP acquired in mid-season trade. Cross-armed, low 3/4s delivery. Changes arm slot often to create deception. Two-seam FB 87-91 with solid arm-side bore. Struggles with command. Average SL, though different angles mean different breaks. Slurve break from 3/4s or sweep from low 3/4s. CU most consistent offering with late fade profile.

Medina,Adonis — SP — Philadelphia
EXP MLB DEBUT: 2020 | H/W: 6-1 185 | FUT: #3 starter | 8B

Thrws R Age 22
2014 FA (DR)
92-95 FB ++++
80-82 SL ++++
86-88 CU +++

Year	Lev	Team	W	L	Sv	IP	K	ERA	WHIP	BF/G	OBA	H%	S%	xERA	Ctl	Dom	Cmd	hr/9	BPV
2015	Rk	GCL Phillies	3	2	0	45	35	2.99	1.20	18.1	248	31	74	2.84	2.4	7.0	2.9	0.2	79
2016	A-	Williamsport	5	3	0	64	34	2.94	1.11	19.4	206	22	76	2.57	3.4	4.8	1.4	0.7	13
2017	A	Lakewood	4	9	0	119	133	3.02	1.19	21.7	235	32	76	2.92	2.9	10.0	3.4	0.5	119
2018	A+	Clearwater	10	4	0	111	123	4.13	1.25	20.6	247	33	69	3.58	2.9	10.0	3.4	0.9	119

Lean righty with a smooth delivery and athleticism in spades. Low-90s heat comes out easy with tons of late movement that has touched 97. Slider has made huge strides with its two-plane depth and is death to RHH, and change-up also is improving. Overall command and sequencing are the next level of polish.

Medina,Luis — SP — New York (A)
EXP MLB DEBUT: 2022 | H/W: 6-1 175 | FUT: Closer | 8E

Thrws R Age 19
2016 FA (DR)
95-99 FB +++++
79-83 CB ++++
90-92 CU +++

Year	Lev	Team	W	L	Sv	IP	K	ERA	WHIP	BF/G	OBA	H%	S%	xERA	Ctl	Dom	Cmd	hr/9	BPV
2017	Rk	Pulaski	1	1	0	23	22	5.09	1.22	15.5	178	23	56	2.20	5.5	8.6	1.6	0.4	25
2018	Rk	Pulaski	1	3	0	36	47	6.25	2.17	15.0	240	35	71	5.64	11.5	11.8	1.0	0.8	-81

Hard-throwing, lean RHP continues to struggle with poor control in rookie ball. Unable to repeat 3/4s delivery with plus-plus arm-speed. FB is high-octane with slight run but lacks plane. 11-to-5 CB is sharp with late, plus-plus break but struggles finishing delivery. CU has plus downward, arm-side run but doesn't maintain FB arm speed.

Mekkes,Dakota — RP — Chicago (N)
EXP MLB DEBUT: 2019 | H/W: 6-7 240 | FUT: Setup reliever | 7C

Thrws R Age 24
2016 (10) Michigan St
88-92 FB +++
79-84 SL +
78-82 CU ++

Year	Lev	Team	W	L	Sv	IP	K	ERA	WHIP	BF/G	OBA	H%	S%	xERA	Ctl	Dom	Cmd	hr/9	BPV
2016	A-	Eugene	1	1	0	17	21	2.12	0.88	7.0	187	27	79	1.56	2.1	11.1	5.3	0.5	161
2017	A	South Bend	3	0	4	31	47	0.58	0.90	6.4	138	24	96	0.84	4.1	13.6	3.4	0.3	154
2017	A+	Myrtle Beach	5	2	3	42	45	1.28	1.07	6.8	174	25	87	1.40	4.3	9.6	2.3	0.0	76
2018	AA	Tennessee	3	0	8	22	30	0.81	1.00	5.3	126	20	95	1.08	5.3	12.2	2.3	0.4	95
2018	AAA	Iowa	1	0	3	31	41	1.45	1.38	5.2	235	36	90	3.17	4.6	11.9	2.6	0.3	107

Large-bodied reliever continues to dominate more with deception than stuff. FB sits at 88-92, topping out at 93 mph but he hides the ball well with a short arm action. Mixes in a SL and CU, but both are below average. Hard to argue with the results, and now owns a career 1.16 ERA, .170 BAA, and 11.6 Dom in 147 IP.

Mella,Keury — SP — Cincinnati
EXP MLB DEBUT: 2017 | H/W: 6-2 200 | FUT: Setup reliever | 7C

Thrws R Age 25
2012 FA (DR)
93-95 FB ++++
79-82 SL ++
82-84 CU +++

Year	Lev	Team	W	L	Sv	IP	K	ERA	WHIP	BF/G	OBA	H%	S%	xERA	Ctl	Dom	Cmd	hr/9	BPV
2017	AA	Pensacola	4	10	1	134	109	4.30	1.33	20.6	263	31	70	4.06	2.9	7.3	2.5	0.9	72
2017	MLB	Cincinnati	0	0	0	4	1	6.75	1.75	9.1	307	28	67	7.05	4.5	2.3	0.5	2.3	-63
2018	AA	Pensacola	7	3	0	85	87	3.07	1.19	21.3	226	29	77	3.11	3.3	9.2	2.8	0.8	95
2018	AAA	Louisville	2	1	0	23	14	2.74	1.13	18.2	236	27	76	2.70	2.3	5.5	2.3	0.4	53
2018	MLB	Cincinnati	0	0	0	9	8	8.90	2.31	11.7	336	34	71	10.48	7.9	7.9	1.0	4.0	-53

Power RHP was starter throughout minors, likely RP long term. Three-pitch pitcher; workhorse is 2-seam FB with solid arm-side bore. Improved the quality of strikes thrown. Best secondary is a late-fading CU. Better consistency needed. CB is a below-average. 12-to-6 shape sometimes slurvy; not a deep break.

Mendez,Yohander — SP — Texas

EXP MLB DEBUT: 2016 | H/W: 6-4 178 | FUT: #4 starter | 7C

Thrws L Age 24
2012 FA (VZ)

91-94	FB	+++
82-84	CU	++++
84-86	SL	++
77-80	CB	++

Year	Lev	Team	W	L	Sv	IP	K	ERA	WHIP	BF/G	OBA	H%	S%	xERA	Ctl	Dom	Cmd	hr/9	BPV
2017	MLB	Texas	0	1	0	12	7	5.21	1.32	7.2	276	27	69	5.46	2.2	5.2	2.3	2.2	51
2018	A+	Down East	1	2	0	31	27	3.48	1.13	24.5	249	30	72	3.30	1.7	7.8	4.5	0.9	112
2018	AA	Frisco	1	1	0	33	32	4.91	1.30	22.7	262	31	68	4.62	2.7	8.7	3.2	1.6	101
2018	AAA	Round Rock	0	7	0	58	50	5.27	1.53	21.1	284	31	72	5.88	3.7	7.7	2.1	2.0	57
2018	MLB	Texas	2	2	0	27	18	5.63	1.58	15.0	267	29	67	5.13	5.0	6.0	1.2	1.3	-9

Tumultuous year included a demotion from MLB club after violation of team rules. At his best, filthy CU is his best pitch and plays off an average FB, but problems locating FB and getting ahead are problem areas. Pitched better in Sept MLB cup of coffee but lacks swing-and-miss stuff and/or reliable breaking ball to make much of a dent.

Mercer,Matt — SP — Arizona

EXP MLB DEBUT: 2021 | H/W: 6-2 180 | FUT: #5 SP/swingman | 7D

Thrws R Age 22
2018 (5) Oregon

92-95	FB	+++
	CB	++
	CU	++

Year	Lev	Team	W	L	Sv	IP	K	ERA	WHIP	BF/G	OBA	H%	S%	xERA	Ctl	Dom	Cmd	hr/9	BPV
2018	NCAA	Oregon	5	7	0	88	86	4.18	1.43	25.0	252	32	71	3.85	4.3	8.8	2.0	0.6	60
2018	Rk	AZL DBacks	0	0	0	2	1	4.50	1.50	8.6	262	18	100	7.85	4.5	4.5	1.0	4.5	-23
2018	A-	Hillsboro	0	0	0	27	37	3.00	0.93	8.4	200	32	67	1.62	2.0	12.3	6.2	0.3	186

High-effort RHP taken in fifth round after three years at Oregon. Pumps 92-95 mph FB with a little in the tank at times but struggles to locate often. Leans heavily on CB for whiffs but backs up on him too often and doesn't display proper feel at times. CU will require work. Some physical projection remaining and could add a tick more in velo.

Mills,McKenzie — SP — Miami

EXP MLB DEBUT: 2020 | H/W: 6-4 205 | FUT: Middle reliever | 6C

Thrws L Age 23
2014 (18) HS (GA)

90-93	FB	+++
72-76	CB	++
78-82	CU	++++

Year	Lev	Team	W	L	Sv	IP	K	ERA	WHIP	BF/G	OBA	H%	S%	xERA	Ctl	Dom	Cmd	hr/9	BPV
2017	A+	Clearwater	0	1	0	15	16	4.74	1.38	21.3	329	43	65	4.84	0.0	9.5		0.6	189
2018	A+	Jupiter	2	5	0	89	85	3.53	1.36	18.6	259	33	75	3.85	3.3	8.6	2.6	0.7	82
2018	A+	Clearwater	2	5	0	89	85	3.53	1.36	18.6	259	33	75	3.85	3.3	8.6	2.6	0.7	82
2018	AA	Jacksonville	0	3	0	16	8	8.33	1.60	17.9	325	34	48	6.40	2.2	4.4	2.0	1.7	38

Big-bodied LHP was acquired in mid-season trade with PHI. Repeatable, stiff, 3/4s delivery not optimal to SP. 3-pitch pitcher. Peppers zone with FB but needs to be fine to survive with limited movement. Fringe CB, struggles with consistent shape and break. CU best pitch w/ plus separation and solid sink, maintains FB arm speed.

Mills,Wyatt — RP — Seattle

EXP MLB DEBUT: 2019 | H/W: 6-3 185 | FUT: Setup reliever | 7D

Thrws R Age 24
2017 (3) Gonzaga

92-95	FB	++++
83-86	SL	++++

Year	Lev	Team	W	L	Sv	IP	K	ERA	WHIP	BF/G	OBA	H%	S%	xERA	Ctl	Dom	Cmd	hr/9	BPV
2017	NCAA	Gonzaga	2	2	12	40	58	1.80	1.10	7.1	261	41	84	2.72	0.9	13.0	14.5	0.2	228
2017	A-	Everett	0	1	2	7	11	2.57	0.86	3.7	132	26	67	0.39	3.9	14.1	3.7	0.0	168
2017	A	Clinton	0	1	4	13	18	1.37	0.84	4.4	119	21	82	0.24	4.1	12.4	3.0	0.0	129
2018	A+	Modesto	6	0	11	42	49	1.92	0.90	4.5	196	29	78	1.43	1.9	10.5	5.4	0.2	155
2018	AA	Arkansas	0	2	0	10	10	10.59	2.16	5.6	385	49	45	7.26	3.5	8.8	2.5	0.0	82

Fast-moving side-armed reliever has moved quickly since pro debut in 2017. True sidewinder delivery minus the knuckle scraping. Very Joe Smith-like delivery. 2-pitch pitcher. Low-to-mid 90s 2-seam FB has plus arm-side run. Sweeping SL has effective drop, making it difficult to lay off, even against LHH.

Mize,Casey — SP — Detroit

EXP MLB DEBUT: 2020 | H/W: 6-3 190 | FUT: #2 starter | 8B

Thrws R Age 21
2018 (1) Auburn

93-96	FB	+++
89-91	SL	+++
86-89	SP	++++

Year	Lev	Team	W	L	Sv	IP	K	ERA	WHIP	BF/G	OBA	H%	S%	xERA	Ctl	Dom	Cmd	hr/9	BPV
2018	NCAA	Auburn	10	6	0	114	156	3.31	0.88	24.8	207	31	64	2.01	1.3	12.3	9.8	0.8	205
2018	Rk	GCL Tigers West	0	0	0	2	4	0.00	0.50	6.6	0	0	100	-1.69	4.5	18.0	4.0	0.0	221
2018	A+	Lakeland	0	1	0	11	10	4.82	1.34	11.6	292	34	69	5.12	1.6	8.0	5.0	1.6	119

Well-proportioned, front-end collegiate starter with sensational command and the best splitter of his draft class. Able to pound the strike zone with a deceptively fluid delivery and a three-pitch mix grading plus or better across the board. Lively fastball complements vicious mid-to-high 80s splitter and slider. Ability to locate sets him apart.

Molina,Marcos — SP — Baltimore

EXP MLB DEBUT: 2019 | H/W: 6-3 188 | FUT: #4 starter | 7D

Thrws R Age 24
2012 FA (DR)

91-94	FB	+++
85-87	SL	++++
84-87	CU	+++

Year	Lev	Team	W	L	Sv	IP	K	ERA	WHIP	BF/G	OBA	H%	S%	xERA	Ctl	Dom	Cmd	hr/9	BPV
2016		Did not pitch - injured																	
2017	A+	St. Lucie	2	3	0	28	23	1.28	0.78	20.3	176	22	86	1.02	1.6	7.3	4.6	0.3	107
2017	AA	Binghamton	3	7	0	78	63	3.92	1.26	24.5	259	31	69	3.49	2.4	7.3	3.0	0.6	83
2018	AA	Binghamton	1	9	0	73	57	6.66	1.79	24.1	331	37	66	7.01	3.6	7.0	2.0	1.7	48
2018	AAA	Las Vegas	0	1	0	8	7	9.88	1.95	19.6	322	38	47	6.66	5.5	7.7	1.4	1.1	8

Oft-injured, former top pitching prospect in NYM system, signed as MiLB FA. Stuff showed signs of recovering during Instructional League. FB still features natural cut but not as explosive. SL is tight with 2-plane break. CU is an average offering. Struggled with consistency and FB command before release. Youth on side.

Moncada,Luis — SP — Tampa Bay

EXP MLB DEBUT: 2022 | H/W: 6-1 150 | FUT: #4 starter | 7D

Thrws L Age 21
2015 FA (VZ)

88-93	FB	++++
77-82	CB	+++
84-85	CU	+

Year	Lev	Team	W	L	Sv	IP	K	ERA	WHIP	BF/G	OBA	H%	S%	xERA	Ctl	Dom	Cmd	hr/9	BPV
2017	Rk	Princeton	4	2	0	38	28	5.65	1.68	13.2	299	33	69	5.91	4.2	6.6	1.6	1.4	22
2018	Rk	Princeton	3	1	0	46	53	3.13	1.13	16.5	208	29	72	2.31	3.5	10.4	2.9	0.4	110

Projectable LHP improved immensely repeating Appy League. Gains in Dom and Cmd aided by better overall stuff. High 3/4s online delivery. Struggles with consistent arm slot. FB ticked up velocity with added strength; plus pitch with solid late run. 1-to-7 CB struggles to maintain true shape. Little feel for CU.

Morales,Francisco — SP — Philadelphia

EXP MLB DEBUT: 2022 | H/W: 6-4 185 | FUT: #2 starter | 9D

Thrws R Age 19
2017 FA (VZ)

92-94	FB	+++
83-86	SL	++++
83-87	CU	++

Year	Lev	Team	W	L	Sv	IP	K	ERA	WHIP	BF/G	OBA	H%	S%	xERA	Ctl	Dom	Cmd	hr/9	BPV
2017	Rk	GCL Phillies	3	2	0	41	44	3.07	1.31	17.0	227	31	75	2.85	4.4	9.6	2.2	0.2	73
2018	A-	Williamsport	4	5	0	56	68	5.29	1.55	18.9	254	35	67	4.49	5.3	10.9	2.1	1.0	71

Broad-shouldered teenager has a workhorse frame already; spent the season tightening up mechanics and driving instead of drifting towards the plate. Command/control improved greatly by the end of the season, though still can lose release point. Low-90s FB; consistent depth on hard SL; CU can be too firm. Raw stuff in place for impact; needs reps.

Moran,Jovani — SP — Minnesota

EXP MLB DEBUT: 2020 | H/W: 6-1 165 | FUT: Middle reliever | 6B

Thrws L Age 21
2015 (7) HS (PR)

90-93	FB	+++
82-84	SL	++
82-84	CU	++++

Year	Lev	Team	W	L	Sv	IP	K	ERA	WHIP	BF/G	OBA	H%	S%	xERA	Ctl	Dom	Cmd	hr/9	BPV
2015	Rk	GCL Twins	0	2	0	19	17	4.22	1.30	13.2	228	30	64	2.64	4.2	8.0	1.9	0.0	48
2016		Did not pitch - injured																	
2017	Rk	Elizabethton	3	1	0	24	45	0.37	0.74	7.8	150	32	100	0.60	2.2	16.7	7.5	0.4	259
2018	A	Cedar Rapids	3	2	4	44	70	2.04	1.18	8.0	167	31	82	1.76	5.5	14.3	2.6	0.2	126
2018	A+	Fort Myers	6	1	4	31	37	2.60	0.90	7.7	185	27	70	1.36	2.3	10.7	4.6	0.3	148

Deceptive, high 3/4s LHP has dominated the lower minors as multi-inning RP. 3-pitch pitcher. Workhorse is a 2-seam FB with solid arm-side bore. Only has handle of pitch to arm-side, struggling with control at times. Renowned for late fading, 82-84 mph CU. Clearly, his best pitch and only swing-and-miss offering. Also features mediocre SL.

Morejon,Adrian — SP — San Diego

EXP MLB DEBUT: 2020 | H/W: 6-0 165 | FUT: #3 starter | 9E

Thrws L Age 20
2016 2016 FA (CU)

90-93	FB	++++
77-79	CB	+++
82-84	CU	+++

Year	Lev	Team	W	L	Sv	IP	K	ERA	WHIP	BF/G	OBA	H%	S%	xERA	Ctl	Dom	Cmd	hr/9	BPV
2017		A-	2	2	0	35	35	3.59	1.14	19.9	272	35	68	3.29	0.8	9.0	11.7	0.5	159
2017	A	Fort Wayne	1	2	0	27	23	4.30	1.51	19.6	267	33	72	4.31	4.3	7.6	1.8	0.7	39
2018	Rk	AZL Padres	0	1	0	2	4	8.18	2.27	11.2	446	69	60	8.83	0.0	16.4		0.0	313
2018	A+	Lake Elsinore	4	4	0	62	70	3.33	1.25	19.5	235	31	76	3.41	3.5	10.1	2.9	0.9	107

Young Cuban LH who spent time on DL with minor injuries. Wields FB that can touch 96 mph and sit 90-93 with some arm-side sink; lacks command of it at present. CB has good 1-to-7 depth and CU flashes above-average fade; both will need to be thrown more when behind in count. Better athlete than thicker build lets on. Chance for three above-average pitches.

Moreno,Erling — SP — Chicago (N)

EXP MLB DEBUT: 2021 | H/W: 6-3 200 | FUT: Setup reliever | 7D

Thrws R Age 22
2014 FA (CB)

92-95	FB	+++
	SL	+
	CU	++

Year	Lev	Team	W	L	Sv	IP	K	ERA	WHIP	BF/G	OBA	H%	S%	xERA	Ctl	Dom	Cmd	hr/9	BPV
2016	Rk	AZL Cubs	2	2	0	32	33	2.80	1.09	20.9	255	34	74	2.71	1.1	9.3	8.3	0.3	154
2016	A-	Eugene	2	1	0	30	22	0.90	0.70	17.6	159	18	95	0.91	1.5	6.6	4.4	0.6	96
2017	A	South Bend	2	4	0	64	57	4.22	1.36	19.1	237	30	68	3.30	4.4	8.0	1.8	0.4	45
2018	Rk	AZL Cubs 2	0	0	0	4	5	0.00	0.24	12.8	78	13	100		0.0	10.7		0.0	211
2018	A	South Bend	2	3	0	67	41	3.88	1.40	23.6	261	31	70	3.47	3.6	5.5	1.5	0.1	19

Slow-developing prospect finally made his full-season debut. 92-94 mph power sinker is best offering, generating tons of GB outs. Secondary pitches include a fringy SL and above-average CU. Throws with some effort and struggles with control. Made 11 starts in 2018, but durability concerns and lack of Dom means his future is likely in relief.

Moreno,Gerson — RP — Detroit

EXP MLB DEBUT: 2021 | H/W: 6-0 175 | FUT: Middle reliever | 7D

Thrws R Age 23
2013 FA (DR)

Velo	Pitch	Grade
93-98	FB	+++
82-85	SL	++
	CU	+

Year	Lev	Team	W	L	Sv	IP	K	ERA	WHIP	BF/G	OBA	H%	S%	xERA	Ctl	Dom	Cmd	hr/9	BPV
2016	A	West Michigan	1	1	11	25	27	1.08	1.08	4.2	212	30	89	1.87	2.9	9.7	3.4	0.0	115
2016	A+	Lakeland	0	3	3	24	27	7.07	1.74	5.2	244	30	61	5.32	7.4	10.0	1.4	1.5	-2
2017	A+	Lakeland	1	0	8	22	30	2.04	1.22	4.3	234	36	85	2.85	3.3	12.2	3.8	0.4	150
2017	AA	Erie	0	3	0	28	36	6.43	1.43	5.9	226	31	56	4.10	5.5	11.6	2.1	1.3	79
2018	AA	Erie	0	1	1	17	21	5.29	1.82	5.6	262	36	72	5.36	7.4	11.1	1.5	1.1	18

High-octane reliever who underwent Tommy John surgery in 2018. Prior to surgery, showed improvements to raw slider. Command inconsistencies still as issue, as have been for the majority of his career. Fastball flashes decent life, slider and changeup struggle to locate. Needs to make offspeed a priority once rehab is complete.

Morgan,Eli — SP — Cleveland

EXP MLB DEBUT: 2021 | H/W: 5-10 175 | FUT: #4 starter | 7B

Thrws R Age 22
2017 (8) Gonzaga

Velo	Pitch	Grade
86-89	FB	+
72-77	CU	+++++
78-80	SL	+++
74-78	CB	+++

Year	Lev	Team	W	L	Sv	IP	K	ERA	WHIP	BF/G	OBA	H%	S%	xERA	Ctl	Dom	Cmd	hr/9	BPV
2017	NCAA	Gonzaga	10	2	0	100	138	2.87	1.11	28.1	221	33	77	2.78	2.8	12.4	4.5	0.8	166
2017	A-	Mahoning Vall	3	2	0	35	58	1.03	0.94	10.1	196	37	88	1.28	2.3	14.9	6.4	0.0	224
2018	A	Lake County	2	0	0	44	56	1.84	0.88	20.4	200	30	81	1.59	1.6	11.4	7.0	0.4	180
2018	A+	Lynchburg	7	7	0	99	100	3.91	1.20	21.0	250	31	70	3.60	2.4	9.1	3.8	1.0	118

Compensates for lack of FB velo with wicked CU that has depth, run, deception, and at times comes out with screwball movement. Average command, will occasionally spin off fastball. Above-average pitchability, willing to quick pitch on FB and CU.

Moss,Scott — SP — Cincinnati

EXP MLB DEBUT: 2020 | H/W: 6-5 210 | FUT: #4 starter | 7C

Thrws L Age 24
2016 (4) Florida

Velo	Pitch	Grade
88-92	FB	+++
80-83	SL	+++
80-83	CU	+++

Year	Lev	Team	W	L	Sv	IP	K	ERA	WHIP	BF/G	OBA	H%	S%	xERA	Ctl	Dom	Cmd	hr/9	BPV
2016	NCAA	Florida	3	0	0	23	31	1.57	1.04	6.3	188	31	83	1.47	3.5	12.1	3.4	0.0	141
2016	Rk	Billings	3	1	0	38	29	2.36	1.29	15.6	246	30	83	3.29	3.3	6.9	2.1	0.5	52
2017	A	Dayton	13	6	0	135	156	3.46	1.20	20.9	230	31	73	3.07	3.2	10.4	3.3	0.7	119
2018	A+	Daytona	15	4	0	132	112	3.68	1.33	21.9	266	32	75	4.06	2.8	7.6	2.7	0.9	80

Big-bodied, command/control oriented LHP had solid 2018. Uses cross-fire delivery to create deception. Features 3 average-to-above-average offerings. Struggled corralling 2-seam FB with average late bore; inconsistent velocity start to start. Sweeping SL is best secondary and best overall pitch. CU rates a tick below average with inconsistent fade.

Muller,Kyle — SP — Atlanta

EXP MLB DEBUT: 2019 | H/W: 6-6 210 | FUT: #4 starter | 7C

Thrws L Age 21
2016 (2) HS (TX)

Velo	Pitch	Grade
91-94	FB	+++
86-88	CT	++
73-77	CB	++
81-83	CU	+++

Year	Lev	Team	W	L	Sv	IP	K	ERA	WHIP	BF/G	OBA	H%	S%	xERA	Ctl	Dom	Cmd	hr/9	BPV
2016	Rk	GCL Braves	1	0	0	27	38	0.66	0.96	10.3	154	27	92	0.88	4.0	12.6	3.2	0.0	137
2017	Rk	Danville	1	1	0	47	49	4.19	1.29	17.6	244	31	70	3.71	3.4	9.3	2.7	1.0	94
2018	A	Rome	3	0	0	30	23	2.40	1.07	19.4	221	25	83	2.82	2.4	6.9	2.9	0.9	77
2018	A+	Florida	4	2	0	80	79	3.25	1.40	24.2	261	35	75	3.52	3.6	8.9	2.5	0.2	81
2018	AA	Mississippi	4	1	0	29	27	3.10	0.97	22.0	212	26	72	2.47	1.9	8.4	4.5	0.9	119

Tall, athletic LHP with a muscular build finally made full-season debut, and advanced to Double-A. Added velo to 2-seam FB with slight arm-side run. Added CT, still work-in-progress. CB has 11-to-5 shape but the break isn't enough to miss bats. CU was revelation with FB arm-speed and fade. Seemingly around the zone, needs to tighten up command.

Munoz,Andres — SP — San Diego

EXP MLB DEBUT: 2019 | H/W: 6-2 165 | FUT: Setup reliever | 8C

Thrws R Age 20
2016 FA (DR)

Velo	Pitch	Grade
95-98	FB	++++
86-88	SL	+++
	CU	+++

Year	Lev	Team	W	L	Sv	IP	K	ERA	WHIP	BF/G	OBA	H%	S%	xERA	Ctl	Dom	Cmd	hr/9	BPV
2016	Rk	AZL Padres	1	1	0	19	26	5.63	1.67	5.4	228	35	65	3.96	7.5	12.2	1.6	0.5	35
2017	A-	Tri-City	3	0	1	23	35	3.88	1.34	4.6	187	30	72	2.91	6.2	13.6	2.2	0.8	95
2017	A	Fort Wayne	0	0	0	2	3	4.29	1.90	3.3	252	41	75	4.43	8.6	12.9	1.5	0.0	18
2018	A-	Tri-City	0	0	0	5	9	0.00	0.38	3.3	0	0	100		3.5	15.6	4.5	0.0	205
2018	AA	San Antonio	2	1	7	19	19	0.95	1.16	3.8	170	24	91	1.60	5.2	9.0	1.7	0.0	39

Electric RH with late-inning relief upside. Short, quick arm action produces upper-90s FB that reportedly hit 101 mph in past, but struggles to locate consistently. Blends in two-plane SL from low 3/4 slot for whiffs. Slim, athletic build and will need to repeat delivery. Still more a "thrower" than a pitcher at this point, but has big-time upside.

Myers,Tobias — SP — Tampa Bay

EXP MLB DEBUT: 2021 | H/W: 6-0 193 | FUT: #4 starter | 7C

Thrws R Age 20
2016 (6) HS (FL)

Velo	Pitch	Grade
91-94	FB	++++
76-80	CB	+++
81-84	CU	++

Year	Lev	Team	W	L	Sv	IP	K	ERA	WHIP	BF/G	OBA	H%	S%	xERA	Ctl	Dom	Cmd	hr/9	BPV
2016	Rk	GCL Orioles	0	0	0	7	4	5.00	1.67	10.8	330	36	73	6.24	2.5	5.0	2.0	1.3	41
2017	A-	Hudson Valley	2	0	0	26	38	3.10	0.80	18.9	188	31	60	1.18	1.4	13.1	9.5	0.3	217
2017	A-	Aberdeen	2	2	0	29	35	4.01	1.16	16.6	254	37	62	2.60	1.8	10.8	5.8	0.0	162
2018	A	Bowling Green	10	6	0	119	101	3.71	1.41	21.9	275	33	76	4.33	3.1	7.6	2.5	0.8	72

Athletic, undersized RHP acquired from BAL in 2017. Crispness of stuff took a step back despite posting good returns in Single-A; overall command suffered. 3/4s cross-fire delivery with terrific extension, which plays up average FB. FB has solid late arm-side run. CB has slurvy shape and is inconsistent. CU is behind CB.

Naile,James — SP — Oakland

EXP MLB DEBUT: 2019 | H/W: 6-4 175 | FUT: Middle reliever | 7C

Thrws R Age 26
2015 (20) Alabama-Birm

Velo	Pitch	Grade
88-90	FB	+++
85-87	CT	+++
	SL	++
	CU	++

Year	Lev	Team	W	L	Sv	IP	K	ERA	WHIP	BF/G	OBA	H%	S%	xERA	Ctl	Dom	Cmd	hr/9	BPV
2017	Rk	AZL Athletics	0	0	0	5	11	1.80	0.80	9.1	221	49	100	2.86	0.0	19.8		1.8	374
2017	A+	Stockton	0	0	0	7	4	5.14	1.43	14.9	313	36	60	4.19	1.3	5.1	4.0	0.0	76
2017	AA	Midland	2	3	0	61	42	3.24	1.18	17.5	242	28	75	3.21	2.5	6.2	2.5	0.7	62
2018	AA	Midland	1	0	0	15	7	3.00	1.27	30.7	287	31	78	3.95	1.2	4.2	3.5	0.6	61
2018	AAA	Nashville	7	10	0	135	77	4.73	1.45	24.1	290	32	68	4.65	2.7	5.1	1.9	0.8	38

Sinkerballer RHP who logged 150+ IP in upper minors in 2018 and is almost ready to contribute. Heavy FB sits high-80s and will top out at 92 mph for high dose of GB outs. Blends in effective CT that neutralizes RHH on inner third of plate. SL/CU are fringe offerings and is most effective with FB/CT combo. Solid middle RP option with low Dom.

Neidert,Nick — SP — Miami

EXP MLB DEBUT: 2019 | H/W: 6-1 180 | FUT: #3 starter | 8C

Thrws R Age 22
2015 (2) HS (GA)

Velo	Pitch	Grade
89-92	FB	+++
83-85	SL	+++
81-83	CU	++++

Year	Lev	Team	W	L	Sv	IP	K	ERA	WHIP	BF/G	OBA	H%	S%	xERA	Ctl	Dom	Cmd	hr/9	BPV
2015	Rk	AZL Mariners	0	2	0	35	23	1.54	0.97	12.1	202	24	85	1.74	2.3	5.9	2.6	0.3	62
2016	A	Clinton	7	3	0	91	69	2.57	0.97	18.1	226	27	77	2.44	1.3	6.8	5.3	0.7	106
2017	A+	Modesto	10	3	0	104	109	2.77	1.08	21.3	244	32	76	2.84	1.5	9.4	6.4	0.6	148
2017	AA	Arkansas	1	3	0	23	13	6.62	1.65	17.2	336	36	62	6.58	1.9	5.1	2.6	1.6	57
2018	AA	Jacksonville	12	7	0	152	154	3.25	1.14	23.2	249	31	76	3.43	1.8	9.1	5.0	1.0	132

Undersized, pitchability RHP enjoyed best season as pro. Repeats jerky 3/4s cross-armed delivery well with great extension, utilizes every inch of body for energy. Peppers lower half of zone with 2-seam FB, which plays up due to funkiness. Maintains FB arm speed and achieves solid separation with late-fading CU. Mixes in 2 types of SL.

Nelson,Nick — SP — New York (A)

EXP MLB DEBUT: 2020 | H/W: 6-1 195 | FUT: #3 starter | 8E

Thrws R Age 23
2016 (4) Gulf Coast St Coll

Velo	Pitch	Grade
94-97	FB	++++
80-82	CB	++++
87-88	CU	++

Year	Lev	Team	W	L	Sv	IP	K	ERA	WHIP	BF/G	OBA	H%	S%	xERA	Ctl	Dom	Cmd	hr/9	BPV
2017	A	Charleston (Sc)	3	12	0	100	110	4.58	1.53	19.8	267	36	69	4.13	4.5	9.9	2.2	0.4	75
2018	A	Charleston (Sc)	1	1	0	24	35	3.72	1.03	18.6	209	34	63	2.03	2.6	13.0	5.0	0.4	182
2018	A+	Tampa	7	5	0	88	99	3.37	1.32	20.2	217	31	72	2.62	4.8	10.1	2.1	0.1	70
2018	AA	Trenton	0	0	0	8	10	5.49	2.32	14.0	302	41	78	7.23	9.9	11.0	1.1	1.1	-51

Lean, Hard-throwing RHP has swing-and-miss profile but struggles with control and repeating 3/4s online delivery. 3-pitch pitcher with two potential plus pitches. Hard-riding FB has late life. Struggles commanding in and out of zone. SL has tight bite and devastating 2-plane movement. CU lags behind rest of arsenal but has improved.

Nix,Jacob — SP — San Diego

EXP MLB DEBUT: 2018 | H/W: 6-3 200 | FUT: #5 SP/swingman | 7C

Thrws R Age 23
2015 (3) UCLA

Velo	Pitch	Grade
91-94	FB	+++
75-78	CB	+++
78-82	CU	+++

Year	Lev	Team	W	L	Sv	IP	K	ERA	WHIP	BF/G	OBA	H%	S%	xERA	Ctl	Dom	Cmd	hr/9	BPV
2017	A+	Lake Elsinore	4	3	0	66	51	4.35	1.33	25.0	295	35	67	4.28	1.4	6.9	5.1	0.7	106
2017	AA	San Antonio	1	2	0	27	22	5.63	1.51	19.6	294	37	59	4.08	3.0	7.3	2.4	0.0	69
2018	AA	San Antonio	2	3	0	52	41	2.07	0.92	21.7	209	25	80	1.95	1.6	7.1	4.6	0.5	103
2018	AAA	El Paso	1	0	0	6	3	0.00	0.83	21.9	228	26	100	1.50	0.0	4.5		0.0	99
2018	MLB	San Diego	2	5	0	42	21	7.05	1.54	20.4	305	31	56	5.96	2.8	4.5	1.6	1.7	24

Big, strong RHP who made MLB debut from rotation in September. Features FB that hums in the low-90s and can peak at 96 mph and shows ability to command it. CB will flash plus depth and bite and mixes in a useable CU as third pitch. Easy, low-effort delivery should allow for plus command moving forward with avg Dom totals.

Nogosek,Steve — RP — New York (N)

EXP MLB DEBUT: 2021 | H/W: 6-1 172 | FUT: Setup reliever | 7D

Thrws R Age 24
2016 (6) Oregon

Velo	Pitch	Grade
93-96	FB	++++
82-85	SL	++
84-86	SP	++

Year	Lev	Team	W	L	Sv	IP	K	ERA	WHIP	BF/G	OBA	H%	S%	xERA	Ctl	Dom	Cmd	hr/9	BPV
2017	A	Greenville	2	3	13	35	45	2.56	1.00	5.8	195	27	81	2.41	2.8	11.5	4.1	1.0	150
2017	A+	St. Lucie	1	1	0	16	15	5.06	1.50	7.7	262	35	63	3.58	4.5	8.4	1.9	0.0	48
2017	A+	Salem	2	1	6	17	18	4.19	1.45	5.7	236	28	77	4.59	5.2	9.4	1.8	1.6	46
2018	A+	St. Lucie	1	1	1	32	37	3.08	1.25	5.7	196	25	81	3.14	5.0	10.4	2.1	1.1	68
2018	AA	Binghamton	0	0	0	20	21	8.10	1.85	5.8	221	27	56	5.19	9.5	9.5	1.0	1.4	-67

High-effort reliever who throws hard but struggles with command and lacks feel for offspeed. Aggressiveness is there, but head whack in delivery makes it unlikely he will ever have a lot of feel. CB is a short slurve and is not reliable. Split is not either.

Norwood,James — RP — Chicago (N) — EXP MLB DEBUT: 2018 — H/W: 6-2 200 — FUT: Setup reliever — 7B

Thrws R Age 25
2014 (7) Saint Louis

Velo	Pitch	Grade
95-98	FB	++++
87-88	SP	+++
85-87	SL	+++
83-85	CU	+

Year	Lev	Team	W	L	Sv	IP	K	ERA	WHIP	BF/G	OBA	H%	S%	xERA	Ctl	Dom	Cmd	hr/9	BPV
2017	A+	Myrtle Beach	3	0	6	39	41	2.31	1.23	5.9	225	31	81	2.63	3.7	9.5	2.6	0.2	89
2017	AA	Tennessee	1	3	1	18	19	5.44	1.70	5.9	300	39	67	5.10	4.5	9.4	2.1	0.5	67
2018	AA	Tennessee	1	2	2	32	36	2.52	1.15	5.1	216	30	80	2.61	3.4	10.1	3.0	0.6	109
2018	AAA	Iowa	1	1	0	17	21	2.62	1.34	4.8	185	27	82	2.68	6.3	11.0	1.8	0.5	46
2018	MLB	Chi Cubs	0	1	0	11	10	4.09	1.73	4.5	311	40	74	4.88	4.1	8.2	2.0	0.0	55

Made his MLB debut after a solid season. Plus FB sits at 95-98, topping at 100 mph with late life. Mixes in a power SL, a SP, and a fringe CU. Four-pitch mix is unusual and allows him to keep hitters off the FB. Stiff mechanics and lack of finesse prevent him from starting, but aggressive approach gives him the tools to make an impact in relief.

Oaks,Trevor — SP — Kansas City — EXP MLB DEBUT: 2018 — H/W: 6-3 220 — FUT: #5 SP/swingman — 6C

Thrws R Age 26
2014 (7) California Baptist

Velo	Pitch	Grade
88-90	FB	++
81-83	SL	+++
85-87	CT	+++
82-83	CU	++

Year	Lev	Team	W	L	Sv	IP	K	ERA	WHIP	BF/G	OBA	H%	S%	xERA	Ctl	Dom	Cmd	hr/9	BPV
2017	Rk	Ogden	0	0	0	5	6	8.65	2.50	13.8	450	56	67	11.18	1.7	10.4	6.0	1.7	158
2017	Rk	AZL Dodgers	0	0	0	2	3	0.00	0.00	5.6	0	0			0.0	13.5		0.0	261
2017	AAA	Oklahoma City	4	3	0	84	72	3.64	1.25	21.4	269	33	71	3.56	1.9	7.7	4.0	0.5	105
2018	AAA	Omaha	8	8	0	128	70	3.23	1.36	24.3	265	30	76	3.63	3.1	4.9	1.6	0.4	23
2018	MLB	KC Royals	0	2	0	13	10	7.50	2.05	16.1	361	42	62	7.18	4.1	6.8	1.7	0.7	30

Fringy, 3/4 slot RHP lives on inducing soft-contact with average to below-average repertoire of four pitches. Made MLB debut. 2-seam FB has solid arm-side run but lacks velocity. SL & CT both effective but neither are swing-and-miss offerings. CU is fringe-average pitch.

Ogle,Braeden — SP — Pittsburgh — EXP MLB DEBUT: 2022 — H/W: 6-2 170 — FUT: Middle reliever — 6C

Thrws L Age 21
2016 (4) HS (FL)

Velo	Pitch	Grade
90-94	FB	+++
83-86	SL	+++
83-85	CU	+++

Year	Lev	Team	W	L	Sv	IP	K	ERA	WHIP	BF/G	OBA	H%	S%	xERA	Ctl	Dom	Cmd	hr/9	BPV
2016	Rk	GCL Pirates	0	2	0	27	20	2.65	1.07	13.2	190	22	78	2.23	3.6	6.6	1.8	0.7	39
2017	Rk	Bristol	2	3	0	43	35	3.14	1.30	17.7	248	31	75	3.11	3.3	7.3	2.2	0.2	59
2018	A	West Virginia	2	0	0	17	21	2.65	1.53	18.5	250	36	84	3.97	5.3	11.1	2.1	0.5	75

Lefty has only thrown 87 innings since being a fourth-round pick out of HS in 2016. Results have been good, other than some wildness, but spent most of 2018 on the DL at Low A West Virginia. Delivery is compact and clean but tends to overthrow, like a lot of young pitchers. SL sharp and short and could play well against LHH. FB and CU show good run.

Ortiz,Luis — SP — Baltimore — EXP MLB DEBUT: 2018 — H/W: 6-3 230 — FUT: #4 starter — 7B

Thrws R Age 23
2014 (1) HS (CA)

Velo	Pitch	Grade
89-94	FB	+++
84-86	SL	+++
84-85	CU	+++

Year	Lev	Team	W	L	Sv	IP	K	ERA	WHIP	BF/G	OBA	H%	S%	xERA	Ctl	Dom	Cmd	hr/9	BPV
2016	AA	Biloxi	2	2	0	23	16	1.95	1.56	16.9	285	33	91	4.82	3.9	6.2	1.6	0.8	25
2017	AA	Biloxi	4	7	0	94	79	4.02	1.23	17.3	229	26	71	3.57	3.5	7.6	2.1	1.1	58
2018	AA	Biloxi	3	4	2	68	65	3.71	1.19	17.0	247	31	72	3.48	2.4	8.6	3.6	0.9	109
2018	AAA	Norfolk	2	1	0	31	21	3.75	1.35	21.7	279	31	76	4.54	2.3	6.1	2.6	1.2	65
2018	MLB	Baltimore	0	1	0	2	0	17.14	4.76	8.0	542	54	60	18.08	12.9	0.0	0.0	0.0	-329

Husky 3/4s RHP suffering from prospect fatigue was acquired in mid-season trade with MIL. Easy, cross-armed delivery. 2-seam FB velocity inconsistent start to start. Commands FB well enough with solid arm-side run. SL hasn't been as tight, struggling with slurvyness. CU took step forward with FB arm-speed and late arm-side fade.

Ortiz,Robinson — SP — Los Angeles (N) — EXP MLB DEBUT: 2022 — H/W: 6-0 180 — FUT: #4 starter — 7D

Thrws L Age 19
2017 FA (DR)

Velo	Pitch	Grade
92-94	FB	+++
	CB	++
	CU	+++

Year	Lev	Team	W	L	Sv	IP	K	ERA	WHIP	BF/G	OBA	H%	S%	xERA	Ctl	Dom	Cmd	hr/9	BPV
2018	Rk	AZL Dodgers	2	2	0	32	42	4.21	1.21	11.8	230	34	65	2.93	3.4	11.8	3.5	0.6	139

Dominican teen held his own in state-side debut. Simple, repeatable mechanics and pounds the strike zone. Solid three-pitch mix is highlighted by a 92-94 mph FB with some arm-side run. CB has good late break, but needs refinement and CU shows above-average to plus. At his size there is projection left and he profiles as a #4 starter.

Oviedo,Johan — SP — St. Louis — EXP MLB DEBUT: 2022 — H/W: 6-6 210 — FUT: #3 starter — 8D

Thrws R Age 21
2016 FA (CU)

Velo	Pitch	Grade
92-95	FB	++++
	CB	+++
	CU	++

Year	Lev	Team	W	L	Sv	IP	K	ERA	WHIP	BF/G	OBA	H%	S%	xERA	Ctl	Dom	Cmd	hr/9	BPV
2017	Rk	Johnson City	2	1	0	27	31	4.96	1.47	19.5	223	32	63	2.98	6.0	10.3	1.7	0.0	42
2017	A-	State College	2	2	0	47	39	4.59	1.51	25.5	285	35	69	4.48	3.4	7.5	2.2	0.6	59
2018	A	Peoria	10	10	1	121	118	4.23	1.54	21.2	240	31	72	3.82	5.9	8.8	1.5	0.4	17

Signed for $1.9 million in 2016 and struggled with control in his state-side debut. Above-average FB sits at 92-95 topping at 98 mph, but FB velo declined as the season progressed. CB flashes plus but needs to be more consistent and shows some feel for CU. Huge frame leaves some projection, but lots of work to do.

Oviedo,Luis — SP — Cleveland — EXP MLB DEBUT: 2023 — H/W: 6-4 170 — FUT: #3 starter — 8D

Thrws R Age 19
2015 FA (VZ)

Velo	Pitch	Grade
91-97	FB	+++
77-78	SL	++
73-78	CB	++
81-84	CU	

Year	Lev	Team	W	L	Sv	IP	K	ERA	WHIP	BF/G	OBA	H%	S%	xERA	Ctl	Dom	Cmd	hr/9	BPV
2017	Rk	AZL Indians	4	2	0	51	70	7.21	1.64	16.3	300	45	52	4.79	3.9	12.3	3.2	0.4	135
2018	A-	Mahoning Vall	4	2	0	48	61	1.88	0.92	19.9	201	29	83	1.84	1.9	11.4	6.1	0.6	173
2018	A	Lake County	1	0	0	9	6	3.00	1.33	18.7	165	21	75	2.01	7.0	6.0	0.9	0.0	-63

A young projection arm who has also shown a high baseline of performance to date. He displayed a lot of promise in short-season ball as an 18-year-old. He has a fairly clean, low-effort delivery and usually stays on line well, which allows him to be an advanced strike thrower.

Paddack,Chris — SP — San Diego — EXP MLB DEBUT: 2019 — H/W: 6-4 195 — FUT: #3 starter — 9C

Thrws R Age 23
2015 (8) HS (TX)

Velo	Pitch	Grade
93-95	FB	++++
78-80	CB	+++
80-82	CU	+++++

Year	Lev	Team	W	L	Sv	IP	K	ERA	WHIP	BF/G	OBA	H%	S%	xERA	Ctl	Dom	Cmd	hr/9	BPV
2016	A	Greensboro	2	0	0	28	48	0.96	0.39	15.0	102	18	89	-0.48	0.6	15.4	24.0	0.6	277
2016	A	Fort Wayne	0	0	0	14	23	0.64	1.00	17.8	218	40	93	1.69	1.9	14.8	7.7	0.0	232
2017		Did not pitch - injury																	
2018	A+	Lake Elsinore	4	1	0	52	83	2.25	0.90	19.4	226	38	77	2.04	0.7	14.3	20.8	0.5	257
2018	AA	San Antonio	3	2	0	37	37	1.94	0.73	18.8	180	24	73	0.84	1.0	9.0	9.3	0.2	153

Strike-thrower who had impressive 2018 campaign back from Tommy John surgery. Tops out at 98 mph and sits 93-95 with plus FB that he manipulates speed and shape of. Owns elite CU that tumbles out of the zone with quality velocity separation. Has tightened up CB; solid-average pitch. Works ahead regularly and is always in control of the game.

Palumbo,Joe — SP — Texas — EXP MLB DEBUT: 2019 — H/W: 6-1 150 — FUT: #4 starter — 7C

Thrws L Age 24
2013 (30) HS (NY)

Velo	Pitch	Grade
92-95	FB	+++
75-79	CB	++++
82-85	CU	++

Year	Lev	Team	W	L	Sv	IP	K	ERA	WHIP	BF/G	OBA	H%	S%	xERA	Ctl	Dom	Cmd	hr/9	BPV
2016	A	Hickory	7	5	8	96	122	2.25	1.11	11.5	208	31	81	2.32	3.4	11.4	3.4	0.5	133
2017	A+	Down East	1	0	0	13	22	0.68	0.61	15.1	97	21	88		2.7	15.0	5.5	0.0	214
2018	Rk	AZL Rangers	0	0	0	9	15	4.00	0.67	10.5	165	28	40	1.18	1.0	15.0	15.0	1.0	261
2018	A+	Down East	1	4	0	27	34	2.67	1.11	17.7	240	33	81	3.22	2.0	11.3	5.7	1.0	168
2018	AA	Frisco	1	0	0	9	10	1.98	0.99	17.3	190	28	78	1.37	3.0	9.9	3.3	0.0	116

Smaller, wiry-built pitcher recovering from Tommy John surgery impressed in his return. Strong three-pitch mix still intact, highlighted by a late-breaking, tightly wound curveball. FB runs up to 95, has life, and he can get it by hitters up in the zone. Change-up flashes average, Compact delivery, clean arm action bodes well for future command.

Pannone,Thomas — SP — Toronto — EXP MLB DEBUT: 2018 — H/W: 6-0 180 — FUT: #5 SP/swingman — 6C

Thrws L Age 24
2013 (9) Coll of So Nevada

Velo	Pitch	Grade
88-91	FB	+++
	CB	++
	CU	++

Year	Lev	Team	W	L	Sv	IP	K	ERA	WHIP	BF/G	OBA	H%	S%	xERA	Ctl	Dom	Cmd	hr/9	BPV
2017	AA	Akron	6	1	0	82	81	2.63	1.07	22.8	224	29	77	2.52	2.3	8.9	3.9	0.5	116
2018	A+	Dunedin	0	1	0	4	1	15.00	2.38	21.8	432	42	33	10.91	2.1	2.1	1.0	2.1	-1
2018	AA	New Hampshire	0	0	0	9	12	3.00	1.56	19.7	262	37	85	4.63	5.0	12.0	2.4	1.0	99
2018	AAA	Buffalo	0	3	0	36	40	4.97	1.30	24.8	282	34	69	5.21	1.7	9.9	5.7	2.0	150
2018	MLB	Toronto	4	1	0	43	29	4.19	1.21	14.4	234	25	71	3.88	3.1	6.1	1.9	1.5	42

Command and control lefty was acquired in the Joe Smith deal and made six late-season starts for the Jays. FB sits at 88-91, topping at 93, but it gets on hitters quickly due to deception. CB and CU are a tick above-average, but leave him little margin for error. Back-end lefty with limited upside.

Pardinho,Eric — SP — Toronto — EXP MLB DEBUT: 2022 — H/W: 6-1 165 — FUT: #3 starter — 8C

Thrws R Age 18
2018 FA (BR)

Velo	Pitch	Grade
90-93	FB	++++
80-83	CB	++++
83-85	SL	++
83-84	CU	++

Year	Lev	Team	W	L	Sv	IP	K	ERA	WHIP	BF/G	OBA	H%	S%	xERA	Ctl	Dom	Cmd	hr/9	BPV
2018	Rk	Bluefield	4	3	0	50	64	2.88	1.06	17.6	208	29	77	2.60	2.9	11.5	4.0	0.9	148

Short, strong-armed hurler was lights-out debut. Compact delivery with an explosive finish results in easy velo. FB sits at 90-93, topping out at 96 relying more on high spin rate than late action. Backs up the heat with a plus CB that has tight spin and late break and a hard SL. CU is shows as above-average with room for more as he matures.

Patino,Luis — SP — San Diego

EXP MLB DEBUT: 2021 | H/W: 6-0 150 | FUT: #3 starter | 9D

Thrws R Age 19 — 2016 2016 FA (CB)

- 93-96 FB ++++
- 77-80 CB +++
- 87-89 SL +++
- 86-88 CU +++

Year	Lev	Team	W	L	Sv	IP	K	ERA	WHIP	BF/G	OBA	H%	S%	xERA	Ctl	Dom	Cmd	hr/9	BPV
2017	Rk	AZL Padres	2	1	0	40	43	2.48	1.20	17.9	221	30	80	2.70	3.6	9.7	2.7	0.5	95
2018	A	Fort Wayne	6	3	0	83	98	2.17	1.07	19.0	217	32	78	2.00	2.6	10.6	4.1	0.1	139

Young, live-armed RH who exploded onto the scene in MWL. Can reach back for 98 mph and comfortably sit mid-90s with lively plus FB and maintains velo deep into starts. CB flashes plus 11-to-5 bend and misses barrels. SL has two-plane movement and CU shows drop required for outs vs. LHH. Good athlete with room to fill out some in upper half.

Paulino,David — RP — Toronto

EXP MLB DEBUT: 2017 | H/W: 6-7 222 | FUT: Setup reliever | 7C

Thrws R Age 25 — 2010 FA (DR)

- 93-96 FB ++++
- 74-76 CB ++++
- 82-85 SL ++
- 84-86 CU ++

Year	Lev	Team	W	L	Sv	IP	K	ERA	WHIP	BF/G	OBA	H%	S%	xERA	Ctl	Dom	Cmd	hr/9	BPV
2017	MLB	Houston	2	0	0	29	34	6.52	1.48	20.8	306	37	63	6.49	2.2	10.6	4.9	2.5	149
2018	Rk	GCL Blue Jays	0	0	0	9	10	3.00	0.89	11.1	216	31	63	1.44	1.0	10.0	10.0	0.0	171
2018	Rk	GCL Astros	0	0	0	9	10	3.00	0.89	11.1	216	31	63	1.44	1.0	10.0	10.0	0.0	171
2018	AAA	Fresno	0	0	0	18	23	5.50	1.17	17.9	240	32	56	3.83	2.5	11.5	4.6	1.5	158
2018	MLB	Toronto	1	0	0	6	6	1.45	1.29	3.6	255	30	100	4.33	2.9	8.7	3.0	1.5	96

Huge fireballer works downhill and comes after hitters with a plus 93-96 FB that tops at 98 in relief. Plus, tight-late breaking CB, SL, and CU give him the tools to start or relieve. Pounds the strike zone and has swing and miss stuff and now owns a career 10.1 Dom and 4.1 Cmd, but command within the zone is fringe and profiles better in relief.

Peacock,Matt — RP — Arizona

EXP MLB DEBUT: 2020 | H/W: 6-0 176 | FUT: Middle reliever | 7C

Thrws R Age 25 — 2017 (23) South Alabama

- 90-92 FB +++
- SL +++
- CU +++

Year	Lev	Team	W	L	Sv	IP	K	ERA	WHIP	BF/G	OBA	H%	S%	xERA	Ctl	Dom	Cmd	hr/9	BPV
2017	NCAA	South Alabama	3	3	10	50	55	2.88	1.16	8.0	225	31	76	2.74	3.1	9.9	3.2	0.5	114
2017	A-	Hillsboro	0	2	1	29	23	2.47	1.10	5.2	226	27	80	2.70	2.5	7.1	2.9	0.6	79
2018	A	Kane County	3	3	2	42	35	3.63	1.26	10.1	261	32	72	3.56	2.3	7.5	3.2	0.6	89
2018	A+	Visalia	4	3	0	56	55	4.66	1.32	21.1	265	33	66	4.08	2.7	8.8	3.2	1.0	103

Control-oriented RHP who split time as RP and SP in full-season debut. Displays plus command of low-90s FB that he locates well low in zone for tons of ground balls. CU/SL are fringe secondaries that will require work in low minors. Chance to stick as back-end SP but could be destined for long relief role.

Pearson,Nate — SP — Toronto

EXP MLB DEBUT: 2020 | H/W: 6-6 245 | FUT: #2 starter | 9D

Thrws R Age 22 — 2017 (1) Florida Internat'l

- 95-98 FB +++++
- 89-94 SL +++
- 73-78 CB ++
- 88-90 CU ++

Year	Lev	Team	W	L	Sv	IP	K	ERA	WHIP	BF/G	OBA	H%	S%	xERA	Ctl	Dom	Cmd	hr/9	BPV
2017	Rk	GCL Blue Jays	0	0	0	1	2	0.00	1.00	3.8	262	55	100	2.23	0.0	18.0		0.0	342
2017	A-	Vancouver	0	0	0	19	24	0.95	0.58	9.2	101	17	82		2.4	11.4	4.8	0.0	159
2018	A+	Dunedin	0	1	0	1	1	15.00	4.17	8.4	596	63	75	25.77	0.0	7.5		7.5	153

Has the best velocity in the system, but missed most of season with a broken arm. Dominates with a double plus 95-98 FB that tops at 102. Relies on downhill tilt from huge frame. Backs up FB with a power SL that shows swing and miss potential. CB and CU are average, but need refinement to reach potential as top-end starter. FB hit 104 mph in AFL.

Pelham,CD — RP — Texas

EXP MLB DEBUT: 2018 | H/W: 6-5 215 | FUT: Setup reliever | 8E

Thrws L Age 24 — 2015 (33) Spartanburg Methodist

- 95-97 FB ++++
- 83-85 SL +++
- 84-86 CU ++

Year	Lev	Team	W	L	Sv	IP	K	ERA	WHIP	BF/G	OBA	H%	S%	xERA	Ctl	Dom	Cmd	hr/9	BPV
2016	A-	Spokane	0	6	2	38	50	6.16	2.08	11.6	251	39	67	4.87	10.2	11.8	1.2	0.0	-44
2017	A	Hickory	4	2	13	62	75	3.19	1.18	6.7	212	29	76	2.91	3.8	10.9	2.9	0.9	112
2018	A+	Down East	0	0	11	27	34	1.99	1.32	4.9	231	35	83	2.70	4.3	11.3	2.6	0.0	104
2018	AA	Frisco	2	0	2	19	19	6.16	1.74	3.6	272	35	63	4.76	6.2	9.0	1.5	0.5	14
2018	MLB	Texas	0	0	0	7	7	7.50	2.22	3.6	371	47	63	7.17	5.0	8.8	1.8	0.0	41

Rode a few extra ticks on his fastball all the way to the majors. Big-framed but very athletic, his control history is troubling, but the strikeouts have piled up and an improved slider/cutter has given him a second potentially plus pitch. Poor change-up will keep him in the bullpen, likely as a left-on-left guy with a chance for more.

Pena,Luis — SP — Los Angeles (A)

EXP MLB DEBUT: 2019 | H/W: 5-11 170 | FUT: Setup reliever | 7D

Thrws R Age 23 — 2014 FA (DR)

- 90-93 FB +++
- SL +++
- CU ++

Year	Lev	Team	W	L	Sv	IP	K	ERA	WHIP	BF/G	OBA	H%	S%	xERA	Ctl	Dom	Cmd	hr/9	BPV
2016	A	Burlington	5	9	1	100	118	4.04	1.32	15.4	240	34	69	3.31	3.9	10.6	2.7	0.5	104
2017	A+	Inland Empire	6	10	0	131	148	5.29	1.50	22.6	272	36	66	4.66	4.0	10.2	2.6	1.0	93
2017	AA	Mobile	1	3	0	20	19	3.15	1.25	20.4	221	26	82	3.69	4.1	8.6	2.1	1.4	63
2018	AA	Mobile	2	4	0	59	63	4.27	1.20	19.8	217	27	67	3.24	3.8	9.6	2.5	1.1	88
2018	AAA	Salt Lake	4	3	0	46	38	5.65	1.71	19.0	265	30	70	5.63	6.2	7.4	1.2	1.6	-17

Compact right-handed starter who progressed well in 2018, splitting the year between Double-A and Triple-A. Delivery and effort level appear to point to a future relief role, as command has been an issue, despite decent offspeed mix. Effective low-90s sinking fastball plays well off above-average slider, while changeup has a ways to go.

Perez,Cionel — RP — Houston

EXP MLB DEBUT: 2018 | H/W: 5-11 170 | FUT: Middle reliever | 7B

Thrws L Age 22 — 2017 FA (CU)

- 95-97 FB ++++
- 83-86 SL +++
- 86-89 CU ++

Year	Lev	Team	W	L	Sv	IP	K	ERA	WHIP	BF/G	OBA	H%	S%	xERA	Ctl	Dom	Cmd	hr/9	BPV
2017	A+	Buies Creek	2	1	0	25	18	2.87	1.27	20.6	276	33	77	3.57	1.8	6.5	3.6	0.4	86
2017	AA	Corpus Christi	0	0	0	13	10	5.54	1.54	14.2	290	34	63	4.75	3.5	6.9	2.0	0.7	49
2018	AA	Corpus Christi	6	1	1	68	83	1.98	1.12	16.8	219	32	84	2.41	2.9	11.0	3.8	0.4	137
2018	AAA	Fresno	1	0	0	5	6	3.53	2.16	6.3	258	37	82	5.16	10.6	10.6	1.0	0.0	-77
2018	MLB	Houston	0	0	0	11	12	4.05	1.17	5.5	161	13	80	3.81	5.7	9.7	1.7	2.4	40

The thin-framed southpaw somehow fires fastballs in the mid-90s with consistency. He backs it up with a two-place slider and a middling changeup. The ingredients are there for a potential starter but his stuff plays up in the bullpen and he might have had trouble holding up in the rotation for a full season.

Perez,Franklin — SP — Detroit

EXP MLB DEBUT: 2020 | H/W: 6-3 197 | FUT: #3 starter | 8D

Thrws R Age 21 — 2014 FA (VZ)

- 91-95 FB ++++
- 81-83 SL +++
- 74-77 CB ++++
- 82-84 CU +++

Year	Lev	Team	W	L	Sv	IP	K	ERA	WHIP	BF/G	OBA	H%	S%	xERA	Ctl	Dom	Cmd	hr/9	BPV
2016	A	Quad Cities	3	3	1	66	75	2.85	1.24	17.9	252	36	75	2.90	2.6	10.2	3.9	0.1	132
2017	A+	Buies Creek	4	2	2	54	53	2.99	1.00	17.2	199	25	72	2.15	2.7	8.8	3.3	0.7	105
2017	AA	Corpus Christi	2	1	1	32	25	3.09	1.38	19.2	268	32	79	3.89	3.1	7.0	2.3	0.6	61
2018	Rk	GCL Tigers	0	1	0	8	5	4.50	0.38	8.5	117	15			0.0	5.6		0.0	119
2018	A+	Lakeland	0	1	0	11	9	8.11	2.07	13.6	324	37	62	7.49	6.5	7.3	1.1	1.6	-26

Legitimate potential as a future big league impact arm. Pounds the zone with a plus fastball. Plus curve creates headaches for hitters on both sides. Change-up and slider are still developing and project as future plus offerings. Sequences extremely well from an athletic, fluid delivery. Health is still a concern after missing much of 2018.

Perez,Freicer — SP — New York (A)

EXP MLB DEBUT: 2020 | H/W: 6-8 190 | FUT: #3 starter | 8E

Thrws R Age 23 — 2015 FA (DR)

- 92-96 FB ++++
- 85-88 SL +++
- 85-86 CB +
- 86 CU ++

Year	Lev	Team	W	L	Sv	IP	K	ERA	WHIP	BF/G	OBA	H%	S%	xERA	Ctl	Dom	Cmd	hr/9	BPV
2016	A-	Staten Island	2	4	0	52	49	4.49	1.46	17.1	258	33	68	3.91	4.3	8.5	2.0	0.5	54
2017	A	Charleston (Sc)	10	3	0	123	117	2.85	1.14	20.4	216	28	75	2.44	3.3	8.5	2.6	0.4	83
2018	A+	Tampa	0	4	0	25	20	7.20	1.88	19.6	284	33	61	5.88	6.8	7.2	1.1	1.1	-37

Big-bodied, tall RHP struggled with injuries in 2018. Repeatable, 3/4s cross-fire delivery has cleaned up. Doesn't use size well in delivery. 2-seam FB overpowers with solid arm-side run. SL projects to be above-average offering with 2-plane break. Struggles replicating FB delivery for CU with solid arm-side fade. CB not a factor.

Perez,Hector — SP — Toronto

EXP MLB DEBUT: 2020 | H/W: 6-3 190 | FUT: #4 starter | 7D

Thrws R Age 22 — 2015 FA (DR)

- 90-95 FB +++
- 82-85 SL +++
- 78-80 CB +++
- 84-85 SP ++

Year	Lev	Team	W	L	Sv	IP	K	ERA	WHIP	BF/G	OBA	H%	S%	xERA	Ctl	Dom	Cmd	hr/9	BPV
2017	A	Quad Cities	1	1	0	18	24	2.50	1.11	17.7	151	21	83	2.18	5.5	12.0	2.2	1.0	86
2017	A+	Buies Creek	6	5	2	89	104	3.64	1.53	18.4	215	30	77	3.60	6.8	10.5	1.6	0.6	24
2018	A+	Buies Creek	3	3	2	72	83	3.86	1.25	17.3	197	27	69	2.69	5.0	10.3	2.1	0.6	70
2018	AA	New Hampshire	0	1	0	25	32	3.93	1.31	17.3	193	29	69	2.54	5.7	11.4	2.0	0.4	69
2018	AA	Corpus Christi	0	1	0	16	18	3.33	1.23	16.4	208	30	70	2.21	4.4	10.0	2.3	0.0	78

Tall, athletic hurler is a late bloomer and signed for $75,000 as an 18-year-old. FB now sits at 90-95, topping at 99 mph and mixes in a SP. SL and CB are above-average on the right night but need consistency. Impressed at three levels, posting a .196 BAA and 10.4 Dom. Command and control need improvement if he is to reach his potential.

Peterson,David — SP — New York (N)

EXP MLB DEBUT: 2020 | H/W: 6-6 215 | FUT: #4 starter | 7B

Thrws L Age 23 — 2017 (1) Oregon

- 88-92 FB +++
- 73-77 CB ++
- 78-81 SL ++
- 79-81 CU +++

Year	Lev	Team	W	L	Sv	IP	K	ERA	WHIP	BF/G	OBA	H%	S%	xERA	Ctl	Dom	Cmd	hr/9	BPV
2017	NCAA	Oregon	11	4	0	100	140	2.52	1.03	25.7	238	38	74	2.20	1.3	12.6	9.3	0.2	208
2017	A-	Brooklyn	0	0	0	3	6	2.81	1.56	4.7	307	57	80	4.32	2.8	16.9	6.0	0.0	246
2018	A	Columbia	1	4	0	59	57	1.83	0.96	24.9	216	29	80	1.78	1.7	8.7	5.2	0.2	129
2018	A+	St. Lucie	6	6	0	68	58	4.35	1.36	21.9	278	35	65	3.59	2.5	7.7	3.1	0.1	88

Sturdy first round pick who is more of a command pitcher than a stuff guy. Similar to Brian Johnson. Knows how to pitch and mix, but no plus pitches. CB and SL blend; needs to find one that works. Command is good but not great; has some deception. Some sink on his FB but nothing special. Will really have to pitch to succeed.

Phillips,Tyler — SP — Texas — EXP MLB DEBUT: 2021 — H/W: 6-5 200 — FUT: #4 starter — 7C

Thrws R Age 23			Year	Lev	Team	W	L	Sv	IP	K	ERA	WHIP	BF/G	OBA	H%	S%	xERA	Ctl	Dom	Cmd	hr/9	BPV
2015 (16) HS (NJ)			2016	A-	Spokane	4	7	0	58	57	6.49	1.68	20.2	322	42	58	5.23	3.1	8.8	2.9	0.3	93
91-93	FB	+++	2017	A-	Spokane	4	2	0	73	78	3.45	1.22	22.7	275	36	73	3.74	1.4	9.6	7.1	0.7	154
80-83	CB	++	2017	A	Hickory	1	2	0	25	15	6.45	1.47	15.4	283	32	54	4.53	3.2	5.4	1.7	0.7	28
79-82	CU	+++	2018	A	Hickory	11	5	0	128	124	2.67	1.02	22.4	245	32	73	2.41	1.0	8.7	8.9	0.3	148
			2018	A+	Down East	1	0	0	5	3	1.80	0.80	18.1	124	15	75	0.25	3.6	5.4	1.5	0.0	18

Broke out in first full-season gig, as both FB velocity and his ability to command the pitch took steps forward. Likewise with his CU, which is currently his best secondary offering. CB currently below average, though could improve due to a great feel for pitching. Workhorse body, though no monster out pitch as of yet.

Pilkington,Konnor — SP — Chicago (A) — EXP MLB DEBUT: 2022 — H/W: 6-3 210 — FUT: #3 starter — 8E

Thrws L Age 21			Year	Lev	Team	W	L	Sv	IP	K	ERA	WHIP	BF/G	OBA	H%	S%	xERA	Ctl	Dom	Cmd	hr/9	BPV
2018 (3) Mississippi St																						
89-92	FB	+++																				
78-81	CB	+++	2018	NCAA	Mississippi St	3	6	0	102	107	4.49	1.36	23.7	269	35	67	3.98	2.9	9.4	3.2	0.7	109
81-83	CU	+++	2018	Rk	Great Falls	0	1	0	12	9	5.25	1.50	8.6	293	34	65	4.75	3.0	6.8	2.3	0.8	59
			2018	Rk	AZL White Sox	0	0	0	2	2	18.00	4.00	6.8	554	66	50	16.51	4.5	9.0	2.0	0.0	59

Tall, big-bodied command/control LHP made professional debut. Cross-fire 3/4s delivery with long arm circle. Has three pitches, all with above-average potential. Sits low 90s with 2-seam FB that features arm-side bore. CB has solid depth and average break; could be plus if depth improves. Has solid feel for CU. Will need to improve consistency.

Pint,Riley — SP — Colorado — EXP MLB DEBUT: 2021 — H/W: 6-4 195 — FUT: #1 starter — 9E

Thrws R Age 21			Year	Lev	Team	W	L	Sv	IP	K	ERA	WHIP	BF/G	OBA	H%	S%	xERA	Ctl	Dom	Cmd	hr/9	BPV
2016 (1) HS (KS)																						
94-98	FB	+++++	2016	Rk	Grand Junction	1	5	0	37	36	5.35	1.78	15.5	292	37	69	5.18	5.6	8.8	1.6	0.5	25
80-83	CB	++	2017	A	Asheville	2	11	0	93	79	5.42	1.67	19.0	268	34	65	4.37	5.7	7.6	1.3	0.3	1
86-88	SL	+++	2018	A-	Boise	0	2	0	8	8	1.13	1.63	11.9	151	22	92	2.56	10.1	9.0	0.9	0.0	-93
85-88	CU	++	2018	A	Asheville	0	1	0	0	0		40.00	4.3	876	88	25	151.13		0.0	0.0	0.0	

4th overall pick in 2016 was limited with forearm tightness and an oblique injury. Still has elite velocity with a high-90s FB that has plus downhill action. SL, CB, and CU all show potential but lack consistency. Biggest downfall to date have been health and abysmal control. At 21, time is still on his side, but must show something in 2019.

Plassmeyer,Michael — SP — Tampa Bay — EXP MLB DEBUT: 2021 — H/W: 6-2 197 — FUT: #4 starter — 7C

Thrws L Age 22			Year	Lev	Team	W	L	Sv	IP	K	ERA	WHIP	BF/G	OBA	H%	S%	xERA	Ctl	Dom	Cmd	hr/9	BPV
2018 (4) Missouri																						
88-93	FB	+++																				
80-82	SL	+++																				
74-78	CB	+++	2018	NCAA	Missouri	5	4	0	91	103	3.06	1.13	25.7	251	34	74	3.04	1.7	10.2	6.1	0.6	156
81-84	CU	+++	2018	A-	Everett	0	1	0	24	44	2.25	0.83	6.7	191	39	74	1.29	1.5	16.5	11.0	0.4	275

Acquired in Mallex Smith trade, command/control LHP stuff took step forward after pro debut; 44 K/ 4 BB. Four average or better pitches. Picked up FB velocity in pros without losing command. CB projects as above-average offering with good shape. SL and CU both project as average pitches.

Plesac,Zack — SP — Cleveland — EXP MLB DEBUT: 2021 — H/W: 6-3 200 — FUT: #4 starter — 7D

Thrws R Age 24			Year	Lev	Team	W	L	Sv	IP	K	ERA	WHIP	BF/G	OBA	H%	S%	xERA	Ctl	Dom	Cmd	hr/9	BPV
2016 (12) Ball St																						
91-94	FB	+++	2017	A-	Mahoning Vall	0	1	0	26	31	1.38	0.85	11.9	160	25	82	0.68	2.8	10.7	3.9	0.0	136
83-84	CU	+++	2017	A	Lake County	1	1	0	25	19	3.60	1.00	15.9	212	25	65	2.38	2.2	6.8	3.2	0.7	83
83-84	SL	++	2018	A+	Lynchburg	8	5	0	122	111	4.05	1.28	22.8	265	33	68	3.63	2.4	8.2	3.4	0.6	100
76-77	CB	+	2018	AA	Akron	3	1	0	22	21	2.45	1.05	21.3	234	30	77	2.46	1.6	8.6	5.3	0.4	128

Good athlete with a smooth, repeatable delivery. Leans heavily on an average FB with solid movement that he can get swings and misses with. Off-speed is work-in-progress, but manages to succeed by locating his fastball and limiting walks. Will likely not be a high K guy if he makes it to the majors, as he lacks a true out pitch.

Poche,Colin — RP — Tampa Bay — EXP MLB DEBUT: 2019 — H/W: 6-3 185 — FUT: Setup reliever — 7B

Thrws L Age 25			Year	Lev	Team	W	L	Sv	IP	K	ERA	WHIP	BF/G	OBA	H%	S%	xERA	Ctl	Dom	Cmd	hr/9	BPV
2016 (14) Arkansas			2017	A	Kane County	2	0	1	24	44	1.12	0.91	6.9	190	40	86	1.11	2.2	16.4	7.3	0.0	252
90-92	FB	++++	2017	A+	Visalia	1	1	2	25	37	1.43	1.07	5.4	165	29	85	1.27	4.6	13.2	2.8	0.0	131
82-85	SL	+++	2018	AA	Montgomery	1	0	1	16	32	0.00	0.38	4.3	81	23	100		1.1	18.0	16.0	0.0	312
			2018	AA	Jackson	0	0	1	11	23	0.00	0.45	4.0	88	27	100		1.6	18.8	11.5	0.0	313
			2018	AAA	Durham	5	0	1	50	78	1.08	0.92	6.7	171	30	91	1.29	3.1	14.0	4.6	0.4	188

Quick-moving LH RP acquired in mid-season trade with ARI. Powerful high-3/4s delivery with plus extension and deception which plays up effectiveness of low-90s 2-seam FB. FB is best pitch, gets on hitters quickly with late arm-side run and is a bat-misser. Dom is elite, could continue in big leagues. SL projects as average pitch in big leagues.

Ponce,Cody — RP — Milwaukee — EXP MLB DEBUT: 2019 — H/W: 6-6 240 — FUT: Setup reliever — 8C

Thrws R Age 24			Year	Lev	Team	W	L	Sv	IP	K	ERA	WHIP	BF/G	OBA	H%	S%	xERA	Ctl	Dom	Cmd	hr/9	BPV
2015 (2) Cal Poly Pomona																						
90-93	FB	+++	2016	A+	Brevard Co	2	8	0	72	69	5.25	1.40	17.9	293	37	62	4.48	2.1	8.6	4.1	0.8	116
87-89	CT	++++	2017	A+	Carolina	8	8	0	120	94	3.45	1.30	22.5	279	32	77	4.32	1.9	7.1	3.8	1.1	94
77-79	CB	++	2017	AA	Biloxi	2	1	0	17	9	1.57	0.87	21.2	171	20	80	0.92	2.6	4.7	1.8	0.0	32
83-85	CU	+++	2018	AA	Biloxi	7	6	0	95	88	4.36	1.28	13.4	247	30	68	3.73	3.2	8.3	2.6	0.9	81

Tall, strong RH who transitioned from SP to RP in AA mid-season. Capable of sitting mid-90s with plus FB out of the bullpen with a sharp late-action CT as primary secondary pitch. CU and CB both grade as average. Has ideal build for workhorse SP but power FB/CT combo could work well from setup relief role as early as 2019.

Poncedeleon,Daniel — RP — St. Louis — EXP MLB DEBUT: 2018 — H/W: 6-4 190 — FUT: #5 SP/swingman — 6B

Thrws R Age 27			Year	Lev	Team	W	L	Sv	IP	K	ERA	WHIP	BF/G	OBA	H%	S%	xERA	Ctl	Dom	Cmd	hr/9	BPV
2014 (9) Arizona																						
93-94	FB	+++	2016	AA	Springfield	9	8	0	151	122	3.52	1.22	22.6	231	28	72	3.04	3.3	7.3	2.2	0.6	59
	SL	++	2017	AAA	Memphis	2	0	0	29	25	2.17	1.14	19.1	197	24	84	2.43	4.0	7.8	1.9	0.6	49
	CU	+	2018	AAA	Memphis	9	4	0	96	110	2.25	1.24	20.5	203	29	83	2.51	4.7	10.3	2.2	0.4	77
			2018	MLB	St. Louis	0	2	1	33	31	2.73	1.12	11.8	205	26	77	2.41	3.5	8.5	2.4	0.5	74

Now fully recovered from a horrific head injury, he was unhittable at Triple-A Memphis and more than held his own in 33 innings in the majors. Mid-90s FB is well located with good late sink and run. Backed up a solid SL and effective CU. Sinker/slider combo works well out of the pen, his logical destination in 2019.

Pop,Zach — RP — Baltimore — EXP MLB DEBUT: 2019 — H/W: 6-4 225 — FUT: Setup reliever — 7D

Thrws R Age 22			Year	Lev	Team	W	L	Sv	IP	K	ERA	WHIP	BF/G	OBA	H%	S%	xERA	Ctl	Dom	Cmd	hr/9	BPV
2017 (7) Kentucky			2017	NCAA	Kentucky	1	1	0	20	20	3.56	1.63	4.1	250	33	78	4.17	6.2	8.9	1.4	0.4	10
94-97	FB	++++	2017	Rk	AZL Dodgers	0	0	0	5	5	0.00	0.80	3.6	124	18	100	0.22	3.6	9.0	2.5	0.0	83
84-86	SL	+++	2018	A	Great Lakes	0	2	0	16	24	2.24	1.18	5.9	209	34	83	2.57	3.9	13.4	3.4	0.6	154
			2018	A+	Rancho Cuca	1	0	7	27	23	0.33	0.70	5.0	146	20	95	0.21	2.0	7.7	3.8	0.0	102
			2018	AA	Bowie	1	1	1	21	17	2.56	0.95	5.7	190	25	70	1.31	2.6	7.3	2.8	0.0	79

Deceptive, hard-throwing RH RP was acquired in mid-season trade with LA. Low 3/4s, cross-arm delivery with some effort. Delivery maximizes movement over control. Two-pitch pitcher. FB has hard arm-side run with sharp drop. Plays down due to poor command. SL is a vertical breaker from the same slot as FB. Difficult to pick up, especially for RHHs.

Povse,Max — SP — Seattle — EXP MLB DEBUT: 2017 — H/W: 6-8 185 — FUT: Setup reliever — 7E

Thrws R Age 25			Year	Lev	Team	W	L	Sv	IP	K	ERA	WHIP	BF/G	OBA	H%	S%	xERA	Ctl	Dom	Cmd	hr/9	BPV
2014 (3) North Carolina-G			2017	AA	Arkansas	3	2	0	39	32	3.46	1.23	17.6	236	30	70	2.79	3.2	7.4	2.3	0.2	64
91-94	FB	+++	2017	AAA	Tacoma	1	4	0	31	29	7.50	1.70	10.8	318	39	54	5.73	3.5	8.4	2.4	0.9	75
76-80	CB	++	2017	MLB	Seattle	0	0	0	3	2	8.44	3.13	6.3	499	53	78	15.16	2.8	5.6	2.0	2.8	43
86-88	CU	+++	2018	AA	Arkansas	4	3	0	60	60	3.44	1.35	25.1	268	35	73	3.55	2.8	9.0	3.2	0.3	103
			2018	AAA	Tacoma	1	6	0	36	45	8.95	1.88	21.3	282	37	52	6.19	7.0	11.2	1.6	1.5	31

Tall, lean RHP continues to struggle through command issues. High-3/4s cross-armed delivery. FB has solid run, but struggles keeping it in lower quadrant of zone. 12-to-6 CB has solid shape but below-average movement. CU comes and goes. Maintains FB arm-speed with mostly late fade.

Poyner,Bobby — RP — Boston — EXP MLB DEBUT: 2019 — H/W: 6-2 175 — FUT: Middle reliever — 6D

Thrws R Age 25			Year	Lev	Team	W	L	Sv	IP	K	ERA	WHIP	BF/G	OBA	H%	S%	xERA	Ctl	Dom	Cmd	hr/9	BPV
2014 (3) Seminole St Coll FL			2016	A	Greenville	4	1	2	52	76	2.07	1.17	7.2	197	32	83	2.20	4.3	13.1	3.0	0.3	137
86-90	FB	++	2016	A+	Salem	0	0	0	18	28	1.00	1.00	8.6	121	24	89	0.64	5.5	14.0	2.5	0.0	122
75-80	SL	++	2017	AA	Portland	5	2	2	49	52	3.12	1.41	5.5	168	21	81	3.05	7.5	9.5	1.3	0.9	-13
82-83	CU	+++	2018	A+	Salem	3	1	5	24	32	3.72	1.45	5.7	276	42	71	3.61	3.3	11.9	3.6	0.0	142
			2018	AA	Portland	2	2	0	36	45	5.98	1.50	8.2	277	37	63	5.16	3.7	11.2	3.0	1.5	119

Deceptive lefty short on athleticism and stuff. Smart and competitive, and commands his pitches well. SL not a plus pitch against LHH and his CU may be his best pitch, so he is more of a reverse platoon type. Since relies on deception, best used in short stints and maybe at short intervals. May not be able to be a consistent MLB pen option.

Puckett,A.J. — SP — Chicago (A)

EXP MLB DEBUT: 2020 | H/W: 6-3 175 | FUT: #5 SP/swingman | 6C

Thrws R Age 23 — 2016 (2) Pepperdine

Velo	Pitch	Grade
90-93	FB	++
77-79	CB	++
80-84	CU	++++

Year	Lev	Team	W	L	Sv	IP	K	ERA	WHIP	BF/G	OBA	H%	S%	xERA	Ctl	Dom	Cmd	hr/9	BPV
2016	Rk	AZL Royals	0	1	0	7	8	3.86	1.14	13.9	288	37	71	4.25	0.0	10.3		1.3	203
2016	A	Lexington	2	3	0	51	37	3.69	1.11	18.3	225	26	68	2.81	2.6	6.5	2.5	0.7	64
2017	A+	Winston-Salem	1	0	0	27	21	4.32	1.48	23.3	314	37	71	4.93	1.7	7.0	4.2	0.7	99
2017	A+	Wilmington	9	7	0	108	98	3.91	1.42	22.9	260	33	73	3.89	3.8	8.2	2.1	0.6	61
2018		Did not pitch - injury																	

Big, strong RHP missed all of 2018 due to Tommy John surgery. Cross-armed, 3/4s delivery creates deception hiding ball in body. 3-pitch pitcher. Heavy-boring 2-seam FB is workhorse. Lives in lower quad but gets hurt when elevated. Best pitch late fading CU with FB arm-action and solid command. CB lacks depth. Maybe need one more pitch to start.

Puk,A.J. — SP — Oakland

EXP MLB DEBUT: 2019 | H/W: 6-6 205 | FUT: #2 starter | 9D

Thrws L Age 23 — 2016 (1) Florida

Velo	Pitch	Grade
93-97	FB	++++
84-86	SL	++++
78-81	CB	++
83-86	CU	++

Year	Lev	Team	W	L	Sv	IP	K	ERA	WHIP	BF/G	OBA	H%	S%	xERA	Ctl	Dom	Cmd	hr/9	BPV
2016	NCAA	Florida	2	3	0	73	101	3.07	1.20	17.3	198	30	77	2.68	4.5	12.4	2.7	0.7	119
2016	A-	Vermont	0	4	0	32	40	3.07	1.09	12.6	202	31	69	1.75	3.4	11.2	3.3	0.0	129
2017	A+	Stockton	4	5	0	61	98	3.69	1.10	17.1	204	37	64	1.91	3.4	14.5	4.3	0.1	187
2017	AA	Midland	2	5	0	64	86	4.36	1.39	20.7	262	40	67	3.53	3.5	12.1	3.4	0.3	141
2018		Did not pitch - injury																	

Towering, high-upside LH who missed all of 2018 due to early April Tommy John surgery. Complements premium mid-90s velocity with plus SL thrown in mid-80s for Ks. Still refining CU; CB is more of show-me fourth pitch right now. Throws downhill with great extension toward plate; produces ground balls regularly. Command isn't great but misses bats.

Quantrill,Cal — SP — San Diego

EXP MLB DEBUT: 2019 | H/W: 6-3 195 | FUT: #4 starter | 8C

Thrws R Age 24 — 2016 (1) Stanford

Velo	Pitch	Grade
92-95	FB	++++
77-81	CB	+++
80-83	CU	++++

Year	Lev	Team	W	L	Sv	IP	K	ERA	WHIP	BF/G	OBA	H%	S%	xERA	Ctl	Dom	Cmd	hr/9	BPV
2017	A+	Lake Elsinore	6	5	0	73	76	3.69	1.39	22.0	274	36	74	4.06	3.0	9.3	3.2	0.6	107
2017	AA	San Antonio	1	5	0	42	34	4.06	1.62	23.3	305	36	78	5.51	3.4	7.3	2.1	1.1	56
2018	AA	San Antonio	6	5	0	117	101	5.15	1.48	22.9	290	35	66	4.81	2.9	7.8	2.7	0.9	79
2018	AAA	El Paso	3	1	0	31	22	3.48	1.42	21.9	308	35	80	5.17	1.5	6.4	4.4	1.2	94

Athletic RH whose K-rate has dropped each year as a pro. Still sits 92-95 mph with plus FB but now plays down due to lack of movement up in zone. Headline pitch is plus CU that is sold well with quality arm speed late tumbling action out of hand. Blends in average CB and occasional SL. Strikes have increased but so too have HR.

Ragans,Cole — SP — Texas

EXP MLB DEBUT: 2022 | H/W: 6-3 190 | FUT: #3 starter | 8D

Thrws L Age 21 — 2016 (1) HS (FL)

Velo	Pitch	Grade
90-94	FB	++++
78-84	CU	+++
75-77	CB	++

Year	Lev	Team	W	L	Sv	IP	K	ERA	WHIP	BF/G	OBA	H%	S%	xERA	Ctl	Dom	Cmd	hr/9	BPV
2016	Rk	AZL Rangers	0	0	0	7	9	5.00	2.36	9.3	351	49	76	7.12	7.5	11.3	1.5	0.0	18
2017	A-	Spokane	3	2	0	57	87	3.63	1.49	18.9	237	38	78	3.91	5.5	13.7	2.5	0.8	116
2018		Did not pitch - injury																	

Lost 2018 to Tommy John surgery, but should be back on the mound by early summer. FB/CU lefty with good velo separation and CB has potential to be an average pitch. Deception in delivery, but has had trouble repeating so control is still raw. Needs innings, but assuming health, could be a riser in another year or so.

Rainey,Tanner — RP — Washington

EXP MLB DEBUT: 2018 | H/W: 6-2 210 | FUT: Setup reliever | 7C

Thrws R Age 26 — 2015 (2) SE Louisiana

Velo	Pitch	Grade
96-99	FB	++++
88-90	SL	++++
90-91	CU	+

Year	Lev	Team	W	L	Sv	IP	K	ERA	WHIP	BF/G	OBA	H%	S%	xERA	Ctl	Dom	Cmd	hr/9	BPV
2016	A	Dayton	5	10	1	103	113	5.59	1.70	16.1	273	36	67	4.95	5.8	9.9	1.7	0.8	40
2017	A+	Daytona	2	2	9	45	77	3.80	0.96	4.4	142	25	62	1.48	4.4	15.4	3.5	0.8	176
2017	AA	Pensacola	1	1	4	17	27	1.59	1.12	4.8	143	22	94	2.15	5.8	14.3	2.5	1.1	118
2018	AAA	Louisville	7	2	3	52	65	2.60	1.17	4.6	146	22	78	1.68	6.2	11.3	1.8	0.3	52
2018	MLB	Cincinnati	0	0	0	7	7	24.43	3.57	5.6	397	41	29	15.91	15.4	9.0	0.6	5.1	-237

Hard-throwing RHP struggled with control and command in 2018 MLB cup-of-coffee. Primarily a 2-pitch pitcher with an occasional CU mixed in. Cross-arm delivery creates deception but causes inconsistent mechanics. Doesn't get much extension, causing high-velocity 2-seam FB to be hittable. SL can be a true 2-plane wipe out pitch with consistency.

Ramirez,Carlos — RP — Oakland

EXP MLB DEBUT: 2017 | H/W: 6-5 205 | FUT: Middle reliever | 8E

Thrws R Age 27 — 2009 FA (DR)

Velo	Pitch	Grade
92-95	FB	++++
82-84	SL	+++

Year	Lev	Team	W	L	Sv	IP	K	ERA	WHIP	BF/G	OBA	H%	S%	xERA	Ctl	Dom	Cmd	hr/9	BPV
2017	MLB	Toronto	0	0	0	16	14	2.78	0.56	4.6	116	9	67	1.10	1.7	7.8	4.7	1.7	113
2018	AAA	Buffalo	0	1	1	8	10	5.56	1.23	4.7	81	13	50	0.89	8.9	11.1	1.3	0.0	-22
2018	AAA	Nashville	2	2	1	40	29	3.13	1.12	6.1	198	23	74	2.47	3.8	6.5	1.7	0.7	32
2018	MLB	Toronto	0	0	0	2	3	4.29	2.86	6.0	144	25	83	5.57	21.4	12.9	0.6	0.0	-329
2018	MLB	Oakland	0	0	0	6	2	3.00	1.00	7.6	106	12	67	0.61	6.0	3.0	0.5	0.0	-90

Big, physical RH features two-pitch power tandem in FB/SL that could play in setup role. Heater will touch 96 mph and sit 92-94 and generate plenty of whiffs when thrown from downhill angle. SL is tight and will be future weapon vs. RHH. Has struggled to throw strikes but has upside if things come around.

Ramirez,Manny — SP — Houston

EXP MLB DEBUT: 2022 | H/W: 5-11 170 | FUT: Closer | 8D

Thrws R Age 19 — 2017 FA (DR)

Velo	Pitch	Grade
94-98	FB	++++
79-80	CB	+++
87-89	CU	+++

Year	Lev	Team	W	L	Sv	IP	K	ERA	WHIP	BF/G	OBA	H%	S%	xERA	Ctl	Dom	Cmd	hr/9	BPV
2018	Rk	GCL Astros	1	1	0	34	46	4.76	1.29	14.0	232	37	59	2.63	4.0	12.2	3.1	0.0	130
2018	A-	Tri City	0	0	0	5	9	0.00	0.98	9.7	65	16	100	0.06	7.1	15.9	2.3	0.0	113

Undersized right-hander with an explosive fastball. Ramirez's development is nascent and his range of outcomes is as wide as the Nile. He was hitting 98 repeatedly by the end of the season but sat 94-96. His curveball flashed above-average with tight spin and break but flashed early. The changeup is firm at present.

Raquet,Nick — SP — Washington

EXP MLB DEBUT: 2020 | H/W: 6-0 213 | FUT: #5 SP/swingman | 7D

Thrws L Age 23 — 2017 (3) North Carolina

Velo	Pitch	Grade
87-90	FB	+++
75-78	CB	++
82-84	SL	++
83-84	CU	

Year	Lev	Team	W	L	Sv	IP	K	ERA	WHIP	BF/G	OBA	H%	S%	xERA	Ctl	Dom	Cmd	hr/9	BPV
2017	NCAA	William/Mary	2	2	0	77	95	4.67	1.61	21.3	267	38	71	4.44	5.3	11.1	2.1	0.6	76
2017	Rk	GCL Nationals	0	0	0	2	2	0.00	1.00	7.6	262	35	100	2.32	0.0	9.0		0.0	180
2017	A-	Auburn	3	2	0	51	22	2.47	1.23	18.8	280	31	80	3.54	1.2	3.9	3.1	0.4	54
2018	A	Hagerstown	4	6	0	67	56	2.81	1.28	23.0	264	33	76	3.19	2.4	7.5	3.1	0.1	88
2018	A+	Potomac	5	3	0	55	36	4.91	1.69	20.7	317	37	70	5.37	3.4	5.9	1.7	0.5	31

Gets impressive downhill plane on pitches despite height due to his straight over-the-top slot. FB barely touches 90 as a starter, but has good sink/run. SL has taken the next step as he's learned to locate it; also has downer action. CB/CU both still in progress; needs one for rotation. Pitchability, but stuff could tick up in relief.

Raudes,Roniel — SP — Boston

EXP MLB DEBUT: 2021 | H/W: 6-1 160 | FUT: Middle reliever | 6D

Thrws R Age 21 — 2014 FA (NI)

Velo	Pitch	Grade
88-92	FB	+++
74-78	CB	++
81-84	SL	++
79-81	CU	+++

Year	Lev	Team	W	L	Sv	IP	K	ERA	WHIP	BF/G	OBA	H%	S%	xERA	Ctl	Dom	Cmd	hr/9	BPV
2016	A	Greenville	11	6	0	113	104	3.66	1.19	18.9	260	33	70	3.38	1.8	8.3	4.5	0.6	118
2017	A+	Salem	4	7	0	116	95	4.50	1.53	22.0	291	34	73	5.11	3.4	7.4	2.2	1.1	59
2018	A+	Salem	2	5	0	54	35	3.67	1.43	20.8	276	32	73	3.93	3.2	5.8	1.8	0.3	38

Heady, thin youngster, who was promising and projectable a couple of years ago, but stuff has not improved and does not have enough command, feel or deception to make it play. FB is average at best, SL and CB lack bite. CU has potential but is not a plus pitch. His best bet is to go the pen where his stuff should play up some.

Reed,Cody — SP — Arizona

EXP MLB DEBUT: 2020 | H/W: 6-3 245 | FUT: #4 starter | 8E

Thrws L Age 22 — 2014 (2) HS (AL)

Velo	Pitch	Grade
90-92	FB	+++
82-84	SL	+++
81-83	CU	+++

Year	Lev	Team	W	L	Sv	IP	K	ERA	WHIP	BF/G	OBA	H%	S%	xERA	Ctl	Dom	Cmd	hr/9	BPV
2016	A	Kane County	5	2	0	39	55	1.84	0.89	20.8	224	36	79	1.74	0.7	12.6	18.3	0.2	227
2016	A+	Visalia	0	5	0	35	29	6.14	1.62	19.5	287	34	62	5.21	4.3	7.4	1.7	1.0	34
2017	A	Kane County	3	2	0	46	49	1.75	0.87	21.3	182	26	79	1.17	2.1	9.5	4.5	0.2	132
2017	A+	Visalia	5	6	0	89	90	3.93	1.39	22.1	272	33	77	4.77	3.0	9.1	3.0	1.4	100
2018		Did not pitch - injury																	

Tall, muscular RHP who missed all of 2018 due to elbow issues. Works downhill and gets good extension on low-90s FB with some late run and sink. Flashes above-average CU with deception and arm speed replication; SL projects as average third pitch. Good athlete who pounds zone regularly but has limited overall Dom/SwK ability.

Reid-Foley,Sean — SP — Toronto

EXP MLB DEBUT: 2018 | H/W: 6-3 216 | FUT: #3 starter | 8D

Thrws R Age 23 — 2014 (2) HS (FL)

Velo	Pitch	Grade
92-95	FB	++++
83-86	SL	++
78-80	CB	++
85-87	CU	++

Year	Lev	Team	W	L	Sv	IP	K	ERA	WHIP	BF/G	OBA	H%	S%	xERA	Ctl	Dom	Cmd	hr/9	BPV
2016	A+	Dunedin	6	2	0	57	71	2.68	0.89	21.2	179	27	69	1.29	2.5	11.2	4.4	0.3	151
2017	AA	New Hampshire	10	11	0	132	122	5.11	1.50	21.1	280	33	70	5.24	3.6	8.3	2.3	1.5	70
2018	AA	New Hampshire	5	0	0	44	52	2.04	1.07	21.4	178	25	84	2.01	4.1	10.6	2.6	0.6	99
2018	AAA	Buffalo	7	5	0	85	98	3.91	1.25	21.6	241	33	68	3.13	3.2	10.4	3.3	0.5	119
2018	MLB	Toronto	2	4	0	33	42	5.17	1.57	20.8	249	33	72	5.09	5.7	11.4	2.0	1.6	69

Tall, workhorse-type had a bounce-back season and made 7 starts for the Jays. Plus 92-95 mph FB has good arm-side run. Power SL has late bite and sink and can be swing-and-miss while CB and CU have a shot at becoming above-average offerings. Works from abbreviated windup with a high leg kick, but struggled with command.

Reyes,Alex — SP — St. Louis
EXP MLB DEBUT: 2016 | H/W: 6-3 185 | FUT: #1 starter | 9C

Thrws R Age 24
2012 FA (DR)

Velo	Pitch	Grade
95-97	FB	+++++
78-81	CB	++++
88-91	CU	+++

Year	Lev	Team	W	L	Sv	IP	K	ERA	WHIP	BF/G	OBA	H%	S%	xERA	Ctl	Dom	Cmd	hr/9	BPV
2018	A	Peoria	1	0	0	5	12	0.00	0.60	17.1	66	32	100		3.6	21.6	6.0	0.0	310
2018	A+	Palm Beach	0	0	0	3	6	0.00	1.61	13.7	314	59	100	4.55	2.9	17.4	6.0	0.0	253
2018	AA	Springfield	1	0	0	7	13	0.00	0.56	24.3	47	12	100		3.8	16.3	4.3	0.0	209
2018	AAA	Memphis	1	0	0	7	13	0.00	0.29	21.7	48	13	100		1.3	16.7	13.0	0.0	284
2018	MLB	St. Louis	0	0	0	4	2	0.00	1.25	16.3	210	24	100	2.33	4.5	4.5	1.0	0.0	-23

When healthy has some of the best raw stuff in the minors. Out in 2017 with Tommy John surgery; torn lat tendon limited him in 2018. Double plus FB sits at 95-97 topping out at 102 mph. Plus 12-to-6 power CB and improved CU give him the tools to dominate. Mechanics are not consistent leading to below-average command and a move to RP seems possible.

Reyes,Denyi — SP — Boston
EXP MLB DEBUT: 2020 | H/W: 6-4 209 | FUT: #5 SP/swingman | 6C

Thrws R Age 22
2014 FA (DR)

Velo	Pitch	Grade
87-90	FB	++
70-73	CB	++
79-83	SL	++
81-82	CU	+++

Year	Lev	Team	W	L	Sv	IP	K	ERA	WHIP	BF/G	OBA	H%	S%	xERA	Ctl	Dom	Cmd	hr/9	BPV
2015	Rk	DSL Red Sox 2	7	1	0	75	63	2.88	1.01	20.5	257	33	68	2.29	0.4	7.6	21.0	0.0	144
2016	Rk	GCL Red Sox	4	1	0	34	25	2.37	0.99	14.5	237	27	81	2.74	1.1	6.6	6.3	0.8	108
2017	A-	Lowell	9	0	0	62	53	1.45	0.95	15.6	229	29	88	2.19	1.0	7.7	7.6	0.4	129
2018	A	Greenville	10	3	0	123	122	1.90	0.85	21.5	209	26	84	2.03	0.9	8.9	9.4	0.8	153
2018	A+	Salem	2	2	0	32	23	2.25	1.13	21.0	250	29	82	3.02	1.7	6.5	3.8	0.6	89

Polished youngster short on stuff but who has a great feel for pitching. Only CU is a true quality MLB offering, but has plus command and an idea. Doesn't walk guys (just 13 in 123.2 Low A innings in 2018). Remains to be seen if arsenal will play at higher levels as a starter. Stuff may play up some in relief.

Reyes,Luis — SP — Washington
EXP MLB DEBUT: 2020 | H/W: 6-2 175 | FUT: #5 SP/swingman | 7D

Thrws R Age 24
2013 FA (DR)

Velo	Pitch	Grade
90-93	FB	+++
73-78	CB	++
83-85	CU	++

Year	Lev	Team	W	L	Sv	IP	K	ERA	WHIP	BF/G	OBA	H%	S%	xERA	Ctl	Dom	Cmd	hr/9	BPV
2016	A+	Potomac	4	8	0	70		5.64	1.64	22.4	258	29	66	4.75	5.9	5.9	1.0	0.9	-35
2017	A+	Potomac	8	13	0	143	133	4.34	1.43	23.4	270	32	73	4.64	3.5	8.4	2.4	1.2	73
2018	Rk	GCL Nationals	0	1	0	4	3	4.50	1.25	8.1	307	38	60	3.63	0.0	6.8		0.0	140
2018	A-	Auburn	0	0	0	7	7	0.00	0.57	11.9	92	14	100		2.6	9.0	3.5	0.0	111
2018	AA	Harrisburg	5	6	0	64	36	5.20	1.54	23.3	270	29	69	5.03	4.5	5.1	1.1	1.3	-12

Simple, athletic delivery with loose arm, he missed time with a mid-season oblique strain. FB/CB/CU mix; neither of secondaries have become MLB average pitches, and FB is straight and hittable. Normally good control, but increased issues with walks at Double-A. Room to add bulk to his frame, though he currently lacks a separator pitch.

Rhame,Jacob — RP — New York (N)
EXP MLB DEBUT: 2017 | H/W: 6-0 222 | FUT: Middle reliever | 7D

Thrws R Age 26
2013 (6) Oklahoma

Velo	Pitch	Grade
93-98	FB	++++
84-87	SL	+++

Year	Lev	Team	W	L	Sv	IP	K	ERA	WHIP	BF/G	OBA	H%	S%	xERA	Ctl	Dom	Cmd	hr/9	BPV
2017	AAA	Oklahoma City	0	2	2	48	55	4.31	1.29	4.8	278	36	70	4.32	1.9	10.3	5.5	1.1	153
2017	AAA	Las Vegas	0	1	0	6	11	1.50	0.33	4.7	106	25	50		0.0	16.5		0.0	315
2017	MLB	NY Mets	1	1	0	9	7	9.00	2.11	4.9	321	35	59	7.90	7.0	7.0	1.0	2.0	-45
2018	AAA	Las Vegas	1	2	11	32	41	3.08	0.93	4.8	196	27	73	2.34	2.2	11.5	5.1	1.1	164
2018	MLB	NY Mets	1	2	1	32	28	5.89	1.43	4.6	296	32	66	6.01	2.2	7.9	3.5	2.2	99

One of many hard-throwing righty relievers the Mets have acquired the last couple of years. Has plus FB and an inconsistent breaker. FB lacks movement and he leaves it up too often. Command and control are concerns, despite his aggressiveness. One of these guys may pop and become dominant. Long-shot that it is him.

Richan,Paul — SP — Chicago (N)
EXP MLB DEBUT: 2023 | H/W: 6-3 200 | FUT: #4 starter | 7C

Thrws R Age 22
2018 (2) San Diego

Velo	Pitch	Grade
90-93	FB	+++
80-83	SL	+++
	CB	++
	CU	++

Year	Lev	Team	W	L	Sv	IP	K	ERA	WHIP	BF/G	OBA	H%	S%	xERA	Ctl	Dom	Cmd	hr/9	BPV
2018	NCAA	San Diego	4	6	0	89	101	4.64	1.26	28.0	282	38	62	3.71	1.3	10.2	7.8	0.5	166
2018	A-	Eugene	0	2	0	29	31	2.16	0.82	10.6	187	25	77	1.51	1.5	9.6	6.2	0.6	148

Polished RHP lacks plus velocity, relying on keeping hitters off-balance. FB sits at 90-93, with arm-side run. Best offering is an above-average SL that holds its shape well with sharp late break. Nothing stands out as plus, but he pounds the strike zone with above-average FB command that should allow him to stick as a starter.

Richardson,Lyon — SP — Cincinnati
EXP MLB DEBUT: 2022 | H/W: 6-2 175 | FUT: #3 starter | 8E

Thrws R Age 19
2018 (2) HS (FL)

Velo	Pitch	Grade
91-94	FB	++++
82-84	SL	++++
73-77	CB	++
81-82	CU	++

Year	Lev	Team	W	L	Sv	IP	K	ERA	WHIP	BF/G	OBA	H%	S%	xERA	Ctl	Dom	Cmd	hr/9	BPV
2018	Rk	Greeneville	0	5	0	29	24	7.14	1.83	12.3	312	37	60	6.02	5.0	7.4	1.5	0.9	18

Raw, athletic FL prep pitcher made professional debut in Appy League. Has room to grow into frame; delivery is raw and FB arm slot creates unfavorable plane. Easy low-to-mid 90s FB has minimal run. Could be plus with added velocity and command. Low 80s SL has swing-and-miss markers. CB and CU both extremely raw.

Rijo,Luis — SP — Minnesota
EXP MLB DEBUT: 2022 | H/W: 5-11 165 | FUT: #4 starter | 7D

Thrws R Age 20
2014 FA (VZ)

Velo	Pitch	Grade
89-93	FB	+++
75-78	CB	+++
83-85	CU	++

Year	Lev	Team	W	L	Sv	IP	K	ERA	WHIP	BF/G	OBA	H%	S%	xERA	Ctl	Dom	Cmd	hr/9	BPV
2017	Rk	GCL Yankees	4	3	0	54	55	3.50	1.11	19.3	251	33	67	2.76	1.5	9.2	6.1	0.3	143
2018	Rk	Pulaski	3	1	0	27	26	2.67	1.07	21.0	269	36	72	2.60	0.3	8.7	26.0	0.0	165
2018	Rk	Elizabethton	5	1	0	48	43	2.06	1.00	18.4	241	31	79	2.21	0.9	8.0	8.6	0.2	138
2018	A-	Staten Island	0	0	0	6	3	3.00	1.67	26.9	321	36	80	4.93	3.0	4.5	1.5	0.0	18
2018	A+	Tampa	1	0	0	6	3	3.00	1.00	22.9	262	30	67	2.36	0.0	4.5		0.0	99

Projectable, 3/4s RHP, acquired mid-season from NYY. Physically lean upper body with room to grow, lower half more mature. 3-pitch pitcher from 3/4s slot. Low 90s FB has late, minimal arm-side run. Commands FB well for level. 11-to-5 CB has a chance of becoming plus offering with solid depth and late break. CU is a work-in-progress.

Riley,Trey — SP — Atlanta
EXP MLB DEBUT: 2022 | H/W: 6-2 200 | FUT: #4 starter | 8E

Thrws R Age 20
2018 (5) Oklahoma St

Velo	Pitch	Grade
93-95	FB	++++
84-86	SL	++++
82-83	CU	+

Year	Lev	Team	W	L	Sv	IP	K	ERA	WHIP	BF/G	OBA	H%	S%	xERA	Ctl	Dom	Cmd	hr/9	BPV
2018	NCAA	Logan College	6	2	0	77	117	1.87	1.01	22.7	174	29	85	1.77	3.7	13.6	3.7	0.6	163
2018	Rk	Danville	0	0	0	9	13	8.00	2.22	7.6	283	42	63	6.59	10.0	13.0	1.3	1.0	-18

Tall, athletic RHP made pro debut in Appy Lg. Athletic, cross-fire delivery achieving plus extension sits mid-90s with 2-seam FB with solid arm-side break. Mid-80s SL is a tight breaker with plus potential. Struggles with CU feel. However, pitch potential plays up due to plus athleticism. Will need to refine delivery to improve FB command.

Rivera,Blake — SP — San Francisco
EXP MLB DEBUT: 2021 | H/W: 6-4 205 | FUT: Setup reliever | 7E

Thrws R Age 21
2018 (4) Wallace St CC

Velo	Pitch	Grade
94-96	FB	++++
82-85	CB	++++

Year	Lev	Team	W	L	Sv	IP	K	ERA	WHIP	BF/G	OBA	H%	S%	xERA	Ctl	Dom	Cmd	hr/9	BPV
2018	NCAA	Wallace St CC	10	0	0	67	98	1.75	0.94	19.4	156	27	82	1.11	3.8	13.2	3.5	0.3	153
2018	A-	Salem-Keizer	0	0	0	19	14	6.16	1.63	9.4	272	31	62	4.96	5.2	6.6	1.3	0.9	-3

Big-bodied, hard-throwing RP dominated JC competition but struggled in pro debut. Overpowers with FB/CB mix. FB is high-octane, exploding late in pitch progression. Struggles with corralling movement. Power CB has solid shape and late, devastating break. It's wildly inconsistent however. Physical delivery. Same college as Craig Kimbrel.

Rivera,Jerryell — SP — Los Angeles (A)
EXP MLB DEBUT: 2022 | H/W: 6-3 180 | FUT: #3 starter | 7B

Thrws L Age 19
2017 (11) HS (PR)

Velo	Pitch	Grade
90-93	FB	+++
73-77	CB	++
	CU	++

Year	Lev	Team	W	L	Sv	IP	K	ERA	WHIP	BF/G	OBA	H%	S%	xERA	Ctl	Dom	Cmd	hr/9	BPV
2017	Rk	AZL Angels	1	0	0	11	11	1.64	0.91	5.1	184	26	80	1.12	2.5	9.0	3.7	0.0	114
2018	Rk	Orem	0	5	0	9	3	14.00	3.78	11.9	387	35	67	15.20	18.0	3.0	0.2	4.0	-414
2018	Rk	AZL Angels	0	3	0	22	19	6.92	1.81	14.6	318	40	58	5.20	4.5	7.7	1.7	0.0	36

Solid, athletic starter with solid projection remaining. Resume currently sits as average, but youth and progression plead the case that he'll continue to sharpen. Loose arm action gives way to clean delivery of a low-90s fastball. Curve can resemble a slider at times and changeup remains a work in progress.

Roberts,Griffin — SP — St. Louis
EXP MLB DEBUT: 2021 | H/W: 6-3 190 | FUT: #3 starter | 7C

Thrws R Age 22
2018 (1) Wake Forest

Velo	Pitch	Grade
90-94	FB	+++
82-85	SL	+++++
	CU	++

Year	Lev	Team	W	L	Sv	IP	K	ERA	WHIP	BF/G	OBA	H%	S%	xERA	Ctl	Dom	Cmd	hr/9	BPV
2018	NCAA	Wake Forest	5	4	0	96	130	3.84	1.21	27.7	223	34	68	2.83	3.6	12.2	3.4	0.6	141
2018	Rk	GCL Cardinals	0	1	1	8	11	6.59	1.22	4.7	206	33	40	2.13	4.4	12.1	2.8	0.0	117
2018	A+	Palm Beach	0	0	0	1	2	0.00	0.00	2.8	0	0			0.0	18.0		0.0	342

Plus 82-85 power slider has late two-plane break was one of the best breaking balls in the 2018 draft. His FB sits at 90-94 as a starter and 94-97 in relief. Strong, athletic frame gives him options in either role. CU lags behind, but FB/SL mix results in lots of swing-and-miss and max-effort mechanics suggest a role in relief.

Robles,Domingo — SP — Pittsburgh

EXP MLB DEBUT: 2021 | H/W: 6-2 170 | FUT: Middle reliever | 6D

Thrws L Age 20 — 2014 FA (DR)

Velo	Pitch	Grade
86-90	FB	++
79-82	SL	++
79-83	CU	+++

Year	Lev	Team	W	L	Sv	IP	K	ERA	WHIP	BF/G	OBA	H%	S%	xERA	Ctl	Dom	Cmd	hr/9	BPV
2016	Rk	GCL Pirates	1	2	1	36	18	4.25	1.22	16.2	283	31	66	3.92	1.0	4.5	4.5	0.8	72
2017	Rk	Bristol	4	8	0	69	51	4.83	1.32	20.4	278	33	63	3.99	2.1	6.7	3.2	0.7	81
2018	A	West Virginia	9	6	0	115	88	2.97	1.25	22.3	267	32	78	3.63	2.0	6.9	3.4	0.6	87
2018	A+	Bradenton	0	3	0	28	19	4.80	1.49	24.2	288	34	66	4.26	3.2	6.1	1.9	0.3	41

Finesse lefty with some feel for pitching, but offerings are not crisp. Breaking stuff is not sharp enough to be quality against LHH. Command and feel are his best attributes but are not good enough to make him anything more than an emergency depth middle reliever.

Rodriguez,Chris — SP — Los Angeles (A)

EXP MLB DEBUT: 2020 | H/W: 6-1 185 | FUT: #3 starter | 8E

Thrws R Age 20 — 2016 (4) HS (FL)

Velo	Pitch	Grade
91-96	FB	+++
78-82	CB	+++
81-84	SL	++
	CU	+++

Year	Lev	Team	W	L	Sv	IP	K	ERA	WHIP	BF/G	OBA	H%	S%	xERA	Ctl	Dom	Cmd	hr/9	BPV
2016	Rk	AZL Angels	0	0	0	11	17	1.62	0.81	5.8	161	30	78	0.57	2.4	13.8	5.7	0.0	200
2017	Rk	Orem	4	1	0	32	32	6.45	1.31	16.6	279	37	46	3.60	2.0	9.0	4.6	0.3	127
2017	A	Burlington	1	2	0	24	24	5.95	1.61	17.9	319	41	61	5.06	2.6	8.9	3.4	0.4	108
2018	--	Did not play - injury																	

Homegrown, athletic starter with deep, developing arsenal to offer. Lively fastball works in two- and four-seam variations with four-seam topping out at 97 mph. Change-up is better of secondary pieces. Good arm speed with repeatable delivery, although command suffers from head snap at his release.

Rodriguez,Elvin — SP — Detroit

EXP MLB DEBUT: 2022 | H/W: 6-3 160 | FUT: #4 starter | 8E

Thrws R Age 21 — 2015 FA (DR)

Velo	Pitch	Grade
89-93	FB	++
75-77	CB	++
	CU	+

Year	Lev	Team	W	L	Sv	IP	K	ERA	WHIP	BF/G	OBA	H%	S%	xERA	Ctl	Dom	Cmd	hr/9	BPV
2016	Rk	AZL Angels	2	2	2	28	23	1.60	0.85	14.8	185	23	83	1.30	1.9	7.3	3.8	0.3	98
2017	Rk	Orem	5	1	0	54	49	2.50	1.04	18.9	228	28	80	2.76	1.8	8.2	4.5	0.8	116
2017	A	Burlington	0	2	0	14	12	4.50	1.64	20.8	336	40	76	6.29	1.9	7.7	4.0	1.3	105
2018	A	West Michigan	8	7	0	113	109	3.34	1.24	21.9	253	32	75	3.47	2.5	8.7	3.4	0.7	105

Long, athletic starter with plenty of projection, but quite raw as a whole. Expected to add velocity as frame fills out. Arm action in need of polish, but shows the instincts that should allow improvements as he continues to mature. Has shown success in locating his curve, while his change-up has struggled to keep up.

Rodriguez,Grayson — SP — Baltimore

EXP MLB DEBUT: 2021 | H/W: 6-5 220 | FUT: #2 starter | 9E

Thrws R Age 19 — 2018 (1) HS (TX)

Velo	Pitch	Grade
91-95	FB	++++
82-84	SL	+++
74-78	CB	+++
80-83	CU	++

Year	Lev	Team	W	L	Sv	IP	K	ERA	WHIP	BF/G	OBA	H%	S%	xERA	Ctl	Dom	Cmd	hr/9	BPV
2018	Rk	GCL Orioles	0	2	0	19	20	1.41	1.26	8.7	240	33	88	2.67	3.3	9.4	2.9	0.0	99

Tall, athletic RHP with projectable physique. High 3/4s delivery with long arm circle. Solid, heavy FB with late run. CB and SL both emerging breakers. Sometimes blends into one another despite velocity differences. Raw fading CU, struggles with consistency.

Rodriguez,Yerry — SP — Texas

EXP MLB DEBUT: 2022 | H/W: 6-2 180 | FUT: #3 starter | 8E

Thrws R Age 21 — 2016 FA (DR)

Velo	Pitch	Grade
91-95	FB	+++
	CU	+++
	CB	++

Year	Lev	Team	W	L	Sv	IP	K	ERA	WHIP	BF/G	OBA	H%	S%	xERA	Ctl	Dom	Cmd	hr/9	BPV
2018	Rk	AZL Rangers	2	2	0	38	55	3.54	1.08	18.6	261	41	65	2.68	0.7	13.0	18.3	0.2	233
2018	A-	Spokane	3	0	0	24	27	1.86	1.12	23.8	244	33	88	3.05	1.9	10.0	5.4	0.7	149

Popped onto map with 82/8 K/BB across two short-season levels. Commands all of FB/CU/CB; change-up flashes plus and flummoxed low-level batters in 2018. Releases ball from a lower slot, which helps fringy CB play up against RHH. Strike-thrower, but mechanics are arm-heavy and he doesn't engage lower half. Raw, but watchable.

Rogers,Trevor — SP — Miami

EXP MLB DEBUT: 2021 | H/W: 6-6 185 | FUT: #4 starter | 7C

Thrws L Age 21 — 2017 (1) HS (NM)

Velo	Pitch	Grade
90-94	FB	+++
81-83	SL	++
83-86	CU	+++

Year	Lev	Team	W	L	Sv	IP	K	ERA	WHIP	BF/G	OBA	H%	S%	xERA	Ctl	Dom	Cmd	hr/9	BPV
2017		Did not play - injury																	
2018	A	Greensboro	2	7	0	72	85	5.86	1.57	18.6	297	41	61	4.70	3.4	10.6	3.1	0.5	118

Tall, lean athletic LHP struggled in full-season debut. Repeatable delivery with 3/4s arm-slot. Easy FB velocity with more in the tank as body fills out. FB lacks horizontal movement. SL profiles as below-average pitch due to lack of vertical movement. CU potentially best pitch. Maintains arm-speed with separation and late sink.

Rolison,Ryan — SP — Colorado

EXP MLB DEBUT: 2021 | H/W: 6-2 195 | FUT: #3 starter | 8C

Thrws L Age 21 — 2018 (1) Mississippi

Velo	Pitch	Grade
91-94	FB	+++
78-81	CB	++++
80-83	CU	++

Year	Lev	Team	W	L	Sv	IP	K	ERA	WHIP	BF/G	OBA	H%	S%	xERA	Ctl	Dom	Cmd	hr/9	BPV
2018	NCAA	Mississippi	10	4	0	97	120	3.71	1.37	23.9	243	35	73	3.41	4.2	11.1	2.7	0.5	106
2018	Rk	Grand Junction	0	1	0	29	34	1.86	0.79	11.6	155	21	81	1.08	2.5	10.6	4.3	0.6	141

Polished collegiate lefty has a solid three-pitch mix and was excellent in his pro debut. FB sits at 90-93 with average to above-average location. Low-80s power CB is his best offering with true swing-and-miss action. CU is a work in progress, but shows potential. Offers simple, repeatable mechanics with some deception and pounds the strike zone.

Romano,Jordan — SP — Texas

EXP MLB DEBUT: 2019 | H/W: 6-6 200 | FUT: Setup reliever | 6C

Thrws R Age 25 — 2014 (10) Oral Roberts

Velo	Pitch	Grade
93-95	FB	++++
82-84	SL	+++
	CB	+
82-85	CU	+

Year	Lev	Team	W	L	Sv	IP	K	ERA	WHIP	BF/G	OBA	H%	S%	xERA	Ctl	Dom	Cmd	hr/9	BPV
2016	A	Lansing	3	2	0	72	72	2.12	1.05	18.6	194	26	81	1.95	3.4	9.0	2.7	0.4	89
2017	A+	Dunedin	7	5	0	138	138	3.39	1.41	20.9	266	36	74	3.54	3.5	9.0	2.6	0.1	85
2018	AA	New Hampshire	11	8	0	137	125	4.14	1.19	22.0	240	29	68	3.43	2.7	8.2	3.0	1.0	93
2018	AAA	Buffalo	1	0	0	5	3	3.60	1.60	22.1	221	26	75	3.33	7.2	5.4	0.8	0.0	-79

Mature hurler closed in college and had Tommy John surgery in 2015. Fully healthy now and features a plus 93-95, topping at 97 with late life and sink. Backs up the heat with an above-average SL, but CB and CU are average at best. Inconsistent mechanics and lack of a quality 3rd offering will likely push him back into relief, but still a useful arm.

Romero,JoJo — SP — Philadelphia

EXP MLB DEBUT: 2019 | H/W: 5-11 190 | FUT: #3 starter | 7B

Thrws L Age 22 — 2016 (4) Nevada

Velo	Pitch	Grade
91-94	FB	+++
80-82	CU	++++
80-85	SL	+++
75-78	CB	++

Year	Lev	Team	W	L	Sv	IP	K	ERA	WHIP	BF/G	OBA	H%	S%	xERA	Ctl	Dom	Cmd	hr/9	BPV
2016	A-	Williamsport	2	2	0	45	31	2.59	1.22	18.2	257	30	79	3.19	2.2	6.2	2.8	0.4	70
2017	A	Lakewood	5	1	0	76	79	2.13	1.08	22.8	221	30	80	2.20	2.5	9.3	3.8	0.2	119
2017	A+	Clearwater	5	2	0	52	49	2.25	1.11	20.5	226	30	80	2.47	2.6	8.5	3.3	0.3	100
2018	AA	Reading	7	6	0	106	100	3.81	1.30	24.3	245	30	74	3.88	3.5	8.5	2.4	1.1	77

Inconsistent year cut short by oblique injury in July. At his best, high marks for pitchability and command; throws quality strikes and mixes pitches well. Change-up is best secondary; can reach back for mid-90s FB but mostly sits 90-92. Compact, repeatable, athletic delivery. Would benefit from SL becoming an out pitch.

Romero,Seth — SP — Washington

EXP MLB DEBUT: 2022 | H/W: 6-1 242 | FUT: #3 starter | 8E

Thrws L Age 22 — 2017 (1) Houston

Velo	Pitch	Grade
91-94	FB	+++
81-83	SL	+++
81-83	CU	+++

Year	Lev	Team	W	L	Sv	IP	K	ERA	WHIP	BF/G	OBA	H%	S%	xERA	Ctl	Dom	Cmd	hr/9	BPV
2017	NCAA	Houston	4	5	0	48	85	3.55	1.37	20.2	253	46	73	3.41	3.7	15.9	4.3	0.4	203
2017	A-	Auburn	0	1	0	20	32	5.40	1.25	13.6	252	44	52	2.76	2.7	14.4	5.3	0.0	204
2018	A	Hagerstown	0	1	0	25	34	3.94	1.12	14.1	220	32	68	3.05	2.9	12.2	4.3	1.1	160

Legion of off-the-field troubles compounded by Tommy John surgery; he will miss all of 2019. His pitches all grade out as at least MLB average, even if stuff backed up some pre-surgery. Is thick-bodied, comes from high 3/4s slot with a rough delivery, but keeps ball hidden and it comes out quick. Layers of risk, however.

Rooney,John — SP — Los Angeles (N)

EXP MLB DEBUT: 2021 | H/W: 6-5 235 | FUT: #4 starter | 6C

Thrws L Age 22 — 2018 (3) Hofstra

Velo	Pitch	Grade
89-93	FB	++
80-83	SL	+++
	CU	++

Year	Lev	Team	W	L	Sv	IP	K	ERA	WHIP	BF/G	OBA	H%	S%	xERA	Ctl	Dom	Cmd	hr/9	BPV
2018	NCAA	Hofstra	8	2	0	95	108	1.23	0.82	26.6	160	23	87	0.89	2.6	10.2	4.0	0.3	133
2018	Rk	AZL Dodgers	0	0	0	5	7	0.00	0.60	8.6	124	22	100		1.8	12.6	7.0	0.0	196
2018	A	Great Lakes	0	0	0	15	14	2.40	1.27	10.2	221	30	79	2.46	4.2	8.4	2.0	0.0	56

He shot up draft boards with a breakout 2018 campaign at Hofstra and then posted a solid pro debut. Works from 3B side of the mound and has simple, repeatable mechanics. Fringe FB sits at 89-93 but with good location. Best offering an above-average SL and CU has good late fade and sink. Profiles as a command and control back-end LHP.

Rucker,Michael | SP | Chicago (N) | EXP MLB DEBUT: 2020 | H/W: 6-1 185 | FUT: #4 starter | 7C

Thrws R	Age 24	Year	Lev	Team	W	L	Sv	IP	K	ERA	WHIP	BF/G	OBA	H%	S%	xERA	Ctl	Dom	Cmd	hr/9	BPV
2016 (11) Gonzaga		2016	Rk	AZL Cubs	3	0	0	8	11	0.00	0.61	5.6	147	25	100		1.1	12.1	11.0	0.0	206
89-93	FB +++	2016	A-	Eugene	0	0	0	4	7	0.00	1.25	8.1	307	54	100	3.54	0.0	15.8		0.0	302
80-83	CU ++	2017	A	South Bend	0	0	1	12	22	1.48	0.57	5.9	169	33	83	0.73	0.0	16.2		0.7	310
75-77	SL +	2017	A+	Myrtle Beach	5	5	1	93	92	2.51	1.11	18.3	238	31	79	2.72	2.0	8.9	4.4	0.5	123
		2018	AA	Tennessee	9	6	0	132	118	3.74	1.13	20.1	229	27	71	3.31	2.6	8.0	3.1	1.2	93

Started pro career as reliever, but moved to starting at High-A. Average 89-93 mph FB plays up due to plus control and command. Improved CU is now above-average while SL is a work in progress. Quick worker, prefers to challenge hitters when behind in the count, adding and subtracting velo on his fastball, but can also result in hard contact against.

Ruiz,Jose | RP | Chicago (A) | EXP MLB DEBUT: 2017 | H/W: 6-1 190 | FUT: Setup reliever | 7C

Thrws R	Age 24	Year	Lev	Team	W	L	Sv	IP	K	ERA	WHIP	BF/G	OBA	H%	S%	xERA	Ctl	Dom	Cmd	hr/9	BPV
2011 FA (VZ)		2017	A+	Lake Elsinore	1	2	2	49	45	6.04	1.67	5.0	291	35	65	5.63	4.6	8.2	1.8	1.3	43
95-98	FB ++++	2017	MLB	San Diego	0	0	0	1	1	0.00	1.00	3.8	0	0	100		9.0	9.0	1.0	0.0	-63
84-87	SL +++	2018	A+	Winston-Salem	0	0	2	13	22	2.75	0.84	4.8	140	21	78	1.70	3.4	15.1	4.4	1.4	197
86-87	CU +	2018	AA	Birmingham	3	1	14	45	55	3.19	1.15	5.4	206	30	72	2.34	3.8	11.0	2.9	0.4	113
		2018	MLB	Chicago (A)	0	0	0	4	6	4.39	1.95	3.3	302	42	86	7.32	6.6	13.2	2.0	2.2	77

Hard-throwing former CA took step forward in development and making it back to big leagues. Physically mature, utilizes 3/4s delivery with a longer arm-circle compared to most converted CA. Three pitches: Mid-to-high 90s FB has late action and misses bats up. SL is wrapped tight with 2-plane movement. CU is not a factor, a show-me pitch.

Rumbelow,Nick | RP | Seattle | EXP MLB DEBUT: 2018 | H/W: 6-0 184 | FUT: Middle reliever | 6B

Thrws R	Age 27	Year	Lev	Team	W	L	Sv	IP	K	ERA	WHIP	BF/G	OBA	H%	S%	xERA	Ctl	Dom	Cmd	hr/9	BPV
2013 (7) Louisiana St		2017	AA	Trenton	0	0	1	11		2.43	0.72	4.9	138	23	63	0.12	2.4	12.2	5.0	0.0	171
92-94	FB +++	2017	AAA	Scranton/WB	5	1	5	29	30	0.62	0.83	6.2	164	24	92	0.69	2.5	9.3	3.8	0.0	119
79-82	CB +++	2018	AA	Arkansas	0	0	0	2	1	0.00	1.00	3.8	262	30	100	2.36	0.0	4.5		0.0	99
86-87	SP +++	2018	AAA	Tacoma	1	0	2	17	25	2.09	1.22	5.3	211	34	85	2.67	4.2	13.1	3.1	0.5	140
		2018	MLB	Seattle	0	0	0	17	16	6.28	1.45	5.7	281	29	68	6.69	3.1	8.4	2.7	3.1	84

Max-effort RH RP made MLB debut after posting solid numbers in Triple-A. Straight-on, high 3/4s delivery achieving plus extension plays up 3-pitch average arsenal. FB is fairly straight but gets on hitters quick. Throws solid 12-to-6 CB with good depth and average break. SP may be best pitch. Change-of-pace pitch with swing-and-miss markings.

Ryder,Ryan | RP | New York (N) | EXP MLB DEBUT: 2019 | H/W: 6-2 205 | FUT: Setup reliever | 7C

Thrws R	Age 23	Year	Lev	Team	W	L	Sv	IP	K	ERA	WHIP	BF/G	OBA	H%	S%	xERA	Ctl	Dom	Cmd	hr/9	BPV
2016 (30) North Carolina		2016	Rk	AZL Indians	0	1	1	18	24	3.96	1.65	5.4	290	42	76	4.79	4.5	11.9	2.7	0.5	111
92-96	FB ++++	2017	A	Lake County	3	4	6	41	49	4.82	1.48	5.4	275	37	68	4.53	3.7	10.7	2.9	0.9	111
84-86	SL +++	2017	A	Columbia	0	0	0	13	13	2.08	0.85	6.0	141	17	80	1.15	3.5	9.0	2.6	0.7	87
83-85	CU ++	2018	A+	St. Lucie	1	0	2	20	23	1.79	0.95	4.7	198	29	79	1.36	2.2	10.3	4.6	0.0	143
		2018	AA	Binghamton	3	3	3	32	36	4.19	1.15	4.9	229	29	69	3.56	2.8	10.1	3.6	1.4	124

Emerged in 2018, showing off his easy, plus FB and an emerging SL. His CU still needs work, and it will determine how effective he is against LHH and maybe how much of a ceiling he has. But a power arm with a pretty clean delivery who should be a solid bullpen piece at MLB level soon.

Sadzeck,Connor | RP | Texas | EXP MLB DEBUT: 2018 | H/W: 6-5 195 | FUT: Setup reliever | 7B

Thrws R	Age 27	Year	Lev	Team	W	L	Sv	IP	K	ERA	WHIP	BF/G	OBA	H%	S%	xERA	Ctl	Dom	Cmd	hr/9	BPV
2011 (11) Howard College		2016	AA	Frisco	10	8	0	140	133	4.17	1.28	23.0	243	29	71	3.85	3.3	8.5	2.6	1.2	82
94-98	FB ++++	2017	AA	Frisco	4	8	0	93	111	6.28	1.53	10.7	284	37	60	5.13	3.8	10.7	2.8	1.3	109
86-89	SL +++	2018	Rk	AZL Rangers	0	0	0	4	10	0.00	0.98	5.2	206	66	100	1.41	2.2	22.0	10.0	0.0	354
77-80	CB ++	2018	AAA	Round Rock	5	3	0	38	43	4.03	1.37	5.0	251	35	70	3.54	3.8	10.2	2.7	0.5	99
		2018	MLB	Texas	0	0	0	9	7	0.99	1.87	3.3	190	24	94	3.62	10.9	6.9	0.6	0.0	-151

Runs fastball up to 98 from a powerful frame, and features a hard slider that combine for a hefty amount of strikeouts. Control, though, has long been a problem, and 11 walks in 9.1 IP was not a good first MLB impression. Harnessing his stuff will be a requirement before finding major league success.

Sanabria,Carlos | RP | Houston | EXP MLB DEBUT: 2021 | H/W: 6-1 193 | FUT: Middle reliever | 7C

Thrws R	Age 23	Year	Lev	Team	W	L	Sv	IP	K	ERA	WHIP	BF/G	OBA	H%	S%	xERA	Ctl	Dom	Cmd	hr/9	BPV
2017 (11) Notre Dame		2017	NCAA	Notre Dame	2	6	0	73	75	5.55	1.67	21.9	282	37	65	4.76	5.1	9.2	1.8	0.5	48
92-94	FB +++	2017	Rk	GCL Astros	1	0	0	4	5	0.00	0.98	7.8	206	31	100	1.52	2.2	11.0	5.0	0.0	156
78-80	CB +++	2017	A-	Tri City	1	1	1	29	37	0.93	0.76	13.0	180	29	86	0.66	1.2	11.4	9.3	0.0	191
84-85	SL ++	2018	A+	Buies Creek	5	3	2	55	74	2.12	1.11	15.5	220	34	81	2.32	2.8	12.1	4.4	0.3	160
83-85	CU ++	2018	AA	Corpus Christi	2	5	0	61	57	2.36	1.21	22.4	232	29	83	3.01	3.2	8.4	2.6	0.6	82

Another in the high-spin mold. Sanabria's fastball sits in the low-to-mid 90s and he rounds out his arsenal with a curveball, slider, and change. He works vertically, from a high slot with the heater, eliciting swings and misses. He'll change eye levels with the curveball, and his slider can be a bit firm and veer into cutter territory.

Sanchez,Ricardo | SP | Seattle | EXP MLB DEBUT: 2019 | H/W: 5-11 225 | FUT: #5 SP/swingman | 7E

Thrws L	Age 21	Year	Lev	Team	W	L	Sv	IP	K	ERA	WHIP	BF/G	OBA	H%	S%	xERA	Ctl	Dom	Cmd	hr/9	BPV
2013 FA (VZ)		2016	A	Rome	7	10	0	119	103	4.76	1.45	21.2	262	31	69	4.46	4.1	7.8	1.9	1.1	48
91-93	FB +++	2017	A+	Florida	4	12	0	100	101	4.95	1.63	20.2	293	37	71	5.20	4.1	9.1	2.2	0.9	70
79-81	CB +++	2018	Rk	GCL Braves	0	0	0	4	4	2.20	0.98	15.6	206	28	75	1.54	2.2	8.8	4.0	0.0	117
84-85	CU +++	2018	Rk	Danville	1	0	0	11	9	3.21	1.25	22.8	258	31	77	3.67	2.4	7.2	3.0	0.8	83
		2018	AA	Mississippi	2	5	0	57	44	4.09	1.56	19.3	287	35	73	4.54	3.8	6.9	1.8	0.5	41

Under-performing, athletic LHP was acquired in trade with ATL. High 3/4s online delivery. Struggles with command despite fairly fluid delivery. 3-pitch pitcher. 2-seam FB has solid arm-side run but doesn't command well, especially to arm-side. CB is slurvy but has solid break. Repeats FB arm speed with late-fading CU.

Sanchez,Sixto | SP | Philadelphia | EXP MLB DEBUT: 2019 | H/W: 5-10 160 | FUT: #1 starter | 9C

Thrws R	Age 20	Year	Lev	Team	W	L	Sv	IP	K	ERA	WHIP	BF/G	OBA	H%	S%	xERA	Ctl	Dom	Cmd	hr/9	BPV
2015 FA (DR)																					
96-99	FB +++++	2016	Rk	GCL Phillies	5	0	0	54	44	0.50	0.76	17.6	178	23	93	0.69	1.3	7.3	5.5	0.0	114
80-82	CB +++	2017	A	Lakewood	5	3	0	67	64	2.41	0.82	18.8	196	26	69	1.16	1.2	8.6	7.1	0.1	140
88-90	CU +++	2017	A+	Clearwater	0	4	0	27	20	4.63	1.32	22.5	260	31	63	3.45	3.0	6.6	2.2	0.3	57
		2018	A+	Clearwater	4	3	0	46	45	2.53	1.08	22.5	230	31	76	2.29	2.1	8.8	4.1	0.2	118

Prized prospect hit an injury speed bump and logged less than 50 IP. Arsenal includes easy high-90s heat along with CB and CU; rare combination of plus stuff and plus command at a young age. Competitive, advanced feel for pitching; athletic and coachable. Injuries highlight durability questions, though bulked up before 2018. Monster potential.

Sandlin,Nick | RP | Cleveland | EXP MLB DEBUT: 2019 | H/W: 5-11 148 | FUT: Setup reliever | 8B

Thrws R	Age 22	Year	Lev	Team	W	L	Sv	IP	K	ERA	WHIP	BF/G	OBA	H%	S%	xERA	Ctl	Dom	Cmd	hr/9	BPV
2018 (2) Southern Miss		2018	NCAA	Southern Miss	10	0	0	102	144	1.06	0.71	24.1	160	27	86	0.50	1.6	12.7	8.0	0.2	204
89-93	FB +++	2018	Rk	AZL Indians	0	0	0	3	4	0.00	0.67	3.5	191	31	100	0.56	0.0	12.0		0.0	234
79-86	SL ++++	2018	A	Lake County	0	0	1	10	15	1.78	0.89	3.7	240	40	78	1.71	0.0	13.4		0.0	259
81-85	CU +++	2018	A+	Lynchburg	1	0	4	6	10	1.48	0.66	3.0	104	22	75		3.0	14.8	5.0	0.0	204
		2018	AA	Akron	1	0	0	4	7	10.98	2.20	4.1	409	64	44	7.79	2.2	15.4	7.0	0.0	235

A pure reliever in the pros, he may be the first one from his draft class to make it to the MLB level. Relies on the run he generates on his FB from a sidearm delivery and a sharp biting SL that could be very tough on RHHs. While he primarily throws from a sidearm slot, he is also able to mix in some other arm angles.

Sandoval,Patrick | SP | Los Angeles (A) | EXP MLB DEBUT: 2020 | H/W: 6-3 190 | FUT: #4 starter | 7C

Thrws L	Age 22	Year	Lev	Team	W	L	Sv	IP	K	ERA	WHIP	BF/G	OBA	H%	S%	xERA	Ctl	Dom	Cmd	hr/9	BPV
2015 (11) HS (CA)		2017	A+	Buies Creek	0	1	0	2	2	12.27	2.27	11.2	392	49	40	7.70	4.1	8.2	2.0	0.0	55
89-93	FB ++	2018	A	Quad Cities	7	1	1	65	71	2.49	1.06	18.0	240	32	78	2.70	1.5	9.8	6.5	0.6	154
77-79	CB +++	2018	A+	Inland Empire	1	0	0	14	21	0.00	0.85	17.3	130	24	100	0.35	3.8	13.3	3.5	0.0	155
81-84	SL ++	2018	A+	Buies Creek	2	0	1	23	26	2.74	0.70	16.2	156	22	60	0.63	1.6	10.2	6.5	0.4	159
80-82	CU ++	2018	AA	Mobile	1	0	0	19	27	1.41	1.04	18.5	181	31	85	1.39	3.8	12.7	3.4	0.0	145

Tall, projectable starter who made a noticeable jump in 2018. Arsenal is led by deep curve with a knack for flashing plus. Fastball survives more off deception than velocity, mixed between an average changeup and slider. Command has improved. Profiles as back-end starter.

Santana,Dennis | SP | Los Angeles (N) | EXP MLB DEBUT: 2018 | H/W: 6-2 160 | FUT: #3 starter | 8D

Thrws R	Age 22	Year	Lev	Team	W	L	Sv	IP	K	ERA	WHIP	BF/G	OBA	H%	S%	xERA	Ctl	Dom	Cmd	hr/9	BPV
2013 FA (DR)		2017	A+	Rancho Cuca	5	6	0	85	92	3.59	1.28	20.5	266	36	72	3.56	2.3	9.7	4.2	0.5	130
91-96	FB ++++	2017	AA	Tulsa	3	1	0	32	37	5.59	1.71	20.8	261	36	66	4.59	6.4	10.3	1.6	0.6	31
84-85	SL +++	2018	AA	Tulsa	0	2	0	38	51	2.59	1.05	18.5	194	29	78	2.22	3.3	12.0	3.6	0.7	145
81-83	CU +	2018	AAA	Oklahoma City	1	1	0	11	14	2.45	1.09	21.5	244	37	75	2.28	1.6	11.5	7.0	0.0	180
		2018	MLB	LA	1	0	0	3	4	14.06	2.19	16.0	399	54	29	7.61	2.8	11.3	4.0	0.0	145

Dynamic RHP has one of the best live arms in the system. Made his MLB debut, but was shutdown in June with a strained rotator cuff. When healthy, FB sits at 93-96 with good sink and is backed up by a plus hard SL, and a below-average CU. Crossfire delivery results in plus movement, but below-average FB command, leading to concerns about durability.

Santillan,Tony — SP — Cincinnati

EXP MLB DEBUT: 2019 | H/W: 6-3 240 | FUT: #3 starter | 8D

Thrws R Age 21
2015 (2) HS (TX)

Velo	Pitch	Grade
92-95	FB	++++
87-90	SL	+++
84-87	CU	++

Year	Lev	Team	W	L	Sv	IP	K	ERA	WHIP	BF/G	OBA	H%	S%	xERA	Ctl	Dom	Cmd	hr/9	BPV
2016	Rk	Billings	1	0	0	39	46	3.92	1.23	19.7	225	30	70	3.27	3.7	10.6	2.9	0.9	109
2016	A	Dayton	2	3	0	30	38	6.88	1.69	19.4	241	34	58	4.61	7.2	11.4	1.6	0.9	29
2017	A	Dayton	9	8	0	128	128	3.38	1.25	20.8	224	29	74	3.04	3.9	9.0	2.3	0.6	74
2018	A+	Daytona	6	4	0	86	73	2.71	1.19	23.1	250	31	79	3.15	2.3	7.6	3.3	0.5	93
2018	AA	Pensacola	4	3	0	62	61	3.62	1.30	23.3	271	33	77	4.30	2.3	8.8	3.8	1.2	115

Big-bodied RHP continues to transition from thrower to pitcher. Known for his high velocity 2-seam FB, it has a hard and late arm-side run. Downward plane helps with sinking action. Hard SL has inconsistent shape; sometimes slurvy, sometimes with cut. CU still work in progress. Lots of reliever risk, especially with command concerns.

Santos,Gregory — SP — San Francisco

EXP MLB DEBUT: 2022 | H/W: 6-2 190 | FUT: #3 starter | 8E

Thrws R Age 19
2015 FA (DR)

Velo	Pitch	Grade
94-97	FB	++++
83-85	SL	++++
83-84	CU	+

Year	Lev	Team	W	L	Sv	IP	K	ERA	WHIP	BF/G	OBA	H%	S%	xERA	Ctl	Dom	Cmd	hr/9	BPV
2018	A-	Salem-Keizer	2	5	0	49	46	4.57	1.61	18.1	316	40	71	5.16	2.7	8.4	3.1	0.5	95

Powerful, athletic RHP pitched outside of complex for the first time. Easy velocity from powerful, durable frame. Struggles repeating 3/4s cross-armed delivery. Does achieve good extension, so stuff plays up. Hard FB has late life; SL has sharp but inconsistent 2-plane break. No feel for CU. Will need to play around with grips.

Santos,Victor — SP — Philadelphia

EXP MLB DEBUT: 2023 | H/W: 6-1 191 | FUT: #4 starter | 8E

Thrws R Age 18
2017 FA (DR)

Velo	Pitch	Grade
91-93	FB	+++
81-82	SL	++
78-80	CU	++++

Year	Lev	Team	W	L	Sv	IP	K	ERA	WHIP	BF/G	OBA	H%	S%	xERA	Ctl	Dom	Cmd	hr/9	BPV
2018	Rk	GCL Phillies	6	1	0	59	65	3.05	1.13	21.2	274	37	75	3.39	0.6	9.9	16.3	0.6	180

Thick-bodied teenager whose arsenal is still developing, but holds some promise. Excellent command and movement on FB, and has shown a very good feel for change-up. Has trouble repeating his delivery, making his K/BB numbers in 2018 (65/4 in 59 IP) even more astounding. A strike-thrower who would benefit from any uptick in velocity.

Sauer,Matt — SP — New York (A)

EXP MLB DEBUT: 2022 | H/W: 6-4 195 | FUT: #4 starter | 7C

Thrws R Age 20
2017 (2) HS (CA)

Velo	Pitch	Grade
91-94	FB	++++
78-79	CB	+++
86-87	CU	+++

Year	Lev	Team	W	L	Sv	IP	K	ERA	WHIP	BF/G	OBA	H%	S%	xERA	Ctl	Dom	Cmd	hr/9	BPV
2017	Rk	GCL Yankees	0	2	0	11	12	5.63	1.88	8.8	292	40	67	4.94	6.4	9.6	1.5	0.0	18
2018	A-	Staten Island	3	6	0	67	45	3.90	1.16	20.5	241	28	65	2.86	2.4	6.0	2.5	0.4	62

Hard-throwing, big-bodied athletic RHP has been eased into pro role. Struggles to repeat max-effort 3/4s delivery. FB velocity backed up a bit, which caused his stuff to play down. FB has moderate break but flatten out in '18. Sticking with 11-to-5 CB with average potential. Maintains FB arm-speed with CU with arm-side run and sink.

Sawyer,Dalton — SP — Oakland

EXP MLB DEBUT: 2020 | H/W: 6-4 190 | FUT: #5 SP/swingman | 7D

Thrws L Age 25
2016 (9) Minnesota

Velo	Pitch	Grade
88-91	FB	++
73-75	CB	+++
81-83	CU	+++

Year	Lev	Team	W	L	Sv	IP	K	ERA	WHIP	BF/G	OBA	H%	S%	xERA	Ctl	Dom	Cmd	hr/9	BPV
2016	A-	Vermont	0	3	3	18	26	3.46	1.37	5.5	226	36	75	3.22	4.9	12.9	2.6	0.5	116
2017	A	Beloit	4	3	1	56	64	2.25	0.98	17.7	177	25	79	1.67	3.4	10.3	3.0	0.5	112
2017	A+	Stockton	5	5	0	66	74	3.68	1.32	21.0	265	33	80	4.68	2.7	10.1	3.7	1.6	126
2017	AAA	Nashville	0	1	0	8	2	12.07	2.20	20.6	342	30	47	9.72	6.6	2.2	0.3	3.3	-120
2018		Did not pitch - injury																	

Tall, lanky southpaw who missed all of 2018 after Tommy John surgery. Relies on deception and timing to throw hitters off fringe 88-91 mph FB. Replicates arm speed well on CU that will flash above-average movement and will mix in an average CB. Works from low 3/4 slot and is tough on LHH. Good athlete and will have plus command.

Sborz,Josh — RP — Los Angeles (N)

EXP MLB DEBUT: 2019 | H/W: 6-3 225 | FUT: Setup reliever | 6C

Thrws R Age 25
2015 (2) Virginia

Velo	Pitch	Grade
91-93	FB	++
77-80	CB	+++
85-87	SL	++
80-83	CU	+

Year	Lev	Team	W	L	Sv	IP	K	ERA	WHIP	BF/G	OBA	H%	S%	xERA	Ctl	Dom	Cmd	hr/9	BPV
2016	A+	Rancho Cuca	8	4	0	108	108	2.66	1.04	20.8	212	27	77	2.39	2.5	9.0	3.6	0.7	112
2016	AA	Tulsa	0	1	1	16	17	3.89	1.42	6.9	271	34	76	4.54	3.3	9.4	2.8	1.1	98
2017	AA	Tulsa	8	8	0	116	81	3.87	1.39	20.4	244	28	73	3.68	4.3	6.3	1.4	0.6	14
2018	AA	Tulsa	3	1	6	16	24	2.80	0.99	4.7	195	32	73	1.94	2.8	13.4	4.8	0.6	184
2018	AAA	Oklahoma City	1	1	0	37	47	4.38	1.43	4.8	267	40	66	3.45	3.6	11.4	3.1	0.0	125

Was moved back to a relief with mixed results. As as starter features a solid 4-pitch mix that includes an average 91-93 mph FB, CB, SL, and CU. Never really developed a feel for the CU; doesn't need it much in refief. Dom spike out of bullpen hints at upside. Funky delivery and short arm action adds deception and FB gets on hitters quickly.

Schaller,Reid — SP — Washington

EXP MLB DEBUT: 2021 | H/W: 6-3 210 | FUT: Setup reliever | 8D

Thrws R Age 22
2018 (3) Vanderbilt

Velo	Pitch	Grade
94-97	FB	++++
86-88	SL	+++
	CU	+

Year	Lev	Team	W	L	Sv	IP	K	ERA	WHIP	BF/G	OBA	H%	S%	xERA	Ctl	Dom	Cmd	hr/9	BPV
2018	Rk	GCL Nationals	0	1	0	11	16	1.61	1.07	8.7	222	34	91	2.69	2.4	12.9	5.3	0.8	184
2018	A-	Auburn	2	2	0	29	16	5.90	1.34	17.3	268	31	51	3.32	2.8	5.0	1.8	0.0	32

Big and strong, he is a hard thrower with a fast arm and fairly clean delivery. Fastball in the mid-90s with a hard cutter/slider hybrid and very occasional change-up. Was reliever in his one year of college, and with two big pitches seems likely that where he stays. Throws strikes.

Scherff,Alex — SP — Boston

EXP MLB DEBUT: 2021 | H/W: 6-2 209 | FUT: Middle reliever | 6C

Thrws R Age 21
2017 (5) HS (TX)

Velo	Pitch	Grade
90-94	FB	+++
75-77	CB	+++
82-85	CU	+++

Year	Lev	Team	W	L	Sv	IP	K	ERA	WHIP	BF/G	OBA	H%	S%	xERA	Ctl	Dom	Cmd	hr/9	BPV
2018	Rk	GCL Red Sox	0	0	0	5	3	1.80	1.20	10.1	262	31	83	2.86	1.8	5.4	3.0	0.0	67
2018	A	Greenville	1	5	0	65	51	4.98	1.40	18.3	271	32	65	4.38	3.2	7.1	2.2	1.0	59

Big starter with a decent 3-pitch mix, but command is an issue because of delivery. Pitches across a firm front leg so his line to the plate suffers. FB, CB and CU are all good when over, but misses his spots too often. Not a lot of feel for his CU but it is deceptive. Stuff could definitely play up out of pen.

Schmidt,Clarke — SP — New York (A)

EXP MLB DEBUT: 2021 | H/W: 6-1 190 | FUT: #3 starter | 8C

Thrws R Age 23
2017 (1) South Carolina

Velo	Pitch	Grade
93-96	FB	++++
81-84	SL	++++
86-88	CU	+++

Year	Lev	Team	W	L	Sv	IP	K	ERA	WHIP	BF/G	OBA	H%	S%	xERA	Ctl	Dom	Cmd	hr/9	BPV
2017	NCAA	South Carolina	4	2	0	60	70	1.35	0.98	25.4	195	28	89	1.83	2.7	10.5	3.9	0.4	134
2018	Rk	GCL Yankees	0	2	0	7	12	7.50	1.39	10.1	283	46	44	4.71	2.5	15.0	6.0	1.3	221
2018	Rk	GCL Yankees W	0	2	0	15	20	4.20	1.07	9.7	221	33	60	2.49	2.4	12.0	5.0	0.6	169
2018	A-	Staten Island	0	1	0	8	10	1.11	0.74	14.4	149	24	83	0.30	2.2	11.1	5.0	0.0	158

2018 draft pick was drafted high despite recent Tommy John surgery, returned late in 2018. Athletic, 3/4s delivery with good extension. 3-pitch pitcher. FB has ticked back up in rehab with solid late run, exploding on hitters. SL has plus profile with tight, sharp break. CU took step forward prior to injury and now profiles as above-average offering.

Schreiber,John — RP — Detroit

EXP MLB DEBUT: 2019 | H/W: 6-3 215 | FUT: Middle reliever | 7C

Thrws R Age 25
2016 (15) NW Ohio

Velo	Pitch	Grade
89-93	FB	++
76-78	SL	+++
80-82	CU	++

Year	Lev	Team	W	L	Sv	IP	K	ERA	WHIP	BF/G	OBA	H%	S%	xERA	Ctl	Dom	Cmd	hr/9	BPV
2016	A-	Connecticut	2	3	0	29	24	2.78	1.10	6.3	219	28	72	2.03	2.8	7.4	2.7	0.0	76
2018	AA	Erie	3	7	18	58	59	2.48	1.14	4.7	223	30	78	2.45	2.9	9.2	3.1	0.3	103

Long, athletic starter with plenty of projection, but quite raw as a whole. Expected to add velocity as frame fills out. Arm action in need of polish, but shows the instincts that should allow improvements as he continues to mature. Has shown success in locating his curve, while his change-up has struggled to keep up.

Schroeder,Jayson — SP — Houston

EXP MLB DEBUT: 2022 | H/W: 6-2 195 | FUT: Middle reliever | 7D

Thrws R Age 19
2018 (2) HS (WA)

Velo	Pitch	Grade
92-94	FB	+++
80-83	SL	+++
74-76	CB	++

Year	Lev	Team	W	L	Sv	IP	K	ERA	WHIP	BF/G	OBA	H%	S%	xERA	Ctl	Dom	Cmd	hr/9	BPV
2018	Rk	GCL Astros	0	0	0	18	18	1.50	1.22	10.4	204	28	86	2.14	4.5	9.0	2.0	0.0	59

Not quite maxed body, but little physical projection left. Sits in the low-90s with sink, and flashes projectable breaking balls due to a quality feel for spin. The slider flashes above-average with run and depth. The curve shows 12-to-6 action.

Seabold,Connor — SP — Philadelphia

EXP MLB DEBUT: 2020 | H/W: 6-2 175 | FUT: #4 starter | 7C

Thrws R Age 23
2017 (3) Cal St Fullerton

Velo	Pitch	Grade
90-92	FB	+++
82-84	SL	++
81-84	CU	++
78-80	CB	++

Year	Lev	Team	W	L	Sv	IP	K	ERA	WHIP	BF/G	OBA	H%	S%	xERA	Ctl	Dom	Cmd	hr/9	BPV
2017	NCAA	Cal St Fullerton	11	5	0	127	122	2.97	1.16	28.1	257	33	74	3.04	1.6	8.6	5.3	0.4	129
2017	A-	Williamsport	2	0	0	10	13	0.90	0.70	7.0	151	25	86	0.20	1.8	11.7	6.5	0.0	180
2018	A+	Clearwater	4	4	0	71	68	3.79	1.00	22.6	221	28	63	2.50	1.8	8.6	4.9	0.8	125
2018	AA	Reading	1	4	0	58	64	4.95	1.27	21.6	251	31	66	4.30	2.9	9.9	3.4	1.5	117

Thinnish frame with some room to add bulk, has a simple delivery with high leg kick and 3/4s release. Control of FB comes and goes, but gets hit hard when leaks out over the plate. Moderate break on slider; at times struggles to stay on top of pitch. No outstanding secondary, and unless FB command improves, could be a bullpen piece.

Seijas,Alvaro — SP — St. Louis

EXP MLB DEBUT: 2022 | H/W: 5-8 175 | FUT: #4 starter | 7D

Thrws R Age 20
2016 FA (VZ)

Velo	Pitch	Grade
92-95	FB	+++
	CB	+++
	CU	+

Year	Lev	Team	W	L	Sv	IP	K	ERA	WHIP	BF/G	OBA	H%	S%	xERA	Ctl	Dom	Cmd	hr/9	BPV
2016	Rk	GCL Cardinals	3	2	0	50	33	3.06	1.22	20.2	254	29	77	3.47	2.3	5.9	2.5	0.7	62
2017	Rk	Johnson City	4	3	0	63	63	4.99	1.57	23.1	307	40	66	4.69	2.9	9.0	3.2	0.3	103
2018	A	Peoria	5	8	1	129	84	4.53	1.63	23.0	290	33	74	5.25	4.3	5.9	1.4	1.0	9

Late developing, projectable RHP saw an uptick in velocity and FB now sits at 92-95 mph with some late life, but below-average control and command. CB can be average but also lacks consistency while CU lags behind. High 3/4 arm slot adds deception. Raw numbers not inspiring, but he has the stuff to make an impact. Very much a work in progress.

Shaffer,Brian — SP — Tampa Bay

EXP MLB DEBUT: 2020 | H/W: 6-5 200 | FUT: #5 SP/swingman | 6C

Thrws R Age 22
2017 (6) Maryland

Velo	Pitch	Grade
90-93	FB	+++
81-83	SL	++
81-84	CU	+++

Year	Lev	Team	W	L	Sv	IP	K	ERA	WHIP	BF/G	OBA	H%	S%	xERA	Ctl	Dom	Cmd	hr/9	BPV
2017	NCAA	Maryland	7	4	0	108		2.66	0.98	25.7	224	28	78	2.63	1.5	9.1	6.1	0.9	141
2017	Rk	AZL DBacks	0	0	0	3	5	3.00	0.33	4.7	106	0		1.63	0.0	15.0		3.0	288
2017	A-	Hillsboro	0	0	0	21	21	3.43	0.90	7.1	233	32	58	1.70	0.4	9.0	21.0	0.0	168
2018	A	Kane County	7	5	0	106	109	2.71	1.08	21.8	239	30	80	3.09	1.8	9.2	5.2	0.9	136
2018	A+	Charlotte	2	2	0	38	16	3.06	1.20	22.0	250	25	80	3.84	2.4	3.8	1.6	1.2	22

Command/control RHP acquired at trade deadline in Matt Andriese trade with ARI. Tall with an average build. 3/4s cross-fire delivery with moderate extension. Fringy pitch profile. Relies on locating pitches to avoid barrels. FB sits low-90s with moderate run. SL consistently only breaks on one plane. CU may be best pitch, with FB arm speed.

Shawaryn,Mike — SP — Boston

EXP MLB DEBUT: 2019 | H/W: 6-2 200 | FUT: #4 starter | 7C

Thrws R Age 24
2016 (5) Maryland

Velo	Pitch	Grade
90-92	FB	+++
84-87	SL	+++
85-86	CU	+++
81-85	CU	+++

Year	Lev	Team	W	L	Sv	IP	K	ERA	WHIP	BF/G	OBA	H%	S%	xERA	Ctl	Dom	Cmd	hr/9	BPV
2016	A-	Lowell	0	1	0	15	22	2.96	1.45	10.8	259	42	77	3.37	4.1	13.0	3.1	0.0	141
2017	A	Greenville	3	2	0	53	78	3.90	1.07	20.7	227	35	65	2.80	2.2	13.2	6.0	0.8	196
2017	A+	Salem	5	5	0	81	91	3.77	1.31	20.9	237	31	75	3.79	3.9	10.1	2.6	1.1	95
2018	AA	Portland	6	8	0	112	99	3.29	1.13	23.3	240	30	72	2.90	2.2	7.9	3.7	0.6	102
2018	AAA	Pawtucket	3	2	0	36	33	3.98	1.13	20.4	227	26	71	3.60	2.7	8.2	3.0	1.5	92

Low-slot 4-pitch righty who relies on plus command of mediocre mix to get hitters out. Think poor man's Aaron Nola. Extreme fly-ball guy so HRs are a concern. Another concern is how he will fair against a lineup loaded with LHH, so pen may be a better option at some point. Showed good makeup and improvement in 2018.

Sheffield,Jordan — RP — Los Angeles (N)

EXP MLB DEBUT: 2021 | H/W: 5-11 162 | FUT: Setup reliever | 8E

Thrws R Age 23
2016 (1) Vanderbilt

Velo	Pitch	Grade
94-97	FB	++++
80-83	SL	+++
87-89	CU	++

Year	Lev	Team	W	L	Sv	IP	K	ERA	WHIP	BF/G	OBA	H%	S%	xERA	Ctl	Dom	Cmd	hr/9	BPV
2016	A	Great Lakes	0	1	0	11	13	4.09	1.55	6.9	262	33	80	5.21	4.9	10.6	2.2	1.6	77
2017	A	Great Lakes	3	7	0	89	91	4.04	1.44	19.0	255	32	74	4.18	4.2	9.2	2.2	0.9	69
2017	A+	Rancho Cuca	0	2	0	18	18	8.00	2.11	17.8	312	39	61	6.79	7.5	9.0	1.2	1.0	-23
2018	Rk	AZL Dodgers	0	0	0	3	4	0.00	1.00	3.8	106	18	100	0.52	6.0	12.0	2.0	0.0	72
2018	A+	Rancho Cuca	1	3	0	34	40	6.88	1.74	11.1	289	36	65	6.53	5.3	10.6	2.0	2.1	66

Former 1st rounder has fallen on hard times. Uses a funky leg-kick to start max-effort delivery. Gets lots of swing-and-miss from a plus 94-97 mph FB, but the pitch lacks movement and he has no idea where the ball is going (career 4.9 Ctl rate). SL shows plus potential, but CU remains fringe. Was moved to relief and looks like future destination.

Sheffield,Justus — SP — Seattle

EXP MLB DEBUT: 2018 | H/W: 5-10 196 | FUT: #2 starter | 9D

Thrws L Age 22
2014 (1) HS (TN)

Velo	Pitch	Grade
92-95	FB	++++
84-87	SL	++++
88-91	CU	+++

Year	Lev	Team	W	L	Sv	IP	K	ERA	WHIP	BF/G	OBA	H%	S%	xERA	Ctl	Dom	Cmd	hr/9	BPV
2017	Rk	GCL Yankees	0	1	0	4	6	2.14	1.19	8.4	252	41	80	2.63	2.1	12.9	6.0	0.0	192
2017	AA	Trenton	7	6	0	93	82	3.19	1.36	22.9	264	31	83	4.54	3.2	7.9	2.5	1.4	75
2018	AA	Trenton	1	2	0	28	39	2.25	1.07	21.8	168	27	79	1.62	4.5	12.5	2.8	0.3	122
2018	AAA	Scranton/WB	6	4	0	88	84	2.56	1.16	17.5	210	28	78	2.34	3.7	8.6	2.3	0.3	73
2018	MLB	NY Yankees	0	0	0	2	0	12.27	3.18	4.4	392	33	67	13.92	12.3	0.0	0.0	4.1	-313

Physically strong, short-stature LHP acquired in off-season trade with NYY. Moderate-effort in cross-fire 3/4s delivery, achieving solid extension. Struggles commanding 2-seam FB with solid late arm-side run. SL took step forward. True, tight 2-plane sharp break. CU fades well with good separation off FB.

Shepherd,Chandler — SP — Boston

EXP MLB DEBUT: 2019 | H/W: 6-3 185 | FUT: Middle reliever | 6C

Thrws R Age 26
2014 (13) Kentucky

Velo	Pitch	Grade
90-93	FB	+++
80-84	SL	++
81-84	CU	++
86-89	CT	+++

Year	Lev	Team	W	L	Sv	IP	K	ERA	WHIP	BF/G	OBA	H%	S%	xERA	Ctl	Dom	Cmd	hr/9	BPV
2015	A+	Salem	0	2	6	52	46	3.63	1.06	7.2	246	31	65	2.74	1.2	7.9	6.6	0.5	128
2016	AA	Portland	1	1	6	30	39	1.80	0.80	4.9	142	19	86	1.21	3.0	11.7	3.9	0.9	148
2016	AAA	Pawtucket	1	2	1	34	23	3.71	1.06	7.3	226	26	67	2.77	2.1	6.1	2.9	0.8	70
2017	AAA	Pawtucket	1	5	2	59	68	4.10	1.30	7.2	261	35	69	3.76	2.7	10.3	3.8	0.8	130
2018	AAA	Pawtucket	7	10	0	129	107	3.90	1.36	21.6	280	33	74	4.36	2.4	7.5	3.1	0.9	88

Triple-A starter who has relieved some and who would be better off in that role, where FB, his best pitch, should play up a grade. Aggressive with stuff, but command inconsistent. Breaking ball is slurvey. Cutter shows potential but is often flat. No strikeout pitch. Middle relief is likely his best role.

Sherfy,Jimmie — RP — Arizona

EXP MLB DEBUT: 2017 | H/W: 6-0 175 | FUT: Setup reliever | 8C

Thrws R Age 27
2013 (10) Oregon

Velo	Pitch	Grade
93-96	FB	++++
76-80	CB	++++
81-83	CU	++

Year	Lev	Team	W	L	Sv	IP	K	ERA	WHIP	BF/G	OBA	H%	S%	xERA	Ctl	Dom	Cmd	hr/9	BPV
2016	AAA	Reno	1	4	12	23	27	6.23	1.43	4.1	235	28	61	4.85	5.1	10.5	2.1	1.9	71
2017	AAA	Reno	2	1	20	49	61	3.12	0.96	4.2	211	29	73	2.58	1.8	11.2	6.1	1.1	170
2017	MLB	Arizona	2	0	1	10	9	0.00	0.69	3.3	148	20	100	0.18	1.8	7.9	4.5	0.0	113
2018	AAA	Reno	5	1	15	45	58	1.60	1.13	4.7	196	30	86	1.99	4.0	11.6	2.9	0.2	119
2018	MLB	Arizona	0	0	0	16	17	1.68	1.12	4.2	150	20	88	1.80	5.6	9.5	1.7	0.6	38

Lean, athletic RP who made debut in 2017 and spent most of 2018 in PCL. Owns plus FB that will sit 93-96 mph with late arm-side life up in zone. CB shows above-average depth to miss bats and will throw it in any count. Control comes and goes but knows how to miss bats regularly. Good athlete who should develop command with more MLB reps.

Shore,Logan — SP — Detroit

EXP MLB DEBUT: 2019 | H/W: 6-2 200 | FUT: #4 starter | 7C

Thrws R Age 24
2016 (2) Florida

Velo	Pitch	Grade
89-93	FB	++
81-85	SL	++
82-84	CU	++++

Year	Lev	Team	W	L	Sv	IP	K	ERA	WHIP	BF/G	OBA	H%	S%	xERA	Ctl	Dom	Cmd	hr/9	BPV
2016	A-	Vermont	0	2	0	21	21	2.57	1.14	11.9	223	30	78	2.57	3.0	9.0	3.0	0.4	99
2017	Rk	AZL Athletics	0	0	0	8	13	0.00	0.25	8.2	81	17	100		0.0	14.6		0.0	281
2017	A+	Stockton	2	5	1	72	74	4.11	1.34	17.7	285	37	70	4.09	2.0	9.2	4.6	0.6	130
2018	A+	Stockton	2	0	0	22	25	1.22	0.90	20.6	224	33	85	1.57	0.8	10.2	12.5	0.0	179
2018	AA	Midland	1	6	0	68	49	5.54	1.52	22.8	307	35	64	5.19	2.5	6.5	2.6	0.9	67

Solidly built starter who makes a living off a combination of a stellar changeup and plus command across the board. Fastball features underwhelming velocity with a max of 93 mph, but his ability to throw strikes makes up for it. Battled back from a lat strain and looks to be back on track with his health.

Singer,Brady — SP — Kansas City

EXP MLB DEBUT: 2020 | H/W: 6-5 210 | FUT: #3 starter | 8B

Thrws R Age 22
2018 (1) Florida

Velo	Pitch	Grade
90-94	FB	++++
80-83	SL	++++
85-87	CU	+++

Year	Lev	Team	W	L	Sv	IP	K	ERA	WHIP	BF/G	OBA	H%	S%	xERA	Ctl	Dom	Cmd	hr/9	BPV
2018		Did not pitch																	

Athletic starter fell in draft due to concerns with workload and his change-up. Cross-fire, lower 3/4s delivery with three pitches. Has above-average command of plus 2-seam FB with late arm-side bore. SL has 2-plane break with devastating late downward movement. CU effectiveness is a question mark due to arm slot, but it has solid fading action.

Smith,Drew — RP — New York (N)

EXP MLB DEBUT: 2019 | H/W: 6-1 170 | FUT: Setup reliever | 7B

Thrws R Age 25
2015 (3) Dallas Baptist

Velo	Pitch	Grade
94-97	FB	++++
79-82	CB	++++
85-86	CU	+++

Year	Lev	Team	W	L	Sv	IP	K	ERA	WHIP	BF/G	OBA	H%	S%	xERA	Ctl	Dom	Cmd	hr/9	BPV
2017	AAA	Durham	0	0	0	1	0	0.00	1.00	3.8	262	26	100	2.41	0.0	0.0		0.0	18
2018	AA	Binghamton	0	0	1	4	6	2.20	0.73	7.3	147	26	67	0.24	2.2	13.2	6.0	0.0	196
2018	AAA	Las Vegas	5	1	2	32	30	2.80	1.18	5.6	223	27	80	3.05	3.4	8.4	2.5	0.8	78
2018	MLB	NY Mets	1	1	0	28	18	3.54	1.43	4.4	301	34	76	4.60	1.9	5.8	3.0	0.6	70

Perhaps the most promising of a slew of RH relievers the Mets have acquired the last couple of years. He has a plus FB and breaking ball combination and has shown enough command and control of them to put himself in line for some late inning use at the MLB level. Needs to reduce walks.

Sobotka,Chad — RP — Atlanta

EXP MLB DEBUT: 2018 | H/W: 6-6 195 | FUT: Setup reliever | 7D

Thrws R	Age 25		Year	Lev	Team	W	L	Sv	IP	K	ERA	WHIP	BF/G	OBA	H%	S%	xERA	Ctl	Dom	Cmd	hr/9	BPV
2014 (4) South Carolina-Upstate			2017	AA	Mississippi	3	1	0	31	23	5.52	1.55	7.5	249	30	62	3.82	5.5	6.7	1.2	0.3	-11
95-98	FB	++++	2018	A+	Florida	2	0	2	20	28	2.24	0.80	5.6	137	24	69	0.30	3.1	12.5	4.0	0.0	159
85-88	SL	++++	2018	AA	Mississippi	2	3	6	28	37	1.93	1.04	4.9	168	26	82	1.54	4.2	11.9	2.8	0.3	119
			2018	AAA	Gwinnett	0	0	3	9	12	1.98	1.54	4.4	163	27	86	2.45	8.9	11.9	1.3	0.0	-9
			2018	MLB	Atlanta	1	0	0	14	21	1.91	0.99	3.8	112	14	92	1.74	5.7	13.4	2.3	1.3	104

Long, tall RHP enjoyed successful MLB cup of coffee. Uneven 3/4s delivery with solid extension. Achieves deception using long limbs to hide ball. Two-pitch pitcher: Four-seam FB has late ride action but struggles commanding, especially to arm-side. SL is mostly tight with plus 2-plane break.

Solis,Jairo — SP — Houston

EXP MLB DEBUT: 2022 | H/W: 6-2 160 | FUT: #4 starter | 7C

Thrws R	Age 19		Year	Lev	Team	W	L	Sv	IP	K	ERA	WHIP	BF/G	OBA	H%	S%	xERA	Ctl	Dom	Cmd	hr/9	BPV
2017 FA (VZ)																						
92-95	FB	++++																				
87-89	SL	+++	2017	Rk	GCL Astros	1	0	0	21	24	3.00	1.24	17.0	243	34	76	3.05	3.0	10.3	3.4	0.4	122
86-87	CU	+++	2017	Rk	Greeneville	1	1	0	14	17	1.93	1.29	14.4	233	35	83	2.64	3.9	10.9	2.8	0.0	111
78-80	CB	++	2018	A	Quad Cities	2	5	0	50	51	3.59	1.61	17.1	257	35	76	3.96	5.7	9.1	1.6	0.2	28

The projectable righty spent the full year at one level just a season after blowing through three. It was an adjustment. When he signed he touched 91, but he now sits 92-95 with late movement. He left his control in short-season ball and as a result couldn't average five innings a start. He rounds out his arsenal with a slider, change, and curve.

Solomon,Peter — SP — Houston

EXP MLB DEBUT: 2020 | H/W: 6-4 185 | FUT: #5 SP/swingman | 7C

Thrws R	Age 22		Year	Lev	Team	W	L	Sv	IP	K	ERA	WHIP	BF/G	OBA	H%	S%	xERA	Ctl	Dom	Cmd	hr/9	BPV
2017 (4) Notre Dame																						
90-94	FB	+++	2017	NCAA	Notre Dame	3	4	3	54		3.83	1.39	10.8	236	33	71	3.25	4.7	10.2	2.2	0.3	75
78-82	CB	++++	2017	Rk	GCL Astros	0	0	0	1	0	0.00	0.00	2.8	0	0			0.0	0.0		0.0	18
83-86	CU	+++	2018	A	Quad Cities	8	1	0	77	88	2.45	1.17	16.2	222	32	78	2.42	3.3	10.3	3.1	0.2	115
85-87	SL	+	2018	A+	Buies Creek	1	0	0	23	26	1.96	0.87	17.0	198	29	75	1.17	1.6	10.2	6.5	0.0	159

Tall and lean RHP who dominated the lower minors while being old for his level. He has a four-pitch mix but might do well to ditch his slider which is well below average at present. The bat-misser is the curveball. A polished arm like his won't be challenged in A-ball, so the upper minors will provide a true test.

Sopko,Andrew — SP — Los Angeles (N)

EXP MLB DEBUT: 2020 | H/W: 6-2 180 | FUT: #5 SP/swingman | 6C

Thrws R	Age 24		Year	Lev	Team	W	L	Sv	IP	K	ERA	WHIP	BF/G	OBA	H%	S%	xERA	Ctl	Dom	Cmd	hr/9	BPV
2015 (7) Gonzaga																						
90-93	FB	++	2016	AA	Tulsa	2	2	0	31	25	4.94	1.48	22.2	286	33	69	4.99	3.2	7.3	2.3	1.2	62
80-83	CB	++	2017	AA	Tulsa	5	7	0	104	74	4.15	1.43	19.3	261	30	73	4.31	3.9	6.4	1.6	1.0	28
73-75	CU	+	2018	A+	Rancho Cuca	3	4	0	64	73	3.23	1.14	21.1	246	34	72	2.97	2.0	10.2	5.2	0.6	149
			2018	AA	Tulsa	3	1	0	53	48	3.90	1.49	16.3	306	36	80	5.63	2.2	8.1	3.7	1.5	105

Stocky RHP uses a three-pitch mix to keep hitters off-balance, but none of his offerings are plus. FB sits at 90-93 but lacks movement. Mid-70s CB has good 12-to-6 action and low-80s SL has ellicts swings and misses. Deliberate mechanics and average arm strength limit him to a back-end role.

Soriano,Jose — SP — Los Angeles (A)

EXP MLB DEBUT: 2021 | H/W: 6-3 168 | FUT: #3 starter | 8E

Thrws R	Age 20		Year	Lev	Team	W	L	Sv	IP	K	ERA	WHIP	BF/G	OBA	H%	S%	xERA	Ctl	Dom	Cmd	hr/9	BPV
2016 FA (DR)																						
92-95	FB	+++																				
80-84	CB	++	2017	Rk	Orem	0	0	0	3	2	2.90	2.58	16.7	314	37	88	7.10	11.6	5.8	0.5	0.0	-191
83-85	CU	++	2017	Rk	AZL Angels	2	2	0	49	37	2.94	1.16	16.3	237	29	75	2.77	2.6	6.8	2.6	0.4	71
			2018	A	Burlington	1	6	0	46	42	4.49	1.50	14.2	207	27	68	3.06	6.8	8.2	1.2	0.2	-19

Projectable starter with developing arsenal. Fastball took big step up to 97 mph in 2018. Frame is projected to bulk up and with it; an easy move to triple digits is expected to follow. Curve stands out more than his change-up at the moment, but his change-up should progress to an average offering. Some mechanical pieces to iron out.

Soroka,Mike — SP — Atlanta

EXP MLB DEBUT: 2018 | H/W: 6-4 195 | FUT: #2 starter | 9C

Thrws R	Age 21		Year	Lev	Team	W	L	Sv	IP	K	ERA	WHIP	BF/G	OBA	H%	S%	xERA	Ctl	Dom	Cmd	hr/9	BPV
2015 (1) HS (AB)			2016	A	Rome	9	9	0	143	125	3.02	1.13	22.6	244	31	72	2.60	2.0	7.9	3.9	0.2	105
91-94	FB	++++	2017	AA	Mississippi	11	8	0	153	125	2.76	1.09	23.0	235	29	76	2.76	2.0	7.3	3.7	0.6	96
84-86	SL	++++	2018	A	Rome	0	0	0	3	3	0.00	0.00	9.0	0	0			0.0	8.4		0.0	170
80-84	CU	+++	2018	AAA	Gwinnett	2	1	0	27	31	2.00	0.96	20.4	208	31	77	1.52	2.0	10.3	5.2	0.0	150
			2018	MLB	Atlanta	2	1	0	25	21	3.57	1.47	21.6	297	37	75	4.35	2.5	7.5	3.0	0.4	86

Pitchability RHP with 2 plus pitches struggled through shoulder injury in 2018. Easy, repeatable 3/4s delivery. Four-pitch pitcher with 2 FB variations. Commands a two-seamer with plus arm-side run; its ahead of four-seamer, which he uses to change eye levels. Has advanced command of sharp, 2-plane SL. CU is average offering with separation off FB.

Soto,Gregory — SP — Detroit

EXP MLB DEBUT: 2020 | H/W: 6-1 180 | FUT: Middle reliever | 7C

Thrws L	Age 24		Year	Lev	Team	W	L	Sv	IP	K	ERA	WHIP	BF/G	OBA	H%	S%	xERA	Ctl	Dom	Cmd	hr/9	BPV
2013 FA (DR)			2015	A-	Connecticut	0	1	0	2	5	22.50	3.50	6.3	151	61	29	7.15	27.0	22.5	0.8	0.0	-306
91-95	FB	+++	2016	A-	Connecticut	3	2	0	71	62	3.04	1.43	20.2	253	33	77	3.42	4.3	7.8	1.8	0.1	43
80-84	SL	+	2017	A	West Michigan	10	1	0	96	116	2.25	1.29	21.9	205	30	83	2.58	5.1	10.9	2.1	0.3	77
74-77	CB	++	2017	A+	Lakeland	2	1	0	28	28	2.25	1.36	23.4	255	34	84	3.42	3.5	9.0	2.5	0.3	85
82-85	CU	+	2018	A+	Lakeland	8	8	0	113	115	4.46	1.51	19.6	241	32	69	3.62	5.6	9.2	1.6	0.3	32

Solidly built rotation arm with valuable lefty velocity. Accessed offspeed more in 2018 than years past, with better shape to curve and the makings of a developing slider. Change-up still lags. Fastball dominates when consistent, but location has continued to be a challenge. Attacks strike zone with good mixing when location is working.

Staumont,Josh — RP — Kansas City

EXP MLB DEBUT: 2019 | H/W: 6-3 200 | FUT: Closer | 8E

Thrws R	Age 25		Year	Lev	Team	W	L	Sv	IP	K	ERA	WHIP	BF/G	OBA	H%	S%	xERA	Ctl	Dom	Cmd	hr/9	BPV
2015 (2) Azusa Pacific			2016	A+	Wilmington	2	10	0	73	94	5.05	1.77	18.6	231	35	70	4.17	8.3	11.6	1.4	0.4	4
95-97	FB	++++	2016	AA	NW Arkansas	2	1	0	50	73	3.05	1.58	20.0	229	37	81	3.64	6.6	13.1	2.0	0.4	75
81-84	CB	++++	2017	AA	NW Arkansas	3	4	0	48	45	4.48	1.58	21.2	236	31	70	3.78	6.3	8.4	1.3	0.4	-2
87-88	CU	+	2017	AAA	Omaha	3	8	0	76	93	6.28	1.67	21.3	230	29	65	5.13	7.5	11.0	1.5	1.7	15
			2018	AAA	Omaha	2	5	1	74	103	3.52	1.50	7.8	220	34	77	3.45	6.3	12.5	2.0	0.5	73

Hard-throwing, physical RHP continues to be on cusp of MLB debut. Struggled as starter, now full-time reliever. Raw, 3/4s delivery better suited for pen. Mid-to-high 90s FB with solid late life. Struggles with FB command, which plays better as RP. Sharp, two-plane slider with devestating break; hard to read out of hand. CU needs work.

Steele,Justin — SP — Chicago (N)

EXP MLB DEBUT: 2020 | H/W: 6-1 180 | FUT: #3 starter | 8D

Thrws L	Age 23		Year	Lev	Team	W	L	Sv	IP	K	ERA	WHIP	BF/G	OBA	H%	S%	xERA	Ctl	Dom	Cmd	hr/9	BPV
2014 (5) HS (MS)			2016	A	South Bend	5	7	0	77	76	5.02	1.71	18.4	300	39	69	4.99	4.6	8.9	1.9	0.4	55
90-94	FB	+++	2017	A+	Myrtle Beach	6	7	0	98	82	2.93	1.38	20.6	265	33	80	3.87	3.3	7.5	2.3	0.5	64
75-78	CB	+++	2018	Rk	AZL Cubs	0	0	0	18	27	1.49	0.72	12.8	150	25	83	0.69	2.0	13.4	6.8	0.5	206
	CU	++	2018	A+	Myrtle Beach	2	1	0	18	19	2.49	0.99	17.3	190	27	72	1.40	3.0	9.4	3.2	0.0	108
			2018	AA	Tennessee	0	1	0	10	7	3.60	1.10	19.6	221	25	70	2.91	2.7	6.3	2.3	0.9	59

Coming off 2017 Tommy John surgery, FB velo was down a tick, but still sat at 90-94 mph and could see more. FB has good late life and sink. Best offering is a plus power CB that features good late break. Improved command was a bonus in limited action. Hard throwing lefties who can find the zone have plenty of value.

Stephen,Trevor — SP — New York (A)

EXP MLB DEBUT: 2019 | H/W: 6-4 210 | FUT: Setup reliever | 7C

Thrws R	Age 23		Year	Lev	Team	W	L	Sv	IP	K	ERA	WHIP	BF/G	OBA	H%	S%	xERA	Ctl	Dom	Cmd	hr/9	BPV
2017 (3) Hill College																						
92-94	FB	++++	2017	Rk	GCL Yankees	0	0	0	2	1	0.00	0.00	5.6	0	0			0.0	4.5		0.0	99
81-84	SL	++++	2017	A-	Staten Island	1	1	0	32	43	1.40	0.81	11.7	181	30	81	0.80	1.7	12.1	7.2	0.0	190
87	CU	++	2018	A+	Tampa	3	1	0	41	49	1.98	0.78	21.1	166	21	85	1.61	2.0	10.8	5.4	1.1	158
			2018	AA	Trenton	3	8	0	83	91	4.55	1.31	20.2	254	34	64	3.50	3.1	9.9	3.1	0.5	111

Big-bodied Texas RHP made it to Double-A in first full pro season. 3/4s, cross-fire delivery using all of his large frame to extending towards the plate. Three-pitch pitcher; best is 2-plane moving SL. Alters grip to create both sweep and tight, sharp break. FB has solid run profile and gets on hitters quick. Slows down arm to throw CU. RP upside.

Stephens,Jordan — SP — Chicago (A)

EXP MLB DEBUT: 2019 | H/W: 6-1 185 | FUT: #4 starter | 7C

Thrws R	Age 26		Year	Lev	Team	W	L	Sv	IP	K	ERA	WHIP	BF/G	OBA	H%	S%	xERA	Ctl	Dom	Cmd	hr/9	BPV
2015 (5) Rice			2015	Rk	AZL White Sox	0	0	0	14	18	0.63	0.63	5.4	149	24	89	0.02	1.3	11.4	9.0	0.0	189
90-93	FB	+++	2016	A+	Winston-Salem	7	10	0	141	155	3.45	1.26	21.3	245	33	75	3.44	3.1	9.9	3.2	0.8	113
87-88	CT	+++	2017	AA	Birmingham	3	7	0	91	83	3.16	1.30	23.5	246	31	76	3.25	3.5	8.2	2.4	0.4	72
77-79	CB	++++	2018	AA	Birmingham	4	3	0	39	40	2.98	1.25	22.8	251	34	75	3.01	2.8	9.2	3.3	0.2	109
80-82	CU	++	2018	AAA	Charlotte	4	7	0	107	99	4.71	1.46	21.8	274	34	69	4.52	3.5	8.3	2.4	0.9	73

Physically-mature RHP continues to advance rapidly. Four pitches: Four-seam FB is workhorse; he struggles to command it away from arm-side and lacks movement. Added CT 2 years ago. Best pitch is 11-to-5 CB; cleaned up loopiness and is now a solid breaker. Threw more CU in 2018; development of the pitch may determine his ceiling.

Stewart,Kohl — SP — Minnesota

EXP MLB DEBUT: 2018 | H/W: 6-3 210 | FUT: #4 starter | 7D

Thrws R Age 24 — 2013 (1) HS (TX)

Velo	Pitch	Grade
90-94	FB	+++
86-88	SL	+++
76-80	CB	++
86-89	CU	+++

Year	Lev	Team	W	L	Sv	IP	K	ERA	WHIP	BF/G	OBA	H%	S%	xERA	Ctl	Dom	Cmd	hr/9	BPV
2017	AA	Chattanooga	5	6	0	77	52	4.09	1.52	20.9	249	29	73	3.92	5.3	6.1	1.2	0.5	-15
2017	AAA	Rochester	1	0	0	5	5	7.20	1.60	22.1	332	40	57	6.58	1.8	9.0	5.0	1.8	131
2018	AA	Chattanooga	3	4	0	68	71	4.76	1.54	21.2	305	40	68	4.68	2.8	9.4	3.4	0.4	112
2018	AAA	Rochester	0	3	0	40	30	4.03	1.42	24.3	284	33	74	4.55	2.7	6.7	2.5	0.9	66
2018	MLB	Minnesota	2	1	0	36	24	3.73	1.44	19.3	250	30	73	3.52	4.5	6.0	1.3	0.2	5

Athletic, former first rounder pick remade self into pitcher, making it to big leagues. Repeatable cross-fire delivery, 3/4s slot. 4-pitch, fringe-average to above-average stuff. Throws sinker and 4-seam FB 70% of the time. Secondaries improved, especially bite to CB. CU became workable pitch while SL used effectively to keep hitters off FB movement.

Stewart,Will — SP — Philadelphia

EXP MLB DEBUT: 2022 | H/W: 6-2 175 | FUT: #4 starter | 7C

Thrws L Age 21 — 2015 (20) HS (AL)

Velo	Pitch	Grade
89-91	FB	+++
80-83	SL	++
75-77	CB	++
82-84	CU	+++

Year	Lev	Team	W	L	Sv	IP	K	ERA	WHIP	BF/G	OBA	H%	S%	xERA	Ctl	Dom	Cmd	hr/9	BPV
2015	Rk	GCL Phillies	1	0	0	20	20	4.90	1.63	7.5	240	29	73	4.88	6.7	8.9	1.3	1.3	-2
2016	Rk	GCL Phillies	2	3	0	44	35	4.08	1.20	16.1	215	27	63	2.43	3.9	7.1	1.8	0.2	42
2017	A-	Williamsport	4	2	0	60	58	4.19	1.48	19.9	274	35	71	4.12	3.7	8.7	2.3	0.4	73
2018	A	Lakewood	8	1	0	113	90	2.07	0.98	21.5	220	27	80	2.11	1.7	7.2	4.3	0.4	102

Short and lean but athletic, he kept SAL hitters off balance all season. Cross-body arm action makes his potentially plus CU all the more difficult to track. Hits spots, commands the FB, changes speeds well, though breaking ball still unreliable. With a touch more strength and velo, would be a high floor/low ceiling type in Marco Gonzales vein.

Stiever,Jonathan — SP — Chicago (A)

EXP MLB DEBUT: 2021 | H/W: 6-1 188 | FUT: #4 starter | 7D

Thrws R Age 21 — 2018 (5) Indiana

Velo	Pitch	Grade
90-93	FB	+++
83-85	SL	++
74-79	CB	+++
84-86	CU	+++

Year	Lev	Team	W	L	Sv	IP	K	ERA	WHIP	BF/G	OBA	H%	S%	xERA	Ctl	Dom	Cmd	hr/9	BPV
2018	NCAA	Indiana	5	6	0	100	97	3.42	1.26	25.5	250	32	74	3.40	2.9	8.7	3.0	0.6	97
2018	Rk	Great Falls	0	1	0	28	39	4.18	1.14	8.5	226	33	66	3.07	2.9	12.5	4.3	1.0	166

High-waisted, athletic RHP made pro debut. Repeatable, 3/4s cross-fire delivery with high leg kick. Pitchability over stuff but stuff has taken step forward. Low-90s FB with arm-side movement early in progression. Best pitch is 11-to-5 CB with swing-and-miss potential. Recently added SL with similar profile as CB. CU flashes average potential.

Suarez,Jose — SP — Los Angeles (A)

EXP MLB DEBUT: 2020 | H/W: 5-10 170 | FUT: #4 starter | 7B

Thrws L Age 21 — 2014 FA (VZ)

Velo	Pitch	Grade
89-93	FB	+++
75-77	CB	++
77-80	CU	+++

Year	Lev	Team	W	L	Sv	IP	K	ERA	WHIP	BF/G	OBA	H%	S%	xERA	Ctl	Dom	Cmd	hr/9	BPV
2017	Rk	AZL Angels	1	0	0	14	19	1.93	1.00	17.8	202	31	85	2.13	2.6	12.2	4.8	0.6	168
2017	A	Burlington	5	1	0	54	71	3.65	1.24	18.3	243	34	75	3.72	3.0	11.8	3.9	1.2	150
2018	A+	Inland Empire	0	1	0	9	18	2.00	0.78	16.2	191	45	71	0.78	1.0	18.0	18.0	0.0	315
2018	AA	Mobile	2	1	0	29	51	3.08	1.44	17.8	292	52	76	3.79	2.5	15.7	6.4	0.0	234
2018	AAA	Salt Lake	1	4	0	78	73	4.49	1.49	19.8	269	34	69	4.18	4.0	8.4	2.1	0.6	61

Compact-sized southpaw who makes a living off movement as opposed to velocity. Fastball will touch mid-90s with good life, complemented by plus change-up with plenty of deception. Curveball is still developing, but flashes as quality offering. Lacks upside, but repeats well with solid instincts and above-average control.

Suarez,Ranger — SP — Philadelphia

EXP MLB DEBUT: 2018 | H/W: 6-0 177 | FUT: #4 starter | 7C

Thrws L Age 23 — 2012 FA (VZ)

Velo	Pitch	Grade
90-93	FB	+++
81-83	SL	+++
84-85	CU	+++

Year	Lev	Team	W	L	Sv	IP	K	ERA	WHIP	BF/G	OBA	H%	S%	xERA	Ctl	Dom	Cmd	hr/9	BPV
2017	A	Lakewood	6	2	0	85	90	1.59	0.89	22.6	178	24	85	1.41	2.5	9.5	3.8	0.4	121
2017	A+	Clearwater	2	4	0	37	38	3.87	1.45	19.9	291	39	72	4.09	2.7	9.2	3.5	0.2	112
2018	AA	Reading	4	3	0	75	54	2.76	1.12	24.6	232	28	74	2.48	2.4	6.5	2.7	0.2	70
2018	AAA	Lehigh Valley	2	0	0	49	31	2.75	1.28	22.4	257	30	79	3.35	2.7	5.7	2.1	0.4	46
2018	MLB	Philadelphia	1	1	0	15	11	5.40	1.80	17.3	332	37	75	7.11	3.6	6.6	1.8	1.8	40

Has touched the mid-90s, but FB settles in at 90-93 and both four-seamer and two-seamer get a lot of GBs. SL/CU round out his arsenal, and has commanded everything in the minors. Gets good extension in delivery with a hint of deception. Will need to get by on pitchability, though, as there's not a lot of room for error. A competitor.

Supak,Trey — SP — Milwaukee

EXP MLB DEBUT: 2020 | H/W: 6-5 210 | FUT: #4 starter | 8D

Thrws R Age 22 — 2014 (2) HS (TX)

Velo	Pitch	Grade
88-92	FB	+++
76-79	CB	+++
	CU	+++

Year	Lev	Team	W	L	Sv	IP	K	ERA	WHIP	BF/G	OBA	H%	S%	xERA	Ctl	Dom	Cmd	hr/9	BPV
2016	A	Wisconsin	2	3	1	44	40	3.88	1.47	17.2	278	35	74	4.33	3.5	8.2	2.4	0.6	71
2017	A	Wisconsin	2	2	0	41	53	1.76	0.76	18.3	154	24	77	0.59	2.2	11.6	5.3	0.2	168
2017	A+	Carolina	3	4	1	72	57	4.62	1.29	19.8	242	27	69	4.21	3.5	7.1	2.0	1.5	52
2018	A+	Carolina	2	1	0	51	48	1.76	1.04	21.9	205	27	84	2.02	2.8	8.5	3.0	0.4	94
2018	AA	Biloxi	6	6	0	86	75	2.92	1.18	21.6	233	29	76	2.81	2.9	7.8	2.7	0.4	80

Large-bodied RHP who logged 137 IP and reached upper minors for the first time. FB can touch 95 mph but operates more around 89-91 mph with ease. Shows aptitude for spinning CB and working on show-me CU. Fills zone regularly and throws downhill from high slot. Frame and ease of delivery project a back-end starter with high floor.

Swanda,John — SP — Los Angeles (A)

EXP MLB DEBUT: 2023 | H/W: 6-2 185 | FUT: #4 starter | 7B

Thrws R Age 20 — 2017 (4) HS (IA)

Velo	Pitch	Grade
90-93	FB	++
74-77	CB	++
80-82	CU	+

Year	Lev	Team	W	L	Sv	IP	K	ERA	WHIP	BF/G	OBA	H%	S%	xERA	Ctl	Dom	Cmd	hr/9	BPV
2017	Rk	AZL Angels	1	2	0	9	6	9.78	2.07	6.4	334	38	50	7.05	5.9	5.9	1.0	1.0	-35
2018	Rk	Orem	0	4	0	30	26	4.50	1.47	12.9	304	36	73	5.25	2.1	7.8	3.7	1.2	102

Solid, athletic starter with projection remaining. Resume currently sits as average, but youth and progression plead the case that he'll continue to sharpen. Loose arm action gives way to clean delivery of a low-90s fastball. Curve can resemble a slider at times and change-up remains a work in progress.

Swanson,Erik — SP — Seattle

EXP MLB DEBUT: 2019 | H/W: 6-3 220 | FUT: Setup reliever | 7C

Thrws R Age 25 — 2014 (8) Iowa Western CC

Velo	Pitch	Grade
92-94	FB	++++
85-87	SL	+++
83-84	CU	++

Year	Lev	Team	W	L	Sv	IP	K	ERA	WHIP	BF/G	OBA	H%	S%	xERA	Ctl	Dom	Cmd	hr/9	BPV
2017	A+	Tampa	7	3	0	100	84	3.96	1.29	20.6	289	35	71	4.30	1.3	7.6	6.0	0.9	120
2018	A-	Staten Island	0	0	0	6	6	4.35	1.29	12.7	314	41	63	3.82	0.0	8.7		0.0	175
2018	AA	Trenton	5	0	0	42	55	0.43	0.88	19.5	156	26	95	0.71	3.2	11.7	3.7	0.0	143
2018	AAA	Scranton/WB	3	2	0	72	78	3.87	1.07	20.0	237	30	69	3.32	1.7	9.7	5.6	1.2	146

Pitchability RHP with stuff and deception was acquired in off-season trade with NYY. Athletic, cross-armed 3/4s delivery with slight back turn and solid extension. Three-pitch pitcher. Four-seam FB has late run, and he commands well within strikezone. Sharp, 2-plane SL is above-average offering. Has feel for CU, struggles maintaining FB arm-speed.

Szapucki,Thomas — SP — New York (N)

EXP MLB DEBUT: 2021 | H/W: 6-2 190 | FUT: #4 starter | 8C

Thrws L Age 22 — 2015 (5) HS (FL)

Velo	Pitch	Grade
93-96	FB	++++
81-84	CB	++++
83-86	CU	+++

Year	Lev	Team	W	L	Sv	IP	K	ERA	WHIP	BF/G	OBA	H%	S%	xERA	Ctl	Dom	Cmd	hr/9	BPV
2015	Rk	GCL Mets	0	0	0	2	3	17.14	2.38	3.6	458	63	20	9.42	0.0	12.9		0.0	249
2016	Rk	Kingsport	2	1	0	29	47	0.62	0.86	21.4	164	29	100	1.30	2.8	14.6	5.2	0.6	205
2016	A-	Brooklyn	2	2	0	23	39	2.35	0.91	21.5	134	28	71	0.53	4.3	15.3	3.5	0.0	176
2017	A	Columbia	1	2	0	29	27	2.79	1.17	19.3	227	30	74	2.30	3.1	8.4	2.7	0.0	85
2018		Did not pitch - injury																	

Missed 2018 after Tommy John surgery. Has had real trouble staying healthy as a pro but has pitched well when he has been. Appears to have the ingredients of a MLB starter - size and strength, a good delivery, and a solid arsenal, but has thrown just 83 innings since being drafted out of HS in 2015, none above Low A. Needs to show; 2019 will be telling.

Tabor,Matt — SP — Arizona

EXP MLB DEBUT: 2021 | H/W: 6-2 160 | FUT: #4 starter | 7C

Thrws R Age 20 — 2017 (3) HS (MA)

Velo	Pitch	Grade
90-92	FB	+++
84-86	SL	+++
82-84	CU	+++

Year	Lev	Team	W	L	Sv	IP	K	ERA	WHIP	BF/G	OBA	H%	S%	xERA	Ctl	Dom	Cmd	hr/9	BPV
2017	Rk	AZL DBacks	0	1	0	4	9	2.14	1.90	5.0	403	74	88	6.89	0.0	19.3		0.0	365
2018	A-	Hillsboro	2	1	0	60	46	3.29	1.20	17.3	258	31	74	3.34	1.9	6.9	3.5	0.6	89

Lean, medium-framed RH with a chance for three solid-average offerings as back-end SP. Works from 3/4 slot and sat easy 90-92 mph in extended spring training with ability to pound zone. SL gets lengthy at times and will need to iron it out. Shows some feel for CU with average fade and depth. Physical projection remaining and could add velocity.

Tarnok,Freddy — SP — Atlanta

EXP MLB DEBUT: 2021 | H/W: 6-3 185 | FUT: #3 starter | 8E

Thrws R Age 20 — 2017 (3) HS (FL)

Velo	Pitch	Grade
91-94	FB	++++
79-82	SL	++++
81-82	CU	++

Year	Lev	Team	W	L	Sv	IP	K	ERA	WHIP	BF/G	OBA	H%	S%	xERA	Ctl	Dom	Cmd	hr/9	BPV
2017	Rk	GCL Braves	0	3	0	14	10	2.57	1.00	6.7	218	27	71	1.77	1.9	6.4	3.3	0.0	82
2018	A	Rome	5	5	0	77	83	3.97	1.44	12.2	244	33	73	3.72	4.8	9.7	2.0	0.6	63

Raw, athletic RHP was eased in to full-season ball. A former SS, he is still relatively new to pitching. Jerky 3/4s delivery with elite arm-speed, but struggles tp rush through delivery. Three pitches: 2-seam FB has solid arm-side run and sink but will unintentionally cut too. Tight, late-breaking SL is best pitch, plus at at maturity. Has some feel for CU.

Tate,Dillon

SP | **Baltimore** | EXP MLB DEBUT: 2019 | H/W: 6-2 185 | FUT: #4 starter | **7B**

Thrws R Age 24
2015 (1) UC-Santa Barbara

Velo	Pitch	Grade
93-96	FB	++++
87-89	SL	+++
85-86	CU	++

Year	Lev	Team	W	L	Sv	IP	K	ERA	WHIP	BF/G	OBA	H%	S%	xERA	Ctl	Dom	Cmd	hr/9	BPV
2016	A	Charleston (Sc)	1	0	0	17	15	3.16	1.58	10.7	303	38	81	4.89	3.2	7.9	2.5	0.5	75
2017	A+	Tampa	6	0	0	58	46	2.63	1.08	25.2	227	27	78	2.67	2.3	7.1	3.1	0.6	84
2017	AA	Trenton	1	2	0	25	17	3.24	1.28	25.6	246	27	79	3.85	3.2	6.1	1.9	1.1	41
2018	AA	Trenton	5	2	0	82	75	3.39	1.12	21.6	224	28	72	2.85	2.7	8.2	3.0	0.8	92
2018	AA	Bowie	2	3	0	40	21	5.82	1.42	24.3	297	33	57	4.56	2.0	4.7	2.3	0.7	48

Was acquired in mid-season trade with NYY; enjoyed best season as pro as set a career high in Dom. Two-seam FB lacks command and overall movement. Two-plane SL is his best secondary; refinement of pitch largely responsible for more Ks. Has a feel for CU but running out of time in development. Heavy RP risk on profile.

Taylor,Curtis

RP | **Tampa Bay** | EXP MLB DEBUT: 2019 | H/W: 6-6 215 | FUT: Setup reliever | **7D**

Thrws R Age 23
2016 (4) British Columbia

Velo	Pitch	Grade
95-98	FB	++++
85	SL	++
87-88	CU	+

Year	Lev	Team	W	L	Sv	IP	K	ERA	WHIP	BF/G	OBA	H%	S%	xERA	Ctl	Dom	Cmd	hr/9	BPV
2016	A-	Hillsboro	1	0	3	16	23	2.24	1.12	3.7	223	37	78	2.06	2.8	12.9	4.6	0.0	174
2017	A	Kane County	3	4	0	62	68	3.33	1.26	19.5	239	32	74	3.19	3.3	9.9	3.0	0.6	105
2018	A+	Charlotte	3	0	2	17	23	3.16	1.23	8.7	261	40	71	2.84	2.1	12.1	5.8	0.0	179
2018	AA	Montgomery	3	4	6	60	74	2.39	1.00	7.7	167	23	81	1.97	3.9	11.1	2.8	0.9	112

Lean, long-limbed RHP became full-time RP in 2018. Athletic, 3/4s online delivery with effort and inconsistency. FB potentially plus-plus at maturity with top shelf velocity and late, unpredictable run. FB command a concern. SL has slurvy shape. Will need to tighten up to reach projection. Firm CU isn't a usable pitch.

Tetreault,Jackson

SP | **Washington** | EXP MLB DEBUT: 2022 | H/W: 6-5 170 | FUT: #4 starter | **7C**

Thrws R Age 22
2017 (7) St Coll of FL, Mana

Velo	Pitch	Grade
89-93	FB	+++
86-89	CT	++
77-79	CB	++
83-84	CU	++

Year	Lev	Team	W	L	Sv	IP	K	ERA	WHIP	BF/G	OBA	H%	S%	xERA	Ctl	Dom	Cmd	hr/9	BPV
2017	Rk	GCL Nationals	0	0	0	2	2	4.50	1.00	7.6	151	0	100	5.22	4.5	9.0	2.0	4.5	59
2017	A-	Auburn	2	2	0	38	36	2.60	1.26	14.1	229	30	79	2.77	3.8	8.5	2.3	0.2	69
2018	A	Hagerstown	3	8	0	110	118	4.01	1.29	22.6	258	34	70	3.76	2.8	9.7	3.5	0.8	117
2018	A+	Potomac	1	1	0	22	20	4.46	1.26	22.7	251	31	65	3.60	2.8	8.1	2.9	0.8	87

Tall and skinny, he improved repeating his delivery in 2018, which resulted in more strikes. FB and CT are main weapons, but both CB and CU have shown promise. Still learning to mix speeds, and lean frame oozes projection. Some added strength to his athleticism could be a recipe for success.

Thomas,Tahnaj

SP | **Pittsburgh** | EXP MLB DEBUT: 2022 | H/W: 6-4 190 | FUT: #3 starter | **8D**

Thrws R Age 19
2017 FA (BM)

Velo	Pitch	Grade
92-96	FB	++++
	CB	++++
	CU	++

Year	Lev	Team	W	L	Sv	IP	K	ERA	WHIP	BF/G	OBA	H%	S%	xERA	Ctl	Dom	Cmd	hr/9	BPV
2017	Rk	AZL Indians	0	3	0	33	29	6.00	1.82	11.8	273	33	68	5.57	6.8	7.9	1.2	1.1	-24
2018	Rk	AZL Indians	0	0	0	19	27	4.69	1.20	9.6	194	29	62	2.80	4.7	12.7	2.7	0.9	119

Traded from Cleveland in off-season in multi-prospect deal. Projection arm with clean mechanics and great extension to plate, reminiscent of Kenley Jansen. Should have enough control and command to be a future starter, shows feel for CB and CU, but both pitches are still works-in-progress.

Thompson,Jake

SP | **Boston** | EXP MLB DEBUT: 2021 | H/W: 6-1 200 | FUT: Middle reliever | **6D**

Thrws R Age 24
2017 (4) Oregon St

Velo	Pitch	Grade
90-93	FB	+++
71-75	CB	++
80-84	SL	++
83-85	SP	+++

Year	Lev	Team	W	L	Sv	IP	K	ERA	WHIP	BF/G	OBA	H%	S%	xERA	Ctl	Dom	Cmd	hr/9	BPV
2017	NCAA	Oregon State	14	1	0	128	119	1.97	0.98	24.3	190	25	81	1.69	2.8	8.4	3.0	0.4	93
2017	A-	Lowell	0	3	0	11	11	3.24	1.44	6.8	242	33	75	3.17	4.9	8.9	1.8	0.0	47
2018	A+	Salem	5	13	0	125	96	5.32	1.56	21.1	295	35	65	4.83	3.4	6.9	2.0	0.6	51

Huge, wide, young starter who is not progressing in that role. Think poor man's Sal Romano. Lacks command and feel to start. Walks have become a major concern. Needs to move to pen where FB and split should play up some.

Thompson,Keegan

SP | **Chicago (N)** | EXP MLB DEBUT: 2020 | H/W: 6-1 208 | FUT: #4 starter | **7C**

Thrws R Age 24
2017 (3) Auburn

Velo	Pitch	Grade
89-92	FB	++
82-84	CB	++
77-79	SL	++
80-83	CU	+++

Year	Lev	Team	W	L	Sv	IP	K	ERA	WHIP	BF/G	OBA	H%	S%	xERA	Ctl	Dom	Cmd	hr/9	BPV
2017	NCAA	Auburn	7	4	0	93	75	2.42	0.90	23.1	203	24	77	1.98	1.6	7.3	4.4	0.7	104
2017	A-	Eugene	1	2	0	19	23	2.37	1.00	10.4	219	31	78	2.18	1.9	10.9	5.8	0.5	163
2018	A+	Myrtle Beach	3	3	0	67	61	3.21	0.92	21.0	205	25	68	2.16	1.7	8.2	4.7	0.8	118
2018	AA	Tennessee	6	3	0	62	54	4.06	1.40	20.1	274	34	70	3.92	3.0	7.8	2.6	0.4	77

Features a four-pitch mix highlighted by an above-average CU. FB lacks plus velo, sitting at 89-92, but is well located with arm-side run and sink. CB is a show-me pitch and lacks depth and SL is the better of the two breaking balls. Biggest asset is his ability to pound the zone and keep hitters off balance.

Thompson,Mason

SP | **San Diego** | EXP MLB DEBUT: 2021 | H/W: 6-7 186 | FUT: #5 SP/swingman | **8D**

Thrws R Age 21
2016 (3) HS (TX)

Velo	Pitch	Grade
90-92	FB	+++
70-73	CB	+++
80-84	CU	+++

Year	Lev	Team	W	L	Sv	IP	K	ERA	WHIP	BF/G	OBA	H%	S%	xERA	Ctl	Dom	Cmd	hr/9	BPV
2016	Rk	AZL Padres	0	0	0	12	12	2.25	1.08	9.4	191	27	77	1.64	3.8	9.0	2.4	0.0	79
2017	A	Fort Wayne	2	4	0	27	28	4.67	1.30	15.9	232	30	64	3.29	4.0	9.3	2.3	0.7	78
2018	A	Fort Wayne	6	8	0	93	97	4.94	1.42	17.9	266	34	65	4.15	3.6	9.4	2.6	0.8	90

Tall, high-waisted RHP who tabbed nearly 100 IP in 2018 after Tommy John surgery back in 2016. Chance for three average-or-better pitches led by 90-92 mph fastball that will flash late life down in zone. CB has more gradual bend; needs to throw it more. Still working on feel for CU but shows arm-side fade. Big build suggests he has a MLB future.

Thornton,Trent

SP | **Toronto** | EXP MLB DEBUT: 2019 | H/W: 6-0 170 | FUT: Middle reliever | **7B**

Thrws R Age 25
2015 (5) North Carolina

Velo	Pitch	Grade
92-95	FB	++++
78-82	CB	++++
88-89	SL	+++

Year	Lev	Team	W	L	Sv	IP	K	ERA	WHIP	BF/G	OBA	H%	S%	xERA	Ctl	Dom	Cmd	hr/9	BPV
2016	A+	Lancaster	7	4	0	89	89	4.14	1.20	21.1	266	32	71	4.20	1.6	9.0	5.6	1.4	136
2016	AA	Corpus Christi	3	1	0	46	35	2.35	1.02	25.2	245	28	83	3.08	1.0	6.8	7.0	1.0	115
2017	AA	Corpus Christi	1	2	0	16	13	6.15	1.55	17.6	355	42	61	6.24	0.0	7.3		1.1	149
2017	AAA	Fresno	8	4	0	115	88	5.09	1.39	23.1	297	35	64	4.71	1.8	6.9	3.8	0.9	93
2018	AAA	Fresno	9	8	0	124	122	4.42	1.20	20.8	252	32	65	3.58	2.2	8.8	3.9	0.9	117

An undersized righty, he excels at high spin rates. His fastball sits in the low-to-mid 90s, and he runs his slider over a range of velocities, with some of the harder variants looking like cutters. His curveball exceeds 3,000 RPMs and the best feature a nasty bite. Despite a full season at AAA, he didn't exceed 130 IP.

Thorpe,Lewis

SP | **Minnesota** | EXP MLB DEBUT: 2019 | H/W: 6-1 160 | FUT: #4 starter | **7B**

Thrws L Age 23
2012 FA (AU)

Velo	Pitch	Grade
89-93	FB	+++
82-85	SL	++
71-75	CB	+++
83-86	CU	++++

Year	Lev	Team	W	L	Sv	IP	K	ERA	WHIP	BF/G	OBA	H%	S%	xERA	Ctl	Dom	Cmd	hr/9	BPV
2017	A+	Fort Myers	3	4	0	77	84	2.69	1.21	19.4	222	31	78	2.64	3.6	9.8	2.7	0.4	97
2017	AA	Chattanooga	1	0	0	6	7	6.00	1.17	23.9	228	23	60	5.10	3.0	10.5	3.5	3.0	126
2018	AA	Chattanooga	8	4	0	108	131	3.58	1.25	20.0	256	35	75	3.87	2.5	10.9	4.4	1.1	147
2018	AAA	Rochester	0	3	0	21	26	3.40	1.23	21.4	251	33	78	3.91	2.5	11.0	4.3	1.3	148

Command/control LHP finally healthy after missing [parts of two seasons with arm injury. High 3/4s slot, easy cross-arm delivery. Commands 2-seam FB with solid bore to both sides of plate. Deceptive CU with late-fading action is swing-and-miss pitch. CB has solid depth, changing eye levels while SL is fringy on a one-plane movement axle.

Tinoco,Justin

SP | **Colorado** | EXP MLB DEBUT: 2019 | H/W: 6-4 190 | FUT: #3 starter | **7D**

Thrws R Age 23
2012 FA (VZ)

Velo	Pitch	Grade
93-96	FB	++++
86-90	SL	+++
78-81	CB	+++
87-90	CU	+

Year	Lev	Team	W	L	Sv	IP	K	ERA	WHIP	BF/G	OBA	H%	S%	xERA	Ctl	Dom	Cmd	hr/9	BPV
2015	A	Asheville	5	0	0	40	37	1.80	1.10	22.4	242	31	86	2.73	1.8	8.3	4.6	0.5	119
2016	A	Asheville	3	8	0	86	53	5.64	1.66	24.1	327	36	67	5.98	2.6	5.5	2.1	1.0	47
2016	A+	Modesto	0	3	0	13	8	15.11	3.05	19.2	500	54	49	14.31	2.1	5.5	2.7	2.1	61
2017	A+	Lancaster	11	4	0	140	107	4.69	1.48	25.1	284	32	71	5.00	3.2	6.9	2.1	1.2	55
2018	AA	Hartford	9	12	0	141	132	4.79	1.33	22.5	273	32	68	4.67	2.4	8.4	3.5	1.5	104

Athletic RHP has a solid four-pitch mix and pounds the strike zone, but inconsistent mechanics results in below-average command within the zone. Walked just 38 in 141 IP, but served up 23 HR. FB sits at 93-96, topping at 98 with good arm-side run and mixes in CB, SL, and below-avg CU. Falls off to 1B side resulting in inconsistent release point.

Torres,Lenny

SP | **Cleveland** | EXP MLB DEBUT: 2023 | H/W: 6-1 190 | FUT: #3 starter | **9D**

Thrws R Age 18
2018 (1) HS (NY)

Velo	Pitch	Grade
92-98	FB	++++
79-83	SL	++++
	CU	+++
	CU	+++

Year	Lev	Team	W	L	Sv	IP	K	ERA	WHIP	BF/G	OBA	H%	S%	xERA	Ctl	Dom	Cmd	hr/9	BPV
2018		Did not pitch																	

He stands out for his athleticism and the life on his potentially plus FB. He has a whippy delivery that allows his FB to sizzle out of his hand and work up in the zone. His offspeed pitches include a SL, CB, and CU, with the SL being the most advanced.

Toussaint,Touki — SP — Atlanta — EXP MLB DEBUT: 2018 — H/W: 6-3 185 — FUT: #2 starter — 9D

Thrws R Age 22	Year	Lev	Team	W	L	Sv	IP	K	ERA	WHIP	BF/G	OBA	H%	S%	xERA	Ctl	Dom	Cmd	hr/9	BPV
2014 (1) HS (FL)	2017	A+	Florida	3	9	0	105	123	5.05	1.36	23.1	254	35	62	3.75	3.6	10.5	2.9	0.7	110
92-95 FB ++++	2017	AA	Mississippi	3	4	0	39	44	3.21	1.33	23.2	213	29	78	3.15	5.1	10.1	2.0	0.7	63
74-77 CB ++++	2018	AA	Mississippi	4	6	0	86	107	2.93	1.19	21.5	214	30	78	2.83	3.8	11.2	3.0	0.7	118
83-86 SP +++	2018	AAA	Gwinnett	5	0	0	50	56	1.44	1.04	24.2	199	29	85	1.60	3.1	10.1	3.3	0.0	117
	2018	MLB	Atlanta	2	1	0	29	32	4.03	1.34	17.3	180	25	68	2.46	6.5	9.9	1.5	0.3	21

Athletic RHP took tremendous step forward in 2018, pitching in postseason. Low-effort, 3/4s delivery with slight turn towards SS creates deception. Struggles repeating mechanics. Four-seam FB is flat but commands better than two-seam FB which has heavy drop but movement hard to corral. 11-to-5 CB & SP are both swing-and-miss pitches.

Tovar,Oscar — RP — Oakland — EXP MLB DEBUT: 2021 — H/W: 6-1 160 — FUT: Middle reliever — 7C

Thrws R Age 21	Year	Lev	Team	W	L	Sv	IP	K	ERA	WHIP	BF/G	OBA	H%	S%	xERA	Ctl	Dom	Cmd	hr/9	BPV
2015 FA (VZ)																				
90-93 FB +++																				
82-84 SL +++	2016	Rk	AZL Athletics	3	2	0	43	31	3.56	1.35	17.9	253	31	71	3.10	3.6	6.5	1.8	0.0	39
CU ++	2017	A-	Vermont	3	2	2	65	45	3.46	1.29	17.8	240	28	74	3.31	3.6	6.2	1.7	0.6	33
	2018	A-	Vermont	4	1	1	26	29	2.06	1.37	6.9	237	34	83	2.92	4.5	10.0	2.2	0.0	77

Strong, medium-framed RHP who transitioned from SP to RP full-time in 2018. Possesses low-90s FB that will touch 94 mph and blend in heavy dose of SL/CU combo, each projecting as average secondary pitches. Has struggled to throw strikes as pro but delivery is compact and simple and should develop his command as he moves up.

Tseng,Jen-Ho — SP — Chicago (N) — EXP MLB DEBUT: 2017 — H/W: 6-1 210 — FUT: #5 SP/swingman — 7D

Thrws R Age 24	Year	Lev	Team	W	L	Sv	IP	K	ERA	WHIP	BF/G	OBA	H%	S%	xERA	Ctl	Dom	Cmd	hr/9	BPV
2014 FA (TW)	2017	AA	Tennessee	7	3	0	90		3.00	1.14	23.8	237	30	76	3.01	2.4	8.3	3.5	0.7	103
90-93 FB ++	2017	AAA	Iowa	6	1	0	55	39	1.80	1.13	24.1	236	27	89	3.09	2.3	6.4	2.8	0.8	71
75-79 CU +++	2017	MLB	Chi Cubs	1	0	0	6	8	7.50	1.17	12.0	228	25	40	5.08	3.0	12.0	4.0	3.0	153
80-83 CB +	2018	AAA	Iowa	2	15	0	136	115	6.28	1.49	22.6	293	34	59	5.26	2.9	7.6	2.6	1.3	76
	2018	MLB	Chi Cubs	0	0	0	2	3	13.50	2.00	9.6	415	53	33	11.68	0.0	13.5		4.5	261

Slender RHP pauses at the top of his delivery before exploding towards the plate. Above-average FB is best offering and sits at 90-93 with arm-side run and sink. Improved 80-83 CU gives him a chance to stick as a starter. Bad luck was partially to explain (.327 BABIP) but so was a career worst 20 HR allowed and too often FB was up in the zone.

Tyler,Robert — RP — Colorado — EXP MLB DEBUT: 2020 — H/W: 6-3 196 — FUT: Setup reliever — 7D

Thrws R Age 23	Year	Lev	Team	W	L	Sv	IP	K	ERA	WHIP	BF/G	OBA	H%	S%	xERA	Ctl	Dom	Cmd	hr/9	BPV
2016 (1) Georgia	2016	NCAA	Georgia	3	5	0	74	89	4.12	1.33	22.0	202	29	69	2.95	5.6	10.8	1.9	0.6	62
95-97 FB ++++	2016	A-	Boise	0	2	0	7	5	6.43	2.57	7.5	92	12	72	4.40	20.6	6.4	0.3	0.0	-422
SL ++	2017		Did not play - injury																	
CU ++++	2018	A	Asheville	4	2	8	38	52	4.02	1.15	4.5	256	37	69	3.71	1.7	12.3	7.4	1.2	194
	2018	A+	Lancaster	0	1	0	9	5	9.89	2.42	4.0	398	42	60	10.09	4.9	4.9	1.0	2.0	-27

Hard-thrower has had a hard time staying healthy, prompting a move to relief. Double plus FB sits at 95-97, topping out at 100 mph with good late life and sink. Backs up the heater with a plus CU and usable SL. Dominated against younger competition in Low-A, but was hit hard when he moved up to High-A.

Uceta,Edwin — SP — Los Angeles (N) — EXP MLB DEBUT: 2022 — H/W: 6-0 155 — FUT: #4 starter — 7D

Thrws R Age 21	Year	Lev	Team	W	L	Sv	IP	K	ERA	WHIP	BF/G	OBA	H%	S%	xERA	Ctl	Dom	Cmd	hr/9	BPV
2016 FA (DR)																				
90-94 FB +++																				
CB ++	2017	Rk	Ogden	2	3	0	56	62	6.59	1.38	16.8	285	36	52	4.79	2.3	10.0	4.4	1.3	137
CU ++++	2018	A	Great Lakes	5	6	0	99	103	3.27	1.19	19.9	245	32	75	3.34	2.4	9.3	3.8	0.8	120
	2018	A+	Rancho Cuca	0	0	0	20	28	7.13	1.44	17.2	230	26	59	5.89	5.3	12.5	2.3	3.1	98

Projectable pitcher dominated in the MWL, but struggled when moved up to A+. Revamped delivery is cleaner and three-pitch mix keeps hitters off-balance despite a fringe low-90s FB. Best offering is a plus CU and dives away from LHB. CB is average but inconsistent. Will need to get stronger and develop a consistent breaking ball to reach full potential.

Underwood,Duane — SP — Chicago (N) — EXP MLB DEBUT: 2018 — H/W: 6-2 205 — FUT: #3 starter — 8D

Thrws R Age 24	Year	Lev	Team	W	L	Sv	IP	K	ERA	WHIP	BF/G	OBA	H%	S%	xERA	Ctl	Dom	Cmd	hr/9	BPV
2012 (2) HS (GA)	2016	A+	Myrtle Beach	0	0	0	4	2	2.14	0.71	14.8	202	23	67	0.88	0.0	4.3		0.0	95
92-95 FB ++++	2016	AA	Tennessee	0	5	0	58	46	4.95	1.67	20.1	287	33	72	5.39	4.8	7.1	1.5	1.1	17
86-88 CT ++	2017	AA	Tennessee	13	7	0	138	98	4.43	1.30	22.8	250	29	67	3.75	3.3	6.4	2.0	0.8	45
76-78 CU ++	2018	AAA	Iowa	4	10	0	119	105	4.53	1.38	18.5	274	34	67	4.02	2.8	7.9	2.8	0.6	85
82-84 CB +++	2018	MLB	Chi Cubs	0	1	0	4	3	2.25	1.25	16.3	151	11	100	3.76	6.8	6.8	1.0	2.3	-43

Has been slow to develop due to injuries and below-average command. Plus FB sits at 92-95, topping at 97 and power CB flashes as plus. Improved CU has late fade and sink and gives him a chance to stick as a SP, but stuff is good enough to be an impact reliever if not.

Valdez,Framber — RP — Houston — EXP MLB DEBUT: 2018 — H/W: 5-11 170 — FUT: Middle reliever — 6B

Thrws L Age 25	Year	Lev	Team	W	L	Sv	IP	K	ERA	WHIP	BF/G	OBA	H%	S%	xERA	Ctl	Dom	Cmd	hr/9	BPV
2015 FA (DR)	2017	A+	Buies Creek	2	3	1	61	73	2.80	1.15	18.6	192	28	76	2.21	4.3	10.8	2.5	0.4	96
92-95 FB ++++	2017	AA	Corpus Christi	5	5	0	49	53	5.88	1.69	18.4	303	40	65	5.34	4.2	9.7	2.3	0.7	79
80-83 CB ++++	2018	AA	Corpus Christi	4	5	1	94	120	4.11	1.29	19.3	257	37	68	3.58	2.8	11.5	4.1	0.7	150
86-88 CU +	2018	AAA	Fresno	2	0	0	8	9	4.39	1.34	17.1	257	36	64	3.10	3.3	9.9	3.0	0.0	107
	2018	MLB	Houston	4	1	0	37	34	2.19	1.24	18.8	174	21	86	2.54	5.8	8.3	1.4	0.7	9

A southpaw with a thick lower half, he pitched at three levels including the majors last year. He is not quite "death on lefties" but has an above-average low-to-mid-90s fastball/plus curveball combo that is difficult to square. He generates a ton of ground balls with his lively, sinking FB.

Vargas,Emilio — SP — Arizona — EXP MLB DEBUT: 2019 — H/W: 6-3 200 — FUT: #4 starter — 7C

Thrws R Age 22	Year	Lev	Team	W	L	Sv	IP	K	ERA	WHIP	BF/G	OBA	H%	S%	xERA	Ctl	Dom	Cmd	hr/9	BPV
2013 FA (DR)	2016	A	Kane County	5	6	0	70	69	3.33	1.15	21.5	241	30	74	3.28	2.3	8.8	3.8	0.9	115
90-94 FB +++	2016	A+	Visalia	0	0	0	15	15	7.80	1.80	17.3	321	40	56	6.34	4.2	9.0	2.1	1.2	67
81-84 SL +++	2017	A	Kane County	5	7	1	100	98	4.04	1.28	19.6	231	29	69	3.29	3.9	8.8	2.3	0.7	72
CU +++	2018	A+	Visalia	8	5	0	108	140	2.50	1.23	21.9	232	34	82	3.03	3.4	11.7	3.4	0.6	136
	2018	AA	Jackson	1	3	0	35	30	4.09	1.11	23.0	238	27	70	3.73	2.0	7.7	3.8	1.5	101

Tall, athletic righty with chance for three average-or-better pitches. FB sits 91-94 mph but is straight and hittable up in zone. Has feel for 11-to-5 SL that is swing-and-miss pitch vs. RHH. CU has progressed and should be useable third pitch vs. LHH. More control than command right now and will need to hit spots as margin for error is fairly low.

Vieaux,Cam — SP — Pittsburgh — EXP MLB DEBUT: 2020 — H/W: 6-5 175 — FUT: #5 SP/swingman — 6C

Thrws L Age 26	Year	Lev	Team	W	L	Sv	IP	K	ERA	WHIP	BF/G	OBA	H%	S%	xERA	Ctl	Dom	Cmd	hr/9	BPV
2016 (6) Michigan St	2016	A-	West Virginia	2	2	0	67	52	3.35	1.25	19.5	250	31	72	3.05	2.8	7.0	2.5	0.3	67
86-90 FB ++	2017	A	West Virginia	2	3	0	62	33	2.75	1.19	22.7	258	30	75	2.92	1.9	4.8	2.5	0.1	53
77-79 CB ++	2017	A+	Bradenton	3	7	0	78	48	4.72	1.43	25.6	288	32	68	4.67	2.6	5.5	2.1	0.9	46
81-84 SL ++	2018	A+	Bradenton	4	1	0	56	52	3.84	1.28	23.0	254	30	76	4.28	2.9	8.3	2.9	1.4	90
78-81 CU +++	2018	AA	Altoona	9	5	0	87	72	3.61	1.10	22.8	243	28	71	3.31	1.8	7.4	4.2	1.0	104

Finesse lefty who lacks plus feel or deception to make stuff play. Throws strikes, has some feel and doesn't beat himself, so has outside shot at being an emergency starter. Lacks good breaking all to be effective left on left reliever.

Villines,Stephen — RP — New York (N) — EXP MLB DEBUT: 2019 — H/W: 6-1 146 — FUT: Middle reliever — 6C

Thrws R Age 23	Year	Lev	Team	W	L	Sv	IP	K	ERA	WHIP	BF/G	OBA	H%	S%	xERA	Ctl	Dom	Cmd	hr/9	BPV
2017 (10) Kansas	2017	Rk	Kingsport	2	1	0	8	11	1.11	1.23	4.1	304	46	90	3.50	0.0	12.2		0.0	238
84-88 FB +++	2017		A-	1	1	1	19	30	1.89	0.74	6.1	195	34	77	1.21	0.5	14.2	30.0	0.5	261
72-76 CB +++	2018	A	Columbia	2	4	6	33	54	4.89	1.15	5.5	261	44	56	3.13	1.4	14.7	10.8	0.5	246
74-76 CU ++	2018	A+	St. Lucie	2	0	4	22	25	0.41	0.59	4.7	101	16	92		2.5	10.2	4.2	0.0	136
	2018	AA	Binghamton	1	0	0	11	17	3.24	0.72	5.6	161	26	57	1.11	1.6	13.8	8.5	0.8	222

Long siderarmer who relies on deception and command. FB is below avg but spots it so well, moving it in and out and up and down. Gets some good sink. CB is a big sweeper, which can play well against RHH. Concern is arsenal and angle against LHH, but should reach MLB bullpen pretty quickly with ability to get RGG out.

Voth,Austin — SP — Washington — EXP MLB DEBUT: 2018 — H/W: 6-1 189 — FUT: Middle reliever — 6A

Thrws R Age 26	Year	Lev	Team	W	L	Sv	IP	K	ERA	WHIP	BF/G	OBA	H%	S%	xERA	Ctl	Dom	Cmd	hr/9	BPV
2013 (5) Washington	2017	A-	Auburn	0	1	0	2	2	13.50	2.50	10.6	415	52	40	8.75	4.5	9.0	2.0	0.0	59
87-90 FB ++	2017	AA	Harrisburg	3	4	0	54	44	5.16	1.40	22.9	292	34	66	5.04	2.2	7.3	3.4	1.3	91
76-79 CB +++	2017	AAA	Syracuse	1	7	0	66	42	6.40	1.80	23.5	313	34	67	6.66	4.6	5.7	1.2	1.6	-4
82-84 CU ++	2018	AAA	Syracuse	6	8	0	125	117	4.38	1.27	21.3	252	31	67	3.75	2.9	8.4	2.9	0.9	92
	2018	MLB	Washington	1	1	0	12	11	6.69	1.49	13.0	260	28	60	5.63	4.5	8.2	1.8	2.2	45

Workhorse finally got some more swings and misses at Triple-A, along with better control, and it resulted in his MLB debut. Still got hit hard upon promotion, as only his CB is a MLB average pitch, but did keep the strikeout rate up. Elevates too many pitches and has a tendency to get hit hard due to batters seeing the ball well.

Waddell,Brandon — SP — Pittsburgh

EXP MLB DEBUT: 2020 | H/W: 6-2 160 | FUT: #5 SP/swingman | 7B

Thrws L Age 24	Year	Lev	Team	W	L	Sv	IP	K	ERA	WHIP	BF/G	OBA	H%	S%	xERA	Ctl	Dom	Cmd	hr/9	BPV
2015 (5) Virginia	2017	Rk	GCL Pirates	1	0	0	3	4	0.00	0.33	9.5	106	18	100		0.0	12.0		0.0	234
88-92 FB +++	2017	A-	West Virginia	1	0	0	9	11	1.00	0.89	16.7	165	22	100	1.78	3.0	11.0	3.7	1.0	135
72-75 CB ++	2017	AA	Altoona	3	3	0	66	56	3.55	1.32	18.2	244	30	73	3.27	3.7	7.6	2.1	0.4	56
81-84 SL ++	2018	AA	Altoona	2	1	0	53	43	2.71	1.09	23.1	206	25	78	2.49	3.2	7.3	2.3	0.7	62
80-84 CU +++	2018	AAA	Indianapolis	5	8	0	81	60	4.21	1.56	18.7	284	34	72	4.39	4.0	6.7	1.7	0.3	30

Heady lefty who has good feel and command but lacks the stuff. Knows what he is doing and mixes pitches well, but does not have a plus pitch or the deception or movement to really be effective. Breaking stuff is not good enough to be a quality left-on-left guy out of pen.

Wahl,Bobby — RP — Milwaukee

EXP MLB DEBUT: 2017 | H/W: 6-3 200 | FUT: Middle reliever | 7D

Thrws R Age 27	Year	Lev	Team	W	L	Sv	IP	K	ERA	WHIP	BF/G	OBA	H%	S%	xERA	Ctl	Dom	Cmd	hr/9	BPV
2013 (5) Mississippi	2017	AAA	Nashville	1	1	3	13	22	4.15	1.38	5.0	262	41	80	5.17	3.5	15.2	4.4	2.1	199
93-96 FB ++++	2017	MLB	Oakland	0	0	0	7	8	5.00	1.67	4.6	283	39	67	4.28	5.0	10.0	2.0	0.0	63
83-84 CB ++	2018	AAA	Nashville	3	2	11	39	65	2.30	0.87	4.3	133	25	75	0.85	3.9	14.9	3.8	0.5	181
87-89 SL ++	2018	AAA	Las Vegas	4	2	12	45	73	2.20	0.87	4.4	136	25	76	0.82	3.8	14.6	3.8	0.4	178
	2018	MLB	NY Mets	0	1	0	5	7	10.59	2.55	3.9	385	49	64	11.53	7.1	12.4	1.8	3.5	50

Came to the Mets in the Jeurys Familia deal and did not pitch well before going on the DL in September with a hamstring injury. Big and strong and has a simple delivery for a reliever, although with some effort. He was dominant in AAA prior to the trade, although with some walk concerns. FB is good, but still searching for reliable secondary.

Warren,Art — RP — Seattle

EXP MLB DEBUT: 2019 | H/W: 6-3 210 | FUT: Closer | 8E

Thrws R Age 26	Year	Lev	Team	W	L	Sv	IP	K	ERA	WHIP	BF/G	OBA	H%	S%	xERA	Ctl	Dom	Cmd	hr/9	BPV
2015 (23) Cincinnati																				
94-97 FB +++++	2016	A	Clinton	9	1	0	74		2.19	1.20	21.3	254	31	81	2.86	2.2	6.7	3.1	0.1	79
78-82 SL ++++	2016	A+	Bakersfield	2	1	0	36	38	5.22	1.93	13.2	291	39	71	5.32	7.0	9.4	1.4	0.2	0
84-87 CB +++	2017	A+	Modesto	3	1	8	64	67	3.08	1.29	6.1	243	32	78	3.45	3.5	9.4	2.7	0.7	92
	2018	AA	Arkansas	1	2	2	15	22	1.78	1.58	4.8	189	32	88	2.83	8.3	13.0	1.6	0.0	29

Hard-throwing RHP struggled with shoulder discomfort throughout 2018. 3-pitch, max-effort pitcher. Has has up-and-down struggles with Ctl throughout career. Explosive, high-octane FB with late life gets swings-and-misses all over the place. SL features sharp, 2-plane break. CB can get slurvy at times but otherwise creates eye-level disruption.

Weathers,Ryan — SP — San Diego

EXP MLB DEBUT: 2021 | H/W: 6-1 200 | FUT: #3 starter | 8C

Thrws L Age 19	Year	Lev	Team	W	L	Sv	IP	K	ERA	WHIP	BF/G	OBA	H%	S%	xERA	Ctl	Dom	Cmd	hr/9	BPV
2018 (1) HS (TN)																				
91-94 FB ++++																				
76-78 CB +++																				
81-83 CU +++	2018	Rk	AZL Padres 2	0	2	0	9	9	3.96	1.21	9.2	238	26	78	4.38	3.0	8.9	3.0	2.0	98
	2018	A	Fort Wayne	0	1	0	9	9	3.00	1.33	12.5	302	40	75	3.75	1.0	9.0	9.0	0.0	153

Strong, thicker LHP taken seventh overall in the 2018 amateur draft. Chance for three above-average pitches with good command of each. Quick arm speed creates low-90s FB that will touch 95 mph. Off-speed stuff is advanced for age; CB will show solid depth and has some feel for fading CU. Throws strikes and projects to have above-average command.

Webb,Braden — SP — Milwaukee

EXP MLB DEBUT: 2020 | H/W: 6-2 190 | FUT: #5 SP/swingman | 7C

Thrws R Age 23	Year	Lev	Team	W	L	Sv	IP	K	ERA	WHIP	BF/G	OBA	H%	S%	xERA	Ctl	Dom	Cmd	hr/9	BPV
2016 (3) South Carolina																				
90-92 FB +++	2016	NCAA	South Carolina	10	6	0	102	128	3.09	1.25	23.1	218	32	76	2.86	4.2	11.3	2.7	0.5	107
CB +++	2017	A	Wisconsin	6	7	3	86	90	4.39	1.29	16.1	229	29	67	3.38	4.1	9.4	2.3	0.8	77
CU ++	2018	A+	Carolina	5	8	0	100	104	4.22	1.45	20.4	240	31	72	3.90	5.0	9.3	1.9	0.8	50
	2018	AA	Biloxi	1	0	0	20	24	1.80	1.15	19.9	187	29	83	1.75	4.5	10.8	2.4	0.0	91

Strong, athletic RH who posted 9.5 Dom across 120 IP in A+/AA in 2018. Delivery has a lot of moving parts and creates deception to the plate. FB sits low-90s and complements it with 12-to-6 CB that will flash plus downward action. CU fades well and will need to be used more in games. Can pitch deep into starts; should fit into #5 SP or long RP role.

Webb,Logan — SP — San Francisco

EXP MLB DEBUT: 2020 | H/W: 6-2 195 | FUT: #3 starter | 8C

Thrws R Age 22	Year	Lev	Team	W	L	Sv	IP	K	ERA	WHIP	BF/G	OBA	H%	S%	xERA	Ctl	Dom	Cmd	hr/9	BPV
2014 (4) HS (CA)	2015	A-	Salem-Kaizer	3	6	0	60	40	4.94	1.53	18.7	310	36	66	4.67	2.4	6.0	2.5	0.3	61
92-95 FB ++++	2016	A	Augusta	2	3	0	42	30	6.21	1.57	20.5	313	35	63	5.95	2.6	6.4	2.5	1.5	64
82-85 SL +++	2017	A-	Salem-Keizer	2	0	0	28	31	2.89	1.18	7.5	248	34	75	2.87	2.3	10.0	4.4	0.3	137
75-78 CB ++	2018	A+	San Jose	1	3	0	74	74	1.82	1.22	14.2	206	28	85	2.37	4.4	9.0	2.1	0.2	62
86-88 CU +++	2018	AA	Richmond	1	2	0	30	26	3.87	1.36	21.0	260	31	76	4.33	3.3	7.7	2.4	1.2	69

Big-bodied, 3/4s RHP fully returned from Tommy John surgery. Jerky delivery with some arm effort. Relies heavily on heavy 2-seam FB with solid arm-side action. Sat mid-90s late in season. Above-average SL presents with 2-plane break. Changes eye levels with 11-to-5 CB. Good separation off FB on arm-side boring CU; above-average pitch at projection.

Weems,Jordan — RP — Boston

EXP MLB DEBUT: 2020 | H/W: 6-5 205 | FUT: Setup reliever | 7D

Thrws R Age 26	Year	Lev	Team	W	L	Sv	IP	K	ERA	WHIP	BF/G	OBA	H%	S%	xERA	Ctl	Dom	Cmd	hr/9	BPV
2012 (4) HS (NC)	2017	AAA	Pawtucket	1	1	0	17	18	7.85	1.80	8.0	302	38	55	5.90	5.2	9.4	1.8	1.0	46
92-97 FB ++++	2018	Rk	AZL Angels	0	0	0	1	3	0.00	0.00	2.8	0	0			0.0	27.0		0.0	504
84-89 SL ++	2018	AAA	Salt Lake	0	1	0	4	7	2.25	0.75	3.6	151	32	67	0.29	2.3	15.8	7.0	0.0	241
86-90 CU ++	2018	AAA	Pawtucket	1	1	1	44	64	2.25	1.14	5.4	225	35	85	2.90	2.9	13.1	4.6	0.8	176
	2018	MLB	LA Angels	0	1	4	16	20	3.35	1.24	4.1	248	37	70	2.72	2.8	11.2	4.0	0.0	144

Converted from CA just a couple of years ago, and looks the part of a dominant late-inning reliever. Tall and long limbed with a clean delivery and throws an easy 95. But FB lacks movement and is often up in the zone. Both SL and CU are below average pitches at this point, so needs something to keep hitters off FB. That could still come, of course.

Weigel,Patrick — SP — Atlanta

EXP MLB DEBUT: 2019 | H/W: 6-6 205 | FUT: #4 starter | 7C

Thrws R Age 24	Year	Lev	Team	W	L	Sv	IP	K	ERA	WHIP	BF/G	OBA	H%	S%	xERA	Ctl	Dom	Cmd	hr/9	BPV
2015 (7) Pacific	2016	A	Rome	10	4	0	129	135	2.51	1.08	22.9	202	27	78	2.20	3.3	9.4	2.9	0.5	99
92-95 FB ++++	2016	AA	Mississippi	1	2	0	20	17	2.23	0.84	24.7	136	15	80	1.30	3.6	7.6	2.1	0.9	58
82-85 SL +++	2017	AA	Mississippi	3	0	0	37	38	2.91	1.16	21.1	234	31	76	2.80	2.7	9.2	3.5	0.5	112
74-77 CB +++	2017	AAA	Gwinnett	3	2	0	41	30	5.27	1.44	21.8	266	30	65	4.54	3.7	6.6	1.8	1.1	36
82-85 CU ++	2018	Rk	GCL Braves	0	0	0	4	6	0.00	0.50	3.3	151	27	100		0.0	13.5		0.0	261

Big-bodied RHP rehabbed after 2017 Tommy John surgery, appearing in 4 complex-level games. Stuff reportedly came back; features a max-effort, 3/4s delivery. Workhorse is 2-seam FB with solid arm-side run. SL is best secondary with sharp 2-plane movement. CB has solid depth but lacks break. Feel for CU comes and goes. RP risk due to delivery.

Wells,Tyler — SP — Minnesota

EXP MLB DEBUT: 2019 | H/W: 6-8 265 | FUT: Setup reliever | 7C

Thrws R Age 24	Year	Lev	Team	W	L	Sv	IP	K	ERA	WHIP	BF/G	OBA	H%	S%	xERA	Ctl	Dom	Cmd	hr/9	BPV
2016 (15) CalSt San Bernardino	2016	Rk	Elizabethton	5	2	0	47	59	3.25	1.21	19.0	231	35	70	2.42	3.2	11.3	3.5	0.0	133
89-93 FB ++++	2017	Rk	GCL Twins	0	2	0	13	16	2.73	1.14	13.1	212	32	73	2.00	3.4	10.9	3.2	0.0	122
73-76 CB +++	2017	A	Cedar Rapids	5	3	0	75	92	3.12	1.13	21.2	229	32	75	2.88	2.6	11.0	4.2	0.7	145
81-83 SL ++	2018	A+	Fort Myers	8	4	0	86	82	2.82	0.89	20.0	198	25	70	1.83	1.8	8.6	4.8	0.6	124
83-84 CU ++	2018	AA	Chattanooga	2	2	1	32	39	1.68	1.15	21.3	202	30	86	2.18	3.9	10.9	2.8	0.3	109

Massive, physically mature RHP dominated two levels in 2018. Low-effort delivery, utilizes lower half well. Pitches from high-3/4s slot. Throws FB with heavy bore and some unintentional cut action. CB is traditional 12-to-6 breaker with solid depth but fringe-average break. SL has one-plane break and fails to throw CU from FB slot.

Wentz,Joey — SP — Atlanta

EXP MLB DEBUT: 2020 | H/W: 6-5 209 | FUT: #3 starter | 8D

Thrws L Age 21	Year	Lev	Team	W	L	Sv	IP	K	ERA	WHIP	BF/G	OBA	H%	S%	xERA	Ctl	Dom	Cmd	hr/9	BPV
2016 (1) HS (KS)																				
89-92 FB +++	2016	Rk	GCL Braves	0	0	0	12	18	0.00	0.67	10.5	81	16	100		3.8	13.5	3.6	0.0	160
73-77 CB +++	2016	Rk	Danville	1	4	0	32	35	5.06	1.59	17.7	256	36	65	3.72	5.6	9.8	1.8	0.0	43
80-83 CU ++++	2017	A	Rome	8	3	0	131	152	2.61	1.11	19.8	211	30	76	2.17	3.2	10.4	3.3	0.3	120
	2018	A+	Florida	3	4	0	67	53	2.28	1.09	16.4	206	25	80	2.23	3.2	7.1	2.2	0.4	59

Tall, athletic LHP struggled through injury-riddled season. High-3/4s, straight on delivery. Struggled repeating delivery dealing with core injuries. Two-seam velocity hasn't taken step forward, possibly due to injury. CB has solid 12-to-6 break and shape. Best pitch may be late-fading CU with FB arm speed & solid separation off FB.

White,Mitchell — SP — Los Angeles (N)

EXP MLB DEBUT: 2019 | H/W: 6-4 205 | FUT: #3 starter | 8D

Thrws R Age 24	Year	Lev	Team	W	L	Sv	IP	K	ERA	WHIP	BF/G	OBA	H%	S%	xERA	Ctl	Dom	Cmd	hr/9	BPV
2016 (2) Santa Clara	2016	A+	Rancho Cuca	1	0	0	2	2	0.00	0.50	6.6	151	22	100		0.0	9.0		0.0	180
94-97 FB ++++	2017	Rk	AZL Dodgers	0	0	0	7	8	0.00	0.57	7.9	92	15	100		2.6	10.3	4.0	0.0	134
86-88 SL +++	2017	A+	Rancho Cuca	2	1	0	38	49	3.77	1.10	16.6	194	31	62	1.69	3.8	11.5	3.1	0.0	124
75-78 CB ++	2017	AA	Tulsa	1	1	0	28	31	2.57	1.07	15.6	177	24	79	2.05	4.2	10.0	2.4	0.6	85
+	2018	AA	Tulsa	6	7	0	105	88	4.54	1.41	20.2	278	33	70	4.55	2.9	7.5	2.6	1.0	75

Has two plus offerings, but below-average command results in too much hard contact. FB sits at 94-97 with late sink and run. SL is also plus and has swing-and-miss action. CB flashes as above-average but is inconsistent while CU lags behind. Had Tommy John surgery in HS and has been held back some, making durability an issue.

White, Owen

SP		Texas		EXP MLB DEBUT:	2024	H/W: 6-3	170	FUT:	#3 starter	8E

Thrws R Age 19
2018 (2) HS (NC)

91-93	FB	+++	
77-81	CB	+++	
83-85	CU	++	

Year	Lev	Team	W	L	Sv	IP	K	ERA	WHIP	BF/G	OBA	H%	S%	xERA	Ctl	Dom	Cmd	hr/9	BPV
2018		Did not pitch																	

Creates deception from a short arm action but quick release; ball gets on the hitter fast. Maintains balance; athleticism bodes well for future, especially in CU development. 91-93 FB and high-70s sharp CB are further along; has also experimented with SL. Promising.

Whitley, Forrest

SP		Houston		EXP MLB DEBUT:	2019	H/W: 6-7	240	FUT:	#1 starter	9B

Thrws R Age 21
2016 (1) HS (TX)

95-97	FB	+++++	
81-83	CB	++++	
81-83	CU	+++++	
85-87	SL	+++	

Year	Lev	Team	W	L	Sv	IP	K	ERA	WHIP	BF/G	OBA	H%	S%	xERA	Ctl	Dom	Cmd	hr/9	BPV
2016	Rk	GCL Astros	0	1	0	4	6	10.98	1.71	6.2	302	47	29	4.64	4.4	13.2	3.0	0.0	137
2017	A	Quad Cities	2	3	0	46	67	2.93	1.37	16.1	244	39	79	3.33	4.1	13.1	3.2	0.4	143
2017	A+	Buies Creek	3	1	0	31	50	3.18	1.19	17.8	242	41	74	3.02	2.6	14.5	5.6	0.6	208
2017	AA	Corpus Christi	0	0	0	14	26	1.90	0.85	13.0	167	33	82	1.29	2.5	16.5	6.5	0.6	246
2018	AA	Corpus Christi	0	2	0	26	34	3.79	1.00	12.5	169	25	63	1.80	3.8	11.7	3.1	0.7	127

Simply put, one of the best pitching prospects in baseball. The tall right-hander boasts at least three plus offerings in his mid-to-upper 90s fastball, hammer curveball, and changeup, and he'll mix in an above-average slider and a useful cutter for good measure. He's the total package and should see MLB time in 2019.

Whitlock, Garrett

SP		New York (A)		EXP MLB DEBUT:	2020	H/W: 6-4	181	FUT:	#4 starter	7C

Thrws R Age 22
2017 (18) Alabama-Birm

92-95	FB	+++	
79-83	SL	+++	
84-87	CU	+++	

Year	Lev	Team	W	L	Sv	IP	K	ERA	WHIP	BF/G	OBA	H%	S%	xERA	Ctl	Dom	Cmd	hr/9	BPV
2017	Rk	Pulaski	1	0	0	5		8.65	1.92	12.3	405	57	56	8.67	0.0	13.8		1.7	267
2017	Rk	GCL Yankees	0	0	0	8	14	1.10	0.49	9.0	147	30	75		0.0	15.4		0.0	295
2018	A	Charleston (Sc)	2	2	0	40	44	1.13	0.75	20.4	169	24	86	0.76	1.6	9.9	6.3	0.2	154
2018	A+	Tampa	5	3	0	70	74	2.44	1.24	20.3	233	32	80	2.78	3.5	9.5	2.7	0.3	96
2018	AA	Trenton	1	0	0	10	4	0.88	1.67	22.9	258	29	94	4.00	6.2	3.5	0.6		-85

Mid-round 2017 draft sleeper put self on map with uptake in stuff and results. Tall, lean physique. Repeatable 3/4s delivery with some funk. Three-pitch pitcher. FB has some natural run but doesn't miss bats. Above-average SL has solid sweeping action and can miss bats. Replicates FB delivery with late-fading CU. Doesn't overpower with anything.

Widener, Taylor

SP		Arizona		EXP MLB DEBUT:	2019	H/W: 6-1	190	FUT:	#4 starter	8C

Thrws R Age 24
2016 (12) South Carolina

91-94	FB	+++	
84-87	SL	+++	
81-84	CU	+++	

Year	Lev	Team	W	L	Sv	IP	K	ERA	WHIP	BF/G	OBA	H%	S%	xERA	Ctl	Dom	Cmd	hr/9	BPV
2016	A-	Staten Island	2	0	1	15	25	0.00	0.40	8.1	45	10	100		2.4	14.9	6.3	0.0	222
2016	A	Charleston (Sc)	1	0	3	23	34	0.78	0.78	11.8	188	30	100	1.54	1.2	13.3	11.3	0.8	226
2017	A+	Tampa	7	8	0	119	129	3.40	1.15	17.5	206	28	70	2.33	3.8	9.7	2.6	0.4	91
2018	AA	Jackson	5	8	0	137	176	2.76	1.04	20.3	204	29	77	2.38	2.8	11.6	4.1	0.8	150

Strong, physical RHP acquired via trade last winter. Works ahead in count and flashes above-average FB command and can spot 91-94 mph heater well vertically. SL command comes and goes but will show above-average tilt to glove side; CU shows glimpses of being dependable third pitch. Repertoire isn't elite but all three should be solid offerings.

Wieck, Brad

RP		San Diego		EXP MLB DEBUT:	2018	H/W: 6-9	255	FUT:	Middle reliever	7B

Thrws L Age 27
2014 (7) Frank Phillips Coll

90-93	FB	+++	
78-82	SL	+++	
83-86	CU	++	

Year	Lev	Team	W	L	Sv	IP	K	ERA	WHIP	BF/G	OBA	H%	S%	xERA	Ctl	Dom	Cmd	hr/9	BPV
2017	AA	San Antonio	2	1	7	30	51	2.68	1.13	3.8	198	37	76	2.04	3.9	15.2	3.9	0.3	187
2017	AAA	El Paso	0	0	0	7	8	10.29	3.00	4.5	358	46	65	10.07	12.9	10.3	0.8	1.3	-144
2018	AA	San Antonio	1	2	10	28	36	1.93	1.00	4.0	202	31	81	1.83	2.6	11.6	4.5	0.3	157
2018	AAA	El Paso	3	0	2	18	34	3.48	1.38	4.5	239	45	78	3.82	4.5	16.9	3.8	1.0	201
2018	MLB	San Diego	0	0	0	7	10	1.29	0.43	4.5	132	17	100	0.53	0.0	12.9		1.3	249

Tall, statuesque RH who was impressive during his short cup of coffee in Sept. Relies on deception and ultra-crossfire delivery to throw hitters off his flat low-90s FB, but is effective up in zone. Two-plane SL produces bulk of whiffs and will sprinkle in show-me CU. More control than command. Extremely effective vs. LHH in short spurts.

Williams, Devin

RP		Milwaukee		EXP MLB DEBUT:	2019	H/W: 6-3	165	FUT:	Middle reliever	8E

Thrws R Age 24
2013 (2) HS (MO)

90-93	FB	+++	
79-81	CB	+++	
82-84	SL	++	
80-82	CU	+++	

Year	Lev	Team	W	L	Sv	IP	K	ERA	WHIP	BF/G	OBA	H%	S%	xERA	Ctl	Dom	Cmd	hr/9	BPV
2015	A	Wisconsin	3	9	0	89	89	3.44	1.25	16.5	230	31	71	2.81	3.6	9.0	2.5	0.3	82
2016	A	Wisconsin	6	3	2	72	74	3.62	1.36	17.7	239	32	73	3.39	4.2	9.2	2.2	0.5	70
2016	A+	Brevard County	1	2	0	25	20	4.32	1.56	21.9	277	33	73	4.63	4.3	7.2	1.7	0.7	31
2017		Did not pitch - injury																	
2018	A+	Carolina	0	3	0	34	35	5.82	1.82	11.3	294	38	67	5.35	5.8	9.3	1.6	0.5	28

Former 2nd-round pick who missed all of 2017 with Tommy John surgery; was eased back into action late in 2018. Lean, quality athlete who struggles to fill the zone consistently. FB sits low-90s with late run and has feel for fading CU. CB/SL overlap and lack quality action. Still has natural ability to miss bats but command has a long way yet to come.

Wilson, Bryse

SP		Atlanta		EXP MLB DEBUT:	2018	H/W: 6-1	224	FUT:	#3 starter	8B

Thrws R Age 21
2016 (4) HS (NC)

93-96	FB	+++	
82-84	SL	++++	
85-88	CU	+++	

Year	Lev	Team	W	L	Sv	IP	K	ERA	WHIP	BF/G	OBA	H%	S%	xERA	Ctl	Dom	Cmd	hr/9	BPV
2017	A	Rome	10	7	0	137	139	2.50	1.04	20.3	214	28	78	2.28	2.4	9.1	3.8	0.5	117
2018	A+	Florida	2	0	0	26	26	0.34	0.88	19.4	178	25	96	0.97	2.4	8.9	3.7	0.0	114
2018	AA	Mississippi	3	5	0	77	89	3.97	1.34	21.3	262	37	69	3.48	3.0	10.4	3.4	0.4	123
2018	AAA	Gwinnett	3	0	0	22	28	5.32	1.05	17.0	244	29	59	4.47	1.2	11.5	9.3	2.5	191
2018	MLB	Atlanta	1	0	0	7	6	6.43	2.00	11.2	288	37	64	5.23	7.7	7.7	1.0	0.0	-51

2016 draft pick shot to MLB in '18 making significant strides with FB movement and velocity. Average 3/4s delivery with solid extension. Three-pitch pitcher. Tinkered with 2-seam FB, found above-average movement while maintaining plus command. Break on 2-plane, tight SL resembled swing-and-miss offering. Maintains FB arm-speed with fading CU.

Winn, Cole

SP		Texas		EXP MLB DEBUT:	2023	H/W: 6-2	190	FUT:	#3 starter	8D

Thrws R Age 19
2018 (1) HS (CA)

91-94	FB	+++	
74-79	CB	++++	
82-85	SL	++	
84-85	CU	++	

Year	Lev	Team	W	L	Sv	IP	K	ERA	WHIP	BF/G	OBA	H%	S%	xERA	Ctl	Dom	Cmd	hr/9	BPV
2018		Did not pitch																	

Rare prep pick that comes with significant polish; throws four pitches and locates well from a delivery that is clean and repeatable. Low-90s FB and 12-to-6 downer CB are the highlights; SL and CU both are potentially average offerings. Has shown a good feel for pitching.

Winn, Keaton

SP		San Francisco		EXP MLB DEBUT:	2022	H/W: 6-4	205	FUT:	Middle reliever	6C

Thrws R Age 21
2018 (5) Iowa Western CC

91-94	FB	+++	
82-84	SL	+++	

Year	Lev	Team	W	L	Sv	IP	K	ERA	WHIP	BF/G	OBA	H%	S%	xERA	Ctl	Dom	Cmd	hr/9	BPV
2018	NCAA	Iowa West CC	4	1	0	36	59	2.24	0.97	7.2	203	38	74	1.44	2.2	14.7	6.6	0.0	222
2018	A-	Salem-Keizer	3	1	0	43	36	4.81	1.44	12.2	288	35	67	4.60	2.7	7.5	2.8	0.8	80

Raw thrower was hittable in pro-debut. 3/4s, straight-on delivery with some effort. Struggles repeating. Two-pitch pitcher, both potentially above-average offerings. FB has solid 2-seam break; commands to both sides of the plate. Struggles to keep SL tight. When it's on, it has 2-plane break profile.

Wong, Jake

SP		San Francisco		EXP MLB DEBUT:	2021	H/W: 6-2	215	FUT:	#3 starter	8E

Thrws R Age 22
2018 (3) Grand Canyon

91-94	FB	++++	
75-77	CB	+++	
82-83	CU	++	

Year	Lev	Team	W	L	Sv	IP	K	ERA	WHIP	BF/G	OBA	H%	S%	xERA	Ctl	Dom	Cmd	hr/9	BPV
2018	NCAA	Grand Canyon	9	3	0	89	88	2.83	1.31	24.6	259	34	79	3.45	2.9	8.9	3.0	0.4	99
2018	A-	Salem-Keizer	0	2	0	27	27	2.32	1.25	10.0	268	35	82	3.36	2.0	9.0	4.5	0.3	126

Hard-throwing RHP had a solid pro debut. 3/4s delivery with good extension and some effort. A three-pitch pitcher, he features a heavy 2-seam FB with solid arm-side run and natural sink. 11-to-5 CB has good shape and complements movement of FB well. Has a feel for developing CU that mimics FB. Solid control carries profile.

Woodford, Jake

SP		St. Louis		EXP MLB DEBUT:	2019	H/W: 6-4	210	FUT:	#5 SP/swingman	7D

Thrws R Age 22
2015 (1) HS (FL)

91-94	FB	+++	
	SL	++	
	CU	++	

Year	Lev	Team	W	L	Sv	IP	K	ERA	WHIP	BF/G	OBA	H%	S%	xERA	Ctl	Dom	Cmd	hr/9	BPV
2016	A	Peoria	5	5	0	108	82	3.33	1.30	21.2	254	30	75	3.54	3.1	6.8	2.2	0.6	58
2017	A+	Palm Beach	7	6	0	119	72	3.10	1.40	21.9	276	31	79	4.07	2.9	5.4	1.8	0.5	36
2018	AA	Springfield	3	8	0	81	56	5.22	1.59	22.3	292	32	71	5.62	3.9	6.2	1.6	1.4	25
2018	AAA	Memphis	5	5	0	64	45	4.50	1.42	22.6	262	30	69	4.07	3.8	6.3	1.7	0.7	29

Tall, durable RHP with average stuff, hit a wall when he reached Double-A. Solid 91-94 mph FB has good late sink, but SL and CU are fringe-average at best. Struggled with control in 2018 leading to a spike in BB% and OppBA. Lacks a swing-and-miss offering and gave up a career-worst 18 HR. Profiles as a back-end starter.

Wright,Kyle — SP — Atlanta
EXP MLB DEBUT: 2018 | H/W: 6-4 200 | FUT: #2 starter | 9D

Thrws R Age 23
2017 (1) Vanderbilt
94-96 FB ++++
83-86 SL ++++
77-81 CB +++
83-85 CU ++

Year	Lev	Team	W	L	Sv	IP	K	ERA	WHIP	BF/G	OBA	H%	S%	xERA	Ctl	Dom	Cmd	hr/9	BPV
2017	Rk	GCL Braves	0	0	0	5	8	1.73	0.96	6.6	170	31	80	1.05	3.5	13.8	4.0	0.0	174
2017	A+	Florida	0	1	0	11	10	3.24	1.08	7.2	204	27	67	1.79	3.2	8.1	2.5	0.0	76
2018	AA	Mississippi	6	8	0	109	105	3.71	1.34	22.7	251	32	72	3.49	3.5	8.7	2.4	0.5	78
2018	AAA	Gwinnett	2	1	0	28	28	2.55	0.82	14.6	159	20	71	1.21	2.6	8.9	3.5	0.6	110
2018	MLB	Atlanta	0	0	0	6	5	4.50	1.67	6.7	191	14	88	5.95	9.0	7.5	0.8	3.0	-90

Lean, athletic hard-throwing RHP made MLB debut. Repeatable, 3/4s delivery with solid extension. Mid-90s 4-seam FB has late, explosive run and misses bats. Can manipulate break of SL with 2-plane, drop-off-the-table break. 11-to-5 CB is workable third pitch with solid shape. Command of CU lags behind rest. Athleticism should play up pitch in future.

Wymer,Sean — SP — Toronto
EXP MLB DEBUT: 2021 | H/W: 6-1 190 | FUT: Setup reliever | 6C

Thrws R Age 22
2018 (4) Texas Christian
91-93 FB +++
80-82 SL ++
84-86 CU ++
++

Year	Lev	Team	W	L	Sv	IP	K	ERA	WHIP	BF/G	OBA	H%	S%	xERA	Ctl	Dom	Cmd	hr/9	BPV
2018	NCAA	Texas Christian	6	3	0	74	69	3.65	1.12	19.4	248	31	70	3.25	1.7	8.4	4.9	0.9	123
2018	A-	Vancouver	4	3	0	35	34	4.87	1.20	10.8	261	33	59	3.53	1.8	8.7	4.9	0.8	126

Short, stocky hurler started and relieved, both in college and pro debut. Average FB sits at 90-93 with good sinking action, hitting 96 in relief. Mixes in SL, CB, and CU all of which are average to above and keep hitters off-balance. Pounds the strike zone, but raw stuff and lack of size make him a back-end starter or setup reliever down the road.

Yamamoto,Jordan — SP — Miami
EXP MLB DEBUT: 2019 | H/W: 6-0 185 | FUT: #5 SP/swingman | 6B

Thrws R Age 22
2014 (12) HS (HI)
87-90 FB ++
69-73 CB +++
77-79 SL ++
80-82 CU +++

Year	Lev	Team	W	L	Sv	IP	K	ERA	WHIP	BF/G	OBA	H%	S%	xERA	Ctl	Dom	Cmd	hr/9	BPV
2016	A	Wisconsin	7	8	0	134		3.83	1.20	20.0	256	35	67	3.11	2.1	10.2	4.9	0.4	145
2017	A+	Carolina	9	4	1	111	113	2.51	1.09	19.7	225	29	80	2.67	2.4	9.2	3.8	0.6	117
2018	Rk	GCL Marlins	1	0	0	11	15	2.45	0.64	12.7	139	20	67	0.69	1.6	12.3	7.5	0.8	195
2018	A+	Jupiter	4	1	0	40	47	1.57	0.85	21.1	187	28	79	0.97	1.8	10.5	5.9	0.0	159
2018	AA	Jacksonville	1	0	0	17	23	2.12	0.94	21.3	200	31	80	1.85	2.1	12.2	5.8	0.5	180

Undersized, athletic RHP playing up pitchability skills to be on cusp of big league debut. Easy, online 3/4s delivery. Commands 5 average or worse pitches. Mixes arm-side running 2-seam and flat 4-seam FB. Throws slow 12-to-6 CB with minimal break. SL is a sweeper and gets some swing-and-miss success. CU mimics 2-seam FB with added fade.

Yan,Hector — SP — Los Angeles (A)
EXP MLB DEBUT: 2022 | H/W: 5-11 180 | FUT: Middle reliever | 7B

Thrws L Age 19
2016 FA (DR)
92-95 FB +++
74-77 CB ++

Year	Lev	Team	W	L	Sv	IP	K	ERA	WHIP	BF/G	OBA	H%	S%	xERA	Ctl	Dom	Cmd	hr/9	BPV
2017	Rk	AZL Angels	0	1	1	16	21	5.03	1.30	6.6	180	29	57	2.05	6.1	11.7	1.9	0.0	63
2018	Rk	Orem	0	4	0	29	29	4.62	1.68	13.1	260	33	74	4.88	6.2	8.9	1.5	0.9	12

Developing arm with experience starting and working from the pen. Compact lefty frame points to a likely future of full time reliever, but the team is still testing him out. Lively fastball has added a few ticks to move to plus. Good swing-and-miss breaking ball that should develop to plus in the end. Biggest roadblock at the moment is command.

Ynoa,Huascar — SP — Atlanta
EXP MLB DEBUT: 2020 | H/W: 6-3 175 | FUT: Closer | 8E

Thrws R Age 20
2014 FA (DR)
92-97 FB ++++
82-85 CB ++++
81-85 CU +

Year	Lev	Team	W	L	Sv	IP	K	ERA	WHIP	BF/G	OBA	H%	S%	xERA	Ctl	Dom	Cmd	hr/9	BPV
2016	Rk	GCL Twins	3	5	0	51	51	3.18	1.10	18.2	234	32	69	2.36	2.1	9.0	4.3	0.2	123
2017	Rk	Elizabethton	0	1	0	25	23	5.36	1.67	18.8	283	36	66	4.63	5.0	8.2	1.6	0.4	31
2017	Rk	Danville	0	3	0	25	27	5.36	1.55	15.7	252	34	63	3.90	5.4	9.6	1.8	0.4	47
2018	A	Rome	7	8	0	91	100	3.65	1.22	20.5	212	28	71	2.86	4.1	9.9	2.4	0.7	84
2018	A+	Florida	1	4	0	24	31	8.18	1.86	18.9	326	46	52	5.77	4.5	11.5	2.6	0.4	105

Brother of Michael Ynoa. Hard-throwing, power RHP dominated at times in full-season debut. 3/4s, cross-fire delivery. Cuts off extension in delivery, relying on arm strength to maximize velocity. Three pitches: FB up to 99 this season with reliever plane and slight, late run. 11-to-5 CB has sharp, late break. Mimimal feel for a CU.

Young,Alex — SP — Arizona
EXP MLB DEBUT: 2019 | H/W: 6-3 180 | FUT: #5 SP/swingman | 7C

Thrws L Age 25
2015 (2) Texas Christian
89-92 FB +++
80-83 SL +++
84-86 CU +++

Year	Lev	Team	W	L	Sv	IP	K	ERA	WHIP	BF/G	OBA	H%	S%	xERA	Ctl	Dom	Cmd	hr/9	BPV
2016	A	Kane County	3	1	0	50	37	2.16	1.10	21.8	217	27	80	2.18	2.9	6.7	2.3	0.2	60
2016	A+	Visalia	2	7	0	68	56	4.62	1.47	24.4	291	34	72	5.17	2.8	7.4	2.7	1.3	76
2017	AA	Jackson	9	9	0	137	103	3.68	1.34	21.1	244	29	74	3.69	3.8	6.8	1.8	0.8	37
2018	AA	Jackson	5	1	0	50	48	3.94	1.29	23.0	257	33	69	3.50	2.9	8.6	3.0	0.5	95
2018	AAA	Reno	5	4	0	80	61	5.96	1.53	17.4	305	35	63	5.56	2.6	6.9	2.7	1.4	72

Up-tempo LHP who split time as SP and RP in PCL. Possesses average FB that tops out at 93 mph but he shows good ability to spot it to all quadrants of zone. CU shows moderate fade and has improved while SL features average 1-to-7 break. Repeats delivery well; good athlete; keeps ball on ground frequently. Back-end SP upside.

Young,Kyle — SP — Philadelphia
EXP MLB DEBUT: 2022 | H/W: 6-11 220 | FUT: #5 SP/swingman | 7D

Thrws L Age 21
2016 (22) HS (NY)
87-90 FB +++
78-81 SL ++
79-81 CU ++

Year	Lev	Team	W	L	Sv	IP	K	ERA	WHIP	BF/G	OBA	H%	S%	xERA	Ctl	Dom	Cmd	hr/9	BPV
2016	Rk	GCL Phillies	3	0	0	27	19	2.67	0.93	11.2	232	29	68	1.76	0.7	6.3	9.5	0.0	114
2017	A-	Williamsport	7	2	0	65	72	2.77	1.12	19.7	240	34	74	2.46	2.1	10.0	4.8	0.1	141
2018	Rk	GCL Phillies W	0	0	0	4	4	0.00	1.00	5.1	151	22	100	0.99	4.5	9.0	2.0	0.0	59
2018	A-	Williamsport	0	0	0	3	2	0.00	0.00	8.5	0	0			0.0	6.0		0.0	126
2018	A	Lakewood	3	3	0	52	44	3.11	1.02	22.2	238	30	69	2.39	1.2	7.6	6.3	0.3	122

Extremely tall with uncanny coordination and body control, he repeats his delivery better than some pitchers 9 inches shorter. Extraordinary extension and lower arm slot play up his currently mediocre arsenal. But room for strength, an if FB ticks up even a bit, and currently sleepy SL gains some bite, he will be an even more intriguing prospect.

Zamora,Daniel — RP — New York (N)
EXP MLB DEBUT: 2019 | H/W: 6-2 185 | FUT: Middle reliever | 6B

Thrws L Age 25
2015 (40) Stony Brook
86-89 FB ++
76-79 CB ++++
84-85 CU +++

Year	Lev	Team	W	L	Sv	IP	K	ERA	WHIP	BF/G	OBA	H%	S%	xERA	Ctl	Dom	Cmd	hr/9	BPV
2016	A	West Virginia	3	2	1	39	45	3.46	1.21	7.5	225	32	71	2.78	3.5	10.4	3.0	0.5	111
2017	A+	Bradenton	2	4	9	53	61	1.86	1.22	5.8	243	34	86	2.93	2.9	10.3	3.6	0.3	126
2017	AA	Altoona	0	0	0	3	2	0.00	1.33	6.2	191	24	100	2.30	6.0	6.0	1.0	0.0	-36
2018	AA	Binghamton	1	1	2	51	69	3.52	1.04	4.9	204	31	66	2.13	2.8	12.1	4.3	0.5	160
2018	MLB	NY Mets	1	0	0	9	16	3.00	1.00	2.1	191	35	75	2.30	3.0	16.0	5.3	1.0	225

Classic old school situational lefty who survives off feel for breaking stuff. Has slot and delivery for the role. Breaker is a plus pitch. He changes break, bite and shape of it well. Has just enough FB and FB command to keep hitters honest, and a good enough CU to survive some AB against RHH. Just needs Tony LaRussa to return as a manager.

Zastryzny,Rob — RP — Chicago (N)
EXP MLB DEBUT: 2017 | H/W: 6-3 193 | FUT: Middle reliever | 6C

Thrws L Age 27
2013 (2) Missouri
90-92 FB ++
80-83 CU +++
77-79 CB +
86-89 CT +

Year	Lev	Team	W	L	Sv	IP	K	ERA	WHIP	BF/G	OBA	H%	S%	xERA	Ctl	Dom	Cmd	hr/9	BPV
2017	Rk	AZL Cubs	0	1	0	8	4	1.10	1.22	11.0	280	32	90	3.17	1.1	4.4	4.0	0.0	67
2017	AAA	Iowa	2	3	1	47	40	5.94	1.36	14.0	274	32	58	4.67	2.7	7.7	2.9	1.3	83
2017	MLB	Chi Cubs	0	0	0	13	11	8.31	2.00	15.7	341	40	58	7.38	4.8	7.6	1.6	1.4	24
2018	AAA	Iowa	3	2	0	56	50	3.86	1.34	7.1	229	28	73	3.51	4.5	8.0	1.8	0.8	41
2018	MLB	Chi Cubs	1	0	0	5	3	5.19	1.92	4.1	290	34	70	5.09	6.9	5.2	0.8	0.0	-75

Older lefty reliever can't seem to stick on the Cubs 25-man roster. Best offering is an average 90-93 mph FB that has late movement but below-average command. High 3/4 delivery and slight crossfire action gives pitches some deception. CU is best secondary and comes from same arm action with good late fade, but CT and CB are below-average.

Zeuch,T.J. — SP — Toronto
EXP MLB DEBUT: 2019 | H/W: 6-7 220 | FUT: #4 starter | 7D

Thrws R Age 23
2016 (1) Pittsburgh
92-94 FB +++
82-84 SL +++
76-78 CB ++
84-86 CU +

Year	Lev	Team	W	L	Sv	IP	K	ERA	WHIP	BF/G	OBA	H%	S%	xERA	Ctl	Dom	Cmd	hr/9	BPV
2016	A	Lansing	0	1	0	8	14	9.00	1.50	17.3	307	51	36	5.23	2.3	15.8	7.0	1.1	241
2017		*Rk*	0	2	0	7	5	5.14	1.57	10.2	313	35	70	5.75	2.6	6.4	2.5	1.3	64
2017	A+	Dunedin	3	4	0	58	46	3.40	1.37	20.3	277	34	75	3.93	2.6	7.1	2.7	0.5	75
2018	A+	Dunedin	3	3	0	36	24	3.49	1.19	24.1	250	28	74	3.61	2.2	6.0	2.7	1.0	65
2018	AA	New Hampshire	9	5	0	120	81	3.08	1.26	23.3	262	31	76	3.49	2.3	6.1	2.6	0.5	65

Uses size to create downhill tilt and sink from high 3/4 arm slot. Above-average FB sits at 92-94, topping at 96. Backs up the FB with an above-average SL, a 12-to-6 CB, and seldom used CU. Relies more on pounding the zone and inducing weak contact than blowing hitters away. Has to stay out of the zone to remain effective.

Zimmerman,Bruce — SP — Baltimore
EXP MLB DEBUT: 2020 | H/W: 6-2 190 | FUT: #5 SP/swingman | 6C

Thrws L Age 24
2017 (5) Mount Olive Coll
87-92 FB ++
83-85 SL +++
78-82 CU +++

Year	Lev	Team	W	L	Sv	IP	K	ERA	WHIP	BF/G	OBA	H%	S%	xERA	Ctl	Dom	Cmd	hr/9	BPV
2017	NCAA	MountOlive Col	9	2	0	99	129	3.18	1.14	26.1	242	36	73	2.89	2.2	11.7	5.4	0.5	170
2017	Rk	Danville	0	1	0	23	28	3.12	1.30	8.6	244	36	73	2.81	3.5	10.9	3.1	0.0	120
2018	A	Rome	7	3	0	84	99	2.78	1.09	23.5	238	33	76	2.71	1.9	10.6	5.5	0.5	157
2018	AA	Mississippi	2	1	0	28	26	3.19	1.56	20.6	239	29	83	4.33	6.1	8.3	1.4	1.0	4
2018	AA	Bowie	2	3	0	21	16	5.12	1.52	18.3	296	35	67	4.93	3.0	6.8	2.3	0.9	60

3/4s LHP acquired in mid-season trade with ATL. Three-pitch pitcher with pitchability. Creates deception with 3/4s delivery, keeping hitters off average package of pitches. 2-seam FB is effective on edges of strike zone with solid 2-seam movement. Gets by with SL, missing barrels. CU is best pitch with deception and velocity separation.

In his 1985 *Baseball Abstract,* Bill James introduced the concept of major league equivalencies. His assertion was that, with the proper adjustments, a minor leaguer's statistics could be converted to an equivalent major league level performance with a great deal of accuracy.

Because of wide variations in the level of play among different minor leagues, it is difficult to get a true reading on a player's potential. For instance, a .300 batting average achieved in the high-offense Pacific Coast League is not nearly as much of an accomplishment as a similar level in the Eastern League. MLEs normalize these types of variances, for all statistical categories.

The actual MLEs are not projections. They represent how a player's previous performance might look at the major league level. However, the MLE stat line can be used in forecasting future performance in just the same way as a major league stat line would.

The model we use contains a few variations to James' version and updates all of the minor league and ballpark factors. In addition, we designed a module to convert pitching statistics, which is something James did not originally do.

Do MLEs really work?

Used correctly, MLEs are excellent indicators of potential. But just like we cannot take traditional major league statistics at face value, the same goes for MLEs. The underlying measures of base skill—batting eye ratios, pitching command ratios, etc.—are far more accurate in evaluating future talent than raw home runs, batting averages or ERAs.

The charts we present here also provide the unique perspective of looking at up to five years' worth of data. Ironically, the longer the history, the less likely the player is a legitimate prospect—he should have made it to the majors before compiling a long history in AA and/or AAA ball. Of course, the shorter trends

are more difficult to read despite them often belonging to players with higher ceilings. But even here we can find small indications of players improving their skills, or struggling, as they rise through more difficult levels of competition. Since players—especially those with any talent—are promoted rapidly through major league systems, a two or three-year scan is often all we get to spot any trends.

Here are some things to look for as you scan these charts:

Target players who...

- spent a full year in AA and then a full year in AAA
- had consistent playing time from one year to the next
- improved their base skills as they were promoted

Raise the warning flag for players who...

- were stuck at a level for multiple seasons, or regressed
- displayed marked changes in playing time from one year to the next
- showed large drops in BPIs from one year to the next

Players are listed on the charts if they spent at least part of 2014-2018 in Triple-A or Double-A and had at least 100 AB or 30 IP within those two levels. Each is listed with the organization with which they finished the season.

Only statistics accumulated in Triple-A and Double-A ball are included (players who split a season are indicated as a/a); Single-A stats are excluded.

Each player's actual AB and IP totals are used as the base for the conversion. However, it is more useful to compare performances using common levels, so rely on the ratios and sabermetric gauges. Complete explanations of these formulas appear in the Glossary.

BATTER	B	Yr	Age	Pos	Lvl	Tm	AB	R	H	D	T	HR	RBI	BB	K	SB	CS	BA	OB	Slg	OPS	bb%	ct%	Eye	PX	SX	RC/G	BPV
Adell, Jo	R	18	19	CF	aa	LAA	63	13	14	6	0	2	6	5	23	2	0	225	285	402	687	8%	63%	0.23	146	109	3.09	20
Alcantara, Sergio	B	18	22	SS	aa	DET	441	45	111	17	3	1	31	35	98	7	5	252	307	310	617	7%	78%	0.36	41	84	2.63	-14
Alemais, Stephen	R	18	23	2B	aa	PIT	402	47	102	15	3	1	29	37	73	13	10	254	316	313	629	8%	82%	0.51	39	101	2.70	8
Alford, Anthony	R	17	23	CF	a/a	TOR	257	38	76	15	0	5	22	33	52	16	3	297	376	412	789	11%	80%	0.63	73	93	5.04	31
		18	24	CF	aaa	TOR	375	45	83	22	1	4	29	26	123	15	8	222	272	319	591	6%	67%	0.21	79	104	2.23	-22
Allen, Austin	L	18	24	C	aa	SD	451	49	115	28	0	17	46	31	112	0	3	254	302	432	733	6%	75%	0.27	113	20	3.69	11
Alonso, Peter	R	17	23	DH	aa	NYM	45	7	13	4	1	2	5	2	8	0	0	290	322	543	865	5%	82%	0.27	138	81	4.96	73
		18	24	1B	a/a	NYM	478	66	110	25	1	25	85	56	154	0	3	229	311	443	754	11%	68%	0.37	142	30	3.86	17
Aquino, Aristides	R	17	23	RF	aa	CIN	459	56	99	20	5	19	58	42	161	9	3	215	281	408	689	8%	65%	0.26	125	114	3.13	12
		18	24	RF	aa	CIN	404	41	87	18	1	18	46	30	129	3	6	216	270	404	675	7%	68%	0.23	123	55	2.94	3
Arozarena, Randy	R	17	22	LF	aa	STL	163	30	38	10	1	3	8	24	35	7	3	236	332	352	684	13%	78%	0.67	73	115	3.14	34
		18	23	LF	a/a	STL	358	49	85	18	0	9	38	26	92	20	9	237	288	361	649	7%	74%	0.28	83	104	2.91	10
Arraez, Luis	L	18	21	2B	aa	MIN	178	21	49	6	0	2	13	11	17	2	0	277	317	337	655	6%	91%	0.63	35	55	3.48	20
Avelino, Abiatal	R	16	21	2B	aa	NYY	127	15	30	11	0	0	14	10	20	1	2	239	295	322	617	7%	84%	0.49	67	57	2.22	23
		17	22	2B	a/a	NYY	291	38	71	12	4	3	32	18	47	7	1	245	288	345	634	6%	84%	0.38	55	121	2.79	29
		18	23	SS	a/a	SF	477	53	119	12	8	10	53	25	113	21	7	249	287	366	653	5%	76%	0.22	66	139	3.05	12
Bannon, Rylan	R	18	22	2B	aa	BAL	98	12	17	5	0	2	8	17	25	0	0	177	297	279	576	15%	74%	0.66	72	31	2.10	-5
Basabe, Luis Alexande	B	18	22	CF	aa	CHW	231	39	55	8	3	6	25	30	84	9	4	239	325	378	703	11%	64%	0.35	98	138	3.44	-1
Bautista, Rafael	R	16	23	CF	aa	WAS	543	67	143	12	2	3	34	40	101	49	11	263	313	310	623	7%	81%	0.40	29	129	3.27	3
		17	24	CF	aaa	WAS	176	19	39	8	1	0	9	7	29	6	5	220	251	273	524	4%	83%	0.18	37	101	1.70	3
		18	25	CF	a/a	WAS	109	9	29	3	1	1	6	6	32	5	2	266	302	325	627	5%	71%	0.18	41	94	2.97	-44
Beaty, Matt	L	17	24	1B	aa	LA	438	50	126	29	1	13	57	27	63	2	3	288	328	444	772	6%	86%	0.42	87	45	4.30	39
		18	25	1B	aaa	LA	101	10	23	9	0	1	9	9	20	0	0	231	291	338	629	8%	80%	0.42	81	27	2.44	10
Bichette, Bo	R	18	20	SS	aa	TOR	539	84	151	45	6	10	66	43	104	28	11	281	333	442	775	7%	81%	0.41	104	140	3.93	65
Biggio, Cavan	L	18	23	2B	aa	TOR	449	68	105	23	4	22	84	84	160	17	9	233	355	450	805	16%	64%	0.53	150	114	4.40	45
Bishop, Braden	R	17	24	CF	aa	SEA	125	15	37	8	1	1	9	13	18	5	1	295	360	390	750	9%	86%	0.71	59	94	4.26	39
		18	25	CF	aa	SEA	345	55	82	17	0	6	26	30	83	4	2	238	299	343	641	8%	76%	0.36	70	78	2.92	1
Boldt, Ryan	L	18	24	RF	aa	TAM	241	33	57	10	5	6	28	20	69	10	2	238	297	390	687	8%	71%	0.29	95	147	3.15	23
Bolt, Skye	B	18	24	CF	aa	OAK	285	32	63	16	3	7	29	20	84	8	1	220	272	370	642	7%	71%	0.24	102	119	2.71	15
Booker, Joel	R	18	25	LF	aa	CHW	267	38	63	11	2	2	15	20	91	11	9	236	290	310	600	7%	66%	0.23	58	119	2.30	-37
Bradley, Bobby	L	17	21	1B	aa	CLE	467	55	112	26	2	20	75	48	116	3	3	241	311	434	744	9%	75%	0.41	114	58	3.77	29
		18	22	1B	a/a	CLE	483	50	102	27	3	23	69	47	158	1	0	212	282	423	705	9%	67%	0.30	142	60	3.24	20
Brigman, Bryson	R	18	23	2B	aa	MIA	42	1	11	2	0	1	5	2	7	2	0	273	302	371	674	4%	84%	0.26	59	31	3.73	1
Castro, Willi	B	18	21	SS	a/a	DET	497	59	124	28	4	8	48	30	117	16	5	250	292	372	664	6%	77%	0.25	80	120	2.99	19
Cecchini, Gavin	R	15	22	SS	aa	NYM	439	55	125	23	3	6	44	36	62	3	4	286	340	395	735	8%	86%	0.58	72	65	3.87	38
		16	23	SS	aaa	NYM	446	49	118	23	1	6	38	33	65	3	1	264	316	359	674	7%	85%	0.51	59	61	3.30	23
		17	24	2B	aaa	NYM	453	48	96	21	2	4	27	31	75	4	5	211	262	295	556	6%	83%	0.41	51	70	1.97	10
		18	25	2B	aaa	NYM	109	9	24	8	1	1	6	5	19	1	1	222	254	345	599	4%	83%	0.25	82	66	2.05	27
Chang, Yu-Cheng	R	17	22	SS	aa	CLE	439	60	92	25	3	21	55	44	129	9	4	210	282	422	705	9%	71%	0.34	131	106	3.16	40
		18	23	SS	aaa	CLE	457	44	108	28	1	10	49	35	158	3	3	236	291	371	662	7%	65%	0.22	105	58	2.90	-20
Chavis, Michael	R	17	22	3B	aa	BOS	248	32	59	20	0	11	32	16	58	1	0	239	287	450	737	6%	77%	0.28	128	46	3.58	37
		18	23	3B	a/a	BOS	155	26	43	10	0	6	20	11	50	2	1	279	327	468	795	8%	68%	0.23	134	72	4.61	16
Ciuffo, Nick	L	17	22	C	aa	TAM	371	37	82	26	1	6	37	38	107	2	0	221	293	343	636	9%	71%	0.35	89	56	2.61	-7
		18	23	C	aaa	TAM	221	22	51	10	0	4	24	11	72	0	0	232	269	332	602	5%	67%	0.15	75	30	2.58	-50
Clement, Ernie	R	18	22	SS	aa	CLE	65	8	15	5	1	0	4	3	7	1	1	238	268	340	608	4%	89%	0.35	68	103	2.03	49
Collins, Zack	L	17	22	C	aa	CHW	34	7	8	2	0	2	5	11	12	0	0	229	421	465	887	25%	64%	0.93	159	25	5.67	44
		18	23	C	aa	CHW	418	54	91	22	1	15	63	97	178	1	1	218	366	382	748	19%	58%	0.55	134	69	3.95	-2
Cozens, Dylan	L	15	21	RF	aa	PHI	40	5	13	2	0	3	7	2	8	2	1	318	358	564	922	6%	80%	0.31	146	54	6.45	67
		16	22	RF	aa	PHI	521	87	132	34	2	37	103	51	210	17	1	254	320	541	862	9%	60%	0.24	217	126	5.27	70
		17	23	RF	aaa	PHI	476	59	91	11	2	25	65	50	221	7	3	192	269	383	652	10%	54%	0.23	141	89	2.95	-25
		18	24	RF	aaa	PHI	297	40	65	14	2	19	47	38	146	7	7	218	306	469	775	11%	51%	0.26	215	91	3.84	27
Craig, Will	R	18	24	1B	aa	PIT	480	60	105	27	2	16	84	35	140	5	3	219	271	384	656	7%	71%	0.25	110	86	2.77	13
Cron, Kevin	R	16	23	1B	aa	ARI	465	53	97	20	1	23	78	29	145	3	1	209	256	408	664	6%	69%	0.20	130	68	2.96	13
		17	24	1B	aa	ARI	515	62	134	33	0	21	75	46	150	1	0	259	320	448	768	8%	71%	0.30	122	35	4.23	10
		18	25	3B	aaa	ARI	392	35	92	22	1	12	59	22	121	1	0	235	276	389	665	5%	69%	0.18	108	39	3.04	-13
Cumberland, Brett	S	18	23	C	aa	BAL	60	5	9	0	0	2	5	4	18	0	0	145	194	265	460	6%	70%	0.20	66	25	1.54	-47
Dalbec, Bobby	R	18	23	3B	aa	BOS	111	11	27	8	1	4	19	5	49	0	0	240	269	447	716	4%	56%	0.09	176	56	3.26	-9
Davis, Jaylin	R	18	24	RF	aa	MIN	240	23	58	12	2	5	27	16	76	4	2	243	291	368	659	6%	69%	0.21	90	83	2.93	-15
Dawson, Ronnie	L	18	23	CF	aa	HOU	114	16	30	5	1	6	13	5	38	5	3	264	297	474	771	4%	67%	0.14	139	120	3.95	25
Daza, Yonathan	R	18	24	CF	aa	COL	219	21	63	17	2	3	23	6	25	3	6	289	307	435	742	2%	89%	0.22	86	82	3.37	55
De La Guerra, Chad	L	17	25	SS	aa	BOS	196	26	48	15	0	3	18	18	53	2	1	246	308	369	677	8%	73%	0.34	90	57	2.99	0
		18	26	2B	a/a	BOS	389	44	83	14	2	12	45	25	132	5	1	212	259	349	608	6%	66%	0.19	94	89	2.57	-20

BATTER	B	Yr	Age	Pos	Lvl	Tm	AB	R	H	D	T	HR	RBI	BB	K	SB	CS	BA	OB	Slg	OPS	bb%	ct%	Eye	PX	SX	RC/G	BPV
Dean, Austin	R	16	23	LF	aa	MIA	480	53	105	22	5	8	59	43	118	1	2	220	283	340	623	8%	75%	0.36	77	74	2.47	4
		17	24	LF	aa	MIA	234	28	60	14	3	4	29	13	53	3	1	257	298	388	686	5%	77%	0.25	80	103	3.10	17
		18	25	LF	a/a	MIA	397	58	116	17	4	9	56	33	67	2	2	292	346	423	769	8%	83%	0.48	73	77	4.42	31
Diaz, Isan	L	18	22	2B	a/a	MIA	431	54	88	20	4	10	48	59	156	12	3	205	301	343	644	12%	64%	0.38	101	117	2.74	-2
Diaz, Yusniel	R	17	21	RF	aa	LA	108	13	33	8	0	3	11	8	32	2	5	309	357	456	813	7%	70%	0.25	104	49	4.19	-5
		18	22	RF	aa	BAL	354	45	90	13	3	9	34	45	71	9	14	253	338	386	724	11%	80%	0.63	75	87	3.38	30
Didder, Ray-Patrick	R	18	24	SS	aa	ATL	131	15	33	6	2	1	15	13	41	8	2	253	322	340	663	9%	69%	0.33	64	128	3.14	-14
Dubon, Mauricio	R	16	22	SS	aa	BOS	251	40	82	21	5	5	34	9	39	5	3	327	351	510	861	4%	85%	0.24	109	130	4.97	74
		17	23	SS	a/a	MIL	492	61	121	26	0	8	47	32	86	31	17	247	293	346	639	6%	83%	0.37	61	100	2.78	23
		18	24	SS	aaa	MIL	108	12	31	8	1	3	12	1	23	4	4	283	292	460	752	1%	79%	0.06	109	119	3.40	43
Dunand, Joe	R	18	23	SS	aa	MIA	217	21	40	11	0	6	25	14	80	0	1	183	232	311	543	6%	63%	0.17	100	38	1.83	-43
Erceg, Lucas	L	18	23	3B	aa	MIL	463	48	109	21	1	13	47	34	91	3	1	236	288	369	657	7%	80%	0.37	78	58	3.08	17
Espinal, Santiago	R	18	24	2B	aa	TOR	147	14	38	9	2	1	17	12	24	2	1	261	315	360	675	7%	83%	0.48	64	84	2.98	27
Estrada, Thairo	R	17	21	SS	NYY		495	70	146	18	3	7	47	33	60	8	12	294	339	385	723	6%	88%	0.55	48	80	3.82	28
		18	22	SS	aaa	NYY	33	1	4	1	0	0	3	0	9	0	0	135	135	161	296	0%	73%	0.00	23	14	0.54	-82
Evans, Phillip	R	16	24	SS	aa	NYM	361	41	104	27	0	7	32	16	71	1	1	289	319	418	737	4%	80%	0.22	88	39	3.89	14
		17	25	3B	aaa	NYM	466	40	101	20	2	8	39	32	100	1	4	217	267	319	586	6%	79%	0.32	62	46	2.27	-8
		18	26	3B	aaa	NYM	219	21	41	6	1	8	24	13	53	2	4	188	235	336	571	6%	76%	0.25	84	61	2.09	2
Filia, Eric	L	18	26	RF	aa	SEA	296	34	66	11	1	2	29	34	38	1	0	224	305	284	589	10%	87%	0.92	38	54	2.42	19
Fox, Lucius	B	18	21	SS	aa	TAM	104	12	21	3	1	1	8	7	23	5	2	201	251	266	517	6%	78%	0.31	40	123	1.82	-3
Friedl, TJ	L	18	23	LF	aa	CIN	261	40	66	9	2	2	14	25	64	16	6	251	316	326	642	9%	76%	0.39	49	137	3.02	2
Garcia, Adolis	R	17	24	RF	a/a	STL	445	53	115	31	2	12	54	27	117	12	10	258	301	415	716	6%	74%	0.23	103	88	3.30	17
		18	25	RF	aaa	STL	406	46	86	21	3	16	53	10	113	7	3	213	232	393	625	2%	72%	0.09	114	110	2.42	20
Garcia, Anthony	R	15	23	LF	a/a	STL	346	43	84	23	1	9	48	37	72	4	3	244	318	397	715	10%	79%	0.52	106	68	3.42	44
		16	24	RF	a/a	STL	340	32	68	15	0	8	33	24	81	2	3	200	253	316	569	7%	76%	0.30	76	46	2.11	-6
		17	25	LF	a/a	STL	386	47	95	17	2	12	58	34	86	7	3	246	308	395	702	8%	78%	0.40	85	81	3.53	21
		18	26	DH	aaa	OAK	480	59	100	27	1	18	69	48	124	1	4	209	281	378	659	9%	74%	0.39	108	45	2.80	17
Garcia, Aramis	R	17	24	C	aa	SF	78	10	20	11	0	0	7	8	24	0	0	257	328	398	726	10%	70%	0.35	128	34	2.89	12
		18	25	C	a/a	SF	339	31	65	13	1	7	28	17	102	0	1	192	230	295	525	5%	70%	0.16	71	50	1.80	-37
Gerber, Mike	L	18	26	CF	aaa	DET	287	29	53	12	2	11	28	18	115	2	2	186	234	357	591	6%	60%	0.16	127	79	2.13	-21
Gimenez, Andres	L	18	20	SS	aa	NYM	137	16	34	8	1	0	14	8	24	9	3	250	291	321	612	5%	82%	0.33	52	120	2.52	20
Gomez, Miguel	B	17	25	2B	aa	SF	308	38	84	17	2	6	33	11	42	0	0	273	298	401	699	3%	87%	0.26	70	60	3.45	29
		18	26	2B	a/a	SF	423	27	102	22	4	4	36	7	75	1	0	241	252	339	592	2%	82%	0.09	62	61	2.27	2
Gonzalez, Luis	R	18	24	SS	aa	CIN	391	39	85	15	1	3	25	15	82	4	4	216	244	278	522	4%	79%	0.18	43	74	1.82	-18
Gordon, Nick	L	17	22	SS	aa	MIN	519	74	136	28	8	8	61	48	135	12	7	262	325	394	719	8%	74%	0.35	83	123	3.41	18
		18	23	SS	a/a	MIN	544	53	125	21	6	6	42	28	116	17	5	230	268	325	594	5%	79%	0.25	58	122	2.38	10
Granite, Zack	L	16	24	CF	aa	MIN	525	68	138	16	6	3	41	32	46	44	16	263	306	336	642	6%	91%	0.71	39	149	3.00	55
		17	25	CF	aaa	MIN	284	42	90	15	4	5	27	21	36	14	7	315	363	443	806	7%	87%	0.59	68	122	4.79	56
Grisham, Trent	L	18	22	RF	aa	MIL	335	42	75	10	2	7	29	59	94	10	3	225	341	330	671	15%	72%	0.62	67	92	3.31	0
Guerrero, Vladimir	R	18	19	3B	a/a	TOR	344	59	132	28	1	19	71	34	38	3	3	383	438	634	1	9%	89%	0.89	133	53	9.64	98
Guillorme, Luis	L	17	23	2B	aa	NYM	481	69	126	18	0	1	42	78	64	4	3	262	365	307	671	14%	87%	1.22	31	52	3.35	17
		18	24	SS	aaa	NYM	247	27	58	12	1	2	22	20	48	1	1	236	294	316	609	8%	81%	0.43	54	63	2.51	2
Gutierrez, Kelvin	R	18	24	3B	aa	KC	472	53	117	14	6	8	53	29	118	16	4	247	291	352	643	6%	75%	0.25	63	128	2.99	3
Haase, Eric	R	16	24	C	aa	CLE	226	24	43	14	1	10	28	14	81	0	2	190	238	393	631	6%	64%	0.17	149	50	2.33	5
		17	25	C	a/a	CLE	339	47	79	17	3	22	48	37	121	3	2	232	307	495	802	10%	64%	0.30	169	90	4.29	41
		18	26	C	aaa	CLE	433	40	88	22	2	15	53	23	167	2	1	203	244	368	612	5%	61%	0.14	125	66	2.39	-22
Hampson, Garrett	R	18	24	2B	a/a	COL	444	57	125	23	6	8	28	36	79	25	6	282	336	412	748	8%	82%	0.46	76	139	4.14	48
Harrison, Monte	R	18	23	CF	aa	MIA	521	73	109	17	2	15	41	38	244	24	10	209	264	338	602	7%	53%	0.16	109	133	2.48	-44
Haseley, Adam	L	18	22	CF	PHI		136	18	38	3	0	5	14	13	22	0	1	282	344	425	769	9%	84%	0.58	74	32	4.72	23
Hayes, Ke'Bryan	R	18	21	3B	aa	PIT	437	56	120	29	6	6	41	49	87	10	5	275	349	410	759	10%	80%	0.57	86	110	3.84	44
Hays, Austin	R	17	22	CF	aa	BAL	261	33	75	10	1	14	46	12	52	1	1	286	317	494	811	4%	80%	0.23	107	57	4.97	33
		18	23	RF	aa	BAL	273	25	57	10	1	10	32	9	64	4	3	209	234	363	597	3%	77%	0.14	89	83	2.30	11
Hermosillo, Michael	R	17	22	CF	a/a	LAA	393	50	90	17	2	7	35	38	115	25	12	229	297	337	634	9%	71%	0.33	71	117	2.73	-6
		18	23	CF	aaa	LAA	273	27	57	11	2	8	29	18	102	6	6	209	259	349	608	6%	63%	0.18	101	102	2.31	-24
Hernandez, Yadiel	L	17	30	RF	aa	WAS	397	41	90	17	1	8	43	41	85	4	3	228	300	335	635	9%	79%	0.48	64	53	2.84	3
		18	31	LF	a/a	WAS	433	46	98	14	1	13	50	41	134	3	3	227	293	356	649	9%	69%	0.31	84	48	3.05	-23
Hilliard, Sam	L	18	24	RF	aa	COL	435	45	108	21	3	8	31	33	157	18	15	247	300	364	664	7%	64%	0.21	89	105	2.79	-25
Hinojosa, C.J.	R	16	22	SS	aa	SF	226	26	54	7	3	2	18	19	47	1	0	238	298	323	621	8%	79%	0.42	51	83	2.71	1
		17	23	SS	aa	SF	373	43	92	15	0	3	32	29	46	5	4	247	301	312	613	7%	88%	0.62	39	58	2.69	15
		18	24	SS	aa	SF	253	22	59	13	1	2	22	20	32	4	3	232	289	315	604	7%	88%	0.65	52	70	2.40	30
Hiura, Keston	R	18	22	2B	aa	MIL	279	34	74	18	2	6	19	21	61	10	5	264	315	408	723	7%	78%	0.34	92	105	3.52	34
Howard, Ryan	L	17	38	DH	aaa	COL	90	4	13	3	0	3	8	1	32	0	0	150	161	277	438	1%	64%	0.04	88	1	1.17	-69

BATTER	B	Yr	Age	Pos	Lvl	Tm	AB	R	H	D	T	HR	RBI	BB	K	SB	CS	BA	OB	Slg	OPS	bb%	ct%	Eye	PX	SX	RC/G	BPV
Ibanez,Andy	R	16	23	2B	aa	TEX	307	33	72	16	2	5	26	22	51	4	2	235	286	348	635	7%	83%	0.43	69	83	2.70	29
		17	24	2B	aa	TEX	310	28	75	13	2	7	25	22	52	5	1	242	292	363	654	7%	83%	0.42	65	83	3.07	25
		18	25	3B	aaa	TEX	463	45	113	19	1	9	40	31	83	1	7	244	291	346	636	6%	82%	0.37	61	30	2.77	0
Jackson,Alex	R	17	22	C	aa	ATL	110	12	25	2	0	5	20	10	36	0	0	232	298	379	677	9%	67%	0.29	90	19	3.53	-36
		18	23	C	a/a	ATL	333	36	61	22	2	7	35	26	130	0	0	185	243	325	568	7%	61%	0.20	116	66	1.87	-27
Jansen,Danny	R	17	22	C	a/a	TOR	246	29	73	20	2	5	28	30	28	1	0	295	373	451	823	11%	89%	1.09	88	60	4.80	67
		18	23	C	aaa	TOR	298	40	77	21	1	11	51	39	53	4	0	260	345	444	789	11%	82%	0.73	109	74	4.44	63
Jimenez,Eloy	R	17	21	RF	aa	CHW	68	11	24	5	0	3	7	5	18	1	1	346	392	556	948	7%	74%	0.30	131	51	7.05	33
		18	22	LF	a/a	CHW	416	58	131	26	3	21	68	30	77	0	1	315	361	544	905	7%	81%	0.39	128	50	6.24	59
Jones,Jahmai	R	18	21	2B	aa	LAA	184	29	41	9	3	2	18	21	56	10	1	223	301	333	635	10%	70%	0.37	77	161	2.72	10
Kelley,Christian	R	18	25	C	aa	PIT	311	29	63	11	2	6	31	20	71	0	0	203	252	310	561	6%	77%	0.28	65	48	2.11	-11
Kieboom,Carter	R	18	21	SS	aa	WAS	248	31	61	15	1	4	20	19	63	3	1	247	300	366	665	7%	75%	0.30	83	77	3.04	4
Knizner,Andrew	R	17	22	C	aa	STL	182	24	56	13	0	3	20	12	28	0	1	305	349	430	780	6%	85%	0.44	76	35	4.52	24
		18	23	C	a/a	STL	335	32	92	16	0	5	35	20	53	0	0	273	315	366	681	6%	84%	0.39	58	23	3.53	3
Kramer,Kevin	L	17	24	2B	aa	PIT	202	27	55	16	3	5	24	15	54	6	2	273	323	452	775	7%	73%	0.28	116	124	3.92	40
		18	25	2B	aaa	PIT	476	57	127	30	2	11	46	29	144	10	6	266	309	408	717	6%	70%	0.20	102	91	3.53	2
Lee,Braxton	L	16	23	CF	aa	TAM	387	28	70	10	2	0	20	24	66	11	11	182	230	220	451	6%	83%	0.37	26	90	1.20	-7
		17	24	CF	aa	MIA	476	77	134	20	2	3	35	63	120	19	15	282	365	351	717	12%	75%	0.52	49	101	3.69	-6
		18	25	RF	a/a	MIA	289	32	55	10	2	1	13	29	66	6	8	190	263	243	506	9%	77%	0.43	37	89	1.51	-15
Lee,Khalil	L	18	20	CF	aa	KC	102	13	24	5	0	2	9	9	28	2	2	234	299	332	631	8%	72%	0.33	72	64	2.64	-16
Lewis,Kyle	R	18	23	CF	aa	SEA	132	15	25	7	0	3	16	14	37	1	0	190	268	318	586	10%	72%	0.38	88	49	2.27	-7
Leyba,Domingo	B	16	21	SS	aa	ARI	156	19	46	7	1	4	18	15	23	4	2	295	359	429	788	9%	85%	0.67	75	84	4.67	46
		17	22	SS	aa	ARI	58	9	15	4	0	2	8	4	6	0	0	263	313	423	736	7%	89%	0.66	87	44	3.84	54
		18	23	2B	aa	ARI	320	35	76	16	2	4	25	29	51	4	2	239	302	334	635	8%	84%	0.57	58	80	2.76	25
Lin,Tzu-Wei	L	15	21	SS	aa	BOS	173	17	33	5	2	0	12	13	28	7	3	193	251	251	502	7%	84%	0.47	38	131	1.54	21
		16	22	SS	aa	BOS	372	33	79	11	4	2	23	28	59	8	7	213	269	277	546	7%	84%	0.49	38	100	1.88	14
		17	23	SS	a/a	BOS	300	36	77	15	4	6	24	27	58	8	6	257	317	389	706	8%	81%	0.46	75	105	3.27	33
		18	24	SS	aaa	BOS	277	28	81	21	2	4	21	19	68	3	4	293	338	424	763	6%	75%	0.28	93	66	3.90	11
Listi,Austin	R	18	25	DH	aa	PHI	217	19	51	7	0	7	29	21	64	0	0	234	302	371	673	9%	71%	0.33	87	14	3.39	-24
Long,Shed	L	17	22	2B	aa	CIN	141	14	32	6	2	4	15	21	34	4	1	230	329	372	701	13%	76%	0.61	82	97	3.39	26
		18	23	2B	aa	CIN	452	64	108	20	4	11	48	50	139	16	7	239	314	375	690	10%	69%	0.36	92	119	3.30	8
Lopez,Nicky	L	17	22	SS	aa	KC	232	23	58	6	1	0	10	14	30	6	4	248	291	284	576	6%	87%	0.47	23	85	2.39	6
		18	23	SS	a/a	KC	504	61	142	14	7	7	43	49	56	12	7	281	345	376	721	9%	89%	0.87	48	104	3.88	45
Lowe,Brandon	L	17	23	2B	aa	TAM	95	7	21	4	1	2	10	2	30	1	1	225	239	339	578	2%	68%	0.06	78	76	2.08	-35
		18	24	2B	a/a	TAM	380	62	98	26	1	18	64	48	122	7	3	258	341	473	814	11%	68%	0.39	150	80	4.62	40
Lowe,Nathaniel	L	18	23	1B	a/a	TAM	288	47	80	15	1	14	50	37	67	1	1	278	360	483	843	11%	77%	0.55	121	56	5.35	45
Lugo,Dawel	R	17	22	3B	aa	DET	516	50	132	24	6	11	56	29	76	3	1	256	295	390	685	5%	85%	0.38	71	79	3.25	34
		18	23	2B	aaa	DET	509	50	128	24	3	3	52	8	69	11	4	251	263	328	591	2%	86%	0.11	49	101	2.38	20
Lund,Brennon	L	17	23	LF	aa	LAA	122	16	33	3	0	1	6	3	38	1	2	267	283	312	596	2%	69%	0.07	33	64	2.65	-71
		18	24	CF	aa	LAA	401	53	92	17	4	7	50	35	118	18	7	230	292	345	637	8%	71%	0.30	77	133	2.74	2
Lux,Gavin	L	18	21	SS	aa	LA	105	17	30	4	1	3	7	10	23	2	2	287	352	424	776	9%	79%	0.47	79	79	4.46	21
Martin,Jason	L	17	22	LF	aa	HOU	300	33	76	22	3	10	32	16	93	6	6	253	292	445	737	5%	69%	0.18	130	98	3.25	21
		18	23	CF	a/a	PIT	468	57	115	16	7	10	45	37	121	10	13	246	301	375	676	7%	74%	0.30	78	108	2.90	8
Martin,Richie	R	17	23	SS	aa	OAK	286	34	57	10	3	2	22	19	60	10	3	198	247	274	521	6%	79%	0.31	46	128	1.77	5
		18	24	SS	aa	OAK	453	53	118	26	7	4	33	33	96	19	11	261	312	379	691	7%	79%	0.35	75	131	3.02	30
Mateo,Jorge	R	17	22	SS	aa	OAK	257	42	70	13	9	6	38	19	68	20	11	272	323	461	783	7%	74%	0.28	108	162	3.59	45
		18	23	SS	aaa	OAK	470	40	98	15	15	2	36	23	149	20	11	209	245	320	565	5%	68%	0.15	70	141	1.72	-18
Mazeika,Patrick	L	17	24	DH	aa	NYM	21	3	6	5	0	0	5	2	7	0	0	300	365	517	882	9%	66%	0.30	208	33	3.99	60
		18	25	C	aa	NYM	295	25	56	10	0	7	30	31	42	0	0	188	266	291	558	10%	86%	0.74	57	18	2.15	15
McCarthy,Joe	L	17	23	1B	aa	TAM	454	66	115	27	6	6	48	79	109	17	6	254	365	379	744	15%	76%	0.73	80	122	3.73	37
		18	24	LF	aaa	TAM	160	26	37	11	1	7	21	21	51	3	1	233	322	435	757	12%	68%	0.41	142	89	3.79	37
McGuire,Reese	L	16	21	C	aa	TOR	319	30	78	19	2	1	37	32	37	5	6	243	312	322	635	9%	88%	0.86	53	73	2.53	38
		17	22	C	aa	TOR	115	17	31	5	1	6	17	14	21	2	1	266	345	470	815	11%	82%	0.68	105	82	4.83	61
		18	23	C	aaa	TOR	322	27	70	9	2	6	33	29	83	3	2	218	283	315	597	8%	74%	0.35	60	61	2.50	-18
McKenna,Ryan	R	18	21	CF	aa	BAL	213	27	45	7	1	3	12	22	59	3	1	213	287	293	580	9%	72%	0.38	54	94	2.33	-18
McKinney,Billy	L	15	21	RF	aa	CHC	274	23	72	25	1	2	31	22	52	0	0	262	318	384	702	8%	81%	0.43	97	30	3.16	28
		16	22	RF	aa	NYY	426	51	103	18	3	4	43	59	105	4	6	241	333	330	663	12%	75%	0.56	61	70	2.92	-3
		17	23	RF	a/a	NYY	441	61	115	26	5	17	59	36	105	2	1	260	316	460	776	8%	76%	0.34	115	83	4.10	39
		18	24	RF	a/a	TOR	294	33	60	12	6	13	34	27	83	1	1	203	270	421	691	8%	72%	0.32	129	88	2.90	35
Mejia,Francisco	B	18	23	C	aaa	SD	427	38	103	25	1	9	48	18	97	0	0	242	272	373	644	4%	77%	0.18	85	38	2.81	-1
Mendoza,Evan	R	18	22	3B	aa	STL	366	28	82	11	1	4	20	23	83	1	1	223	268	290	558	6%	77%	0.27	43	46	2.21	-29
Miller,Brian	L	18	23	LF	aa	MIA	262	25	62	7	2	0	12	16	44	18	8	235	279	274	553	6%	83%	0.35	26	116	2.20	1

BATTER	B	Yr	Age	Pos	Lvl	Tm	AB	R	H	D	T	HR	RBI	BB	K	SB	CS	BA	OB	Slg	OPS	bb%	ct%	Eye	PX	SX	RC/G	BPV
Miller, Ian	L	15	23	CF	aa	SEA	347	33	77	12	3	0	19	23	61	24	14	223	271	275	546	6%	83%	0.38	37	130	1.89	13
		16	24	CF	aa	SEA	430	60	100	7	5	0	26	41	63	46	3	232	299	274	572	9%	85%	0.65	23	169	2.78	30
		17	25	CF	a/a	SEA	512	69	133	18	3	3	28	27	124	35	6	261	297	329	626	5%	76%	0.21	45	143	3.09	-6
		18	26	CF	aaa	SEA	422	44	88	13	2	1	30	32	112	24	11	210	266	260	526	7%	74%	0.29	37	120	1.91	-24
Miroglio, Dominic	R	18	23	C	aa	ARI	78	2	16	4	1	0	8	1	13	0	1	206	214	275	489	1%	83%	0.06	46	59	1.30	-9
Mondou, Nate	L	18	23	3B	aa	OAK	165	12	37	6	0	0	11	15	28	2	1	222	286	260	546	8%	83%	0.52	30	41	2.06	-14
Mountcastle, Ryan	R	17	20	3B	aa	BAL	153	16	28	8	0	3	13	3	39	0	0	181	196	283	479	2%	74%	0.07	68	49	1.42	-28
		18	21	3B	aa	BAL	394	49	105	16	3	11	46	20	84	2	0	267	302	406	708	5%	79%	0.24	81	77	3.71	15
Mundell, Brian	R	17	23	1B	aa	COL	172	25	51	12	0	3	16	21	26	1	1	297	373	415	788	11%	85%	0.81	73	44	4.60	36
		18	24	1B	aa	COL	441	38	109	24	1	6	32	42	80	1	3	247	313	347	660	9%	82%	0.53	65	33	2.96	9
Murphy, Sean	R	17	23	C	aa	OAK	191	20	35	6	0	3	18	16	36	0	0	183	248	261	509	8%	81%	0.46	47	34	1.76	-10
		18	24	C	a/a	OAK	265	42	66	23	2	6	34	20	55	2	0	248	301	416	717	7%	79%	0.36	110	101	3.26	52
Naylor, Josh	L	17	20	1B	aa	SD	156	17	39	9	0	2	18	15	37	2	1	247	312	341	653	9%	77%	0.41	65	53	2.97	-6
		18	25	3B	aa	CIN	221	30	51	9	0	5	21	26	51	2	0	230	311	344	655	11%	77%	0.51	71	56	3.17	5
Neuse, Sheldon	R	17	23	3B	aa	OAK	67	7	22	4	0	0	5	5	23	0	0	335	379	390	769	7%	66%	0.21	53	24	4.86	-71
		18	24	3B	aaa	OAK	499	38	114	23	3	4	43	25	191	3	1	228	264	307	572	5%	62%	0.13	69	74	2.18	-64
Newman, Kevin	R	16	23	SS	aa	PIT	233	35	60	10	2	2	24	21	26	5	3	258	321	333	654	8%	89%	0.84	45	98	3.00	40
		17	24	SS	a/a	PIT	509	57	124	27	4	3	36	26	66	10	3	245	281	331	612	5%	87%	0.39	52	105	2.52	33
		18	25	SS	aaa	PIT	437	57	113	26	2	3	27	24	56	22	13	258	297	345	642	5%	87%	0.42	57	114	2.72	41
Nido, Tomas	R	17	23	C	aa	NYM	367	40	79	17	1	8	59	32	73	0	0	215	278	334	612	8%	80%	0.44	70	39	2.55	6
		18	24	C	a/a	NYM	232	18	51	16	1	3	22	7	46	0	0	218	240	339	578	3%	80%	0.15	81	36	2.05	5
Nottingham, Jacob	R	16	21	C	aa	MIL	415	43	95	14	0	11	35	28	145	9	2	228	277	337	614	6%	65%	0.19	79	77	2.82	-39
		17	22	C	aa	MIL	325	37	68	21	2	10	48	37	93	7	3	210	291	382	673	10%	71%	0.40	112	93	2.86	25
		18	23	C	aaa	MIL	178	22	42	9	1	7	24	9	68	1	1	235	273	422	695	5%	62%	0.14	136	85	3.20	-7
Nunez, Dom	L	17	22	C	aa	COL	297	31	60	10	1	10	24	45	80	6	1	203	308	350	658	13%	73%	0.56	86	75	3.10	12
		18	23	C	aa	COL	324	27	69	12	0	8	34	37	74	6	6	212	294	321	615	10%	77%	0.50	67	47	2.57	-1
Ockimey, Josh	L	17	22	1B	aa	BOS	103	10	27	8	0	2	9	14	34	0	0	261	350	403	753	12%	67%	0.41	107	14	3.97	-17
		18	23	1B	a/a	BOS	404	44	93	21	2	16	58	56	157	1	1	229	323	408	732	12%	61%	0.35	136	46	3.68	-7
Pache, Cristian	R	18	20	CF	aa	ATL	104	9	27	3	1	1	7	4	29	0	2	256	287	329	616	4%	72%	0.16	49	66	2.54	-41
Paredes, Isaac	R	18	19	3B	aa	DET	131	18	41	9	0	3	20	17	22	1	0	311	389	441	830	11%	83%	0.77	82	42	5.43	36
Patterson, Jordan	L	15	23	RF	aa	COL	185	21	50	18	0	6	26	9	44	7	4	271	304	473	777	5%	76%	0.20	149	81	3.79	60
		16	24	RF	aaa	COL	427	55	115	22	7	11	46	34	120	7	0	270	324	434	758	7%	72%	0.29	106	130	4.06	29
		17	25	1B	aaa	COL	484	53	122	29	6	20	63	25	134	2	6	253	289	460	750	5%	72%	0.18	126	80	3.52	25
		18	26	1B	aaa	COL	413	47	92	19	2	17	46	26	143	4	2	224	270	404	674	6%	65%	0.18	125	75	3.05	-2
Pentecost, Max	R	18	25	C	aa	TOR	344	32	77	16	2	8	42	12	101	1	0	224	251	352	603	3%	71%	0.12	87	62	2.45	-20
Perez, Yanio	R	18	23	3B	aa	TEX	44	6	9	1	0	0	4	6	16	0	0	207	301	229	529	12%	64%	0.37	22	44	2.01	-89
Peters, DJ	R	18	23	CF	aa	LA	491	59	99	20	2	22	45	32	219	1	2	201	250	383	633	6%	55%	0.15	146	62	2.62	-29
Peterson, Dustin	R	16	22	LF	aa	ATL	524	65	142	37	2	11	88	46	112	4	1	271	330	414	744	8%	79%	0.41	95	73	3.90	30
		17	23	LF	aaa	ATL	314	30	65	10	1	1	26	25	92	1	2	207	265	250	515	7%	71%	0.27	34	51	1.78	-59
		18	24	LF	aaa	ATL	406	37	96	21	0	9	44	23	107	2	0	237	278	354	632	5%	74%	0.21	81	49	2.84	-14
Peterson, Kort	L	18	24	RF	aa	KC	166	19	34	8	3	5	22	10	66	5	3	206	249	380	630	5%	60%	0.14	129	135	2.27	-3
Polo, Tito	R	17	23	CF	aa	CHW	127	23	39	8	3	1	23	11	26	13	4	308	364	440	803	8%	80%	0.43	78	166	4.54	48
		18	24	CF	aa	CHW	163	20	36	5	3	1	7	11	39	14	4	223	273	306	579	7%	76%	0.29	51	160	2.25	8
Potts, Hudson	R	18	20	3B	aa	SD	78	4	11	0	0	2	4	9	35	1	0	142	229	207	435	10%	55%	0.25	45	31	1.45	-112
Pujols, Jose	R	18	23	RF	aa	PHI	89	9	21	2	0	3	14	11	41	2	2	235	319	370	688	11%	54%	0.27	106	39	3.44	-64
Raley, Luke	L	18	24	1B	aa	MIN	484	62	118	17	6	16	54	28	150	3	0	244	284	404	688	5%	69%	0.18	101	111	3.32	3
Ramirez, Tyler	L	17	22	LF	aa	OAK	208	24	58	10	1	3	20	23	56	2	3	279	350	380	730	10%	73%	0.41	68	65	3.81	-12
		18	23	LF	aa	OAK	512	58	129	32	4	7	63	48	162	4	4	253	317	372	689	9%	68%	0.30	91	78	3.12	-11
Ramos, Roberto	L	18	24	1B	aa	COL	199	20	43	9	0	13	27	21	78	2	1	216	290	453	743	9%	61%	0.27	169	31	3.81	9
Ray, Corey	L	18	24	CF	aa	MIL	532	77	121	31	6	26	67	54	198	23	8	227	297	457	754	9%	63%	0.27	164	155	3.77	49
Read, Raudy	R	17	24	C	aa	WAS	411	36	95	22	1	13	50	22	89	2	0	232	271	386	658	5%	78%	0.25	91	43	2.99	11
		18	25	C	a/a	WAS	197	13	48	10	1	2	21	10	43	0	0	244	279	345	624	5%	78%	0.22	66	40	2.65	-12
Reed, Buddy	S	18	23	CF	aa	SD	179	18	28	6	0	1	13	10	71	15	3	158	202	206	409	5%	61%	0.14	46	130	1.19	-69
Rengifo, Luis	S	18	21	SS	a/a	LAA	341	55	84	16	6	4	36	35	60	14	9	246	317	364	681	9%	82%	0.59	68	147	2.91	49
Reyes, Pablo	R	17	24	2B	aa	PIT	420	54	105	19	3	8	44	45	75	18	16	250	323	369	693	10%	82%	0.60	67	103	3.13	35
		18	25	LF	a/a	PIT	401	43	98	20	3	6	32	25	85	13	8	245	290	357	646	6%	79%	0.30	71	103	2.75	17
Riley, Austin	R	17	20	3B	aa	ATL	178	29	53	6	1	8	28	22	56	2	0	296	372	467	839	11%	69%	0.39	103	81	5.81	5
		18	21	3B	a/a	ATL	390	51	109	27	2	16	59	29	130	1	0	280	329	484	813	7%	67%	0.22	144	65	4.73	17
Rios, Edwin	L	16	22	3B	aa	LA	122	13	29	7	0	5	16	7	34	0	0	240	281	416	697	5%	72%	0.20	116	23	3.39	2
		17	23	1B	a/a	LA	475	58	131	32	0	20	75	27	126	1	2	276	315	473	787	5%	73%	0.21	122	31	4.42	13
		18	24	3B	aaa	LA	309	35	80	22	0	8	42	17	129	0	1	260	298	407	705	5%	58%	0.13	130	32	3.38	-41
Robinson, Errol	R	17	23	SS	aa	LA	227	29	55	8	1	2	12	22	57	9	3	242	310	309	619	9%	75%	0.39	44	106	2.81	-13
		18	24	SS	aa	LA	433	39	89	12	1	7	37	26	121	13	10	205	250	287	538	6%	72%	0.21	54	77	1.94	-33

BATTER	B	Yr	Age	Pos	Lvl	Tm	AB	R	H	D	T	HR	RBI	BB	K	SB	CS	BA	OB	Slg	OPS	bb%	ct%	Eye	PX	SX	RC/G	BPV
Robles, Victor	R	17	20	CF	aa	WAS	139	21	43	12	1	3	12	11	23	10	3	307	356	455	811	7%	83%	0.45	91	118	4.76	57
		18	21	CF	aaa	WAS	158	22	42	10	1	2	9	16	27	13	6	264	332	369	700	9%	83%	0.58	68	115	3.31	40
Rodgers, Brendan	R	17	21	SS	aa	COL	150	17	39	5	0	6	15	7	34	0	2	263	295	412	707	4%	77%	0.20	83	33	3.62	-5
		18	22	SS	a/a	COL	426	39	107	26	2	14	49	23	93	9	3	250	289	416	705	5%	78%	0.25	102	84	3.39	32
Rodriguez, Alfredo	R	18	24	SS	aa	CIN	26	3	4	0	0	0	0	2	8	0	0	170	221	170	390	6%	69%	0.21	0	59	1.15	-92
Rogers, Jake	R	18	23	C	aa	DET	352	47	69	14	1	14	46	33	118	6	1	197	266	362	628	9%	66%	0.28	111	95	2.72	2
Rooker, Brent	R	18	24	1B	aa	MIN	503	56	113	28	3	18	62	43	164	5	1	224	285	398	683	8%	67%	0.26	121	85	3.10	10
Sanchez, Jesus	L	18	21	RF	aa	TAM	98	12	19	7	0	1	10	10	24	1	1	191	263	290	553	9%	76%	0.40	76	65	1.75	3
Sanchez, Jose	L	17	23	LF	aa	KC	29	2	4	1	0	0	1	2	5	0	0	130	178	165	343	6%	82%	0.33	27	30	0.68	-29
Schales, Brian	R	18	22	3B	aa	MIA	422	45	97	24	2	8	43	51	120	3	2	230	313	352	665	11%	71%	0.42	87	64	2.97	-2
Schrock, Max	L	16	22	2B	aa	OAK	23	2	8	1	0	0	2	0	0	0	1	357	357	399	756	0%	###	0.00	28	51	4.06	40
		17	23	2B	aa	OAK	417	45	119	17	1	5	37	27	45	3	2	286	329	369	698	6%	89%	0.60	46	57	3.75	25
		18	24	2B	aaa	STL	417	31	89	19	0	3	32	18	40	8	6	212	245	278	523	4%	90%	0.45	42	63	1.79	24
Senzel, Nick	R	17	22	3B	aa	CIN	209	42	72	14	1	12	36	28	47	5	4	345	423	588	1	12%	78%	0.61	137	86	8.04	72
		18	23	2B	aaa	CIN	171	19	48	11	1	5	21	16	45	7	2	280	342	457	799	9%	74%	0.36	114	99	4.57	36
Seymour, Anfernee	B	18	23	RF	aa	MIA	51	5	11	3	0	1	4	5	10	3	1	222	294	337	631	9%	80%	0.51	78	82	2.68	27
Shaw, Chris	L	16	23	1B	aa	SF	232	24	54	15	5	4	28	19	61	0	0	233	291	393	684	8%	74%	0.31	105	78	2.74	20
		17	24	LF	a/a	SF	469	50	120	32	1	17	68	33	151	0	0	257	306	438	744	7%	68%	0.22	124	30	3.84	-6
		18	25	LF	aaa	SF	394	38	81	17	2	14	46	15	170	0	0	204	233	363	596	4%	57%	0.09	127	53	2.32	-46
Short, Zack	R	18	23	SS	aa	CHC	436	58	89	25	2	15	50	73	149	7	3	205	319	372	690	14%	66%	0.49	121	83	3.11	15
Siri, Jose	R	18	23	CF	aa	CIN	253	36	53	7	7	11	29	21	102	12	5	211	271	426	697	8%	59%	0.20	147	151	2.92	18
Solak, Nick	R	17	22	2B	aa	NYY	119	15	33	8	1	2	9	10	26	1	1	275	330	416	746	8%	78%	0.37	89	75	3.77	23
		18	23	2B	aa	TAM	478	77	120	15	2	16	65	58	131	18	7	250	331	389	720	11%	73%	0.44	85	112	3.92	15
Sosa, Edmundo	R	18	22	SS	a/a	STL	452	51	108	27	1	9	46	17	101	5	4	238	265	359	625	4%	78%	0.17	81	69	2.56	5
Stallings, Jacob	R	15	26	C	aa	PIT	265	19	60	12	1	2	24	11	74	3	1	228	258	300	558	4%	72%	0.15	60	64	2.13	-35
		16	27	C	aaa	PIT	257	19	46	15	0	5	24	9	75	0	1	181	209	292	500	3%	71%	0.12	83	34	1.49	-32
		17	28	C	aaa	PIT	216	28	54	14	0	3	30	14	35	1	2	251	296	356	652	6%	84%	0.39	66	50	2.82	17
		18	29	C	aaa	PIT	256	26	57	17	1	2	28	11	63	1	3	222	253	320	573	4%	75%	0.17	74	59	1.96	-11
Stewart, Christin	L	16	23	LF	aa	DET	87	14	17	2	0	5	15	10	27	0	0	192	275	375	650	10%	69%	0.36	112	42	3.08	-1
		17	24	LF	aa	DET	485	55	109	25	3	23	71	47	151	2	0	225	293	433	726	9%	69%	0.31	130	76	3.58	22
		18	25	LF	aaa	DET	444	59	105	19	3	20	65	56	118	0	0	236	322	426	749	11%	73%	0.48	114	50	3.97	24
Stewart, DJ	L	17	24	LF	aa	BAL	457	65	104	14	1	17	64	57	105	16	5	229	314	379	693	11%	77%	0.55	82	101	3.60	28
		18	25	RF	aaa	BAL	421	48	86	20	1	11	45	44	114	9	5	205	280	336	616	9%	73%	0.38	86	87	2.51	7
Stokes Jr., Troy	R	17	21	LF	aa	MIL	135	19	35	9	0	7	18	16	36	9	3	256	336	479	815	11%	73%	0.45	136	88	4.71	52
		18	22	LF	aa	MIL	467	69	107	23	6	19	54	60	159	18	2	228	317	426	743	11%	66%	0.38	133	142	3.84	38
Straw, Myles	R	17	23	CF	aa	HOU	46	8	10	0	0	0	3	6	10	2	0	214	303	214	516	11%	77%	0.56	0	86	2.30	-40
		18	24	CF	a/a	HOU	516	74	126	14	4	1	24	55	119	55	10	244	317	291	608	10%	77%	0.46	32	150	3.02	0
Stubbs, Garrett	L	16	23	C	aa	HOU	120	18	35	8	1	3	13	11	13	4	0	289	349	457	805	8%	89%	0.87	93	105	4.91	82
		17	24	C	a/a	HOU	340	34	65	15	0	3	27	31	71	8	0	191	258	261	519	8%	79%	0.43	47	86	1.87	-1
		18	25	C	aaa	HOU	297	41	72	15	3	3	26	23	64	4	0	244	299	346	645	7%	78%	0.36	66	115	2.83	17
Tatis Jr., Fernando	R	17	18	SS	aa	SD	55	6	15	1	0	1	6	2	16	3	0	268	294	341	634	3%	71%	0.12	45	81	3.60	-48
		18	19	SS	aa	SD	353	70	97	21	3	14	39	30	115	14	5	274	331	472	803	8%	67%	0.26	136	145	4.53	39
Taylor, Logan	R	18	25	3B	a/a	SEA	230	20	52	7	1	5	24	16	85	0	0	228	279	338	617	7%	63%	0.19	80	35	2.76	-57
Tebow, Tim	L	18	31	LF	aa	NYM	271	22	55	11	1	4	25	16	138	1	0	203	248	292	540	6%	49%	0.12	91	53	1.99	-101
Tellez, Rowdy	L	16	21	1B	aa	TOR	438	63	126	30	2	22	72	56	100	4	3	288	369	518	887	11%	77%	0.56	141	59	5.72	63
		17	22	1B	aaa	TOR	445	44	99	31	1	6	55	46	100	6	1	223	296	339	635	9%	78%	0.46	78	73	2.62	15
		18	23	1B	aaa	TOR	393	38	100	22	0	11	44	35	80	6	4	254	315	398	713	8%	80%	0.44	89	50	3.59	23
Thaiss, Matt	L	17	22	1B	aa	LAA	178	28	49	13	0	1	24	35	56	4	3	277	396	367	763	17%	69%	0.63	77	60	3.99	-11
		18	23	1B	a/a	LAA	525	54	122	28	5	12	56	31	120	6	5	233	276	372	648	6%	77%	0.26	87	91	2.70	19
Thompson, David	R	17	24	3B	aa	NYM	476	59	114	26	1	16	65	42	109	8	7	240	301	400	701	8%	77%	0.39	95	66	3.33	23
		18	25	3B	aaa	NYM	66	6	13	4	0	1	3	3	25	1	2	193	224	279	503	4%	63%	0.11	78	78	1.33	-54
Toro-Hernandez, Abrah S		18	22	3B	aa	HOU	178	15	38	14	2	2	20	15	50	3	3	211	273	337	610	8%	72%	0.30	96	83	2.04	7
Travis, Sam	R	15	22	1B	aa	BOS	243	29	70	18	2	3	31	27	36	7	6	287	359	413	772	10%	85%	0.76	88	85	3.94	59
		16	23	1B	aaa	BOS	173	25	47	11	0	5	28	15	43	1	0	272	328	431	759	8%	75%	0.34	106	53	4.23	20
		17	24	1B	aaa	BOS	304	35	79	15	0	5	21	33	61	5	2	260	333	361	694	10%	80%	0.55	63	60	3.57	10
		18	25	1B	aaa	BOS	361	29	86	13	0	6	36	24	97	1	2	238	285	328	613	6%	73%	0.24	61	27	2.72	-37
Trevino, Jose	R	17	25	C	aa	TEX	402	33	86	10	0	6	35	16	49	1	2	215	245	285	531	4%	88%	0.33	37	33	2.01	1
		18	26	C	aa	TEX	184	14	37	6	1	2	12	10	31	0	1	201	243	281	524	5%	83%	0.34	47	43	1.79	-3
Tucker, Cole	B	17	21	SS	aa	PIT	167	23	42	4	5	2	17	19	31	10	3	251	330	364	694	10%	81%	0.62	55	142	3.28	34
		18	22	SS	aa	PIT	517	66	124	20	6	4	38	47	109	30	13	240	304	326	629	8%	79%	0.43	53	135	2.70	17
Tucker, Kyle	L	17	20	CF	aa	HOU	287	35	72	20	1	15	42	19	71	7	4	251	299	481	780	6%	75%	0.28	136	83	3.97	50
		18	21	RF	aaa	HOU	407	63	116	23	2	19	69	35	95	15	4	284	340	486	826	8%	77%	0.36	120	109	5.10	53
Urena, Jhoan	B	17	23	1B	aaa	NYM	44	4	8	0	1	2	6	3	19	1	0	185	239	362	601	7%	57%	0.16	113	84	2.60	-43
		18	24	RF	aa	NYM	421	37	92	17	1	11	50	32	132	2	5	219	275	344	618	7%	69%	0.24	85	45	2.55	-28

BATTER	B	Yr	Age	Pos	Lvl	Tm	AB	R	H	D	T	HR	RBI	BB	K	SB	CS	BA	OB	Slg	OPS	bb%	ct%	Eye	PX	SX	RC/G	BPV
Urias, Luis	R	17	20	SS	aa	SD	442	74	130	20	3	3	36	63	66	7	5	294	382	373	756	13%	85%	0.96	48	89	4.23	32
		18	21	2B	aaa	SD	450	60	114	26	5	6	32	48	123	1	1	252	325	368	693	10%	73%	0.39	81	83	3.20	1
Urias, Ramon	R	18	24	2B	a/a	STL	311	36	79	24	0	9	33	18	65	1	2	254	294	421	715	5%	79%	0.27	108	40	3.35	27
Verdugo, Alex	L	16	20	CF	aa	LA	477	56	126	23	1	13	61	39	71	2	6	264	320	398	718	8%	85%	0.55	77	39	3.65	31
		17	21	CF	aaa	LA	433	56	123	26	2	5	52	40	56	8	3	285	345	392	737	8%	87%	0.72	63	87	3.94	44
		18	22	CF	aaa	LA	343	36	101	18	0	8	36	26	52	6	2	294	343	416	759	7%	85%	0.50	72	58	4.53	30
Wade, LaMonte	L	17	23	LF	aa	MIN	424	68	118	21	3	6	61	67	73	8	2	278	377	386	763	14%	83%	0.92	63	98	4.36	40
		18	24	LF	a/a	MIN	424	45	99	10	3	9	40	52	80	8	3	234	318	340	658	11%	81%	0.65	57	87	3.18	20
Wall, Forrest	L	18	23	CF	aa	TOR	299	39	65	13	3	6	21	25	95	15	7	217	278	336	614	8%	68%	0.27	83	131	2.48	-4
Walton, Donnie	L	18	24	2B	aa	SEA	208	18	42	12	1	1	18	17	41	2	1	200	261	276	536	8%	81%	0.42	55	71	1.76	4
Ward, Drew	L	16	22	3B	aa	WAS	178	17	37	7	0	2	21	20	53	0	1	208	287	288	575	10%	70%	0.37	60	29	2.24	-41
		17	23	3B	aa	WAS	413	39	87	18	0	8	44	46	145	0	0	210	289	311	600	10%	65%	0.32	75	21	2.49	-52
		18	24	1B	a/a	WAS	374	53	83	16	3	11	48	51	128	1	2	221	314	367	681	12%	66%	0.40	102	71	3.11	-8
Ward, Taylor	R	17	24	C	aa	LAA	119	13	31	3	0	3	18	20	20	0	0	260	367	351	719	14%	83%	1.02	47	17	4.16	7
		18	25	3B	a/a	LAA	375	48	106	21	0	10	43	45	115	13	4	283	359	418	778	11%	69%	0.39	97	76	4.71	1
White, Eli	R	18	24	2B	aa	OAK	504	63	134	27	7	6	43	47	130	14	10	266	328	386	715	9%	74%	0.36	80	118	3.34	15
Wiel, Zander	R	18	25	1B	a/a	MIN	437	47	116	24	2	8	53	35	105	7	5	265	319	389	708	7%	76%	0.33	82	80	3.51	10
Williams, Justin	L	16	21	RF	aa	TAM	148	17	32	5	2	5	23	4	33	0	1	219	241	377	618	3%	77%	0.13	91	82	2.41	15
		17	22	RF	aa	TAM	366	47	100	19	2	12	64	33	78	5	2	274	335	437	771	8%	79%	0.43	93	85	4.36	33
		18	23	RF	aaa	STL	425	38	93	18	0	8	44	23	107	3	4	218	258	319	577	5%	75%	0.21	67	45	2.24	-22
Wong, Kean	L	16	21	2B	aa	TAM	446	44	111	19	2	4	47	26	80	8	11	249	290	326	616	6%	82%	0.33	50	74	2.52	3
		17	22	2B	a/a	TAM	422	44	101	20	0	4	43	34	98	15	10	240	297	318	614	7%	77%	0.35	54	77	2.60	-10
		18	23	2B	aaa	TAM	451	56	113	20	2	8	43	35	131	6	3	250	304	356	660	7%	71%	0.26	73	87	3.08	-15
Zagunis, Mark	R	16	23	LF	a/a	CHC	358	47	91	22	4	8	38	41	89	4	2	255	332	407	739	10%	75%	0.46	100	93	3.65	31
		17	24	LF	aaa	CHC	330	45	74	18	1	10	42	55	109	3	3	225	335	373	708	14%	67%	0.50	102	57	3.38	-2
		18	25	RF	aaa	CHC	371	46	83	14	0	5	29	53	118	8	1	224	321	304	625	13%	68%	0.45	60	75	2.90	-30

PITCHER	Th	Yr	Age	LvL	Org	W	L	G	Sv	IP	H	ER	HR	BB	K	ERA	WHIP	BF/G	OBA	bb/9	k/9	Cmd	hr/9	H%	S%	BPV
Acevedo, Domingo	R	17	23	a/a	NYY	6	2	16	0	92	95	37	12	27	78	3.68	1.33	23.8	269	2.7	7.6	2.9	1.2	32%	77%	72
		18	24	aa	NYY	3	3	14	0	66	63	29	4	22	44	3.88	1.28	19.4	252	3.0	6.0	2.0	0.6	29%	70%	65
Adams, Chance	R	16	22	aa	NYY	8	1	13	0	70	44	23	8	27	63	3.01	1.01	20.5	182	3.4	8.1	2.4	1.0	21%	75%	87
		17	23	a/a	NYY	15	5	27	0	150	129	57	16	63	117	3.41	1.27	22.8	233	3.8	7.0	1.9	1.0	27%	77%	60
		18	24	aaa	NYY	4	5	27	0	113	122	78	22	62	96	6.24	1.63	18.6	277	4.9	7.6	1.5	1.8	31%	65%	25
Adams, Spencer	R	16	20	aa	CHW	2	5	9	0	55	64	27	2	10	24	4.39	1.34	25.6	291	1.7	3.9	2.4	0.4	32%	66%	59
		17	21	aa	CHW	7	15	26	0	153	206	102	25	45	103	6.03	1.65	26.2	324	2.7	6.0	2.3	1.5	36%	66%	30
		18	22	a/a	CHW	7	13	28	0	161	189	85	25	62	85	4.73	1.55	25.2	294	3.4	4.7	1.4	1.4	31%	74%	12
Adcock, Brett	L	18	23	aa	HOU	4	2	9	0	40	40	19	2	22	24	4.25	1.55	19.5	261	5.0	5.4	1.1	0.5	30%	72%	41
Agrazal, Dario	R	18	24	aa	PIT	5	6	15	0	87	108	48	10	14	42	4.93	1.40	24.5	305	1.4	4.3	3.1	1.0	33%	66%	54
Akin, Keegan	L	18	23	aa	BAL	14	7	25	0	139	128	57	18	57	117	3.68	1.32	23.1	245	3.7	7.5	2.1	1.2	28%	77%	59
Alcala, Jorge	R	18	23	aa	MIN	2	7	14	1	62	69	36	6	31	48	5.14	1.60	19.6	281	4.5	7.0	1.6	0.8	33%	68%	49
Alcantara, Sandy	R	17	22	aa	STL	7	5	25	0	125	146	76	14	55	88	5.43	1.60	22.1	292	3.9	6.3	1.6	1.0	33%	67%	38
		18	23	aaa	MIA	6	3	19	0	117	119	56	9	38	76	4.33	1.34	25.7	265	2.9	5.8	2.0	0.7	30%	68%	57
Allard, Kolby	L	17	20	aa	ATL	8	11	27	0	150	174	72	13	49	120	4.34	1.49	24.0	292	3.0	7.2	2.4	0.8	35%	72%	68
		18	21	aaa	ATL	6	4	19	0	113	114	40	6	32	77	3.16	1.29	24.4	263	2.5	6.1	2.4	0.5	31%	76%	75
Allen, Logan	L	18	21	a/a	SD	14	6	25	0	150	116	44	10	47	134	2.62	1.09	23.5	215	2.8	8.0	2.9	0.6	27%	78%	102
Almonte, Yency	R	16	22	aa	COL	3	1	5	0	30	28	15	6	18	17	4.58	1.53	26.1	250	5.3	5.2	1.0	1.8	25%	77%	2
		17	23	a/a	COL	8	4	22	0	111	124	51	16	57	72	4.15	1.63	22.5	283	4.6	5.9	1.3	1.3	31%	78%	22
		18	24	aaa	COL	3	5	18	1	45	50	31	9	14	26	6.26	1.43	10.7	283	2.8	5.3	1.9	1.8	29%	60%	14
Alvarez, Yadier	R	17	21	aa	LA	2	2	7	0	33	32	15	1	22	32	4.02	1.64	21.0	255	6.0	8.7	1.4	0.3	34%	74%	78
		18	22	aa	LA	1	2	17	1	49	39	26	2	38	46	4.73	1.56	12.7	220	6.9	8.4	1.2	0.3	29%	68%	76
Alzolay, Adbert	R	17	22	aa	CHC	0	3	7	0	33	32	14	0	13	26	3.92	1.37	19.5	257	3.5	7.3	2.1	0.0	33%	68%	91
		18	23	aaa	CHC	2	4	8	0	41	47	23	4	13	23	5.06	1.47	22.1	290	2.8	5.0	1.8	0.9	32%	66%	37
Anderson, Drew	R	17	23	a/a	PHI	9	4	22	0	114	101	55	17	43	82	4.30	1.25	21.2	238	3.4	6.4	1.9	1.3	26%	70%	46
		18	24	aaa	PHI	9	4	19	0	106	109	57	18	30	73	4.80	1.32	23.1	268	2.6	6.2	2.4	1.5	29%	68%	44
Anderson, Ian	R	18	20	aa	ATL	2	1	4	0	20	16	6	0	9	21	2.87	1.24	20.4	222	3.9	9.5	2.4	0.0	31%	74%	118
Anderson, Shaun	R	18	24	a/a	SF	8	7	25	0	142	159	66	12	33	105	4.17	1.35	23.7	284	2.1	6.7	3.2	0.8	33%	70%	83
Anderson, Tanner	R	17	24	aa	PIT	10	8	30	0	133	166	68	7	36	77	4.62	1.52	19.3	306	2.4	5.2	2.1	0.5	35%	69%	56
		18	25	aaa	PIT	3	2	39	6	62	77	22	2	16	39	3.17	1.49	6.9	305	2.2	5.6	2.5	0.3	35%	78%	71
Armenteros, Rogelio	R	16	22	aa	HOU	2	0	3	0	18	19	5	1	4	12	2.23	1.24	24.8	267	1.9	5.7	3.0	0.6	31%	84%	82
		17	23	a/a	HOU	10	4	24	1	124	98	29	8	35	130	2.14	1.07	20.1	219	2.6	9.4	3.7	0.6	29%	83%	129
		18	24	aaa	HOU	8	1	22	1	118	111	48	14	43	112	3.66	1.31	22.1	250	3.3	8.6	2.6	1.1	31%	76%	79
Bachlor, Tyler	R	18	25	aa	NYM	0	3	20	7	24	16	8	2	13	25	3.08	1.21	4.8	194	4.8	9.4	2.0	0.8	25%	77%	91
Baez, Michel	R	18	22	aa	SD	0	3	4	0	19	25	18	4	12	18	8.33	1.92	22.6	315	5.6	8.7	1.6	1.9	37%	58%	19
Baez, Sandy	R	18	25	aa	DET	1	9	33	1	105	140	85	23	49	67	7.31	1.80	14.7	321	4.2	5.7	1.4	2.0	34%	62%	-5
Bailey, Brandon	R	18	24	aa	HOU	1	0	5	1	26	25	14	6	9	19	4.88	1.32	21.7	255	3.2	6.6	2.1	2.1	26%	72%	24
Banda, Anthony	L	16	23	a/a	ARI	10	6	26	0	150	165	58	11	55	129	3.49	1.47	24.7	281	3.3	7.7	2.3	0.7	34%	77%	74
		17	24	aaa	ARI	8	7	22	0	122	136	77	15	48	96	5.70	1.51	24.0	284	3.6	7.1	2.0	1.1	33%	63%	49
		18	25	aaa	TAM	4	3	8	0	42	52	22	3	19	42	4.67	1.70	23.7	306	4.1	9.0	2.2	0.7	39%	73%	72
Beede, Tyler	R	15	22	aa	SF	3	8	13	0	72	73	54	4	37	43	6.67	1.52	24.1	263	4.6	5.3	1.2	0.5	30%	53%	44
		16	23	aa	SF	8	7	24	0	147	165	63	9	57	117	3.82	1.51	26.6	284	3.5	7.1	2.0	0.6	34%	75%	67
		17	24	aaa	SF	6	7	19	0	109	140	70	13	40	70	5.74	1.66	25.7	314	3.3	5.7	1.7	1.0	35%	66%	31
		18	25	aaa	SF	4	9	33	0	74	90	61	8	54	61	7.46	1.95	10.7	302	6.6	7.4	1.1	1.0	36%	61%	34
Bielak, Brandon	R	18	22	aa	HOU	2	5	11	0	62	60	20	5	22	50	2.88	1.32	23.4	256	3.2	7.2	2.3	0.7	31%	80%	74
Black, Ray	R	16	26	aa	SF	1	4	35	6	31	22	24	1	37	43	6.92	1.87	4.2	199	10.6	12.3	1.2	0.3	31%	60%	104
		18	28	a/a	SF	3	0	36	5	37	23	12	2	13	50	3.00	0.98	3.9	182	3.1	12.1	3.9	0.4	28%	69%	159
Blackham, Matt	R	18	25	aa	NYM	1	2	22	0	27	21	12	2	18	30	3.90	1.43	5.2	215	6.0	10.0	1.7	0.7	29%	74%	86
Blewett, Scott	R	18	22	aa	KC	8	6	26	0	149	190	98	12	49	84	5.91	1.60	25.4	311	3.0	5.1	1.7	0.7	34%	62%	37
Bostick, Akeem	R	17	22	aa	HOU	6	6	18	0	80	111	49	8	20	53	5.54	1.62	19.8	328	2.2	5.9	2.7	0.9	37%	66%	55
		18	23	a/a	HOU	2	5	22	3	98	99	44	8	35	90	4.01	1.36	18.6	263	3.2	8.2	2.6	0.8	33%	72%	83
Brigham, Jeff	R	18	26	a/a	MIA	9	3	16	0	91	96	31	8	24	72	3.02	1.31	23.5	271	2.3	7.1	3.1	0.8	32%	80%	84
Brown, Zack	R	18	24	aa	MIL	9	1	22	0	127	122	50	12	40	98	3.52	1.27	23.7	253	2.9	6.9	2.4	0.8	30%	75%	72
Brubaker, JT	R	17	24	aa	PIT	7	6	26	0	130	186	88	11	49	87	6.08	1.81	23.1	337	3.4	6.0	1.8	0.7	39%	66%	39
		18	25	a/a	PIT	10	6	28	0	154	180	60	9	46	103	3.51	1.47	23.6	293	2.7	6.0	2.2	0.5	34%	76%	64
Burdi, Nick	R	15	22	aa	MIN	3	4	30	2	44	44	25	3	30	45	5.06	1.70	6.6	263	6.3	9.3	1.5	0.6	34%	70%	72
		17	24	aa	MIN	2	0	14	1	17	12	1	1	6	16	0.77	0.93	4.6	194	2.3	8.3	3.6	0.7	24%	99%	122
Burdi, Zack	R	16	21	a/a	CHW	2	0	42	16	64	35	25	4	42	83	3.56	1.20	6.1	164	5.8	11.7	2.0	0.6	24%	71%	116
		17	22	aaa	CHW	0	4	29	7	33	33	17	2	18	46	4.64	1.53	5.0	262	4.8	12.4	2.6	0.6	39%	69%	113
Burke, Brock	L	18	22	aa	TAM	6	1	9	0	56	44	14	2	14	64	2.28	1.03	24.0	218	2.2	10.3	4.6	0.3	31%	78%	161
Burr, Ryan	R	18	24	a/a	CHW	4	3	37	2	52	41	18	4	28	44	3.18	1.32	5.8	220	4.8	7.5	1.6	0.7	27%	78%	69
Burrows, Beau	R	17	21	aa	DET	6	4	15	0	76	90	48	5	33	63	5.70	1.61	22.5	294	3.9	7.5	1.9	0.6	36%	64%	62
		18	22	aa	DET	10	9	26	0	134	145	75	14	56	105	5.06	1.50	22.3	278	3.8	7.1	1.9	0.9	33%	67%	54
Burrows, Thomas	L	18	24	aa	ATL	0	0	15	6	19	12	4	0	6	22	1.96	0.98	4.8	188	2.9	10.5	3.6	0.0	28%	78%	155

PITCHER	Th	Yr	Age	LvL	Org	W	L	G	Sv	IP	H	ER	HR	BB	K	ERA	WHIP	BF/G	OBA	bb/9	k/9	Cmd	hr/9	H%	S%	BPV
Cabrera, Genesis	L	17	21	aa	TAM	5	4	12	0	65	85	31	6	27	46	4.36	1.74	24.6	318	3.8	6.4	1.7	0.9	37%	76%	39
		18	22	a/a	STL	8	9	27	0	141	122	69	13	65	125	4.41	1.33	21.7	235	4.2	8.0	1.9	0.8	29%	68%	72
Canning, Griffin	R	18	22	a/a	LAA	4	3	23	0	106	100	47	8	37	100	4.02	1.29	19.0	251	3.1	8.4	2.7	0.6	32%	69%	93
Carroll, Cody	R	17	25	aa	NYY	2	5	26	5	47	47	21	6	25	49	3.98	1.53	7.9	261	4.8	9.3	1.9	1.2	33%	78%	63
		18	26	aaa	BAL	4	0	37	9	47	40	20	0	25	45	3.74	1.37	5.3	230	4.7	8.5	1.8	0.0	31%	70%	98
Castellani, Ryan	R	17	21	aa	COL	9	12	27	0	157	207	127	24	52	106	7.29	1.65	26.1	319	3.0	6.1	2.0	1.4	35%	56%	28
		18	22	aa	COL	7	9	26	0	135	167	116	21	77	74	7.76	1.81	24.1	305	5.2	4.9	1.0	1.4	32%	57%	1
Castillo, Jesus	R	17	22	aa	LAA	0	2	5	0	24	32	11	2	6	20	4.07	1.63	21.1	327	2.3	7.5	3.2	0.9	39%	77%	75
		18	23	aa	LAA	9	5	21	0	99	114	68	8	31	52	6.20	1.47	20.2	291	2.8	4.7	1.7	0.7	32%	56%	38
Cease, Dylan	R	18	23	aa	CHW	3	0	10	0	53	37	14	4	25	68	2.33	1.16	21.1	198	4.2	11.5	2.8	0.7	29%	83%	122
Civale, Aaron	R	18	23	aa	CLE	5	7	21	0	107	141	63	15	23	66	5.27	1.53	22.2	318	1.9	5.5	2.9	1.3	35%	68%	47
Clarke, Taylor	R	16	23	aa	ARI	8	6	17	0	98	123	54	12	23	61	5.00	1.49	24.7	308	2.1	5.6	2.7	1.1	34%	68%	52
		17	24	a/a	ARI	12	9	27	0	145	143	65	17	52	114	4.03	1.35	22.4	259	3.3	7.1	2.2	1.1	30%	73%	60
		18	25	aaa	ARI	13	8	27	0	152	153	63	9	40	101	3.72	1.27	23.0	263	2.4	6.0	2.5	0.5	31%	71%	75
Clifton, Trevor	R	17	22	aa	CHC	5	8	21	0	100	132	75	9	48	76	6.73	1.80	22.1	319	4.3	6.8	1.6	0.8	37%	62%	40
		18	23	a/a	CHC	7	7	26	0	128	121	57	9	54	85	3.97	1.36	20.6	250	3.8	6.0	1.6	0.6	29%	71%	56
Clouse, Corbin	L	17	22	aa	ATL	3	4	16	1	22	26	10	2	15	24	4.02	1.84	6.4	294	6.0	9.6	1.6	1.0	38%	80%	59
		18	23	a/a	ATL	6	2	45	4	65	59	18	0	25	70	2.47	1.29	5.9	244	3.4	9.6	2.8	0.0	34%	79%	123
Conlon, PJ	L	17	24	aa	NYM	8	9	28	1	136	169	77	20	48	95	5.09	1.59	21.4	306	3.2	6.3	2.0	1.3	34%	71%	33
		18	25	aaa	NYM	4	9	23	0	114	152	78	17	37	69	6.12	1.66	22.2	321	2.9	5.4	1.9	1.3	35%	65%	23
Crowe, Wil	R	18	24	aa	WAS	0	5	5	0	27	37	23	5	16	12	7.53	1.97	26.0	325	5.5	4.1	0.7	1.5	33%	63%	-16
De La Cruz, Oscar	R	18	23	aa	CHC	6	7	16	0	78	90	57	9	33	62	6.56	1.57	21.5	289	3.8	7.1	1.9	1.1	34%	58%	47
De Los Santos, Enyel	R	17	22	aa	SD	10	6	26	0	150	159	86	14	49	117	5.16	1.39	24.3	273	3.0	7.0	2.4	0.8	32%	63%	67
		18	23	aaa	PHI	10	5	22	0	128	121	46	15	44	98	3.20	1.29	24.0	251	3.1	6.9	2.2	1.0	29%	80%	61
Deetz, Dean	R	17	24	a/a	HOU	7	6	25	0	85	80	43	8	47	84	4.56	1.50	14.6	251	5.0	8.9	1.8	0.8	32%	71%	70
		18	25	a/a	HOU	2	0	24	0	39	27	3	1	18	46	0.78	1.15	6.5	199	4.0	10.5	2.6	0.2	29%	95%	126
Diehl, Phillip	L	18	24	aa	NYY	0	1	14	1	28	22	5	3	12	25	1.74	1.21	8.1	219	3.8	7.8	2.0	0.9	26%	92%	73
Diplan, Marcos	R	18	22	aa	MIL	2	6	12	0	57	70	41	8	39	50	6.43	1.91	22.5	304	6.1	7.9	1.3	1.3	36%	68%	29
Dunn, Justin	R	18	23	aa	NYM	6	5	15	0	91	95	47	7	38	92	4.67	1.45	26.0	269	3.7	9.0	2.4	0.7	35%	68%	86
Dunning, Dane	R	18	24	aa	CHW	5	2	11	0	62	72	27	0	26	59	3.87	1.58	24.8	290	3.8	8.6	2.2	0.0	38%	73%	95
Dunshee, Parker	R	18	23	aa	OAK	7	4	12	0	82	66	21	5	13	67	2.25	0.97	26.0	222	1.5	7.4	5.0	0.5	27%	79%	144
Duplantier, Jon	R	18	24	aa	ARI	5	1	14	0	67	61	24	4	29	56	3.27	1.34	19.9	244	3.9	7.6	1.9	0.5	30%	76%	76
DuRapau, Montana	R	16	24	aa	PIT	3	3	50	22	49	51	25	6	19	41	4.52	1.42	4.2	267	3.5	7.4	2.1	1.1	31%	71%	56
		17	25	a/a	PIT	3	2	42	15	53	44	17	2	22	48	2.83	1.26	5.1	228	3.8	8.2	2.2	0.4	29%	78%	92
		18	26	a/a	PIT	1	2	19	2	32	34	23	7	11	29	6.42	1.40	7.1	274	3.0	8.2	2.7	1.9	31%	57%	51
Eckelman, Matt	R	18	25	aa	PIT	1	1	23	11	26	22	6	1	16	13	2.21	1.44	4.9	228	5.5	4.6	0.8	0.4	26%	86%	43
Elledge, Seth	R	18	22	aa	STL	3	1	13	4	18	14	8	3	5	17	4.14	1.06	5.4	212	2.7	8.4	3.1	1.3	24%	66%	88
Escobar, Luis	R	18	22	aa	PIT	4	0	7	0	37	34	22	4	21	21	5.26	1.48	22.9	246	5.1	5.1	1.0	0.9	26%	66%	27
Faedo, Alex	R	18	23	aa	DET	3	6	12	0	60	64	42	17	22	48	6.24	1.43	21.3	273	3.4	7.2	2.1	2.6	28%	65%	10
Fernandez, Junior	R	18	21	aa	STL	0	0	16	0	21	20	12	1	14	15	5.33	1.64	5.9	252	6.2	6.2	1.0	0.4	30%	66%	52
Ferrell, Riley	R	17	24	aa	HOU	2	2	36	4	52	61	28	2	14	48	4.78	1.44	6.2	292	2.5	8.3	3.4	0.4	37%	65%	105
		18	25	a/a	HOU	4	3	43	9	53	55	30	5	33	55	5.00	1.66	5.5	268	5.6	9.3	1.6	0.9	34%	71%	64
Festa, Matthew	R	18	25	aa	SEA	5	2	44	20	49	59	18	7	13	57	3.35	1.46	4.8	300	2.3	10.5	4.6	1.2	39%	82%	117
Flexen, Chris	R	17	23	aa	NYM	6	1	7	0	49	36	13	6	9	45	2.46	0.91	25.9	206	1.6	8.3	5.2	1.1	25%	80%	142
		18	24	aaa	NYM	6	7	18	0	92	110	41	9	29	67	4.03	1.51	22.1	299	2.8	6.5	2.3	0.9	34%	75%	57
Funkhouser, Kyle	R	18	24	a/a	DET	4	7	19	0	99	118	58	12	52	76	5.22	1.71	23.7	296	4.7	6.9	1.5	1.1	34%	71%	35
Gallen, Zac	R	17	22	a/a	STL	5	6	17	0	92	108	46	11	25	54	4.54	1.44	23.1	294	2.4	5.3	2.2	1.0	32%	71%	42
		18	23	aaa	MIA	8	9	25	0	134	165	61	13	48	117	4.08	1.59	23.6	304	3.2	7.9	2.5	0.9	37%	76%	66
Garcia, Bryan	R	17	22	a/a	DET	2	1	31	8	32	20	10	2	17	30	2.89	1.15	4.1	182	4.7	8.5	1.8	0.7	23%	77%	88
Garcia, Rico	R	18	24	aa	COL	6	2	11	0	67	70	25	12	23	48	3.38	1.38	25.6	269	3.1	6.4	2.1	1.6	29%	83%	36
Gatto, Joe	R	18	23	aa	LAA	3	4	16	0	78	100	62	9	36	42	7.13	1.74	22.3	313	4.2	4.9	1.2	1.1	34%	59%	14
Gohara, Luiz	L	17	21	a/a	ATL	4	3	19	0	87	86	36	7	37	99	3.75	1.41	19.4	259	3.8	10.2	2.7	0.7	35%	74%	101
		18	22	a/a	ATL	3	5	13	0	60	68	39	10	17	50	5.76	1.42	19.7	287	2.6	7.5	2.9	1.5	33%	62%	58
Gonsalves, Stephen	L	16	22	aa	MIN	8	1	13	0	74	49	18	1	36	74	2.19	1.14	22.7	190	4.3	8.9	2.1	0.1	26%	80%	110
		17	23	a/a	MIN	9	5	20	0	110	119	59	15	33	95	4.80	1.39	23.2	278	2.7	7.8	2.8	1.2	33%	68%	70
		18	24	a/a	MIN	12	3	23	0	122	94	50	10	69	97	3.67	1.33	22.0	213	5.1	7.1	1.4	0.7	25%	74%	62
Gonsolin, Tony	R	18	24	aa	LA	6	0	9	0	45	35	13	3	15	41	2.58	1.10	19.7	217	2.9	8.3	2.8	0.6	27%	79%	103
Gonzalez, Luis	L	18	26	a/a	BAL	2	3	42	9	72	73	32	6	28	66	4.05	1.40	7.3	263	3.5	8.2	2.3	0.8	32%	72%	76
Gonzalez, Merandy	R	18	23	aa	MIA	3	6	14	0	73	77	41	7	33	41	5.04	1.51	22.6	272	4.1	5.0	1.2	0.8	30%	67%	31
Green, Nick	R	18	23	aa	NYY	1	2	3	0	18	15	9	3	7	8	4.64	1.22	24.4	222	3.7	3.9	1.0	1.4	21%	66%	14
Greene, Conner	R	15	20	aa	TOR	3	1	5	0	25	28	16	1	12	14	5.78	1.61	22.2	287	4.3	5.0	1.2	0.4	32%	62%	39
		16	21	aa	TOR	6	5	12	0	69	66	40	6	34	43	5.31	1.45	24.5	255	4.4	5.7	1.3	0.8	28%	63%	40
		17	22	aa	TOR	5	10	26	0	133	166	101	9	86	80	6.84	1.90	24.1	308	5.8	5.4	0.9	0.6	35%	62%	28
		18	23	a/a	STL	4	5	40	0	90	83	43	3	59	57	4.33	1.57	9.9	246	5.9	5.7	1.0	0.3	29%	71%	52
Gutierrez, Vladimir	R	18	23	aa	CIN	9	10	27	0	147	167	94	24	41	126	5.78	1.41	23.1	287	2.5	7.7	3.1	1.4	33%	61%	66

PITCHER	Th	Yr	Age	LvL	Org	W	L	G	Sv	IP	H	ER	HR	BB	K	ERA	WHIP	BF/G	OBA	bb/9	k/9	Cmd	hr/9	H%	S%	BPV
Hamilton, Ian	R	17	22	aa	CHW	1	3	14	1	19	32	15	0	9	20	7.18	2.15	6.7	372	4.3	9.4	2.2	0.0	48%	63%	82
		18	23	a/a	CHW	3	2	43	22	53	45	13	3	17	54	2.18	1.18	4.9	232	2.9	9.1	3.1	0.4	31%	83%	116
Hanhold, Eric	R	18	25	a/a	NYM	5	3	31	8	45	50	24	2	16	43	4.78	1.47	6.2	283	3.2	8.7	2.7	0.4	37%	66%	97
Hansen, Alec	R	18	24	aa	CHW	0	4	9	0	37	38	36	4	48	30	8.81	2.30	21.2	264	11.6	7.2	0.6	1.0	31%	60%	29
Hartman, Ryan	L	18	24	aa	HOU	11	4	25	0	122	125	47	14	27	120	3.43	1.25	19.9	267	2.0	8.8	4.5	1.0	33%	76%	118
Harvey, Hunter	R	18	24	aa	BAL	1	2	9	0	33	41	23	3	9	24	6.31	1.51	15.9	306	2.4	6.6	2.7	0.9	35%	58%	61
Hatch, Thomas	R	18	24	aa	CHC	8	6	26	0	145	153	79	19	67	97	4.89	1.51	24.2	272	4.1	6.0	1.4	1.2	30%	70%	32
Hearn, Taylor	L	18	24	aa	TEX	4	8	24	0	129	128	67	14	53	113	4.67	1.40	22.7	260	3.7	7.9	2.1	1.0	31%	68%	66
Helsley, Ryan	R	17	23	a/a	STL	3	1	7	0	39	37	15	4	18	37	3.48	1.44	23.5	256	4.3	8.7	2.0	0.9	32%	79%	69
		18	24	a/a	STL	5	3	12	0	69	54	34	7	28	63	4.47	1.17	23.0	215	3.6	8.2	2.3	0.9	26%	63%	83
Herget, Jimmy	R	17	24	a/a	CIN	4	4	52	25	62	66	29	7	24	62	4.18	1.46	5.1	274	3.5	9.0	2.6	1.0	34%	74%	77
		18	25	a/a	CIN	3	3	50	0	61	72	30	7	23	54	4.42	1.56	5.4	295	3.4	8.0	2.4	1.0	36%	73%	65
Hernandez, Carlos	L	15	28	a/a	COL	3	1	8	0	41	72	33	12	8	18	7.30	1.97	24.3	385	1.8	3.9	2.1	2.8	38%	70%	-37
		16	29	a/a	COL	6	11	28	0	130	267	113	17	24	64	7.79	2.23	23.5	421	1.6	4.4	2.7	1.1	45%	65%	19
Hernandez, Jonathan	R	18	22	aa	TEX	4	4	12	0	64	68	45	7	39	48	6.33	1.68	24.0	275	5.5	6.7	1.2	1.0	32%	62%	35
Holmes, Clay	R	16	23	aa	PIT	10	9	26	0	136	160	78	10	63	82	5.13	1.64	23.4	293	4.2	5.4	1.3	0.7	33%	68%	36
		17	24	aaa	PIT	10	5	25	0	113	118	57	5	64	79	4.54	1.62	20.0	271	5.1	6.3	1.2	0.4	32%	71%	53
		18	25	aaa	PIT	8	3	22	0	96	111	44	4	41	79	4.10	1.59	19.2	291	3.9	7.4	1.9	0.4	36%	73%	69
Holmes, Grant	R	17	21	aa	OAK	11	12	29	0	148	163	83	14	57	126	5.05	1.49	22.0	281	3.5	7.6	2.2	0.8	34%	66%	65
Honeywell, Brent	R	16	21	aa	TAM	3	2	10	0	59	57	17	4	14	48	2.62	1.18	23.7	253	2.1	7.2	3.5	0.6	30%	80%	103
		17	22	a/a	TAM	13	9	26	0	137	156	67	13	36	154	4.40	1.41	22.2	288	2.4	10.2	4.2	0.9	38%	70%	121
Houser, Adrian	R	15	22	aa	MIL	5	3	14	0	70	88	48	15	23	48	6.14	1.57	22.1	306	3.0	6.2	2.1	1.9	33%	65%	18
		16	23	aa	MIL	3	7	13	0	70	96	59	7	25	47	7.59	1.72	24.5	326	3.2	6.1	1.9	0.9	37%	54%	41
		18	25	a/a	MIL	2	4	21	0	80	114	54	11	26	55	6.05	1.74	17.4	335	2.9	6.2	2.1	1.2	38%	67%	33
Houston, Zac	R	18	24	a/a	DET	1	2	46	10	56	34	13	4	27	64	2.15	1.09	4.8	178	4.3	10.2	2.4	0.6	24%	83%	113
Howard, Brian	R	18	23	aa	OAK	4	4	12	0	68	73	30	7	22	52	3.93	1.40	23.9	275	2.9	6.9	2.4	0.9	32%	74%	64
Howard, Sam	L	16	23	aa	COL	5	6	16	0	90	148	62	17	32	52	6.20	1.99	27.1	367	3.2	5.1	1.6	1.7	39%	72%	-4
		17	24	aa	COL	5	8	24	0	127	145	68	16	48	79	4.84	1.51	23.0	287	3.4	5.6	1.6	1.1	31%	70%	32
		18	25	aaa	COL	3	8	21	0	96	124	64	15	35	61	6.02	1.66	20.5	314	3.3	5.7	1.7	1.4	34%	66%	20
Hudson, Dakota	R	17	23	a/a	STL	10	5	25	0	153	172	64	8	50	78	3.75	1.45	26.1	286	2.9	4.6	1.6	0.4	32%	74%	45
		18	24	aaa	STL	13	3	19	0	113	120	35	1	37	71	2.77	1.39	25.1	274	2.9	5.6	1.9	0.1	32%	78%	72
Irvin, Cole	L	17	23	aa	PHI	5	3	13	0	84	83	46	14	24	58	4.92	1.27	26.6	259	2.6	6.2	2.4	1.5	28%	66%	45
		18	24	aaa	PHI	14	4	26	0	162	161	58	14	37	114	3.21	1.22	25.2	260	2.0	6.3	3.1	0.8	30%	76%	83
James, Josh	R	17	24	aa	HOU	4	8	21	3	76	94	46	1	33	63	5.51	1.66	16.2	305	3.9	7.4	1.9	0.1	38%	64%	75
		18	25	a/a	HOU	6	4	23	1	117	90	47	10	48	140	3.58	1.18	20.4	214	3.7	10.7	2.9	0.7	30%	71%	115
Jay, Tyler	L	18	24	aa	MIN	4	5	38	2	61	88	35	8	20	39	5.15	1.77	7.4	337	3.0	5.8	1.9	1.2	37%	73%	27
Jewell, Jake	R	17	24	aa	LAA	7	8	24	0	125	170	93	17	44	70	6.73	1.72	23.6	326	3.2	5.0	1.6	1.2	35%	61%	16
		18	25	a/a	LAA	3	4	26	5	38	43	14	3	18	29	3.38	1.60	6.5	285	4.3	6.9	1.6	0.7	34%	81%	51
Jones, Connor	R	18	24	a/a	STL	6	5	26	0	112	129	57	5	62	67	4.53	1.71	19.6	290	5.0	5.3	1.1	0.4	33%	72%	40
Keller, Mitch	R	17	21	aa	PIT	2	2	6	0	35	29	16	2	11	38	4.05	1.18	23.1	232	3.0	9.8	3.3	0.6	31%	65%	119
		18	22	a/a	PIT	12	4	24	0	139	138	63	10	53	111	4.10	1.38	24.3	261	3.4	7.2	2.1	0.7	31%	71%	70
Kent, Matt	L	18	26	a/a	BOS	11	8	28	0	150	194	87	16	39	99	5.19	1.55	23.5	314	2.4	6.0	2.5	1.0	35%	67%	52
Kilome, Franklyn	R	17	22	aa	PHI	1	3	5	0	30	28	14	2	15	18	4.33	1.46	25.4	253	4.5	5.4	1.2	0.7	28%	71%	41
		18	23	aa	NYM	4	9	26	0	140	141	73	10	62	109	4.71	1.45	23.0	264	4.0	7.0	1.8	0.6	31%	67%	62
King, Michael	R	18	23	aa	NYY	10	2	18	0	121	102	31	10	20	92	2.33	1.01	25.7	230	1.5	6.9	4.6	0.7	27%	81%	125
Kline, Branden	R	15	24	aa	BAL	3	3	8	0	39	43	22	5	21	22	4.93	1.62	21.8	280	4.7	5.1	1.1	1.2	30%	72%	15
		18	27	aa	BAL	4	4	32	15	45	39	11	4	16	36	2.23	1.22	5.7	235	3.2	7.2	2.3	0.7	28%	85%	77
Kopech, Michael	R	17	21	a/a	CHW	9	8	25	0	134	106	53	7	70	156	3.57	1.31	22.2	218	4.7	10.5	2.2	0.5	31%	73%	107
		18	22	aaa	CHW	7	7	24	0	127	115	62	11	62	151	4.39	1.39	22.3	242	4.4	10.7	2.4	0.7	33%	69%	100
Kremer, Dean	R	18	22	aa	BAL	5	2	9	0	53	45	14	3	19	54	2.46	1.21	23.8	231	3.3	9.1	2.8	0.6	30%	82%	105
Lakins, Travis	R	17	23	aa	BOS	0	4	8	0	30	41	27	2	22	16	8.13	2.08	18.6	323	6.6	4.6	0.7	0.7	35%	59%	13
		18	24	a/a	BOS	3	2	36	3	55	47	19	4	19	46	3.11	1.20	6.1	232	3.1	7.5	2.4	0.6	28%	75%	87
Lambert, Jimmy	R	18	24	aa	CHW	3	1	5	0	25	25	11	3	7	26	4.04	1.28	20.5	263	2.5	9.2	3.7	1.0	33%	71%	107
Lambert, Peter	R	18	21	a/a	COL	10	7	26	0	150	175	67	14	28	87	4.01	1.35	24.1	292	1.7	5.2	3.1	0.8	32%	72%	69
Littrell, Zack	R	17	22	aa	MIN	10	0	14	0	86	86	32	5	27	70	3.38	1.32	25.3	262	2.8	7.3	2.6	0.5	32%	75%	85
		18	23	a/a	MIN	6	9	24	0	129	154	75	10	49	107	5.25	1.57	23.6	298	3.4	7.4	2.2	0.7	36%	66%	66
Loaisiga, Jonathan	R	18	24	aa	NYY	3	1	9	0	35	46	20	9	7	34	5.23	1.49	16.8	316	1.7	8.7	5.2	2.2	36%	73%	86
Lopez, Yoan	R	15	22	aa	ARI	1	6	10	0	48	54	32	5	24	28	6.04	1.63	21.4	286	4.5	5.2	1.1	0.9	31%	63%	25
		16	23	aa	ARI	4	7	14	0	62	83	53	13	34	30	7.68	1.89	20.9	322	5.0	4.4	0.9	1.9	33%	62%	-20
		18	25	aa	ARI	2	6	45	12	63	45	25	4	27	70	3.54	1.15	5.6	203	3.9	9.9	2.5	0.6	28%	70%	110
Lovelady, Richard	L	17	22	aa	KC	3	2	21	3	33	34	11	1	13	30	2.93	1.42	6.7	265	3.6	8.1	2.2	0.3	34%	79%	89
		18	23	aaa	KC	3	4	46	9	73	62	25	3	21	58	3.03	1.13	6.3	230	2.6	7.2	2.8	0.4	28%	73%	99
Luzardo, Jesus	L	18	21	a/a	OAK	8	4	20	0	96	91	37	7	23	89	3.47	1.19	19.3	251	2.2	8.3	3.8	0.6	32%	72%	116
Maples, Dillon	R	17	25	a/a	CHC	2	3	31	10	32	28	11	1	24	46	3.16	1.60	4.6	234	6.7	13.0	2.0	0.3	38%	80%	118
		18	26	aaa	CHC	2	3	41	10	40	26	14	1	42	60	3.16	1.68	4.4	185	9.3	13.3	1.4	0.2	32%	80%	121

PITCHER	Th	Yr	Age	LvL	Org	W	L	G	Sv	IP	H	ER	HR	BB	K	ERA	WHIP	BF/G	OBA	bb/9	k/9	Cmd	hr/9	H%	S%	BPV
Martin, Corbin	R	18	23	aa	HOU	7	2	21	0	103	99	43	8	28	82	3.76	1.24	19.9	254	2.5	7.2	2.9	0.7	30%	71%	86
May, Dustin	R	18	21	aa	LA	2	2	6	0	35	28	14	0	10	25	3.67	1.10	22.9	222	2.7	6.4	2.4	0.0	28%	63%	99
McCreery, Adam	L	18	25	a/a	ATL	4	10	84	4	112	126	58	2	76	114	4.67	1.79	6.2	284	6.1	9.1	1.5	0.2	38%	72%	79
McKay, David	R	18	23	a/a	SEA	5	1	36	1	53	40	16	3	21	63	2.70	1.15	5.9	212	3.5	10.7	3.0	0.5	30%	78%	124
McKenzie, Triston	R	18	21	aa	CLE	7	4	16	0	92	75	36	10	30	76	3.49	1.13	22.8	224	2.9	7.4	2.6	1.0	26%	73%	80
McRae, Alex	R	16	23	aa	PIT	8	6	16	0	88	132	57	7	25	54	5.82	1.77	25.4	346	2.5	5.5	2.2	0.7	39%	67%	44
		17	24	aa	PIT	10	5	27	0	150	211	82	11	39	71	4.94	1.67	24.9	333	2.4	4.3	1.8	0.6	36%	70%	33
		18	25	aaa	PIT	3	10	26	1	117	158	75	10	52	82	5.80	1.80	20.8	324	4.0	6.3	1.6	0.7	37%	67%	39
McWilliams, Sam	R	18	23	aa	TAM	6	7	19	0	101	128	68	14	40	84	6.02	1.67	23.9	310	3.6	7.4	2.1	1.2	36%	65%	44
Medeiros, Kodi	L	18	22	aa	CHW	7	7	27	0	139	146	74	17	73	125	4.79	1.58	22.7	271	4.8	8.1	1.7	1.1	32%	72%	52
Mekkes, Dakota	R	18	24	a/a	CHC	4	0	41	11	55	42	8	2	31	59	1.37	1.31	5.6	212	5.0	9.6	1.9	0.4	29%	91%	100
Mella, Keury	R	17	24	aa	CIN	4	10	27	1	134	184	106	23	53	94	7.09	1.77	22.8	327	3.5	6.3	1.8	1.6	36%	61%	18
		18	25	a/a	CIN	9	4	21	0	108	111	48	12	41	84	4.01	1.41	21.8	268	3.4	7.0	2.1	1.0	31%	74%	57
Mendez, Yohander	L	16	21	a/a	TEX	8	2	17	0	78	58	22	2	31	58	2.55	1.15	18.2	210	3.6	6.7	1.9	0.3	26%	77%	85
		17	22	a/a	TEX	7	8	24	0	138	138	79	29	47	104	5.17	1.34	23.9	263	3.0	6.8	2.2	1.9	28%	68%	33
		18	23	a/a	TEX	1	8	18	0	92	116	66	23	37	67	6.46	1.66	22.9	309	3.6	6.6	1.8	2.2	33%	67%	4
Mills, McKenzie	L	18	23	aa	MIA	0	3	4	0	18	25	18	3	4	7	8.64	1.59	20.1	327	2.0	3.4	1.7	1.5	33%	44%	2
Molina, Marcos	R	17	22	aa	NYM	3	7	13	0	78	96	49	7	25	58	5.68	1.56	26.3	304	2.9	6.7	2.3	0.8	35%	63%	58
		18	23	aa	NYM	1	10	16	0	83	118	63	13	32	56	6.80	1.81	24.1	335	3.5	6.0	1.7	1.4	37%	64%	17
Moreno, Gerson	R	17	22	aa	DET	0	3	20	0	28	26	24	4	17	30	7.84	1.56	6.1	250	5.5	9.7	1.7	1.4	31%	49%	57
		18	23	aa	DET	0	1	14	1	17	20	13	2	14	17	6.67	2.02	5.9	295	7.6	9.0	1.2	1.2	36%	68%	39
Muller, Kyle	L	18	21	aa	ATL	4	1	5	0	29	26	13	4	6	23	4.06	1.10	22.7	241	1.8	7.2	4.0	1.1	28%	67%	100
Munoz, Andres	R	18	19	aa	SD	2	1	20	7	19	12	2	0	10	18	1.06	1.17	3.8	181	4.9	8.3	1.7	0.0	25%	90%	105
Naile, James	R	16	23	a/a	OAK	2	2	5	0	28	36	20	2	8	12	6.36	1.58	24.7	314	2.6	4.0	1.5	0.7	34%	58%	28
		17	24	aa	OAK	2	3	14	0	62	63	26	5	17	33	3.80	1.30	18.2	267	2.5	4.9	2.0	0.7	29%	72%	51
		18	25	a/a	OAK	8	10	26	0	152	204	92	13	42	67	5.43	1.62	26.0	322	2.5	4.0	1.6	0.8	34%	66%	24
Neidert, Nick	R	17	21	aa	SEA	1	3	6	0	23	37	20	4	5	12	7.70	1.79	17.9	360	1.9	4.5	2.4	1.7	38%	58%	11
		18	22	aa	MIA	12	7	26	0	154	158	63	16	31	136	3.67	1.22	24.0	266	1.8	7.9	4.4	1.0	32%	73%	113
Nix, Jacob	R	17	21	aa	SD	1	2	6	0	28	38	23	0	9	19	7.47	1.72	20.9	330	3.0	6.1	2.0	0.0	39%	52%	69
		18	22	aa	SD	3	3	10	0	60	47	13	8	8	39	1.89	0.92	22.5	216	1.3	5.8	4.6	0.4	25%	81%	131
Norwood, James	R	17	24	aa	CHC	1	4	14	1	19	27	15	1	10	16	7.14	1.98	6.4	340	4.8	7.7	1.6	0.6	41%	62%	50
		18	25	a/a	CHC	2	3	40	2	53	43	17	3	26	46	2.90	1.29	5.5	221	4.4	7.8	1.8	0.6	27%	79%	78
Oaks, Trevor	R	16	23	a/a	LA	13	2	20	0	126	139	44	9	17	74	3.16	1.24	25.6	282	1.2	5.3	4.4	0.7	32%	76%	102
		17	24	aaa	LA	4	3	15	0	84	99	39	5	16	61	4.16	1.37	23.5	294	1.8	6.5	3.7	0.6	35%	69%	96
		18	25	aaa	KC	8	8	22	0	129	158	59	5	46	55	4.11	1.58	25.8	302	3.2	3.8	1.2	0.4	33%	73%	32
Ortiz, Luis	R	16	21	aa	MIL	3	6	15	1	63	89	32	6	19	44	4.61	1.71	19.0	335	2.7	6.2	2.3	0.9	38%	75%	47
		17	22	aa	MIL	4	7	22	0	94	100	63	19	41	70	6.01	1.50	18.5	274	3.9	6.6	1.7	1.8	29%	64%	21
		18	23	a/a	BAL	5	5	22	2	101	112	50	13	26	71	4.44	1.37	19.3	282	2.3	6.3	2.7	1.2	32%	71%	57
Paddack, Chris	R	18	22	aa	SD	3	2	7	0	39	26	9	1	4	33	2.16	0.76	20.1	190	0.9	7.5	8.3	0.2	24%	71%	228
Pannone, Thomas	L	17	23	aa	TOR	7	3	20	0	117	118	50	18	31	94	3.85	1.27	23.9	263	2.4	7.2	3.1	1.4	30%	75%	70
		18	24	a/a	TOR	0	3	8	0	47	60	31	11	13	43	5.82	1.54	25.7	310	2.4	8.1	3.3	2.1	35%	68%	49
Paulino, David	R	18	24	aaa	HOU	0	0	4	0	18	17	11	3	5	19	5.39	1.18	18.0	249	2.3	9.6	4.3	1.4	31%	57%	111
Pelham, CD	L	18	23	aa	TEX	2	0	24	2	19	24	17	1	14	16	8.08	2.02	3.8	310	6.8	7.4	1.1	0.6	38%	57%	43
Pena, Luis	R	17	22	aa	LAA	1	3	4	0	20	19	9	4	9	17	4.21	1.42	21.2	254	4.2	7.7	1.8	1.6	29%	77%	41
		18	23	a/a	LAA	6	7	23	0	107	100	60	15	52	87	5.03	1.42	19.8	249	4.4	7.3	1.7	1.2	28%	67%	48
Perez, Cionel	L	18	22	a/a	HOU	7	1	20	1	75	63	18	3	26	78	2.18	1.19	15.1	230	3.1	9.3	3.0	0.4	31%	82%	117
Perez, Hector	R	18	22	aa	TOR	0	2	10	0	43	35	21	1	24	43	4.43	1.37	18.1	223	5.1	8.9	1.8	0.2	30%	65%	94
Poche, Colin	L	18	24	a/a	TAM	6	2	66	39	7	2	20	96	1.02	0.89	6.1	173	2.7	13.1	4.9	0.3	29%	91%	192
Ponce, Cody	R	17	23	aa	MIL	2	1	3	0	18	13	5	0	6	8	2.34	1.06	22.8	207	2.9	4.0	1.4	0.0	24%	75%	66
		18	24	aa	MIL	7	6	29	0	95	113	67	15	38	74	6.37	1.59	14.4	296	3.6	7.1	2.0	1.4	34%	61%	37
Poncedeleon, Daniel	R	16	24	aa	STL	9	8	27	0	151	151	73	11	59	106	4.35	1.39	23.5	262	3.5	6.3	1.8	0.6	30%	69%	59
		17	25	aaa	STL	2	0	6	0	29	24	9	2	14	19	2.74	1.30	19.9	227	4.2	6.0	1.4	0.7	26%	81%	56
		18	26	aaa	STL	9	4	19	0	97	81	28	4	50	86	2.61	1.35	21.3	228	4.7	7.9	1.7	0.4	29%	81%	81
Pop, Zach	R	18	22	aa	BAL	1	1	14	1	22	15	7	0	6	14	2.72	0.95	6.0	198	2.3	5.8	2.5	0.0	24%	68%	102
Povse, Max	R	16	23	aa	ATL	4	1	11	0	71	77	33	5	13	43	4.20	1.27	26.3	278	1.7	5.4	3.2	0.6	31%	67%	80
		17	24	a/a	SEA	4	6	22	0	71	87	49	4	26	53	6.27	1.60	14.2	304	3.3	6.7	2.0	0.6	36%	59%	59
		18	25	a/a	SEA	5	9	18	0	100	119	70	9	49	90	6.28	1.67	25.0	296	4.3	8.0	1.8	0.8	36%	61%	59
Poyner, Bobby	L	17	25	aa	BOS	0	1	27	9	38	24	5	2	12	41	1.28	0.94	5.3	180	2.9	9.6	3.4	0.6	24%	91%	131
		18	26	a/a	BOS	0	0	34	6	44	57	21	5	12	28	4.36	1.56	5.7	314	2.5	5.7	2.3	1.0	35%	74%	44
Puk, A.J.	L	17	22	aa	OAK	2	5	13	0	64	71	35	2	24	71	4.95	1.48	21.2	282	3.3	10.0	3.0	0.3	39%	64%	114
Quantrill, Cal	R	17	22	aa	SD	1	5	8	0	42	63	26	6	16	29	5.51	1.88	24.9	346	3.5	6.1	1.7	1.3	39%	73%	22
		18	23	a/a	SD	9	6	28	0	148	189	85	15	41	106	5.16	1.55	23.1	312	2.5	6.5	2.6	0.9	36%	68%	59
Rainey, Tanner	R	17	25	aa	CIN	1	1	14	4	17	11	5	3	14	23	2.68	1.47	5.2	188	7.3	12.1	1.7	1.8	24%	92%	71
		18	26	aaa	CIN	7	2	44	3	51	31	20	3	39	53	3.54	1.38	4.9	179	6.9	9.4	1.4	0.5	24%	74%	90

PITCHER	Th	Yr	Age	LvL	Org	W	L	G	Sv	IP	H	ER	HR	BB	K	ERA	WHIP	BF/G	OBA	bb/9	k/9	Cmd	hr/9	H%	S%	BPV
Ramirez, Carlos	R	17	26	a/a	TOR	3	0	25	3	38	21	0	0	12	36	0.00	0.87	5.6	166	2.8	8.6	3.1	0.0	23%	100%	139
		18	27	aaa	OAK	2	3	33	2	49	37	24	3	27	37	4.46	1.30	6.1	212	4.9	6.9	1.4	0.6	25%	65%	66
Reed, Cody	L	15	22	aa	CIN	8	4	13	0	78	76	29	6	25	72	3.32	1.28	24.7	255	2.9	8.2	2.9	0.6	32%	75%	95
		16	23	aaa	CIN	6	4	13	0	73	88	35	8	22	58	4.27	1.51	24.3	299	2.7	7.2	2.6	1.0	35%	74%	62
		17	24	aaa	CIN	4	9	21	0	106	126	54	9	66	88	4.54	1.80	23.4	295	5.6	7.4	1.3	0.8	36%	76%	46
		18	25	aaa	CIN	4	8	18	0	107	134	60	17	34	88	5.05	1.56	26.1	306	2.8	7.4	2.6	1.4	35%	71%	50
Reid-Foley, Sean	R	17	22	aa	TOR	10	11	27	0	133	171	96	27	55	106	6.49	1.70	22.2	314	3.7	7.2	1.9	1.8	35%	66%	21
		18	23	a/a	TOR	12	5	24	0	131	123	61	9	52	126	4.20	1.34	22.7	250	3.6	8.6	2.4	0.6	32%	69%	88
Reyes, Alex	R	16	22	aaa	STL	2	3	14	0	65	68	39	6	31	84	5.33	1.51	20.2	269	4.2	11.6	2.7	0.8	38%	64%	105
		18	24	a/a	STL	2	0	2	0	16	2	0	0	4	21	0.00	0.37	25.9	047	2.1	11.7	5.5	0.0	8%	100%	232
Reyes, Denyi	L	16	23	aa	BOS	5	4	13	0	65	86	44	7	29	47	6.06	1.76	23.0	318	4.0	6.5	1.6	0.9	37%	66%	38
		17	24	a/a	BOS	11	8	26	0	145	153	76	16	62	125	4.69	1.48	24.0	272	3.8	7.7	2.0	1.0	33%	70%	60
		18	25	aaa	BOS	5	5	16	0	88	92	42	13	28	92	4.28	1.36	23.0	270	2.8	9.4	3.3	1.3	33%	73%	87
Reyes, Luis	R	18	24	aa	WAS	5	6	12	0	65	80	47	10	33	30	6.45	1.73	24.7	303	4.6	4.1	0.9	1.4	31%	65%	-5
Rhame, Jacob	R	15	22	aa	LA	3	3	39	2	50	39	21	6	18	50	3.74	1.14	5.1	217	3.3	9.0	2.8	1.1	27%	71%	92
		16	23	aaa	LA	1	7	54	7	63	60	27	6	25	60	3.81	1.35	4.9	252	3.6	8.5	2.4	0.8	32%	74%	82
		17	24	aaa	NYM	0	3	45	2	54	59	25	6	10	58	4.23	1.28	4.9	279	1.7	9.7	5.5	1.0	36%	70%	143
		18	25	aaa	NYM	1	2	25	11	33	23	10	3	8	34	2.79	0.92	4.9	196	2.0	9.3	4.5	0.9	25%	74%	140
Romano, Jordan	R	18	25	a/a	TOR	12	8	26	0	143	157	88	19	49	103	5.55	1.44	23.5	280	3.1	6.5	2.1	1.2	32%	63%	47
Romero, JoJo	L	18	22	aa	PHI	7	6	18	0	108	106	50	15	40	91	4.14	1.35	25.0	258	3.3	7.5	2.3	1.2	30%	73%	61
Rucker, Michael	R	18	24	aa	CHC	9	6	26	0	134	134	71	20	42	98	4.77	1.31	21.3	261	2.8	6.6	2.3	1.3	29%	67%	51
Ruiz, Jose	R	18	24	aa	CHW	3	1	33	14	46	41	22	3	22	47	4.38	1.37	5.9	242	4.2	9.2	2.2	0.5	32%	67%	91
Rumbelow, Nick	R	15	24	aaa	NYY	2	3	37	8	53	58	34	5	14	48	5.73	1.37	6.0	280	2.4	8.2	3.4	0.9	34%	58%	91
		17	26	a/a	NYY	5	1	25	6	40	28	7	0	13	36	1.65	1.00	6.2	196	2.8	8.1	2.9	0.0	26%	82%	125
		18	27	a/a	SEA	1	0	15	2	21	18	5	1	9	21	2.11	1.27	5.8	234	3.7	9.0	2.5	0.5	31%	85%	99
Sadzeck, Connor	R	15	24	aa	TEX	1	1	7	0	20	26	25	1	17	13	11.55	2.19	14.1	316	8.0	6.0	0.8	0.5	37%	42%	29
		16	25	aa	TEX	10	8	25	0	141	159	89	22	59	106	5.67	1.55	24.6	286	3.8	6.8	1.8	1.4	32%	66%	34
		17	26	aa	TEX	4	8	38	0	94	137	96	18	46	86	9.26	1.95	11.8	342	4.4	8.2	1.9	1.7	40%	52%	24
		18	27	aaa	TEX	5	3	32	0	38	46	23	3	19	32	5.41	1.69	5.4	299	4.4	7.7	1.7	0.6	37%	67%	60
Sanchez, Ricardo	L	18	21	aa	ATL	2	5	13	0	59	77	34	4	24	38	5.17	1.70	20.6	315	3.6	5.8	1.6	0.5	36%	69%	44
Sandoval, Patrick	L	18	22	aa	LAA	1	0	4	0	21	14	4	0	8	24	1.58	1.02	20.4	188	3.3	10.1	3.0	0.0	28%	83%	141
Santana, Dennis	R	17	21	aa	LA	3	1	7	0	33	35	23	2	20	33	6.25	1.70	21.1	277	5.6	9.1	1.6	0.6	36%	62%	70
		18	22	a/a	LA	1	3	10	0	51	38	15	3	14	57	2.59	1.03	19.7	210	2.5	10.1	4.0	0.5	29%	76%	143
Santillan, Tony	R	18	21	aa	CIN	4	3	11	0	63	76	32	10	17	55	4.54	1.46	24.6	299	2.4	7.8	3.3	1.4	35%	74%	68
Sborz, Josh	R	16	23	aa	LA	0	1	10	1	17	20	9	2	6	15	4.93	1.57	7.3	302	3.1	7.8	2.5	1.3	36%	72%	54
		17	24	aa	LA	8	8	24	0	117	123	60	9	52	68	4.61	1.50	21.0	272	4.0	5.3	1.3	0.7	30%	69%	39
		18	25	a/a	LA	4	2	46	6	54	56	26	1	19	59	4.29	1.38	4.9	267	3.1	9.8	3.1	0.2	37%	66%	121
Schreiber, John	R	18	24	aa	DET	3	7	49	18	58	57	21	2	20	47	3.20	1.32	4.9	257	3.1	7.3	2.4	0.4	32%	75%	86
Seabold, Connor	R	18	22	aa	PHI	1	4	11	0	60	60	35	11	18	58	5.29	1.30	22.6	261	2.7	8.7	3.2	1.7	30%	64%	71
Sheffield, Justus	L	17	21	aa	NYY	7	6	17	0	93	115	46	21	35	73	4.43	1.61	24.3	303	3.4	7.0	2.1	2.0	33%	81%	20
		18	22	a/a	NYY	7	6	25	0	116	96	41	5	52	108	3.18	1.28	19.0	227	4.0	8.4	2.1	0.4	29%	75%	91
Shepherd, Chandler	R	16	24	a/a	BOS	2	3	40	7	64	54	29	7	20	51	4.07	1.15	6.4	229	2.8	7.2	2.6	1.0	26%	67%	76
		17	25	aaa	BOS	1	5	34	2	60	79	42	7	21	54	6.38	1.68	7.9	320	3.2	8.1	2.5	1.0	39%	62%	61
		18	26	aaa	BOS	7	10	25	0	131	190	86	17	39	82	5.87	1.74	24.0	339	2.7	5.7	2.1	1.2	38%	68%	30
Sherfy, Jimmie	R	14	23	aa	ARI	3	1	37	1	38	40	26	5	18	38	6.16	1.52	4.5	270	4.3	8.9	2.1	1.1	34%	60%	65
		15	24	aa	ARI	1	6	44	2	50	61	48	4	29	41	8.75	1.83	5.2	305	5.3	7.5	1.4	0.7	37%	49%	47
		16	25	aa	ARI	3	4	40	22	43	31	21	7	19	47	4.50	1.16	4.3	205	3.9	9.9	2.5	1.5	25%	66%	82
		17	26	aaa	ARI	1	1	44	20	49	42	19	6	10	48	3.45	1.06	4.3	234	1.8	8.9	4.9	1.2	29%	73%	130
		18	27	aaa	ARI	5	1	38	15	45	33	8	1	19	45	1.54	1.16	4.7	208	3.8	9.0	2.4	0.2	28%	87%	113
Shore, Logan	R	18	24	aa	OAK	1	6	13	0	70	97	49	7	19	40	6.29	1.65	24.2	330	2.4	5.1	2.1	0.9	36%	61%	38
Smith, Drew	R	17	24	a/a	NYM	3	2	15	0	20	12	4	1	6	15	1.71	0.89	4.9	176	2.6	6.8	2.6	0.5	21%	84%	100
		18	25	a/a	NYM	5	1	25	3	39	31	11	3	13	30	2.62	1.11	6.2	216	3.0	6.9	2.3	0.6	26%	79%	83
Sobotka, Chad	R	17	24	aa	ATL	3	1	18	0	31	37	28	1	22	20	8.07	1.92	8.2	298	6.5	5.8	0.9	0.4	35%	54%	38
		18	25	a/a	ATL	2	3	31	9	38	26	11	1	23	39	2.51	1.27	5.0	194	5.3	9.3	1.7	0.3	27%	80%	100
Sopko, Andrew	R	16	22	aa	LA	2	2	6	0	31	41	22	5	10	22	6.31	1.66	23.2	320	3.0	6.3	2.1	1.4	36%	64%	31
		17	23	aa	LA	5	7	23	0	105	118	56	12	41	64	4.83	1.52	19.8	286	3.5	5.5	1.6	1.0	31%	70%	32
		18	24	aa	LA	3	1	14	0	54	73	25	9	12	41	4.12	1.56	16.9	322	2.0	6.8	3.4	1.5	36%	79%	58
Soroka, Mike	R	17	20	aa	ATL	11	8	26	0	154	159	64	11	37	117	3.75	1.28	24.2	268	2.2	6.8	3.1	0.7	32%	72%	88
		18	21	aaa	ATL	2	1	5	0	27	22	7	0	6	27	2.34	1.03	20.8	227	1.9	8.9	4.8	0.0	31%	75%	164
Staumont, Josh	R	16	23	aa	KC	2	1	11	0	50	51	23	2	38	60	4.05	1.77	21.0	264	6.9	10.7	1.6	0.4	37%	77%	87
		17	24	a/a	KC	6	12	26	0	125	130	103	18	102	111	7.45	1.86	22.5	270	7.4	8.0	1.1	1.3	32%	60%	34
		18	25	aaa	KC	2	5	41	1	75	72	37	4	55	81	4.45	1.68	8.2	252	6.5	9.7	1.5	0.5	34%	73%	79
Stephens, Jordan	R	17	25	aa	CHW	3	7	16	0	92	109	47	6	43	70	4.60	1.65	25.6	296	4.2	6.9	1.6	0.6	35%	72%	55
		18	26	a/a	CHW	8	10	28	0	148	192	95	16	62	114	5.76	1.71	24.0	314	3.8	6.9	1.8	1.0	37%	67%	42

PITCHER	Th	Yr	Age	LvL	Org	W	L	G	Sv	IP	H	ER	HR	BB	K	ERA	WHIP	BF/G	OBA	bb/9	k/9	Cmd	hr/9	H%	S%	BPV
Stewart, Kohl	R	16	22	aa	MIN	9	6	16	0	92	104	37	4	43	39	3.66	1.59	25.4	286	4.2	3.8	0.9	0.4	31%	77%	28
		17	23	a/a	MIN	6	6	17	0	82	100	57	7	50	46	6.28	1.83	22.4	303	5.4	5.0	0.9	0.7	34%	65%	22
		18	24	a/a	MIN	3	7	21	0	110	159	73	9	35	81	5.95	1.76	24.0	338	2.8	6.6	2.3	0.7	40%	65%	55
Suarez, Jose	L	18	20	a/a	LAA	3	5	24	0	110	118	49	5	37	113	4.00	1.41	19.4	274	3.0	9.2	3.0	0.4	36%	70%	107
Suarez, Ranger	L	18	23	a/a	PHI	6	3	21	0	125	128	45	5	35	76	3.22	1.30	24.6	266	2.5	5.4	2.1	0.3	31%	75%	69
Supak, Trey	R	18	22	aa	MIL	6	6	16	0	88	90	38	6	30	66	3.87	1.36	23.0	265	3.1	6.7	2.2	0.6	32%	72%	71
Tate, Dillon	R	17	23	aa	NYY	1	2	4	0	25	29	13	5	10	15	4.65	1.55	27.3	291	3.6	5.3	1.5	1.7	30%	76%	10
		18	24	aa	BAL	7	5	22	0	124	131	66	12	34	77	4.80	1.33	23.4	273	2.5	5.6	2.3	0.8	31%	64%	57
Taylor, Curtis	R	18	23	aa	TAM	3	4	30	6	62	39	19	6	26	66	2.80	1.05	8.0	183	3.8	9.5	2.5	0.9	23%	78%	100
Thompson, Jake	R	14	20	aa	TEX	4	1	9	0	47	43	19	4	22	44	3.74	1.39	21.8	245	4.3	8.6	2.0	0.7	31%	74%	79
		15	21	aa	PHI	11	7	24	0	133	137	60	11	41	102	4.09	1.34	23.0	269	2.8	6.9	2.5	0.8	32%	71%	73
		16	22	aaa	PHI	11	5	21	0	130	131	52	15	41	78	3.61	1.33	25.6	264	2.8	5.4	1.9	1.0	29%	76%	44
		17	23	aaa	PHI	5	14	22	0	118	161	88	15	49	79	6.67	1.77	24.7	325	3.7	6.0	1.6	1.1	36%	63%	26
		18	24	aaa	MIL	1	2	33	3	53	50	25	5	27	47	4.32	1.46	6.9	251	4.6	7.9	1.7	0.9	30%	72%	62
Thompson, Keegan	R	18	23	aa	CHC	6	3	13	0	62	78	35	3	23	46	5.15	1.62	21.2	308	3.3	6.6	2.0	0.5	37%	67%	61
Thornton, Trent	R	16	23	aa	HOU	3	1	7	0	46	47	14	6	5	31	2.72	1.14	26.0	268	1.0	6.0	6.2	1.1	30%	82%	133
		17	24	a/a	HOU	9	6	25	0	131	178	82	14	22	88	5.59	1.52	22.8	324	1.5	6.0	4.1	0.9	37%	64%	83
		18	25	aaa	HOU	9	8	24	0	125	126	61	12	28	100	4.39	1.24	21.2	264	2.0	7.2	3.5	0.9	31%	66%	92
Thorpe, Lewis	L	18	23	a/a	MIN	8	7	26	0	131	151	67	20	37	129	4.62	1.43	21.5	289	2.6	8.8	3.5	1.4	35%	72%	82
Tinoco, Justin	R	18	23	aa	COL	9	12	26	0	141	188	109	33	43	105	6.94	1.64	24.2	321	2.7	6.7	2.5	2.1	35%	62%	19
Touki, Toussaint	R	18	22	a/a	ATL	9	6	24	0	137	117	45	8	51	139	2.95	1.23	23.1	232	3.4	9.1	2.7	0.5	31%	77%	105
Tseng, Jen-Ho	R	16	22	aa	CHC	6	8	22	0	113	154	62	13	32	61	4.96	1.64	23.0	325	2.5	4.8	1.9	1.1	35%	72%	27
		17	23	a/a	CHC	13	4	24	0	145	146	49	13	39	105	3.04	1.27	24.8	262	2.4	6.5	2.7	0.8	30%	79%	74
		18	24	aaa	CHC	2	15	26	0	137	179	107	21	45	95	7.03	1.63	23.5	316	3.0	6.3	2.1	1.4	35%	57%	33
Underwood, Duane	R	16	22	aa	CHC	0	5	13	0	59	74	37	8	31	41	5.68	1.78	20.8	308	4.7	6.2	1.3	1.2	35%	70%	22
		17	23	aa	CHC	13	7	25	0	138	157	90	16	54	85	5.85	1.53	24.0	287	3.5	5.5	1.6	1.0	32%	62%	33
		18	24	aaa	CHC	4	10	27	0	120	143	68	8	38	87	5.07	1.51	19.2	297	2.8	6.5	2.3	0.6	35%	66%	65
Valdez, Framber	L	17	24	aa	HOU	5	5	12	0	49	71	40	5	23	46	7.38	1.93	19.4	340	4.3	8.5	2.0	0.8	42%	61%	54
		18	25	a/a	HOU	6	5	22	1	105	114	53	8	31	106	4.57	1.38	20.1	278	2.7	9.0	3.4	0.6	36%	67%	105

ORGANIZATION RATINGS/RANKINGS

Each organization is graded on a standard A-F scale in four separate categories, and then after weighing the categories and adding some subjectivity, a final grade and ranking are determined. The four categories are the following:

Hitting: The quality and quantity of hitting prospects, the balance between athleticism, power, speed, and defense, and the quality of player development.

Pitching: The quality and quantity of pitching prospects and the quality of player development.

Top-End Talent: The quality of the top players within the organization. Successful teams are ones that have the most star-quality players. These are the players who are a teams' above average regulars, front-end starters, and closers.

Depth: The depth of both hitting and pitching prospects within the organization.

Overall Grade: The four categories are weighted, with top-end talent being the most important and depth being the least.

TEAM	Hitting	Pitching	Top-End Talent	Depth	Overall
San Diego Padres	A-	A	A	A	A
Tampa Bay Rays	A	A-	A	A	A
Chicago White Sox	A	B	A	B+	A-
Toronto Blue Jays	A	B-	A	B	B+
Atlanta Braves	B	A	A-	B	B+
Minnesota Twins	A-	B	A-	C+	B
Cincinnati Reds	B	C+	A-	B	B
Philadelphia Phillies	C	B	B	B+	B
Los Angeles Dodgers	B+	B-	B	B+	B
Colorado Rockies	B	B-	B-	A-	B
Houston Astros	B-	B	A-	C	B-
Detroit Tigers	B-	B+	B	B-	B-
Kansas City Royals	B-	A-	B	C+	B-
New York Yankees	C+	B+	B-	A-	B-
Texas Rangers	C	B-	B-	B	B-
St. Louis Cardinals	B-	C+	B-	B	B-
Baltimore Orioles	B-	C+	B-	C	C+
Boston Red Sox	C	B	C	C+	C+
Oakland Athletics	C+	C	B-	C+	C
Milwaukee Brewers	B-	C-	B-	C	C
San Francisco Giants	C+	C	B-	C-	C
Los Angeles Angels	B-	B-	C+	C+	C
Seattle Mariners	C	B-	C+	D	C
Miami Marlins	C	C	C-	C+	C
Pittsburgh Pirates	B	D	C	C	C
Washington Nationals	C	D	B-	D	C-
New York Mets	C-	C+	C-	C	C-
Arizona Diamondbacks	D+	C-	D+	C	D+
Cleveland Indians	C-	D+	D	D+	D+
Chicago Cubs	C-	C	D	D	D+

This section of the book may be the smallest as far as word count is concerned, but may be the most important, as this is where players' skills and potential are tied together and ranked against their peers. The rankings that follow are divided into long-term potential in the major leagues and shorter-term fantasy value.

ORGANIZATIONAL: Lists the top 15 minor league prospects within each organization in terms of long-range potential in the major leagues.

POSITIONAL: Lists the top 15 prospects, by position, in terms of long-range potential in the major leagues.

TOP POWER: Lists the top 25 prospects that have the potential to hit for power in the major leagues, combining raw power, plate discipline, and at the ability to make their power game-usable.

TOP BA: Lists the top 25 prospects that have the potential to hit for high batting average in the major leagues, combining contact ability, plate discipline, hitting mechanics and strength.

TOP SPEED: Lists the top 25 prospects that have the potential to steal bases in the major leagues, combining raw speed and base-running instincts.

TOP FASTBALL: Lists the top 25 pitchers that have the best fastball, combining velocity and pitch movement.

TOP BREAKING BALL: Lists the top 25 pitchers that have the best breaking ball, combining pitch movement, strikeout potential, and consistency.

2019 TOP FANTASY PROSPECTS: Lists the top 40 minor league prospects likely to have the most value to their respective fantasy teams in 2019, then 35 more players to consider who could get the call and have the skills to produce. Remember that this section addresses 2019 value, not long-term value.

TOP 100 ARCHIVE: Takes a look back at the top 100 lists from the past eight years.

The rankings in this book are the creation of the minor league department at BaseballHQ.com. While several baseball personnel contributed player information to the book, no opinions were solicited or received in comparing players.

T.G.I.F. just got an upgrade.

Break through the noise at your transaction deadline with BaseballHQ Friday, a FREE weekly newsletter from fantasy baseball's #1 premium information source. Each issue is your link to exclusive insights from the experts at BaseballHQ.com.

Every Friday, beginning in late January, you'll receive:
- Comprehensive player analyses
- Cutting-edge statistical insight
- Innovative game strategies
- Master Notes from trusted HQ writers
- Reviews, discounts and more!

And there's no obligation. It's FREE. Sign up TODAY at:
www.baseballhq.com/friday

TOP PROSPECTS BY ORGANIZATION

AL EAST

BALTIMORE ORIOLES
1. DL Hall, LHP
2. Yusniel Diaz, OF
3. Ryan Mountcastle, 3B
4. Grayson Rodriguez, RHP
5. Austin Hays, OF
6. Ryan McKenna, OF
7. Luis Ortiz, RHP
8. Hunter Harvey, RHP
9. Adam Hall, SS
10. Blaine Knight, RHP
11. Keegan Akin, LHP
12. Dillon Tate, RHP
13. Jean Carlos Encarnacion, 3B
14. Dean Kremer, RHP
15. Richie Martin, 2B/SS

BOSTON RED SOX
1. Bobby Dalbec, 3B
2. Michael Chavis, 1B/3B
3. Jason Groome, LHP
4. Triston Casas, 3B
5. Mike Shawaryn, RHP
6. Josh Ockimey, 1B
7. Matt Kent, LHP
8. Durbin Feltman, LHP
9. Darwinzon Hernandez, LHP
10. Travis Lakins, RHP
11. Jarren Duran, 2B/OF
12. CJ Chatham, SS
13. Tanner Houck, RHP
14. Jordan Weems, RHP
15. Alex Scherff, RHP

NEW YORK YANKEES
1. Estevan Florial, OF
2. Jonathan Loaisiga, RHP
3. Albert Abreu, RHP
4. Everson Pereira, OF
5. Clarke Schmidt, RHP
6. Roansy Contreras, RHP
7. Anthony Seigler, C
8. Delvi Garcia, RHP
9. Antonio Cabello, OF
10. Michael King, RHP
11. Luis Gil, RHP
12. Luis Medina, RHP
13. Domingo Acevedo, RHP
14. Matt Sauer, RHP
15. Josh Breaux, C

TAMPA BAY RAYS
1. Wander Franco, SS
2. Brent Honeywell, RHP
3. Brendan McKay, LHP/1B
4. Jesus Sanchez, OF
5. Vidal Brujan, 2B
6. Ronaldo Hernandez, C
7. Matthew Liberatore, LHP
8. Lucius Fox, SS
9. Nathaniel Lowe, 1B
10. Shane Baz, RHP
11. Shane McClanahan, LHP
12. Brandon Lowe, 2B/3B/OF
13. Miguel Gomez, OF
14. Josh Lowe, OF
15. Garrett Whitley, OF

TORONTO BLUE JAYS
1. Vladimir Guerrero, 3B
2. Bo Bichette, SS
3. Nate Pearson, RHP
4. Danny Jansen, C
5. Jordan Groshans, 3B/SS
6. Kevin Smith, 3B/SS
7. Eric Pardinho, RHP
8. Anthony Alford, OF
9. Sean Reid-Foley, RHP
10. Cavan Biggio, 1B/2B/3B
11. Griffin Conine, OF
12. Miguel Hiraldo, 3B
13. Hector Perez, RHP
14. Elvis Luciano, RHP
15. Rowdy Tellez, 1B

AL CENTRAL

CHICAGO WHITE SOX
1. Eloy Jimenez, OF
2. Michael Kopech, RHP
3. Dylan Cease, RHP
4. Nick Madrigal, 2B
5. Luis Robert, OF
6. Dane Dunning, RHP
7. Luis Gonzalez, OF
8. Micker Adolfo, OF
9. Blake Rutherford, OF
10. Zack Burdi, RHP
11. Luis Alexander Basabe, OF
12. Steele Walker, OF
13. Jake Burger, 3B
14. Zack Collins, C
15. Konnor Pilkington, LHP

CLEVELAND INDIANS
1. Triston McKenzie, RHP
2. Ethan Hankins, RHP
3. Nolan Jones, 3B
4. Yu-Cheng Chang, SS
5. Bo Naylor, C
6. George Valera, OF
7. Oscar Mercado, OF
8. Bobby Bradley, 1B
9. Luis Oviedo, RHP
10. Sam Henteges, LHP
11. Lenny Torres, RHP
12. Richard Palacios, 2B
13. Bryan Rocchio, SS
14. Tyler Freeman, SS
15. Eli Morgan, RHP

DETROIT TIGERS
1. Casey Mize, RHP
2. Matt Manning, RHP
3. Daz Cameron, OF
4. Isaac Paredes, SS
5. Franklin Perez, RHP
6. Beau Burrows, RHP
7. Willi Castro, SS
8. Kyle Funkhouser, RHP
9. Parker Meadows, OF
10. Jake Rogers, C
11. Wenceel Perez, SS
12. Kody Clemens, 2B
13. Christin Stewart, OF
14. Alex Faedo, RHP
15. Logan Shore, RHP

KANSAS CITY ROYALS
1. Khalil Lee, OF
2. Daniel Lynch, LHP
3. MJ Melendez, C
4. Nicky Lopez, 2B/SS
5. Brady Singer, RHP
6. Yefri Del Rosario, RHP
7. Jackson Kowar, RHP
8. Seuly Matias, OF
9. Nick Pratto, 1B
10. Kyle Isbel, OF
11. Carlos Hernandez, RHP
12. Michael Gigliotti, OF
13. Josh Staumont, RHP
14. Kris Bubic, LHP
15. Brewer Hicklen, OF

MINNESOTA TWINS
1. Royce Lewis, SS
2. Alex Kirilloff, OF
3. Brusdar Graterol, RHP
4. Wander Javier, SS
5. Trevor Larnach, OF
6. Brent Rooker, 1B/OF
7. Blayne Enlow, RHP
8. Jhoan Duran, RHP
9. Lewis Thorpe, LHP
10. Gilberto Celestino, OF
11. Yunior Severino, 2B
12. Nick Gordon, 2B/SS
13. Ryan Jeffers, C
14. Luis Rijo, RHP
15. Jorge Alcala, RHP

AL WEST

HOUSTON ASTROS
1. Kyle Tucker, OF
2. Forrest Whitley, RHP
3. Josh James, RHP
4. Yordan Alvarez, OF
5. J.B. Bukauskas, RHP
6. Corbin Martin, RHP
7. Freudis Nova, SS
8. Brandon Bielak, RHP
9. Rogelio Armenteros, RHP
10. Seth Beer, 1B/OF
11. Jairo Solis, RHP
12. Joe Perez, 3B
13. Bryan Abreu, RHP
14. Ronnie Dawson, OF
15. Alex McKenna, OF

LOS ANGELES ANGELS
1. Jo Adell, OF
2. Jahmai Jones, 2B
3. Kevin Maitan, 3B/SS
4. Brandon Marsh, OF
5. Matt Thaiss, 1B
6. Griffin Canning, RHP
7. Chris Rodriguez, RHP
8. Michael Hermosillo, OF
9. Leonardo Rivas, SS
10. Jesus Castillo, RHP
11. Jose Suarez, LHP
12. Jose Soriano, RHP
13. Stiward Aquino, RHP
14. Livan Soto, SS
15. Trent Deveaux, OF

OAKLAND ATHLETICS
1. Jesus Luzardo, LHP
2. A.J. Puk, LHP
3. Kyler Murray, OF
4. Sean Murphy, C
5. Lazaro Armenteros, OF
6. Austin Beck, OF
7. Jameson Hannah, OF
8. Jorge Mateo, SS
9. Grant Holmes, RHP
10. James Kaprielian, RHP
11. Sheldon Neuse, 3B
12. Daulton Jefferies, RHP
13. Greg Deichmann, OF
14. Jeremy Eierman, SS
15. Tyler Ramirez, OF

SEATTLE MARINERS
1. Jarred Kelenic, OF
2. Justus Sheffield, LHP
3. Justin Dunn, RHP
4. Julio Rodriguez, OF
5. Logan Gilbert, RHP
6. Evan White, 1B
7. Kyle Lewis, OF
8. Braden Bishop, OF
9. Josh Stowers, OF
10. Cal Raleigh, C
11. Jake Fraley, OF
12. Erik Swanson, RHP
13. Sam Carlson, RHP
14. Dom Thompson-Williams, OF
15. Art Warren, RHP

TEXAS RANGERS
1. Hans Crouse, RHP
2. Bubba Thompson, OF
3. Leody Taveras, OF
4. Julio Pablo Martinez, OF
5. Cole Winn, RHP
6. Anderson Tejeda, SS
7. Taylor Hearn, LHP
8. Jonathan Hernandez, RHP
9. Chris Seise, SS
10. A.J. Alexy, RHP
11. Jonathan Ornelas, 3B
12. Cole Ragans, LHP
13. Mason Englert, RHP
14. Eli White, 2B/SS
15. Joe Palumbo, LHP

TOP PROSPECTS BY ORGANIZATION

NL EAST

ATLANTA BRAVES
1. Ian Anderson, RHP
2. Mike Soroka, RHP
3. Austin Riley, 3B
4. Touki Toussaint, RHP
5. Kyle Wright, RHP
6. William Contreras, C
7. Bryse Wilson, RHP
8. Cristian Pache, OF
9. Luiz Gohara, LHP
10. Drew Waters, OF
11. Greyson Jenista, 1B/OF
12. Joey Wentz, LHP
13. Kolby Allard, LHP
14. Freddy Tarnok, RHP
15. C.J. Alexander, 3B

MIAMI MARLINS
1. Monte Harrison, OF
2. Sandy Alcantara, RHP
3. Conner Scott, OF
4. Edward Cabrera, RHP
5. Nick Neidert, RHP
6. Jose Devers, SS
7. Braxton Garrett, LHP
8. Jorge Guzman, RHP
9. Isan Diaz, 2B
10. Will Banfield, C
11. Osiris Johnson, SS
12. Tristan Pomey, OF
13. Tommy Eveld, RHP
14. Brian Miller, 1B/OF
15. Trevor Rogers, LHP

NEW YORK METS
1. Peter Alonso, 1B
2. Andres Gimenez, SS
3. Thomas Szapucki, LHP
4. David Peterson, LHP
5. Will Toffey, 3B
6. Anthony Kay, LHP
7. Drew Smith, RHP
8. Franklyn Kilome, RHP
9. Ronny Mauricio, SS
10. Mark Vientos, 3B
11. Ryan Ryder, RHP
12. Shervyen Newton, SS
13. Tomas Nido, C
14. Luis Guillorme, SS
15. Steve Nogosek, RHP

PHILADELPHIA PHILLIES
1. Sixto Sanchez, RHP
2. Alec Bohm, 3B
3. Adonis Medina, RHP
4. Luis Garcia, SS
5. Spencer Howard, RHP
6. Francisco Morales, RHP
7. Adam Haseley, OF
8. JoJo Romero, LHP
9. Jhailyn Ortiz, OF
10. Mickey Moniak, OF
11. Rafael Marchan, C
12. Ranger Suarez, LHP
13. Enyel De Los Santos, RHP
14. Simon Muzziotti, OF
15. Mauricio Llovera, RHP

WASHINGTON NATIONALS
1. Victor Robles, OF
2. Carter Kieboom, SS
3. Luis Garcia, 3B/SS
4. Mason Denaburg, RHP
5. Jake Irvin, RHP
6. Wil Crowe, RHP
7. Tim Cate, LHP
8. Seth Romero, LHP
9. Yasel Antuna, SS
10. Raudy Read, C
11. Reid Schaller, RHP
12. Tanner Rainey, RHP
13. Telmito Agustin, OF
14. Jackson Tetreault, RHP
15. Kyle Johnston, RHP

NL CENTRAL

CHICAGO CUBS
1. Miguel Amaya, C
2. Adbert Alzolay, RHP
3. Brailyn Marquez, LHP
4. Nico Hoerner, SS
5. Alex Lange, RHP
6. Justin Steele, LHP
7. Aramis Ademan, SS
8. Duane Underwood, RHP
9. Cole Roederer, OF
10. Brennen Davis, OF
11. Brendon Little, LHP
12. Oscar De La Cruz, RHP
13. Richard Gallardo, RHP
14. Michael Rucker, RHP
15. Keegan Thompson, RHP

CINCINNATI REDS
1. Nick Senzel, 2B
2. Taylor Trammell, OF
3. Jonathan India, 3B
4. Hunter Greene, RHP
5. Shed Long, 2B
6. Tony Santillan, RHP
7. Mike Siani, OF
8. Jose Siri, OF
9. Tyler Stephenson, C
10. Mariel Bautista, OF
11. Jacob Heatherly, LHP
12. Stuart Fairchild, OF
13. Vladimir Gutierrez, RHP
14. Jose Garcia, 2B/SS
15. Aristides Aquino, OF

MILWAUKEE BREWERS
1. Keston Hiura, 2B
2. Corey Ray, OF
3. Brice Turang, SS
4. Joe Gray, OF
5. Tristen Lutz, OF
6. Lucas Erceg, 3B
7. Mauricio Dubon, SS
8. Larry Ernesto, OF
9. Zack Brown, RHP
10. Trey Supak, RHP
11. Payton Henry, C
12. Aaron Ashby, LHP
13. Caden Lemons, RHP
14. Troy Stokes Jr., OF
15. Marcos Diplan, RHP

PITTSBURGH PIRATES
1. Mitch Keller, RHP
2. Ke'Bryan Hayes, 3B
3. Oneil Cruz, SS
4. Travis Swaggerty, OF
5. Kevin Newman, SS
6. Kevin Kramer, 2B
7. Cole Tucker, SS
8. Brandon Waddell, LHP
9. Luis Escobar, RHP
10. Calvin Mitchell, OF
11. Brian Reynolds, OF
12. Montana DuRapau, RHP
13. Dario Agrazal, RHP
14. Jason Martin, OF
15. Pablo Reyes, 3B/OF

ST. LOUIS CARDINALS
1. Alex Reyes, RHP
2. Nolan Gorman, 3B
3. Dakota Hudson, RHP
4. Randy Arozarena, OF
5. Elehuris Montero, 3B
6. Ryan Helsley, RHP
7. Andrew Knizner, C
8. Dylan Carlson, OF
9. Justin Williams, OF
10. Griffin Roberts, RHP
11. Genesis Cabrera, LHP
12. Luken Baker, 1B
13. Adolis Garcia, OF
14. Conner Capel, OF
15. Edmundo Sosa, SS

NL WEST

ARIZONA DIAMONDBACKS
1. Jon Duplantier, RHP
2. Jazz Chisholm, SS
3. Taylor Widener, RHP
4. Daulton Varsho, C
5. Pavin Smith, 1B
6. Kristian Robinson, OF
7. Alek Thomas, OF
8. Jake McCarthy, OF
9. Marcus Wilson, OF
10. Drew Ellis, 3B
11. Matt Tabor, RHP
12. Emilio Vargas, RHP
13. Yoan Lopez, RHP
14. Andy Yerzy, C
15. Kevin Cron, 1B

COLORADO ROCKIES
1. Brendan Rodgers, 2B/3B/SS
2. Colton Welker, 3B
3. Garrett Hampson, 2B/SS
4. Grant Lavigne, 1B
5. Ryan Rolison, LHP
6. Riley Pint, RHP
7. Peter Lambert, RHP
8. Tyler Nevin, 1B
9. Ryan Vilade, SS
10. Ryan Castellani, RHP
11. Sam Hilliard, OF
12. Reid Humphreys, RHP
13. Terrin Vavra, SS
14. Ben Bowden, LHP
15. Robert Tyler, RHP

LOS ANGELES DODGERS
1. Alex Verdugo, OF
2. Keibert Ruiz, C
3. Gavin Lux, SS
4. Dustin May, RHP
5. Will Smith, C/3B
6. Tony Gonsolin, RHP
7. DJ Peters, OF
8. Jeter Downs, 2B/SS
9. Dennis Santana, RHP
10. Mitchell White, RHP
11. Yadier Alvarez, RHP
12. Jeren Kendall, OF
13. Michael Grove, RHP
14. Diego Cartaya, C
15. Edwin Rios, 1B

SAN DIEGO PADRES
1. Fernando Tatis Jr., SS
2. MacKenzie Gore, LHP
3. Chris Paddack, RHP
4. Francisco Mejia, C
5. Luis Urias, SS
6. Adrian Morejon, LHP
7. Michel Baez, RHP
8. Ryan Weathers, LHP
9. Luis Patino, RHP
10. Logan Allen, LHP
11. Cal Quantrill, RHP
12. Esteury Ruiz, 2B
13. Anderson Espinoza, RHP
14. Jeisson Rosario, OF
15. Xavier Edwards, SS

SAN FRANCISCO GIANTS
1. Joey Bart, C
2. Heliot Ramos, OF
3. Alexander Canario, OF
4. Logan Webb, RHP
5. Ray Black, RHP
6. Shaun Anderson, RHP
7. Sean Hjelle, RHP
8. Jalen Miller, 2B
9. Jake Wong, RHP
10. Gregory Santos, RHP
11. Chris Shaw, OF
12. Tyler Beede, RHP
13. Melvin Adon, RHP
14. Aramis Garcia, C
15. Heath Quinn, OF

TOP PROSPECTS BY POSITION

CATCHER
1   Joey Bart, SF
2   Keibert Ruiz, LA
3   Francisco Mejia, SD
4   Danny Jansen, TOR
5   Sean Murphy, OAK
6   MJ Melendez, KC
7   Ronaldo Hernandez, TAM
8   Miguel Amaya, CHC
9   William Contreras, ATL
10 Andrew Knizner, STL
11 Daulton Varsho, ARI
12 Will Smith, LA
13 Bo Naylor, CLE
14 Rafael Marchan, PHI
15 Tyler Stephenson, CIN

FIRST BASEMEN
1   Peter Alonso, NYM
2   Brendan McKay, TAM
3   Nathaniel Lowe, TAM
4   Josh Naylor, SD
5   Brent Rooker, MIN
6   Evan White, SEA
7   Nick Pratto, KC
8   Matt Thaiss, LAA
9   Grant Lavigne, COL
10 Pavin Smith, ARI
11 Kevin Cron, ARI
12 Bobby Bradley, CLE
13 Josh Ockimey, BOS
14 Rowdy Tellez, TOR
15 Seth Beer, HOU

SECOND BASEMEN
1   Nick Senzel, CIN
2   Keston Hiura, MIL
3   Luis Urias, SD
4   Nick Madrigal, CHW
5   Vidal Brujan, TAM
6   Jahmai Jones, LAA
7   Esteury Ruiz, SD
8   Kevin Kramer, PIT
9   Richard Palacios, CLE
10 Brandon Lowe, TAM
11 Eli White, TEX
12 Isan Diaz, MIA
13 Cavan Biggio, TOR
14 Shed Long, CIN
15 Jalen Miller, SF

SHORTSTOP
1   Fernando Tatis Jr., SD
2   Royce Lewis, MIN
3   Bo Bichette, TOR
4   Wander Franco, TAM
5   Brendan Rodgers, COL
6   Carter Kieboom, WAS
7   Andres Gimenez, NYM
8   Luis Garcia, WAS
9   Gavin Lux, LA
10 Jazz Chisholm, ARI
11 Oneil Cruz, PIT
12 Garrett Hampson, COL
13 Xavier Edwards, SD
14 Ronny Mauricio, NYM
15 Tyler Freeman, CLE

THIRD BASEMEN
1   Vladimir Guerrero Jr., TOR
2   Austin Riley, ATL
3   Jonathan India, CIN
4   Ke'Bryan Hayes, PIT
5   Nolan Gorman, STL
6   Alec Bohm, PHI
7   Nolan Jones, CLE
8   Ryan Mountcastle, BAL
9   Colton Welker, COL
10 Bobby Dalbec, BOS
11 Michael Chavis, BOS
12 Hudson Potts, SD
13 Jordan Groshans, TOR
14 Elehuris Montero, STL
15 Triston Casas, BOS

OUTFIELDERS
1   Eloy Jimenez, CHW
2   Victor Robles, WAS
3   Kyle Tucker, HOU
4   Alex Kirilloff, MIN
5   Jo Adell, LAA
6   Taylor Trammell, CIN
7   Alex Verdugo, LA
8   Luis Robert, CHW
9   Jesus Sanchez, TAM
10 Yordan Alvarez, HOU
11 Yusinel Diaz, BAL
12 Jarred Kelenic, SEA
13 Estevan Florial, NYY
14 Leody Taveras, TEX
15 Julio Pablo Martinez, TEX
16 Cristian Pache, ATL
17 Khalil Lee, KC
18 Heliot Ramos, SF
19 Drew Waters, ATL
20 Kristian Robinson, ARI
21 Travis Swaggerty, PIT
22 Daz Cameron, DET
23 Brandon Marsh, LAA
24 Bubba Thompson, TEX
25 Trevor Larnach, MIN
26 Blake Rutherford, CHW
27 George Valera, CLE
28 Seuly Matias, KC
29 Austin Beck, OAK
30 Monte Harrison, MIA
31 Austin Hays, BAL
32 Kyler Murray, OAK
33 Adam Haseley, PHI
34 Corey Ray, MIL
35 Tirso Ornelas, SD
36 Luis Gonzalez, CHW
37 Anthony Alford, TOR
38 Tristen Lutz, MIL
39 DJ Peters, LA
40 Ryan McKenna, BAL
41 Kyle Lewis, SEA
42 Lazaro Armentero, OAK
43 Julio Rodriguez, SEA
44 Conner Scott, MIA
45 Alexander Canario, SF

STARTING PITCHERS
1   Forrest Whitley, HOU
2   Jesus Luzardo, OAK
3   Michael Kopech, CHW
4   MacKenzie Gore, SD
5   Sixto Sanchez, PHI
6   Casey Mize, DET
7   Dylan Cease, CHW
8   Mike Soroka, ATL
9   Alex Reyes, STL
10 Ian Anderson, ATL
11 Brent Honeywell, TAM
12 Mitch Keller, PIT
13 Chris Paddack, SD
14 Hunter Greene, CIN
15 A.J. Puk, OAK
16 Kyle Wright, ATL
17 Triston McKenzie, CLE
18 Touki Toussaint, ATL
19 Matt Manning, DET
20 Adrian Morejon, SD
21 Justus Sheffield, SEA
22 Jon Duplantier, ARI
23 Luis Patino, SD
24 Adonis Medina, PHI
25 Michel Baez, SD
26 Brusdar Graterol, MIN
27 Matthew Liberatore, TAM
28 Dustin May, LA
29 Josh James, HOU
30 Jonathan Loaisiga, NYY
31 Brady Singer, KC
32 Dane Dunning, CHW
33 Nate Pearson, TOR
34 Hans Crouse, TEX
35 DL Hall, BAL
36 Franklin Perez, DET
37 Griffin Canning, LAA
38 Bryse Wilson, ATL
39 Logan Allen, SD
40 Justin Dunn , SEA
41 Dakota Hudson, STL
42 Daniel Lynch, KC
43 Alex Faedo, DET
44 Luiz Gohara, ATL
45 Jason Groome, BOS
46 Cole Winn, TEX
47 Albert Abreu, NYY
48 Sandy Alcantara, MIA
49 Shane Baz, TAM
50 Taylor Widener, ARI
51 Beau Burrows, DET
52 Luis Oviedo, CLE
53 Peter Lambert, COL
54 Ryan Weathers, SD
55 Kolby Allard, ATL
56 Yefry Del Rosario, KC
57 Grayson Rodriguez, BAL
58 Francisco Morales, PHI
59 Braxton Ashcraft, PIT
60 Lenny Torres, CLE

61 Brailyn Marquez, CHC
62 Adbert Alozay, CHC
63 Taylor Hearn, TEX
64 Corbin Martin, HOU
65 Spencer Howard, PHI
66 J.B. Bukauskas, HOU
67 Jonathan Hernandez, TEX
68 Shane McClanahan, TAM
69 Delvi Garcia, NYY
70 Blaine Knight, BAL
71 Eric Pardinho, TOR
72 Ryan Rolison, COL
73 Logan Gilbert, SEA
74 Logan Webb, SF
75 Nick Neidert, MIA

RELIEF PITCHERS
1   Zack Burdi, CHW
2   Nick Sandin, CLE
3   Yoan Lopez, ARI
4   Cody Ponce, MIL
5   Jimmie Sherfy, ARI
6   Reid Humphreys, COL
7   Bryan Garcia, DET
8   Tommy Eveld, MIA
9   Bryan Abreu, HOU
10 Jason Foley, DET
11 Ian Hamilton, CHW
12 Maurico Llovera, PHI
13 Ray Black, SF
14 Art Warren, SEA
15 Junior Fernandez, STL

TOP PROSPECTS BY SKILLS

2019 TOP FANTASY IMPACT

TOP POWER
Vladimir Guerrero, Jr., 3B, TOR
Eloy Jimenez, OF, CHW
Peter Alonso, 1B, NYM
Bobby Dalbec, 3B, BOS
Joey Bart, C, SF
Nolan Gorman, 3B, STL
Alec Bohm, 3B, PHI
Seuly Matias, OF, KC
Dylan Cozens, OF, PHI
Alex Kirilloff, OF, MIN
Nick Senzel, 2B, CIN
Kyle Tucker, OF, HOU
Austin Riley, 3B, ATL
Jarred Kelenic, OF, SEA
Bo Bichette, SS, TOR
Brendan Rodgers, SS, COL
Fernando Tatis, Jr., SS, SD
Jonathan India, 3B, CIN
Wander Franco, SS, TAM
Sherten Apostel, 3B, TEX
Ronaldo Hernandez, C, TAM
Jhailyn Ortiz, OF, PHI
Oneil Cruz, SS, PIT
Triston Casas, 3B, BOS
Grant Lavigne, 1B, COL

TOP SPEED
Victor Robles, OF, WAS
Royce Lewis, SS, MIN
Vidal Brujan, 2B, TAM
Lucius Fox, SS TAM
Anthony Alford, OF, TOR
Buddy Reed, OF, SD
Jorge Mateo, SS, OAK
Jonathan Macado, OF, STL
Anfernee Seymour, OF, MIA
Miles Straw, OF, HOU
Nick Madrigal, 2B, CHW
Taylor Trammell, OF, CIN
Jo Adell, OF, LAA
Bubba Thompson, OF, TEX
Kyler Murray, OF, OAK
Oneil Cruz, SS, PIT
Estevan Florial, OF, NYY
Garrett Hampson, SS, COL
Andres Gimenez, SS, NYN
Nicky Lopez, 2B/SS, KC
Cristian Pache, OF, ATL
Oscar Mercado, OF, CLE
Mauricio Dubon, SS, MIL
Drew Waters, OF, ATL
Richard Palacios, 2B, CLE

TOP BREAKING BALL
Forrest Whitley, RHP, HOU
Michael Kopech, RHP, CHW
Hunter Greene, RHP, CIN
Alex Reyes, RHP, STL
Josh James, RHP, HOU
Luis Medina, RHP, NYY
MacKenzie Gore, LHP, SD
Brusdar Graterol, RHP, MIN
Jhoan Duran, RHP, MIN
Yadier Alvarez, RHP, LA
Jonathan Loaisiga, RHP, NYY
Kyle Wright, RHP, ATL
Shane McClanahan, LHP, TAM

TOP BA
Vladimir Guerrero, Jr, 3B, TOR
Alex Kirilloff, OF, MIN
Royce Lewis, SS, MIN
Nick Madrigal, 2B, CHW
Bo Bichette, SS, TOR
Wander Franco, SS, TAM
Keston Hiura, 2B, MIL
Victor Robles, OF, WAS
Nick Senzel, 2B, CIN
Kyle Tucker, OF, HOU
Eloy Jimenez, OF, CHW
Jarred Kelenic, OF, SEA
Peter Alonso, 1B, NYM
Brendan Rodgers, SS, COL
Taylor Trammell, OF, CIN
Luis Garcia, SS, WAS
Ronaldo Hernandez, C, TAM
Vidal Brujan, 2B, TAM
George Valera, OF, CLE
Alex Verdugo, OF, LA
Franciso Mejia, C, SD
Luis Urias, 2B, SD
Ke'Bryan Hayes, 3B, PIT
Colton Welker, 3B, COL
Keibert Ruiz, C, LA

TOP FASTBALL
Forrest Whitley, RHP, HOU
Sixto Sanchez, RHP, PHI
Hunter Greene, RHP, CIN
Michael Kopech, RHP, CHW
Alex Reyes, RHP, STL
Nate Pearson, RHP, TOR
Ethan Hankins, RHP, CLE
Zack Burdi, RHP, CHW
Ian Anderson, RHP, ATL
Yadier Alvarez, RHP, LA
Dylan Cease, RHP, CHW
Josh James, RHP, HOU
Jorge Guzman, RHP, MIA
Luis Medina, RHP, NYY
Art Warren, RHP, SEA
Junior Fernandez, RHP, STL
MacKenzie Gore, LHP, SD
Jesus Luzardo, LHP, OAK
Ray Black, RHP, SF
Dillon Maples, RHP, CHC
Brendan McKay, LHP, TAM
Justin Tinoco, RHP, COL
Brusdar Graterol, RHP, MIN
Melvin Adon, RHP, SF
Jhoan Duran, RHP, MIN

Spencer Howard, RHP, PHI
J.B. Bukauskas, RHP, HOU
Yoan Lopez, RHP, ARI
Sandy Alcantara, RHP, MIA
A.J. Puk, LHP, OAK
Bryse Wilson, RHP, ATL
Clarke Schmidt, RHP, NYY
Michel Baez, RHP, SD
Jonathan Hernandez, RHP, TEX
Jon Duplantier, RHP, ARI
Jason Groome, LHP, BOS
Triston McKenzie, RHP, CLE

THE TOP 40 · RANKED
1 Victor Robles (OF, WAS)
2 Nick Senzel (2B, CIN)
3 Vladimir Guerrero, Jr. (3B, TOR)
4 Garrett Hampson (2B, COL)
5 Kyle Tucker (OF, HOU)
6 Eloy Jimenez (OF, CHW)
7 Brandon Lowe (2B, TAM)
8 Alex Verdugo (OF, LA)
9 Peter Alonso (1B, NYM)
10 Keston Hiura (2B, MIL)

11 Danny Jansen (C, TOR)
12 Luis Urias (2B, SD)
13 Bo Bichette (SS, TOR)
14 Francisco Mejia (C, SD)
15 Christin Stewart (OF, DET)
16 Austin Hays (OF, BAL)
17 Kevin Newman (SS, PIT)
18 Alex Reyes (RHP, STL)
19 Austin Riley (3B, ATL)
20 Fernando Tatis, Jr. (SS, SD)

21 Anthony Alford (OF, TOR)
22 Brent Honeywell (RHP, TAM)
23 Jesus Luzardo (LHP, OAK)
24 Brendan Rodgers (SS, COL)
25 Chris Shaw (OF, SF)
26 Jonathan Loaisiga (RHP, NYY)
27 Touki Toussaint (RHP, ATL)
28 Mike Soroka (RHP, ATL)
29 Stephen Gonsalves (LHP, MIN)
30 Justus Sheffield (LHP, NYY)

31 Forrest Whitley (RHP, HOU)
32 Mitch Keller (RHP, PIT)
33 Luiz Gohara (LHP, ATL)
34 Sandy Alcantara (RHP, MIA)
35 Kolby Allard (LHP, ATL)
36 Kyle Wright (RHP, ATL)
37 Yordan Alvarez (OF, HOU)
38 Yusniel Diaz (OF, BAL)
39 Jon Duplantier (RHP, ARI)
40 Luis Ortiz (RHP, BAL)

THE NEXT 35 · ALPHA ORDER
Albert Abreu (RHP, NYY)
Logan Allen (LHP, SD)
Ian Anderson (RHP, ATL)
Beau Burrows (RHP, DET)
Daz Cameron (OF, DET)
Griffin Canning (RHP, LAA)
Dylan Cease (RHP, CHW)
Michael Chavis (3B, BOS)
Zack Collins (C, CHW)
Alex Faedo (RHP, DET)
Nick Gordon (SS/2B, MIN)
Monte Harrison (OF, MIA)
Ke'Bryan Hayes (3B, PIT)
Dakota Hudson (RHP, STL)
Josh James (RHP, HOU)
Carter Kieboom (SS, WAS)
Kevin Kramer (2B, PIT)
Peter Lambert (RHP, COL)
Shed Long (2B, CIN)
Nathaniel Lowe (1B, TAM)
Corbin Martin (RHP, HOU)
Jorge Mateo (SS, OAK)
Triston McKenzie (RHP, CLE)
Ryan Mountcastle (3B, BAL)
Sean Murphy (C, OAK)
Josh Naylor (OF, SD)
Cristian Pache (OF, ATL)
Chris Paddack (RHP, SD)
A.J. Puk (LHP, OAK)
Cal Quantrill (RHP, SD)
Corey Ray (OF, MIL)
Dennis Santana (RHP, LA)
Will Smith (C, LA)
Dillon Tate (RHP, BAL)
Bryse Wilson (RHP, ATL)

TOP 100 PROSPECTS ARCHIVE

2018

1. Ronald Acuna (OF, ATL)
2. Victor Robles (OF, WAS)
3. Vladimir Guerrero Jr. (3B, TOR)
4. Eloy Jimenez (OF, CHW)
5. Gleyber Torres (SS, NYY)
6. Brendan Rodgers (SS, COL)
7. Nick Senzel (3B, CIN)
8. Alex Reyes (RHP, STL)
9. Walker Buehler (RHP, LA)
10. Michael Kopech (RHP, CHW)

11. Fernando Tatis Jr. (SS, SD)
12. Kyle Tucker (OF, HOU)
13. Bo Bichette (SS, TOR)
14. Lewis Brinson (OF, MIL)
15. Brent Honeywell (RHP, TAM)
16. MacKenzie Gore (LHP, SD)
17. Forrest Whitley (RHP, HOU)
18. Willy Adames (SS, TAM)
19. Leody Taveras (OF, TEX)
20. Royce Lewis (SS, MIN)

21. Mitch Keller (RHP, PIT)
22. Francisco Mejia (C, CLE)
23. Kyle Wright (RHP, ATL)
24. A.J. Puk (LHP, OAK)
25. Sixto Sanchez (RHP, PHI)
26. Hunter Greene (RHP, CIN)
27. Franklin Barreto (SS, OAK)
28. Juan Soto (OF, WAS)
29. Triston McKenzie (RHP, CLE)
30. Luiz Gohara (LHP, ATL)

31. Alex Verdugo (OF, LA)
32. Franklin Perez (RHP, DET)
33. Luis Robert (OF, CHW)
34. Keston Huira (2B, MIL)
35. Ryan McMahon (1B, COL)
36. Scott Kingery (2B, PHI)
37. Mike Soroka (RHP, ATL)
38. Willie Calhoun (OF/2B, TEX)
39. Kolby Allard (LHP, ATL)
40. Austin Hays (OF, BAL)

41. Jack Flaherty (RHP, STL)
42. J.P. Crawford (SS, PHI)
43. Anthony Alford (OF, TOR)
44. Austin Meadows (OF, PIT)
45. Brendan McKay (1B/LHP, TAM)
46. Luis Urias (2B/SS, SD)
47. Kyle Lewis (OF, SEA)
48. Taylor Trammell (OF, CIN)
49. Yadier Alvarez (RHP, LA)
50. Estevan Florial (OF, NYY)

51. Jay Groome (LHP, BOS)
52. Cal Quantrill (RHP, SD)
53. Nick Gordon (SS, MIN)
54. Jesus Sanchez (OF, TAM)
55. Chance Adams (RHP, NYY)
56. Jorge Mateo (SS, OAK)
57. Ian Anderson (RHP, ATL)
58. Michel Baez (RHP, SD)
59. Alec Hansen (RHP, CHW)
60. Monte Harrison (OF, MIL)

61. Keibert Ruiz (C, LA)
62. Carson Kelly (C, STL)
63. Kevin Maitan (3B, LAA)
64. Riley Pint (RHP, COL)
65. Anderson Espinoza (RHP, SD)
66. Matt Manning (RHP, DET)
67. Austin Beck (OF, OAK)
68. Dylan Cease (RHP, CHW)
69. Jorge Alfaro (C, PHI)
70. Justus Sheffield (LHP, NYY)

71. Blake Rutherford (OF, CHW)
72. Chance Sisco (C, BAL)
73. Ryan Mountcastle (3B, BAL)
74. Corbin Burnes (RHP, MIL)
75. Jake Bauers (OF/1B, TAM)
76. Pavin Smith (1B, ARI)
77. Adonis Medina (RHP, PHI)
78. Jon Duplantier (RHP, ARI)
79. Heliot Ramos (OF, SF)
80. Adrian Morejon (LHP, SD)

81. Dustin Fowler (OF, OAK)
82. Mickey Moniak (OF, PHI)
83. Shane Baz (RHP, PIT)
84. Yusniel Diaz (OF, LA)
85. Jesse Winker (OF, CIN)
86. Stephen Gonsalves (LHP, MIN)
87. Isan Diaz (2B, MIL)
88. Joey Wentz (LHP, ATL)
89. Tyler O'Neill (OF, STL)
90. Alex Faedo (RHP, DET)

91. Jo Adell (OF, LAA)
92. Austin Riley (3B, ATL)
93. Corey Ray (OF, MIL)
94. Brandon Woodruff (RHP, MIL)
95. Mitchell White (RHP, LA)
96. Yordan Alvarez (1B, HOU)
97. Michael Chavis (3B, BOS)
98. Jose De Leon (RHP, TAM)
99. Christian Arroyo (3B, TAM)
100. Chris Shaw (1B, SF)

2017

1. Yoan Moncada (2B, CHW)
2. Andrew Benintendi (OF, BOS)
3. Dansby Swanson (SS, ATL)
4. Alex Reyes (RHP, STL)
5. Lucas Giolito (RHP, CHW)
6. Victor Robles (OF, WAS)
7. J.P. Crawford (SS, PHI)
8. Tyler Glasnow (RHP, PIT)
9. Brendan Rodgers (SS, COL)
10. Austin Meadows (OF, PIT)

11. Gleyber Torres (SS, NYY)
12. Amed Rosario (SS, NYM)
13. Rafael Devers (3B, BOS)
14. Lewis Brinson (OF, MIL)
15. Anderson Espinoza (RHP, SD)
16. Willy Adames (SS, TAM)
17. Eloy Jimenez (OF, CHC)
18. Manuel Margot (OF, SD)
19. Ozzie Albies (2B, ATL)
20. Clint Frazier (OF, NYY)

21. Bradley Zimmer (OF, CLE)
22. Franklin Barreto (SS, OAK)
23. Brent Honeywell (RHP, TAM)
24. Cody Bellinger (1B, LAD)
25. Francis Martes (RHP, HOU)
26. Reynaldo Lopez (RHP, CHW)
27. Jose De Leon (RHP, LAD)
28. Mickey Moniak (OF, PHI)
29. Ian Happ (2B, CHC)
30. Kyle Tucker (OF, HOU)

31. Nick Senzel (3B, CIN)
32. Michael Kopech (RHP, CHW)
33. Aaron Judge (OF, NYY)
34. Josh Bell (1B, PIT)
35. Kyle Lewis (OF, SEA)
36. Hunter Renfroe (OF, SD)
37. Jorge Mateo (SS, NYY)
38. Amir Garrett (LHP, CIN)
39. Corey Ray (OF, MIL)
40. Jeff Hoffman (RHP, COL)

41. Tyler O'Neill (OF, SEA)
42. Josh Hader (LHP, MIL)
43. Kolby Allard (LHP, ATL)
44. Jason Groome (LHP, BOS)
45. Jorge Alfaro (C, PHI)
46. Nick Williams (OF, PHI)
47. Nick Gordon (SS, MIN)
48. Sean Newcomb (LHP, ATL)
49. Alex Verdugo (OF, LAD)
50. Blake Rutherford (OF, NYY)

51. Carson Fulmer (RHP, CHW)
52. Vladimir Guerrero, Jr. (3B, TOR)
53. David Paulino (RHP, HOU)
54. Mitch Keller (RHP, PIT)
55. Riley Pint (RHP, COL)
56. Francisco Mejia (C, CLE)
57. Brady Aiken (LHP, CLE)
58. Yulieski Gurriel (3B, HOU)
59. Braxton Garrett (LHP, MIA)
60. Tyler Jay (LHP, MIN)

61. A.J. Puk (LHP, OAK)
62. Kevin Newman (SS, PIT)
63. Robert Stephenson (RHP, CIN)
64. Sean Reid-Foley (RHP, TOR)
65. Matt Manning (RHP, DET)
66. Anthony Alford (OF, TOR)
67. Jesse Winker (OF, CIN)
68. Dominic Smith (1B, NYM)
69. Raimel Tapia (OF, COL)
70. Zack Collins (C, CHW)

71. James Kaprielian (RHP, NYY)
72. Erick Fedde (RHP, WAS)
73. Luis Ortiz (RHP, MIL)
74. Phil Bickford (RHP, MIL)
75. Jake Bauers (OF, TAM)
76. Justus Sheffield (LHP, NYY)
77. Matt Chapman (3B, OAK)
78. Luke Weaver (RHP, STL)
79. Grant Holmes (RHP, OAK)
80. Bobby Bradley (1B, CLE)

81. Ronald Acuna (OF, ATL)
82. Derek Fisher (OF, HOU)
83. Brett Phillips (OF, MIL)
84. Yadier Alvarez (RHP, LAD)
85. Leody Taveras (OF, TEX)
86. Yohander Mendez (LHP, TEX)
87. Kevin Maitan (SS, ATL)
88. Triston McKenzie (LHP, CLE)
89. Willie Calhoun (2B, LAD)
90. Ryan McMahon (3B, COL)

91. Isan Diaz (2B, MIL)
92. Ian Anderson (RHP, ATL)
93. Trent Clark (OF, MIL)
94. Alex Kirilloff (OF, MIN)
95. Harrison Bader (OF, STL)
96. Tyler Beede (RHP, SF)
97. Richard Urena (SS, TOR)
98. Mike Soroka (RHP, ATL)
99. Dylan Cease (RHP, CHC)
100. Stephen Gonsalves (LHP, MIN)

TOP 100 PROSPECTS ARCHIVE

2016

1. Byron Buxton (OF, MIN)
2. Corey Seager (SS, LAD)
3. Lucas Giolito (RHP, WAS)
4. J.P. Crawford (SS, PHI)
5. Alex Reyes (RHP, STL)
6. Julio Urias (LHP, LAD)
7. Yoan Moncada (2B, BOS)
8. Tyler Glasnow (RHP, PIT)
9. Joey Gallo (3B, TEX)
10. Steven Matz (LHP, NYM)

11. Rafael Devers (3B, BOS)
12. Jose Berrios (RHP, MIN)
13. Orlando Arcia (SS, MIL)
14. Blake Snell (LHP, TAM)
15. Trea Turner (SS, WAS)
16. Bradley Zimmer (OF, CLE)
17. Jose De Leon (RHP, LAD)
18. Brendan Rodgers (SS, COL)
19. Dansby Swanson (SS, ATL)
20. Robert Stephenson (RHP, CIN)

21. Nomar Mazara (OF, TEX)
22. Victor Robles (OF, WAS)
23. Aaron Judge (OF, NYY)
24. Manuel Margot (OF, SD)
25. Clint Frazier (OF, CLE)
26. Lewis Brinson (OF, TEX)
27. Alex Bregman (SS, HOU)
28. Jon Gray (RHP, COL)
29. Ryan McMahon (3B, COL)
30. Austin Meadows (OF, PIT)

31. Nick Williams (OF, PHI)
32. Franklin Barreto (SS, OAK)
33. David Dahl (OF, COL)
34. Brett Phillips (OF, MIL)
35. Gleyber Torres (SS, CHC)
36. Sean Newcomb (LHP, ATL)
37. Carson Fulmer (RHP, CHW)
38. Ozhaino Albies (SS, ATL)
39. Dillon Tate (RHP, TEX)
40. Andrew Benintendi (OF, BOS)

41. Jameson Taillon (RHP, PIT)
42. Raul Mondesi (SS, KC)
43. Archie Bradley (RHP, ARI)
44. Tim Anderson (SS, CHW)
45. Kolby Allard (LHP, ATL)
46. Jake Thompson (RHP, PHI)
47. Dylan Bundy (RHP, BAL)
48. Willy Adames (SS, TAM)
49. Anderson Espinoza (RHP, BOS)
50. Aaron Blair (RHP, ATL)

51. A.J. Reed (1B, HOU)
52. Jeff Hoffman (RHP, COL)
53. Jesse Winker (OF, CIN)
54. Brent Honeywell (RHP, TAM)
55. Josh Bell (1B, PIT)
56. Anthony Alford (OF, TOR)
57. Tyler Kolek (RHP, MIA)
58. Max Kepler (OF, MIN)
59. Hunter Renfroe (OF, SD)
60. Mark Appel (RHP, PHI)

61. Kyle Zimmer (RHP, KC)
62. Jose Peraza (2B, CIN)
63. Kyle Tucker (OF, HOU)
64. Cody Reed (LHP, CIN)
65. Billy McKinney (OF, CHC)
66. Nick Gordon (SS, MIN)
67. Braden Shipley (RHP, ARI)
68. Jorge Lopez (RHP, MIL)
69. Touki Toussaint (RHP, ATL)
70. Hector Olivera (3B, ATL)

71. Derek Fisher (OF, HOU)
72. Jorge Alfaro (C, PHI)
73. Raimel Tapia (OF, COL)
74. Grant Holmes (RHP, LAD)
75. Dominic Smith (1B, NYM)
76. Daz Cameron (OF, HOU)
77. Alex Jackson (OF, SEA)
78. Sean Manaea (LHP, OAK)
79. Amed Rosario (SS, NYM)
80. Reynaldo Lopez (RHP, WAS)

81. Javier Guerra (SS, SD)
82. Hunter Harvey (RHP, BAL)
83. Luis Ortiz (RHP, TEX)
84. Brady Aiken (LHP, CLE)
85. Matt Olson (1B, OAK)
86. Jorge Mateo (SS, NYY)
87. Daniel Robertson (SS, TAM)
88. Taylor Guerrieri (RHP, TAM)
89. Amir Garrett (LHP, CIN)
90. Willson Contreras (C, CHC)

91. Renato Nunez (3B, OAK)
92. Tyler Jay (LHP, MIN)
93. Tyler Stephenson (C, CIN)
94. Christian Arroyo (SS, SF)
95. Josh Naylor (1B, MIA)
96. Brian Johnson (LHP, BOS)
97. Tyler Beede (RHP, SF)
98. Garrett Whitley (OF, TAM)
99. Cody Bellinger (1B, LAD)
100. Michael Fulmer (RHP, DET)

2015

1. Kris Bryant (3B, CHC)
2. Byron Buxton (OF, MIN)
3. Carlos Correa (SS, HOU)
4. Addison Russell (SS, CHC)
5. Corey Seager (SS, LAD)
6. Francisco Lindor (SS, CLE)
7. Joc Pederson (OF, LAD)
8. Miguel Sano (3B, MIN)
9. Lucas Giolito (P, WAS)
10. Joey Gallo (3B, TEX)

11. Dylan Bundy (P, BAL)
12. Jorge Soler (OF, CHC)
13. Archie Bradley (P, ARI)
14. Julio Urias (P, LAD)
15. Jon Gray (P, COL)
16. Daniel Norris (P, TOR)
17. Carlos Rodon (P, CHW)
18. Tyler Glasnow (P, PIT)
19. Noah Syndergaard (P, NYM)
20. Blake Swihart (C, BOS)

21. Aaron Sanchez (P, TOR)
22. Henry Owens (P, BOS)
23. Jameson Taillon (P, PIT)
24. Robert Stephenson (P, CIN)
25. Andrew Heaney (P, LAA)
26. David Dahl (OF, COL)
27. Jose Berrios (P, MIN)
28. Jorge Alfaro (C, TEX)
29. Hunter Harvey (P, BAL)
30. Alex Meyer (P, MIN)

31. Kohl Stewart (P, MIN)
32. J.P. Crawford (SS, PHI)
33. Alex Jackson (OF, SEA)
34. Jesse Winker (OF, CIN)
35. Raul Mondesi (SS, KC)
36. D.J. Peterson (3B, SEA)
37. Austin Meadows (OF, PIT)
38. Josh Bell (OF, PIT)
39. Kyle Crick (P, SF)
40. Luis Severino (P, NYY)

41. Nick Gordon (SS, MIN)
42. Kyle Schwarber (OF, CHC)
43. Aaron Nola (P, PHI)
44. Kyle Zimmer (P, KC)
45. Alex Reyes (P, STL)
46. Braden Shipley (P, ARI)
47. Albert Almora (OF, CHC)
48. Clint Frazier (OF, CLE)
49. Tyler Kolek (P, MIA)
50. Mark Appel (P, HOU)

51. Rusney Castillo (OF, BOS)
52. Sean Manaea (P, KC)
53. A.J. Cole (P, WAS)
54. Matt Wisler (P, SD)
55. Raimel Tapia (OF, COL)
56. C.J. Edwards (P, CHC)
57. Dalton Pompey (OF, TOR)
58. Hunter Renfroe (OF, SD)
59. Hunter Dozier (3B, KC)
60. Brandon Nimmo (OF, NYM)

61. Tim Anderson (SS, CHW)
62. Maikel Franco (3B, PHI)
63. Mike Foltynewicz (P, HOU)
64. Nick Kingham (P, PIT)
65. Eddie Butler (P, COL)
66. Steven Matz (P, NYM)
67. Domingo Santana (OF, HOU)
68. Aaron Judge (OF, NYY)
69. Daniel Robertson (SS, OAK)
70. Stephen Piscotty (OF, STL)

71. Kyle Freeland (P, COL)
72. Kevin Plawecki (C, NYM)
73. Lucas Sims (P, ATL)
74. Yasmany Tomas (OF, ARI)
75. Jose Peraza (2B, ATL)
76. Eduardo Rodriguez (P, BOS)
77. Max Fried (P, ATL)
78. Manuel Margot (OF, BOS)
79. Matt Olson (1B, OAK)
80. Ryan McMahon (3B, COL)

81. Alex Gonzalez (P, TEX)
82. Tyler Beede (P, SF)
83. Alen Hanson (SS, PIT)
84. Grant Holmes (P, LAD)
85. Aaron Blair (P, ARI)
86. Michael Taylor (OF, WAS)
87. Trea Turner (SS, SD/WAS)
88. Christian Bethancourt (C, ATL)
89. Marco Gonzales (P, STL)
90. Michael Conforto (OF, NYM)

91. Sean Newcomb (P, LAA)
92. Alex Colome (P, TAM)
93. Jeff Hoffman (P, TOR)
94. Luke Jackson (P, TEX)
95. Lewis Brinson (OF, TEX)
96. Willy Adames (SS, TAM)
97. Jake Thompson (P, TEX)
98. Nick Williams (OF, TEX)
99. Colin Moran (3B, HOU)
100. Bradley Zimmer (OF, CLE)

TOP 100 PROSPECTS ARCHIVE

2014

1. Byron Buxton (OF, MIN)
2. Oscar Taveras (OF, STL)
3. Xander Bogaerts (SS, BOS)
4. Taijuan Walker (RHP, SEA)
5. Miguel Sano (3B, MIN)
6. Francisco Lindor (SS, CLE)
7. Javier Baez (SS, CHC)
8. Archie Bradley (RHP, ARI)
9. Carlos Correa (SS, HOU)
10. Gregory Polanco (OF, PIT)

11. Addison Russell (SS, OAK)
12. Jameson Taillon (RHP, PIT)
13. Kris Bryant (3B, CHC)
14. Dylan Bundy (RHP, BAL)
15. George Springer (OF, HOU)
16. Nick Castellanos (3B, DET)
17. Noah Syndergaard (RHP, NYM)
18. Kevin Gausman (RHP, BAL)
19. Carlos Martinez (RHP, STL)
20. Robert Stephenson (RHP, CIN)

21. Yordano Ventura (RHP, KC)
22. Jonathan Gray (RHP, COL)
23. Kyle Zimmer (RHP, KC)
24. Albert Almora (OF, CHC)
25. Mark Appel (RHP, HOU)
26. Aaron Sanchez (RHP, TOR)
27. Travis d'Arnaud (C, NYM)
28. Kyle Crick (RHP, SF)
29. Joc Pederson (OF, LA)
30. Alex Meyer (RHP, MIN)

31. Garin Cecchini (3B, BOS)
32. Jorge Soler (OF, CHC)
33. Jonathan Singleton (1B, HOU)
34. Maikel Franco (3B, PHI)
35. Lucas Giolito (RHP, WAS)
36. Eddie Butler (RHP, COL)
37. Andrew Heaney (LHP, MIA)
38. Jackie Bradley (OF, BOS)
39. Taylor Guerrieri (RHP, TAM)
40. Corey Seager (SS, LA)

41. Adalberto Mondesi (SS, KC)
42. Billy Hamilton (OF, CIN)
43. Clint Frazier (OF, CLE)
44. Tyler Glasnow (RHP, PIT)
45. Kolten Wong (2B, STL)
46. Henry Owens (LHP, BOS)
47. Gary Sanchez (C, NYY)
48. Jorge Alfaro (C, TEX)
49. Austin Meadows (OF, PIT)
50. Austin Hedges (C, SD)

51. Alen Hanson (SS, PIT)
52. Marcus Stroman (RHP, TOR)
53. Kohl Stewart (RHP, MIN)
54. Max Fried (LHP, SD)
55. Jake Odorizzi (RHP, TAM)
56. Michael Choice (OF, TEX)
57. C.J. Edwards (RHP, CHC)
58. Trevor Bauer (RHP, CLE)
59. Julio Urias (LHP, LA)
60. Jake Marisnick (OF, MIA)

61. Jesse Biddle (LHP, PHI)
62. Eddie Rosario (2B, MIN)
63. Lucas Sims (RHP, ATL)
64. Lance McCullers (RHP, HOU)
65. A.J. Cole (RHP, WAS)
66. Rougned Odor (2B, TEX)
67. Colin Moran (3B, MIA)
68. Mike Foltynewicz (RHP, HOU)
69. Allen Webster (RHP, BOS)
70. Chris Owings (SS, ARI)

71. Eduardo Rodriguez (LHP, BAL)
72. Miguel Almonte (RHP, KC)
73. Blake Swihart (C, BOS)
74. Jose Abreu (1B, CHW)
75. Zach Lee (RHP, LA)
76. Danny Hultzen (LHP, SEA)
77. Matt Wisler (RHP, SD)
78. Matt Barnes (RHP, BOS)
79. James Paxton (LHP, SEA)
80. Rosell Herrera (SS, COL)

81. Erik Johnson (RHP, CHW)
82. David Dahl (OF, COL)
83. Hak-Ju Lee (SS, TAM)
84. D.J. Peterson (3B, SEA)
85. Luke Jackson (RHP, TEX)
86. Delino DeShields (OF, HOU)
87. Brian Goodwin (OF, WAS)
88. Hunter Dozier (SS, KC)
89. Matt Davidson (3B, CHW)
90. Anthony Ranaudo (RHP, BOS)

91. Jimmy Nelson (RHP, MIL)
92. Bubba Starling (OF, KC)
93. Christian Bethancourt (C, ATL)
94. Courtney Hawkins (OF, CHW)
95. Domingo Santana (OF, HOU)
96. Kaleb Cowart (3B, LAA)
97. Jose Berrios (RHP, MIN)
98. Braden Shipley (RHP, ARI)
99. Justin Nicolino (LHP, MIA)
100. Alex Colome (RHP, TAM)

2013

1. Jurickson Profar (SS, TEX)
2. Dylan Bundy (RHP, BAL)
3. Wil Myers (OF, TAM)
4. Gerrit Cole (RHP, PIT)
5. Oscar Taveras (OF, STL)
6. Taijuan Walker (RHP, SEA)
7. Trevor Bauer (RHP, CLE)
8. Jose Fernandez (RHP, MIA)
9. Travis d'Arnaud (C, NYM)
10. Miguel Sano (3B, MIN)

11. Zack Wheeler (RHP, NYM)
12. Christian Yelich (OF, MIA)
13. Tyler Skaggs (LHP, ARI)
14. Francisco Lindor (SS, CLE)
15. Javier Baez (SS, CHC)
16. Shelby Miller (RHP, STL)
17. Nick Castellanos (OF, DET)
18. Xander Bogaerts (SS, BOS)
19. Jameson Taillon (RHP, PIT)
20. Danny Hultzen (LHP, SEA)

21. Jonathan Singleton (1B, HOU)
22. Mike Zunino (C, SEA)
23. Billy Hamilton (OF, CIN)
24. Anthony Rendon (3B, WAS)
25. Mike Olt (3B, TEX)
26. Byron Buxton (OF, MIN)
27. Nolan Arenado (3B, COL)
28. Carlos Correa (SS, HOU)
29. Archie Bradley (RHP, ARI)
30. Julio Teheran (RHP, ATL)

31. Matt Barnes (RHP, BOS)
32. Gary Sanchez (C, NYY)
33. Jackie Bradley (OF, BOS)
34. Carlos Martinez (RHP, STL)
35. Bubba Starling (OF, KC)
36. Jake Odorizzi (RHP, TAM)
37. Jedd Gyorko (3B, SD)
38. Alen Hanson (SS, PIT)
39. George Springer (OF, HOU)
40. Nick Franklin (2B, SEA)

41. Aaron Sanchez (RHP, TOR)
42. Albert Almora (OF, CHC)
43. Kaleb Cowart (3B, LAA)
44. Taylor Guerrieri (RHP, TAM)
45. Kyle Zimmer (RHP, KC)
46. Noah Syndergaard (RHP, NYM)
47. Kolten Wong (2B, STL)
48. Tyler Austin (OF, NYY)
49. James Paxton (LHP, SEA)
50. Rymer Liriano (OF, SD)

51. Jake Marisnick (OF, MIA)
52. Trevor Story (SS, COL)
53. Kevin Gausman (RHP, BAL)
54. Trevor Rosenthal (RHP, STL)
55. Alex Meyer (RHP, MIN)
56. Jorge Soler (OF, CHC)
57. Matt Davidson (3B, ARI)
58. Brett Jackson (OF, CHC)
59. Michael Choice (OF, OAK)
60. David Dahl (OF, COL)

61. Mason Williams (OF, NYY)
62. Robert Stephenson (RHP, CIN)
63. Chris Archer (RHP, TAM)
64. Oswaldo Arcia (OF, MIN)
65. Zach Lee (RHP, LA)
66. Tony Cingrani (LHP, CIN)
67. Jesse Biddle (LHP, PHI)
68. Gregory Polanco (OF, PIT)
69. Addison Russell (SS, OAK)
70. Robbie Erlin (RHP, SD)

71. Courtney Hawkins (OF, CHW)
72. Brian Goodwin (OF, WAS)
73. Martin Perez (LHP, TEX)
74. Luis Heredia (RHP, PIT)
75. Yasiel Puig (OF, LA)
76. Wilmer Flores (3B, NYM)
77. Justin Nicolino (LHP, MIA)
78. Max Fried (LHP, SD)
79. Adam Eaton (OF, ARI)
80. Gary Brown (OF, SF)

81. Casey Kelly (RHP, SD)
82. Lucas Giolito (RHP, WAS)
83. Wily Peralta (RHP, MIL)
84. Michael Wacha (RHP, STL)
85. Austin Hedges (C, SD)
86. Kyle Gibson (RHP, MIN)
87. Hak-Ju Lee (SS, TAM)
88. Dan Straily (RHP, OAK)
89. Kyle Crick (RHP, SF)
90. Avisail Garcia (OF, DET)

91. Cody Buckel (RHP, TEX)
92. Tyler Thornburg (RHP, MIL)
93. Allen Webster (RHP, BOS)
94. Jarred Cosart (RHP, HOU)
95. Bruce Rondon (RHP, DET)
96. Delino DeShields (2B, HOU)
97. A.J. Cole (RHP, OAK)
98. Manny Banuelos (LHP, NYY)
99. Yordano Ventura (RHP, KC)
100. Trevor May (RHP, MIN)

TOP 100 PROSPECTS ARCHIVE

2012

1. Bryce Harper (OF, WAS)
2. Matt Moore (LHP, TAM)
3. Mike Trout (OF, LAA)
4. Julio Teheran (RHP, ATL)
5. Jesus Montero (C, NYY)
6. Jurickson Profar (SS, TEX)
7. Manny Machado (SS, BAL)
8. Gerrit Cole (RHP, PIT)
9. Devin Mesoraco (C, CIN)
10. Wil Myers (OF, KC)

11. Miguel Sano (3B, MIN)
12. Jacob Turner (RHP, DET)
13. Anthony Rendon (3B, WAS)
14. Trevor Bauer (RHP, ARI)
15. Nolan Arenado (3B , COL)
16. Jameson Taillon (RHP, PIT)
17. Shelby Miller (RHP, STL)
18. Dylan Bundy (RHP, BAL)
19. Brett Jackson (OF, CHC)
20. Drew Pomeranz (LHP, COL)

21. Martin Perez (LHP, TEX)
22. Yonder Alonso (1B, SD)
23. Taijuan Walker (RHP, SEA)
24. Danny Hultzen (LHP, SEA)
25. Gary Brown (OF, SF)
26. Anthony Rizzo (1B, CHC)
27. Bubba Starling (OF, KC)
28. Travis d'Arnaud (C, TOR)
29. Mike Montgomery (LHP, KC)
30. Jake Odorizzi (RHP, KC)

31. Hak-Ju Lee (SS, TAM)
32. Jonathan Singleton (1B, HOU)
33. Garrett Richards (RHP, LAA)
34. Manny Banuelos (LHP, NYY)
35. James Paxton (LHP, SEA)
36. Jarrod Parker (RHP, OAK)
37. Carlos Martinez (RHP, STL)
38. Jake Marisnick (OF, TOR)
39. Yasmani Grandal (C, SD)
40. Trevor May (RHP, PHI)

41. Gary Sanchez (C, NYY)
42. Mike Olt (3B, TEX)
43. Wilin Rosario (C, COL)
44. John Lamb (LHP, KC)
45. Francisco Lindor (SS, CLE)
46. Dellin Betances (RHP, NYY)
47. Michael Choice (OF, OAK)
48. Arodys Vizcaino (RHP, ATL)
49. Trayvon Robinson (OF, SEA)
50. Matt Harvey (RHP, NYM)

51. Will Middlebrooks (3B, BOS)
52. Jedd Gyorko (3B, SD)
53. Randall Delgado (RHP, ATL)
54. Zack Wheeler (RHP, NYM)
55. Zach Lee (RHP, LA)
56. Tyler Skaggs (LHP, ARI)
57. Nick Castellanos (3B, DET)
58. Robbie Erlin (LHP, SD)
59. Christian Yelich (OF, MIA)
60. Anthony Gose (OF, TOR)

61. Addison Reed (RHP, CHW)
62. Javier Baez (SS, CHC)
63. Starling Marte (OF, PIT)
64. Kaleb Cowart (3B, LAA)
65. George Springer (OF, HOU)
66. Jarred Cosart (RHP, HOU)
67. Jean Segura (2B, LAA)
68. Kolten Wong (2B, STL)
69. Nick Franklin (SS, SEA)
70. Alex Torres (RHP, TAM)

71. Rymer Liriano (OF, SD)
72. Josh Bell (OF, PIT)
73. Leonys Martin (OF, TEX)
74. Joe Wieland (RHP, SD)
75. Joe Benson (OF, MIN)
76. Wily Peralta (RHP, MIL)
77. Tim Wheeler (OF, COL)
78. Oscar Taveras (OF, STL)
79. Xander Bogaerts (SS, BOS)
80. Archie Bradley (RHP, ARI)

81. Kyle Gibson (RHP, MIN)
82. Allen Webster (RHP, LA)
83. C.J. Cron (1B, LAA)
84. Grant Green (OF, OAK)
85. Brad Peacock (RHP, OAK)
86. Chris Dwyer (LHP, KC)
87. Billy Hamilton (SS, CIN)
88. A.J. Cole (RHP, OAK)
89. Aaron Hicks (OF, MIN)
90. Noah Syndergaard (RHP, TOR)

91. Tyrell Jenkins (RHP, STL)
92. Anthony Ranaudo (RHP, BOS)
93. Jed Bradley (LHP, MIL)
94. Nathan Eovaldi (RHP, LA)
95. Andrelton Simmons (SS, ATL)
96. Taylor Guerrieri (RHP, TAM)
97. Cheslor Cuthbert (3B, KC)
98. Edward Salcedo (3B, ATL)
99. Domingo Santana, OF, HOU)
100. Jesse Biddle (LHP, PHI)

2011

1. Bryce Harper (OF, WAS)
2. Domonic Brown (OF, PHI)
3. Jesus Montero (C, NYY)
4. Mike Trout (OF, LAA)
5. Jeremy Hellickson (RHP, TAM)
6. Aroldis Chapman (LHP, CIN)
7. Eric Hosmer (1B, KC)
8. Dustin Ackley (2B, SEA)
9. Desmond Jennings (OF, TAM)
10. Julio Teheran (RHP, ATL)

11. Mike Moustakas (3B, KC)
12. Brandon Belt (1B, SF)
13. Freddie Freeman (1B, ATL)
14. Michael Pineda (RHP, SEA)
15. Matt Moore (LHP, TAM)
16. Mike Montgomery (LHP, KC)
17. Brett Jackson (OF, CHC)
18. Nick Franklin (SS, SEA)
19. Jameson Taillon (RHP, PIT)
20. Jacob Turner (RHP, DET)

21. Shelby Miller (RHP, STL)
22. Martin Perez (LHP, TEX)
23. Wil Myers (C, KC)
24. Kyle Gibson (RHP, MIN)
25. Lonnie Chisenhall (3B, CLE)
26. Tyler Matzek (LHP, COL)
27. Brett Lawrie (2B, TOR)
28. Yonder Alonso (1B, CIN)
29. Jarrod Parker (RHP, ARI)
30. Jonathan Singleton (1B, PHI)

31. Tanner Scheppers (RHP,TEX)
32. Kyle Drabek (RHP, TOR)
33. Jason Knapp (RHP, CLE)
34. Manny Banuelos (LHP, NYY)
35. Alex White (RHP, CLE)
36. Jason Kipnis (2B, CLE)
37. Wilin Rosario (C, COL)
38. Manny Machado (SS, BAL)
39. Chris Sale (LHP, CHW)
40. Devin Mesoraco (C, CIN)

41. Tyler Chatwood (RHP, LAA)
42. John Lamb (LHP, KC)
43. Danny Duffy (LHP, KC)
44. Trevor May (RHP, PHI)
45. Mike Minor (LHP, ATL)
46. Jarred Cosart (RHP, PHI)
47. Tony Sanchez (C, PIT)
48. Brody Colvin (RHP, PHI)
49. Zach Britton (LHP, BAL)
50. Dee Gordon (SS, LA)

51. Miguel Sano (3B, MIN)
52. Grant Green (SS, OAK)
53. Danny Espinosa (SS, WAS)
54. Simon Castro (RHP, SD)
55. Derek Norris (C, WAS)
56. Chris Archer (RHP, CHC)
57. Jurickson Profar (SS, TEX)
58. Zack Cox (3B, STL)
59. Billy Hamilton (2B, CIN)
60. Gary Sanchez (C, NYY)

61. Zach Lee (RHP, LA)
62. Drew Pomeranz (LHP, CLE)
63. Randall Delgado (RHP, ATL)
64. Michael Choice (OF, OAK)
65. Nick Weglarz (OF, CLE)
66. Nolan Arenado (3B, COL)
67. Chris Carter (1B/OF, OAK)
68. Arodys Vizcaino (RHP, ATL)
69. Trey McNutt (RHP, CHC)
70. Dellin Betances (RHP, NYY)

71. Aaron Hicks (OF, MIN)
72. Aaron Crow (RHP, KC)
73. Jake McGee (LHP, TAM)
74. Lars Anderson (1B, BOS)
75. Fabio Martinez (RHP, LAA)
76. Ben Revere (OF, MIN)
77. Jordan Lyles (RHP, HOU)
78. Casey Kelly (RHP, SD)
79. Trayvon Robinson (OF, LA)
80. Craig Kimbrel (RHP, ATL)

81. Jose Iglesias (SS, BOS)
82. Garrett Richards (RHP, LAA)
83. Allen Webster (RHP, LA)
84. Chris Dwyer (LHP, KC)
85. Alex Colome (RHP, TAM)
86. Zack Wheeler (RHP, SF)
87. Andy Oliver (LHP, DET)
88. Andrew Brackman (RHP,NYY)
89. Wilmer Flores (SS, NYM)
90. Christian Friedrich (LHP, COL)

91. Anthony Ranaudo (RHP, BOS)
92. Aaron Miller (LHP, LA)
93. Matt Harvey (RHP, NYM)
94. Mark Rogers (RHP, MIL)
95. Jean Segura (2B, LAA)
96. Hank Conger (C, LAA)
97. J.P. Arencibia (C, TOR)
98. Matt Dominguez (3B, FLA)
99. Jerry Sands (1B, LA)
100. Nick Castellanos (3B, DET)

GLOSSARY

AVG: Batting Average (see also BA)

BA: Batting Average (see also AVG)

Base Performance Indicator (BPI): A statistical formula that measures an isolated aspect of a player's situation-independent raw skill or a gauge that helps capture the effects of random chance has on a skill. Although there are many such formulas, there are only a few that we are referring to when the term is used in this book. For pitchers, our BPI's are control (bb%), dominance (k/9), command (k/bb), opposition on base average (OOB), ground/line/fly ratios (G/L/F), and expected ERA (xERA). Random chance is measured witih the hit rate (H%) and strand rate (S%).

***Base Performance Value (BPV):** A single value that describes a pitcher's overall raw skill level. This is more useful than any traditional statistical gauge to track performance trends and project future statistical output. The BPV formula combines and weights several BPIs:

(Dominance Rate x 6) + (Command ratio x 21) – Opposition HR Rate x 30) – ((Opp. Batting Average - .275) x 200)

The formula combines the individual raw skills of power, command, the ability to keep batters from reaching base, and the ability to prevent long hits, all characteristics that are unaffected by most external team factors. In tandem with a pitcher's strand rate, it provides a complete picture of the elements that contribute to a pitcher's ERA, and therefore serves as an accurate tool to project likely changes in ERA. **BENCHMARKS:** We generally consider a BPV of 50 to be the minimum level required for long-term success. The elite of bullpen aces will have BPV's in the excess of 100 and it is rare for these stoppers to enjoy long-term success with consistent levels under 75.

Batters Faced per Game *(Craig Wright)*

((IP x 2.82) + H + BB) / G

A measure of pitcher usage and one of the leading indicators for potential pitcher burnout.

Batting Average (BA, or AVG)

(H/AB)

Ratio of hits to at-bats, though it is a poor evaluative measure of hitting performance. It neglects the offensive value of the base on balls and assumes that all hits are created equal.

Batting Eye (Eye)

(Walks / Strikeouts)

A measure of a player's strike zone judgment, the raw ability to distinguish between balls and strikes. **BENCHMARKS:** The best hitters have eye ratios over 1.00 (indicating more walks than strikeouts) and are the most likely to be among a league's .300 hitters. At the other end of the scale are ratios

less than 0.50, which represent batters who likely also have lower BAs.

bb%: Walk rate (hitters)

bb/9: Opposition Walks per 9 IP

BF/Gm: Batters Faced Per Game

BPI: Base Performance Indicator

***BPV:** Base Performance Value

Cmd: Command ratio

Command Ratio (Cmd)

(Strikeouts / Walks)

This is a measure of a pitcher's raw ability to get the ball over the plate. There is no more fundamental a skill than this, and so it is accurately used as a leading indicator to project future rises and falls in other gauges, such as ERA. Command is one of the best gauges to use to evaluate minor league performance. It is a prime component of a pitcher's base performance value. **BENCHMARKS:** Baseball's upper echelon of command pitchers will have ratios in excess of 3.0. Pitchers with ratios under 1.0 — indicating that they walk more batters than they strike out — have virtually no potential for long term success. If you make no other changes in your approach to drafting a pitching staff, limiting your focus to only pitchers with a command ratio of 2.0 or better will substantially improve your odds of success.

Contact Rate (ct%)

((AB - K) / AB)

Measures a batter's ability to get wood on the ball and hit it into the field of play. **BENCHMARK:** Those batters with the best contact skill will have levels of 90% or better. The hackers of society will have levels of 75% or less.

Control Rate (bb/9), or Opposition Walks per Game

BB Allowed x 9 / IP

Measures how many walks a pitcher allows per game equivalent. **BENCHMARK:** The best pitchers will have bb/9 levels of 3.0 or less.

ct%: Contact rate

Ctl: Control Rate

Dom: Dominance Rate

Dominance Rate (k/9), or Opposition Strikeouts per Game

(K Allowed x 9 / IP)

Measures how many strikeouts a pitcher allows per game equivalent. **BENCHMARK:** The best pitchers will have k/9 levels of 6.0 or higher.

*Expected Earned Run Average (Gill and Reeve)

(.575 x H [per 9 IP]) + (.94 x HR [per 9 IP]) + (.28 x BB [per 9 IP]) - (.01 x K [per 9 IP]) - Normalizing Factor

"xERA represents the expected ERA of the pitcher based on a normal distribution of his statistics. It is not influenced by situation-dependent factors." xERA erases the inequity between starters' and relievers' ERA's, eliminating the effect that a pitcher's success or failure has on another pitcher's ERA.

Similar to other gauges, the accuracy of this formula changes with the level of competition from one season to the next. The normalizing factor allows us to better approximate a pitcher's actual ERA. This value is usually somewhere around 2.77 and varies by league and year. BENCHMARKS: In general, xERA's should approximate a pitcher's ERA fairly closely. However, those pitchers who have large variances between the two gauges are candidates for further analysis.

Extra-Base Hit Rate (X/H)

(2B + 3B + HR) / Hits

X/H is a measure of power and can be used along with a player's slugging percentage and isolated power to gauge a player's ability to drive the ball. BENCHMARKS: Players with above average power will post X/H of greater than 38% and players with moderate power will post X/H of 30% or greater. Weak hitters with below average power will have a X/H level of less than 20%.

Eye: Batting Eye

h%: Hit rate (batters)

H%: Hits Allowed per Balls in Play (pitchers)

Hit Rate (h% or H%)

(H—HR) / (AB – HR - K)

The percent of balls hit into the field of play that fall for hits.

hr/9: Opposition Home Runs per 9 IP

ISO: Isolated Power

Isolated Power (ISO)

(Slugging Percentage - Batting Average)

Isolated Power is a measurement of power skill. Subtracting a player's BA from his SLG, we are essentially pulling out all the singles and single bases from the formula. What remains are the extra-base hits. ISO is not an absolute measurement as it assumes that two doubles is worth one home run, which certainly is not the case, but is another statistic that is a good measurement of raw power. BENCHMARKS: The game's top sluggers will tend to have ISO levels over .200. Weak hitters will be under .100.

k/9: Dominance rate (opposition strikeouts per 9 IP)

Major League Equivalency (Bill James)

A formula that converts a player's minor or foreign league statistics into a comparable performance in the major leagues. These are not projections, but conversions of current performance.

Contains adjustments for the level of play in individual leagues and teams. Works best with Triple-A stats, not quite as well with Double-A stats, and hardly at all with the lower levels. Foreign conversions are still a work in process. James' original formula only addressed batting. Our research has devised conversion formulas for pitchers, however, their best use comes when looking at BPI's, not traditional stats.

MLE: Major League Equivalency

OBP: On Base Percentage (batters)

OBA: Opposition Batting Average (pitchers)

On Base Percentage (OBP)

(H + BB) / (AB + BB)

Addressing one of the two deficiencies in BA, OBP gives value to those events that get batters on base, but are not hits. By adding walks (and often, hit batsmen) into the basic batting average formula, we have a better gauge of a batter's ability to reach base safely. An OBP of .350 can be read as "this batter gets on base 35% of the time."

Why this is a more important gauge than batting average? When a run is scored, there is no distinction made as to how that runner reached base. So, two thirds of the time—about how often a batter comes to the plate with the bases empty—a walk really is as good as a hit. BENCHMARKS: We all know what a .300 hitter is, but what represents "good" for OBP? That comparable level would likely be .400, with .275 representing the level of futility.

On Base Plus Slugging Percentage (OPS): A simple sum of the two gauges, it is considered as one of the better evaluators of overall performance. OPS combines the two basic elements of offensive production — the ability to get on base (OBP) and the ability to advance baserunners (SLG). BENCHMARKS: The game's top batters will have OPS levels over .900. The worst batters will have levels under .600.

Opposition Batting Average (OBA)

(Hits Allowed / ((IP x 2.82) + Hits Allowed))

A close approximation of the batting average achieved by opposing batters against a particular pitcher. BENCHMARKS: The converse of the benchmark for batters, the best pitchers will have levels under .250; the worst pitchers levels over .300.

Opposition Home Runs per Game (hr/9)

(HR Allowed x 9 / IP)

Measures how many home runs a pitcher allows per game equivalent. BENCHMARK: The best pitchers will have hr/9 levels of under 1.0.

Opposition On Base Average (OOB)

(Hits Allowed + BB) / ((IP x 2.82) + H + BB)

A close approximation of the on base average achieved by opposing batters against a particular pitcher. BENCHMARK: The best pitchers will have levels under .300; the worst pitchers levels over .375.

Opposition Strikeouts per Game: See Dominance Rate.

Opposition Walks per Game: See Control Rate.

OPS: On Base Plus Slugging Percentage

RC: Runs Created

RC/G: Runs Created Per Game

Runs Created *(Bill James)*

(H + BB - CS) x (Total bases + (.55 x SB)) / (AB + BB)

A formula that converts all offensive events into a total of runs scored. As calculated for individual teams, the result approximates a club's actual run total with great accuracy.

Runs Created Per Game *(Bill James)*

Runs Created / ((AB - H + CS) / 25.5)

RC expressed on a per-game basis might be considered the hypothetical ERA compiled against a particular batter. **BENCHMARKS:** Few players surpass the level of a 10.00 RC/G in any given season, but any level over 7.50 can still be considered very good. At the bottom are levels below 3.00.

S%: Strand Rate

Save: There are six events that need to occur in order for a pitcher to post a single save...

1. The starting pitcher and middle relievers must pitch well.
2. The offense must score enough runs.
3. It must be a reasonably close game.
4. The manager must choose to put the pitcher in for a save opportunity.
5. The pitcher must pitch well and hold the lead.
6. The manager must let him finish the game.

Of these six events, only one is within the control of the relief pitcher. As such, projecting saves for a reliever has little to do with skill and a lot to do with opportunity. However, pitchers with excellent skills sets may create opportunity for themselves.

Situation Independent: Describing a statistical gauge that measures performance apart from the context of team, ballpark, or other outside variables. Strikeouts and Walks, inasmuch as they are unaffected by the performance of a batter's surrounding team, are considered situation independent stats.

Conversely, RBIs are situation dependent because individual performance varies greatly by the performance of other batters on the team (you can't drive in runs if there is nobody on base). Similarly, pitching wins are as much a measure of the success of a pitcher as they are a measure of the success of the offense and defense performing behind that pitcher, and are therefore a poor measure of pitching performance alone.

Situation independent gauges are important for us to be able to separate a player's contribution to his team and isolate his performance so that we may judge it on its own merits.

Slg: Slugging Percentage

Slugging Percentage (Slg)

(Singles + (2 x Doubles) + (3 x Triples) + (4 x HR)) / AB

A measure of the total number of bases accumulated per at bat. It is a misnomer; it is not a true measure of a batter's slugging ability because it includes singles. SLG also assumes that each type of hit has proportionately increasing value (i.e. a double is twice as valuable as a single, etc.) which is not true. **BENCHMARKS:** The top batters will have levels over .500. The bottom batters will have levels under .300.

Strand Rate (S%)

(H + BB - ER) / (H + BB - HR)

Measures the percentage of allowed runners a pitcher strands, which incorporates both individual pitcher skill and bullpen effectiveness. **BENCHMARKS:** The most adept at stranding runners will have S% levels over 75%. Once a pitcher's S% starts dropping down below 65%, he's going to have problems with his ERA. Those pitchers with strand rates over 80% will have artificially low ERAs, which will be prone to relapse.

Strikeouts per Game: See Opposition Strikeouts per game.

Walks + Hits per Innings Pitched (WHIP): The number of baserunners a pitcher allows per inning. **BENCHMARKS:** Usually, a WHIP of under 1.20 is considered top level and over 1.50 is indicative of poor performance. Levels under 1.00 — allowing fewer runners than IP — represent extraordinary performance and are rarely maintained over time.

Walk rate (bb%)

(BB / (AB + BB))

A measure of a batter's eye and plate patience. BENCHMARKS: The best batters will have levels of over 10%. Those with the least plate patience will have levels of 5% or less.

Walks per Game: See Opposition Walks per Game.

WHIP: Walks + Hits per Innings Pitched

Wins: There are five events that need to occur in order for a pitcher to post a single win...

1. He must pitch well, allowing few runs.
2. The offense must score enough runs.
3. The defense must successfully field all batted balls.
4. The bullpen must hold the lead.
5. The manager must leave the pitcher in for 5 innings, and not remove him if the team is still behind.

X/H: Extra-base Hit Rate

*xERA: Expected ERA

* Asterisked formulas have updated versions in the Baseball Forecaster. *However, those updates include statistics like Ground Ball Rate, Fly Ball Rate or Line Drive Rate, for which we do not have reliable data for minor leaguers. So we use the previous version of those formulas, as listed here, for the players in this book.*

TEAM AFFILIATIONS

TEAM	ORG	LEAGUE	LEV	TEAM	ORG	LEAGUE	LEV
Aberdeen	BAL	New York-Penn League	SS	Columbus	CLE	International League	AAA
Akron	CLE	Eastern League	AA	Connecticut	DET	New York-Penn League	SS
Albuquerque	COL	Pacific Coast League	AAA	Corpus Christi	HOU	Texas League	AA
Altoona	PIT	Eastern League	AA	Danville	ATL	Appalachian League	Rk
Amarillo	SD	Texas League	AA	Dayton	CIN	Midwest League	A-
Arkansas	SEA	Texas League	AA	Daytona	CIN	Florida State League	A+
Asheville	COL	South Atlantic League	A-	Delmarva	BAL	South Atlantic League	A-
Auburn	WAS	New York-Penn League	SS	Down East	TEX	Carolina League	A+
Augusta	SF	South Atlantic League	A-	Dunedin	TOR	Florida State League	A+
AZL Angels	LAA	Arizona League	Rk	Durham	TAM	International League	AAA
AZL Athletics	OAK	Arizona League	Rk	El Paso	SD	Pacific Coast League	AAA
AZL Brewers	MIL	Arizona League	Rk	Elizabethton	MIN	Appalachian League	Rk
AZL Cubs	CHC	Arizona League	Rk	Erie	DET	Eastern League	AA
AZL Diamondbacks	ARI	Arizona League	Rk	Eugene	CHC	Northwest League	SS
AZL Dodgers	LAD	Arizona League	Rk	Everett	SEA	Northwest League	SS
AZL Giants	SF	Arizona League	Rk	Fayetteville	HOU	Carolina League	A+
AZL Indians	CLE	Arizona League	Rk	Florida	ATL	Florida State League	A+
AZL Mariners	SEA	Arizona League	Rk	Fort Myers	MIN	Florida State League	A+
AZL Padres	SD	Arizona League	Rk	Fort Wayne	SD	Midwest League	A-
AZL Rangers	TEX	Arizona League	Rk	Frederick	BAL	Carolina League	A+
AZL Reds	CIN	Arizona League	Rk	Fresno	WAS	Pacific Coast League	AAA
AZL Royals	KC	Arizona League	Rk	Frisco	TEX	Texas League	AA
AZL White Sox	CHW	Arizona League	Rk	GCL Astros	HOU	Gulf Coast League	Rk
Batavia	MIA	New York-Penn League	SS	GCL Blue Jays	TOR	Gulf Coast League	Rk
Beloit	OAK	Midwest League	A-	GCL Braves	ATL	Gulf Coast League	Rk
Billings	CIN	Pioneer League	Rk	GCL Cardinals	STL	Gulf Coast League	Rk
Biloxi	MIL	Southern League	AA	GCL Marlins	MIA	Gulf Coast League	Rk
Binghamton	NYM	Eastern League	AA	GCL Mets	NYM	Gulf Coast League	Rk
Birmingham	CHW	Southern League	AA	GCL Nationals	WAS	Gulf Coast League	Rk
Bluefield	TOR	Appalachian League	Rk	GCL Orioles	BAL	Gulf Coast League	Rk
Boise	COL	Northwest League	SS	GCL Phillies East	PHI	Gulf Coast League	Rk
Bowie	BAL	Eastern League	AA	GCL Phillies West	PHI	Gulf Coast League	Rk
Bowling Green	TAM	Midwest League	A-	GCL Pirates	PIT	Gulf Coast League	Rk
Bradenton	PIT	Florida State League	A+	GCL Rays	TAM	Gulf Coast League	Rk
Bristol	PIT	Appalachian League	Rk	GCL Red Sox	BOS	Gulf Coast League	Rk
Brooklyn	NYM	New York-Penn League	SS	GCL Tigers East	DET	Gulf Coast League	Rk
Buffalo	TOR	International League	AAA	GCL Tigers West	DET	Gulf Coast League	Rk
Burlington	KC	Appalachian League	Rk	GCL Twins	MIN	Gulf Coast League	Rk
Burlington	LAA	Midwest League	A-	GCL Yankees East	NYY	Gulf Coast League	Rk
Carolina	MIL	Carolina League	A+	GCL Yankees West	NYY	Gulf Coast League	Rk
Cedar Rapids	MIN	Midwest League	A-	Grand Junction	COL	Pioneer League	Rk
Charleston	NYY	South Atlantic League	A-	Great Falls	CHW	Pioneer League	Rk
Charlotte	CHW	International League	AAA	Great Lakes	LAD	Midwest League	A-
Charlotte	TAM	Florida State League	A+	Greeneville	HOU	Appalachian League	Rk
Chattanooga	CIN	Southern League	AA	Greensboro	PIT	South Atlantic League	A-
Clearwater	PHI	Florida State League	A+	Greenville	BOS	South Atlantic League	A-
Clinton	MIA	Midwest League	A-	Gwinnett	ATL	International League	AAA
Columbia	NYM	South Atlantic League	A-	Hagerstown	WAS	South Atlantic League	A-

TEAM	ORG	LEAGUE	LEV	TEAM	ORG	LEAGUE	LEV
Harrisburg	WAS	Eastern League	AA	Pensacola	MIN	Southern League	AA
Hartford	COL	Eastern League	AA	Peoria	STL	Midwest League	A-
Hickory	TEX	South Atlantic League	A-	Portland	BOS	Eastern League	AA
Hillsboro	ARI	Northwest League	SS	Potomac	WAS	Carolina League	A+
Hudson Valley	TAM	New York-Penn League	SS	Princeton	TAM	Appalachian League	Rk
Idaho Falls	KC	Pioneer League	Rk	Pulaski	NYY	Appalachian League	Rk
Indianapolis	PIT	International League	AAA	Quad Cities	HOU	Midwest League	A-
Inland Empire	LAA	California League	A+	Rancho Cucamonga	LAD	California League	A+
Iowa	CHC	Pacific Coast League	AAA	Reading	PHI	Eastern League	AA
Jackson	ARI	Southern League	AA	Reno	ARI	Pacific Coast League	AAA
Jacksonville	MIA	Southern League	AA	Richmond	SF	Eastern League	AA
Johnson City	STL	Appalachian League	Rk	Rochester	MIN	International League	AAA
Jupiter	MIA	Florida State League	A+	Rocky Mountain	MIL	Pioneer League	Rk
Kane County	ARI	Midwest League	A-	Rome	ATL	South Atlantic League	A-
Kannapolis	CHW	South Atlantic League	A-	Round Rock	HOU	Pacific Coast League	AAA
Kingsport	NYM	Appalachian League	Rk	Sacramento	SF	Pacific Coast League	AAA
Lake County	CLE	Midwest League	A-	Salem	BOS	Carolina League	A+
Lake Elsinore	SD	California League	A+	Salem-Keizer	SF	Northwest League	SS
Lakeland	DET	Florida State League	A+	Salt Lake	LAA	Pacific Coast League	AAA
Lakewood	PHi	South Atlantic League	A-	San Antonio	MIL	Pacific Coast League	AAA
Lancaster	COL	California League	A+	San Jose	SF	California League	A+
Lansing	TOR	Midwest League	A-	Scranton/Wilkes-Barre	NYY	International League	AAA
Las Vegas	OAK	Pacific Coast League	AAA	South Bend	CHC	Midwest League	A-
Lehigh Valley	PHI	International League	AAA	Spokane	TEX	Northwest League	SS
Lexington	KC	South Atlantic League	A-	Springfield	STL	Texas League	AA
Louisville	CIN	International League	AAA	St. Lucie	NYM	Florida State League	A+
Lowell	BOS	New York-Penn League	SS	State College	STL	New York-Penn League	SS
Lynchburg	CLE	Carolina League	A+	Staten Island	NYY	New York-Penn League	SS
Mahoning Valley	CLE	New York-Penn League	SS	Stockton	OAK	California League	A+
Memphis	STL	Pacific Coast League	AAA	Syracuse	NYM	International League	AAA
Midland	OAK	Texas League	AA	Tacoma	SEA	Pacific Coast League	AAA
Mississippi	ATL	Southern League	AA	Tampa	NYY	Florida State League	A+
Missoula	ARI	Pioneer League	Rk	Tennessee	CHC	Southern League	AA
Mobile	LAA	Southern League	AA	Toledo	DET	International League	AAA
Modesto	SEA	California League	A+	Trenton	NYY	Eastern League	AA
Montgomery	TAM	Southern League	AA	Tri-City	HOU	New York-Penn League	SS
Myrtle Beach	CHC	Carolina League	A+	Tri-City	SD	Northwest League	SS
Nashville	TEX	Pacific Coast League	AAA	Tulsa	LAD	Texas League	AA
New Hampshire	TOR	Eastern League	AA	Vancouver	TOR	Northwest League	SS
New Orleans	MIA	Pacific Coast League	AAA	Vermont	OAK	New York-Penn League	SS
Norfolk	BAL	International League	AAA	Visalia	ARI	California League	A+
Northwest Arkansas	KC	Texas League	AA	West Michigan	DET	Midwest League	A-
Ogden	LAD	Pioneer League	Rk	West Virginia	PIT	New York-Penn League	SS
Oklahoma City	LAD	Pacific Coast League	AAA	West Virginia	SEA	South Atlantic League	A-
Omaha	KC	Pacific Coast League	AAA	Williamsport	PHI	New York-Penn League	SS
Orem	LAA	Pioneer League	Rk	Wilmington	KC	Carolina League	A+
Palm Beach	STL	Florida State League	A+	Winston-Salem	CHW	Carolina League	A+
Pawtucket	BOS	International League	AAA	Wisconsin	MIL	Midwest League	A-

LIVE EVENTS — THIS SPRING!

"An unforgettable experience"

Get a head start on the 2019 season with a unique opportunity to go one-on-one with some of the top writers and analysts in the fantasy baseball industry. First Pitch Forums are coming to top US cities for lively and informative draft prep seminars.

Winning strategies! Player pool insights! Sleepers! Mock draft exercises! You will come away with the tools you need to win in 2019!

BaseballHQ.com founder Ron Shandler, and GMs Brent Hershey and Ray Murphy bring a dynamic energy to each event. They are joined by BaseballHQ analysts and experts from ESPN.com, MLB.com, RotoWire, The Athletic.com, FanGraphs, Baseball Prospectus, Mastersball, and more.

2019 Schedule:

February 23: Chicago
February 24: Atlanta

March 8: Boston
March 9: New York/NJ
March 10: Baltimore/DC

For complete details visit *www.firstpitchforums.com* and follow *@BaseballHQ* on Twitter

Plus, don't forget "the best weekend of the year":
First Pitch Arizona in Phoenix at the Arizona Fall League.
October 31-November 3, 2019. Save the date!

Get Baseball Insights
Every Single Day.

The *Minor League Baseball Analyst* provides a head-start in evaluating and selecting up-and-coming prospects for your fantasy team. You can maintain that edge all season long.

From spring training to the season's last pitch, BaseballHQ.com covers all aspects of what's happening on and off the field—all with the most powerful fantasy slant on the Internet:

- Nationally-renowned baseball analysts.
- MLB news analysis; including anticipating the next move.
- Dedicated columns on starting pitching, relievers, batters, and our popular Fact or Fluke? player profiles.
- Minor-league coverage beyond just scouting and lists.
- FAAB targets, starting pitcher reports, strategy articles, daily game resources, call-up profiles and more!

Plus, **BaseballHQ.com** gets personal, with customizable tools and valuable resources:

- Team Stat Tracker and Power Search tools
- Custom Draft Guide for YOUR league's parameters
- Sortable and downloadable stats and projection files
- Subscriber forums, the friendliest on the baseball Internet

Visit **www.baseballhq.com/subscribe**
to lock down your path to a 2019 championship!

Full Season subscription **$89**
(prorated at the time of order; auto-renews each October)

Draft Prep subscription **$39**
(complete access from January through April 30, 2019)

Please read our Terms of service at www.baseballhq.com/terms.html

Minor League Baseball Analyst & BaseballHQ.com:
Your season-long championship lineup.

2018 Projected Skills Comps vs Market				ASSETS								LIABILITIES						
TARGETS		**BATTER**	Pos	Tm	PT	Pw	Sp	Av	*	Pk	Rg	Av	Inj	Ex	Nw	Pk	Ag	Rg
ADP	R$	**PITCHER**	Pos	Tm	PT	Er	K	Sv		Pk	Rg	Er	Inj	Ex	Nw	Pk	Ag	Rg
49	$ 20	Hoskins,Rhys	73	PHI	F	P+		a	*					EX				
183	$ 7	Carpenter,Matt	3	STL	F	P+		a	*									
304	$ 2	Belt,Brandon	3	SF	F	P+		a	*				INJ					
196	$ 6	Conforto,Michael	78	NYM	M	P+		a	*				INJ	e				
198	$ 6	Thames,Eric	37	MIL	M	P+		a	*									

If you love the Forecaster, you gotta meet BABS

After the Forecaster, continue to follow Ron's latest groundbreaking work online. His new roster construction process, the Broad Assessment Balance Sheet (BABS) is an innovation that is rapidly catching on with fantasy league winners. He writes about it exclusively at his current home, **RonShandler.com**.

A one-year membership to **RonShandler.com** includes *"The BABS Project"* eBook (pdf version), plus all this:

- *BABS Project* updates and ongoing analysis
- BABS ratings, asset group rankings and cheat sheets for 2019 drafts
- Custom reports from the BABS Database
- Ron's insights, including all his *ESPN Insider* columns
- BABS ratings for RotoLab software
- BABS minor league ratings
- BABS fantasy baseball leagues
- Members-only message boards
- Commentary, polls, contests and more

Annual membership. $19.95

For more information:

- Visit **RonShandler.com.** Sign up for membership or free email updates.
- "Like" Ron's Facebook page: **facebook.com/ronshandler.baseball**
- Follow Ron on Twitter: **@RonShandler**

RotoLab
Draft Software

RotoLab is both a draft preparation program and an in-draft management tool. Just make the roster moves and player selections, and the program handles the rest... automatically! All budget calculations, inflation changes, player lists, team stats and standing totals are a single mouse click away. And... **RotoLab comes loaded with industry-leading player projections from BaseballHQ.com!**

FREE DEMO at www.rotolab.com
HUGE discount for Baseball HQ subscribers!

- Easy to use interface
- Sort, search and filter data at the click of a mouse
- Five years of historical and projected stats
- User notes for each player
- Drag-and-drop player moves
- Two-click operation to draft players
- Flexible league setup options
- Customizable valuation process
- User-definable player list
- Roster management from a single screen
- Cheat Sheet and full stat views to draft from

RON SHANDLER'S 2019
BASEBALL FORECASTER

RON SHANDLER'S 2019
BASEBALL FORECASTER
AND ENCYCLOPEDIA OF FANALYTICS

The Industry's Longest-Running Publication for Baseball Analysts & Fantasy Leaguers • Est. 1986

33RD EDITION, FROM
BASEBALL HQ.COM

BRENT HERSHEY &
RAY MURPHY, EDITORS

BRANDON KRUSE &
RYAN BLOOMFIELD,
ASSOCIATE EDITORS

• The first to develop sabermetric applications for fantasy league play
• Accurate projections, fully supported and intuitively logical
• The source used by MLB GMs, the media and other fantasy services
• Innovators of proven strategies like the LIMA Plan, Mayberry Method, MP3 and Xtreme Regression Drafting

Everything you need to draft and run your team:

Stats and sabermetrics • Leaderboards
Research abstracts • Encyclopedia of Fanalytics
Leading indicators and projections • Injury logs

**FREE 2019 Projections Update ...
Available March 1 for book buyers only**

$26.95 plus $6.00 Priority Mail S&H. To order:

http://www.baseballhq.com/baseball-forecaster

BASEBALL HQ.COM
RADIO

Fantasy Sports Writers Association
Podcast of the Year (2013)

Join host **Patrick Davitt**, BaseballHQ.com's top analysts and other industry experts for interviews, news and insights on how to win your league.

These FREE twice-weekly (Tue/Fri) podcasts are each 45-80 minutes, and available via download or subscription through iTunes.

Guests who appeared on BaseballHQ Radio in 2018 include:

• Ron Shandler, Baseball Forecaster
• Todd Zola, Mastersball.com
• Joe Sheehan, JoeSheehan.com
• Derek Carty, ESPN.com
• Scott Pianowski, Yahoo! Sports
• Gene McCaffrey, Wise Guy Baseball
• Jeff Zimmerman, FanGraphs.com
• Jason Collette, RotoWire
• Mike Gianella, BaseballProspectus.com
• Paul Sporer, FanGraphs.com

LISTEN to the PODCAST NOW
— It's FREE! —
baseballhq.com/ radio/